Roosevelt
and
Frankfurter
Their Correspondence
1928 - 1945

ATLANTIC–LITTLE, BROWN BOOKS
ARE PUBLISHED BY
LITTLE, BROWN AND COMPANY
IN ASSOCIATION WITH
THE ATLANTIC MONTHLY PRESS

Published simultaneously in Canada
by Little, Brown & Company (Canada) Limited

PRINTED IN THE UNITED STATES OF AMERICA

Felix Frankfurter
(Portrait by Gardner Cox)

Roosevelt
and
Frankfurte

Their Correspond
1928 ~ 194

Annotated by MAX

PU

wi

Ar

LITTLE, BI

For
Caroline

Acknowledgments

IN PREPARING even a partial list of those who helped me with this book, I must begin with the many veterans of the New Deal, in Washington and elsewhere, who have so generously shared with me their knowledge and experience of the Roosevelt era. I must also record my gratitude, with equal emphasis, to that galaxy of scholars and historians who have done so much to re-create the Roosevelt years and illuminate their meaning.

My debt to the various historians of the Roosevelt era is beyond my power of acknowledgment, reinforced as it is in many instances by feelings of personal friendship. Without attempting an exhaustive list, I would like in particular to thank Mr. Frank Freidel, Mr. James MacGregor Burns, Mr. Eric Goldman, Mr. Irving Brant, Sir D. W. Brogan, Mr. Allan Nevins, Mr. Henry Steele Commager, Mr. Max Beloff, Mr. John Morton Blum, Mr. Samuel Eliot Morison, Mr. Alpheus T. Mason, Mr. Bernard Bellush, Mr. William E. Leuchtenburg, Mr. Daniel R. Fusfeld, Mr. Basil Rauch. I should like to thank especially Mr. Arthur M. Schlesinger, Jr., and Mr. Barry Karl who read the proofs of this book and made many helpful suggestions. It would be the final satisfaction for me if these scholars, and others like them, would find in these pages some clues to a more detailed understanding of various passages in Roosevelt's Presidency.

My debt to many libraries is also copious and important. First in importance is the Franklin D. Roosevelt Library at Hyde Park. Its director, Mrs. Elizabeth Drewry, and her staff of courteous and tireless assistants, have perfected a tradition which enables them to convert the drudgeries of research into the arts of friendship. I must acknowledge as well the help given me by the Library of Congress, and especially by Mr. David Mearns, the director of its precious manuscripts division. My thanks also go to the Supreme Court library and in particular to Miss Helen Lally; to the Athenaeum Library in Boston; the Public Library in Boston; and the Public Library in Washington, D.C.

But my greatest debt of all must go to my friend and editor, Mr. Edward Weeks of the Atlantic Monthly Press, and to all the members of his staff, for patient encouragement and for intelligent incentives which I can never repay. It is with much more than a casual or routine word of thanks that I convey my gratitude to Mr. James Messett for his admirable typing and general assistance; to Miss Albee for her benevolent reminder of deadlines; to Mrs. Marguerite Sheffield for her laborious and exact copy editing; to Mr. Upton Brady and Mr. Peter Davison for the gift of courage in the occasional dark hour.

Mr. LaRue Brown was particularly helpful in reconstructing Frankfurter's years in Boston.

As always, I have gained guidance and inspiration from my friendship with Mr. Paul Freund of the Harvard Law School and Mr. Frank Buxton, one of the oldest of Frankfurter's friends.

Finally, I want to acknowledge the constant and unmeasured help given me by Mrs. Elsie Douglas, Frankfurter's confidential secretary, and by Mr. Donald Hiss, the legal executor of his estate. Without their assistance this book would never have been completed.

Most of the merits of this book belong to all these friends and colleagues. Its faults and shortcomings rest on me alone.

M.F.

Biographical Notes

Franklin Delano Roosevelt (1882-1945). Attended Groton, Harvard, Columbia Law School. In 1910 elected to the State Senate of New York. In 1913 became Assistant Secretary of the Navy in Wilson's Administration. In 1920 chosen as the Democratic candidate for Vice-President on the Cox-Roosevelt ticket. In August 1921, at age of thirty-nine, stricken with infantile paralysis while at Campobello Island in New Brunswick. Legs paralyzed, he began his slow and painful struggle against becoming a permanent invalid. In 1924, with his "Happy Warrior" speech, he nominated Alfred E. Smith as the Presidential candidate but the Democrats at a deadlocked convention finally selected John W. Davis. In 1928 he nominated Al Smith for the Presidency and was elected as Governor of New York while Smith was being defeated by Herbert Hoover. In 1930 re-elected as Governor by a huge majority and became a strong candidate for the Presidential nomination. In 1932 elected as President for the first time; he was to become the only man in American history to be elected to four terms in the White House, defeating President Hoover, Landon, Willkie, and Dewey. He died at the age of sixty-three on April 12, 1945, at Warm Springs, Georgia.

Eleanor Roosevelt. His wife, and in her own right a major national figure.

James Roosevelt. Their oldest son.

Felix Frankfurter (1882-1965). Born in Austria the same year that Roosevelt was born at Hyde Park, he came to New York in 1894 at the age of twelve, speaking not a word of English, but twelve years later, in 1906, he was graduated from the Harvard Law School with an academic record of supreme distinction. For the next five years, 1906-1911, he served as chief assistant to Henry L. Stimson, who was then the District Attorney for the Southern District of New York. In 1911, in the Taft Administration, he became special counsel to Secretary of War Stimson and also law officer of the Bureau of Insular Affairs. In 1914, almost thirty-two, he joined the faculty of the Harvard Law School and remained there until 1939, with periodic interruptions for service in Washington. In 1917, at the request of Newton D. Baker, Secretary of War in Wilson's Administration, he became secretary and counsel to the President's Mediation Commission on labor problems, and later chairman of the War Labor Policies Board. At the Paris Peace Conference after the First World War, he, as the representative of Dr. Chaim Weizmann, negotiated the Zionist-Arab agreement with Lawrence of Arabia as the representative of King Faisal. He was one of the founders of the Civil Liberties Union, served as counsel for the National Consumers League, and was a legal adviser to the National Association for the Advancement of Colored People. In 1927 he found himself the center of a strenuous controversy when he intervened in the Sacco-Vanzetti case with the argument, based on a detailed analysis of the judicial record, that the two men, regardless of their guilt or innocence, had been denied a fair trial. In 1933 he turned down President Roosevelt's offer to become the Solicitor General. In 1939, aged fifty-six, he became an Associate Justice of the Supreme Court of the United States in succession to Mr. Justice Benjamin Cardozo. In August 1962, after serving on the Supreme Court for twenty-four terms, he resigned for reasons of health. On February 22, 1965, at the age of eighty-two, he died in Washington.

Marion Denman Frankfurter.   His wife and often his literary adviser.

Dean Acheson.   Undersecretary of the Treasury, 1933; Assistant Secretary of State, 1941-1945; later, Secretary of State.

Hamilton Fish Armstrong.   Editor, *Foreign Affairs* quarterly.

Arthur A. Ballantine.   Undersecretary of the Treasury in the Hoover Administration and friend of both Roosevelt and Frankfurter.

Bernard M. Baruch.   Financier and Presidential adviser; adviser to war mobilization director after 1943.

Adolf A. Berle, Jr.   Special counsel, Reconstruction Finance Corporation; Assistant Secretary of State, 1938-1944.

Francis Biddle.   Solicitor General, 1940; Attorney General, 1941-1945.

Hugo L. Black.   Democratic Senator from Alabama, 1927-1937; Roosevelt's first appointment to the Supreme Court, 1937.

William E. Borah.   Republican Senator from Idaho, 1903-1940; chairman, Senate Foreign Relations Committee.

Louis D. Brandeis (Isaiah).   Associate Justice of the Supreme Court, 1916-1939.

McGeorge Bundy.   Author of important book on Stimson; later national security adviser to Presidents Kennedy and Johnson.

James F. Byrnes.   Democratic Senator from South Carolina, 1931-1941; Associate Justice of the Supreme Court, 1941-1942; director of economic stabilization and later of war mobilization.

C. C. Burlingham.   Revered lawyer in New York; exemplar of responsible citizenship.

Frank Buxton. Editor, Boston *Herald.*

Benjamin V. Cohen. Presidential adviser and major figure in the New Deal.

Thomas G. Corcoran. Equally important member of famous Corcoran-Cohen team.

Sir Stafford Cripps. Labour member of Churchill's cabinet during the Second World War.

Homer Cummings. Attorney General, 1933-1939.

Thomas E. Dewey. Governor of New York, 1942-1954; defeated by Roosevelt in 1944 Presidential election.

William O. Douglas. Commissioner and chairman, Securities and Exchange Commission, 1936-1939; Associate Justice of the Supreme Court since 1939.

Stephen T. Early. Assistant secretary to Roosevelt, 1933-1937; secretary, 1937-1945.

James A. Farley. Chairman, Democratic National Committee, and Roosevelt's campaign manager; Postmaster General, 1933-1940.

William Green. President, American Federation of Labor, 1924-1952.

Learned Hand. Famous member, Court of Appeals for the Second Circuit.

Robert E. Hannegan. Chairman of the Democratic National Committee in 1940 when Roosevelt was nominated for third term.

W. Averell Harriman. Administrative officer, National Recovery Administration; member, Business Advisory Council, Department of Commerce, 1933-1939; Ambassador to the Soviet Union.

Leon Henderson. With NRA, 1934-1935; WPA, 1936-1938; SEC commissioner, 1939-1941; administrator, Office of Price Administration, 1941-1942.

Sidney Hillman. Trade union leader; Presidential adviser.

Harry L. Hopkins. Director, Federal Emergency Relief Administration, 1933-1935; Works Progress administrator, 1935-1938; Secretary of Commerce, 1938-1940; later a leading Presidential adviser and assistant.

Charles Evans Hughes. Chief Justice of the United States, 1930-1941.

Cordell Hull. Secretary of State, 1933-1946.

Harold L. Ickes. Secretary of the Interior, 1933-1946.

Robert H. Jackson. Assistant Attorney General, 1936-1938; Solicitor General, 1938-1939; Associate Justice of the Supreme Court, 1941-1954.

Hugh S. Johnson. Administrator, National Industrial Recovery Administration, 1933-1934.

Joseph P. Kennedy.   Chairman, Securities and Exchange Commission, 1935; Ambassador to Great Britain, 1937-1941.

John Maynard Keynes.   Most influential economist of this century; friend of Frankfurter since Paris Peace Conference.

James M. Landis.   Member, Securities and Exchange Commission, 1934-1937; later, dean of the Harvard Law School.

Alfred M. Landon.   Governor of Kansas, 1933-1937; defeated by Roosevelt in 1936 Presidential election.

Harold J. Laski.   Prominent British Socialist; member of Fabian Society and executive committee of the Labour Party; professor of political science, University of London; connected with the London School of Economics; one of Frankfurter's greatest friends.

Marguerite A. LeHand (Missy).   Roosevelt's personal secretary and close friend.

John L. Lewis.   President, United Mine Workers of America.

Walter Lippmann.   Editor, columnist, publicist.

Lord Lothian.   British Ambassador in Washington.

Marvin H. McIntyre.   Presidential assistant and appointments secretary, 1933-1942.

Archibald MacLeish.   Lawyer, poet, playwright; Librarian of Congress, 1939-1944; Assistant Secretary of State, 1944-1945.

George C. Marshall.   Chief military adviser to Roosevelt in Second World War; Secretary of State, 1947-1950; Secretary of Defense, 1950-1951.

Raymond Moley.   Assistant Secretary of State, 1927-1932; important member of the original Brain Trust; Presidential speech writer.

Ogden L. Mills (Oggie).   Undersecretary (1927-1932) and later Secretary of the Treasury in the Hoover Administration.

Henry Morgenthau, Jr.   Chairman, Federal Farm Board, 1933; Undersecretary of the Treasury, 1934; Secretary of the Treasury, 1934-1945.

Frank Murphy.   Mayor of Detroit, 1930-1933; Governor General and later High Commissioner to the Philippines, 1934-1936; Governor of Michigan, 1936-1938; Attorney General, 1939-1940; Associate Justice of the Supreme Court, 1940-1949.

Philip Murray.   Trade union leader.

George W. Norris.   Republican Senator from Nebraska, 1913-1943; long-time friend of Roosevelt and Frankfurter.

Geoffrey Parsons.   Editor, New York *Herald Tribune.*

Frances Perkins. Secretary of Labor, 1933-1945; only woman member of Roosevelt's cabinet.

Sam Rayburn. Democratic Congressman from Texas; Speaker of the House of Representatives, 1940-1952.

Stanley F. Reed. Solicitor General, 1935-1938; Associate Justice of the Supreme Court, 1938-1957.

Donald R. Richberg. Labor expert; adviser to Roosevelt; temporary chairman, National Industrial Recovery Board, 1935.

Owen J. Roberts. Associate Justice of the Supreme Court, 1930-1945.

Samuel I. Rosenman. Counsel to Roosevelt as Governor of New York; chief Presidential speech writer.

Alfred E. Smith. Governor of New York, 1919-1920 and 1923-1928; defeated by Hoover in 1928 Presidential race.

Henry L. Stimson. Secretary of State under Hoover; Secretary of War under Roosevelt.

Harlan F. Stone. Associate Justice of the Supreme Court, 1925-1941; Chief Justice of the United States, 1941-1946.

Arthur Hays Sulzberger. Publisher, New York *Times*, 1935-1961.

Dorothy Thompson. Distinguished journalist and occasional speech writer for Roosevelt; famed for her early opposition to Hitler.

Rexford G. Tugwell. Member of the first Brain Trust; Assistant Secretary of Agriculture, 1933; Undersecretary of Agriculture, 1934-1937.

Grace Tully. The President's personal secretary after Miss LeHand's stroke in the summer of 1941.

Robert F. Wagner. Democratic Senator from New York, 1927-1949; leading supporter of New Deal legislation.

James J. Walker. Mayor of New York, forced to resign by Governor Roosevelt.

Henry A. Wallace. Secretary of Agriculture, 1933-1940; Vice-President of the United States, 1941-1945; Secretary of Commerce, 1945-1946.

General Edwin M. "Pa" Watson. Presidential assistant and intimate friend.

Chaim Weizmann. Leader of World Zionist Movement.

Burton K. Wheeler. Isolationist Senator (Democratic) from Montana, 1923-1947, with progressive voting record on domestic legislation; deeply involved in court-packing controversy of 1937.

William Allen White. Editor, Emporia (Kansas) *Gazette*.

Wendell L. Willkie.   Defeated by Roosevelt in 1940 Presidential race.

John G. Winant.   Governor of New Hampshire, 1925-1926 and 1931-1934; labor mediator; Ambassador to Great Britain, 1941-1946.

Laurence Winship.   Managing editor, Boston *Globe.*

William Woodin.   First Secretary of the Treasury under Roosevelt, 1933-1934.

Contents

Photographs appear between pages 398 and 399

Introduction

THIS correspondence is a record of friendship, a chronicle of the New Deal, a manual on the high art of political leadership, and a testament of citizenship. In its pages are clues to many puzzling episodes in the Roosevelt years. No one else quite filled Frankfurter's role, for he was outside the Administration but always within Roosevelt's confidence. He could speak to the President with the authority of an expert and the intimacy of a friend.

The initial attempt to publish this correspondence, if only in fragmentary form, was made as long ago as 1949 on the initiative of Mr. Arthur M. Schlesinger, Jr., then at work on the first of his volumes on the Age of Roosevelt. On August 5, 1949, he wrote this letter to Frankfurter:

Poughkcepsie, N.Y., August 5, 1949

Dear Mr. Justice:

A slumbering intention to write to you was awakened today when I read your excellent draft for the platform of 1936. It is a fine document and still would make a good party platform.

In other words, the FDR papers are beginning to be opened up; and I am spending the summer here, burrowing through them. The quantity is so staggering that I feel rather like a mole attacking the Great Pyramid. But it is very exciting work. I look forward to a moment when I can talk over a good many things with you.

I have asked my publishers to send you a copy of my forthcoming book, to be called *The Vital Center* (a publisher's title). It is to come out on the 8th September. It is a political tract, designed to get my private political views out of my system so that they won't get in my way when I write the New Deal book.

I saw Isaiah [Berlin] leave with bitter regret. What an indispensable person he is! I hope you will use your influence with Oxford and Harvard to make sure that he is back here regularly. Perhaps Dean [Acheson] could be induced to count him as reverse-ERP [European Recovery Program and the Marshall Plan].

Please give my very best to Mrs. F.

Yours ever,
ARTHUR S.

He followed up this appeal with another letter:

Poughkeepsie, N.Y., August 6, 1949

Dear Mr. Justice:

It occurred to me that my letter of yesterday might be open to misinterpretation. I read your draft for a 1936 platform in a folder devoted to platform suggestions; your own letters to FDR, I regret to say, have not been opened for research. I can understand why this should be, particularly in the case of a sitting justice of the Supreme Court. But, at the same time, as a historian, I feel unhappy to have so much rich material withdrawn from view.

I have accordingly suggested today to Mr. Herman Kahn, the very efficient head of the Roosevelt Memorial Library, that he ask you whether you would examine the material with an eye to releasing as much as possible to scholars. I hope more than I can say that you will see your way to doing something of this sort, not only in justice to your own role in those exciting days, but also because I am certain (having been the fortunate recipient of occasional letters from you) that your letters will throw indispensable light on the great issues of the New Deal. This, I am sure, is true, not only because of your own more philosophical approach to the issues, but also because geographical separation made letters more important in your relationship with F.D.R. than they were in the case of people who were in Washington throughout the period.

If this letter is improper, I know that you will know that it is motivated by the purest historical passion. I doubt very much whether an adequate history of the New Deal can be written without the Frankfurter-Roosevelt letters of 1933-38. You yourself should choose what should be reserved for the ultimate historian; but in the meantime I hope something may be turned over to us proximate fellows!

Very sincerely yours,
ARTHUR S.

Mr. Schlesinger's parents were two of Frankfurter's most cherished friends, and he had known "little Arthur" since he was a child. Naturally, Mr. Schlesinger's two letters were treated very seriously. Frankfurter turned for advice to Mr. Dean Acheson, Judge Learned Hand, Mr. C. C. Burlingham in New York, and Mr. Justice Stanley Reed of the Supreme Court. But the advice which weighed most heavily with him came from Mr. McGeorge Bundy, then working on the papers of Henry L. Stimson, Secretary of War under Roosevelt. Mr. Bundy wrote:

Council on Foreign Relations, Inc.
New York, N.Y., August 15, 1949

Dear Mr. Justice:

I don't know what to say. This problem is one which I have just come from discussing with Colonel Stimson, in so far as it applies to his own papers; and no matter what the circumstances, there never seems to be any perfect solution.

In the case of the Roosevelt collection there is a serious difficulty which does not apply to the Stimson papers. Our general solution in the latter case has been to make available whatever is already accessible and catalogued (so far this means the Diary only) to individuals, judged as individuals, for their free use, but with a right of review held by me as trustee for the Colonel before anything is published. This solution separates the sheep from the goats among investigators and allows to the approved investigators that freedom of search which is a necessary part of really scholarly work.

The problem of the Roosevelt papers seems to me to have a double difficulty as compared with our method. As I understand it, what is opened there must be opened to all, with the result that there can be no discrimination between what would be valuable for Arthur and what would be manhandled by Westbrook Pegler. On the other hand, since it is clear that not all of the papers can be uncovered, even the responsible scholar must be satisfied with an incomplete investigation. In such circumstances a wise solution becomes vastly difficult.

Of course, I do not know at all what is contained in your correspondence with F.D.R., but I find it difficult to believe that you always wrote with an eye to the prevention of misinterpretation by men who are eager to misinterpret. I think, therefore, that a very rigorous selective process would be required before you could properly open your papers at this stage to indiscriminate investigation. This is so, not merely because of your present responsibility, but perhaps almost more because of your unusually intimate connection with a man who does not yet belong to the ages. It would be necessary, therefore, to reduce the correspondence to a fragment, perhaps a large one but more probably a rather devitalized remainder. Such a fragment would hardly be of major value to a responsible student and it would certainly be used even in all its innocence by the modern men with a muckrake. What good would that do?

Arthur's work has been undertaken in so fine a spirit that it would be a great pity not to give him such help as you can — and I know better than most how much your help means. But I wonder if the sealed folders at Hyde Park are a vital component of that assistance. Do they contain both the originals and the carbons of your correspondence? There is surely no objection — except that of the drain on your time and office strength — to your opening your own papers to anyone you choose and only to those you choose. And as one who has observed your memory and then checked it against documents, I incline to believe that you can do the bulk of the job in conversation.

So my own ignorant vote would be very strongly against any decision to open any part of your private correspondence now at Hyde Park. You cannot open it all; the part that you can open would necessarily be of less value to those who deserve help than to those who do not. The materials remaining under your direct personal control should be sufficient for the guidance of those you wish to guide. This is not an anti-historical position, and in so far as it lays any burdens upon qualified students in the field, they are the burdens which should be expected by men who attempt the writing of history at a time when feeling has not cooled and many of the men concerned are still on stage. The responsibility to history is, as Arthur recognizes, a responsibility to the "ultimate historian." That responsibility, as I have suggested to you before, includes a strong obligation to do at some stage, if strength allows, the sort of thing Mr. Churchill has always done; but that is a job which one does not suggest in proximate terms to a front-line fighter in a summer rest area.

I have tried to answer in reasoned argument; I have omitted and now put in only as an apostrophe my personal feeling that the trained historian — and I would include myself if I had the training — has a remarkable lack of appreciation for the simple values of privacy. Their profession is the reading of other people's mail, and the best of them accept in their work a standard of snooping which they would indignantly reject in daily life. Your letters to F.D.R. are still a part of the daily life of many people; to such letters surely one should apply not the standard of even the finest premature historian, but the standard of ordinary good manners.

I return the papers you sent me, and I will of course keep my trap shut.

The Colonel and Mrs. Stimson sent you both messages of affection — from the Ausable Club, St. Hubert's P.O., Essex County, N.Y. — if you have time a letter from you would be worth a box of pills from the best of specialists. I think he is really getting better, and with a fair breeze and good friends, there is real hope that he may be more actively interested this year than he has been since 1947. The general public value of such a new lease on life I find difficult to overestimate, and of course its meaning for all his friends hardly needs discussion.

My love to you both.

As ever,
MAC

P.S.   I see on rereading that I start "not knowing what to say" and wind up saying a lot of fairly dogmatic things. I'm sorry to have made up my mind so fully on a subject I know so little about — and I have certainly presumed, to lecture you on a topic you have thought about much more than I. But the only thing to do when asked for comment is to comment — you know of course that I am not of those who consider it an outrage if a request for advice is not followed by blind obedience.

On reflection, Frankfurter decided, with reluctance, to deny Mr. Schlesinger's request. It was self-evident that numerous problems would arise if this correspondence were published while Frankfurter was still on the Supreme Court. Frankfurter was also convinced that a small volume of selected letters would be superficial and misleading. Mr. Schlesinger would have to see the entire correspondence for the Presidential years or none of it. He decided that for the time being all his letters to Roosevelt, starting with the first term, should be closed to historians and research workers. They remained thus sealed and inaccessible at the Roosevelt Memorial Library in Hyde Park until he removed the ban to make possible this book. Roosevelt's own letters, of course, have been open to scholarly research.

Frankfurter thought the publication of his correspondence on a generous scale would help put Roosevelt's policies in a fresh light. It had always been a matter of deep personal sadness to him that Roosevelt, during all his years in the White House, had been compelled to endure more criticism and abuse than any President since Lincoln. The unique relationship between Frankfurter and Roosevelt enabled him to see the development of the President's programs from a point of view not always available to the family of official advisers; and he gradually became persuaded that the President's reputation, already secure, was entitled to this additional testimony which he alone could bring.

Nor was Frankfurter indifferent to the fact that his voice, speaking as it were from beyond the grave, would call upon men to consider old prejudices in a new perspective and with much greater knowledge. No other private citizen had been exposed to such pitiless criticism, at once extensive and offensive. He was accused of seeking power without responsibility, of trying to rule from behind the scenes, of warping official policy to his personal ends through the influence of his friends whom he had placed in strategic positions throughout the Administration. General Hugh S. Johnson, the NRA Administrator, wrote with venomous bitterness about Frankfurter in 1935, blaming the Administration's misfortunes on "the Harvard crowd" and "Happy Hot Dogs" and denouncing Frankfurter as "the most influential single individual in the United States."

Mr. George Peek, an authority on farm policy, declared that "a plague of young lawyers settled on Washington. They all claimed to be friends of somebody or other and mostly of Felix Frankfurter and Jerome Frank. They floated airily into offices, took desks, asked for papers, and found no end of things to be busy about. I never found out why they came, what they did, or why they left." Actually, things were even worse than Mr. Peek realized, for Jerome Frank was a friend of Frankfurter and shared many of his objectives.

Nor did the personal criticism cease when Frankfurter became a member of the Supreme Court. "In the writing of Felix Frankfurter," said Mr. Westbrook Pegler, "the Supreme Court last week issued to labor unions a special license to commit crimes against individuals and thus against the community. The fact that labor unions are private associations and may be utterly corrupt was not touched upon, but deserves consideration by the

layman and Congress. This decision is consistent with the New Deal philosophy, which itself was derived from Justice Frankfurter, through his con-
tamination of mischievous cub lawyers who, in turn, have polluted the
thought of the government on the subject of the rights of industry and of
the individual citizen."

Not everyone was ready to echo the generous judgment of Mr. Arthur
Schlesinger, Jr., who wrote: "Small, quick, articulate, jaunty, Frankfurter
was inexhaustible in his energy and his curiosity, giving off sparks like an
overcharged electric battery. He loved people, loved conversation, loved influence, loved life. Beyond his sparkling personal qualities, he had an eru-
dite and incisive legal intelligence, a resourceful approach to questions of
public policy, and a passion for raising the standards of public service. And,
to make these things effective, he had what Mr. Justice Holmes had not
unkindly described in 1920 as 'an unimaginable gift of wiggling in wherever
he wants to!' " Many others looked at Frankfurter and returned a different
and hostile verdict.

In view of the repeated accusations that Frankfurter delighted in packing
the Administration with his friends and disciples, it is rather astonishing to
find him, on February 5, 1938, beginning a letter to Roosevelt with these
words: "I have just learned that Hamilton Fish Armstrong's name is under
consideration for the Vienna post, and venture to trouble you, for the first
time since March 4, 1933, with an uninvited suggestion for one of your
appointments." By the time this letter is reached, the reader has seen
Frankfurter make many recommendations for appointments to the President, and he may be pardoned for feeling a sense of perplexity at this declaration. What is the explanation?

The key phrase is "uninvited suggestion." Frankfurter to the very end
insisted that he almost never offered a suggestion for filling an office in the
Administration unless he had first been asked to do so by the President; and
the available record of his meetings and talks with Roosevelt, apart from
their correspondence, confirms his statement. But that is not the whole
explanation. Once he had been asked for a recommendation or had been
informed of a vacancy, Frankfurter often gave the President five or six
names, when only one was needed, and it was not unusual to find all of
them, before very long, ending up as officials in the Administration. But
this same procedure had been followed by Frankfurter with other Presidents; the only difference was that Roosevelt was more responsive to his
suggestions. He had sent bright young men to the Harding, Coolidge, and
Hoover administrations from the Harvard Law School; and he sent more
of them to the Roosevelt Administration because the times were desperate
and trained minds were urgently needed in Washington.

He judged his success as a teacher at the Harvard Law School, to no small degree, by the number of men who went into some form of public service instead of going at once into a big law firm at a large salary. The depression, he believed, imposed an obligation of public service on all who were capable of meeting the highest standards, for otherwise our civilization might collapse or explode into revolution. "In this fourth winter of our discontent," he wrote in 1933, "it is no longer ignorant to believe that this depression has a significance very different from prior economic stresses in our national history. The more things change the more they remain the same is an epigram of comfortable cynicism. There are new periods in history, and we are in the midst of one of them." Acting on this conviction, and knowing more outstanding lawyers than anyone else in the country, he thought it was his duty in a period of profound strain and misery to do what he could to persuade his friends to work for the government. But many people, now as then, are skeptical of this philosophy and see in Frankfurter a secret and unavowed craving for an empire of personal power in Washington. Those who take this view will agree with the New York *American* that Frankfurter was "the Iago of this Administration" — but they will also reject the evidence contained in this correspondence.

It must be emphasized, of course, that this book provides only one important window on the vast and extensive domain of the New Deal, Roosevelt had other problems and other advisers. By the same token, this correspondence shows us only one fragment of Frankfurter's crowded and intense life. He too had other interests and other friends. But no such prolonged and intimate correspondence between a President and a private adviser can be found elsewhere in American politics; and that, for all its limitations, explains its unique and central importance in the history of the New Deal.

Frankfurter wrote his first personal letter to Roosevelt after the First World War on January 4, 1921, welcoming him back to the practice of law in New York. He suspected, however, that Roosevelt would return to public life before very long. "In that mess of a New York," he told Roosevelt, "you are much needed."

When Roosevelt, in the late summer of 1921, was disabled by his attack of infantile paralysis at Campobello and began his heroic struggle for recovery, Frankfurter thought this meant the end of Roosevelt's public career. He had already seen and admired the compassion which Roosevelt always displayed when confronted with evidence of the rough injustices of industrial society, and he applauded the courage with which Roosevelt battled for reform. He looked upon Roosevelt, even at this early stage, as a Democrat who could be a formidable ally of Alfred E. Smith in reforming the legislative practices of New York. Roosevelt could accomplish this task with certain assets denied even to Al Smith, a gallant figure to Frankfurter, who regarded him as the embodiment of many virtues essential to the attainment of clean and progressive government in state legislatures. For Roosevelt had no links with Tammany Hall, and his personal distinction set him apart from other men in public life. The possibility that Roosevelt might be driven from politics by a physical incapacity seemed to Frankfurter an intolerable stroke of malicious fortune. He spoke of it sadly to friends at Harvard, wrote to Al Smith expressing his sorrow over the affliction suffered by his colleague, and watched Roosevelt's painful struggle to regain his strength with sympathy and with admiration.

During a visit to New York, when Roosevelt had begun to make his slow recovery, Frankfurter called on him and, to his surprised delight, found himself talking not to an invalid but to an eager and undaunted politician waiting almost serenely for a return to the surge and thunder of political controversy. This personal experience confirmed Frankfurter's belief that Roosevelt carried heavy armor, and had the staying power necessary for greatness. He had expected to engage in a brief courtesy visit but found himself involved in a serious and wide-ranging political discussion.

The Presidential campaign of 1920, otherwise so disastrous to Frankfurter's hopes, had provided the most dramatic proof that Roosevelt would not shrink from being the advocate of a lost cause, an essential weapon in a reformer's armory. Roosevelt, as the Vice-Presidential candidate on the Cox-Roosevelt ticket, had gone down to a resounding defeat under the avalanche of votes which had swept Warren Harding into office. But Roosevelt had never lacked the courage to praise President Woodrow Wilson, then extremely unpopular, and to support the League of Nations, then a forlorn hope. Frankfurter admired Roosevelt's robust independence, even though he had reservations on Wilson's greatness, and deplored the League's entanglement with the ill-omened Versailles settlement. He liked a political leader who respected his conscience and refused to feed popular prejudices.

It is not surprising that Frankfurter never met Roosevelt during their years at Harvard. The exacting discipline of the Law School absorbed Frankfurter's time and energy, while Roosevelt as an undergraduate glittered in Harvard's exclusive clubs. Mr. Grenville Clark, who had been Frankfurter's classmate at the Law School, introduced the two young lawyers late in 1906 at a luncheon in New York. Roosevelt had gone to the Columbia Law School. Frankfurter recalled years afterwards that in their first conversation he and Roosevelt had exchanged memories of their experiences at the Harvard Law School and the Columbia Law School, and then had gone on to talk about books. He had advised Roosevelt not to mutilate a book by underlining it but to follow instead the example of Macaulay and draw a line in the margin to mark a significant passage. Perhaps the authority of Macaulay was unnecessary, but Roosevelt in later years often drew lines in books and memoranda. They were Franklin and Felix to one another almost from the start — and Roosevelt as President insisted that Frankfurter should call him Frank unless a third person in the room made the formal title unavoidable. In these early New York years they became easy acquaintances rather than intimate friends.

Their acquaintance ripened into friendship in the Wilson Administration when they worked for a time on the same floor of the old State-Army-Navy building, now the Executive Office building next to the White House. Roosevelt, then Assistant Secretary of the Navy, formed the habit of looking in on him for a brief visit. In the spring of 1913 Mr. Arthur Ballantine, a Harvard friend of both Roosevelt and Frankfurter, wrote Roosevelt from Boston that the Navy Department was making a mistake in eliminating two naval branches in the Hull Division since they were being run very efficiently. He also asked Frankfurter, an attorney in the Bureau of Insular Affairs of the War Department, to discuss this problem with Roosevelt. At that time a system for the scientific use of manpower in large industrial concerns, known as the Taylor System, was being actively discussed and Frankfurter was interested in it without being converted to it. Ballantine thought the Taylor System should be examined more sympathetically by the Navy Department. After his conference, Frankfurter, with Roosevelt's approval, sent this telegram to Ballantine:

HAD VERY SATISFACTORY TALK WITH ROOSEVELT. FEAR AS TO LOSS OF GOVERN-
MENT SERVICE OF MEN IN QUESTION ENTIRELY IDLE. DEPARTMENT ANXIOUS
FOR EFFICIENCY AND ECONOMY, AS WELL AS PERMANENTLY SOUND LABOR CON-
DITIONS. OPPOSED TO TAYLOR SYSTEM AS SUCH, BUT EXPERIMENTING IN OTHER
YARDS WITH VIEW TO ARRIVING AT OTHER ADEQUATE SYSTEM.

This was the first of many messages to be prepared by Frankfurter over the next thirty years in consultation with Roosevelt.

In 1914 Frankfurter left Washington to become a professor at the Harvard Law School but he was back in the War Department in 1917. Roosevelt took pride always in the labor relations of the Navy Department, particularly the absence of strikes, and he often discussed these problems with Frankfurter, who had already begun his lifelong absorption with the trade union movement. Frankfurter's duties swiftly broadened and he found a congenial task in becoming Chairman of the War Labor Policies Board, with Roosevelt representing the Navy. In actual fact, Roosevelt attended the full meetings of the Board only rarely, perhaps no more than three times, being usually represented by a proxy. This arrangement was very satisfactory to Frankfurter, who had agreed with Roosevelt that he would bring naval matters and general questions of policy directly to him as the Assistant Secretary of the Navy. Frankfurter estimated that during these crowded months of the First World War, from 1917 on, scarcely a day passed when he did not have a conference with Roosevelt or talk with him on the phone. This was the formative period of their friendship.

While Frankfurter, after the war, concentrating on national affairs, was supporting first the Progressive Movement as led by Senator Robert M. La Follette and later the Presidential ambitions of Governor Alfred E. Smith, the stricken Roosevelt could do nothing more than maintain his tenuous links with Democratic leaders and await a more fortunate hour. But Frankfurter never despaired that his old friend would yet command a vital influence in the development of national policy. His hopes were strengthened when Roosevelt at the 1924 Democratic Convention made his eloquent address in nomination of Al Smith, the speech which lives in political history as the "Happy Warrior" speech. The nomination at that convention, caught in a bruising and interminable stalemate, escaped Al Smith and went instead to Mr. John W. Davis, a barren prize, for the divided and quarrelsome Democrats could not hope to defeat President Coolidge. But the convention had rescued Roosevelt from the shadows and placed him before the nation as a man of destiny. Four years later he would again nominate Al Smith and would himself be elected as Governor of New York while Smith was losing to Herbert Hoover. Profoundly impressed by the buoyant courage and verbal grace of the "Happy Warrior" speech, Frankfurter told Roosevelt that the 1924 convention had produced two speeches worthy of "an enduring place in the treasury of American eloquence" — his own, and Newton D. Baker's impassioned but unavailing defense of Woodrow Wilson's dedication to the League of Nations.

This, then, is the general background to the friendship of Roosevelt and Frankfurter as revealed and expressed in this book. It is a friendship based upon ideas, upon a shared philosophy of public life, upon similar convictions of social justice and world order. For over fifty years a letter addressed "Felix, U.S.A." would inevitably have reached Frankfurter, as the old Boston editor, Mr. Frank Buxton, has so wisely said; and the use of "Franklin" or "Frank," even in the Presidential years, was in obedience to Roosevelt's own wishes. This informality enabled them more easily to make their correspondence an exploration and illumination of men and events deeply set in the history of our times.

Very few letters are given here relating to the period 1928-1932, for Roosevelt as Governor of New York had of necessity to concentrate on state problems. Even during these years, however, Frankfurter and Roosevelt kept their friendship in repair, with Frankfurter often offering advice both on men and on policies. But these years, though important, formed only the prelude to their cooperation during the Presidential years, the substance of this book.

There are many revelations in these pages. It is difficult to believe, for example, that the legend can survive that Roosevelt and Keynes were unable to understand each other, the famous politician being baffled by the famous economist, and the economist being perplexed by the politician. The evidence presented in these letters destroys that legend. The President and John Maynard Keynes, brought together by Frankfurter, liked each other and worked hard to sustain their relationship. Keynes, indeed, could be described by Frankfurter as the most important defender in England of the New Deal; and the ideas and doctrines of Keynes ran through the philosophy of the New Deal.

While Frankfurter was a visiting professor at Oxford in the early stages of the New Deal, he sent to Roosevelt a memorandum prepared by some young Oxford economists, several of them later destined to be among the foremost leaders of economic thought in Britain. This memorandum, which analyzed the major problems of the American economy, was carefully studied by the President and his chief advisers. It is altogether unusual, of course, to find a group of British professors giving advice to an American President. But the depression was a most unusual event, and it prescribed its own duties.

Roosevelt was grateful for any ideas, no matter where they came from, that would put men and women back to work. The British economists knew that their own country and the entire world economy could not recover until the United States had conquered the depression. Hence their eagerness to get their ideas to the President. It should cause regret rather than surprise that intellectual cooperation of this kind between friendly nations should await a war or a depression.

While in England, Frankfurter lectured at the Royal Institute of International Affairs, clashing at question time with George Bernard Shaw in a memorable debate. Harold J. Laski, writing to Mr. Justice Holmes, has described that encounter:

> The main thing of which to tell you this week is Felix's address to the Institute of International Affairs — a body half-eminent, half-expert to which it is far from easy to speak. It was a discussion of the Roosevelt experiment and the Constitution, and I thought it about as masterly a job as I have ever heard. He had great clarity, simplicity, and directness. But, even more, in the discussion, in which there was much criticism and no little hostility, he really scored a triumph. He knew, of course, infinitely more than his critics; but to keep the audience in a mood where its sym-

pathy was always on his side, and to show tact, and charm, and discretion
in keeping the ball rolling always to your opponents' goal isn't easy; but
Felix did it like a great artist and I sat there, as you would have done,
bubbling with pride. It's not everybody who can make an audience feel
that e.g. poor Bernard Shaw is, of course, very bright and brilliant as a rule,
but that this is one of his off-days, and the lecturer, who is a very kind
person, is letting him off nicely because he is an old man. I wish you could
have heard it and rejoiced with me in its consummate mastery and artistic
excellence. . . .

Actually, the debate was more dramatic and Frankfurter's triumph even
more decisive than Laski had indicated. Frankfurter had spent most of his
time explaining the principles of the American federal system, and showing
how the New Deal had to be worked out within these restraints. The discussion was opened by Sir William Beveridge, former head of the London
School of Economics and years later, as author of the Beveridge report on
social security from the cradle to the grave, a principal architect of the
Welfare State. Just back from a visit to America, Beveridge referred in
passing to the difficulty of accommodating the Constitution to Roosevelt's
economic experiments.

Later in the discussion Shaw picked up Beveridge's remark and made it
the text of his own rollicking speech. Shaw ridiculed the American Constitution as a weary anachronism that would have to go if freedom were to
breathe and expand.

As Shaw went on, Frankfurter leaned over to the chairman, Lord Eustace Percy, and whispered, "The Lord hath delivered him into my hands."

Frankfurter began his reply by observing that on a thousand subjects he
would take Shaw's word without further question. But when the matter at
issue involved the American Constitution, he thought he had a right to be
heard. He then scorched and withered Shaw's argument by a devastating
analysis of its deficiencies. He treated Shaw as if he were a not very bright
boy at the Harvard Law School.

When a summary of the meeting was prepared, Shaw had his name covered with a white piece of paper on which was written "a Member." Shaw
knew that his debate with Frankfurter had not been his finest evening.

Perhaps the biggest single revelation in this book is the evidence of
Frankfurter's active and continuous role in the Supreme Court–packing
controversy of 1937. This compels a complete reversal of accepted versions,
including the version of total neutrality which Frankfurter himself had
spread. Roosevelt asked Frankfurter for help, and Frankfurter gave it, copi-
ously and energetically, despite many misgivings about the way the President had conducted his quarrel with the Supreme Court.

When Frankfurter early in 1939 agreed to appear before the Senate Judiciary Committee which was considering his nomination to the Supreme Court, he anticipated some awkward questions about this 1937 controversy. With the help of Mr. Acheson, his counsel at the hearing, he prepared this statement:

> I have not expressed an opinion on the President's Court proposals. I was importuned to state my views by both advocates and opponents. I refrained from doing so. I have found generally that as a law teacher I can be more helpful by drawing people's attention to relevant considerations which should guide them in reaching their own conclusions than by attempting to influence them by mine.
>
> I think in private conversation I went so far as to say that I thought the Court proposals were matters on which men equally patriotic could reasonably differ. In the heat of the controversy I had to remind friends on both sides of the issue that freedom of thought, as Mr. Justice Holmes used to remind us, was freedom not only for the ideas we like but for the ideas which we despise.
>
> I am very glad to be interrogated by this committee on anything which I have said or done, but I feel very strongly the impropriety of a nominee for the Supreme Court expressing thoughts or opinions which are intended to be indicative of his future attitude as a member of the Court or which may even remotely involve questions that may come before the Court.

As the hearing continued, it proved to be unnecessary to use this prepared statement in this form. But it is impossible to reconcile this claim of neutrality with his persistent advice to the President in the Court-packing fight. There is nothing wrong with what Frankfurter did; there is a good deal wrong, however, with being a secret partisan while wearing the disguise of public neutrality. This discrepancy weighed on Frankfurter's conscience, and explains his eagerness to publish the documentary evidence which at last can put his role in its true light.

Frankfurter always believed that William Allen White of the Emporia *Gazette*, perhaps the most beloved editor in America, had correctly found the origins of the Court-packing controversy in Roosevelt's triumphant reelection in 1936 with an overpowering majority. White was convinced that Roosevelt took that election to mean that the Supreme Court had to get out of his way because the people had armed him with their mandate. On October 11, 1937, looking back on the savage months of controversy, White wrote to Frankfurter:

> I have always feared the moron minority in this country more than the predatory group. I realize, of course, that much of the predatory groups is also moronic, but a lot of it is devastatingly acute.
>
> For a long time I have been itching to write to you. I am deeply disturbed by the obvious tendencies of the President. He is taking too many

short cuts, making too many snap judgments, apparently confusing himself with the Party or Group of Parties which won at the election.

As I see it, the November result came through the assemblage of half a dozen minorities, some of which are quite antagonistic to others. But the farmers, the city Tammanies, the yellow dog Democrats, the Negroes, Labor, and the unemployed all bestowed their ballots upon Mr. Roosevelt. There was no definite mandate in the bestowal. He had no right to assume a personal mandate, which would crack up his largest minority, which I feel was the Democratic Party — a vague and somewhat indefinite group, but probably the most tangible element politically in his victory.

If ever a winner in an election should have gone slow, called in counsel, moved only with his official advisers, his Party leaders, that winner was Franklin Roosevelt last fall. He was leader by the Grace of God, and the landslide swept away the wires to God, leaving him two alternatives: To call for help or to follow his hunches. He followed his hunches. It was appalling that he should do so. If he expected to maintain a monolith party in a democracy, he should have reinforced it with steel rods of counsel! Otherwise a monolith party either crumbles, or, if maintained, is not a democratic institution. It is something else again! Dunt esk! It indicated some basic megalomania, some ruthless self-confidence that was not pleasant to observe.

It has been evident for ten or a dozen years that the Supreme Court, not only now with its nine old men, but always, has lagged too far but not so terribly far behind public opinion as manifest in Congressional majorities that have piled up again and again — favoring a good proposition. I have always felt that the Court as an institution should have certain veto powers upon clamor but not upon settled public opinion. I think, as I have indicated, that the Court has not been, in years past, crassly and terribly out of line with public opinion, but it has, as a matter of fact, lagged too tardily several times.

Last November, George Norris was trying to work out some formula to take up the slack, a formula which provided for a Constitutional amendment. In the course of a desultory lifetime correspondence, based upon affectionate admiration, I have written to him and he has written to me about passing events. So it happened that he sent me a rough draft of what was in his mind. I suggested strongly that it should include some provision which would always give the Supreme Court the right to veto Congressional measures abridging or denying the rights set forth in what we know as the Bill of Rights. I believe I wrote to him that the whole amendment should be studied with that end in view: forbidding Congress to pass laws annulling a specific definite provision of the Constitution, and limiting the right of the courts to pass on those laws only which did annul definite Constitutional provisions, and finally *specifying* those rights, privileges and immunities set forth in the so-called Bill of Rights.

I know that George Norris was in hopes to present his plan when the President jumped in with his Court plan, and a lot of men of his liberal character and ideals felt as Norris did. Norris and his kind were well worth respecting. They had been in the fight when he was a young man. To break their heart and drive them away from his leadership was a tragedy. They will come back, but not with the same full faith in his judgment that we had before.

White's letter had a sequel, without precedent or parallel in this entire correspondence. Frankfurter sent it to Roosevelt who returned it without one word of acknowledgment. Never again did anything like that happen.

Sometimes the excitement in these letters comes from the sudden entrance of a name resonant with achievement in the New Deal. That is true of Frankfurter's introduction of Mr. Benjamin V. Cohen and Mr. Thomas G. Corcoran to Roosevelt. For these two men Frankfurter had an affection and admiration that touched the superlative. His ultimate estrangement from Mr. Corcoran caused him the sort of pain which it takes years to ease. I must add, in fairness to Mr. Corcoran, that I have never heard him utter one word of reproach against Frankfurter, even after this harsh and painful severance.

In this whole correspondence, on the political side, few things are more moving than Roosevelt's discovery as early as 1935 that he might be a hero to the majority of Americans but he was a hero doomed to lead a divided party. It is also easy to understand why Frankfurter's eloquent memorandum in 1940 did so much to persuade Roosevelt to run for a Third Term.

The day after Roosevelt was inaugurated as President in 1933 Hitler grasped supreme power in Nazi Germany. Thus began one of the fateful encounters in world history. From the start, Roosevelt saw the menace of dictators to peace and freedom. His task was to remain ahead of American opinion without being repudiated by a lethargic and bewildered public, ready to endure many injustices rather than to drift into war.

In this task of leadership Roosevelt had a faithful and vigilant ally in Frankfurter. From 1934 on, Frankfurter never swerved from the conviction that Churchill was the only European leader who, in cooperation with Roosevelt, could save the world from war. He exalted Churchill even in those lost years when he was being derided and rejected in England. In 1936 Frankfurter ordered an old friend out of his house because he had spoken critically of Churchill. That will indicate the intensity of Frankfurter's opposition to the danger and folly of appeasement. He sent the President a steady stream of articles from the European press to emphasize the dangers to peace, despite the assurances often given by the dictators. He used this material, too voluminous to be reproduced in its entirety here, as a warning to the President to avoid excessive reliance on official soothsayers who predicted that all would yet be well in Europe.

Within this larger tragedy which darkened our age were many personal tragedies of men and women broken by brutal cruelty. It is not surprising that Frankfurter, who had been an indispensable figure in bringing Albert Einstein to this country, should also have been so active in arranging sanctuary for Sigmund Freud in England after the Nazi occupation of Austria. Few men were more diligent than Frankfurter in seeking opportunities to bring scholars and writers out of Nazi Europe into freedom. He helped not only the famous and the heroic. He deserves far more honor for helping the obscure and the frightened.

The publication of this book wipes an undeserved stain from Frankfurter's name and gives us a chance to make some reparation for a wrong done him. During all the years of the Nazi terror, Frankfurter was criticized in Jewish circles for being too timid and hesitant and conventional in his protests against this organized barbarism. He was accused of putting his personal safety ahead of the safety of the Jewish people. He grieved over these attacks; they hurt him deeply; but he offered neither defense nor explanation. We now can see that Frankfurter did not hoard his influence for reasons of personal security. He used it with the President and other senior officials whenever he could redress an injustice or bring hope to those who felt forsaken. This record is impressive. Still more impressive was his constant recognition that Nazi Germany was not only the enemy of the Jewish people but the enemy of world peace. It was on this larger issue, and ultimately on the fate of freedom itself, that Frankfurter concentrated as he presented his case to a deeply responsive Roosevelt.

The evidence provided in these letters shows that he helped Roosevelt to avoid the perils of neutrality and to bring aid to the British people during the Battle of Britain before it was too late. Nor did he forget France. He gave Roosevelt a memorandum from Jean Monnet, one day to be the father of the Common Market, on the dangers to Europe of Hitler's "New Order." He also gave him a top secret report on events inside Vichy France, and on a confidential French mission that led to negotiations with Churchill himself. He warned Roosevelt, weeks before Pearl Harbor, that the Japanese diplomatic mission had not been sent to Washington to negotiate in good faith. He was wrong, completely wrong, about the prospects for a postwar partnership with Russia but he did not stand alone in making that mistake. He made the suggestion that persuaded Roosevelt to place Mr. Henry L. Stimson and Mr. Robert Patterson in charge of the War Department. He played the vital role in the transaction which led to Mr. Justice Byrnes's resignation from the Supreme Court and his appointment as Director of Economic Mobilization. He gave the President an early and prophetic report by Niels Bohr of Denmark on nuclear policy as it would affect the general problems of foreign policy and our relations with Russia.

But he failed where he had every right to succeed. Supported by Mr.

Byrnes, he urged Roosevelt to appoint Judge Learned Hand of New York to the vacant seat on the Supreme Court as the one jurist of this century worthy of being compared with Holmes, Brandeis, and Cardozo. With Roosevelt's approval, Frankfurter had actually drafted the Presidential announcement of the appointment. Then at the last moment Roosevelt balked. He sadly said he could not make the appointment because he was trapped by his own words about the danger of having old men on the Supreme Court. It was a needless anxiety. Judge Hand was not that old and, as his later judicial career showed, he had many years of most distinguished service left in him. Thus is history swayed by a trifle.

*   *   *

A few weeks before his death on February 22, 1965, Mr. Justice Felix Frankfurter told me that he had at last decided what should be done with his correspondence with President Franklin D. Roosevelt. He had intended to go over this correspondence with me letter by letter, explaining the background, weighing the importance of the various issues, evaluating the men who had shaped these decisions. But lack of time, and later a lack of energy, had kept him from this patient reconstruction of the past. As he felt the end coming near, he said he had decided to turn the task over to me, with one word of advice and one word of warning.

The advice was that I was to remember that there was nothing in American history that quite resembled this correspondence between a President and a law professor who later became a member of the Supreme Court of the United States.

In one of his letters Frankfurter told Roosevelt that he regarded himself as an "outside insider"; he knew, in turn, that the President looked on him as a trusted and confidential adviser on a wide range of public issues even though he was not a member of the Administration. Indeed, a cluster of infamous rumors had spread over this relationship for many years, with Frankfurter being denounced as a sinister figure in the shadows, using his personal influence with the President to satisfy purposes remote from the national interest.

These accusations had never bothered Frankfurter during his years of public service, and he ignored them during his brief years of retirement. But he advised me to remember that if ignorant malice required no answer, we all owed an obligation to the truth and should never hesitate to satisfy the claims of history.

He told me that truth alone could disarm these evil whispers. Let the full story be told; let the American people see what he was doing and hear what he was telling the President; let them have all the facts that would enable them to reach their own independent and accurate judgment. He awaited that judgment with equanimity, just as he was sure his reputation would survive it with honor. But to provide a basis for fair judgment, one should publish the correspondence in bulk so that the entire relationship between Roosevelt and Frankfurter could be seen in an intelligent and responsible setting which did justice to both men.

Then, with equal gravity, he turned to the warning.

Frankfurter had hesitated to consent to the publication of these letters because so many of them had been written while he was on the Supreme Court. Should a Justice of the Supreme Court have interested himself so actively in controversial public issues? He always thought this was a fair question to which honorable men could return different answers.

It seemed to Frankfurter that no answer could be either honest or persuasive if it failed to give full weight to these two essential points. In the first place, it should be remembered that Frankfurter never gave advice while on the Court on narrow partisan issues of a political kind that could come before that Court for judgment. The questions which absorbed his mind and conscience were questions which stood above the contentions of normal political strife and touched the national destiny. Secondly, it should also be remembered that less than nine months after Frankfurter had taken his seat on the Supreme Court, war had broken out in Europe; England and France had finally resolved to meet the Nazi challenge; and the United States was moving in troubled neutrality in a world of peril with freedom itself under siege.

Was it possible for normal rules to prevail in such a time of upheaval? Did Frankfurter cease to be a citizen when he became a Justice? Is the Supreme Court a monastery?

Frankfurter answered all these questions in the proud faith that he had acted in the great tradition of American citizenship. He was certain that he had said or done nothing which profaned "the majestic integrity of the Supreme Court" — his own phrase — or disturbed its appointed place in the American system of government. He conceded that some Americans, with all the evidence before them, might wish that he had been a less strenuous adviser of the President in these judicial years. But he hoped that even these critics would recognize that he had asked for no special favors, sought no special privileges, served no selfish causes. His one cause was the public interest, and to be its advocate to the President was his constant purpose.

Perhaps he sometimes made mistakes. He never claimed that no blemishes existed in this record. He mocked people with ambitions to infallibility, and he once said of himself with pride that he was not "that monster of perfection, a man without prejudices." He had his prejudices, ardent and combative, but he made them feel the restraints of the public interest; and especially in the war years, his conduct was a model of responsible citizenship. Surveying the record as a whole, and admitting the occasional blunder and blemish, one feels that few readers of this correspondence will wish to condemn the values and objectives which guided his conduct, even when they cannot always agree with his specific policies.

The fairest and most accurate judgment on the propriety of Frankfurter's advice to Roosevelt while he was on the Supreme Court has been given by Judge Samuel I. Rosenman. Himself a friend of the President, and his most accomplished speech-writer, Judge Rosenman could testify from personal experience on the exact nature and significance of Frankfurter's role. Writing in his admirable book, *Working with Roosevelt*, Judge Rosenman, in a discussion of Roosevelt's decision to accept the nomination in 1940 for a third term, summed up the general Roosevelt-Frankfurter relationship in these words:

> On Thursday, Justice Felix Frankfurter came to swear in Colonel Frank Knox as Secretary of the Navy. We talked at length then and again the next day, and he mentioned some points he thought the President ought to make in his acceptance speech.
>
> Frankfurter was a reliable source of ideas and language. Before he was appointed to the Supreme Court, Corcoran, Cohen and I used to consult him frequently on all kinds of matters, and I am told that Moley did also. After he became a member of the Bench his activities were necessarily circumscribed, and no one who knew him was left in doubt about his scrupulous observance of the restrictions of the Supreme Court Bench. But he continued to be very helpful to the President — and also to Sherwood and me — in many ways. Frequently, while a speech was in the discussion stage, we would drive out to his home in Georgetown to exchange ideas about what it should contain. Our sessions often lasted until the early hours of the morning, and they were always fruitful. Occasionally, when speeches were in the writing stage, we sent him drafts for suggestion and criticism.
>
> We were always careful — as was the President — never to discuss with him anything that might later embarrass him in his judicial capacity. I never knew him to offer any advice — or to be consulted — on any political question or on any matter that might possibly come before him later for judicial review.

One unforgettable story will reveal the extent to which Frankfurter refused to use his friendship with Roosevelt for his own benefit.

Frankfurter almost never talked of his family or his relatives. There were two exceptions: his mother and a cherished uncle who was head of the National Library in Vienna. Praise of his mother never ceased on his lips. Whenever he met an eminent man or someone who had filled the world with his deeds, he always remarked, with great seriousness, "He must have had a mother." Only one scale lower in his ardent affection was his favorite uncle. Yet he made no appeal for help to President Roosevelt when the

Nazis, after their occupation of Austria, forced his uncle, then an extremely old man, into a concentration camp. Instead, he asked Lady Astor in London to intervene with her German friends and plead for mercy. Lady Astor, with characteristic kindness and courage, told the German Ambassador what she thought of a nation which persecuted unoffending and aged scholars. Frankfurter's uncle finally was released from the concentration camp, but the agony of his confinement never left him, and brought him more swiftly to the grave.

Roosevelt heard of this entire episode only after the uncle had died when he read an obituary notice in the American press. He rebuked Frankfurter for refusing to ask his own American government for help. But Frankfurter with shy pride was always glad that he had not bothered Roosevelt with his personal grief.

In 1950, some months after his correspondence with Mr. Schlesinger and Mr. Bundy, by arrangement with the Franklin D. Roosevelt Library at Hyde Park, Frankfurter had sealed his correspondence with Roosevelt and had forbidden scholars and research workers to have access to these documents without his knowledge and consent. He had originally intended to be rather generous in granting this permission to scholars interested in one particular subject but something happened in 1952 which made him change his mind. Once his suspicions had become alert, he could not put off the conviction that the correspondence, in the wrong hands, would be used to discredit him and cheapen the President. The correspondence therefore remained completely sealed until he turned it over to me.

What had happened that made him so anxious to protect the President from unfair attack?

On January 10, 1952, Frankfurter wrote to Mrs. Frida Laski, the widow of Harold J. Laski, about the biography of Laski then being written by Mr. Kingsley Martin. He was particularly concerned about the use that might be made of Laski's correspondence with Roosevelt. Even without having seen this correspondence, he had no objection to its publication, provided it reached the public in full. He had agreed with Mr. Mark De Wolfe Howe of the Harvard Law School that there should be no editing out in the Holmes-Laski correspondence, although there might be some people, like Mr. Roscoe Pound, the former dean of the Law School, who might feel hurt by an occasional expression. But Frankfurter thought totally different influences had to be considered where Roosevelt was concerned.

He told Mrs. Laski that she would be surprised and distressed by the amount of "distortion and misrepresentation and plain lying" being turned against Roosevelt's reputation. Laski would have shrunk in horror from being made an unwitting instrument in furthering this campaign of vilification. Kingsley Martin could not possibly know the base uses to which the Roosevelt-Laski letters would be put "in the passionate and poisonous atmosphere" of the 1952 Presidential campaign.

Frankfurter was troubled that Roosevelt's patriotism and loyalty would be challenged for partisan reasons in an election campaign, once it was discovered that Roosevelt had enjoyed a long political correspondence with Laski, one of the acknowledged leaders of Socialist thought and a former chairman of the British Labour party. He therefore asked Mrs. Laski and Mr. Martin to consult him before they decided what letters they would use. His advice was taken, and the material was used with dignity and responsibility.

There are letters in this book which show that Roosevelt and Frankfurter never hesitated to disagree with Laski's Socialism, though Roosevelt admired Laski and Frankfurter loved him. But if Laski could get Roosevelt into trouble, what about Frankfurter?

The legend persisted, over the years, that Frankfurter was a dangerous radical in politics. Actually, he was not even a Democrat. Roosevelt, with great precision and affectionate banter, had called him "an independent pig." His first leader was President Theodore Roosevelt, a Republican. Mr. Henry L. Stimson, another Republican, remained forever the model of the courageous and responsible citizen in action. He had supported Robert M. La Follette as leader of the Progressive Movement. He gave to Al Smith the generous admiration which he had never been able to give to President Wilson. And his friendship with Franklin D. Roosevelt had known every triumph, had suffered no intermission, had prevailed over every ordeal, and was stronger at the end than at the beginning. Naturally he hesitated to expose to the public a book which revealed his deepest private loyalties as well as his detailed views on public questions; but his obligation to history prevailed with him, and finally conquered all doubts.

In talking with me about this book, Frankfurter insisted that I must explain Mr. Justice Brandeis's relationship to President Roosevelt and to the New Deal. This is indeed one of the most important points to emerge from this correspondence.

Most people, including attentive students of the Supreme Court, will be surprised by the persistent and unbroken involvement of Justice Brandeis in the New Deal. For Brandeis had an austere, self-effacing, and monastic philosophy of the freedom permitted him as a member of the Supreme Court. He sometimes went to the White House to see the President, beginning in 1917 with the Balfour Declaration, on matters affecting the future of the Zionist Movement. Otherwise he was silent. He gave no interviews. He wrote no articles. He made no speeches. Yet the originating and liberating mind of Brandeis permeated Washington with its influence. To his apartment came many of the most gifted men and women in the Administration for counsel and inspiration.

All this has long been known. Mr. Schlesinger, in his indispensable three books on the Age of Roosevelt, carried the analysis of Brandeis's influence to a new and unexpected height by depicting him as the central intellectual force behind the second New Deal. Mr. Schlesinger argued that the first New Deal, begun in 1933, had tried to use political power to control and direct the concentrations of economic power for the public good. The second New Deal, starting in 1935, placed more emphasis on a competitive society in an expanding economy than on a national plan for an organic economy. The aims and human values remained constant; but the techniques were different.

Mr. Schlesinger saw the differences between 1933 and 1935 in the men who molded policies for the President. He listed the main figures of the first New Deal as Raymond Moley, Rex Tugwell, Adolf Berle, Donald Richberg, General Hugh Johnson. The leading figures of the second New Deal were Frankfurter, Thomas Corcoran, Ben Cohen, James M. Landis, Marriner Eccles, William O. Douglas, Leon Henderson, and Lauchlin Currie. He said the shift in TVA from Arthur Morgan, the biographer of Edward Bellamy, to David Lilienthal, the protégé of Frankfurter, was symptomatic. Summing up, Mr. Schlesinger concluded that "the second New Deal was eventually a coalition between lawyers in the school of Brandeis and economists in the school of Keynes."

Despite the scholarship and eloquence with which Mr. Schlesinger presented this interpretation, Frankfurter never accepted it. He thought it was at once too tidy and logical an explanation of decisions that often were extorted by the pressure of a relentless crisis. But he never questioned the importance of Mr. Schlesinger's interpretation. He knew that it had permeated a large part of the scholarly writing of our time on the problems and achievements of Roosevelt's four terms.

In view of these facts, I think it will be universally conceded that Mr. Schlesinger has acted in the highest tradition of responsible scholarship in asking me to use the following letter from Frankfurter to him, even though it challenges and repudiates a thesis central to his entire study of Roosevelt. The letter, dated June 18, 1963, was written to Mr. Schlesinger after a lunch at the White House with President Kennedy and reads as follows:

Dear Arthur:

After leaving the White House on Monday, which was indeed an extremely pleasant occasion, and the President could not have been more gracious and agreeable, I reflected on the inadequacies of the answer I made to his question as to why I disagreed with your view on the Roosevelt

Administration in the 30s, and more particularly that there were two New Deals. I did not tell him my basic reason for disagreement. It is that from your several references to your private interviews with Thomas G. Corcoran I gathered they had a considerable influence on the interpretation you give in your book about the two New Deals, for Tommy is a very persuasive raconteur.

I did not say what I wanted to say, for I did not think the occasion was an appropriate time for what might have turned into an argumentative discussion, especially since my doctor has restricted my engaging in controversial talk. But I feel free, indeed feel compelled, by my view of things to tell you that Tommy Corcoran's fairy tales are not a good source for historical writing. I so characterize his talks because by temperament he is a romantic and uncritical spinner of yarns. I say this after much experience with him and I am confident that Dean Acheson would not disagree in this estimate of Corcoran. As I have already indicated, he is a very persuasive talker and raconteur.

When you asked me if I would read the manuscript of your book since I am involved in much of it, it was for that reason that I felt compelled to decline to read it, because I have strong views that the undertow of personal interest disables a man to sit in disinterested judgment upon himself.

There are a few more things to be said. I must reject your assumption that there was a real clash of views between Moley-Tugwell and F.F.-Brandeis. This assumes that the respective parties had coherent and systematic views on some of the problems that are involved in Roosevelt's policies.

You are also wrong in assuming that I saw completely eye to eye with Brandeis on socio-economic matters, any more than it is true that I was an echo of his outlook on the law, particularly constitutional law. Of course there is no doubt that Brandeis had a very important influence on me, particularly in his austere moral views, in matters where moral issues do not lie on the surface, for everybody, as for instance in the Profumo affair. A good illustration of Brandeis's moral austerity and the expression he gave to his moral views was his vigorous protest to President Lowell against the continued retention in Harvard's portfolio of New Haven securities after evidence established financial misconduct by the New Haven.

As for myself, undoubtedly both Holmes and Brandeis influenced me in my constitutional outlook, but both of them derived theirs from the same source from which I derived mine, namely, Professor James Bradley Thayer, with whom both had personal relations but whose views influenced me only through his writings, as was indirectly true of the man who taught me constitutional law at Harvard Law School, namely, Professor Wambaugh, a pupil of Thayer. Moreover, Thayer's views were in the air at the Law School while I was there and I undoubtedly imbibed that atmosphere.

As for my general outlook on matters sociological and economic, I am by temperament not an ideologue but a stark empiricist.

One of these days, when my doctor's orders make it free for me to see you, I should like to tell you the extent to which Brandeis disciplined himself to carry out in his own conduct of life the definition I gave the President and you of what he thought judgment involved: 'the almost instinctive correlation of a thousand imponderables.' I should like to tell you how he safeguarded and disciplined himself to make sure that he penetrated the imponderables on matters that called for his judgment when the imponderables did not lie on the surface. I think I could interest you by what I would tell you.

I am so grateful to you for seeing to it that I had a word with your father on Monday and I am also indebted to you for the genuine pleasure which I derived from my visit to the White House.

With warm regards to you and affectionate regards to your Marion,

Very sincerely yours,

Felix Frankfurter

That does not end the story. When I asked Frankfurter about this letter, he said it was very important as an expression of his views on the meaning of the New Deal. Then, in a spirit of historical candor, and with a respect for scholarship equal to Mr. Schlesinger's own high standards, he directed my attention to an exchange of letters with Mr. Raymond Moley. The exchange took place more than a year before the date assigned by Mr. Schlesinger to the coming of the second New Deal.

Frankfurter had written to Mr. Moley to protest, with the firmness of affectionate friendship, against the repeated stories reaching him that he was the voice of Brandeis and had filled the Administration with his disciples. Mr. Moley replied, with equal friendship but with even more firmness, that it was possible for Frankfurter to refuse to consider himself as the master but it was quite impossible to make these men refuse to regard themselves as his disciples. Then, on the question of Brandeis's influence, Mr. Moley went on to say that he would have to repudiate the testimony of his own eyes and ears if he failed to emphasize that he had heard Frankfurter quote Brandeis's opinions as the ultimate authority at conferences too numerous for cataloging.

My own judgment is that Brandeis's influence was by no means as starkly doctrinaire as Mr. Schlesinger suggests but it began earlier and lasted longer. It must be added with the utmost emphasis that there is nothing in the unpublished record that casts the slightest stain or discredit on Brandeis's place among the supreme jurists in our history. He often as a Justice voted against New Deal legislation which had been discussed with him while it was being formulated. Frankfurter did directly, mainly in a time of war, what Brandeis did indirectly, in a time of peace. This point, crucial to our understanding of the New Deal, will be discussed with documentary evidence in my forthcoming biography of Frankfurter. Meanwhile the important point for us to remember, as we think of his letters to Mr. Schlesinger and Mr. Moley, is that Frankfurter is not trying to make a case for himself or to score debater's points. He is content to let the facts judge him. He has nothing to hide, nothing to withhold. That is precisely the spirit in which he wished this entire correspondence with Roosevelt to be judged.

As one would expect, the letters from Frankfurter are far more numerous. He often asked Roosevelt not to reply. The business of many letters would be taken care of by Roosevelt in a long telephone call or by a conference in the White House. Roosevelt did not like to pour out his mind on paper. The liberating phrase rarely came to him in a letter though it often gleamed in a speech.

All the letters by Frankfurter and Roosevelt given here are given as written. A volume of equal size could be published by using every Frankfurter letter on the drafts of legislation, his reports on officials to be given jobs in the Administration, and his enclosures dealing with foreign policy. But nothing would be gained by this endless accumulation of detail. It would merely repeat the themes on which we have ample evidence now. Nothing essential has been omitted. Nothing has been left out to protect anyone or to avoid controversy.

Frankfurter certainly was never reticent of praise when he wrote to Roosevelt. It may even be said that he was an artist in adulation; and sometimes, forgetting the artistry, he laid on flattery with a trowel. Sometimes the flattery, it must be admitted, may seem excessive and repugnant. It would have been better for Frankfurter's reputation if he had indulged in less of it. But before we stress this charge we must remember the relationship between these two men. Frankfurter never wavered in his faith that Roosevelt ranked with Washington and Lincoln. Years after Roosevelt's death, Frankfurter's eyes would sometimes fill with tears of affection and admiration as he described Roosevelt's greatness. These letters of praise were the ones which Roosevelt was swift to answer. He could have stopped such letters with one gesture of disapproval, one statement that he did not like them. Instead, he welcomed and encouraged them over a long span of years and to the very end. Roosevelt needed this praise and Frankfurter thought he deserved it. That is their defense, if any defense is needed.

Fluent and accomplished as a letter-writer, Frankfurter shrank from a letter of condolence to Mrs. Roosevelt and the children. Though he sent a broken note, he expressed his grief during a visit to the bereaved family. He himself received nearly five hundred messages of condolence, for people knew he too had been stricken and bereaved. In a special place of honor, to the last hour, he kept what his old friend Admiral Samuel Eliot Morison, the famous historian, had written near Okinawa on April 13, 1945, the day after Roosevelt's death. Entitled simply "Franklin Delano Roosevelt, 1882-1945," Morison's tribute and assessment read as follows:

I have lost one whom I had come to regard as a dear personal friend. The Navy has lost its greatest champion. The United States has lost a statesman who restored her economy and her self-confidence, warned and prepared her against the greatest menace to her existence, and led her through infinite trials and tribulations to the very eve of victory. The world has lost the one man since the Emperor Augustus who had a fair chance of giving it another *Pax Romana*.

He was a statesman partly in the Jeffersonian, partly the Cromwellian tradition; a background of democratic principle yet a great opportunist. A flair for the possible and attainable, rather than, like Wilson, for the ideal. An aristocrat by breeding, birth and training, he devoted his gifts and attainments to the commonwealth. A democrat in that he had no class or race prejudice, and liked all kinds of people. A patriot so wise that he could look ahead beyond narrow nationalism and see that America's fate was bound up with the world. A great capacity to take advice; equally good as a listener and a talker. I have sometimes regretted his vindictiveness against political and personal opponents; but he met opposition more often with laughter and ridicule than by anger. Nor did he raise up anyone capable of succeeding him worthily. A tremendous courage and energy that triumphed over crippling disease enabled him to carry for twelve years the greatest burden any statesman in history has been called upon to bear. Always loyal to Church, country, family, friends, state, college, club. Of broader vision than Churchill, though not so eloquent; a greater power than Stalin, though not so ruthless, and not like him independent of criticism and above representative government. The constitutional framework within which he had to operate was often irksome to him, as to other strong men, but he accepted its limitations; and if the representative part of the federal system was less powerful at his death than at his accession, the factiousness and incompetence of legislators were the cause, not he. In the crises of his administration he realized that the attitude "it can't be done" was a menace to the constitution; he always found a way, and thus increased the prestige of the constitution among average citizens.

He lacked Lincoln's humility but he was not an egotist like Wilson, still less a megalomaniac like Napoleon; greater than either and the author of more enduring good to humanity than any statesman since Lincoln. Like most great men he was perfectly conscious of his own powers and eager to exercise them. Well read and cultured in the deepest sense, with an excellent memory and a capacity for reflecting on what he read. And he always retained a boyish zest for life, appetite for knowledge, capacity for friendship, love of adventure. He lived joyously and dangerously, and died at the summit of achievement.

Grant him O Lord eternal peace, let everlasting light shine upon him.

A day or two after the death of Mrs. Roosevelt in 1964, Mr. Phil Elman was visiting the sick and disabled Frankfurter. As he lay in bed, Frankfurter slowly and solemnly spoke these words as if bidding farewell to Mrs. Roosevelt:

> Dear Eleanor, your life was full of beauty and achievement. In the words of Milton, there should be no tears, no wailing, for your life was not wasted. You were a vital part of Franklin's life, and he was a vital part of my life, and when you died, part of me died with you.

Professor to Governor

1928 – 1932

1928

April 13 — Frank Kellogg, Secretary of State, prepares plan to outlaw war as an instrument of national policy.

April 21 — Aristide Briand, for the French government, outlines his proposal for the renunciation of war.

August 27 — Kellogg-Briand Pact signed in Paris.

October 1 — The first Five Year Plan begins in the Soviet Union.

November 6 — Herbert Hoover elected President with 21,392,190 votes to Al Smith's 15,016,443.

1929

January 19 — Appointment of committee headed by Owen D. Young to review the reparations problem.

February 11 — Lateran treaties concluded with the Papacy, making Vatican City an independent state.

March 4 — Herbert Hoover inaugurated.

May 30 — The Labour party wins the British general election, with Ramsay MacDonald becoming the Prime Minister.

August 6-13 — Hague conference on the Young plan. Germany's acceptance of this plan led to the evacuation of the Rhineland by French troops.

September 28 — November 1 — Prime Minister Ramsay MacDonald visits United States and Canada.

October 23-24 — Wall Street crash begins as the grim prelude to the Great Depression.

1930

January 21 — April 22 — London Naval Conference at which Great Britain, United States, France, Italy, and Japan agree to regulate submarine warfare and limit the size and firing power of submarines.

January 28 — Primo de Rivera, the strong man of Spain, resigns.

February 6 — Mussolini signs a treaty of friendship with Austria.

June 10   *The Simon report on India, a landmark on India's road to independence, but condemned by Gandhi as tardy and inadequate.*

June 17   *President Hoover signs the Smoot-Hawley tariff act despite the protests of one thousand American economists that it will produce a dangerous experiment in economic nationalism.*

September 14   *The German election suddenly raises Hitler's Nazi party to the status of a major political force. Hitler now has 107 seats in the Reichstag as against his previous 12 seats.*

November 6 —
December 9   *The Preparatory Commission on Disarmament holds its final meetings.*

December 12   *Allied troops evacuate the Saar.*

1931

May 4   *Failure of leading Austrian banks creates financial crisis in Central Europe.*

June 20   *President Hoover proposes a moratorium of one year on all intergovernmental debts, including reparations and war debts.*

August 24   *Resignation of Labour government in London over gathering financial crisis.*

August 25 —
October 27   *National coalition government formed in Britain. The bulk of the Labour party did not follow MacDonald into the coalition government but he remained as Prime Minister.*

September 18   *Japan invades Manchuria.*

September 21   *Bank of England quits the gold standard.*

1932

January 4   *Japan controls South Manchuria.*

January 7   *Henry L. Stimson, Secretary of State, declares that the United States "will not recognize any situation, treaty, or agreement which may be brought about by means contrary to the covenants and obligations of the Pact of Paris." This declaration, known as the Stimson doctrine, was made in protest against Japan's occupation of Manchuria.*

January 29   *Shanghai is attacked by Japan.*

February 2   *Reconstruction Finance Corporation established. At Geneva, sixty nations gather for World Disarmament Conference.*

March 3   *Chinese forces driven from Shanghai by Japanese attacks.*

March 13   *In the German presidential election, out of a total vote of 37,660,000, Von Hindenburg receives 18,662,000, and Adolf Hitler, the runner-up in a four-way contest, 11,328,000.*

March 16   *Prime Minister Ramsay MacDonald, head of Britain's national coalition government, proposes a reduction in the national armies of Europe. Japan withdraws her troops from Shanghai after mediation by the League of Nations.*

June 16   *Lausanne Conference opens for the revision of the Young plan for reparations payments. This is the first international economic conference since the crash of 1929.*

July 21   *Imperial Economic Conference begins in Ottawa and raises tariffs against countries outside the British Empire.*

September 19   *Russia joins the League of Nations.*

October 4   *The Lytton report, on behalf of the League of Nations, condemns Japan's aggression in Manchuria but tempers this criticism by proposing that Japan be granted certain preferred rights in an autonomous Manchuria. Japan serves notice of her withdrawal from the League of Nations.*

November 8   *Franklin D. Roosevelt elected President with 27,831,857 votes to Herbert Hoover's 15,761,841.*

December 19   *Japan denounces the naval agreements signed at the disarmament conferences of 1922 and 1930.*

D URING *the years of Roosevelt's Governorship in New York, Frankfurter was in rather frequent touch with him, by phone or letter,
on several recurrent issues. The most important of these was public power. We have forgotten the intense battles fought over this issue because the campaign for public power has ceased to be a hot one. But at
this time power was the pivot of the political debate. For their stand on this
issue largely determined whether political leaders would support public regulation of all utilities or would leave them to be owned and controlled by
private financial groups whose wealth exceeded their social conscience.
That is the way Roosevelt and Frankfurter both saw the problem. Frankfurter was convinced that what happened in the public power controversy
in New York would influence the entire nation. So it turned out to be, for
Roosevelt, with Frankfurter playing an active but minor role, defined the
issues in a way which established the differences on power policy not only
with the Republican party in New York but with the Hoover Administration in Washington. It was this preliminary battle which prepared Roosevelt for his later campaign in support of Senator George Norris's effort to
establish the Tennessee Valley Authority.*

*Allied with the struggle over public power was the continuing dispute
over the place of public utilities in the American economy. The legal problems associated with public utilities absorbed a good deal of Frankfurter's
time at the Harvard Law School, and he placed his technical knowledge at
Roosevelt's service. Serious scandals in the management of utilities, in the
Samuel Insull empire and elsewhere, had shown the sinister connection
between political corruption and high rates. Thus what would otherwise
have been a dull and technical controversy suddenly was charged with
moral significance. By speech and magazine articles Roosevelt, with Frankfurter's constant encouragement and occasional help, staked out his own
position in the Democratic party as an advocate of increased public control
of utilities.*

*A third issue which united the two men was a shared interest in obtain-
ing far more stringent regulations over the sale of securities and the general*

management of the stock market to ensure greater protection for the public interest. Their experiences in this early campaign helped them to work together in effortless harmony in the first days of the New Deal when the regulation of the securities market assumed critical importance.

A fourth issue was the general question of reform — including reforms in prison administration, reforms in the methods of judicial appointments, and reforms in civil service administration. Frankfurter declined to serve on various commissions on the ground that his duties at the Harvard Law School were too exacting for him to accept an additional formal assignment; but he agreed to act as an informal adviser, to recommend various people to Governor Roosevelt, and to write an occasional memorandum for him.

A fifth issue concerned the scandals of Mayor Walker's administration. It was Frankfurter who worked out for Roosevelt the legal formula under which Mayor Walker and other officials were required to explain and justify the sources of their wealth, which was out of all proportion to their official salaries. Under this formula, it was not necessary to prove actual corruption, something which might be difficult to establish in a court of law. It was enough, in an inquiry conducted by Governor Roosevelt himself, to create a presumption of guilt unless the Mayor could give frank and adequate answers. The formula was justified by success. For Roosevelt's cross-examination forced Mayor Walker to resign.

The sixth and greatest issue which bound the two men in a working partnership was the tragic suffering caused by the depression and their conviction that the Hoover Administration was debarred, by its economic and political philosophy, from doing anything effective about it. But one must not exaggerate Roosevelt's role, at this stage of his career. He was still a Governor, absorbed with the problems of New York, including the problems of relief for the unemployed. His best way to show the difference between his philosophy and Mr. Hoover's philosophy was by pointing to what was being done in Albany and was not being done in Washington. This primarily affected problems of administration and policy inside New York, thus reducing the scope and effectiveness of Frankfurter's assistance.

Moreover, Governor Roosevelt still had to be nominated for the Presidency. In preparation for this national campaign, Roosevelt formed his Brain Trust, drawn largely from Columbia University and organized by Mr. Raymond Moley. The Brain Trust consulted Frankfurter on occasion but it had plenty of ideas of its own. Frankfurter was slightly more active during the Presidential campaign itself.

In this book many letters and memoranda relating to this period have been omitted because they deal with what are now dead issues or with personalities of no living significance. Something had to be eliminated to keep the volume within tolerable limits, and the best place to make these omissions seemed to be here. The important point that emerges from the 1928-1933 period is that Roosevelt and Frankfurter, friends for a long time, had established an easy partnership on public issues that enabled them to work far more closely together once Roosevelt took office as President and faced national and international problems on which Frankfurter's advice could be helpful and sometimes indispensable.

Two examples will indicate the kind of relationship they had formed.

Just before he took the oath of office on March 4, 1933, Roosevelt wrote:

> *The quality of National politics, viewed as a science which is capable of affecting for the better the lives of the average man and woman in America, is the concern of National leadership — particularly in such years as these when the hand of discouragement has fallen upon us, when it seems that things are in a rut, fixed, settled, that the world has grown old and tired and very much out of joint. That is the mood of depression, of dire and weary depression which, if the quality of our political leadership is right, should vanish so utterly that it will be difficult to reconstruct the mood. . . .*
>
> *Yet wild radicalism has made few converts, and the greatest tribute I can pay my countrymen is that in these days of crushing want, there persists an orderly and hopeful spirit on the part of the millions of our people who have suffered so much. To fail to offer them a new chance is not only to betray their hopes but to misunderstand their patience.*

Frankfurter had these words framed and kept them on his desk until he left late in 1933 for his academic year in England at Oxford. He used to tell friends and visitors that Roosevelt's words gave a "faultless definition" of his own philosophy and hopes.

The second episode shows that Roosevelt and Frankfurter could meet on the intimate questions of taste in literature as well as on the exacting issues of public policy.

On February 15, 1929, H. M. Tomlinson, the British essayist and novelist, delivered a lecture on "War Books" at Manchester University. The next year the lecture was printed in this country in an edition limited to 215 copies. Frankfurter read with dismay Tomlinson's denunciation of Churchill's The War Crisis *as a supremely bad book on the 1914-1918 war. For Frankfurter could not remember the time when he had not admired Churchill as a statesman and as a writer. But he also, quite rightly, regarded Tomlinson as a master of prose. What was he to do? He had often urged Roosevelt to read Churchill, and now he went to him for comfort and advice. He took the book with him on an early visit to Roosevelt and they discussed at length this offending passage from Tomlinson's criticism:*

Is wisdom there? It looks to me as though there were a lack of control, which is not wise. Is light there? Yes, of a kind — the kind which comes in chromatic beams from the wings to give an object on the stage an appearance it does not own. It is, for me, eloquence in an Eton collar on Speech Day. . . . If we think we ought to be eloquent because the subject deserves it, and try to be, then we are not. The test for a book about the war is the same as that for any other sort of book. . . . For the truth is simple. It is of the heart; the mind will give it form, but had better not attempt to improve too much the simple nature of the truth. From the desire to heighten and improve it came the books about the war which we will not read now, though once we thought they were wonderful. It is a sad mistake to suppose you may reproduce the sound of drum-fire by words resembling the roll of drums.

According to Frankfurter's recollection, he and Roosevelt gave Churchill something better than a suspended sentence as a writer. In view of their later friendship and partnership, which probably saved the freedom of mankind, it is not without interest to find Roosevelt in 1930 showing this concern with Churchill's style. When Evelyn Waugh wrote his scornful dismissal of Churchill's prose as "mock-gothic," Frankfurter writhed as if in pain; but Roosevelt was no longer here to comfort him.

The correspondence of these early years, though abbreviated, is given in sufficient volume to show the flowering of the Roosevelt-Frankfurter relationship. Perhaps the best measure of their intimacy is provided by the fact that Roosevelt in 1932 interrupted his flight to the Democratic National Convention in Chicago, where he was to receive the Presidential nomination, so that he could have a long telephone conversation with Frankfurter, who had been given a judicial appointment in Massachusetts by Governor Ely. This appointment was later declined.

Cambridge, Mass., October 9, 1928

My dear Franklin Roosevelt —

Your nomination is, of course, occasion for national rejoicing. But I am still a New Yorker in spirit and so find special reasons for self-satisfaction. It gives one new strength when such pure-mindedness and real public zeal find popular acclaim. As a Jew I am particularly happy that your nomination prevented the New York contest from degenerating into an unworthy competition for the "Jewish vote." Now all good and wise citizens ought to be drawn to your standard.

With all good wishes,

Very sincerely,

FELIX FRANKFURTER

Roosevelt had been nominated as the Democratic candidate for the Governorship of New York. Frankfurter had spent his boyhood and youth and early working years in New York. Roosevelt carried New York against Albert Ottinger while Alfred E. Smith was losing that state to Herbert Hoover in the 1928 Presidential campaign.

Cambridge, Mass., November 8, 1928

Dear Franklin:

Your victory is a great source of consolation and hope. To have the direction of New York affairs in your hands in immediate succession to Smith assures such momentum to those standards of government which Smith and you typify as to secure for them almost the force of a tradition. For you have, as Smith has, the conception of government which seems to me indispensable to the vitality of a democratic government, namely, the realization that the processes of government are essentially educational processes. And so I shall continue to be heartened by what will come out of Albany. I know you will satisfy my own loyalty as a New Yorker, for spiritually I continue to feel that the Governor of New York is my Governor.

With the deepest good wishes for your continued strength, and with congratulations and regards to your wife,

Very sincerely yours,
FELIX FRANKFURTER

Cambridge, Mass., November 21, 1928

Dear Franklin:

I wonder if, when you come North, you could conveniently stop off at Washington for a talk with Mr. Justice Brandeis. On two questions of considerable public importance, he has suggestions which you will want to consider very early at Albany, and perhaps even in part deal with in your first message to the legislature. If talking with him is not feasible, I shall be glad on your return to New York to come down and see you and put the matters he has in mind to you. Of course, I think it would be much better if he could put his views to you directly, but that may not be workable. If so, I am at your disposal.

Faithfully yours,
F.F.

Brandeis was eager to give Roosevelt his views on public utilities and on judicial reform. This is the first reference in the correspondence to the influence of Brandeis, an influence almost always invisible, but pervasive and important. He is often referred to as Isaiah in tribute to his moral force.

Warm Springs, Ga., November 24, 1928

Dear Felix: —

I did think of the possibility of stopping in Washington on my way North, about December tenth, but I have given up the idea, as it would be construed as some kind of a bid for national leadership and I am stepping on any such idea with both feet.

I shall be in New York practically all of the time between December twelfth and December twenty-first, and am keen to have a good long talk with you. Do run down at that time and, of course, if Mr. Justice Brandeis goes back to Boston for the Christmas season, I should love to see him on his way through New York.

As you know, I put into my campaign a very definite plea for judicial reform and that is a subject on which I need much help!

Always sincerely,
F.D.R.

In response to growing criticisms of the Public Service Commission, the New York legislature, with its Republican majority, had reluctantly agreed to the appointment of a nine-member investigating commission. The composition of the commission made certain that the majority report would favor existing practices, for six members were Republicans, the other three being appointed by Governor Roosevelt. Since he could expect nothing more than a minority report to present his views, he was determined that his three appointees would be men of such stature that their recommendations and criticisms would command great support. He obtained men of this caliber by appointing Frank P. Walsh, later to be chairman of the New York Power Authority; Professor James C. Bonbright of Columbia University; and Donald C. Adie, who served as secretary to the commission. Frankfurter had written to Roosevelt: "By the way, if you are thinking of a disinterested financial man for your commission of utilities inquiry, I hope you will canvass the qualities of Professor James Bonbright of Columbia. I don't know anybody, certainly in New York, who has a more penetrating understanding of the fundamental problems relating to utilities and utilities regulation, nor one who would bring a more disinterested expert attitude to bear on these problems." During the writing of their minority report, the three men consulted frequently with Frankfurter.

Two separate developments had raised the questions of power development and utilities regulation to critical importance in New York. In the first place, the Public Service Commission, under the chairmanship of William A. Prendergast, consistently handed down rulings favorable to the utilities, both on rates and on profits. The central issue concerned profits. Both Roosevelt and Frankfurter argued in favor of the principle that all profits should be regulated by a "reasonable return" on the original investment. Chairman Prendergast, sheltering behind a succession of court opinions, argued that the real principle should be that profits should reflect "present-day" values. The difference between these two principles could be measured in many millions of dollars, and in important variations of rates to the consumer.

The second development was an organized effort by the financial interests controlled by J. P. Morgan and Andrew W. Mellon to dominate the development of New York's power resources. This threat gave Roosevelt the chance to portray the issue as a clash between public and private power, and to enlist the attention of the nation in the struggle in New York.

Roosevelt did not win the battle for public control of utilities at one stroke, but he gained most of his objectives gradually. Even a hostile and torpid legislature could no longer tolerate the abuses which had stirred up such a ferment of criticism, and Roosevelt kept up a steady campaign for more reform, prodding the legislature to be more active. More important still, he was able to infuse the Public Service Commission and the New York Power Authority with a new respect for the public interest by his own appointments. Thus he achieved the substance of his program, though falling short of all his hopes, by a characteristic fusion of public education and executive action — a technique to become very familiar during his years in the White House.

Albany, N.Y., July 5, 1929

Dear Felix: —

Our Public Service Investigations Committee met yesterday in Albany. As you know, the six Republican members are three Senators and three Assemblymen — all of them not merely conservative but definitely reactionary. All that my three appointees can do is to make the scope of the investigation as broad and as fundamental as possible and see to it that the progressive side of the case obtains adequate publicity.

I asked Walsh to get in touch with you in order to obtain full information about what is going on in Massachusetts.

Where are you going to be this summer? I wish much we might have a talk some day. I expect to be away on inspection trips and the Governors' Conference until about the first of August.

Very sincerely yours,
F.D.R.

Cambridge, Mass., July 13, 1929

Dear Frank —

You will be glad to hear that Frank Walsh promptly communicated with me. He came up here and spent a whole day, during which we went over the scope of the inquiry, and ways and means of carrying it out effectively. Even though the public has only three representatives out of nine, the public group, I am confident, can rip the situation wide open.

Always yours,

FELIX FRANKFURTER

An outbreak of prison riots had awakened a belated sense of the need for reform in prison administration throughout New York State. Since his youth, Frankfurter had shown an unswerving interest in developing more humane standards of administration for both state and federal prisons. He was delighted to find that Roosevelt shared this interest.

One of the complications in New York was the existence of the Baumes Law, named after state Senator Caleb H. Baumes, forcing a life term to be imposed on fourth offenders. The rigor of this law drove third offenders still engaged in crime to the commission of desperate acts since they had very little to lose, if caught, as they would automatically go to jail for the rest of their lives. Roosevelt, among other reforms, wanted this law greatly modified.

Dr. Raymond F. C. Kieb, Commissioner of Correction, had investigated the riots in the Dannemora and Auburn prisons. His rather complacent comments unwittingly emphasized the desirability of a broad-gauged inquiry.

In 1931 Roosevelt was awarded a gold medal by the National Committee on Prisons and Prison Labor for his "outstanding service" in the cause of prison improvement.

Cambridge, Mass., July 29, 1929

Dear Frank:

I assume that you will appoint a very strong commission of inquiry into prison administration. I venture to suggest the inclusion into membership of such a commission of Sanford Bates, Superintendent of United States Prisons. Bates was until recently the head of the Department of Correction here, and would bring to the investigation wide knowledge, ample familiarity with penological advances the world over, and level-headedness. I realize that the members of such a commission are usually residents of the state. But in as much as the United States sends prisoners to some of the New York institutions (at least, it did so in the days when I was in the United States Attorney's office), the United States itself has an immediate interest in New York prison administration, and this would furnish relevance for the Bates appointment. Even if this is no longer so, you can easily justify the appointment of the Federal Prisons Superintendent! I venture to make the suggestion because I know he would bring a good deal of authority to the results of such an investigation.

Dr. Kieb's comment, as reported in this morning's *Times*, opens up a number of very important lines for fundamental inquiry.

Faithfully yours,
F.F.

Albany, N.Y., August 5, 1929

Dear Felix:

I have not yet made up my mind in regard to the appointment of a commission of inquiry into the prison situation. It is far more than a matter of inquiring into the prison administration; it goes into the whole question of the Baumes Law, parole, etc. The mere matter of administration can be improved as to food, exercise, etc., etc. without a commission of inquiry outside of existing officials.

In regard to a general inquiry, I hesitate chiefly because there have been inquiries of this nature almost every year for the last twenty or twenty-five years. We have volumes of reports from expert penologists. Almost every penologist has an individual theory and it is difficult to get any unanimity of opinion.

My present inclination is to appoint no new commission but to ask the existing Baumes Commission to reopen the whole subject of life sentences for fourth offenders, especially where the offenses are committed against property and not against persons, and to hold hearings and let everybody talk.

Our chief immediate problem in the state is a physical one — the building of more prisons to take care of the overcrowding and to eliminate the use of the present antiquated cell accommodations. One new prison will be started this autumn but it will take two years before we can actually get into it.

As ever, yours,
F.D.R.

A new phase opened in the power controversy when Floyd L. Carlisle, chairman of the Niagara-Hudson Power Corporation, suggested that negotiations with Governor Roosevelt could lead to a settlement. This overture in time produced a Republican offer in the legislature for the appointment of a commission with a broad mandate to examine all plans for the development of hydroelectric power on the St. Lawrence River. Roosevelt joined with Frankfurter in hailing this offer as a victory for his cause, for he would appoint all the five commissioners and presumably their report would em-

*body his philosophy on public power. But his jubilation was premature.
The Republicans had not agreed to surrender; they merely wished to re-
move the power issue from the 1930 election. Obstinate negotiations with
Republican leaders and with "the Carlisle crowd" had still to take place.*

Cambridge, Mass., January 17, 1930

Dear Frank:

All too often public men compromise essentials on a vital issue, accept
stone for bread, and then comfort themselves with the metaphor that half a
loaf is better than none. By holding out on your water power policy for
New York, you have vindicated courage in government. You have also
achieved the indispensable, correct first step in working out a socially sound
water power policy. The Republican bill gives you what you want, and now
men of the calibre of Al Smith will be able to put their disinterested minds
to proving, as we believe they can prove, that the greatest natural resource
owned by the State can be used predominantly for the public welfare and
not for profit. Your achievement means, I believe, everything for the future
water power policy of the whole country. Once New York establishes that
power can not only be developed but developed with due regard to the
public interest, the unimaginative and selfish claims elsewhere will find an
effective reply in the New York example.

Altogether, your success at the crucial stage of the fight — insistence
that we begin right in regard to water power development — is a great triumph. It ought to encourage all who care about the public good to continue to apply alert energy in garnering the fruits of your efforts. I am very
happy about your accomplishment.

Faithfully yours,
F.F.

Albany, N.Y., January 24, 1930

Dear Felix:

I have waited to thank you for your nice note until I could be reasonably certain that the Republican offer is genuine. Apparently this is the case.
Now comes the most difficult part of all. I am taking the position that in
view of the fact that the bill sets up a policy (even though it may be merely
a temporary policy), it allows me to appoint commissioners and directs that
these commissioners bring in, if possible, a plan based on this policy. It is, I
think, right for me to appoint as commissioners men who will be sympathetic to the whole basic principle. The Republican press is howling for the
appointment of "non-partisan" commissioners: i.e., people who have no
preconceived notions whatsoever. In the first place, nobody with any real
intelligence has gotten this far without having some preconceived notions.

In the second place, I think it is right to appoint people who will work day and night to bring in a plan based on the policy.

Think over the many people you know and let me have any suggestions in regard to personnel. Residence in New York is desirable but not essential for all members of the commission.

Do come and see us soon.

Always sincerely yours,
F.D.R.

In June 1930 Walter Lippmann wrote an article for Harper's *magazine on "The Peculiar Weakness of Mr. Hoover." After discussing the article with Roosevelt, Frankfurter wrote the following letter to Lippmann, expressing the most powerful criticisms of President Hoover as national leader. This letter is very important as an index to Roosevelt's own thinking: it is clear from Frankfurter's argument that as early as 1930, before the depression had deepened to its full intensity, Roosevelt had lost confidence in Hoover's ability to grapple with the economic crisis. During all this period Frankfurter often presented Roosevelt's case to Lippmann, arguing with a freedom which the Governor hesitated to exercise.*

June 22, 1930

Dear Walter:

On two grounds I am grateful for your piece on Hoover. In the first place, by a critical discussion of the President's performances you help restore the all-essential condition of a democratic society, namely, the free and aggressive practice of scrutinizing the conduct of our rulers. As you well know, during the post-war period, following the systematic censorship of the war, a contrary tradition of subservience to those in authority and particularly of presidential immunity from criticism was in danger of growing up. Such a tendency must effectively be smashed, and your piece helps towards a healthy return of earlier days.

Secondly, you perform an important educational task in making clear once again that government is not business, that government is quite an art in itself. Hoover unwittingly may render a great service in driving home that truth by his very failures. For, as you point out, there was a peculiarly favorable conjunction of man and circumstances in putting the engineering and business theory of politics to the test through Hoover's presidency. The professionalism of politics was one of my themes in one of the Dodge lectures and I am very much delighted to have your own illuminating analysis of the matter. Reiteration is the essence of political education.

On the merits, I agree with your analysis of Hoover's "peculiar weakness" but my own view of him finds his weakness more far-reaching. I believe that not only is his conduct "that of a weak man," but that he is "really a weak man." In finding his past performances "bold," I think you look at the facts of the past in part through the glasses of that very legend which you so keenly expose. In other words, I think you take too much for granted our old views of his past about the circumstances of which we know much less than we know concerning the circumstances of his first year in office. I am not eager to diminish his past glory. But I merely suggest that the weakness of his presidential conduct may well call for a reconsideration of prior assumptions in regard to the qualities of his past performance.

Thus, specifically, I do not believe that Hoover falters "only when he has to act in the medium of democracy." Do you think his performances were essentially different when he acted in the medium of authority, of autocracy, of negotiation, having nothing to do with the hurly-burly of the democratic process? Isn't he true to form compared with his attitude and his conduct whenever he encountered opposition? He has always quarreled when he did not have his own way, or, rather, he can perform only when he has his own way. I don't call that boldness; I call that egregious egotism and appetite. You remember his remark, "I don't see why they can't cooperate with me in my own way."

Really the Belgian work and the food administration during the war were not achievements of a bold man or at all on the scale of two pieces of work about which I happen to know a good deal — Goethals' work at Panama and Crowder's organization and administration of the draft. Both of these tasks involved many more resistances and enjoyed far less immunity than Hoover's work. His Belgian relief work, after all, enlisted the tenderest interests of mankind and, so far as both England and Germany were concerned, had the great advantage of the desire of both these countries not to antagonize the United States on so sensitive a feeling as feeding women and children. And as for Hoover's food administration, what real sacrifice was he called upon to ask of the American people? How much did Americans really have to forego during the war, compared with the rationing, let us say, of the English in the later stages of the war? Moreover, as food administrator, he already was the legendary figure of Belgian relief.

We repeat unquestioningly that Hoover is a great engineer. Is he? Do you really know a first-rate engineer who will on his conscience testify that Hoover is a great engineer? Just what great engineering achievement can you name to his credit? Isn't he rather a great promoter and a successful promoter? I think the matter is important because while he talks the language of engineering, the language of fact, the language of dependence on objective proof, there are too many instances within my knowledge to make me have any confidence that he has the habits of engineering accuracy. You will recall his reckless disregard of fact in regard to the rubber controversy, and I know, as a result of painful investigation, that his alleged facts in regard to unemployment and interstate power were thoroughly unreliable. And I was not at all surprised in reading Sir William Beveridge's book on British food control during the war (in the Carnegie series) that Hoover as food administrator said a lot of things and gave a lot of figures that weren't so. And consider how he has perverted the great fact-finding commission on crime into a political device. Such a series of instances reveals, I believe, a far-reaching tendency in him — the tendency of a promoter who uses all things that come within his scope for the success of his promotion.

I am not a romantic about democracy, but it ought not to carry a heavier load than it has to carry. And I think that the difficulty with Hoover is not at all that he is unaccustomed to the hurly-burly of politics, and can only work with precision on facts uninfluenced by human deflection, particularly the deflections of democracy. Do you really believe that Hoover, had he been in Owen Young's place, could have worked out the reparations problem or could have done what Dwight Morrow did in Mexico in negotiating a settlement between church and state? At neither of those tasks would he have been working "in the medium of democracy." He would have failed at those jobs for the same reason that he got into rows with the Interstate Commerce Commission when he was Secretary of Commerce, dealing with problems as to which the public was wholly ignorant, and neither public nor Congress were butting in. Of course, Hoover has abilities, but he has lacks of inner security and the self-confidence that come from encountering equals with open-mindedness, and his judgment is constantly thwarted by inordinate ambition.

However, I did not mean to write a whole essay.

Yours always,
F.F.

Beginning in January 1930, Thomas C. T. Crain, district attorney for New York, a Democrat, began an investigation of the New York courts. Roosevelt was critical of the lack of vigor with which Crain had examined charges against Judge Bertini, appointed by Roosevelt as a Special Sessions Court judge, and against Judge Crater, who had disappeared. It was charged that both appointments had been made with the connivance of Tammany Hall, which had arranged for ten-thousand-dollar payoffs to various officials. In August, Crain announced that no indictments had been brought by the grand jury.

Roosevelt, who had ordered the minutes of the grand jury brought to him for review, had then assigned the case to the state attorney general, Hamilton Ward, a Republican. Hiram C. Todd, another Republican, became special assistant to Ward. They were both strongly supported by

Charles H. Tuttle, United States Attorney for the New York District, who became the unsuccessful Republican candidate for Governor against Roosevelt in 1930.

Todd, who wished to widen the investigation into a general inquiry into bribery and corruption, gave frequent interviews to the press in which he made damaging accusations without citing any proof that his charges were valid. Frankfurter contrasted this reckless procedure with the restraint and responsibility which had guided Emory R. Buckner as special prosecutor of Municipal Malefactors. Buckner had served earlier with Frankfurter as an Assistant United States Attorney under Henry L. Stimson.

Repeatedly, Tuttle demanded that Roosevelt ask for Bertini's resignation. Bertini was still under investigation when he died in March 1931.

Albany, N.Y., October 16, 1930

Dear Felix:

I only have time for a line. You are quite right that the atmosphere in New York City is not what it should be, but I can't help it if editors deliberately misrepresent my acts.

1. I started the Special Grand Jury within twenty-four hours of Crain's failure.

2. I forced through the Appellate Division investigation of the Magistrates' Courts.

3. I did not decline to extend the powers of the Special Grand Jury. They have complete power to investigate what you or I eat for breakfast or anything else. I did decline to extend the Attorney General's power before the Special Grand Jury until and unless they give me something more than the general statement that they believe crookedness to exist.

I simply must have something to go on before I go through with that excellent idea of yours about the appointment of a perfectly independent person to investigate the Supreme Court judges themselves. The Attorney General's plea of lack of funds is, of course, dishonest for he has the whole huge staff of his office to work with.

You are right about Buckner. Nevertheless I declined to make merely a grand stand play for the sake of votes. The present investigations are proceeding smoothly and effectively except that Todd, before the Grand Jury, is violating every legal ethic twice a day when he talks to the press.

As ever yours,

F.D.R.

Walter Lippmann at this time was editor of the New York World.

The New York Herald Tribune *had run a box listing the eleven most prominent officials charged with corruption. Hence the reference to the "Eminent Eleven."*

Charles S. Whitman, district attorney for New York City from 1910 to 1914, used the publicity gained in part from his self-serving use of evidence gathered by grand juries to help him become Governor of New York from 1915 to 1918.

What most impressed Frankfurter about Buckner was the fairness with which he prosecuted even a man like Daugherty, notorious in American history as the corrupt Attorney General of the Harding Administration. Miller was one of his associates. "Buckner," said Frankfurter, "realized that he who wields the instruments of criminal justice wields the most terrible instruments of government. In order to assure their just and compassionate use, a prosecutor must have an almost priest-like attitude toward his duties. Buckner practiced this attitude without deviation."

Frankfurter also showed Roosevelt his letter to Lippmann dated October 23, 1930. It is worth considerable emphasis that Frankfurter had no hesitation in showing this letter to Roosevelt despite the critical references in the last paragraph. Louis Waldman was an independent labor candidate.

Cambridge, Mass., October 17, 1930

Dear Frank:

You may be interested in this letter of mine to Walter Lippmann.

Yours always,
F.F.

Cambridge, Mass., October 17, 1930

Dear Walter:

I don't have to tell you my feelings about judicial corruption or about Tammany and all its works. And I should probably find my vocabulary of contempt inadequate if I tried to express my opinion of the Eminent Eleven. So that while Bertini's fate is as much a matter of indifference to me as that of an anonymous ant, the issue which he raises in regard to the conduct by prosecutors of grand juries is one of profound importance, despite the fact that he raises it.

There are deep grounds of policy behind the tradition and the legal doctrine of secrecy regarding proceedings before a grand jury. I speak as an old prosecutor, and know what every prosecutor knows, that grand juries are pliable instruments in the control of prosecutors. The avoidance of grand juries as instruments of oppression, of political partisanship, of passion, and the corresponding protection of men's reputations and the community's goodwill are therefore in the keeping solely of the austere good faith and disinterestedness of the prosecutors. One of the most fastidiously moral men that I know has had his life permanently scarred and marred because Charlie Whitman, for reasons of self-seeking, indulged in publicity regarding alleged misconduct on the part of the man in question (a most honorable lawyer), while the matter was still under investigation and should have been kept a complete secret. The charge was later completely dispelled.

I know that you are wholly familiar with these generalities, but don't dismiss them as irrelevant in the present situation. That there are crooks on and off the bench in Tammany Hall, I have no doubt. But there is no less doubt that Tuttle and Todd have been wholly disloyal to the standards that should govern prosecutors and their responsibility to the grand jury and the public. Nor have you and I any doubt that they have been preoccupied with political and personal preferment. And there are particular reasons for calling a sharp halt to Todd's performance even though perchance some Tammany crooks may be beneficiaries. His past record as a prosecutor disentitles him to confidence. He it was who, as counsel for the United States, first investigated the Daugherty-Miller affairs before the federal grand jury. The result of his conduct was an indictment against Miller and the clearance of Daugherty. Buckner then became United States Attorney; the history of what followed, you know. The grand jury under his guidance found that the indictment against Miller brought in by Todd was an inadequate basis for prosecution, and a new indictment was found against Miller, from which a conviction resulted. Under Buckner's guidance the grand jury also indicted Daugherty, whom, at the second trial, eleven jurors found guilty. It needs only to be added that Todd was an associate and an appointee of Daugherty's.

I underline every word you wrote in your editorial yesterday on gangs and city governments. We are dealing with a rotten system. Somewhere, however, the vicious circle must be broken. Perhaps it is my personal experience with the awful power that prosecutors wield and the terrible instruments that they control, that makes me feel that as good a place to begin as any, as important an insistence as any, is the integrity of our prosecutorial agency. For my part, the supine incompetence of Crain is not a whit more dangerous to the public well-being than the misuse of grand jury machinery, as feeders for political publicity by Tuttle when he was United States Attorney, and now by Todd.

Always yours,
FELIX FRANKFURTER

October 23, 1930

Dear Walter:

Many thanks for your letter. I believe I understand not inadequately the difficulties that confront you in regard to the gubernatorial election. In writing you the other day I did not mean to suggest any choice, certainly not on your part. And the last thing in the world that I want is the softening of blows against judicial crookedness. If my letter appeared one-sided it is because I was dealing with one side of the problem, *i.e.*, the relation of prosecutorial standards to civic decencies.

What I wrote was called forth by your editorial on Bertini. A daily paper of course must be concerned with individual Bertinis. I did not mean to crowd out the immediate issues of Bertini's or Roosevelt's conduct. What I was suggesting was another, and I believe larger, issue that also concerns newspapers — at least a paper like the *World*. I have been watching rather closely New York politics for thirty years, and for the last decade have had to deal intimately with the functions of a prosecutor's office, and its operations, in the United States. And it is my profound conviction that not until our prosecutorial mechanism ceases to be the football of politics will we make appreciable, permanent advancement in the administration of criminal justice and in the elimination of such evils as those which are now again to the fore in New York City.

You may say these are generalities too remote from the immediacies. But the bottom factor in all large American cities is the lack of confidence in the disinterestedness of the prosecution. And justly so. So long as prosecutors use their office for personal or party advantage, so long will you find the cynicism and distrust about prosecutions, particularly where political offenses are involved, that now generally pervade American cities. You will recall that the first MacDonald Government was driven from power, despite Asquith's great unwillingness to do so, because it was widely believed that it exerted political pressure, in a single case, upon the Director of Public Prosecutions. Nothing reveals more deeply the differences between criminal justice in England and here than the status of the Director of Public Prosecutions.

Nor am I talking about Utopia. I feel as strongly as I do about this not merely because I have been academically worrying over these problems for many years. My convictions come primarily from seeing two standards of prosecution contemporaneously in action — Stimson's conduct of the United States Attorney's office and Whitman's behavior as county district attorney. In a matter where public feelings ran strong, Stimson refused to be hurried in finding an indictment although importuned to do so by President Roosevelt. Conversely, he insisted on going forward with a prosecution which Hearst had initiated, and was exploiting personally as a candidate against Hughes, although Stimson was again importuned by intimate party leaders to postpone action until after the 1906 election.

Now Tuttle's career as United States Attorney has been a denial of all these standards of prosecutorial disinterestedness and fair-play. In Buckner's private words to me, Tuttle "has perverted all the right traditions of a prosecutor's office, not only during the last six months but for the last three years." I believe that the insistence on these standards goes deeper than the immediate case of a Bertini, because the extent to which we adhere to these standards determines what happens when a Bertini case arises, if indeed it does not measurably affect, as I am sure it does, the range and nature of official and private crookedness in a community.

All this is surely relevant, however, also upon the election. For Tuttle has himself been guilty of the very wrongs against which he is crusading. I know that weighty evidence of criminal misconduct by a Federal judge was submitted to him in a responsible form, and he has delayed and delayed and shilly-shallied over two years because it involved offending his party in general and the Westchester Republican organization in particular.

So that were I in New York I should vote against Tuttle, not only with ease but with enthusiasm, for he has prostituted the very law which he champions. For me the most distasteful politician is the pious fraud.

I can easily see how you would say "Plague on both your houses," and vote for Waldman. Despite all, I should vote for Roosevelt. I know his limitations. Most of them derive, I believe, from lack of an incisive intellect and a kind of optimism that sometimes makes him timid, as well as an ambition that leads to compromises with which we were familiar in Theodore Roosevelt and Wilson. But on the whole he has been a very good governor, and on the whole I feel less strongly than you do about looking to Albany in cleaning up messes in our municipalities. This opens up a long story, but I think we are too prone to despair of local obstacles against cleaning up undesirable situations, and appealing to external forces which in the long run do not furnish permanent remedies.

Always yours,

FELIX FRANKFURTER

There is no doubt that Roosevelt assigned Walter Lippmann a high place among his "deliberate editorial cads." That is why he encouraged Frankfurter to argue the Roosevelt case with Lippmann in repeated letters. But these letters will be searched in vain for any admission that Frankfurter was acting as Roosevelt's advocate, though Lippmann probably suspected it. Apparently the scope of caddishness was rather wider than Roosevelt and Frankfurter, in this instance, were ready to concede.

Cambridge, Mass., November 11, 1930

Dear Frank —

What a crashing victory it was! And never did a statesman receive a more unequivocal vindication from his people. New York wants a continuation of the kind of government you have been giving them, because you educated them to want such a government and to understand that they were getting it. And your friends rightly believe that the forthrightness and standards which made you a leader, over-night, in the fight against things that twenty years ago were symbolized by "Blue-eyed" Billy Sheehan, guide you also today.

And so the electorate has given you more power for your qualities than ever before.

With warm good wishes,

Yours always,
F.F.

In 1928 Roosevelt had been elected with a plurality of only 25,564 votes, with his opponent waiting twelve days before he finally conceded defeat; in 1930 he was re-elected with a majority of 725,000 votes. In 1911 as a young member of the New York legislature in Albany, F.D.R. first showed his ability in controversy when he led the fight against the designation of William F. Sheehan as United States Senator. He opposed Sheehan as a creature of Tammany and as a symbol of boss rule.

Warm Springs, Ga., December 1, 1930

Dear Felix:

Many thanks for your mighty nice letter which has been forwarded to me down here. I am getting some exercise and at least a partial holiday.

I wish when I get back you would run over to Albany and spend the night with us. I want to talk to you of many things — water power, public utilities, New York City judges, deliberate editorial cads, and other choice subjects. Where are you going to be in the Christmas holidays? It would be great if you could spend a night with me in Albany or at Hyde Park where we shall be the Saturday, Sunday and Monday after Christmas.

As ever yours,
F.D.R.

Cambridge, Mass., December 10, 1930

Dear Frank:

That's a tempting invitation of yours and I am eager to "jaw" with you (to use the Chaucerian English of Justice Holmes) about a number of the subjects which you enumerate. I am afraid I am tied up for the Christmas season. But if you can have me early or late in January on any Wednesday or Thursday (except January 14 and 15), I should be glad to come to Albany.

Now that you have a Democratic Attorney General, may I refresh your recollection of the message that Brandeis sent you, as to the inadequate representation of the state of New York in important cases before the Supreme Court.

With holiday greetings from my wife and myself,

Yours always,
F.F.

Albany, N.Y., January 10, 1931

Dear Felix:

Ever so many thanks for sending me the copy of *The Public and Its Government*. Some day when you are here you must write your name in it.

I am looking forward to reading it.

As ever yours,
F.D.R.

This book contains the text of Frankfurter's Dodge lecture at Yale. Roosevelt particularly liked the phrase that in a democracy the expert must always be on tap but never on top. (Frankfurter, at 1 A.M. on August 30, 1934, while staying up with Roosevelt at Hyde Park, inscribed the book: "To F.D.R., with old affection and new respect. F.F.")

On January 21, 1931, Professor James C. Bonbright had written a long letter to Frankfurter on several questions relating to public power. Two days later, Frankfurter had replied to express agreement with the tactics which Bonbright had urged on the St. Lawrence Commission. He went on to say: "The longer I live the more truth do I find in the idea underlying a remark of J. M. Keynes, 'Diplomacy is too much for man.' In other words, I think the strength of the public position is not in finessing or skillful maneuvering." He added that the Carlisle crowd "cannot be beaten in that game. The public's case ought to rest on facts and arguments that can be frankly avowed. I am against dealing with these matters as though they were old-fashioned horse trades." Roosevelt's letter shows that he agreed with Frankfurter's strategy.

Albany, N.Y., January 28, 1931

Dear Felix: —

I entirely agree with you and Bonbright. One trouble with some of the Commission was that they thought they could play politics both with the Legislature and the Carlisle crowd. I told them to let me do the political fencing for them and, without taking undue credit unto myself, I think I am a better trader in this kind of work than they are! As a matter of fact, I find the best kind of trading is to go after the objective in the simplest and clearest way.

I am sorry Bonbright is going abroad just at this time. I should have liked to have had his advice on the form of legislation.

> Always sincerely,
> F.D.R.

Cambridge, Mass., June 13, 1931

Dear Frank:

1. I feel as I suspect many a girl must have felt on finding herself engaged without ever having said "yes" to the suitor. But I am in for it, and I need hardly tell you how profoundly important I regard the work of any commission charged with the duty of proposing a more civilized system of legal justice, particularly for New York. Even your persuasiveness would not have led me to go on your Commission did I not know of your deep interest in the subject.

2. In case you cannot get Percy Straus, or in any event in case you have a place free, I should like to urge on you the appointment of Charles A. Beard. He would bring great qualities. I think you can get him to serve, and I would bring to bear my influence with him.

3. With all due modesty, I know not a little about the history of the various movements which have produced the English system of legal administration, — a system, which, with all its defects, is so much more civilized than any we have in this country. Indispensable to the success of the Royal Commissions, which have produced the British reforms, have been first-class secretaries who have had the laboring oar in the details of the enterprise. If you are to come even measurably close to your desires and to achieve what you want to achieve, you ought to have such a first-class secretary.

I know of no man more suited to the task than Max Lowenthal. He has real generalship in organizing large inquiries, is familiar with the materials and the personnel in the field, has unusual capacity for organizing complicated and elusive data and an obstinate will in bringing the right thing to pass. With him as secretary, I would feel confident that your Commission would set a landmark in the history of legal reform in the United States. I don't know whether you can get him to do this work. I am sure you ought to insist on getting him.

It was a joy to see you so fit and eager.

> Yours always,
> F.F.

P.S.   Lowenthal is ever so much better than Greenbaum. He has more drive, imagination, knowledge and insight.

Telegram to Roosevelt

Cambridge, Mass., June 19, 1931

ON FULL RECONSIDERATION BELIEVE STRONGLY THAT MY CIRCUMSTANCES DO
NOT ENABLE ME TO GIVE SERVICES THAT EFFECTIVE ACCOMPLISHMENT OF THE
WORK OF YOUR COMMISSION REQUIRES. REGRETFULLY ASK YOU THEREFORE NOT
TO APPOINT ME. MUST LEAVE IN TEN DAYS FOR CALIFORNIA AND WILL BE GONE
TILL MIDDLE OF SEPTEMBER. AT BEGINNING OF NEW ACADEMIC YEAR WILL BE
ESPECIALLY TIED DOWN HERE. THEREFORE WILL BE DISABLED FROM PERSONAL
ATTENDANCE EXCEPT MOST RARELY. DURING NEXT SIX MONTHS COMMISSION
OUGHT TO HAVE MORE ACTIVE MEMBER, SOMEBODY LIKE DEAN YOUNG SMITH
OF COLUMBIA. AM CONFIDENT I CAN CONTRIBUTE WHATEVER HELP I CAN BE
THROUGH CONSULTATIVE WAYS ALTHOUGH NOT MEMBER COMMISSION. MY
DEEP INTEREST IN YOUR AIMS FOR PROCEDURAL REFORMS UNABATED AND AM
SURE YOU KNOW I WANT TO DO EVERYTHING IN MY POWER TO HELP YOU, BUT
IT WILL NOT DO TO HAVE OFFICIAL RESPONSIBILITY WHICH TIME AND DISTANCE
MAKE IT IMPOSSIBLE TO PERFORM.

FELIX FRANKFURTER

Cambridge, Mass., June 27, 1931

Dear Frank:

It was a pleasure to inscribe the fly-leaf of *Mr. Justice Holmes*.

I wonder if you have received a copy of my little volume of lectures
delivered at Yale, entitled *The Public and Its Government*. I know you
have a thing or two to do, but I should like you somehow or other, sometime or other, to steal three-quarters of an hour to read the last essay in it,
"Expert Administration and Democracy."

A very good summer to you! And I hope to see you in the fall.

Yours always,
F.F.

*Frankfurter's inscription on the fly-leaf of his book on Mr. Justice
Holmes reads: "Dear Frank, not the least tie between us is the meaning
that Mr. Justice Holmes has for us. Affectionately, Felix Frankfurter, June
26, 1931." He had evidently forgotten that Roosevelt had acknowledged
The Public and Its Government the previous January.*

*The New York legislature, in a surprise move, ordered an inquiry into
corruption in New York, with primary emphasis on the activities of Tammany Hall and Mayor Walker. The inquiry was directed by Judge Samuel
Seabury, a fearless prosecutor. Slow in gathering momentum, the investigation reached its climax on the eve of the Democratic National Convention
of 1932.*

In the summer of 1931 the New York Power Authority engaged in a public correspondence with President Hoover on the development of public power along the St. Lawrence. The exchange of letters revealed Hoover's sympathy with the "Carlisle crowd" in their defense of private power.

Laguna Beach, Cal., August 28, 1931

Dear Frank —

I'm a long way from my "spiritual home" — New York — and so the full news of things reaches me slowly. I have only now read your message to the Special Session, and should like you to know how much I rejoice over the way you have handled the New York City situation and the backing you're giving to Seabury. It's the same old Tiger!

I have left no opportunity unavailed out here to tell them about your work in detail — especially your knowing and aggressive leadership on Power and Unemployment.

The Hoover-Castle performance regarding the St. Lawrence was pretty bad — and I expect very little from Washington these days.

Hope you had a not too hot summer.

Always yours,
F.F.

Albany, N.Y., September 7, 1931

Dear Felix: —

You do not say how long you are remaining in Hollywood, for I take it that Laguna Beach is a suburb. You did not tell me that you were making a film! In any event it will be good to get you east again and I do wish you could run in or stop off in Albany before you become a Professor again.

I am getting much joy out of these active days but still I hope to go to Warm Springs the twenty-first of this month for a three weeks' holiday.

As ever yours,
F.D.R.

Cambridge, Mass., September 14, 1931

Dear Frank:

Were I to write you in appreciation of all your deeds these days that excite my enthusiasm, you would be the victim of a new daily dozen. But I certainly cannot forego to tell you that you have never done anything that hit me more where I live than in your forthright statement comparing the financing methods of "the greatest Secretary of the Treasury since Hamilton" with the policy on which you insist. I cannot characterize the attempts of the Administration to deal with its deficits without increasing taxation as otherwise than cowardly fear. The New York situation furnished you an admirable opportunity for making clear to the nation a much-needed lesson on public finance. But nothing surprises this particular observer of national events more than the way public men pass up opportunities made to order for them — they are so scared by the so-called prudences. But you *are* seizing your opportunities. And so I rejoice deeply over the leadership which you have asserted on these basic public questions and the lucid education to which you are subjecting the public in what usually are the mysteries of finance.

Keep it up!

Always yours,
F.F.

The derisive reference is to Andrew Mellon, Hoover's Secretary of the Treasury, whom Frankfurter loathed. Roosevelt had accused the Hoover Administration of hiding essential financial information from the public.

Cambridge, Mass., Sept. 20, 1931

Dear Frank:

The special session is off your hands, but your good deeds survive. I think you showed real statesmanship in the issues you put to the Legislature and dogged leadership in making your will prevail. And in New York the donkey should be the symbol of the GOP.

Now take a good vacation in Warm Springs.

Always yours,
F.F.

Cambridge, Mass., October 27, 1931

Dear Frank:

The enclosed letter may interest you, in view of your vigorous efforts earlier in the year to persuade the Legislature to throw adequate safeguards around savings bank deposits.

If those fellows on Fourteenth Street, or wherever Tammany Hall may now be, persist in their way, they may give you the Presidency in a walk. Anyhow, all good luck to you!

Always yours,
F.F.

NEW YORK *HERALD TRIBUNE*, MONDAY, OCTOBER 19, 1931

THREE BANKING FUNCTIONS
Professor Frankfurter Notes That They Are Too Often Confused

To the New York *Herald Tribune*:

It is the current fashion to charge our present difficulties to "psychology." Doubtless this is a correct diagnosis, if "psychology" is a comprehensive term for beliefs and mental attitudes. Certainly nothing will be gained by an ostrich policy. The winds of truth must blow freely and publicly, even though they may touch the sensitive system of banking and finance. It should, therefore, be deemed a distinct public service for correspondents to write as frankly as did Mr. Lawrence J. Anhalt in yesterday's *Herald Tribune* regarding the causes for lack of confidence in bankers.

I should like to raise, however, issues of even more far-reaching and more impersonal import than the banking practices to which Mr. Anhalt referred. In recent years it has become increasingly evident that the basic difficulty with our banks is the confusion of three functions which ought to be kept fastidiously segregated:

1. Savings banking. It is the obligation of the savings bank man to take practically no risk. His prime duty is to promote safety.

2. Commercial banking. The financial needs of merchants and manufacturers make it necessary to take business risks. Banks should not avoid these risks, but know whom and when to trust.

3. Security banking — buying and selling. This involves not only knowledge of fundamental merits, but also knowledge of markets, of social and political movements, etc.

By combining these three functions our banking men have not only dulled and confused their banking wits. They have also — unless all one hears is wholly without foundation — too often confused the funds of the three departments of banking and thereby disregarded trust obligations. Everyone, of course, eagerly welcomes constructive efforts toward starting again healthy economic currents. But if the above brief analysis regarding banking functions and tendencies be sound, one wonders to what extent it was heeded in the recent scheme for increasing bank aggregations.

FELIX FRANKFURTER

Cambridge, Mass., October 16, 1931

Albany, N.Y., November 4, 1931

Dear Felix:

It is good to get your note and I like your clear distinction in regard to banking functions. There is one other fundamental of the present situation which has been overlooked — the growing of the practice of corporations during the past twenty years to retain and refund their bonded debts instead of amortizing and paying them off at maturity. In other words, the whole trend has been towards an overloading of mortgages. Credit of all kinds is necessary, but not unnecessary credit. Put your mighty mind to work on this.

When am I going to see you? I go to Warm Springs for a couple of weeks on November eighteenth, but I do hope that you will arrange to run up to Albany or Hyde Park during the Christmas holidays.

As ever yours,
F.D.R.

Albany, N.Y., December 29, 1931

Dear Felix:

The article from the *New Republic* of December twenty-third is based upon an error of fact. The action of the Insurance Commissioners was not the arbitrary substitution of June thirtieth valuation of securities in place of December thirty-first valuation. The precise action is set forth in the resolution of the Convention which I am herewith enclosing. You will see that the objective was a *fair valuation of securities as of December thirty-first:* that the average of a period was deemed a more accurate standard than the valuation as reflected by sales on the Exchange on any particular day. That the average over five quarters happened to coincide generally with the values as reflected by the sales on June thirtieth, and that reference to June thirtieth as the day's figures to be taken was merely as a convenient way of ascertaining the average in view of the coincidence.

These reports of companies required to be made as of December thirty-first are not alone for the information of the public in the matter of its dealings with insurance companies. If that were all, of course the more conservative the report the better, and no harm would occur. In addition to the public information feature these reports must be acted upon by the respective Insurance Departments under the mandatory requirements for liquidation of companies in case of insolvency or impairment. The liquidation of a company is a serious matter for policyholders. The potential assets of policyholders should not be needlessly sacrificed. To insist upon a company's showing a financial condition worse than it really is would result in needless loss and hardship to policyholders and aggravate the depression by forced sale of securities and additional unemployment.

The Superintendent of Insurance of New York, Mr. George S. Van Schaick, gave careful attention to the question. His letter to the New York *Times*, explaining the position of the Department, is sent you herewith. There is also sent you an editorial from the *World-Telegram* of New York which was carried, I believe, by all of the Scripps Howard papers. The attitude of the Gannett papers is shown by the enclosed editorial from the Rochester *Times-Union*.

In these troublesome times, it is not always easy to adopt a policy that fits. In view of this reply to your inquiry, both Mr. Van Schaick and I would be pleased to have your further comment. Do you think Mr. Van

Schaick should give the *New Republic* an article setting forth the reasons for the action, or do you think it better to drop the press discussion?

Always sincerely yours,
F.D.R.

The following telegram related to a message of support for the Presidential nomination which Frankfurter was authorized to convey to Roosevelt on behalf of a group of Democratic Governors and Senators from the Western states. These Democrats offered the advice that Roosevelt should criticize the Hoover Administration in a series of speeches well timed to attract national attention. Frankfurter also reported to Roosevelt that he had more support in these Western states than along the Atlantic seaboard.

Telegram to Miss LeHand
Cambridge, Mass., January 4, 1932

HAVE IMPORTANT INFORMATION FOR F.D.R. CAN I PHONE HIM TONIGHT AND IF SO WHEN? . . . WILL BE AT MY HOUSE 192 BRATTLE STREET, CAMBRIDGE, ALL DAY EXCEPT LUNCH TIME. PHONE NUMBER PORTER 3699. HAPPY NEW YEAR TO YOU.

FELIX FRANKFURTER

Cambridge, Mass., January 24, 1932
Dear Frank:

Judge Irving Lehman has just asked me to the dinner that he is planning on February 9th for you and the Court of Appeals, and I thought I should like to go if I could take the occasion for a visit with you. I simply have had to put off your various cordial invitations in the past, but if you could have me for the 9th I could plan to stay over to the 10th. That would give us a chance for real talk. I write you thus freely because I count on you being equally blunt if the time should not be convenient for you.

I have been delaying outrageously a reply to your recent letter in regard to the valuation of securities by insurance companies. In view of the facts which you set forth and your specific inquiries, I thought I ought to inform myself before attempting a letter to you. And that has taken a little time, but I hope to write you again before very long.

I am perfectly delighted with the way your legislative program is moving.

Always yours,
F.F.

Cambridge, Mass., February 16, 1932
Dear Frank:

It is silly to urge on you the appointment of Cuthbert Pound as Chief Judge as soon as Cardozo is confirmed, for of course you will do that. But I should like to say a word just to satisfy my own feelings, and I write as one who has been studying intimately for years not only the work of the New York Court of Appeals but Pound's part in it. He is really one of the big judges of our land and seems less big merely because he has very consciously concealed himself behind the shadow of Cardozo. Indeed almost from the moment that Cardozo came to the Court of Appeals, Pound has been eager to have him become Chief Judge, and probably more than any one single person Pound brought it to pass that both parties should unite on Cardozo. He, as a senior Republican judge, would have had claims on his party's nomination, but I happen to know personally how hard he worked to bring about the circumstances that made Cardozo Chief.

Always yours,
F.F.

Mr. Justice Cardozo had been nominated by President Hoover to fill the seat on the Supreme Court made vacant by Mr. Justice Holmes's resignation.

On April 22, 1932, Walter Lippmann sent Frankfurter a quotation from a letter by Bernard Berenson, the famous authority on art. Commenting on the Hoover Administration and the depression, Berenson wrote: "My own position is not like yours, one of natural sympathy with the loaded ass fording a raging torrent. I am more inclined to discuss why he did not cross earlier, why he allowed the torrent to get so dangerous, or failed to plan how to dry it up altogether by and by." Once again Frankfurter wrote to Lippmann as an interpreter and exponent of Roosevelt's philosophy. After reading this letter, Roosevelt told Frankfurter that he particularly liked the characterization of the Hoover Administration as one "of panic and timidity." He thought those were the notes to strike in his own criticisms. It is not altogether without interest to find Frankfurter as early as 1932 referring to "the problems of the Great Society"; his reference was to Graham Wallas's book of 1914, The Great Society: A Psychological Analysis — *a book dedicated to Walter Lippmann. Edmund Wilson, now honored as a literary critic and historian, was also at this time a penetrating analyst of the blunders and mischances that marked official policy in these depression years.*

Roosevelt, of course, had little reason to like Lippmann, who was critical of many things in his record as Governor and opposed his Presidential nomination. Writing on January 8, 1932, Lippmann said "the art of carrying water on both shoulders is highly developed in American politics, and Mr. Roosevelt has learned it." He went on to say that "Franklin D. Roosevelt is a highly impressionable person, without a firm grasp of affairs and without

*very strong convictions." Then he remarked that "Franklin D. Roosevelt is
an amiable man with many philanthropic impulses, but he is not the dangerous enemy of anything. He is too eager to please." Not content with this
criticism, he insisted that "Mr. Roosevelt is, as a matter of fact, an exces-
sively cautious politician. He has been Governor for three years and I doubt
whether anyone can point to a single act of his which involved any political
risk." He summed up his criticism as follows: "Franklin D. Roosevelt is
no crusader. He is no tribune of the people. He is no enemy of entrenched
privilege. He is a pleasant man who, without any important qualifications
for the office, would very much like to be President." No wonder Roosevelt
preferred to deal with Lippmann not directly but through Frankfurter as an
intermediary.*

May 31, 1932

Dear Walter:

It gives me truly deep satisfaction not to have you join the pharisaic
outburst against the moral obtuseness of New York's Jimmie. The intensity
and, frequently, venom with which these laxities of Jimmie Walker have
been condemned remind me of nothing so much as the effort of the children of Israel to relieve themselves of responsibility through a scapegoat.
Curse Jimmie hard enough and the curser will forever be purged, seems to
have been the governing psychological practice of the "great and the good."
I speak of Jimmie's "laxities" not because I want to minimize their qualities
but because I want to avoid, if I can, that very self-righteousness with
which most of my friends these days seem to be forgetting the moral climate in which they lived so happily prior to the great crash and which was
generated so largely by the most influential in the land.

I have long, long since dissociated myself from all the forces of the past
through which belief in supernatural influences appear as belief in some
form of God. But like the elder Huxley — and to no small extent because
of him — I have never doubted that there were laws of cause and effect in
this universe. The behavior of those who determined the standards of society during the mad years preceding the October crash was bound to be
followed by the long course of wreckage through which we are now living.
Seeing life, as I do, so largely through the effects of men and measures upon
the minds of generous, able and ambitious youth, I could see, as though it
were a visible object, the directions in which they were pushed by those
who set directions for them—those who are conventionally recognized and
esteemed as the most successful in our society. "We live by symbols," says
Holmes. The symbols for these lads here during the post-war period were
the Coolidges and Mellons, the Hoovers and Hugheses, the Youngs and
Bakers. And I ask you in all sadness of heart what directions and standards

did these men set for the young? What examples of courage in speech and action did these men set before them, what criteria of "success" did they represent?

I am grateful, therefore, to have you put the Jimmie Walker business in its appropriate perspective. The cheap Jimmie Walker never set the pace for the students of the Harvard Law School. But men in the highest posts who were complacent towards corruption and leaders of my profession who either participated in stock jobbing or helped others to do so, did create the dominant environment.

Always yours,
F.F.

The following letter, shown to Roosevelt, indicates the growing bitterness with which Frankfurter and Roosevelt contemplated the Hoover Administration. For a full appreciation of Frankfurter's devotion to Roosevelt, it is necessary to remember not only how much he liked Roosevelt but also how much he disliked Hoover.

Sir Arthur Salter's book, Recovery — the Second Effort, *analyzed the economic dislocation which had followed the First World War and the measures, both private and governmental, which had produced a measure of recovery. He had a far more comprehensive grasp of the measures needed to break the back of the depression than was possible, for example, to an economist like Professor Frank Taussig of Harvard, with his belief in wider international trade as the best prescription for recovery.*

Bruce Barton and Ivy Lee were symbols of what would now be called "the Madison Avenue technique."

April 12, 1932

Dear Walter:

Many thanks for your letter.

We are, I believe, of one mind regarding the intensity of the "fever" from which the world is suffering and "the necessity of stopping the decay." Mine has been a very sombre outlook for a long time, and it has been unrelieved sadness that events have not falsified my pessimism. I have felt — and continue to feel — in this mood because my analysis of the situation has been in substance that of Salter (though of course not with the detailed thoroughness of his grasp) except that I have been much more convinced than his book seems to indicate of the necessity of enormous scaling down and correspondingly less hopeful of lifting the price levels. So far as prices are concerned, I was educated by Brandeis's opinion nearly ten years ago and the study of the problem and attention to events since. (The other day when my teasing side wearied of Frank Taussig's charming stuffiness in regard to the causes of the depression, I suggested that the real cause was the prejudice of economists and business leaders against footnotes and their resulting neglect of what Brandeis had put to them in the famous *South Western Bell Telephone* case decided May 1, 1923. You may be interested in reading that footnote now.)

Having had for some time the general Salter estimates about affairs, I have been pessimistic in my outlook because of my lack of confidence in those who are at the direction of affairs in government and in finance. The Administration leaders, and especially the President, and the dominant influences in finance, seem to me by their past performances to have shown either lack of insight or lack of courage to act on their insight. Surely it was plain — or should have been—to the most Pollyannish temperament nearly two years ago that we were in for a very heavy deficit for '30-'31 and a still heavier one for '31-'32. The financial advisers of the Administration were urged certainly a year and a half ago to plan to balance the budget by heavier taxes. (I shan't take the time to look over our old correspondence, but I think I am not mistaken in being under the impression that I wrote you on that subject some two years ago in the light of the revenue receipts that were then being published in little items on the back pages of the papers.) The attitude of the Administration was that it wasn't necessary to balance the budget — that we had over-payed off the war bonds in the past and could afford now to run into debt to meet current needs for a while. And I do not recall any insistence then on a balanced budget from our financial or business leaders.

Strangely enough, the Hoover moratorium made me gloomy rather than happy as soon as I saw that it was limited to one year. My pessimism wasn't alleviated when I had good reason to infer that it had been suggested to the President to make it a two-year moratorium but that he had cut it down to one year. I felt as I did, of course, because I discounted the ability of the French and Germans to reach an accord for a permanent decent settlement within the year and equally thought it hopeless to expect Germany's recovery for the resumption of reparation payments. And since the year's respite would bring the matter into our Presidential campaign, my settled opinion about Hoover's timidity made me tolerably certain that he would not dare renew the moratorium or take some other positive step of direction in the European imbroglio. And the Hoover-Laval conversation almost broke my heart. To expect the French and Germans to work things out and to have the most powerful and most disinterested nation retire, seemed to me pitiable abdication of responsibility. I know the essential basis that moved the President — or rather the essential concern, namely, that we had our domestic troubles and they needed attention. But this of course is the essential fallacy of his whole recent outlook — that we have a "war" on a domestic front rather than an interdependent world maladjustment.

The whole policy of the government in its recent emergency measures is based on the assumption that by restoring confidence in the banking situation here and creating easy money, substantial improvement can be achieved here even though conditions abroad remain unimproved. This of course leaves out of account the price-debt problem, the whole price movement of products which sell in the international market and whose prices are internationally determined, and leaves European countries to fight out debts-reparations for themselves even though experience shows how far they can and have gone in destroying their credit position in order to prove that they cannot pay debts. I know, of course, the embarrassment of Congressional attitude as a great, perhaps even deciding, factor in the President's mind. But you and I are agreed that ever since the moratorium he has failed to realize his responsibility for (a) working out a necessary program and (b) aggressively taking such a program to the country. Hence it is that the Congressional obstructions to a wise dealing with the international situation have not seemed to me of major importance, provided wisdom and guts dwelt in the White House. In the present distracted and floundering state of the American people, the one prophecy about which one can be dogmatic is that the nation would respond to a President who had self-mastery and was ready to impose his mastery upon the country.

I recount all this because of its relevance to my general outlook upon the specific proposals that emanate from the White House and from Wall Street. (I use Wall Street of course in the sense in which the English speak of the City.) Starting with lack of confidence in the far-sightedness or serene disinterestedness of mind and temper of those who initiate the various proposals to deal with the "fever," naturally I deem it most important to subject their improvisations to the closest, tough-minded scrutiny, just because I too am concerned with the immediate. You know me well enough to know hat temperamentally the ivory tower is not my congenial habitat. But I do not think that the philosophy of the godseekers is the most promising attitude towards the specific proposals that have been emanating from Washington and rather slavishly been sponsored in the press. I have felt nothing but a feverish temper of mind on the part of our leaders for these many months. And I submit that the physicians that deal with the fever ought not to deal with it feverishly. One measure after another has been concocted and hurriedly concocted as though it were an injection that would save life, and indeed one by one they have been advertised as saviors of life. I distrust this attitude, and on the whole it obstructs clear thinking about government, especially at times of great stress, to think about it in figures of speech. As each one of the Washington remedies have been concocted they have been denominated emergency efforts, and any plea for deliberation, for detailed discussion, for exploration of alternatives, has been regarded as obstructive or doctrinaire or both. It is in connection with the means of dealing with the immediate rather than the fact of dealing with it, that I ventured to suggest that you are too much concerned with these matters "from the point of view of the immediate actors in affairs and the immediate play of political forces," rather than giving us the benefit of what I believe is more needed than anything else — a cool, well matured projection of the isolated and unrelated immediate factors in the perspective of deeper causes and tendencies. We have had too much government by tricks and by Bruce Barton–Ivy Lee advertising and publicity stunts. Never has Brandeis been more vindicated in his favorite quotation from Euripides: "The worldly-wise are not wise." And so consistently with insistence on balancing the budget, we ought not to be compelled to accept at face value that it's a sales tax or a deficit; consistently with the relief for a financial panic, we ought not to be told there isn't time to write a Reconstruction Finance Act that will avoid obvious ambiguities and thereby avoid obvious future difficulties; consistently with a wise railroad policy, we ought not to have all thought or criticism outlawed because the President is full of dogmas on the subject.

Take the subjects that you enumerate as requiring attention for an effective reconstruction — reform of the banking structure, control of investment, extension of public control over public services. Of course this isn't the time to propose comprehensive reforms. But surely in so far as these problems are dealt with in their immediate aspects — and they are — the bearing of the immediate proposal upon furtherance or retardation of what is conceived to be the general healthy economic development of the country, becomes of prime importance, and to that extent the immediate cannot be isolated from its implications. Take the President's recurring angers and excitements about short selling; the Glass-Steagall Bill; loans to railroads which are engaged in efforts towards illegal consolidation or intercorporate relationships through holding companies that defeat the regulatory powers of the Commission. How can you deal with these specific questions directed to the immediate without stopping long enough to take soundings and see whither you are going in the inevitable general direction? Yet every time there is new stress or a new sense of stress — every time the Administration discovers something it should have known a year ago and quickly concocts a potion for the patient — the regimented spokesmen of the White House and the press of New York and the big cities generally, partly because they are baffled, partly because they suspect any questioning by those who aren't regular, make slavish belief in that potion a test of confidence in one's country. That's precisely what happened in regard to the tax debate in the House as to which I believe the country was infinitely more hysterical than even the shallowest Congressman. And it was hysterical because those who give the lead most powerfully to opinion struck the keynote. The notion that the only way to balance the budget is by a sales tax is to me the last word in foolishness. If you tell me that that was the only practical way, I'll say to you that prophecy of what is practical is not my test of what a public critic should urge. I am not having in mind your own writings, for I know you were away during the essential stages of the tax fight in the House. I am speaking generally. Again and again and again wisdom goes by default because we make a private discount that this or that wise measure isn't practical, *i.e.*, our fellow citizens couldn't be brought to the level of wisdom or fairness on which we move. Well, we don't know about that until we have tried to urge them to that level. What kind of a lead has the President or the Treasury given towards widening the base of the income tax and reducing its exemptions? Of course the generality it has thrown out in an occasional speech. But why should it find response when it is accompanied by what is to me an outrageous policy of immunity in the heavy and inordinate income brackets? And what I had in mind was that you are in a singularly free position not to be bound by the calculations of those who see only in front of their noses as to what is or isn't feasible when judged by the taking of a vote tomorrow afternoon. What does need and need cryingly your help, is the education of the public and public men, in a hard, critical and detached judgment upon the proposals and lack of proposals that are chargeable to our present political and financial guides.

Perhaps I have conveyed to you the general direction of my mind and my judgment on men and tendencies. Out of these come some of the specific opinions which from time to time I have expressed to you.

Always yours,
F.F.

Enclosure

Engineers testifying in recent rate cases have assumed that there will be a new plateau of prices. In *Galveston Electric Co.* v. *Galveston*, 258 U.S. 388, the company contended that a plateau 70 per cent. above the price level of 1914 should be accepted, and a plateau 33⅓ per cent. above was found probable by the master and assumed to be such by the lower court. In *Bluefield Water Works & Improvement Co.* v. *Public Service Commission*, 679, *post*, one 50 per cent. above the 1914 level was contended for; in the case at bar a plateau 25 per cent. above. But for the assumption that there will be a plateau there is no basis in American experience. The course of prices for the last 112 years indicates, on the contrary, that there may be a practically continuous decline for nearly a generation; that the present price level may fall to that of 1914 within a decade; and that, later, it may fall much lower. Prices rose steadily (with but slight and short recessions) for the 20 years before the United States entered the World War. From the low level of 1897 they rose 21 per cent. to 1900; then rose further (with minor fluctuations, representing times of good business or bad) and reached in 1914 a point 50 per cent. above the 1897 level. Then the great rise incident to the war set in. "Wholesale Prices, 1890 to 1921," U.S. Department of Labor, Bureau of Labor Statistics, Bulletin No. 320, pp. 9-26. These are averages of the wholesale prices of all commodities. In the Bureau chart the 1913 prices are taken as the datum line (100). As compared with them the 1897 level was 67, the 1900 level 81. The chart on page 10 of the pamphlet entitled "Price Changes and Business Prospects," published by the Cleveland Trust Company, gives price fluctuations for the 110 years prior to 1921. It shows three abrupt rises in the price level, by reason of war; and some less abrupt falls, by reason of financial panic. These may be called abnormal. But the normal has never been a plateau. The chart shows that the peak price levels were practically the same during the War of 1812, the Civil War, and the World War; and it shows that practically continuous declines, for about 30 years, followed the first two wars. The experience after the third may be similar.

> Mr. Justice Brandeis, dissenting, in *Southwestern Bell Telephone Co.* v. *Public Service Commission,* 262 U.S. 276, 304-305, n. 16 (1923).

April 27, 1932

Dear Walter:

Thank you for letting me see B.B.'s pungent passage.

Having talked not a little about the past, I have not unnaturally given you the impression that I am chiefly concerned with it, or, in the alternative, with the more remote future. But unlike B.B., I am neither historian nor philosopher. If I have any temperament at all, it is that of the statesman who seeks to bring things to pass here and now, in the near future. But that presupposes a little knowledge of history and some philosophy. And therefore it is that I deem the past and its meaning of considerable importance in guiding my thinking about men who are responsible for measures for working out of the depression. Like you, I too want "the loaded ass" to cross the torrent. But to me it is important not to forget that he is an ass, and the enterprise of crossing must not too readily and completely be left to his devising. I distrust figures of speech in politics — perhaps because I am no good at inventing them — and so I will say in plain English that the past performances of our leaders in business, finance and politics, particularly in finance, for they have had direction of things, seem to me most important in the kind of confidence that we ought to repose in them now. In short, I do not think that we should surrender independent and critical judgment on the panaceas that they hastily and hopefully devise.

I am not merely standing on the sidelines with a remote interest in, or disdain of, the passing show. For more than a year I have spent not a little time and energy on concrete problems that confront the Administration. I am just back from Washington in response to a summons to help on some of the fiscal problems of the government. I don't know what impression you brought back, but I felt I was breathing an atmosphere of panic and timidity. On what seems to me the core of the present world situation practically nothing is being done. So far as I can make out, the President thinks all the reparations-debt talk is "propaganda emanating from Wall Street." But even on the major assumption of their effort — that we can work things out, or at least must, at home without reference to Europe — I discerned no long-range thinking, no realization of the truly constructive things that ought to be attempted, in addition to the preventive measures. Panic and even terrorism operate in connection with the new economy program. The balanced budget became a symbol, and most thinking stopped as to the manner of balancing. Economy has become a symbol, and any slicing anywhere, no matter what its consequences, is the order of the day to such an extent that Congressmen and Senators don't dare call their souls their own. Some of the things that are being done in the name of economy in Washington just now make one really despair of the candor and courage, or even the humor of those who rule us. And all of it is whipped up by the business and financial leaders, who stimulate the press and the influential forces in the communities in response to which "the Hill" is going to commit all sorts of foolishness.

It is against this kind of folly and unthinking activism — let's do something without recking consequences — that I think it is so essential to be on guard. The general history of the last twenty or twenty-five years is an experience that we ought not to forget. When I first came out of Law School and found myself at once pitched into work with Stimson on prosecutions for rebates by railroads and big shippers, on the sugar fraud cases, the bank manipulations and commodity cornerings revealed in the panic of 1907, I was still innocent and assumed that those manifestations were merely the pathology of big business. But in the years that followed I naturally began to wonder to what extent what I had theretofore regarded as aberrations and incidents were really organic. The resistance to, even more than the disclosures of, Brandeis regarding waste and exploitation in railroad management, the relation of the bankers to these abuses, the far-reaching implications of banker control and big business as analyzed by Brandeis in his *Other People's Money* in 1914, the passionate intensity of the opposition to his appointment in 1916 on the part of finance and big business and their retainers, the accentuation of motives of greed after the

War, the subversion of even the most established banking traditions to recklessness and gambling parading under the new devices of pyramiding and affiliates — all this and more took me out of my age of innocence. And I am not talking in generalities. It has been part of my job here to study in detail these manifestations, because they fell directly within the subject matter of the so-called "courses" for which I was responsible. I mean specifically such affairs as the St. Paul [railway] reorganization and the relation of Kuhn, Loeb thereto, the Alleghany Company and J. P. Morgan, the whole miserable story of utility valuation, and the share that our most eminent lawyers have had in all these doings.

Mine being a pragmatic temperament, all my scepticism and discontent with the present order and tendencies have not carried me over to a new, comprehensive scheme of society, whether socialism or communism. Or, perhaps, ten years in government, and as many more of intensive study of its problems, have made me also sceptical of any full-blown new scheme and left me most conscious of the extraordinary difficulties of the problems of the Great Society. Not that I do not wonder sometimes whether the thorough-going integrity of an artist like Edmund Wilson, with all his innocence or perhaps because of it, does not go to the root of things more trenchantly and more fearlessly than I do. At all events, I do not embrace, and indeed distrust, a full-blown, "rational" counter-system. But I should be disloyal to all my experience if I did not rigorously keep to the foreground my bottom conviction, as pithily expressed by a recent writer in the *Commonweal*, that "greed is the witch," and more particularly my distrust of the capacity for disinterested insight and courageous thinking on the part of those who have had the dominant direction of affairs during the last decade or so. That's why I deem it so profoundly important to exert an uncompromising critical spirit upon their doings and their proposals. I think you will agree that those were wrong who insisted that during the War we must do nothing except think about fighting the War, and postpone considerations regarding the peace until after the War was over. That was not Lincoln's way. All through the Civil War he thought of the days of peace, for he knew well that the way in which the War was conducted and more particularly the feelings that were released or checked, would determine the aftermath of the War. So also, I think it was an act of great statesmanship on the part of Stanley Baldwin during the General Strike to concentrate not merely on putting down the Strike but also on the state of mind which would be left by the Strike.

In the same way, as I have heretofore put it to you, none of these so-called emergency measures — apart perhaps from immediate relief work — are merely emergency measures without effect upon the future. And that is why I am so insistent that all the proposals be canvassed with adequate opportunity for deliberation, even during the emergency, and that opposition or criticism be not met, as it has been all too much met, with the spirit of resentment against critics and questioners. And it is essential to bring into the open and keep them there, matters that Washington and high finance either neglect or oppose. For it is not at all impossible that as a result of the depression our social situation will have been worsened, not merely because of the impoverishment of vast numbers of our fellow beings, but even more so because when the tide will have turned, a greater percentage of the wealth of the country will be found to have come into the control of even a smaller percentage of the population than was the case before the depression. And if that be so, those of us who, by temperament or habit of conviction, believe that we do not have to make a sudden and drastic break with the past but by gradual, successive, although large, modifications may slowly evolve out of this profit-mad society, may find all our hopes and strivings indeed reduced to a house of cards.

Always yours,
F.F.

In the summer of 1932, Governor Ely, without consulting Frankfurter in advance, nominated him for the Supreme Judicial Court of Massachusetts. Former Governor Fuller, who had been Governor of Massachusetts when Frankfurter intervened in the Sacco-Vanzetti case, at once issued a statement which made no attempt to hide its anger. "With Ely pardoning murderers and Frankfurter an open sympathizer with murderers on the supreme bench," said Fuller, "I see no reason why murder should not flourish in Massachusetts. Were I a member of the Governor's Council, I would cut off my right hand before I would vote to confirm Frankfurter." Statements in praise of Frankfurter and in support of the nomination were made, among others, by Newton D. Baker, former Secretary of War; Judge George W. Anderson, retired, United States Circuit Court of Appeals; Judge Robert P. Patterson of the United States district court of New York; and Robert J. Watt, secretary-treasurer of the Massachusetts branch, American Federation of Labor.

The nomination was announced on June 22, 1932. Frankfurter told the Governor that he was reluctant to accept, and on June 29 he submitted a formal letter declining the nomination. The letter was given to the press by the Governor on July 12. News of Frankfurter's declination was in the meantime withheld at the Governor's request, because of his desire to have further opportunities to persuade Frankfurter to accept. Confirmation of the nomination had been assured. Frankfurter's letter of June 29 sets forth the reasons for his declination.

Cambridge, Mass., June 29, 1932

My dear Governor Ely:

Your Excellency's nomination of me for the Supreme Judicial Court has presented the most difficult decision of my professional life. While I knew that my name was mentioned for the vacancy created by Mr. Justice Carroll's death, I did not feel called upon then to make a decision. I was confident that as a matter of course I would have an opportunity for reflection, in case you were to consider me for another vacancy, before a nomination was made. Your Excellency's action in naming me for Mr. Justice Sanderson's place therefore found me completely unprepared.

The choice could not be easy. You have offered me an opportunity that comes to very few lawyers. To join the bench which can draw upon the spirit of Shaw and Holmes for the creative tasks of judicial administration in our day, is a call of high honor and of profound importance to the well-being of the Commonwealth. Your confidence in me, confirmed by the widest expression of professional opinion, makes any words of gratitude seem feeble and irrelevant.

But I have other responsibilities to the law which, after much anguish of mind, I feel I ought not now to sever. As against the opportunities for immediate achievement on the bench, the long-term effects of legal education make their claim. The grave problems already upon us and those looming on the horizon require as never before a courageous and learned bar. And from such a bar alone can come an enlightened judiciary. The future direction of bar and bench will be determined by the quality of our law schools. Moreover, the fabric of the law, particularly our public law, we have been told repeatedly by the most far-sighted in the profession, must be designed chiefly by the law schools. This work must go forward, and I cannot bring myself to believe that I should prematurely abandon my share in it, however great and honorable the opportunity you offer me. I should have less confidence in the rightness of this decision did not the admonitions of colleagues make me feel that to leave this School now would be a kind of desertion.

Most respectfully,
FELIX FRANKFURTER

While going by air to the Chicago Democratic Convention to accept the Presidential nomination, Roosevelt paused in his journey to engage in a long telephone conversation with Frankfurter. Sworn to secrecy by Governor Ely, Frankfurter could not tell Roosevelt that his congratulations came too late, for the judicial appointment had already been declined in private. Then the conversation shifted to political matters, and the help which Governor Ely could give Roosevelt in carrying the New England states.

The long telephone conversation was summarized by Frankfurter in the following memorandum.

Memorandum of telephone conversation between Felix Frankfurter and Governor Roosevelt, July 2, 1932

R.: Well, Felix, I am glad to hear your voice. I haven't been able to tell you how happy I am that you got your big chance. I wish it were the Supreme Court of the United States — that's where you belong. Do you have trial work?

F.: It's like your Court of Appeals.

R.: They told me it was like our Supreme Court.

F.: They're wrong; don't take any more advice from the people who told you that.

R.: Rosenman told me that on the plane on the way out to Chicago.

F.: So that's all you fellows had to talk about on the way out. No — it's the court on which Holmes and Shaw sat.

R.: That's fine. Well, I want to see you.

F.: Listen, I don't have to tell you that you got off on the right foot at Chicago.

R.: Yes, I think we got off on the right foot. It helped to straighten things out.

F.: Now what I called you for is something very specific. I could not get hold of your wife or Rosenman, and I have an important suggestion that I want to put to you at once. It concerns Massachusetts and Ely. I wish you would write a rather personal note to Governor Ely, asking him to come down to see you as soon as his public business permits. You could say that you are asking him to do what you would have done if Fate had reversed the roles.

R.: There is a limit to what a fellow will do to turn the other cheek.

F.: But I wish you would write him, not as Governor but as National Committeeman. Remember he is that.

R.: Yes, that's true. But he must be an awful ass.

F.: No, he's a novice in politics, certainly in national politics. I don't think you appreciate the intense bitterness up here, not only in Massachusetts but in Rhode Island. Ely is National Committeeman of Massachusetts and it is very important that other fellows don't run away with the position. I don't think it would in the slightest impair the dignity of your position or your native dignity to say that as National Committeeman of Massachusetts you hoped he would come down to see you. I really think it would be all right to do it.

R.: But of course I've already done a lot of turning the other cheek.

F.: I have never heard Ely say an unkind thing about you.

R.: My Lord, he did it on the air. I heard his speech at the primaries convention.

F.: Of course his nominating speech wasn't written by him.

R.: But the way it was written was even worse. They wanted him to talk with Hague and he wouldn't stand for it. [*Frank Hague was "boss" of the Democratic party in New Jersey.*]

F.: He's an upstate Springfield fellow. You will be able to play ball with him, and you can afford to be generous. I'm sure no one would misunderstand it or think badly of it.

R.: Only two people over-stepped the bounds of decency at the Convention: Frank Hague and Ely.

F.: Because of his speech?

R.: Things he said to the delegates.

F.: When? That surprises me.

R.: I wish you would talk to Jimmy [Roosevelt] about things out there. He will give you the picture. He could run out to see you today or tomorrow.

F.: I tried to get hold of Jimmy. I wired and phoned Rye Beach and got no answer.

R.: He may be sleeping, but I'm sure you can get him in Boston.

F.: I don't see how you stood it all. The freshness of your voice over the radio was grand.

R.: All right, was it?

F.: It pulled a pretty difficult situation quickly together. You got the jump on them then and there. Now keep it. To return to Ely — as to turning the other cheek, you know the Jew is supposed to be the only man in Christendom to turn the other cheek. You really can afford to take the initiative with Ely.

R.: People don't see it in that light.

F.: I'm sure you could write a letter consistent with your position as well as your nature. I have seen Ely three times. He is a simple country fellow.

R.: I've seen him at Governor's conventions and elsewhere.

F.: He's really a simple nature.

R.: How do you mean "simple"? There are two meanings, you know.

F.: I think he is both. But remember this: from the word go, he said you would be his second choice. Then things got messed up; things here are all snarled up in local bitterness.

R.: That's Boston. New York is all smoothed out.

F.: It isn't merely local — even New Hampshire and Rhode Island are involved. Ely and his following count there.

R.: Even Maine.

F.: Massachusetts, Rhode Island, Connecticut and New York are very important, and Ely is outstanding among Smith people now.

R.: I'll start something right away. It may not be exactly what you suggest.

F.: That's fine, and I'll get hold of Jimmy. I was sitting next to him (Ely) not so long ago at lunch; he didn't say a thing then about you that couldn't have been taken down and published.

R.: He'll be all right.

F.: You see things here all snarled up by the local situation and the Governorship.

R.: No doubt.

F.: Feeling is intensely bitter here. But you can break it. Ely would have to come to Canossa — to Albany.

R.: Walsh has been fine. [*Senator Walsh of Massachusetts earned Roosevelt's gratitude for not working for Al Smith.*]

F.: The peg you can hang your letter to Ely on is that he is National Committeeman; that gives you an official relationship.

R.: Yes, I'll do something. I am going on a cruise next week, going to Little Boar's Head. Maybe you can come out there.

F.: I'm going to be here right along. As soon as I get your free mind, I have some things of immediate importance to tell you in regard to the finances of this Government.

R.: I wish you would see Colonel House [*former advisor to President Wilson*] and ask him for a document on things economic that I mailed to him this morning. It was drawn up by Tugwell, Berle and Moley. [*Rexford Tugwell, Adolf Berle, and Raymond Moley were all members of the Brain Trust.*]

F.: Remember this in your speeches about a balanced budget: When you are in the White House you'll be confronted with a deficit next year probably as big as this year's.

R.: Just about.

F.: It's very important to remember that in what you say and don't say. That's what they'll leave for you. There are some specific things I want to talk to you about later.

R.: That's good. I hope I'll see you soon.

F.: You think about my first question.

R.: I'll start something right away.

F.: Keep your health, Frank. Good luck.

Frankfurter had a long talk with James Roosevelt about the political situation in Massachusetts and throughout New England. As a result of this conversation, and of an early meeting with Roosevelt, Frankfurter began an intensive campaign, ultimately successful, to persuade Al Smith to drop his sulky anger and openly support Roosevelt for the Presidency. In the campaign itself Al Smith was very helpful in swinging his powerful following in New England behind Roosevelt.

Albany, N. Y., July 14, 1932

Dear Felix:

I want to send you this line to thank you for your awfully nice telegram about Jimmy. I am anxious to have a talk with you as soon as we can get together.

Always sincerely yours,
F.D.R.

Cambridge, Mass., July 18, 1932

Dear Molly Dewson:

You see one of the gains from not having gone on the Massachusetts Court is that I can be alive during the campaign.

I am trying to acquire detailed knowledge about Roosevelt's work as Governor. If you have any material on the following please send it along:

1. Financial policy, including taxation
2. Social legislation
3. Unemployment relief and future planning against unemployment
4. Water power
5. Other public utilities
6. Agricultural development and its relation to industrial development
7. Penal and correctional reform
8. Standards of appointment to office
9. General administration

You did a grand job in Chicago.

Ever yours,
FELIX FRANKFURTER

July 21, 1932

Dear Governor —

Here is a real asset. Frankfurter is known favorably by hundreds of law school men. He is a marvelous speaker and writer.

My best
MOLLY DEWSON

Mary (Molly) Dewson had worked with Frankfurter, years before, in preparing a brief for the Consumer's League on minimum wages for

*women and children in the District of Columbia. The Supreme Court in
the Adkins case struck down the minimum wage law. In the 1932 campaign
she was director, Women's Division, Democratic National Campaign Committee, an important job in which she persuaded women voters to support
Roosevelt. This letter indicates the range of subjects on which Frankfurter
concentrated during the Presidential campaign.*

Cambridge, Mass., July 22, 1932

Dear Frank:

Since even during your flight to Chicago, you found time to learn
about my nomination to the Supreme Judicial Court, you may have since,
in the calm way in which you manage to do things, have noticed that I
declined Ely's nomination. I couldn't tell you about it when we talked
because I was under the obligation of silence. The fact of the matter is that
Ely named me without prior consultation because, as he told me since, "I
did not want to give you a chance to say 'no.' " Well, I did say "no" very
early, but Ely asked me to keep mum because he was trying for more than
two weeks to persuade me to accept. I declined, in essence, because it was
perfectly clear that I could be much more useful both to the law and to the
country where I am than to go on the Massachusetts Court.

And one of the things I am free to do now is to do my small share to
turn out Hoover and help elect you. I have your note saying that you are
anxious to have a talk with me, and I am at your disposal at any time or
place, beginning with Friday morning the 29th. I plan to loaf for a few
days.

There are a number of important matters about which I have some
things to say, but won't bother you on paper.

Always yours,
F.F.

Telegram to Frankfurter

Albany, N.Y., July 28, 1932

CONFIRMING TELEPHONE CALL THIS AFTERNOON, GOVERNOR ROOSEVELT DE-
LIGHTED TO HAVE YOU AND MRS FRANKFURTER COME TO ALBANY SATURDAY
AFTERNOON FOR DINNER AND SPEND THE NIGHT.

GUERNSEY T. CROSS, Secretary to the Governor

*Despite charges of corruption, James J. Walker, the friend and cham-
pion of Tammany, had been re-elected Mayor of New York in 1929 with
a 500,000 majority. Roosevelt had always been suspicious of Jimmy Walker
but for a time he had entered into an uneasy political alliance with him. In
1928, in an eloquent speech, Walker had nominated Roosevelt for the*

Governorship. Four years later Roosevelt was to force Walker to resign in disgrace as Mayor.

The corruption which ran through the Walker administration soon became a public scandal. Business groups campaigned in vain for reform. Two great religious orators, Rev. John Haynes Holmes and Rabbi Stephen S. Wise, denounced Mayor Walker as if he were a wise-cracking devil — and the people listened. Roosevelt had a premonition that disaster awaited the debonair Mayor. He told William Randolph Hearst that "our little Mayor can save much trouble in the future by getting on the job, cleaning his own house, and stopping wise-cracks. If he does not do all this, he can have only himself to blame if he gets into trouble."

Some observers, including Walter Lippmann, then with the New York World, thought Roosevelt was too patient with the spectacular wrongdoing of Walker. It was the memory of these years, in part, that led Mr. Lippmann to prefer Newton D. Baker to Roosevelt as the Democratic Presidential candidate in 1932.

Early in 1931 the New York legislature appointed a committee, under the chairmanship of Samuel H. Hofstadter, to examine the civic government of New York and of courts within the area of the city. The committee counsel was Samuel Seabury, and under his leadership, the exposure of corruption went on at an urgent pace, so that the Seabury investigation became a classic example of a fearless public inquiry. But Walker remained nonchalant and apparently invulnerable, even though the net steadily tightened over more of his friends and colleagues.

Finally Seabury presented a report that in effect accused Mayor Walker of flagrant and persistent corruption, and of the manifold abuse of his office. Using a rarely exercised prerogative, Governor Roosevelt decided to sit in judgment on the Walker case himself, to examine the Mayor personally, and to remove him from office if the evidence justified such severe action.

Great interests were at stake. Roosevelt was on the eve of his own Presidential campaign, and the whole country was waiting to see what he would do in New York. He might outrage and alienate powerful figures in the Democratic party if he struck at Tammany by pulling down Walker in shame and disgrace. On the other hand, any truce with evil would tarnish and destroy his credentials as a reformer.

Roosevelt never hesitated. His cross-examination of Walker in the executive chamber at Albany lasted several days and was devastating. He broke the Mayor's gay façade and reduced him to bewildered futility. Walker appealed to the courts to save him from this ordeal, arguing that the Governor had no power to remove him. The court upheld the Governor's power of removal as constitutional. Crushed and afraid, Walker shrank

*from again answering Roosevelt's penetrating questions and abruptly re-
signed.*

*Roosevelt always regarded his dramatic and courageous victory over
Mayor Walker as a landmark in his own career.*

Cambridge, Mass., August 5, 1932

Dear Frank:

Since leaving Albany I have thought a great deal about the Walker
situation. I have read carefully Seabury's original specifications in his letter
of June 8th, the Mayor's reply, and now Seabury's answer to the Mayor. I
have not read the record of the hearings before the Hofstadter Committee
but I did read Walker's testimony before the Committee as printed in the
New York *Times*. If Seabury accurately represents the record — that is, if
he not only quotes accurately but gives the quotations and their context,
and makes no vital omissions — then it seems to me that the facts ineluc-
tably compel removal of the Mayor.

I speak as one who spent nearly six years as a prosecutor when I say
that certainly some of the charges would warrant action by the Grand Jury;
I do not say conviction by a petty jury. But the criteria for criminal prosecutions are not applicable, and to think about them is only likely to confuse.
What Cardozo said about the responsibility of officers of the court, i.e.,
lawyers, is of course applicable to public officials generally and especially the
chief executive of the nation's metropolis. "The Grand Jury," Chief Judge
Cardozo wrote in the Karlin Case, "inquires into crimes with a view to
punishment or correction through the sanction of the criminal law. There
are, however, many forms of professional misconduct that do not amount
to crimes. Even when they do, disbarment is not punishment within the
meaning of the criminal law" (*People ex rel. Karlin* v. *Culkin*, 248, N.Y.,
465, 470). To paraphrase Cardozo, there are many forms of official misconduct that do not amount to crimes but do call for removal.

Surely the Sisto matter, the Equitable Bus franchise affair, the Equitable Trust Company letter of credit transaction, standing unexplained,
make out a clear case of the acceptance of substantial favors by the Mayor
at the hands of people who are seeking favors from the Mayor and towards
whom he should have been in a position of austere indifference and impar-
tiality. Taken in their cumulative effect they show the Mayor to have been
a person of what, in the days of Victorian morality in the case of women,
used to be called "easy virtue." Not only does the Mayor not adequately
explain the case against him made by these transactions, but his explanations are contradictory, evasive, and — coming from a man of his intellectual skill and alertness — incredible. And when all this is coupled with
Sherwood's role and the Mayor's relation to Sherwood, no other reasonable

conclusion is possible except that the Mayor has not met those standards of rectitude and propriety which surely must be exacted from the Mayor of New York.

It is not as though Walker was "let in" by happy-go-lucky friends who liked his company and simply paid tribute to good fellowship. The inescapable fact is that he was the beneficiary of sizable money favors from those who themselves had substantial money interests in having the Mayor as a friend, in being "solid" with the Mayor who had enormous power in the dispensation of enormous public concessions of one sort or another. The situations in which the Mayor was entangled are of course complicated and without precedent. But at bottom it reduces itself to a relatively simple matter, namely, whether the removing power extends to a series of instances in which the Mayor of New York was the beneficiary of sizable sums from people who contemporaneously were interested in official actions to be taken by the Mayor in matters of great monetary interest.

I have no doubt that the kind of an opinion that you would write would put the matter so simply and in language of such unanswerable austerity that it will not be possible to put any other interpretation upon your action than as the performance of a sad but inescapable duty.

Always yours,
F.F.

J. A. Sisto represented a taxicab holding company interested in limiting the number of taxicabs in New York. He gave the Mayor various bonds worth more than $25,000. The Equitable Bus Company, without funds and without experience, tried to use the Mayor's influence to establish a monopoly over the City's bus transportation. J. Allan Smith, an Equitable agent who had provided Walker with a letter of credit, later paid off a $3,000 overdraft for the Mayor. Russell T. Sherwood, once a $60-a-week bookkeeper and later a financial agent for the Mayor, had $961,000 in his bank account, with more than $700,000 of this amount in cash.

Cambridge, Mass., August 5, 1932

Dear Frank:

I wonder if you have seen the enclosed article by Charles Merz in regard to the loss of our foreign trade. Merz deals with the matter very neutrally. I believe you could present in dramatic form the responsibilities of the President for the loss of our export trade.

I do not mean, of course, general talk such as the threats now centering in Ottawa. I mean a factual marshalling of what has appeared in the daily news during the last two or three years — the actual events showing, from day to day, how in some country or other by governmental action or mercantile arrangement some outlet for American goods has been closed. Some of your research men could without difficulty dig out this material from the New York *Times* and the *U. S. Daily* and shape up a very telling indictment against the policies of the present Administration.

We had a grand visit with you. Marion came away quite excited by the vitality and good humor and confidence with which you are leading the fight.

Always yours,
F.F.

Charles Merz's article appeared in the New York World. *The Ottawa Conference was preparing to raise tariffs by all members of the British Empire and Commonwealth against the rest of the world.*

Albany, N.Y., August 7, 1932

Dear Felix:

Thanks much for letting me see this interesting letter from Frank Bolen. In Philadelphia they are faced with the difficult problem of a perfectly impossible local organization as in other places, but they should recognize that the issue is the Presidency rather than Philadelphia city government!

Your letter about the Walker case is grand. I shall have a bad time if Walker insists on calling and cross-examining all the witnesses, etc., put on. I have, of course, complete discretion, but it is my feeling that if Walker gives specific reasons to cross-examine definite witnesses on definite points, I must summon them in order to avoid the obvious effort to make it appear that he is about to be convicted after the prosecution has been heard, without opportunity for him to cross-examine. I wish you would give me your slant on this.

I am delighted to see that article by Charles Merz. I am working on it.

It was grand to see you both last week. You stimulate me enormously. Repeat the dose again.

As ever yours,
FRANKLIN D. ROOSEVELT

It is difficult, at this point in time, to realize that Roosevelt, before the beginning of the 1932 campaign, feared the strength of President Hoover in the great industrial states of the East. This feeling was due not to Hoover's own appeal but to the soreness and divisions in the Democratic party. Roosevelt was not yet the hero of the Democratic party; he was resented by some leaders for having thrust Al Smith into political oblivion and by others for having struck a cynical political bargain by choosing John Nance

Garner of Texas as his Vice-Presidential running mate. These crosscurrents swirled in angry confusion in Pennsylvania politics, with its important electoral college vote, and Roosevelt was grateful for Frank Bolen's careful and documented analysis of the situation.

Cambridge, Mass., August 8, 1932

Dear Frank:

I spent a very interesting evening with David Sarnoff, the President of the Radio Corporation, with whom I happen to have very pleasant relations. Confidentially, he is as critical of the President — born of knowledge extending for over many years — as you and I. I do not know whether under any circumstances he would publicly break his party ties — he is a traditional Republican — but I think it would be a very considerable help to have him know you, to get the feel of you, and to convey that to the many, many people with whom he comes in contact. As a matter of fact, he has been infected with some of the New York poison and I spent many hours in making him see a very different picture. My own account, based on personal experiences in official life, left, I believe, a considerable impression.

He was, as you know, at Owen Young's side in the formulation of the Young Plan and has very trenchant and discerning views regarding international trade and the bearing thereon of debts and reparations. It occurs to me that it would be appropriate for you to invite him to Albany and have him put to you his views on the business aspects of our international relations, and thus have him gain a first-hand glimpse of you. He would, I am sure, cordially respond to such an invitation.

Always yours,
F.F.

Owen D. Young, an enlightened business executive, president of the General Electric Company, had been active in trying to settle Europe's war debts, and in showing the disastrous effects of reparations payments on world trade.

Cambridge, Mass., August 12, 1932

Dear Frank:

In the President's speech of acceptance, there appears the following sentence on the subject of prohibition:

> "Our opponents pledge the members of their party to destroy every vestige of constitutional and effective Federal control of the [liquor] traffic."

I need not tell you what a perversion this is of the repeal plank in the Democratic platform. But it is also a crass misrepresentation of legal history and a disregard of the constitutional situation as well as of the legislative condition that would remain were the 18th Amendment repealed tomorrow. I refer, of course, to the regulatory power conferred by the Commerce Clause, exercised through the Webb-Kenyon Act of 1913 and now subsisting regardless of the 18th Amendment. For in a unanimous decision of the Supreme Court rendered on May 16 last, the court speaking through Chief Justice Hughes held that the Webb-Kenyon Act continued in full vitality despite the adoption of the 18th Amendment. I quote from the case of *McCormick & Co.* v *Brown* which will be officially reported in 185 U.S.:

> "Prior to the adoption of the 18th Amendment, the Congress, exerting its constitutional power of regulation, had prohibited the movement of intoxicating liquors in interstate commerce into any state for purposes prohibited by the State law. . . . The Congress has not expressly repealed that Act and there is no basis for an implication of repeal."

And so the President's proposal insofar as it requires "absolute guarantees in the Constitution of the United States to protect each state from interference and invasion by its neighbors" would merely write into the Constitution the Webb-Kenyon Act when as a matter of fact the power to pass such protection is already included in the Commerce Clause and can be exercised, as it has been exercised since 1913, if a majority of the Congress deems such protection by the states necessary or desirable.

Of course, this does not touch the question of the saloon. But every state has complete control to deal with the problem of the saloons within its borders. To write provisions into the Constitution of the United States dealing with saloons opens up a new Pandora's box of difficulties regarding Federal regulation of local conditions. The power of the states to deal with this problem is ample; the power of the Federal government to protect the states in the enforcement of their state policies is equally ample without further constitutional provision.

Always yours,
F.F.

Frankfurter believed that President Hoover, in 1932 as in the 1928 campaign, would try to divide the Democrats on the issue of prohibition. Hence this warning letter to Roosevelt.

Albany, N.Y., August 24, 1932

Dear Felix:

It is certainly good to get your fine note and before that your telegram.

The Walker hearing drags on, but I am confident that it is best I should not give them any chance to say that I am railroading the case.

When the hearing is over I hope much that you will run over here to talk with me in strict confidence about the ethics and the law involved.

Very sincerely yours,
F.D.R.

Telegram to Roosevelt
Center Lovell, Me., September 2, 1932

WARM CONGRATULATIONS. RESIGNATION IS CONCESSION AND COMPLETE VINDICATION OF YOUR FIRMNESS, SKILL AND FAIRNESS AS CHIEF EXECUTIVE.

FELIX FRANKFURTER

This refers to Mayor Walker's resignation.

Albany, N.Y., September 6, 1932

Dear Felix: —
Ever so many thanks for your wire. Your opinion means a great deal to me.

Always sincerely yours,
F.D.R.

Cambridge, Mass., September 10, 1932

Dear Frank:
(1) Perhaps on the train you will find time to read the enclosed illuminating discussion of the share that restricted purchasing power had in causing the depression — the author is an economist at Ohio State University — and the lesson that teaches us for the future. See the quotation from Vanderlip and the confirmation, as to auto sales, in a recent clipping from the New York *Tribune*.

(2) If there is time, you might find it very profitable to have Commissioner Eastman of the Interstate Commerce Commission see your railroad speech before it's delivered.

(3) Finally, all good luck and my best wishes for the trip.

Ever yours,
F.F.

Writing to Roosevelt on the campaign train Frankfurter enclosed Gordon Hage's article in the New Republic *June 3, 1931, on* Credit and Prosperity, *showing that 65 per cent of auto sales in the United States went to incomes of $3,000 and less. He always reminded Roosevelt of the importance of people with small incomes in stimulating the process of recovery and breaking the depression. Joseph Eastman, a hero to Frankfurter, was* *the supreme authority in the country on railroad policy as it affected the public interest.*

Telegram to Roosevelt
Care Roosevelt Special
Via Southern Pacific, San Francisco, Cal.

Cambridge, Mass., September 22, 1932

YOUR RAILROAD AND POWER SPEECHES ARE ADMIRABLE ANALYSES OF PROB-
LEMS AND WISE FORMULATION OF APPLICABLE PRINCIPLES. ALL YOUR TALKS
ARE TRULY EDUCATIONAL AND FORECAST HOW EFFECTIVELY YOU WILL TAKE
THE WHOLE NATION TO SCHOOL WHEN YOU ARE IN THE WHITE HOUSE. THE
OMENS ARE MOST ENCOURAGING. WITH ALL GOOD WISHES.

FELIX FRANKFURTER

Walter Lippmann, knowing of Frankfurter's efforts to keep Al Smith committed to Roosevelt, described a long interview with Smith in which the rejected Democratic leader was plainly in a mood of truculent irritation with Roosevelt. It was after this letter from Lippmann that Frankfurter renewed his efforts with Smith, who finally agreed to speak in Boston. Frankfurter described this speech as "Al Smith at his golden best."

John J. Raskob, who played a central role in organizing Smith's Presidential campaign in 1928, also intervened to end Smith's sulking. Although out of sympathy with Roosevelt's outlook, Raskob was interested in efforts to strengthen party harmony. Bernard Baruch thought all differences should be subordinated to the task of removing Hoover from the White House. The World Economic Conference did not take place until Roosevelt was President in 1933. Phillip Littell had been one of the early editors of the New Republic.

September 28, 1932

Dear Walter:

That's a very poignant account you give of Al Smith's mood, and plainly enough it is a deep mood. I fear that he is in the grip of primitive emotions, for of course the ordinary play of politics and the rules of the game in no wise would explain his behavior since Chicago.

Because primitive feeling dictates his present attitude only a counter feeling equally deep-rooted can, I suspect, pull him out of the "bog" in which you found him. A strong personal intimacy will alone be able to dissolve his present rigidity. I have gathered from time to time that between no person and Al Smith is there a deeper elemental intimacy than between him and Jakie Raskob. I think Raskob is the fellow who can move him. And isn't Barney Baruch the one to make Raskob see the devastating personal and historic injury that would befall Al Smith if he remains Achilles in his tent? What say you to this?

I have excellent reasons to believe — though my information does not come from the State Department — that the World Economic Conference has been put off to the Greek kalends — at least until next spring or summer. Do you know anything about this? It seems to me an ominous delay.

Ever yours,

F.F.

P.S.   I thought you said some things that needed to be said about Hoover's courage. To me he is the most timid man who has been in the White House since Buchanan. And I speak, as I need hardly tell you, not from speculation but from intimate details of his relations to some of the most important people in his administration. Years ago Phil Littell said were he to write an epitaph of Hoover, he would write: "Here lies the man whose dominant passion was fear." I think that I would modify that to read: "Here lies a man of over-weening ambition yoked to fear."

Chicago, Ill., October 1, 1932

Dear Felix:

I just want to send you this line to thank you for your telegram.

I really think the trip has been highly successful from all points of view. I want to see you when I get back.

With best wishes to you,

Sincerely,

F.D.R.

Telegram to Mr. and Mrs. Frankfurter

Hyde Park, N.Y., October 4, 1932

HOPE YOU BOTH CAN SPEND SATURDAY NIGHT HERE WITH ME AT HYDE PARK. IT WILL BE GRAND TO SEE YOU.

FRANKLIN D. ROOSEVELT

Reply Wire

MANY THANKS. . . . WE SHALL BE DELIGHTED TO TURN UP SATURDAY AFTERNOON.

FELIX FRANKFURTER

Telegram to Roosevelt

Cambridge, Mass., October 5, 1932

YOUR TRIUMPH IN SECURING LEHMAN'S NOMINATION IS FITTING CLIMAX TO ACHIEVEMENTS OF YOUR TRIP.

F.F.

*Herbert Lehman — "my good right arm," Roosevelt called him — had
been nominated to succeed Roosevelt as Governor of New York.*

Telegram to Roosevelt
Cambridge, Mass., October 7, 1932

SUBMIT FOR YOUR CONSIDERATION DESIRABILITY OF RELEASING BONUS STATE-
MENT FOR NEXT MONDAY MORNING. FULLY CONFIDENT, HOWEVER, OF YOUR
SURE TOUCH AS TO TIME AND CIRCUMSTANCES FOR SUCH MATTER.

F.F.

Telegram to Roosevelt
Cambridge, Mass., October 9, 1932

ACCORDING TO YOUR MESSAGE THROUGH SAYRE AM DRAFTING MEMORANDUM
ON FEDERAL COURTS. YOU'LL HAVE IT IN TWO OR THREE DAYS.

FELIX FRANKFURTER
Cambridge, Mass., October 12, 1932

Dear Frank:

Unfortunately Frank Sayre gave me only the meagerest indication of
what you wanted in regard to the federal courts — indeed, gave me no
intimations of the direction in which your own mind was running. But, as
you may know, federal jurisdiction happens to be one of my specialities,
and I have written a book on *The Business of the Supreme Court.* I have
therefore outlined in the enclosed what seemed to me to be the outstanding problems calling for attention in the present jurisdiction and position of
the federal courts, that also happen to be matters of real practical public
interest and concern. If there are other things you have in mind, regarding
which I can be of use, of course do let me know.

Continued good luck to you! In wishing you good luck, I don't mean
to overlook the wise judgments all along the line by you which have the
appearance of luck.

A good trip to you.

Faithfully yours,
F.F.

Enc.

*The enclosed memorandum has not been found among the Roosevelt
papers, and Frankfurter kept no copy.*

Telegram to Roosevelt
Cambridge, Mass., October 12, 1932

ON FRIDAY MORNING THE PAPERS WILL CARRY YOUR VIEWS ON RELIEF, WHICH
NECESSARILY WILL INVOLVE A SPENDING PROGRAM, THEREFORE SUGGEST FOR
YOUR CONSIDERATION THE ADVANTAGE OF APPEARING IN THE SATURDAY MORN-

ING PAPERS WITH THE BONUS STATEMENT TO SHOW YOUR AWARENESS OF THE OTHER SIDE OF THE PROBLEM. THIS WILL ALSO AVOID APPEARANCE OF THAT STATEMENT AS RESPONSE TO REPUBLICAN DEMAND, FOR HOOVER PROBABLY WILL MAKE REFERENCE TO THE SUBJECT IN HIS CLEVELAND SPEECH SATURDAY NIGHT.

FELIX FRANKFURTER

Thousands of veterans had come to Washington in June to petition for the passage of the bonus bill which would place an estimated additional $2 billion in circulation. While opposed to the bonus bill, Roosevelt, for political reasons, hedged his opposition. On October 13, after a telephone conversation with the campaigning Roosevelt, Frankfurter wrote to Lippmann in defense of the candidate's conduct. The relevant portion of this letter follows.

October 13, 1932

Dear Walter:

Roosevelt's performance on the bonus sheds interesting light on his alleged indecisiveness. I had talk with him about it — or rather he brought up the subject — nearly three months ago. His views were as clear and definite as you and I would wish. And they have, I believe, remained so ever since. Despite pressure from powerful members of his party — and some who ought to know better — he decided weeks ago to express his views, and as you know, actually formulated them about two weeks ago. After your phone, I urged him to come out last Monday, and later suggested — after I had learned what Coolidge was going to say at the Tuesday meeting — that he forestall Cal. But he couldn't be moved. He has his own sense of time and timeliness, as I have experienced in other matters. Had I been in his place, I would have disposed of the bonus business long ago — at least I think I would have, though God only knows what a candidature would do to a man. And so he may well be subject to criticism for biding his time in the way he does. But it has nothing to do with lack of decision or conviction. In fact, it is one form that his decisiveness takes. And what has struck me in the limited knowledge I have had of some of his campaign decisions is that he makes his own. With all of his attachment to Colonel House and regard for the latter's advice, I happen to know that he disregarded an urgent importunity of House's, reinforced by that of another Wilson leader, and followed his independent judgment. The event, I believe, vindicated Roosevelt. But whether or no, I was interested in the independence of his judgment and the confidence that he has in it, alongside of the eager accessibility of his mind. . . .

F.F.

Telegram to Roosevelt
Care of Roosevelt Special
Indianapolis, Ind.

Cambridge, Mass., October 20, 1932

HAVE JUST HEARD YOUR PITTSBURGH SPEECH. AN EXTRAORDINARILY EFFECTIVE
AND DEVASTATING PRESENTATION OF NATIONAL FINANCE UNDER HOOVER RULE.
YOUR BONUS TREATMENT COULD NOT HAVE BEEN BETTER DONE. IT PUTS THE
BUSINESS IN ITS RIGHT PERSPECTIVE. THE WHOLE SPEECH MOST EDUCATIVE
AND POWERFUL. WARM CONGRATULATIONS AND GOOD WISHES.

FELIX FRANKFURTER

*Frankfurter had reason to regret this enthusiastic telegram. To begin
with, he really wished that Roosevelt had been much bolder in dealing with
the bonus problem — a point of view which Roosevelt later accepted. In
addition, and far more important, this Pittsburgh speech with its emphasis
on economy, reduced expenditures, and a balanced budget proved an embarrassment to Roosevelt once he became President.*

*On October 26, Frankfurter wrote to Lippmann on various themes, in-
cluding the bonus issue which had become a test question in the campaign.
Frankfurter said:*

If Roosevelt is elected, I think he will often do the right things, as it were,
on inadequate and not wholly sturdy grounds. That's what I feel about his
bonus statement. That issue, in Al's phrase, is out of the window now. I
think he did well to discuss the whole bonus issue in the perspective of a
financial analysis of the government, and the conditions that he laid down
put the ki-bosh on the bonus. Of course Cleveland would have done it
otherwise — but then Cleveland, with all his forthrightness, Nevins not-
withstanding, did two of the most lastingly hurtful things to the well-being
of this country and this country's relation to the peace of the world as well.
I mean of course the Debs injunction and Venezuela. Franklin's accommodating spirit has of course its outs, but also its ins. I don't expect heroic
action from him, and when I think of the high-minded men who counsel
him to say nothing about the bonus — of course I think they were wholly
wrong — I don't feel too badly about the way in which he handled it, for,
as I have indicated, I expect him to do many things that will be wise in the
result in ways that will, from his point of view, arouse as little ill-feelings as
he likes to arouse.

Enroute Roosevelt Special, October 25, 1932

Dear Felix: —

That was an awfully nice telegram and while I am on the trip I want to
let you know how much I appreciate your wiring me.

I am more than glad that you approve of my bonus statement.
Raymond Moley is here with me and joins me in best wishes.

Always sincerely,
F.D.R.

Cambridge, Mass., October 26, 1932

Dear Frank:

After our telephone conversation the other day, I promptly communicated with Louis B. I have heard from him, and at the next opportunity for talk I shall give you his message.

Your second trip, like the first, was an unqualified success. You have probably heard John Davis' remark that it is a wonderful campaign speech that loses no votes. Your speeches held and gained votes.

Always yours,
F.F.

Louis B. is Mr. Justice Brandeis. John W. Davis, a leader of the American bar, was the Democratic Presidential candidate in 1924. This was one of Frankfurter's favorite quotations, perhaps too often used.

Telegram to Roosevelt

Cambridge, Mass., October 28, 1932

AFTER FURTHER REFLECTION CANNOT URGE TOO STRONGLY GREAT IMPORTANCE OF VERY SOLID SPEECH HERE.

FELIX FRANKFURTER

He wanted Roosevelt to make an impressive speech in Boston where there was some anti-Roosevelt sentiment because Al Smith was not the candidate.

Once he decided to enter the campaign on behalf of Roosevelt, Al Smith spoke with all his famous vigor and incisiveness. He derided Ogden Mills's administration of the Treasury Department in the Hoover Administration as a grotesque exhibition of timidity masked by a pretense to superior knowledge. Still interested in completely mending the breach between Roosevelt and Smith, Frankfurter hoped that Herbert Bayard Swope, an intimate friend of Bernard Baruch, could be enlisted in this cause. This letter, like the others to Lippmann, was written with Roosevelt's approval.

October 28, 1932

Dear Walter:

1. Al Smith handed Oggie a few last night — and used all his dramatic skill with great effectiveness. And this morning he would be groggy, were he

less thick-skinned, from the wallop with which you pasted him. I speak of that gent with such assurance, for I know him well. We were at Law School together, and I used to see him rather at close range in my early years in New York. But if you want to get a real insight into the irresponsibility and recklessness of his financial administration, as well as his unreliability, ask Baruch to tell you his story of his talk with Mills after Mills submitted his estimates last December. For the enlightenment of the American public, that story ought to be publicly told, but Baruch is, of course, a gentleman. But you ought to have it in the back of your head, particularly if Hoover were to be elected, with all the power that that would bring to Mills now and in '36.

2. Al's speech here was extremely effective for the particular audience for which it was intended. If I had to bet, I should bet Massachusetts would go for Hoover. But of course one can't tell how deep the tide is if the *Lit. Dig.* figures should turn out to be fair indices. Al was at his very best. And the outpouring of affection and devotion to him both at Providence and here had a quality about it such as I have never seen given to any American political figure. He touches their human qualities, that makes one realize how starved the American people are for a rich political personality. I think his bitterness is largely deflated. I had some frank talk with him in New York, and he got it all out of his system. Even then it wasn't directed personally against Roosevelt. Yesterday he was quite devoid of it — he was serene, full of good humor and bent on the job of bringing as much aid as he possibly could to the ticket. He did it so far as it was in him to do it.

3. There seems to be a good deal of touchiness on both sides as between Al and Franklin — each wants the other to make the overtures, each apparently is eagerly waiting for the other to take the old, vigorous, friendly step. I wish there were more fellows like Herbert Swope, who acutely see the qualities of both men and very actively play for the strength between them instead of emphasizing the differences and the tensions. Every time I see Herbert I am more impressed with the extraordinary powers of detachment, the gay objectivity, that one so seldom finds in so lusty a nature. I am for him strong. If I had a few spare millions, I'd make him run a paper with it — provided he ran the paper and nothing else.

4. Soon the show will be over. It does seem to me a gruelling process to everybody concerned. Al is of course dead right that the Conventions ought to be held in September and the campaign last not more than two months.

Yours always,
F.F.

On November 5, 1932, on Roosevelt's entreaty, Frankfurter entered the Presidential campaign personally and delivered a radio speech in support of his candidacy. Frankfurter said President Hoover "has demonstrated that he is devoid of the art of governing." He added that "Mr. Hoover has tragically failed as a political and popular leader because he distrusts the democratic process of reasoning with equals."

Then he said that "in Governor Roosevelt's administration of the greatest state in the union, he has shown that he is alive to the problems of the new day, and that he has both the will and the capacity to deal with them in the light of the new day. His financial administration, his early alertness to problems of relief, his refusal to starve social services on the false plea of economy, his reliance on associates like Miss Frances Perkins, the ablest industrial commissioner in the country, all give proof that as President he will endeavor to translate into action that philosophy of government so ably expressed in his speech before the Commonwealth Club of San Francisco and in his address on social justice in Detroit.

"His success in wresting wise measures of taxation, power regulation, and unemployment relief from Republican legislatures has demonstrated those qualities of effective persuasion which are the essence of political leadership.

"Governor Roosevelt's outlook and achievements, and the courage and hope of which his life is a triumph, justify us in following his lead. Supported by the liberal and progressive sentiment of the country, he can help us out of our present moral and material morass and start new ways of thought into new deeds of action. And so his election on Tuesday next may well be the augury of better days."

Telegram to Roosevelt
Cambridge, Mass., November 7, 1932

YOUR CAMPAIGN HAS EDUCATED THE HOPES OF THE NATION AND INVIGORATED ITS FAITH. AS A RESULT, NOT SINCE WILSON'S CAMPAIGN IN 1912 HAS THE PUBLIC TEMPER BEEN MORE RIPE TO SUPPORT THE PROGRESSIVE LEADERSHIP WHICH YOU HAVE ESPOUSED. THE MORROW WILL CALL THAT LEADERSHIP TO POWER. AFTER THE FOURTH OF MARCH YOU WILL BE ABLE TO MOBILIZE, AS HAS NO PRESIDENT SINCE WILSON, THE WILL AND WISDOM OF THE NATION FOR YOUR SUCCESSFUL VINDICATION OF THE CONCERT OF INTERESTS. TO THAT END MY DEVOTED WISHES. FAITHFULLY YOURS.

Felix Frankfurter

Cambridge, Mass., November 10, 1932

Dear Frank:

The end crowns all and a glorious end it is — a very great beginning.

Apart from all else, you will carry to the White House an equipment of transcendent importance. No predecessor of yours, not even T.R., I believe, brought to the Presidency so extensive and intimate a knowledge of his countrymen as you have. You will thus be the comprehending expression of the diverse interests, feelings, hopes and thoughts of the multiple forces which are unified into the nation. Pervasive confidence is bound to be the fruit of your wide and deep understanding of our national life, just as the overwhelming vote now makes you the embodiment of the nation's will.

Faithfully yours,
Felix Frankfurter

Cambridge, Mass., November 12, 1932

Dear Frank:

Just a word about the question you put to me after your Boston Arena speech. I am sure my observations are superfluous, for I assume that you have already decided against the trip. But I write because you asked me to tell you my views. Here they are, after mature reflection.

It is my clear conviction that a trip abroad would be a very, very serious mistake. In the first place, you would be dogged during your whole Administration by silly talk capable however of influencing naive public opinion, that those clever devils in Europe hornswoggled you. Every action or proposal looking towards international appeasement would be entangled with reference to the "secret diplomacy" of European conversations. The difficulties in the way of converting Americans to necessary action in the international field are sufficiently formidable. They ought not to be further complicated. (From that angle, I hope that no foreign potentates will be encouraged to come here.)

There is another aspect about the trip abroad. The hard winter ahead makes it most desirable for you to continue to represent to the people a simple, unostentatious life. A European trip would absolutely preclude that and it would introduce, with its inescapable "royal" entertainments, a damaging element into the situation.

Faithfully yours,
F.F.

P.S.   Mr. Justice Brandeis strongly concurs in the above.

The following memorandum by Frankfurter, which breaks off here in the middle of the first paragraph, was prepared for President-elect Roosevelt to give him guidance on his relations with President Hoover. Frankfurter had tried his hand on the kind of statement which Roosevelt might make after seeing the President. Hoover raised many difficulties, and Roosevelt began

to fear that Hoover wanted not consultation but commitments. Later Frank-
furter was instrumental in arranging frank talks between Roosevelt and
Secretary of State Stimson to ease the problems of transition.

November 14, 1932

Memorandum

Cooperation implies common purposes and the desire to find effective means for achieving them. In my talk with the President and in my notes I have emphasized my entire agreement with the need for immediate and thorough exploration of the facts bearing on inter-allied debts and world economic recuperation. I have clearly expressed the necessary stages in such a survey in view of the Constitutional situation which leaves the executive responsibility with Mr. Hoover (till I can. . . .)

Telegram to Roosevelt

Cambridge, Mass., November 15, 1932

YOUR REPLY TO PRESIDENT HOOVER ADMIRABLE AND NOT THE LEAST YOUR LAST SENTENCE AND YOUR INSISTENCE ON MAKING MEETING WHOLLY IN-FORMAL AND PERSONAL.

FELIX FRANKFURTER

Cambridge, Mass., November 16, 1932

Dear Frank:

Perhaps you can find time to read the enclosed, written by Sir W. T. Layton, the editor of the *London Economist,* in the latest issue that has reached me.

Layton, as you probably know, is at the very forefront of British econo-mists. He is that rare thing, an economic thinker who combines scientific distinction with unusual experience in practical affairs of Government. He has been one of the chief experts of the British Government ever since the War and the kind of expert who tells his government even unpleasant truths. You may recall that very recently he resigned as an English expert on the preparatory committee of the World Economic Conference in pro-test against the Ottawa Agreements.

Ever yours,
F.F.

The Layton article warned against the dangers of economic nationalism
and the strangulation of world trade.

Albany, N.Y., November 17, 1932

Dear Felix:

You are absolutely right about the trip. It is already out of my mind.

I had a real old-fashioned 100% attack of flu and am weak as a kitten, but it has given me the chance to "lay abed" and is a blessing in disguise.

Thank you ever so much for your nice telegrams. I hope I shall see you soon.

Always sincerely yours,
F.D.R.

Cambridge, Mass., November 24, 1932

Dear Frank:

Your handling of the debt situation was more than well adopted to the immediate situation. It announces a policy of executive power which serves as an admirable assertion of Presidential leadership, and at the same time escapes sterile deadlock between the President and Congress. This illustrates a technique which in your hands will, I am confident, often break the ice without trying to hammer it to pieces. By seeking right objectives through other means than those around which hostile emotion has clustered, right ends will be accomplished and wrong feelings will not be stirred.

But the really important thing for the country now is for you to have a decent kind of holiday. I was much distressed to have you tell me you had had old-fashioned flu. I know what that is. I was a victim of the flu epidemic in Paris in 1919, and know what debilitation that miserable bug can leave behind even in the firmest vitality. So have at least a few days of real loafing and relaxation.

With good wishes,

Faithfully yours,
FELIX FRANKFURTER

Cambridge, Mass., November 28, 1932

Dear Frank:

The other day over the phone you indicated your desire to see me during the week-end of December 10th. This is merely to say that I await your pleasure and that I am at your disposal at the time and at the place to be designated by you.

Faithfully yours,
F.F.

Telegram to Roosevelt

Cambridge, Mass., December 12, 1932

IS THIS SATURDAY OR SUNDAY CONVENIENT FOR YOU TO SEE ME? SOME OF THE MATTERS WILL REQUIRE, SHOULD THEY APPEAL TO YOU, TIME FOR PREPARATION WHICH, IF POSSIBLE, SHOULD BE UNDER WAY BY CHRISTMAS.

FELIX FRANKFURTER

Roosevelt had asked Frankfurter to give him his views on the new legislative program, and on its scale of priorities, after Roosevelt's Inaugural.

Professor to President

January 1933 – September 1933

1933

January 30	Adolf Hitler becomes Chancellor of Germany.
March 4	President Franklin D. Roosevelt begins his first term. In the 1932 election Roosevelt had received 472 electoral college votes, with Hoover getting 59 votes. In the 1928 election Hoover had defeated Alfred E. Smith by 444 votes against 87 votes in the electoral college.
March 6	By a Presidential proclamation, the banks in the United States remained closed for four days.
March 9	Emergency Banking Act is passed.
March 31	Civilian Conservation Corps is established.
May 10	Nazi book-burnings in Germany.
May 12	Federal Emergency Relief Act and Agricultural Adjustment Act are passed.
May 18	Tennessee Valley Authority is established.
May 27	Truth in Securities Act is passed.
June 5	Joint Resolution of Congress nullifies the gold clause in private and public contracts.
June 12 — July 27	World Economic Conference meets in London.
June 26	National Industrial Recovery Act is passed.

Memorandum by Frankfurter

Cambridge, Mass., January 4, 1933

About 3:45 P.M. today, Secretary Stimson phoned and said he was able to report progress regarding the President-elect's invitation to see him. He did not have an opportunity until last night to talk with the President. All that is necessary now to bring about the meeting is the observance of a little formality customary in such situations. If Mr. Roosevelt will write or wire — preferably write — a note to the President, saying that he would like to discuss with the Secretary of State certain matters affecting the State Department and hopes that the President has no objections, the President will respond favorably. Thereupon Stimson would be glad to come to New York to suit Mr. Roosevelt's convenience. The suggested formality is settled tradition. When Mr. Hoover was President-elect and desired to confer with Secretary Kellogg, he too wrote to President Coolidge to ask whether Mr. Coolidge had any objections to his seeing Secretary Kellogg.

Stimson said that Roosevelt's letter to him, dated December 24, was very kind and extremely helpful in easing matters at Washington, and he thought that Roosevelt would appreciate the situation. [*This letter had been written by Frankfurter for Roosevelt.*] He is anxious to talk with Roosevelt as soon as possible. He will come to New York or he will come to Hyde Park, if that is the pleasure of Roosevelt.

I told Stimson that I would phone Roosevelt that night and later phone him between ten and eleven.

About 9 P.M. I talked with Roosevelt in response to Miss LeHand's wire to phone him between 8:30 and 10:00. I gave Roosevelt a summary of my talk with Stimson. He took it very good-naturedly, saw the humor of the business. I told him it all made me feel like an eighteenth-century minuet, to which he replied it was eighteenth century all right but he didn't know if it were a minuet. I emphasized the eagerness of Stimson to see him, and said, "You can appreciate the psychology of the man in the White House. Of course you will write him and get the silly nonsense over with." To which he countered, "Tell me what to write — dictate right now the note that you think I ought to send him," which I did, in substance repeating what Stimson thought should be in the note. Roosevelt took it down and said he would write it to the President. I asked him when. He said he would put it in the mails tonight. I suggested he special delivery it. I then asked him to give alternative dates to Stimson. I reminded him that Stimson would be glad to come to Hyde Park, which I assumed would be a better place than New York, crowded with visitors. He said I could phone Stimson that he would be glad to have him lunch at Hyde Park this coming Saturday or Monday next — there was a train leaving New York for Pough- keepsie at 9 A.M., getting there 10:45, and that would give them an ample stretch of time. In his characteristically boyish way, he added with laughter, "I don't suppose he wants to come Sunday. Gifford Pinchot will be there then." I told him how much Stimson appreciated his note and how much it helped Stimson, adding, "Stimson, you know, is a very different fellow from Hoover." To which Roosevelt replied, "That's been very evident through- out this affair." Since Roosevelt does not know Stimson except through some casual meeting, I told him to remember that Stimson is rather slow- minded, methodical, single-trackminded like Wilson and not quick and darting as he is, and that he will therefore have to give Stimson ample time to let him lay out all that is in his mind. He said he would.

At about 10:45 P.M. I phoned Stimson and told him the conclusion of my talk with Roosevelt. He was much pleased by Roosevelt's attitude and very eager to know when the letter would reach the White House. I gave him the alternative dates, adding as an element for his judgment, that if he went on Monday Roosevelt would be returning to New York City immedi- ately after lunch and that therefore there might be a more unlimited time on Saturday. He said he thought he would go up on Saturday, and per my arrangement with Roosevelt, would wire Roosevelt of his choice.

Stimson sounded a little bit tired and tense and a little anxious about his meeting with Roosevelt. He asked me for any suggestions I had regard- ing the meeting and I told him the important thing to remember is that Roosevelt has confidence in him and really wants to be informed and that he should go to the meeting in a wholly relaxed frame of mind and talk with Roosevelt as two gentlemen who care about the same things and have confidence in each other's talk; that Roosevelt has a very friendly and boy- ish nature and that he, Stimson, should meet him in that spirit. With evi- dent gravity he said, "I am very glad to hear that." It was perfectly plain to me, in the light of my previous talks with Stimson, that he has been filled full of all sorts of fearsome nonsense regarding Roosevelt. I went on to say that I expect him to be of considerable influence on matters of interna- tional relations dear to his heart during the next four years, living as he will at Woodley [in Washington]. I added, "Indeed, it is not unlikely that out of office you will have more influence with the next Administration than you did with this one." At which he laughed heartily and added, "You always were an optimistic boy," and I rejoined, "These are terrible days and I had supposed that determination and optimism are not offenses but needs." He was very warm in his appreciation of the whole business and extremely grateful and expressed, for him, almost sentimental gratitude "for what you have done in this matter."

F.F.

During the interregnum between Roosevelt's election and his inaugura-tion as President, there was naturally much speculation about the members of his cabinet. At one point a fairly strong movement developed in support of Norman H. Davis, Undersecretary of the Treasury in the Wilson Ad-ministration, for the position of Secretary of State. But a shadow rested on his name. The Supreme Court had upheld a judgment against him, the LAS OVAS case, for having violated a position of financial trust in Cuba in the First World War, being guilty of fraud, and having taken secret profits.

On January 9, 1933, Lippmann sent Frankfurter a letter and a memoran-dum dealing with the LAS OVAS case from Allen Dulles, then a lawyer in New York and many years later the director of the Central Intelligence Agency. Lippmann said Frankfurter was free to show this material to Presi-dent-elect Roosevelt. He added that he had discussed the LAS OVAS case with Judge Learned Hand, who had read the opinions and who felt that even on the facts as set forth in the judgment no final condemnation would be warranted. Judge Hand believed that if he personally wanted Davis for the cabinet, other things being equal, this case would not stop him from appointing him. Lippmann emphasized that he did not wish to be associ-ated either with spreading stories about a friend or in trying to help that friend to be appointed to an office.

The next day Frankfurter, after a telephone conversation with Roosevelt, wrote to Lippmann:

When I saw Roosevelt recently I did not initiate the reference to Davis; Roosevelt mentioned him in connection with a general problem. I did not bring knowledge of the LAS OVAS case to Roosevelt; he had it. (This ought not to be surprising, judging from the number of people who have talked about it, and the case is a leading one on promoters' liabilities in corporation casebooks.) Norman Davis has ties of long standing with Roosevelt; I have none with Davis. You will agree, therefore, that it would be officious of me to be the conduit of the Dulles Memorandum to Roose-velt or, indeed, to take any initiative in discussing Davis with Roosevelt.

When I first learned about this case I was naturally interested and read the opinions, both in the Court of Appeals and in the Supreme Court. Beyond that I have not gone. You are amateur lawyer enough to know that if one is to travel outside judicial opinions for one's judgment of a case one has to make extensive investigation, beginning with the record and briefs. I cannot now command the time to do this. (I have just looked at the record and find it is a volume of 254 pages.) I have therefore no views on the case beyond what the court opinions generate, and I have no responsibility for obtaining any views.

In fact, when the point of decision was reached, Frankfurter took the lead in urging Roosevelt not to appoint Davis, primarily because his economic outlook and general philosophy would make him an awkward colleague in a New Deal cabinet. Cordell Hull became Secretary of State.

Telegram to Hon. F. H. La Guardia
House of Representatives, Washington, D.C.

Cambridge, Mass., January 12, 1933

ANY NEW PROVISION FOR RAILROAD REORGANIZATION SHOULD BE KEPT IN SEPARATE BILL AND NOT MADE PART OF GENERAL BANKRUPTCY MEASURE. VITAL POWER FOR PROTECTION OF PUBLIC AND MINORITY INTERESTS IN RAILROAD REORGANIZATION IS POWER TO FORMULATE AND CONTROL REORGANIZATION PLAN. IN VIEW OF PAST EXPERIENCE, THAT POWER SHOULD NOT BE ALLOWED TO INSIDERS OR THOSE WHO IN THE PAST HAVE FINANCIALLY MISMANAGED RAILROADS. SEE JUSTICE STONE'S OPINION IN ST. PAUL CASE TWO EIGHTY TWO U.S., PARTICULARLY PAGE THREE-THIRTY-SEVEN. SUCH POWER OF FORMULATION SHOULD BE VESTED IN THE INTERSTATE COMMERCE COMMISSION. TO GIVE COMMISSION MERELY POWER TO APPROVE PLANS PREVIOUSLY FORMULATED BY INSIDERS IS LIKELY TO BE LOCKING THE STABLE AFTER THE HORSE IS STOLEN. IT MAKES ALL THE DIFFERENCE IN THE WORLD WHETHER REORGANIZATION BEGINS OR ENDS WITH THE COMMISSION. COMMISSION MUST BE GIVEN NECESSARY MEANS AND POWER TO FORMULATE ANY REORGANIZATION PLAN. IT WOULD BE GRAVE SACRIFICE OF PUBLIC INTEREST TO LEAVE THAT POWER WITH INSIDERS. IT IS BETTER TO LEAVE SITUATION AS IT IS THAN TO STILL FURTHER STRENGTHEN PRACTICAL CONTROL NOW RESTING WITH INSIDERS. PUBLIC INTEREST AT STAKE IS TOO GREAT TO JUSTIFY THIS BEING PUSHED THROUGH AS EMERGENCY MATTER.

FELIX FRANKFURTER

A copy of this telegram was sent to Roosevelt. In the St. Paul case, according to Justice Stone, the question before the Supreme Court was "whether the salutary provisions" of the Interstate Commerce Commission could be avoided. Can "an issue of securities to defray excessive reorganiza-

tion expenses" be withdrawn from the Commission's control? The majority of the Supreme Court decided that by astuteness in the drafting of documents the bankers' lawyers had deprived the Commission of power to enforce necessary public safeguards. As a result, Frankfurter said, the reorganization managers of the St. Paul secured for themselves over a million dollars, and half a dozen New York law firms, an amount estimated by one of the managers to be between two-thirds of a million and a million.

Warm Springs, Ga., January 23, 1933

Dear Felix:

I was sorry not to have an opportunity to talk with you on the telephone the other night, but my last few days were a nightmare of callers, dinners, etc. If you want to call me here you will find me safely in the Cottage every evening.

Always sincerely yours,
F.D.R.

Cambridge, Mass., January 28, 1933

Dear Frank:

There are several items about which I will speak briefly:

1. First and foremost, let me express gratification at the way you have propelled two vital matters in world affairs. The impact of your support of Stimson on the "Manchurian business" is of importance not merely on that specific issue, difficult as that it. It contributed and will continue to contribute much in making for coherence and common effort among the Western peoples generally.

Guessing, as I can somewhat, the many difficulties, personal and political, in which the debt problems are entangled, I can appreciate all the more how much progress you have already made and the shoals and reefs which you have already avoided. The reins are now definitely in your hands, even though others are plainly enough trying to pull them this way and that. Nor has Neville Chamberlain's speech helped matters. It seems to me increasingly clear that your job is largely to be the broker between the two countries, between the two great English-speaking peoples. For you must find substantial ground for the British, in view of the actualities of the situation, and something equally palatable for this country. I am happy in the thought not only that the opinion of our own people is more liquid than it has ever been and more ready to be led by him whom they have so overwhelmingly chosen as their leader, but also that there is a growing and educable realization of the relation of the debts to price recovery and a general revival.

2. Agreeable to your suggestion, I spent an evening with Pelley, and I

liked him a lot. He has, it seems to me, a real public understanding, an understanding, that is, of the public responsibilities and the public implications of the railroads. His attitude towards the Interstate Commerce Commission was gratifying. "I am a strong Commission man," he told me. We canvassed many problems including questions concerning the Commission's reorganization. I have thought much about the questions regarding the reorganization of the various commissions which you put to me in our Albany talk, and I have also exchanged ideas with Eastman and McNinch and with Justice Brandeis who knows most about the work of the Interstate Commerce Commission and the effective methods for discharging its tasks. I shall be glad to be at your disposal for talk on these matters at your convenience. Let me now only express a *caveat* against any early conclusion which would involve mingling of Power matters with jurisdiction as to other utilities. I think there are very serious reasons for keeping Power concentrated in a single agency, but such an agency I do not believe calls for more than three Commissioners rather than the present composition of five.

3. I have also thought a good deal about your question regarding the early calling up by you of a Governors' Conference. I had a chance to discuss it yesterday with Frances Perkins, who is here on the Interstate Conference for Uniform Labor Laws. We agreed that labor matters should certainly form one of the very few items which such a conference should be restricted to if it is to be effective. More than that, we agreed that the labor agenda should be itself closely defined and strictly related to the immediately essential aspects of the depression and means for recovery. In other words, the Governors' Conference should be focused on the emergency. The work of the Interstate Conference here, Frances Perkins and I agreed, ought to be the starting point of detailed preparation for your Conference, if you decide to have one.

I wonder if the only other subject for such a Conference should not be taxation, also closely confined to a consideration of problems common between the States and the National Government, on an exploration of ways and means to avoid needless friction and a proper allocation between States and the Nation in the tapping of revenue.

4. I enclose two more comments on Guy Thompson from solid and dependable lawyers.

5. I hope the days in Warm Springs aren't as madly hectic as were your New York days, and that you are getting some breathing spell. But I am particularly glad, when I think what is ahead of you, that you are to have a really relaxed time of it on your cruise.

Faithfully yours,

FELIX FRANKFURTER

Stimson, as Secretary of State in the Hoover Administration, had developed the doctrine of "parallel association" with the League of Nations in resistance to Japanese aggression in Manchuria, even though the United States was not a member of the League. Chamberlain, not yet Prime Minister but the rising man in the British government, had argued that Britain could waive reparation payments from Germany only if Britain's war debts to the United States were reduced or canceled.

Joseph B. Eastman (1882–1944) was chairman of the Interstate Commerce Commission and one of the greatest public servants of this century. Frankfurter had discussed with Brandeis, and others, the various problems which would face Roosevelt in strengthening the regulatory agencies as guardians of the public interest. McNinch was a member of the Federal Power Commission.

Frances Perkins, an old friend of Frankfurter, was to serve as Secretary of Labor in Roosevelt's cabinet.

Guy Thompson of St. Louis had been president of the American Bar Association. Roosevelt had asked Frankfurter to collect confidential estimates on Thompson's fitness for a high office in the government.

Telegram to Roosevelt
Cambridge, Mass., February 3, 1933

YOUR DEVELOPMENT PLAN AND POLICY IS THE BEST NEWS SINCE ELECTION.

FELIX FRANKFURTER

Roosevelt had given the country his first tentative plan for the development of unused resources to reduce the burdens of unemployment.

Cambridge, Mass., February 19, 1933

Dear Frank:

No one who knew you even slightly could possibly have expected any other attitude and action than those which you manifested at Miami. But nevertheless one is proud, very proud, not merely as one is for a friend but for the national symbol that you now are.

I happened to be at the Executive Mansion Wednesday night, and you can about imagine the feelings that went through the place when Herbert Lehman told us the news as it came to him over the phone from the A.P. I felt something subtler and deeper than mere relief and the poignant sense of gratitude. I can't quite put it into words, but the utterances and the silences of the various retainers in the Mansion, that night and next morning at breakfast, somehow conveyed to me the most eloquent meaning of the devotion and affection and hopes for the country that you now embody.

Considering the jitters that so many of our so-called leaders have these days, your self-possession and serenity, your prompt and continuing attention to the business at hand, your calm refusal to be deflected by the irrational mischances of life have given to the country the lesson that it needs perhaps above all others these days.

With warm regards,

Always yours,

F.F.

On February 15, 1933, President Roosevelt went ashore at Miami and then drove in a motorcade through the city. While he was talking with Mayor Anton Cermak of Chicago, a figure in the crowd, Joe Zangara, an unemployed bricklayer, suddenly began firing shots at the Presidential party. Roosevelt was unharmed, but Cermak was hit and died a few days later, and four others were wounded. Roosevelt's courage and dignity during this tragic ordeal greatly impressed the nation.

Cambridge, Mass., February 23, 1933

Dear Frank:

I congratulate you heartily on the ensemble of your Cabinet — and to achieve the right ensemble was, I venture to believe, the most important and most difficult of your tasks. For it was essential to secure effective representation of the diverse and not always parallel forces expressed in your election. And now you have done it. But you have done more. You have picked — so far as I am entitled to personal judgment — four men peculiarly fitted for their posts. Cordell Hull seems to me to have just the right temperament and outlook. Woodin I have met only once but was captivated by him. Tom Walsh of course is the very embodiment of Justice. And Frances Perkins is not only the best possible woman for your Cabinet but the best man for her job. From all I hear of Wallace he is no less ideal.

A Cabinet is like a symphony orchestra — the qualities that come out of the individual members depend to no small extent upon the qualities which the leader draws out of them. The New York Philharmonic is a very different thing when Toscanini leads rather than someone else. And so, under you, this Cabinet will be even better than they are as individuals.

You have got the essentials under way. Now I look forward to having your Inaugural modify greatly the defeatist attitude so sedulously cultivated recently. I hope in your own happy way you will find enduring expression for the transcendent need of the hour — some felicitous way of indicating that our greatest need is to resume employment, and the way to resume employment is to resume employment. The budget will be balanced when business recovers rather than this foolish theory of magic that business will recover by balancing the budget.

Always with good wishes,

Faithfully yours,
F.F.

Frankfurter's praise of Cordell Hull was deliberately moderate. He thought Hull was the best available candidate for the position of Secretary of State, and supported his appointment, but he never believed that Hull would give a creative impetus to American foreign policy. That leadership would have to come primarily from Roosevelt himself. Frankfurter was greatly impressed by the courage with which William Woodin bore his heavy burdens as Secretary of the Treasury during 1933, despite illness and fatigue. Woodin resigned at the beginning of 1934. An early death prevented Senator Tom Walsh from leaving his mark as Attorney General. He was succeeded by Homer Cummings. Frances Perkins was an invaluable member of the Cabinet as Secretary of Labor. Until he felt he had a call to higher duties, Henry A. Wallace was equally useful as Secretary of Agriculture.

The next letter is Frankfurter's message of good wishes as Roosevelt prepares for his First Inaugural ceremony.

Cambridge, Mass., March 1, 1933

Dear Frank,

As you go forth to take the helm of the Ship of State, I bid you — godspeed.

Never was gay and gallant command more needed; never has it been entrusted into more auspicious hands. May Providence continue to smile on you, and thereby on your country and the world.

Most sincerely and faithfully yours,

Felix Frankfurter

The White House, March 7, 1933

Dear Felix: —

Your letters are always a joy — saying so much in so few words. You know how much I appreciate your good wishes. I shall see you soon.

Always sincerely,
F.D.R.

This is Roosevelt's first letter to Frankfurter from the White House, written three days after the Inaugural ceremonies.

Memorandum by Frankfurter of a visit with
Roosevelt on March 8, 1933, when the President
asked Frankfurter to become Solicitor General

In response to his invitation some weeks before, I was lunching with Mr. Justice Holmes on March 8, 1933, the occasion of his ninety-second birthday. There were present the Justice's secretary, Donald Hiss, and Thomas Corcoran, one of his earlier secretaries now at the Reconstruction Finance Corporation. I had been called to the phone during the course of the lunch and therefore told Hiss that if there were any more phone calls for me not to tell me about them until after lunch — I did not want to disturb the Justice. There was a telephone call and Hiss attended to it. After lunch, about three o'clock, Hiss told me that the White House had called in an endeavor to locate me. He reported Colonel McIntyre, the President's secretary, as saying that I had been expected to lunch at the White House, that the President had been waiting for me since 1:30 and desired me to call at once. I phoned McIntyre, and he opened up with, "You were expected here since 1:30 — where are you?" I pleasantly replied, "I am at a better place. I am at Mr. Justice Holmes'. My arrangement to lunch with him has been of long standing, but in any event I could not have been at the White House at 1:30 because your phone message was the first news I've had that I am expected there." McIntyre said there must have been a slip-up, that Moley or Miss LeHand had undertaken to get word to me at ten in the morning. He said he was glad to have the episode happen because it would help to straighten out matters and get right habits at the White House. "You'd better come over here as soon as you can; the President is anxious to see you and has been waiting for you since 1:30." I told him I would get there just as soon as I could decently disengage myself from the Justice.

I told the conversation to the Justice, who genially remarked, "Usually," with an innuendo, "the White House has the right of way, but it's rather amusing to put the President's nose out of joint." I said to the Justice, "Apart from all else, I shall tell the President, when I make my explanation, that there was a conclusive reason for lunching with you rather than with him." "What kind of a conclusive reason have you?" "Well, I shall say to the President, 'Could you have furnished me fizz water at luncheon?' " (We had sauterne as well as champagne at the Justice's luncheon, and he drank about three or four glasses of champagne.) At which the Justice looked at me with simulated sternness and said, "Young fellow, I don't want you to misunderstand things: I do not deal with bootleggers but I am open to corruption."

I got to the White House about 3:30, saw McIntyre, who in a few minutes ushered me into the President's office, with which McIntyre's room immediately connects. The President stretched out his hand with a warm welcome in his eager, boyish voice, and playfully said, "Well, Felix, they'll make a banker of me yet." He beckoned me to sit down, and I said, "Before I sit down, Frank (I checked myself and added) I'll have to learn not to call you Frank, (which he pleasantly waved aside saying, "Of course, continue to call me Frank, except in the presence of others.") before I sit down I should like to tell you that while I cared deeply about T.R.'s Administration, and my loyalty was heavily engaged by Woodrow Wilson, I care even more about the success of your Administration." The President replied, "I know that, and I want you to be a part of it. I want you to be Solicitor General."

This took me completely off my feet. It was the first reference, directly or obliquely, that Roosevelt had ever made to me about my holding any office, although at Albany and over the phone he had discussed with me and very intimately questions of personnel for the Cabinet and other places in the Government. I started to speak, but he stopped me with, "I want to talk before you say anything." He then said, "I have wanted you to be Solicitor General ever since November." He said he had talked with "poor Tom Walsh" about it, and that Walsh was very eager to have me, and that it "just awaited the formalities." "When Attorney General Walsh died I had to act quickly, and I put Homer Cummings in. Homer was scheduled to go to the Philippines, and he wants to go there still. I think he's a shrewd, level-headed fellow, and he's all right. I have talked to him about you; he said he thinks he met you only once, but knows all about you and admires you greatly and is most enthusiastic about having you as Solicitor General. Now I want you down here, because I need you for all sorts of things, and in all sorts of ways. As you know, we are going in heavily for utility regulation, reorganization of the various Commissions, amendment to the Sherman Law and a lot of other things. I need your help on all those matters, and I want you to come very much." This accurately conveys the substance of the President's remarks in stating his desire in wanting me to be Solicitor General.

I said to him, in substance, that he would understand if I didn't put in words how I felt about what was implied in his desire to have me as Solicitor General. I said, "To a lawyer it is professionally the most interesting job. But confronted as I am with the situation, I have to decide whether I ought to come down and give myself up completely to being a technical lawyer, exciting as it would be to have charge of the Government's cases before the Supreme Court." The President interrupted to say that I could free myself for other work, there would be adequate help in the Department, etc., etc., to which I replied, "If you don't mind my saying so, I think

I know the demands of that office perhaps more completely than there is any reason for your knowing them. I have known about the work of that office almost from the time that I left the Law School. It is exciting and profoundly important professional work. But if a man is to be Solicitor General, he must make up his mind that it will absorb sixteen hours of the day." I briefly tried to indicate the nature of the duties of the Solicitor General's office and why it would preclude participation in working out his Presidential policies. I then proceeded, "It is my genuine conviction — I am sure it is so — that I can do much more to be of use to you by staying in Cambridge than by becoming Solicitor General. The fact of the matter is that I could not have anything to do on any of the matters on which you would want my help and do my job as Solicitor General — it just can't be done. I am due to go to Oxford next fall. I won't urge that as an excuse, for while of course I am obligated, and it would disarrange matters if I didn't go, considering the exigencies of the time, I have no doubt I could be released if there were a compelling public duty. But I do want to say that no matter who will be your ambassadors abroad, I think I can be of use to you even while I am abroad, and of more use to you than as Solicitor General."

Having listened eagerly and with sympathy, the President made the following reply: "I think there is a great deal in what you say. I'm not at all sure it isn't true that you can be of more use to my Administration outside of office than you could as Solicitor General. But there is another consideration, and I am going to talk Dutch to you. I am going to talk to you frankly, as a friend. You ought to be on the Supreme Court, and I want you to be there. One can't tell when it will come — it may come in my time or not — but that's the place where you ought to be. Now you have, of course, a national reputation, a national recognition. But you know — and I said I was going to talk Dutch to you — that there are also objections to you. For a good many years now you have been a professor (smiling), you haven't actively practiced law, you've never held judicial office (again smiling), you've been the man who has refused to be a judge, then there is the Sacco and Vanzetti case (again smiling) and (this time with a grave countenance) your race. I can't put you on the Supreme Court from the Harvard Law School. But once you are Solicitor General, these various objections will be forgotten or disappear. I talk to you this way because I think for once you have a right to think selfishly, to think about yourself and not exclusively of the public interest."

My reply was: "Of course I very deeply appreciate not only what you say but the friendship that makes you say it. You know what any American lawyer thinks about the Supreme Court and a place on it, but so far as that goes, that matter will have to take care of itself, if ever the time may come.

It's clear to me that from the point of view of such usefulness as I may have, I ought not to abandon what I am doing and can do to become Solicitor General, and I do not think it is a wise way of life to take a job I don't want because it may lead to another, which also I'm not at all sure I'd want. All that must be left to the future. I really don't think I ought to take a post at which I know I cannot be of the use that I can be in remaining where I am, simply because it may promote my going elsewhere."

After a pause, the President said, "Well, there's no hurry about this. I tell you what I want you to do. I sometimes find it useful, and you might find it useful — I wish you would talk to your Mrs. about it. And I repeat that for once you have a right to think a little bit selfishly." I said that of course I would, and he added, "You are going to see Brandeis before very long. I suggest you talk with him about it." I said that I would. He then added, "I have not wanted to see Brandeis. I thought it would be unwise, before I had seen the Chief Justice. I am hoping to have Hughes and Mrs. Hughes to lunch before very long, and then I can see Brandeis."

"Speaking of the Supreme Court," I went on, "are you aware that before very long you are likely to have two vacancies to be filled west of the Mississippi?" I then told him that I had been advised that Congress had passed the Act giving full retirement allowances to the Justices of the Supreme Court, and that I had good reason to believe that Van Devanter and Sutherland would retire before next Term of Court. That took him by surprise. "I hadn't realized that. But when is McReynolds going to retire — isn't he going to resign?" I told him I feared not. "There is one man who can't retire," said the President, "and that's Brandeis — I won't accept his resignation." During the course of the talk, which lasted about half an hour, the Secretary came in several times, to say that either the Secretary of the Treasury or Secretary of State was on the wire. Throughout the President was at ease and concentrated on the matter at hand between us. I started to go once or twice, but he indicated a desire to go on, and finally said, "I'll see you at tea at Holmes', won't I?" I told him he would. So I turned up at Holmes' at 5:30 when President and Mrs. Roosevelt and James came to call.

I drove back with the President to the White House to talk about a matter affecting the Treasury, at Undersecretary Ballantine's request. As the President alighted at the White House he asked me where I was staying, and I said, pausing a moment, "Now don't you draw any inference from my answer. I am staying at Solicitor General Thacher's — he is an old friend of mine." The President laughed heartily and said, "Well, you don't have to be so proud. I know him too; he was the same year at Yale as I was at Harvard." The President then asked how long I was to be in Washington. I told him I had to leave the next day. He said, "I'd like to see you very soon again," to which I replied, "I am at your call any time you want to see me here." He laughingly remarked, "I wish that were true — you mean it's true subject to a single exception," whereat we parted in the pleasantest fashion.

I told the substance of the above (omitting reference to the Supreme Court) to Mr. Justice Brandeis and to Judge Thacher. Brandeis said for me to take the Solicitor Generalship would be "absurd." I told the fact of the offer and declination very confidentally to Cardozo, who expressed deep disappointment, "not merely because of the arguments that the Court would have from you, but because of the importance of just having you down here these days. I seem to meet hardly anybody who is capable of thinking on these socio-economic matters, hardly anybody except Brandeis and you, and you ought to be down here." I told him in brief that precisely because I was interested in those problems I did not think I ought to sink myself in the work of the Solicitor Generalship. Later, on Thursday, the 9th, I told Mr. Justice Holmes of the offer and the declination, and he said, "You did well, and I'm glad you declined. I think it would have been unwise for you to accept." To neither Holmes nor Cardozo did I tell the President's references to the Supreme Court.

On March 14th I wrote the President a formal letter of declination, of which a copy is appended.

The foregoing was dictated March 15, 1933. It is, I believe, a very accurate account of what transpired between the President and me, for the interview lay, of course, very vividly in my mind, and I repeated it promptly to Brandeis and to Marion on my return.

FELIX FRANKFURTER

Telegram to Marvin H. McIntyre
New York, N.Y., March 10, 1933

PLEASE TELL THE PRESIDENT HOW DEEPLY I REJOICE WITH THE REST OF THE COUNTRY OVER THE LEADERSHIP AGAIN MANIFESTED BY HIS MESSAGE TODAY.

FELIX FRANKFURTER

The message dealt with the banking crisis and the Emergency Banking Act. Banking operations in the United States ceased on March 3. The object of the legislation was to secure the reopening of the banks and to keep them open. Congress passed the emergency act, and the President signed it, that same day.

In some respects this exchange of letters with Lippmann contains the most unexpected material in the whole correspondence. For it shows Frankfurter, writing with Roosevelt's approval, deploring any abdication of power by Congress, while recognizing the need for immediate action in the supreme emergency of the banking crisis and the collapse of confidence. With a prophetic instinct, Roosevelt, in the very act of using all the powers appropriate to the crisis, anticipated the charge that would one day resound through the land that he was greedy for the powers of a dictator. Frankfurter, in obedience to his lifelong philosophy, wanted nothing done in this emergency that would reduce the power of Congress to compel the White House to meet the most detailed and voluminous criticisms of the legislative branch. Lippmann, despite his personal doubts about Roosevelt, doubts revived and expressed in every Presidential election in which he ran, was governed by an equally strong belief in executive action and never managed to shake off his resentment at the claims of Congress to be an equal branch of government.

After studying this correspondence with great care, and being totally unimpressed by Lippmann's present support, Roosevelt told Frankfurter that Lippmann's philosophy of government and of social organization would make him a determined opponent of the New Deal, and all his talk about the necessity of strong Presidential leadership would not prevent his ultimate divergence and opposition. Frankfurter agreed with the assessment and with the prediction. But they both kept this agreement a secret from Lippmann.

The reference in Lippmann's first paragraph is to an offer by Roosevelt in June 1932 to have Frankfurter work directly with him in the Presidential campaign and then become an important member of his Administration. Frankfurter agreed to help in many ways but insisted that his primary base must remain the Harvard Law School.

Charles E. Mitchell of the National City Bank in New York had become a classic example of the failure of leaders in Wall Street either to explain or to justify their financial manipulations when they were compelled to testify under oath in the Pecora investigations.

March 11, 1933

Dear Walter:

Ours is not the responsibility for immediate action in these exigent and hectic days, and so we can pursue the luxury — I am inclined to think of it as a necessity — of thinking beyond the immediate moment and debating the implications of events and policies.

After all, I have spent about half of my mature life in the harness of office, in three departments of the government, have been from time to time consultant of some of the other departments and independent Agencies of the government as well as of committees of Congress and leading Senators. I have known more or less intimately the official ways and methods of five Presidents. And I have spent the whole of my life as a rather close student of the contemporary political affairs not only of our own country but of Great Britain. Government therefore is not alien to me, and I am no stranger to its mysteries. Of course there are times for summary action and the pace for devising policies is properly more rapid at one time than at another. But all this is a very different thing from educating the public into the psychology of dictatorship. I know your phrase has been concentration of authority, but the result is the same. We have not, and ought not to have, government by Presidential decree — which is the essence of the theory and practice of continental dictatorship. And I am very strongly against encouraging the forces that push towards such political habits of mind in this country. The last week of course called for rapidity of deliberation and decision. But I think nothing but harm comes from talking about dictatorship, however euphemistically phrased, when all that we mean is responsibility appropriate to the specific situations. Before very long we shall, I think, be confronting this problem very concretely in the potential danger of too-hasty, too-ill-considered reorganizations of different activities of the government, derived too much from short-sighted notions of economy and too little heedful of their deeper meaning. After all, the Lord doesn't create people sufficiently capacious in wisdom and detachment — no matter how disinterested — to run these vast organisms, whether of government or of finance, without ample opportunity for the corrective judgment of the deliberative process. And I strongly deplore the current tendency to assume that power as such generates wisdom and that the deliberative processes are drags upon wise action. I know these are generalities, but I think they are generalities of a profound importance. And they aren't worth a damn if they are scrapped at the first test. In a word, I think the public needs education most vitally in the factors relevant to wise decisions rather than to have dinned in its ear as the dominant need of the hour abdication of everybody's reason. Especially is this true for a President of Roosevelt's temperament and for an Administration committed to his general policies.

Of course I do not believe that vice inheres in the rich and virtue in the poor. But for too long we have been largely operating on the assumption that the converse is the truth, and more particularly that the rich are the guardians of wisdom and should control affairs. I don't think I have any animus against Mitchell — I care as little about him as I did about Jimmie Walker. The crux of the business is not the wickedness of the Mitchells but the power which is wielded by concentration of financial power which they are wholly unworthy — no matter who they are — to wield because of the obfuscations and the arrogances which power almost invariably generates. Again I say the Lord hasn't created anybody competent to rule wisely the kind of a thing that the Chase Bank was. It's absurd, tragically absurd, that the House of Morgan should be exercising the power it is exercising, not because they are wicked but because a long term of years, and particularly the last few years, has shown that they are singularly unknowing, and do not even understand the meaning of their own actions. And that is penetrating into the marrow of people to an extent that profoundly affects the whole task of reconstruction. Brandeis saw it all with a seer's discernment more than twenty years ago, and everything that he prophesied since has been vindicated with an almost tragic uncanniness.

Yes, I know the old Adam is in all of us, and the poor are greedy and the veterans are selfish and the farmers want pap. But I really think you underestimate the extent to which decency and fairness and live-and-let-live can be won from the great masses so long as they don't feel that they are the victims of great inequalities. Compare, for instance, the immediate occasion that produced the Pullman strike in '94 with the lack of strikes in this depression. And since writing you last, quite unrelatedly of course to our correspondence, Buxton, the hard-boiled editor of the Republican Boston *Herald*, was telling me that Legion people in his composing room have been saying to him they are quite ready to forego "theirs" if they are sure that the big fellows are not getting theirs. But over and beyond these problems of the moral infection of bad example is the great problem of concentrated power, and the part the huge fortunes play in our society.

The "New Deal" may be a phrase but it may also be translated into realities. And I have very high hopes that circumstances are cooperating with Roosevelt's temperament and desires for a less greedy, a less jug-handled society.

Always yours,
F.F.

March 14, 1933

Dear Felix:

I suppose I am entitled to regard your remark about having no responsibility for immediate action to mean that the reports about your taking an office in the Administration are conclusively untrue. Naturally I have thought about them a good deal and my own conclusion was that I wanted you not to take an office. The reasons which held last June seem to me still to hold, and I rejoice in your holding to the way of life you have chosen.

I fully appreciate your own experience in government and I know it's been much greater than my own. But I have some acquaintance with the way public opinion works, and relying upon that, the only comment I would make upon what you say in your letter is that it leaves me with a feeling that you are a little bit hesitant about breaking the eggs to make the omelet. I take it from your letter that you approve of what's been done during the past ten days, but that you deplore the arousing of the public which has accompanied it. Aren't you a little bit in the position of desiring the end but being hesitant to will the means?

Of course the means are rough and, to a degree, irrational. But the process of reason in public affairs is necessarily a very slow process, and in an acute emergency you have either to choose the means that will procure the end or forego attaining it.

I recognize fully the "potential" danger of too hasty, too ill-considered reorganization, but what would you have done in the circumstances of the last two or three weeks? Do you really think, for example, that I should have urged Congress to consider carefully and attempt to understand thoroughly the provisions of the banking bill before passing it, or was it right to call upon Congress to take the thing on faith, suspending debate, suspending the process of education, suspending the deliberative method? I faced that choice honestly in my own mind, and I am prepared to risk the potential dangers which you point out for the sake of averting the much more actual dangers which were right upon us.

I agree with you that the public needs education in the factors relevant to wise decisions. But frankly I do not believe it's possible to educate the people on all the factors that are relevant to all the wise decisions that have got to be made in the next few weeks. It is utterly impossible to perform such a feat of education. The matters are too intricate, prejudices are too deep and complex, the necessary technical knowledge is too lacking.

Yours ever,
W.L.

March 15, 1933

Dear Walter:

Your letter of the 14th has come, and for the moment I am going to ask you to let me withhold comment on your personal reference, only adding that I don't want you to draw any inference from that one way or the other. To envelop myself in seeming mystery is not congenial to me, but I'll say no more.

Not even adjudication need be leaden-footed to be deliberative, or at least to be not arbitrary. Neither does legislation. The actions of Congress at this session offend none of my prejudices regarding the appropriate scope for reason in government or the appropriate role of Congress in our scheme of things. What I object to — and it goes to the very root of my political convictions — is the building up of opinion hostile to the need for Congress as a policy-making organ and as a critic of executive measures. It is one thing, in a time of great danger, to exact concentrated attention and a complete disregard of irrelevant or minor motives. It is quite another thing to ask Congress to abdicate its judgment. During a good part of the Hoover Administration it was deemed almost treason to question the legislative proposals from the White House. You and I had some correspondence on that subject, and more particularly on what is now patent to all — the ill-conceived aspects of the Reconstruction Finance Corporation legislation.

Specifically, what troubled me in your recent writings is the general impression that was undoubtedly fostered in the minds of your readers — if some very intelligent numbers of them who spoke to me about it are fair samples — that Congress is an awful nuisance, and that that Jack-in-the-Box ought to be shut up. It ought all to be left to the Great White Father.

Now it so happens that I very much believe in, and have believed in, the present White Father. Not the least of the reasons for my wanting to leave room for the deliberative and corrective processes of Congress is knowledge of the hurried and scurried way in which legislative recommendations and administrative regulations have been coming to pass and will come to pass. Precisely because I greatly want success for Roosevelt — and all that it implies for the country and the world — I want not abdication of Congress but true collaboration. I call the debate in the Senate on the Economy Bill all to the good. That the hardened feelings of hundreds of thousands of our people, who in their nature are no more grafters than you and I are, should be considerately dissolved instead of steam-rollered into sullen discontent, is to me the kind of a national good which, in multitudinous other instances, it will be important to secure. And particularly so because I am so confident that on a vast scale sacrifices — the disappointment of expectancies — will have to be made. I do not mind hurried action in the Senate or the House, nor do I mind either body acting solely because it has confidence in the representations made to it by leaders like Senator Glass who do happen to know the meaning of technical legislation.

I venture to suggest that the important thing is to explain, at least in the large outlines, the reasons behind various proposals, rather than to inculcate the simple habit of expecting the White House to pull rabbits out of a hat. If for no other reason, because the rabbit-pulling process is not likely to be of long duration. If we don't look out, the conflicts of interest now brewing beneath the surface will break out, and not too pleasantly, before this Administration has run its term. I have not the slightest fear

that that tendency will be encouraged by Roosevelt himself. By temperament and experience he knows the importance of carrying the consent of
the country — as far as may be — along with him, not merely generally and
vaguely but by specific appeal on specific policies.

Always yours,
F.F.

Cambridge, Mass., March 14, 1933

Dear Mr. President:

Let me tell you at the outset, however awkwardly, how deeply I was
moved by your talk last Wednesday afternoon. I have no vocabulary of
gratitude adequate for such an impressive manifestation of confidence and
for such generous friendship.

While T.R. and Woodrow Wilson strongly engaged my devotion,
about the success of neither — as I told you — did I care as deeply as I do
about your Administration. I have reflected much on all you said, and discussed the matter not only with my wife but also, very confidentially, with
Holmes and Brandeis. They are clear that I can be of more use to the
public and to you by not becoming Solicitor General.

No man can do his duty as Solicitor General without exclusive attention to the vast technical law business of that office. I shall not burden you
with the details of the work of the Solicitor General's Office, but it will give
you some indication, in the concrete, of its necessary professional absorption if I state that at the last Term of the Supreme Court 39% of all the
appellate dispositions of the Court were Government cases, and that up to
last week of this Term the Solicitor General was responsible for the preparation of briefs and memoranda in 323 cases, exclusive of the burden of oral
arguments running into scores of cases. In addition to this, of course, it is
his duty to determine when appeals should be taken, in the hundreds of
cases decided against the Government in the lower courts, as well as his
task to prepare and supervise the opinions rendered by the Attorney General.

In the light of all this, and in view of the weightiest counsel that I have
had, I am compelled to say that the attitude which I expressed to you when
I saw you remains my deepest conviction. I should nevertheless like to feel
that I am part of your Administration even outside of office.

Let me take this occasion to rejoice over the momentum of achievement and good will which you have been accumulating within only a few
days. No one who has followed your life in crucial matters, since those early
Billy Sheehan days, could have had any doubt of the results when the testing time came. But the effectiveness of your action and the serenity of your

spirit, in the most trying times of the country since the Civil War, are precisely the invigoration of will and spirit which the country needs.

Faithfully yours,
FELIX FRANKFURTER

Cambridge, Mass., March 13, 1933

Dear Mac:

All sorts of letters which come my way reflect the confidence that the President has aroused throughout the land. One of these I should like to quote to you. You may pass it on the President, for it comes from a singularly brave and beautiful character. In a letter which has just come to me Will Scarlett, the Bishop Coadjutor of Missouri, writes the following:

"We are greatly heartened out here by Mr. Roosevelt's Inaugural Address, and by the way he has taken hold of this situation, and I find rising courage on every side."

It was a great joy to see you in the flesh again, and to see you where you ought to be.

With warm regards,

Very sincerely yours,
FELIX FRANKFURTER

Hon. Marvin H. McIntyre, The White House

Cambridge, Mass., March 18, 1933

Dear Mr. President:

Opinion on the merits of the Farm Relief Bill is beyond my competence, but I do know a first-rate Presidential message when I see it. I have read Presidents' messages regularly since I first entered the Government service in 1906, and I have read scores of them back of that, in Richardson's *Messages*. None has ever excited me more than your short message in submitting the Farm Relief Bill; none was ever better calculated to give the country the right temper of mind on an important and complex national question. The lesson in candor and in the necessary experimental attitude towards problems the answers to which nobody knows and which must be achieved by trial and error may, in the long run, be even more important than the solution of the specific agricultural difficulties.

It really was a gem of an utterance.

Faithfully yours,
FELIX FRANKFURTER

Cambridge, Mass., March 22, 1933

Dear Mr. President:

1. Of course I rejoice over your message on unemployment relief. The emergency measures of your first few days were indispensable. But putting

men to work — gradual but steady re-employment — is the ultimate objective, and your new proposals start us on that road. You will have to educate Green *et al* — but you will.

2. If, as I assume, George Otis Smith will go, there is opportunity for saving by reducing the Power Commission to three members. They could do the job at least as well as a Commission of five. I hope it may commend itself to you not to merge the Power Commission at present with anything else, nor to put upon it new duties, like regulating communications. During the last Administration that Commission substantially marked time because of internal conflicts. Under your leadership they should go ahead aggressively. But it would arrest progress on power problems for the Commission to be thrown into the hopper of a general reorganization. Psychologically, it may also detract from the dramatic attention that power should have for some time if any Commission has only divided and not exclusive responsibility for power.

3. Speaking of regulatory commissions, I should like to say a word about Ray Stevens, in view of our talk about him at Albany. I wonder if you know that there has been a change in Stevens' arrangements, and that he is now able to leave Siam on relatively short notice. He is, of course, admirably suited for the Trade Commission, of which he was once counsel, or for any one of the other regulatory commissions.

But I should like to suggest his fitness for another post. If, as I assume, Cummings will remain where he is, does not Ray Stevens to an unusual degree possess a combination of qualities peculiarly fitting for the Governor-Generalship of the Philippines? He combines deep simplicity of nature, love of his kind, complete disinterestedness and shrewd Yankee wisdom. Because of these qualities he has kept the confidence of all the contending elements during the recent turmoil in Siam. I have known half a dozen of the advisers to the King of Siam — for that post, as you know, has from the beginning been filled by Harvard Law School men — and I have good reason for believing that not one of them has been as successful and as beloved by the people of Siam as has been Stevens. Stevens is equally at home with prince and peasant. He would become beloved of the Filipinos, and at the same time sail with care and safety in the troubled waters of the East.

4. Let me quote from two letters I've just had, which were not intended for your eyes. The first is from Gus Hand — Judge Augustus N. Hand:

> F.D.R. is doing wonderfully, — 100%. It is good that we at last have a President who has political skill and experience, and a party divorced from control by Big Business. I believe F.D.R. has ability to ride this painful storm and do something to relieve the world. Brandeis said to me two years ago that he was sick of having a President who didn't understand

politics. They are all praising everything now, — but wait until F.D.R. does something besides open banks and spank veterans, and see what they will say.

The second comes from a very able young lawyer, who is associated with one of the big legal-financial firms:

> When the Administration locks horns with Wall Street, it will have much more support than Roosevelt I ever had when he went trust-busting. Because now also conservative elements are lined up against the bankers: every industrialist whose program for development was retarded by lack of credit facilities; every rentier to whom the National City Co. sold sour bonds; every professional man who lost his shirt in the market; every die-hard who took a trimming (& most of them did) will be solidly lined up against the "money power." After all, when so thoroughgoing an arch-tory as your classmate ——— rehearses the evils of interlocking banking and investment directorates, it's a pretty significant straw to indicate the direction of the hurricane.

With warm regards,

Faithfully yours,
F. F.

William Green was president of the American Federation of Labor. George Otis Smith was chairman of the Federal Power Commission from December 1930–November 1933.

Telegram to Roosevelt

Boston, Mass., March 25, 1933

SIXTIETH ANNIVERSARY DINNER OF CRIMSON NOW IN PROGRESS. IT WOULD OF COURSE CHEER UNDERGRADUATES, GRADUATES AND GUESTS IMMENSELY IF A WORD OF GREETING CAME FROM YOU. AFFECTIONATELY YOURS,

FELIX FRANKFURTER

Telegram to the President, Harvard Crimson
Cambridge, Mass.

The White House, March 25, 1933

MY AFFECTIONATE GREETINGS TO ALL THE EDITORS OLD AND YOUNG. KEEP THE OLD SHEET FLYING.

FRANKLIN D. ROOSEVELT

The White House, April 5, 1933

Dear Felix:

Keep on writing me even if I do not reply. You are right about George Otis Smith. I am trying to find out if its membership can be reduced to three, leaving it an independent Commission. I think McNinch is all right.

I am glad you reminded me of Ray Stevens. He would be splendid on the Trade Commission. I seriously think of Frank Murphy, Mayor of Detroit, for the Philippines — young, red-headed, idealistic, but at the same time an interpreter of warring elements. What do you think?

I have not yet forgiven you. How can I find anybody else with just your qualifications to appear on behalf of the government before the Supreme Tribunal? You are an independent pig and that is one reason why I cannot blame you!

As ever yours,
F.D.R.

Cambridge, Mass., March 28, 1933

Dear Mr. President:

The following comes to me from an English friend who happens to know intimately the ins and outs of English politics and the drift of English opinion, but who has also a discerning knowledge of the currents of continental politics. It speaks for itself:

> My impression is very definite that the United States does not wholly realize how much the European future turns upon the decisive action taken by your President and the Secretary of State. No doubt for public purposes debts and disarmament must be kept apart. But in the private discussions I hope it will be emphasized by your people that Great Britain is expected to make a determined and definite effort at Geneva to disarm and that this will smooth the paths to a debt agreement. English public opinion is aware of the need for a drastic programme and is gravely troubled by its absence. The difficulties in the way of action are that (i) the technicians in the service departments are hostile; (ii) certain cabinet members are hostile; (iii) the cabinet members who favour an advance are merely general instead of specific. Your people, if they so will, can lift the whole discussion on to a new plane. But it will need the kind of resolution and courage the President has shown in your domestic affairs. Effectively the need is for America to reinforce those elements in English public life which have the will to righteousness without the power to act upon their will. They require the stimulus of American urgency — twice as effective now because of the immense impression made by the new President. I emphasize urgency because no one not in Europe can realize how near our feet lie to the abyss; failure at Geneva may well mean the end of disarmament for a decade. The people are hungry for leadership. It is in the power of America to speak in their name and thereby to change the whole outlook and the dearest hopes of a generation.

Always faithfully yours,
F.F.

P.S.   That was a gracious wire you sent to the *Crimson* dinner. Warranted warm cheers.

The English friend was S. K. Ratcliffe, the veteran British journalist.

Cambridge, Mass., April 14, 1933

Dear Mr. President:

Three things:

1. You may be interested in the analysis, below, of Ramsay MacDonald's mental habits and ways as a negotiator. It comes to me from a trusted English friend of great discernment, who has intimately watched for years MacDonald's ways, and whose desires are for the things we care about. What he writes will, in general, not be news to you, but it may help in formulating a picture of MacDonald as negotiator. Here it is:

> Mr. MacDonald's ability in the realm of diplomatic negotiation lies in what may be termed its rhetorical aspect. He has considerable skill in contributing an atmosphere of general good will and of large principle. He likes to lay down issues in such a fashion as to maximise possible agreement. His mind is not a concrete mind, and he therefore likes to concern himself with the approach rather than the detail, the drift of the conclusions rather than the conclusions themselves. He has very considerable dexterity in the handling of men, and this enables him to effect compromises for the sake of agreement the value of which (e.g. the Young Plan) becomes much more dubious when it is analysed in cold objectivity. He is, alas, ill-equipped to deal with economic issues; though he is, to some extent, balanced on this side by the considerable competence of his technical adviser, Sir F. Leith-Ross. He has confidence in his own powers as a negotiator, and this gives him a doggedness and persistence to which real value must be attached. He can irritate by being vague; and he likes formulae of this character which make a popular appeal. He does not easily reveal his own mind, largely because he is in himself indecisive; and he dislikes being pushed towards the definite and the concrete. Mr. Henderson once said that the only way to deal with Mr. MacDonald was to insist at the outset on specific conclusions and then drive him to them one by one. His elusiveness does not make this easy; but long experience indicates that it is much the most helpful technique if one is to arrive at definite conclusions with him.

2. Your message to the Governors urging minimum wage legislation was most gratifying. It was an effective because concrete way of driving home the President's influence over state legislation through the prestige of his office, and his party leadership. It emphasizes the national importance of minimum wage standards as part of a comprehensive program for restoring purchasing power and putting the brake on further deflation. Finally, it

will encourage Herbert Lehman to realize that fighting has its rewards as well as its joys, by giving nationwide recognition to his accomplishment. You would have been amused at the session Frances Perkins, Molly Dewson and I had with Lehman to persuade him to take the lead for the New York Minimum Wage Law. Especially would you have chortled had you heard Molly Dewson reading him the riot act. He finally came across handsomely.

3. I treasure your "independent pig" as more of an accolade than had I been awarded what I am told is one of the most prized distinctions in the world, the Turkish Order of Chastity of the Second Class. Seriously, I will not trust to words to tell you how deeply moving and how heartening are the implications of generosity and confidence that lie behind that facetious characterization of yours.

That the mental climate of the country has been greatly changed since March 4th you know full well, and that it has been changed by you is a matter of history. It was to me a great joy to see you as fit and as serene as ever. Your buoyancy and determination are widely infectious. And it was a great pleasure to have been at that Sunday night supper.

With warm regards.

Faithfully yours,
F.F.

This analysis of Prime Minister Ramsay MacDonald's habits as a negotiator came from Harold J. Laski, a candid and critical friend of the British Labour leader. Arthur Henderson, the Foreign Secretary, had gifts of character that made him a more formidable figure than the more eloquent and accomplished MacDonald.

Although they liked Governor Herbert Lehman, both Roosevelt and Frankfurter felt he would never fulfill his capacity as a reform governor unless he developed a greater willingness to fight hard in a just cause. There is no doubt that Lehman met this test successfully in the next few years.

Cambridge, Mass., April 17, 1933

Dear Mr. President:

1. Considering its source and the nature of the subject matter, I thought I ought to send the enclosed letter from Mr. Justice Stone directly to you. Incidentally you are, I am sure, aware that he has genuine sympathies on the essential issues of the day. He is one of the really dependable liberals on the Court.

2. My warmest thanks for your personal intervention with Rayburn on the Securities Bill. It came at a crucial moment and was decisive. I am

keeping in close telephonic touch with the situation, and there is every reason to believe that an effective and carefully-safeguarded bill will emerge. The House legislative counsel is very persnickety, and so the process is a bit slow. I don't have to tell you that the subject is very complicated, with many ramifications, raising a number of difficult drafting problems. On some of these problems I have, happily, been able to tap the most authoritative and socially-minded experience that is available.

3. The appointment of John Collier as Indian Commissioner is, if I may say so, a combination of courage and wisdom. My concern with Indian matters goes back to the T.R. days, when the dearest friend I ever had — Robert G. Valentine '96 — was Assistant Commissioner and later Commissioner. Collier's appointment means not only a truly new deal for the Indians but a new vindication of Uncle Sam's old but neglected duties as trustee for the Indians. What a great engine for public service the Department of Interior will be, before you get through with it.

Always yours,
F.F.

Mr. Justice Stone had written to Frankfurter that it was essential for Roosevelt to make the maximum use of his Presidential powers during his first months in office, that the country desperately wanted him to do so, and that he should be neither discouraged nor dismayed by charges that he wished to exercise arbitrary power.

Representative Sam Rayburn, later Speaker of the House of Representatives for a record number of years, was the principal legislative architect of the Securities Bill, which stood at the center of the President's program to place the vagaries of speculation in Wall Street and the power of corporate finance under some measure of public regulation. Frankfurter was the main author of the Securities Bill, working with James M. Landis and Benjamin V. Cohen to assist Rayburn.

John Collier, as Frankfurter predicted, proved to be an outstanding Indian Commissioner, with a reputation for lasting achievement that time has done nothing to dim.

Grappling with the confusion and urgency of the problems created by the depression, Roosevelt turned increasingly to Frankfurter for advice on appointments. He greatly approved of this letter to Lippmann.

Joseph P. Cotton, one of the great figures in the history of the American bar, had left his immensely lucrative law practice in New York and, at Frankfurter's urging, had become Undersecretary of State to Mr. Stimson in the Hoover Administration. Charles Hill Howland had left the law to begin a career filled with distinction in the State Department.

April 17, 1933

Dear Walter:

Yes, you have put your finger on the greatest immediate need — qualified men for key jobs. I can only speak with confidence about members of my own profession. Nothing more devastatingly proves the golden calf pursuit which has corrupted this country, in the subtlest forms of corruption, during the last two or three decades, than lack of capable, free men among lawyers of parts between the ages of thirty and fifty odd. By "free" I mean especially the resiliency of mind and judgment — like Joe Cotton's — that is ready to take in new facts and new forces and to realize that new accommodations have to be made, though made in the organic unfolding of valid past traditions and techniques. And the reason that that is so, is well illustrated by Joe Cotton. I could not name half a dozen other lawyers of even comparable ability to Joe who were as free as he — who did not sell their clients their opinions and their feelings as well as their skill. It is not without interest that of those who are like him several left the law, and they left it precisely because of its unconscious enslavement. I have in mind a few like Howland.

The difficulty, therefore, is not that argumentatively such men are politically vulnerable but that they are intrinsically in the grip of conventions and biases that would make them obstructive to the doing of what needs to be done — through lack of courage or insight or the dominance of old habits, but obstructive in any event.

Of the disinterestedness of such men I have no doubt. But disinterestedness is not enough. During the last few weeks I have had occasion to talk with a number of them — men very able, very eager for public service and aware that something new is stirring in the world. And yet they are really a hindrance rather than a help in the solution of our difficulties. They made me realize anew that men may be public-spirited without being — to use the jargon — progressive.

Some time ago I wrote you about the effect that post-war America, especially, was having upon the generous young lawyers whom I happen to know intimately. I believe it would be an eye-opener even to you if I showed you letters that have come to me during recent years from some of the ablest younger lawyers in the big New York offices, or listened to the talk that I hear from them when they come, as it were, to confessional. Literally by the score they are sick of it all. That's one of the heartening things about the times — that the Government can avail itself of an abler lot of younger lawyers for key junior positions than has been true at any time since I left the Law School.

Always yours,
F.F.

Memorandum for Felix Frankfurter

The White House, April 22, 1933

I think you can assure our friend, whose letter I am returning, that it is all right about Edgar Hoover. Homer Cummings agrees with me.

All well here. I wish you could be sitting at my side when I "take on" the Prime Minister, etc.

F.D.R.

Frankfurter had reported a rumor that the young J. Edgar Hoover of the FBI was unhappy with the new Administration and wished to leave.

Prime Minister Ramsay MacDonald of Great Britain was coming to Washington to urge a far-ranging world economic conference upon the President. But the President at this stage was thinking primarily of a national approach. He took the United States off the gold standard while the Prime Minister was still crossing the Atlantic.

Cambridge, Mass., April 26, 1933

Dear Mr. President:

Many thanks for your chit regarding Edgar Hoover. I have taken the liberty of passing the comforting message on to our friend.

I know your gracious and generous habit of making those of us who have the welfare of your Administration so deeply at heart feel as though we were part of the official family. Yet your kind expression, in your note of the 22nd, that you wished I "could be sitting" at your side when you "take on" the Prime Minister tempts me to say that I hope you know that I am always available for any *ad hoc* jobs, whenever you think I can be of the slightest use. So summon me at any time you think I can be of any particular help.

For the rest, it seems to me that you have "taken on" MacDonald and Herriot with admirable effectiveness and success. The crucial condition for wise action is the generation of the right atmosphere out of which right action flows. You certainly have achieved that in abundance — you have set in motion currents which are bound to lead not only our own ship of state, but the ship of the world state, with you at the helm, into safe harbor.

And how I rejoice that Oggie has so early taken the field against you! !

With warm regards,

Always yours,

F.F.

Herriot, the Prime Minister of France, wanted assurances of American support for France's national security and for a French plan, vague and general, for the revival of trade.

"Oggie" is Ogden Mills, Secretary of the Treasury in the Hoover Admin-
istration, who had taken the field against the New Deal even at this early
stage and who grew steadily more critical with the passage of time.

Washington, D.C., May 2, 1933

My dear Frankfurter:

Thank you for your note and the enclosed memorandum, which I return herewith.

The writer of the memorandum said the same thing to me at the
White House the other evening. It is reassuring to realize that matters of
this kind get to the President and receive his personal attention. I think it is
enormously important for sound administration that such things should
happen.

With best regards, I am,

Yours sincerely,
HARLAN STONE

Frankfurter sent this note to the President. Mr. Justice Stone wanted to
make certain that the President had a system of checking on administrative
decisions, since such decisions could sometimes be as important as policy
directives.

Cambridge, Mass., May 9, 1933

Dear Mr. President:

1. When Woodrow Wilson was taunted with being a professor I ventured the remark — and it was before I was tarred with the professorial
stick — that all the great Presidents of the United States have essentially
been educators. You are again proving that. Sunday night you again took
the nation to school — as I hope you will, from time to time, take it to
school. With admirable simplicity and lucidity you are making known to
the nation what you are doing. But you are also making the people feel —
and nothing is more important for a democracy — that in a true sense of
the word it is *their* government, and that *their* interests and *their* feelings
are actively engaged.

2. You might like to have your recollection refreshed with the exact
words of George Washington to which I referred the other night: "Let us
raise a standard to which the wise and the honest can repair. The event is in
the hand of God."

They were used by Washington at the Philadelphia Convention when
lesser and less daring men than he opposed proposals for an effective Constitution.

3. I was, and still am, excited by your suggestion of appealing, through

the heads of states, to the peoples of Europe to save the Disarmament Conference. There is every reason for hoping that the peoples of Europe will respond, as our people are responding, to an appeal by you. I am confident that the governments of Europe are much more timid and lethargic about daring action than their peoples. These governments are apparently willing to take all the risks of non-action and timid action. But they are unwilling to take risks for peace and recovery, although Europe stands at the edge of an abyss. An appeal such as you outlined Sunday afternoon — and I am not concerned with the details now — would touch the imagination and hopes of men everywhere.

I was particularly heartened by your remark that it would not matter if you did "fail." Such an appeal could not in any true sense of the word "fail." You may not secure the adoption of a particular proposal. In any event you would tap new forces for peace and recovery. Such courageous assertion of leadership in behalf of right and reason would set in motion the latent forces of right and reason in men. You would thus give coherence and organization to the scattered feelings and purposes of men. I profoundly hope, therefore, that you too will raise a standard "to which the wise and honest can repair."

Always faithfully yours.
FELIX FRANKFURTER

Frankfurter is referring here to Roosevelt's second "fireside chat," delivered on Sunday, May 7, 1933. He had seen the President that afternoon to look at the advance text, on which some work still had to be done, and to discuss various issues of foreign policy particularly the question of disarmament. The quotation from George Washington was one which Frankfurter often used when discussing public issues with Roosevelt. Every appeal by Roosevelt, both public and private, failed to save the Disarmament Conference.

Cambridge, Mass., May 15, 1933

Dear Mac:

A sceptic like you may need reassurance that everything that is happening in Washington is constitutional. So glance at the enclosed. I don't need to bring reassurance to the President on that score, but even he might like to run his eye down the column.

With warm regards,

Always yours,
F.F.

Hon. Marvin H. McIntyre

BOSTON *GLOBE*, MAY 15, 1933
FRANKFURTER ON AIR UPHOLDS NEW DEAL
Harvard Man Says Program of F.D.R. Is Constitutional

The constitutionality of the Roosevelt program was defended last night in an address over station WNAC by Felix Frankfurter, Harvard Law School professor, who asserted that the Constitution is quite flexible enough to meet the new needs of America.

Prof. Frankfurter declared that "vague clauses" have been employed in the past to support countless important practices in industry, and advised that the constitutionality of a practice be determined, not by the letter of the law, but by the needs of society.

JUSTICES MUST READ LIFE
"The justices of the Supreme Court," he said, "are in fact arbiters of social policy. They are so because their duties make them so. The words of the Constitution are usually so unrestrained by their intrinsic meaning, or by their history, or by prior decision, that they leave the individual justice free, if indeed they do not compel him to gather meaning, not from reading the Constitution, but from reading life.

"The Constitution has ample resources within itself to meet the changing needs of successive generations, for it was made for an undefined and expanding future, and for a people gathered from many nations, and of many tongues.

"If the court, aided by an alert and public-spirited bar has access to the facts and follows them, the Constitution is flexible enough to meet all the new needs of our society."

Prof. Frankfurter said that terms like "due process of law" are of a convenient vagueness to meet the shifting circumstances of our dynamic society. "Of necessity," he asserted, "the content of our laws is derived from without, not revealed within the clauses of the Constitution."

DUE PROCESS IMPORTANT
"The meaning that is put upon these phrases controls the Nation's effort to meet the task. The capacity of our State to control or mitigate unemployment, to assure a fair wage, to clear the slums, to distribute fairly the burden of taxation, the discharge of these, and like responsibilities of modern government, depends on the Supreme Court's reading of the 'due process' clause.

"There have been various attempts in the past to subject the great economic agencies to social responsibilities. These depended upon the interpretation of the 'commerce clause.' The interpretation, of course, in turn depended upon who interpreted, as much as on what was being interpreted."

The speaker said that the flexibility of clauses in the Constitution has been continually used to settle industrial policies, even controversies affecting business combinations and trade unions. He suggested, in conclusion, that there is support for new policies within the Constitution.

The White House, May 22, 1933

Dear Felix:

In the first place, I am not a sceptic, and in the second, I need no assurances.

However, there are lots of sceptics who do need assurances; therefore, thanks.

Hope the President will also like it.

Sincerely yours,
M. H. McINTYRE

Roosevelt had addressed a solemn appeal to sovereigns and presidents for peace by disarmament and for international action to end economic chaos. He pointed out that the World Economic Conference would soon meet. With grave emphasis, he also pointed out that the disarmament conference had already labored for more than a year without having reached any satisfactory results.

Telegram to Roosevelt

Cambridge, Mass., May 16, 1933

YOU DID A VERY GREAT THING IN APPEALING DIRECTLY TO THE CONSCIENCE OF ALL THE PEOPLES ON BEHALF OF THE COMMON INTEREST OF HUMANITY.

FELIX FRANKFURTER

Telegram to Roosevelt

Cambridge, Mass., May 23, 1933

WARM APPRECIATION FOR YOUR EFFECTIVE SUPPORT WITHOUT WHICH THERE WOULD NOT HAVE BEEN AN ADEQUATE SECURITIES BILL CARRYING OUT THE PURPOSES OF YOUR MESSAGE.

FELIX FRANKFURTER

Cambridge, Mass., May 24, 1933

Dear Mr. President:

The passage of the Securities Bill again vindicates your leadership. Through your impulse, the need for correcting abuses in the flotation of security issues was recognized in the Chicago platform, your message to Congress made the legislation part of the Administration's program, and at crucial stages of the legislative process your support was essential in finally bringing an adequate bill into port.

In the enactment of so complicated a measure as the Securities Bill, particularly one that is directed against entrenched abuses, the energetic and intelligent help of members of Congress is indispensable. A number of the Senate and House members did yeoman's work — the leader of the Senate, Joe Robinson, for instance, helped greatly. But I do not think it is invidious to single out for special mention Chairman Rayburn of the House Committee. He gave himself completely to effectuating the purposes of your message. He worked indefatigably for a law that should be fair to the legitimate interests of finance, while at the same time protecting the exploitation of the credulity and limited knowledge of investors; and the qualities of courage that he showed were no less striking. He was keenly aware of the subtle forces trying to defeat your purposes and was effectively on guard against them. I say all this out of a sense of gratitude for an unusually effective piece of legislative leadership.

Always with warm regards,

Faithfully yours,
F.F.

Cambridge, Mass., May 29, 1933

Dear Mr. President:

I hope my hurried reply to your question last Saturday regarding Dr. Splawn was not so hurried as to leave any doubt about my high opinion of Dr. Splawn's qualifications. My contacts with Splawn have been entirely through common interests and activities on the public side of railroad and utility problems, and I have followed intimately his work for the House Committee on Interstate Commerce, the Interstate Commerce Commission, and the Federal Power Commission. On the basis of that knowledge, I have acquired a very high regard for Splawn's technical equipment and social outlook. He has a sophisticated understanding of corporate and utility finance, a balanced judgment and a habit of fairness that is always regardful of the comprehensive national interest in the solution of the complicated railroad and power problems. On the Interstate Commerce Commission he would be a real accession to the purposes of the Administration.

And I am very happy about your contemplated nomination of Ray Stevens for the Trade Commission. I hope he will be put in special charge of the enforcement of the Securities Act. That Act will be merely a piece of paper unless it is administered by a man of courage, imagination, understanding and complete disinterestedness. Ray Stevens combines those qualities to an unusual degree. His appointment will, I am sure, meet with high favor among the liberals in and out of the Democratic Party.

Always faithfully yours,
F.F.

Walter Marshall Splawn, president of the University of Texas 1924–1927, was appointed to the Interstate Commerce Commission in 1934. He later served as Commission chairman. Ray Stevens was appointed.

Cambridge, Mass., May 29, 1933

Dear Mr. President:

Herewith is a clean draft of the Bill to correct the abuses of contingent fees in tax and other claims against the Government, about which we talked on Saturday and which you are planning to have put through as part of the Administration's program at this session. I am also enclosing a copy of the supporting memorandum, which you scanned.

L.D.B. thinks — this is of course solely for your own ears — that large losses to the revenue are directly traceble to evils connected with contingent fees in tax and other suits against the Government and that this Bill will plug up at least some of the holes that should be plugged up.

This is, of course, the most opportune time to secure this legislation.

Always faithfully yours,

F.F.

P.S.   It was most cheering to find your tremendous drive unabated.

The text of the bill, drafted by Frankfurter in consultation with Mr. Justice Brandeis (L.D.B.), is omitted here for reasons of space. Frankfurter was never satisfied with the restraints imposed on lawyers engaged in suits against the government on a contingent fee basis. The memorandum explains his reasoning.

Memorandum in Support of Bill

1. *Policy.* Except for the prohibition of fee-splitting, this bill merely makes general a policy that has long been applied in a multitude of special classes of cases.[1] The purpose, as is indicated in the title of the bill, and as was recognized by Mr. Justice Brandeis in *Calhoun* v. *Massie* with reference to an earlier statute, is "in part to protect just claimants from extortion or improvident bargains, and in part to protect the Treasury from frauds and imposition." It recognizes "that the causes which gave rise to laws against champerty and maintenance are persistent."[2] Just claims against the government should of course be paid. The limitation on contingent fees and the prohibition of fee-splitting are founded on sad and very costly experience. They seek to protect the Treasury from depredations due to enormous rewards gained by stirring up litigation and astute prosecution of flimsy claims. When counsel fees for recovery of taxes, in individual cases, run into the millions — as they notoriously have — litigation is

bound to be fomented and every device and ingenuity will be exploited to withdraw vast sums from the Treasury.

2. *Constitutionality.* The constitutionality of this bill is not open to question. Broad powers of Congress over the enforcement of claims against the United States have been recognized from the beginning of our government. In 1792 Congress restricted assignments of pension claims;[3] in 1828 it prohibited both transfers and attachments of certain payments made to Revolutionary War veterans.[4] In 1853 Congress imposed stringent regulations upon the assignment of all claims against the United States[5] and this statute is still in effect.[6] In *United States* v. *Hall*,[7] the Supreme Court held that even the power to define embezzlement of pension money after payment was within the Congressional domain. The validity of statutes limiting attorneys' fees in certain classes of claims has been determined upon several occasions.[8] In one of the earliest cases, *Frisbie* v. *United States*, Mr. Justice Brewer, while conceding "that, generally speaking, among the inalienable rights of the citizen is that of the liberty of contract," [9] stated that "Congress being at liberty to give or withhold a pension, may prescribe who shall receive it, and determine all the circumstances and conditions under which any application therefor shall be prosecuted. No man has a legal right to a pension, and no man has a legal right to interfere in the matter of obtaining pensions for himself or others. The whole control of that matter is within the domain of Congressional power. Having power to legislate on this whole matter, to prescribe the conditions under which parties may assist in procuring pensions, it has the equal power to enforce by penal provisions compliance with its requirements." [10] In the most recent case upon the subject the Court, speaking unanimously through Mr. Justice McReynolds, dismissed the argument as to constitutionality with the statement: "The validity of Section 13, construed as above indicated, we think is not open to serious doubt." [11]

3. *Specific Provisions.*

(*a*) The requirement of filing fee agreements adapts and enlarges upon the present law as to pension claims.[12] The device of enforcing this requirement by a refusal to recognize agents or attorneys who have not complied is suggested by several provisions now in force refusing absolutely to recognize agents or attorneys in certain cases.[13] The power to enact such a provision follows readily from its legitimacy as a means of insuring the observance of Section 2. The validity of similar provisions with regard to pension claims and services to Indians has not been questioned.[14]

(*b*) The limitation of fees to twenty *per centum* follows the percentage set in the Omnibus Claims Act of 1915.[15] The limitation to $2500 is included in recognition of the fact that as to large claims a fee of 20%

would be exorbitant. Allowance of any fees above that amount should depend upon explicit permission of the tribunal. Allowance of a charge, even though the proceeding is unsuccessful, is essential; so long as the charge is slight there is no reason why it can not be made without the assistance of the tribunal. But inasmuch as there is no means of controlling more substantial charges directly by statute it seems wise to require resort to the tribunal whenever any considerable charge is to be made. The use of the tribunal to regulate fees is well established by earlier statutes.[16]

(c) The provision as to fee-splitting has been adapted from the statutes in New York[17] and Wisconsin[18] and the American Bar Association's canons of professional ethics.[19] It follows, primarily, the New York statute which has been in successful operation since 1876.[20] Although it is new to the laws of the United States, its constitutionality is uncontestable.

(d) Section 5 is not essential, inasmuch as it is not likely that this act could be regarded as inconsistent with existing special provisions. But it avoids possible controversy to be explicit.

1. See 8 U.S.C. sec. 63 (colored soldiers' pay); 10 U.S.C. sec. 867 (arrearages in soldiers' pay); 25 U.S.C. sec. 82 (services to Indians); 38 U.S.C. secs. 111, 112, 114, 116, 244, 286, 324, 325, 326, 361, 619 (all pensions); 43 U.S.C. secs. 842, 843 (bounty lands); 26 Stat. 822 (refund of direct tax); 26 Stat. 851, 854 (claims for Indian depredations); 38 Stat. 989 (Omnibus Claims Act); 40 Stat. 102, 104 (war risk insurance).

2. See 253 U.S. 170, 173, 174.

3. Act of March 23, 1792, c. 10, sec. 6, 1 Stat. 245.

4. Act of May 15, 1828, c. 53, sec. 4, 4 Stat. 270.

5. Act of Feb. 26, 1853, c. 81, sec. 1, 10 Stat. 170.

6. 31 U.S.C. sec. 203.

7. 98 U.S. 343.

8. Frisbie v. United States, 157 U.S. 160; Hall v. Halsell, 161 U.S. 72; Calhoun v. Massie, 253 U.S. 170; Margolin v. United States, 269 U.S. 93; cf. Yeiser v. Dysart, 267 U.S. 540; see Note (1924).

9. See 157 U.S. 160 at 165.

10. See 157 U.S. 160 at 166.

11. See Margolin v. United States, 269 U.S. 93, 102.

12. 38 U.S.C. 114.

13. 38 U.S.C. secs. 286, 325, 326, 363.

14. See 38 U.S.C. sec. 114; cf. 25 U.S.C. sec. 82.

15. Act of March 4, 1915, c. 140, sec. 4, 38 Stat. 989.

16. See Act of May 20, 1918, c. 77, sec. 1, 40 Stat. 555; 38 U.S.C. sec. 111, 43 U.S.C. 842; cf. 38 U.S.C. secs. 286, 324, 326, 361, 363.

17. N.Y. Penal Code, sec. 274 (2).

18. Wis. Laws of 1827, c 459, p. 670.

19. Canon 34.

20. See N.Y. Laws of 1876, c. 448, sec. 74.

Cambridge, Mass., June 6, 1933

Dear Mr. President:

You could not, I believe, have given Mr. Morgan a better associate on the Tennessee Valley Authority than Lilienthal. That's a team that is bound to produce great results. They assure the soundest possible promise for the realization of the manifold national purposes that lie behind the Tennessee Valley development. Not often does one get such a combination of training, courage, understanding and youthful ardor as Lilienthal represents. It is a truly great appointment.

Always yours,
F.F.

P.S.   Of course I'm watching your management of "The Hill" with eagerness and confidence.

Arthur E. Morgan was chairman of the Tennessee Valley Authority, later resigning from that position after a controversy over policy and administration. David Lilienthal, who succeeded Morgan in 1941 and to whom Frankfurter was devoted, will always be linked with the greatness of TVA.

Frankfurter's abiding interest in tax reform was sharpened by the revelations that some of the wealthiest men in the country had escaped the bulk of their income tax payments by taking advantage of legal loopholes. The investigation of Wall Street, known as the Pecora investigation, revealed that J. P. Morgan, by thoroughly legal means, had avoided all federal income taxes in the United States for 1930, 1931, and 1932, though he paid his taxes in England for these years. Colonel McCormick of the Chicago Tribune placed a value of only $25,250 on his personal property, a valuation which required a tax of $1,515. A tax of $90 was paid by Louis Florsheim of Florsheim Shoes. The chairman of the S. W. Straus investment and banking firm did even better: his tax came to $18. Shares in the Alleghany Corporation, a Van Sweringen holding company, were sold at a discount far below their market value to a private preferred list which included, among others, General Pershing, Charles A. Lindbergh, Owen D. Young, William G. McAdoo. In dealing with these tax abuses and market irregularities, Frankfurter had the continuous advice and help of Mr. Justice Brandeis.

Cambridge, Mass., July 10, 1933

Dear Mr. President:

I am burdening you with this letter and its enclosures because of serious matters affecting the financial administration of the government which I think I ought to bring to your attention.

1. I have been waiting until you had Congress off your hands and had returned from your vacation before sending you the enclosed letter from Judge Green. It came to me out of a clear sky, for I have not the personal acquaintance of the Judge. Considering its source, the views expressed in this letter appear very important. As you probably know, Judge Green was on the Ways and Means Committee and its chairman for five years, chairman of the Joint Tax Committee of the House and Senate, and as a member of the Court of Claims — who is, I know, well thought of by the Supreme Court — has had ample opportunity for a dispassionate judgment on the quality of our tax administration. Especially significant is it that Judge Green should be "firmly of the opinion" that through effective administration of our revenue laws "at least $50,000,000 a year and probably $100,000,000 a year more would be realized in taxes." This is a striking confirmation of figures of avoidable losses through ineffective enforcement which, when once or twice I put them to you, may have seemed rather tall.

2. Just before he left Washington, Mr. Justice Stone wrote me a long-hand letter expressing views which he asked me to keep "strictly confidential" but which I know he would not mind my passing on to you. I quote him:

> You know that more money can be lost to the government in a single badly conducted case than Douglas can save in a year. And the President's whole program will be put to the test through the activities of his law officers. Thoroughgoing building up of the Department of Justice by the appointment of capable young men ought to go forward without delay.

Both Brandeis and Stone feel very strongly the importance of retaining in the Solicitor General's office two young men of really unusual ability who have been especially successful in the argument of tax cases before the Supreme Court. They are Erwin N. Griswold and Paul D. Miller. Not only the liberal minority of the Court, but also some of the others, have been full of praise for the arguments of these men. I happen to know that both of them are being strongly tempted by outside offers. To lose the services of these men would really be a heavy blow not only to the government's law business but to its finances. I have urged both of them — they happen to be former students of mine — for the present at least to turn down the private offers.

3. In addition it would be an immense reinforcement for the government in a much-needed field if William A. Sutherland of the Atlanta bar, a man older than Miller and Griswold, were drawn into the tax work. He combines courage, ability and experience as to tax litigation. The subtleties of tax law — with its complicated statutory and constitutional problems —

require seasoned skill. Seldom is that at the service of the public, because
the slant of those who are skilled is usually anti-government. Fortunately
Sutherland has both the ability and the right public slant.

4. Finally, as to the need of a thorough re-examination of our tax laws.
You may recall that we had a talk about this when I last saw you, before
Christmas, in Albany. May I ask you to run your eye over the enclosed brief
memorandum which may have gained more immediate practical importance from the recent disclosures as to the workings of our revenue measures.

Always your,
F.F.

*Lewis W. Douglas was budget director at this time. Erwin N. Griswold
years later became the dean of the Harvard Law School.*

Frankfurter Memorandum on
Scrutiny of Existing Tax Legislation and Its Interpretation

1. A very careful survey of existing revenue measures should be made
in the interest of increasing the revenue. Obviously this must be made by
someone not connected with the Treasury and perhaps best by an entirely
fresh mind which has not become accustomed to glaring defects or wrongs
in past legislation and administration made in the interest particularly of
the heavy taxpayer.

2. Some of these will seem like corrections of detail and will not involve increase of rates, and might be put over without a great fight. For
instance:

(1) Those relating to deductions from gross income. Under the
Revenue Act and its practices, as I understand, deductions logically applicable to the whole of a taxpayer's income are applied wholly to that part of
the income which is taxable. Thus the taxpayer's expenses incident to taking care of his property (like commissions and expenses of his man of business) although properly applicable to the whole estate or income are in fact
deducted from the taxable income before figuring the tax.

(2) Similarly, the 13% deduction on account of gifts to chari-
table purposes are apparently deducted from the taxable part of the income
and not apportioned between taxable and non-taxable.

(3) There is no doubt that a careful study of the Act, in connection with past decisions of the courts and rulings of the Treasury Department and of the Board of Tax Appeals, would uncover possibilities of stopping revenue leaks aggregating hundreds of millions of dollars. This would
require the skillful formulation of amendments needed to overcome strained

interpretations of the Supreme Court, and resourcefulness in steering round some of its holdings of unconstitutionality.

December 20, 1932

Washington, D.C., June 9, 1933

My dear Professor Frankfurter:

I trust you will pardon any seeming presumption in a letter being addressed to you by one who knows you only by reputation, but I was very much interested in reading your recent article in the *Yale Review* and I can write you confidentially as to matters upon which some persons might think one who was in my position ought not to express an opinion, although he could not help having one.

It is quite true that there are some Judges who seem to think that the Constitution embodies their own ideas with reference to political economy, and that any legislation which is contrary thereto violates that venerated document and is unconstitutional. Perhaps in the march of events we will some day get back to what I think is the true principle; namely, that the courts have no power to set aside the economic policies of a legislative body simply because the Judges consider such policy unwise. This feeling on the part of Judges with reference to the wisdom of a statute has often resulted in having tax laws declared to be arbitrary, capricious, and that if enforced would show a want of "due process of law." In this way many provisions have been so characterized which in England no one would ever think of attacking.

It should be observed in this connection, however, that the Supreme Court is much more liberal than the Federal District courts with which the Court of Claims is often in conflict. If the District courts had their way there would be little left of the income and estate tax provisions which could not be evaded.

As the situation stands, in my opinion, the Government suffers more from the lack of administration of proper enforcement of our revenue laws than in any other way. Unfortunately there is no way to make the situation known except by thorough congressional investigation guided by some attorney who is skilled in technical tax law and imbued with an interest for the public. The seat of the trouble is in the Bureau of Internal Revenue where, in my opinion, settlements are continually being made contrary to the public interest. The Mitchell case is an example. Mitchell seems to have disclosed to the Bureau at least enough of the facts in the case to enable it to get to the very bottom of the matter with very little trouble and I am informed reliably as I think that his case is but one of hundreds, perhaps thousands, of others who were equally culpable and whose cases ought to have been investigated by the Bureau, but in which the returns made by the taxpayer were blindly accepted. I am firmly of the opinion that with the proper Commissioner in charge of the Bureau and a competent Solicitor who would enforce the law regardless of how much he might come into conflict with what is commonly called "big interests," at least $50,000,-000 a year and probably $100,000,000 a year more would be realized in taxes. You may possibly recollect that I was about five years the chairman of the Committee on Ways and Means and chairman of the Joint Tax Committee of the House and Senate, and I may say also that the greater portion of the business of the court with which I am now connected is cases in which the plaintiff seeks to have taxes refunded. Consequently I have had much experience in these matters.

All that I have written above however is but preliminary to another important matter to which I hoped you might give some attention and bring about some government action if you finally concluded the case was a proper one.

You probably have noticed that in the examination of Van Sweringen before the Senate Committee, he testified in substance that the Geneva Corporation was organized for the purpose of making it unnecessary to pay income taxes on a profit which was made by the General Securities Corporation and that Mr. Pecora, referring to the method taken, said "It was lawful," but afterwards seemed to qualify the remark. That the Government was defrauded at least in a moral sense, there is no doubt and I am inclined to think also in a legal sense although that can only be determined after a somewhat close investigation of the matter.

You are aware of the rules laid down by the courts when puppet corporations are organized to conceal the identity of some persons who pull the strings and cause them to operate, and also as to the effect under certain situations of actions of a corporation whose identity through stock ownership is practically the same as another which controls it, and other decisions which prevent an individual or corporation being shielded by another corporation which is used simply as a mask for the operations of the first party. I think that where a corporation is organized wholly for the purpose of avoiding a tax and is controlled entirely by the persons who would pay the tax, the whole matter becomes simply a fraudulent device which will not avail the taxpayer. Of course you have no personal interest in the matter but you have often interested yourself in public matters where there was no possibility of gain to yourself and I thought possibly you might be inclined to give some attention to this matter if you have not already done so and make your conclusions public. I would not write you about it but for the fact that while the matter could not in any event come before the court of which I am a member there are many people that would criticize my making any investigation and public comment in relation to a case of this kind.

I desire in conclusion to express my hope that in any event you will continue to publish articles of the nature of the one to which I have referred. Coming from one who has so high a standing as a lawyer, I think these articles will have some effect on the courts which have already to some extent modified their former decisions.

With great esteem, I remain

Very truly yours,
WM. R. GREEN

Frankfurter's article in the Yale Review *dealt with social issues before the Supreme Court, and opposed all efforts to convert that Court into a super-legislature.*

Charles E. Mitchell of the National City Bank in New York admitted under questioning by Ferdinand Pecora for a Congressional investigating committee that he had avoided all income tax payments in 1929 by selling stock to a relative at a loss and then buying it back later. Defending the Pecora investigation against the charge that it was destroying the nation's confidence in bankers, Roosevelt said the bankers "should have thought of that when they did the things that are being exposed now."

Cambridge, Mass., July 6, 1933

My dear Judge Green:

Your letter, which has been left unacknowledged too long, has given me the greatest possible encouragement. You were generous to write me. That one with your long experience in the legislative and judicial branches should so authoritatively confirm some of the views I had reached, however reluctantly, makes me indeed have confidence in those views.

I, too, have spent a good part of my mature life in government — almost half of it. It has left me with the conviction that, on the whole, government suffers ever so much more from apathy and lack of energy and of imagination on the part of administrators than from corruption. Your intimation that the government is losing $50 to $100 million yearly through lax enforcement of our internal tax laws vindicates my own guess in the matter — I say "guess" when in fact a good deal of very dependable information underlies the judgment. One could not have better authority for this judgment than that which comes from your unparalleled experience on the Ways and Means Committee and more recently, from your judicial coign of observation.

The matter has been of grave concern to me for some time, and I have tried to make those who have the ultimate responsibility see the enormous leakages involved in our tax administration. By cheese-paring a few millions yearly are saved, while through ineffectual legal enforcement or through failure to plug up obvious holes in our tax measures, hundreds of millions are lost by the Government.

Your views ought to help secure ways for the correction of the great evils to which you call attention. I am therefore grateful to you for writing. You may, of course, trust my discretion as to your communication.

With appreciation and high esteem,

Sincerely yours,

FELIX FRANKFURTER

A copy of this letter was sent by Frankfurter to Roosevelt.

Office of the Attorney General, Washington, D.C., July 19, 1933

My dear Mr. President:

This answers your memorandum relative to the letter of Professor Frankfurter, dated July 10, and the enclosed letter from Judge William R. Green, both of which I return herewith.

1. The matters referred to in paragraph one, and in Judge Green's letter, present once again a subject which I have been considering for a considerable period of time. I have received innumerable suggestions along these same lines and have given the matter some independent study. The suggestions, for the most part, refer to the administration of the existing laws by the Treasury Department and affect the Department of Justice only collaterally. I have long felt the need of closer cooperation between the Departments and have been working on plans to bring this about.

2. It is, as suggested, highly important that tax cases in the Department of Justice should be properly studied and presented. This also is a problem with which I am dealing. Messrs. Griswold and Miller have been in the Solicitor General's office for several years. They are both good men. I think Judge Biggs would like to keep both of them, at least for a considerable period of time.

3. Mr. Sutherland would not meet the situation at all and it is rather too bad that this is so because, within certain limits, he is a man of very excellent attainents.

4. This is an important subject, requiring careful study. I had assumed, however, that the Treasury Department was already considering this matter; if not, I think, it might be well to have someone assigned to the task who is available both in the matter of ability and time.

Respectfully yours,

HOMER CUMMINGS

Attorney General

Telegram to Roosevelt

Cambridge, Mass., June 10, 1933

AM TICKLED PINK BY STEVENS APPOINTMENT. THAT IS REALLY FIRST RATE.

FELIX FRANKFURTER

Ray Stevens was appointed to the Trade Commission as recommended by Frankfurter.

Telegram to Roosevelt

Cambridge, Mass., June 10, 1933

DEVOTED WOMEN SUPPORTERS OF ADMINISTRATION REPRESENTING INFLUENTIAL NATIONAL ORGANIZATIONS INSIST ON BELIEVING THAT CURTAILMENT OF PRESENT SCOPE OF CHILDREN'S BUREAU IS THREATENED AS PART OF REORGANIZATION SCHEME. I TOLD THEM I REFUSED BELIEVE THAT YOU WOULD SANCTION INROADS UPON EXTRAORDINARILY FINE ACHIEVEMENTS CHILDREN'S BUREAU BECAUSE OF ANY ALLEGED CLAIM OF ABSTRACT LOGIC REGARDING DIVISION OF FUNCTIONS BETWEEN CHILDREN'S BUREAU AND PUBLIC HEALTH SERVICE. VENTURE TO BELIEVE THAT NOT ANOTHER AGENCY OF GOVERNMENT HAS FINER RECORD FOR ECONOMY AND EFFICIENCY THAN CHILDREN'S BUREAU NOR IS ANY MORE WARMLY ENTRENCHED IN LOYALTY OF WOMEN AND LIBERAL SENTIMENT OF COUNTRY.

FELIX FRANKFURTER

The White House, June 10, 1933

Dear Felix: —

As you will know by the time this reaches you, the reports of the illness or death of the Children's Bureau have been grossly exaggerated! As a matter of fact, some day and somehow we have got to do something to tie a lot of these loose ends in together but I have not been able to get to it at this session and nothing will be done until January.

Yesterday some of them came to see me and I started to tell them to keep their shirts on but thought better of it!

Always sincerely,

F.D.R.

Cambridge, Mass., June 12, 1933

Dear Mr. President:

Your very kind letter about the Children's Bureau again proves that for you time is not of limited duration but is a psychological equipment. It is hardly believable that you should have managed to squeeze in that letter to me despite the terrific pressure of the close of the session. But please let

me say that no communication of mine ever carries with it the need or
expectation of a reply, which makes me all the more appreciate that you
should have written me about the Children's Bureau.

Now that the sands of the special sessions have about run out, what an
extraordinary achievement these last few months have recorded. Enduringly extraordinary the achievement will remain.

And now get the refreshment of letting the government run itself for a
few days. It has plenty of momentum to permit you to indulge in a wholly
carefree loaf.

Always faithfully yours,
F.F.

*The British government on June 14, 1933, announced the payment to the
United States of $10 million on war debts with a note emphasizing that this
amount was to be considered "as an acknowledgement of the debt pending
a final settlement." Roosevelt in reply said that he did not regard Britain as
being in default. He said it is "vitally necessary," during these opening days
of the World Economic Conference, to avoid "difficult and possibly protracted discussions" of the debt problem.*

Telegram to Roosevelt

Cambridge, Mass., June 15, 1933

YOUR DEBT STATEMENT ADMIRABLY EASES TENSION ON BOTH SIDES OF OCEAN
AND GREATLY PROMOTES PROCESS OF DEFINITIVE SOLUTION.

FELIX FRANKFURTER

Telegram to Roosevelt

Cambridge, Mass., June 16, 1923

HOW WISE YOU WERE TO BRING CONGRESS AROUND BY SKILLFUL PATIENCE
RATHER THAN TO INTENSIFY FEELINGS BY APPEALING TO COUNTRY AGAINST
CONGRESS. NO ONE MORE EARNED A GOOD HOLIDAY THAN THAT I HOPE YOU
WILL NOW HAVE.

FELIX FRANKFURTER

The White House, June 17, 1933

My dear Dr. Frankfurter:

Just before leaving for his little vacation, the President asked me to tell
you that he was delighted to have your generous message of approval you
sent him yesterday, and to thank you very warmly for it.

Very sincerely yours,
M. H. McINTYRE

The following brief note to McIntyre was clipped to the letter to F.D.R.

Say, Mac, if you are going to "Dr." me — I'll begin to feel stuffy!

F.F.

Cambridge, Mass., July 6, 1933

Dear Mr. President:

1. A good holiday for you is really a good thing for the country, and you give every sign of having had a refreshing holiday.

2. Ray Stevens talked with me over the phone late last night. You certainly invigorated him immensely. He needed precisely the transfusion of strength and optimism which you gave him. The poor fellow needs a good holiday. In time he will be very fit and eager for the fray that is ahead — for fray indeed is ahead in the administration of the Securities Act. There are still too many in "the Street" who think that what Joe Cotton used to call the "green goods business" — when he passed on securities issues for his notable clients — will flourish as of old. It is hard for some folk to realize that new social and economic standards ever come into play.

Ray Stevens was perfectly delighted with the vigorous support which you are giving him to secure key men, especially Mathews, who seems unusually equipped for the direction of the Securities Division.

3. I have felt for some years that Keynes is the best economic bet, and so I was delighted with his enthusiastic support of your forthright rejection of that London formula, with all its mischievous ambiguities — a literary shell-game if there ever was one.

4. I read with satisfaction this morning that you are *not* aiming for the 1926 level. Confidentially, L.D.B., whom I saw over the weekend, thinks the 1926 prices were much too inflated.

With warm regards,

Always yours,
F.F.

Frankfurter cherished the memory of Joseph Cotton as one of the supreme lawyers in American history.

George C. Mathews was appointed a member of the Securities and Exchange Commission a year later.

John Maynard Keynes, the famous economist, had met Frankfurter at the Paris Peace Conference of 1919–1920, and they remained close friends. He supported Roosevelt's refusal to accept the gold standard in preference to nationally managed currencies. He wrote that Roosevelt's message to the World Economic Conference in London was "a challenge to us to decide whether we propose to tread the old, unfortunate ways, or to explore new

paths; paths new to statesmen and to bankers, but not new to thought."
Others blamed Roosevelt for having destroyed the hopes of the conference.
L.D.B. is Brandeis.

Hyde Park, N.Y., July 11, 1933

Dear Felix:

That was a perfectly splendid telegram you sent me about the message to London. My grateful thanks to you for it.

Very sincerely yours,
F.D.R.

Cambridge, Mass., July 14, 1933

Dear Mr. President:

You were very kind to send me the Regulations and the form of the Registration Statement (Form A-1) promulgated by the Trade Commission under the Securities Act, and to invite my views thereon.

1. The Commission has had to deal with new and intricate problems under great pressure of time and seriously handicapped through lack of an organization technically equipped for this new work. The Commission has wisely, therefore, emphasized the provisional and empiric character of its rules. There will be need for revision of the Rules and the Form in the light of experience gained in the practical operation of technical details. Improvements will only come from a consciously critical attitude on the part of the administrators. The heart of the business, therefore, is the quality of the men who will be entrusted, by day-to-day administration, with effectuating in the concrete the purposes at which you aimed in the Securities Act. Thus, for instance, I am not entitled to express a judgment on the workability of the important accounting provisions required by the Commission. But I do know that courageous and imaginative accounting skill will be required from the staff, supported by the Commission, if the Securities Act is to accomplish what you wanted it to accomplish.

2. About one matter in the Commission's regulations I am concerned, namely, the extent to which information called for by the Registration Statement may be omitted in the prospectus. I am rather fearful of the authorization of an abbreviated prospectus as well as the permission to omit from the prospectus entirely certain items called for by the Registration Statement. I am particularly troubled by the total omission from the prospectus of items (17), (28), (38), (39) and (46) of Form A-1. Furthermore, certainly some summary of the profit and loss statement for the three preceding years should be included in the prospectus. It must be recalled that the Act permits dispensation in the prospectus of information required

in the Statement only where "not" necessary or appropriate in the public interest or for the protection of investors. We must therefore abandon the notion, so fruitful of mischief in the past, that a prospectus should be short and easily read. We ought to learn from English experience the dangers of allowing abbreviated prospectuses. There is little reason for omitting from the prospectus items other than bulky exhibits required in the Registration Statement. The prospectus is all that the average investor will see, and all the important information should be in the prospectus.

3. Modern business enterprise being as complicated as it is, the task of the Commission in dealing with it will be correspondingly difficult. In some instances experience may, perhaps, indicate the need for simplification; in others there will be need for greater refinement. Granted intelligent and vigilant administration of the Securities Act by the Commission and the increasing insight that will come therefrom, one has every right to expect great results from the Securities Act.

Faithfully yours,
F.F.

Cambridge, Mass., July 17, 1933
Dear Mr. President:

The following comes from L.D.B.: "That was a superb order of F.D.R.'s *re* postmasters. I had been specially eager for that since the Myers Case. I hope F.D.R. will act similarly on some offices in the Treasury."

The Myers Case (272 U.S. 52) held, as you probably know, that the President's power of removal is part of the prerogative of the Executive and cannot be limited by requiring the concurrence of the Senate in its exercise.

Faithfully yours,
F.F.

President Machado of Cuba had been forced to resign on August 12, 1933, after an uprising by Cuban officers. Roosevelt without delay declared that "armed intervention by the United States in Cuba was unequivocally forbidden. The vessels were sent to protect American lives if necessary; but I made it clear that there could not possibly be any intervention by us in the internal affairs of Cuba." On January 23, 1934, the United States government recognized the government of Colonel Mendieta. That same year Roosevelt moved to abrogate the treaty of 1903, with its Platt Amendment under which Cuba, in certain specified circumstances, had agreed to United States intervention. Roosevelt denounced the amendment as an "anachronism."

Telegram to Roosevelt

Windsor, Vt., August 13, 1933

WARM CONGRATULATIONS ON SUCCESS OF YOUR NON-INTERVENTION POLICY IN
CUBA.

FELIX FRANKFURTER

Telegram to Roosevelt

Windsor, Vt., August 19, 1933

HOORAY! EVIDENTLY THOSE STEEL FELLOWS CAN UNDERSTAND YOU WHEN YOU
TALK DUTCH TO THEM AND SO WILL THE OTHERS.

FELIX FRANKFURTER

*Roosevelt on August 19 had issued an executive order establishing a code
of fair competition for the iron and steel industry.*

Cambridge, Mass., September 5, 1933

Dear Mr. President:

On the 24th of this month I am sailing for Oxford and of course very
much want to see you before leaving. So, although I am not without some
realization of the pressure upon your time, I am venturing to hope that you
will be able to find it possible to see me. I am holding myself at your disposal and can take the night train on short notice at any time between now
and the 22nd.

Always faithfully yours,
F.F.

*He was going to spend an academic year at Oxford as the Visiting East-
man Professor from the United States.*

Memorandum by Felix Frankfurter

September 6, 1933

Just as Mrs. Roosevelt had seated herself in the drawing room and we
were settling down in groups to talk, the President's secretary came to the
door and beckoned me into the passage. The President wants to know if
you'd care to sit in on his Conference with the Coal Operators. "Are you
sure I shan't be in the way?" "He says you are to come along."

I went in to the room where the Conference was to be held to find the
President chatting with General Johnson, Mr. Hopkins, and Mr. Richberg.

"Come along," said the President, "how'd you like to act as Secretary
and sit in that corner?" "If you're sure it's all right," I said, snatching a pad
off the desk, "I'm happy to take on the job." "Go to it," he said.

A few minutes later there entered the representatives of the Coal Operators and of the Mine Workers Union. I hardly dared look up and most

of them could hardly see that I was there. Messrs. Morrow, Francis, O'Neill and Taggart represented the Operators and, as far as I could gather, Mr. John L. Lewis was the only man who spoke for the Mine Workers.

"Come along and sit ye down," said the President, "let's make it a family party. I thought that when Cuba blew up yesterday it was about the only thing I was to have trouble with, so it's up to you to help clear this thing up. Remember Cuba only affects 3 million folk, but coal affects 25 million and we've got to straighten this situation out *quick*. We can't let this go on. I know a few of the details, so I'm depending on you to fill in the rest and if I can give any help on the contract end, I'll be happy to do so. If you want my help, I'll fix 'em! Will some one tell me what this difficulty is about in simple language? Now don't all speak at once, make yourselves at home and have a cigar."

General Johnson dropped the remark that "These operators are all too intense and they insist on filling up the NRA code with unnecessary language."

"Let me tell you a story," the President said. "The newspaper men wanted to add in their code the first clause of the American Constitution and to add that nothing in that clause was to be limited or abrogated." My answer was, "You can't do it, not unless you add the whole of the rest of the Constitution and then I shall put in the Ten Commandments as well. I'm opposed to surpluses of language. All our quarrels arise out of these struggles over vague terms and unnecessary language."

At this moment one of the Operators spoke up. "Mr. President, one week ago we were agreed on the principles behind this code. We agreed to let the open shop go. The operators wanted the same clause the automobile men had and we agreed to leave out all mention of the open and the closed shop, but the mine workers want a moral victory over us. We know that many of them are in the Amalgamated Mine Workers but we object to a clause which would suggest that every mine worker had to be in the A.M.W. We accepted General Johnson's amendment, but we're disinclined to give away moral rights.

"In some of our districts we've had the open shop for four to five years and in others from thirty to forty years. We admit that Mr. Lewis's organization represents most of the men, but I want protective measures to prevent the rest of the men being pushed into Mr. Lewis's scheme. There are between ten to fifty thousand men not in Lewis's organization and I think they need protection. I think Mr. Lewis feels too strongly on this. It is our feeling that a workman should have a right to join and a right not to join."

"All right," said the President, "why don't you let me say that?"

"We'll want the printed contract to be in every man's hand, and if anything is said outside that, it's sure to get lost."

"But I'll see that the code will be read alongside my statement and it will say that the Government is a party to this contract and will see that each side gets a fair interpretation. The contract you suggest and your contracts are drafted in an English that 9/10ths of the miners can't understand — they simply won't read it."

"The Aluminum Companies," went on the President, "came out with a fifteen-page contract which included their own interpretation and distributed it around their employees with an order at the end, 'Please vote yes or no tomorrow.' A friend of mine sent me one of these with a little note saying, 'What the Hell's it all about?' That sort of thing is not good. I want a contract that Mr. Lewis and the owners can interpret and that the NRA and Johnson or I can add our confirmation too if you and Lewis are once agreed on the intent. But if you put this language of yours into the code," — here he read out the owners suggested clause — "well, I don't know what it means. I tried hard for ten minutes to make it out and if I, as a lawyer, can't figure it out — well that language is obscure. Why not let me, as President, put it plainer, what you want to say is that a man shall have the right to work without being a member of a union. Neither Johnson nor I are happy about these weasel words that were put into the auto codes. They will always add difficulties and finally land us in an endless mess."

"Well," said one of the owners, "it's no use having to come back here over and over again, let's get it clear now."

"Then," said the President, "let me see to it, you'll get more men to recognize it if you let me say it in a foreword than if the owners try to put it into the contract."

"We've ruled out mention of the closed shop as well as of the open shop, but we do want a contract that will be fair to men who are not in the union."

At this point Mr. Lewis, who by a crane of the neck I was suddenly able to recognize, sitting straight opposite the President, said: —"As far as we know everyone in the Appalachians has joined the Union. Where are these 10,000 miners?"

"There was a time," said the President, "when T.R. saved the situation that had nearly run away from him by saying he'd call out the Army. We don't want anything of that kind in these days. There are a thousand of you operators, all educated men, and there are 250,000 to 300,000 mine workers and you've gone ahead and put down here language that they won't understand. Let me clarify it for both of you and put in my own explanation at the head of the contract."

"The United Mine Workers will accept your good offices, Mr. President, and trust you to clarify it."

"What these men have done, Mr. President, is admirable," added General Johnson.

"Can you put your explanation alongside the contract, Mr. President?" asked Mr. O'Neill, for the operators.

"I've done it elsewhere."

"The sanctity of President Roosevelt's signature carries a lot of weight — we'd want the language tomorrow morning."

"There's one other matter," added the President. "Mr. Hopkins, here, is head of our Relief Programme and he's given me many examples of a miner, because he's in debt to the company, not receiving any pay for his work — not a red cent. Legally, this may be one thing, but from a human point of view, it is quite another. If the country were told the facts tomorrow, there'd be an awful explosion. We have examples everywhere. I know of a case where a man has worked for two months and received nothing in cash. You can't explain that kind of thing away. I know that where a mine is short of cash there are difficulties and the mine will want to cut down the debts of its store department."

"The trouble is, Mr. President, that employment is spread too thin in the coal mines. These deductions are against previous advances. It is unfortunate, but half a loaf is better than no bread."

"I realize how much there is to be said," said the President, "but I want you to see that in checking off, he gets something."

"We know," said one of the operators, "that there have been abuses and we hope that the code and the union will help to rectify these — but what has this to do with the contract? Wages will in some cases be increased 50%."

"Even then," said the President, "only to a certain extent will troubles be eliminated. There will be many mines not running at all and we've got to limit production to consumption. It is up to the operators to lend a hand as much as to the Union and the Workers. In the old days, did my family think anything of the miners very much when they closed down a mine? But today 100,000 miners with their families have to be moved out of mining and you've got to help me. Does Lewis agree with me?"

"Yes, Mr. President."

"We've a lot of wreckage to clean up and we shall have to sell bonds to the public to get the land back and to take over areas with the help of the Government. Do you think we could agree on a price? Would you rather take bonds or go on paying taxes on the land? Of these surplus miners, some we can re-employ. Why, some of your state taxes are terrible. What are you going to do with these people?"

"Some companies are going to take on a lot more miners."

"Yes, but remember quite a lot of that country was farm country in 1810, but the top soil has been running off it since the mines opened and it's all in the creek bottoms and that land will have to go back to forest. There used to be 20,000 farm families in Harlan County. It dropped to 10,000 and coal jumped it up to 50,000. They came in from the valleys and have been getting poorer and poorer. It is a very difficult problem."

"We've no greater surplus," said Mr. O'Neill, "than anywhere else."

"That may be, but the move out is a lot slower in coal. You know the saying 'once a miner, always a miner,' and it's darned hard to get a miner to do anything else or to change his point of view. Same with the railways. Look at Lewis!" Everyone laughed and Lewis, turning to O'Neill, said, "and look at O'Neill, he was once a miner and one of our fair-haired boys — an official in our union."

"Yes, that's true," said O'Neill.

"Well," said the President, suddenly switching back to the main point, "can we write out something to suit everybody?"

"This is it," said Johnson, leaning over with a slip of paper to the President, who read it out aloud.

"They may ask you, Mr. President, to explain what it means," said Mr. O'Neill.

"Oh," said another of the operators, a little bitterly, "he'll call in Mr. Richberg. Mr. Richberg can explain anything."

"Can you sign up for General Johnson tonight?" asked the President.

"No, we've got 1000 other generals to deal with, but we might get through with it in the morning."

"We'd waive our right to check off, if something were done about deductions," said Mr. Lewis. "There are many extreme cases. I know of a man who has earned $600 in two years and in the last 24 months, he's never seen a cent of it. That man is no better than an indentured servant of the old days. And remember, with his debt hanging over him he can't go and get employment elsewhere. We can collect our own dues. Participation in the check off would simplify our collection of dues and we shall lose some of our money without it but we're ready to waive that. I know the operators have their convictions about that, but the whole question of deductions should be referred to a joint committee. It is the extreme deductions we're against, we're not opposed to the stores."

"We want to straighten out the public mind in this matter," added the President. "I've prevented, during the last six weeks, five or six sensational stories about this check-off trouble being written up in the press. I said to the pressmen don't run them, till we have tried to settle this thing and let's avoid an attack in public."

"I don't know how we're to get this price fixing done and to set up the new machinery," interjected one of the operators.

"You get that contract written up tomorrow, and if you've anything else on your minds, just let me know. Goodnight," were the final words of the President.

Mr. Hopkins came across to me. "What's the betting," he said, "50-1 against?" "No, I don't see why they shouldn't come across," I answered, "but you know them."

The President settled down to twenty minutes' discussion with Commander Byrd after that and it was midnight before we said goodnight to everyone.

General Hugh Johnson was head of the National Recovery Administration (NRA) and Donald Richberg of Chicago was his chief assistant. Harry Hopkins was to become the President's intimate friend and adviser. At this time he was head of the relief program. The President's intervention resulted in the agreement being signed.

Telegram to Roosevelt
Cambridge, Mass., September 7, 1933

REJOICE OVER YOUR CONSULTATION WITH LATIN AMERICAN DIPLOMATS. ITS IMPLICATIONS ARE FINE OMENS FOR ANY EVENTUALTIES.

FELIX FRANKFURTER

As evidence of his "Good Neighbor" policy, Roosevelt had invited the Latin American ambassadors to a general review of problems in this hemisphere, including the continued unrest in Cuba.

The White House, September 7, 1933

My dear Mr. Frankfurter:

The President asked me to thank you much for your telegram of September seventh, and to tell you that he thinks it was very good of you to send it.

Very sincerely yours,
LOUIS McH. HOWE

Telegram to Miss LeHand
Cambridge, Mass., September 13, 1933

IF IT IS POSSIBLE FOR THE PRESIDENT TO SEE ME AT ANY TIME BEFORE TWENTY-THIRD, FOR I SAIL FROM BOSTON TWENTY-FOURTH, WOULD IT BE

FEASIBLE NOW TO FIX TIME? I TROUBLE YOU ABOUT THIS BECAUSE ALL MY
OTHER MOVEMENTS ARE CONTINGENT UPON WASHINGTON TRIP.

FELIX FRANKFURTER

Telegram to Frankfurter
The White House, September 13, 1933
PRESIDENT HOPES YOU CAN COME TO WASHINGTON ON THURSDAY THE FOUR-
TEENTH FOR DINNER AND THE NIGHT.

M. A. LEHAND

Telegram to Roosevelt
Cambridge, Mass., September 19, 1933
COAL CODE IS HAPPY RESULT OF YOUR MASTERFUL HANDLING OF CONFERENCE
LAST THURSDAY NIGHT.

FELIX FRANKFURTER

Cambridge, Mass., September 23, 1933
Dear Miss LeHand:

If the letters about me to the various embassies, which the President so
kindly volunteered to send — more particularly to make available to me the
channel of the diplomatic pouch, in writing to him — have not yet gone,
may I trouble you to have them sent to my Oxford address, for we are
sailing tomorrow. I think I left my Oxford address with you; but if not, it
is: Eastman House, Norham Gardens, Oxford, England.

You know how deep and continuous will be my good wishes for the
White House. With personal regards to you, in which my wife joins (she
much appreciated your message to her),

Very cordially yours,
FELIX FRANKFURTER

Cambridge, Mass., September 24, 1933
Dear Miss LeHand,

I venture to give this note to a very dear friend of mine, Thomas G.
Corcoran, and at present an assistant to the Secretary of the Treasury. He
is a most valuable public servant and one of the most indefatigable workers
for the success of this administration. From time to time he may come to
you about matters, and I commend him to you warmly. He is a person of
entire dependability.

Very cordially yours,
FELIX FRANKFURTER

*This is the first reference in this correspondence to Thomas (the Cork)
Corcoran, one of the central figures in the New Deal, and for long and busy*

years an admired friend of Frankfurter and trusted collaborator with him on many public causes.

Radiogram to Roosevelt

M.V. *Britannic,* September 26, 1933

LANDIS HAS UNIQUE EQUIPMENT FOR FAIR EFFECTIVE ADMINISTRATION SECURITIES ACT DURING CRUCIAL MONTHS. DEVOTED GREETINGS.

FELIX FRANKFURTER

This telegram, sent from the ship on which Frankfurter was bound for an academic term at Oxford, urged the appointment of James M. Landis of the Harvard Law School as a member of the Securities and Exchange Commission. Later, Landis was to become chairman of that commission in succession to Mr. Joseph P. Kennedy.

M. V. *Britannic*
October 1, 1933

Dear Mr. President:

First and foremost, let me tell you how exhilarating and invigorating an experience was my over-night with you. I could not have had a better send-off for the months to come — a richer opportunity for understanding the energy and hope and wisdom that are now directing America. You yourself I have not seen fitter looking for many a year; you seemed as mobilized and as full of reserves as when I saw you in the early days of the Wilson Administration. That in itself augurs greatly for the nation. And your handling of the coal conflict that Thursday night was a superb manifestation of the New Deal and of the new personality in action — a keen eye on the desired direction, resoluteness in pursuing it and achieving it within our democratic traditions, that is, through consent, however stimulated by the pressure of need, rather than through the arbitrary imposition of will. I am very grateful to you for letting me be present to see and feel the purposes that move you and the means by which you are vindicating them.

And you were most kind to let me canvass with you aims and achievements of the Administration, in all their varied ramifications, and to let me see how the course of events and their significance, since you came to the Presidency, lay in your own mind. The English, as you know, are greedy in their eagerness for knowledge about your Administration, and they are hopefully anxious about its meaning for them. In all sorts of quiet ways they will want to know, and it will be of inestimable value for my interpretation to be able to draw on what you were kind enough to put in the back of my head.

My Washington visit filled me with buoyancy and confidence, and not the less so because of the evidence that came to me, during the week before my departure, that the forces of opposition — business, financial and political forces — are stirring beneath the surface, ready to become overt as soon as they think they dare encounter the unparallelled tide of popular favor now running in your direction. You, of course, know much more about these hostilities and machinations than I do. But it may not be without interest to you, as straws in the wind, for me to enumerate three items of information that came to me, quite unconnectedly, on three successive days just before sailing:

1. The man in charge of the Boston *Herald* editorial page — not Buxton, who is away for a time — told an intimate friend of mine that he was regretfully aware of a decision on the part of those who controlled the *Herald* — the strongest banking and financial interests in Boston — that "the time has come to open up on the Administration and to take the offensive, that they have let it alone long enough."

2. A responsible business man told me that, on going to his lawyers to arrange for some refinancing, "they filled me full of fears and told me to forget all about refinancing until after Congress repealed or substantially modified the Securities Act; that it was desired not to have any respectable financing done during the next few months, so as to show that the Securities Act makes desirable financing impossible. There is no question but that leading bankers and the big law firms are trying to create a bankers' strike." The law firm in question was none other than Ropes, Grey, Boyden and Perkins. Jack Richardson, a member of that firm, is, as you know, one of Hoover's intimates and Republican National Committeeman for Massachusetts, and he has quietly in the last few weeks been despairing of the Republic because of your policies.

3. You may know that Archibald MacLeish, the poet, who is now one of the editors of *Fortune*, is at work on an interpretive piece on you for the December *Fortune*. Archie is one of my old students — he was an excellent lawyer — and he had a long talk with me about you and the meaning of your policies. He told me that "the big, rich fellows in New York," whom he has been seeing in the course of his study, are almost without exception privately hostile and awaiting ripe opportunities publicly to oppose the New Deal, whatever may be their public professions or their public display of the Blue Eagle of the NRA.

None of which, as I said, will be news to you, and all of which and more will, I am sure, only whet your appetite for the joy of battle, and still more stiffen your purposes. That the great body of the nation will rally to your side, as the fight stiffens and the lines will be drawn, I have not a shadow of doubt. You will have the support not only of the great rank and file, but also of thoughtful and solid citizens who are not Bourbon in their habits and whom the recent years have torn from their conventional party moorings. The views of Mr. Justice Stone — considering that he is an old-line Republican, a member of Sullivan & Cromwell before he became Coolidge's Attorney General — seem to me in this connection very significant. Let me quote from a letter which I had from him shortly before leaving.

> The new Securities Act promises well and undoubtedly will prevent some of the fraudulent schemes which have been common in the past, especially in marketing bonds. There is another like evil that must ultimately be reached, and that is the creation of boom markets for stocks through wash sales on the Exchange.
>
> I have been hoping, and still hope, to see the Administration deal with the question of the recognition of Russia on the merits and in accordance with the principles of international law and common sense, unaffected by the obsession which seems to have obscured it since our present policy was adopted in the Harding Administration.

You greatly excited me by your plan of getting the important appropriation committees of Congress to work during December, so as to have the appropriation bills in shape for action very early after Congress meets, thereby, and through your skillful suggestiveness with the leaders of Congress, to get through with the business of Congress by May 1. This is only another illustration — for I am sure you will be able to make your plans prevail — of how much can be done towards governmental competence and cooperation within the framework of our constitutional system, if there is real leadership at the head.

You were most kind to suggest that I write you from time to time, and I shall avail myself of the kind privilege you extended to me to send letters through the pouch.

Every good wish for your continued well-being and the success of your efforts.

Faithfully yours,
FELIX FRANKFURTER

Hyde Park, N.Y., October 2, 1933

My dear Mr. Ambassador:

I am giving this letter to my old friend, Mr. Felix Frankfurter, who is proceeding abroad and who expects to visit London during his travels. I have asked Mr. Frankfurter to call upon you while in England and I would appreciate any courtesies or facilities you may extend to him while there, including the use of the diplomatic pouch in the event of his desiring to send any communications to me through that channel.

Very sincerely yours,

FRANKLIN D. ROOSEVELT

The Honorable Robert Worth Bingham
American Ambassador
London, England

Similar letters were sent by Roosevelt to other American Ambassadors in Europe.

Oxford to Washington

October 1933 – June 1934

1933

October 14   Germany announces her withdrawal from the League of Nations and the Disarmament Conference.

November 1   Recognition by the United States of the Soviet Union.

1934

May 29 —

June 11   World Disarmament Conference ends in failure.

June 14   Blood purge of Nazi leaders in Germany on Hitler's orders.

Oxford, England, October 9, 1933

Dear Mr. President:

My grateful congratulations on the Landis and Mathews appointments, of which I have just been informed by wire. How thereby you have again proved your eagerness to have brains, disinterestedness and social purpose in your Administration.

The English papers, as you know, are inadequate in reporting American news. But they have given enough account of your utterances and actions since I left to indicate that a real captain is at the helm.

Faithfully yours,

FELIX FRANKFURTER

George C. Mathews had been moved by Roosevelt from the Federal Trade Commission to the Securities and Exchange Commission. The Chairman of the SEC was Joseph P. Kennedy, with the other members being James M. Landis, Ferdinand Pecora, Mathews and Robert Healy of Vermont. The Commission administered the Securities Act of 1933 and the Securities Exchange Act of 1934. An early recruit was William O. Douglas of the Yale Law School, later Mr. Justice Douglas of the Supreme Court.

Oxford, England, October 11, 1933

Dear Mr. President:

The American papers have come, bringing a full text of your Chicago speech. For the life of me I cannot understand why, as the papers say, you were dissuaded by friends from going to Chicago. In any event, what a fortunate thing that you disregarded their advice, for the speech was, as the New York *Times* well put it, a triumph of geniality combined with firmness. It was more than that in bringing out into the open the basic necessity of subordinating sectional and group interests to the common good. That seems to me the chief task that confronts you on almost all the major questions — how to make the various groups see their group interests in the perspective of the national whole. From time to time that will necessitate the use of your great powers and prestige in the open — by such a speech as the one at Chicago.

Always with good wishes,

Faithfully yours,

FELIX FRANKFURTER

Oxford, England, October 17, 1933

Dear Mr. President:

1. Many thanks for your kind letters of introduction to the Ambassadors and Minister Wilson.

2. Dodd is, of course, keeping you fully apprised on Germany. Yet I venture to send you the enclosures — a letter to the *Times* from a distinguished British soldier (Major General Sir Neill Malcolm) and Garvin's leader in the last issue of the *Observer* — as illuminating glimpses into the violence and madness now dominating in Germany. Developments make it abundantly clear that the significance of Hitlerism far transcends ferocious anti-semitism and fanatical racism. Dr. Alice Hamilton is right in insisting that the attack against the Jew is merely an index to the gospel of force and materialism that explains the present rulers of Germany.

3. The air here is charged, albeit in a sober kind of way, with the kind of feeling that preceded 1914. I think I can say without exaggeration that I have followed English public opinion rather closely for more than twenty years, and never has it seemed to me to be so essentially united on any issue as it is in its present feeling towards Hitlerism. During the last few days I have seen a number of distinguished German exiles. They are men of great culture, of balanced judgment and of passionate German patriotism, but they all agree that the international behavior of Berlin towards the Disarmament Conference is largely explained by domestic considerations — an effort to divert attention from economic difficulties, the growing fiasco of the Reichstag fire trial, and internal dissensions. They are also agreed that the forces of violence and chauvinism of the Hitler regime will be accelerated and intensified.

4. Have you thought of broadcasting in German, and saying some plain things that need to be said? Perhaps the most stark fact about the present German situation is that its people live in darkness. Not until one meets in the flesh highly educated Germans and realizes how completely they have been barred from knowledge of the outside world can one adequately appreciate how all the channels of light are shut from them. No other voice in the world would carry such weight as yours, and a broadcast from you to the world could not possibly be kept out of Germany — though a regime that reviles Goethe as not having been a patriotic German makes idle any prophecy about its future foolishness. Such a speech may do very little in Germany, and I am not at all hopeful that it would. But by such an act you would become the rallying center of the world's sanity.

Ever with warm regards and good wishes,

Faithfully yours,
FELIX FRANKFURTER

Hugh R. Wilson was the American Minister at Bern, Switzerland.

Ambassador William Edward Dodd had begun to report on the long shadow cast by the Nazi government in Germany.

Dr. Alice Hamilton, the sister of Edith Hamilton, the classical scholar, was one of Frankfurter's most cherished friends and an authority on industrial medicine.

Oxford, England, October 29, 1933

Dear Mr. President:

1. The enclosed leader strikes me as an unusually perceptive analysis, at least for this side, of what you are trying to do, and so it may interest you. On the whole, the press despatches from America are inadequate and misleading. Partly this is due to the meagreness of the cables — a brevity induced, I suppose, by economy — partly to the usual desire of the press to give the polemical aspects of a situation. But I believe the chief factor of inadequacy lies elsewhere. Since the most important news from America these days concerns finance, the slant of the financial community is predominant. And so the news that comes here is tinctured, however unconsciously, with the Wall Street bias — its hostility and its doubts. This news naturally has the greatest influence with powerful financial interests here, which in turn considerably affects the general currents of opinion. I ought to say that two of the news services make a reasonably successful effort to give a comprehensive insight into our total situation. Willmot Lewis does very well for *The Times*, although even he is not free from accentuating the elements of financial opposition and scepticism about your program; and the Manchester *Guardian* is true to its traditions of fairness and liberalism. It is because the enclosed article goes beneath the shallow surface of the news that comes here, and aims at a real understanding of your objectives, that I am sending it.

2. I find here a pervasive interest in our affairs and an astonishing amount of goodwill. I am rather struck with that — with the feeling of eagerness that we should succeed because at the helm in the United States is resourceful determination to evolve order and well-being out of economic anarchy and competitive greed. Dons and students, editors of financial papers and trade union officials, M.P.s of every shade of political opinion want to know what is happening and to understand the directions we are taking. On the part of the masses here there is an immense amount of identification of their hopes with your endeavor.

3. My wire about your exchange with Kalinin was an intimation of my enthusiasm for your Russian policy. Apart from beneficial economic consequence, your termination of the hostile and anomalous relations between Russia and the United States may, in view of the new constellation of the Great Powers, be of really momentous significance to the world's peace.

There surely can be little doubt that Germany and Japan are moving on converging lines, full of ominous significance to the growing tension between Russia and Japan. And so, strange as it may seem to some of the politically myopic opponents of your Russian policy, your note to Kalinin is calculated to mark the beginning of a most important chapter in the pursuit of world peace.

4. I wonder if Tom Thacher might not be of use to you in Russian matters. You know, don't you, that he went to Russia with Raymond Robbins and Allen Wardwell for the Red Cross in 1918 and came back convinced that the Soviet regime would endure and that we ought to get into prompt and beneficial relations with them. I remember Lord Reading saying to me at the time that Thacher's discussion of the Russian problem was the most intelligent he had heard from anyone. Thacher's interest in Russian problems has continued, he knows the Soviet representatives and has their goodwill. You could count on Thacher's full sympathy with your objectives. Also, he would bring knowledge of large affairs and, in a pleasant way, would brook no nonsense. That he is a good Republican and a "Wall Street lawyer" would only add, I believe, to his usefulness to you for this particular work.

5. The impact of events on this side makes one thing more clear than ever to me — that the guidance of foreign relations must substantially be in your own hands. In the first place, there is such interaction among various issues that do not seem immediately related that vital decisions must be made by one who sees these interconnections and is not too immersed in the specific problems as they arise from day to day. Secondly these are not days for cautious and conventional conceptions of foreign relations and hampering preoccupations with formalities and precedents quite inapplicable to present-day exigencies and complexities.

6. There was one statement in your broadcast last Sunday that especially delighted me, namely, the candor with which you told the country that your price aims and the related monetary policy cannot be accomplished overnight and may take years for realization. When I last saw you, I ventured to tell you that not the least important basis for your hold on the people is their feeling that you are a truth-teller and not a miracle-worker—that you are promising them not rabbits out of a hat, but unceasing devotion and the exploration of every expedient for righting economic wrong. The public will continue to behave like grown men so long as the appeal is made to them as grown men, and they will continue to believe in you because their confidence is enlisted for reason, intelligent effort and fair-mindedness. The rest is with God.

    Always with warm regards,   Faithfully yours,

                                                FELIX FRANKFURTER

The enclosed article from the Week-end Review *said: "What makes it so difficult for Wall Street or the City to understand the President's standpoint is that they instinctively assume their own survival in more or less their present form, whereas Mr. Roosevelt does not assume it, and so far as Wall Street is concerned, contemplates eventual changes which will be most unattractive to the banking and stockbroking community."*

Sir Willmot Lewis was the veteran Washington correspondent of the London Times.

Roosevelt's exchange of telegrams with President Kalinin of the Soviet Union was part of the procedure for recognizing the Russian government. Frankfurter had always been an active and vocal opponent of the policy of non-recognition.

Judge Thomas D. Thacher had been one of Frankfurter's friends when he went to Washington in the First World War. He was Solicitor General from 1930 until early 1933. In 1943 he became counsel for New York City, and from 1943 until his retirement in 1948 he was a member of the New York State Court of Appeals.

Oxford, England, November 23, 1933

Dear Mr. President:

1. A leading Oxford don, speaking for an influential group of Oxford economists who are deeply sympathetic with your financial and economic objectives and look to you as a stimulus to motion by the British Government, came to ask me whether it would be deemed impertinent for them to express their views to you in a private communication. I replied that one of your chief characteristics is accessibility of mind to suggestions, particularly from those in general agreement with your purposes. He then asked whether there were any likelihood of such a communication reaching you, and I volunteered to undertake its transmission.

Such is the explanation of the origin of the enclosed letter. I felt I ought to serve as the post-office, as it were, for this letter because the writers have been strong supporters of your policies, and have refused to be worshippers of the golden calf theory of currency and have vainly struggled for action by their government along your expansionist lines. As I wrote you in one of my earlier letters, a good deal of "sound," conservative financial opinion in this country complacently hopes that your efforts will not prevail because success in America would react against British conservatism. The writers of this letter represent quite the opposite body of opinion, one that is most eager that the American effort should succeed and serve as a propelling example against the negativistic British policy, which relies on things just happening.

2. I am also sending you a letter which has just come from J. G. Mc-

Donald, the League High Commissioner for German Refugees. I dare say that Dodd has informed you of these matters directly, but since McDonald writes me with great perturbation, you might like to see the letter.

3. Your Russian recognition shows how, with careful handling, even the most passionate feeling evaporates, or, at least, that action sensibly grounded silences even noisy opposition. It is a little amusing to find not a few of the English papers belaboring MacDonald for his dilatory incompetence in not concluding a trade agreement with Russia and thereby letting you beat him to it.

4. You may be interested in summary extracts from an address of mine here in which I attempted to set forth the achievements and the directions of your Administration.

5. This letter will reach you after Thanksgiving, but I hope the memory of turkey dinner will still be fresh enough to make holiday good wishes not too irrelevant.

Faithfully yours,
FELIX FRANKFURTER

The "leading Oxford don" was Roy Harrod of Christ Church, years later to be the biographer of Keynes.

The letter from McDonald, given here, was prophetic in its scarcely concealed fear that the Western governments would never grasp the dimensions and significance of the German refugee problem in time to take effective international action on a large scale.

Frankfurter's address set the New Deal in the background of American history to explain why Roosevelt commanded such popular support.

The following memorandum, prepared by distinguished Oxford economists, had an immense influence in Washington, for it provided an impartial and well-informed judgment, from friendly outside sources, on almost every major economic problem facing the Administration. Roosevelt discussed and examined this memorandum with his most responsible advisers. Its technical character should not disguise its importance, nor the range of its influence.

PRIVATE AND CONFIDENTIAL

To the President of the U.S.A.

Sir,

We, the signatories of this letter, occupy official positions as teachers of economics, in the University of Oxford. We wish first to state our grounds for venturing to write to you.

We are all interested in the question of monetary policy and have, as a matter of professional duty, followed the events of the recent depression closely. We feel strongly that this problem is not to be solved by the method of waiting for it to solve itself. We believe that a deliberate policy of expansion is desirable, both to hasten the amelioration of present troubles and also to lay the foundations of policy designed to prevent the recurrence of similar troubles in future.

We have expressed in public our views regarding the application of these ideas to British policy. We have throughout the depression remained convinced that counter-acting measures of expansion should be adopted, on principles which have in our judgment remained fundamentally unchanged.

We believe that positive measures are even more important in the U.S.A. than here. We therefore welcomed with enthusiasm the indications which came to us that an expansionist policy was likely to be pursued and that a programme of Public Works was to play a prominent part in it. We welcomed with enthusiasm your statement to the World Economic Conference of July 1, which rendered a joint attempt to buttress up the old system out of the question. We also welcomed with enthusiasm your statement of October 22 "that a resolute attempt would be made to raise commodity prices in the U.S.A. to a specified level and thereafter to prevent fluctuations in the commodity value of the dollar." We believe that the policy of which these statements contain the promise might if wisely pursued usher in a new era of prosperity, and that some such policy is a matter of urgency if western civilization is to be maintained. We think that this is a great opportunity for the U.S.A. to assume leadership in these matters.

It is our intention in the following paragraphs to outline as briefly as possible the means by which such a policy would in our judgment be rendered effective.

We believe that inflation of a kind likely to increase output and raise prices can only be produced by an increase of *incomes* which is *not accompanied by* an equivalent increase in the costs of producing the goods which these incomes are used to buy. We lay stress on the increase of incomes by contrast with (1) an increase of money in circulation and (2) an increase in the liquidity of corporation assets.

We suggest four ways in which such an increase of incomes may be brought about.

1. An increased production of capital goods increases the incomes and expenditure of those engaged on their production without increasing the quantity of consumable goods on the market. It thus tends to raise the price level of those consumable goods.

The increased production of capital goods may be stimulated by low interest rates, especially a low long-term rate. For this reason it is important that in their open market policy the Federal Reserve Banks should be encouraged to purchase long-dated securities. The stimulus given by a low rate in favour of an easy money policy is not enough. It requires the assistance of other measures.

2. We believe that the principal weapon in raising prices should be a great campaign of Public Works. In addition to the direct employment given, Public Works also give employment in the first instance to the trades producing the necessary raw materials and capital equipment.

But they have a further repercussion, which is of the first importance in considering a policy of raising commodity prices. The wages, salaries, etc., paid out to those engaged in the employment already mentioned will be largely expended on consumable goods. Thus the desired effect of a rise in the purchasing power devoted to consumable goods, unaccompanied by an increase in the gross costs of producing them, is secured. Thus a force is set up tending to raise commodity prices and to expand the output of consumable goods. In our opinion this measure should take priority of all others and the whole strength and ingenuity of the Administration should be put behind an immediate attempt to give effect to it.

3. Another means of raising purchasing power without increasing costs, is to distribute incomes by way of unemployment relief and other social services with borrowed money. It is essential that these schemes should not be financed by taxation. If they are, the income that is put into one pocket is taken out of another, and there is no net increase of purchasing power nor tendency for prices to rise. We therefore recommend a great drive for relieving distress through the agencies of the federal, state or municipal administrations on borrowed money.

4. All methods of encouraging private enterprise in constructional work should be explored. We may mention as instances (a) special assistance in railway construction (b) the guarantee of interest on new issues for approved purposes and (c) subsidies for these purposes.

5. We believe that it is important that the borrowing incurred for purposes 2, 3 and 4 should not be allowed to raise the long-term interest rate. It is desirable that the Federal Reserve Banks should make such purchases of long-dated securities as are necessary to prevent rates rising and ensure that funds are available for government borrowing. This conforms to the principles laid down in our first recommendation.

We also feel it desirable to refer to certain expedients that cannot be relied on as the principal weapons in the specific task of restoring the volume of output and employment. We do not wish to affirm that there is nothing to be said in favour of these expedients or that they have no positive merits of their own.

1. We do not believe that relief should be sought in the first instance by measures designed to increase the quantity of money. We do not believe

that resort to the printing press in the literal sense would be of value. Nor do we believe that there is much to be gained through the further injection of credit by open market operations of the Federal Reserve System on a large scale. This is not to deny that the purchases in the spring of 1932 were highly beneficial. It is essential that money should be kept as easy as possible and the indebtedness of the member banks to the Federal Reserve Banks should be kept at a low level. If sufficient purchases are made to satisfy these two conditions, further additional purchases would not of themselves necessarily have an expansionary effect.

It is to be observed, however, that both the issue of additional currency and further purchases by the Federal Reserve System may subsequently become necessary again, as ancillaries to the other measures of internal expansion which were recommended above. Much use of the printing press does not, however, seem likely to be required.

2. We regard with profound respect your intentions in instituting the industrial codes. We appreciate that the new deal with labour was conceived as a great piece of humane and progressive statesmanship and that it may be regarded by future historians as an important landmark in American progress towards more rational relations between employers and employees, between the rich and poor.

We are bound to say, however, while recognising the great merits of this legislation so conceived, that it is not specifically conducive to quickening economic activity.

If a rise in money wage rates is initiated, it is essential that it should be accompanied by a sufficient rise of prices to cover the increased costs consequential upon it. But it must be noted that the rise of wage rates cannot be relied on to secure this, in the absence of other measures for increasing purchasing power.

Any labour measures tending to raise employers' costs give rise to similar difficulties. Here again their presence makes it all the most necessary to execute simultaneously other policies of expansion.

3. We do not think that loans to corporations by such bodies as the Reconstruction Finance Corporation, even if financed by "inflationary money" necessarily tend to quicken activity. The test here is whether they are used to finance the output of new capital goods. If they are merely used to enable corporations to liquify their assets, they may have little or no effect in reviving activity. Such loans may often be justifiable. But there is danger that too much "inflationary money," the creation of which must after all be of a finite amount, may be used for this purpose, and too little left over for use in ways which would cause an actual expansion of activity.

4. We do not condemn schemes for regulating the output of raw products which have fallen to specially low values. But we point out that

this cannot take us far in solving the general problem. Such schemes may enable farmers to keep in line with the restrictive policy of manufacturers and so improve their relative position. But the main objective is a reversal of restriction all round. Moreover it is doubtful if much can be done, through restrictions, to increase the purchasing power of farmers except with international cooperation. Farmers are, however, directly benefited in so far as restriction among manufacturers gives place to expansion, since the demand for their products is thereby improved.

5. We do not believe that the purchasing power of the dollar can be effectively reduced, by depreciating its value either in terms of other currencies or of gold.

It does not follow that dollar devaluation in terms of other currencies must be ruled out. On the contrary it may be desirable. But what is essential is that it should follow as a corollary from internal inflation and not be used as a lever for producing internal inflation. If used in the latter way it is likely to be ineffective in the U.S.A. and detrimental elsewhere. But if the U.S.A. embarks on measures of genuine internal inflation of the kind mentioned above, and if the other countries do not fall into line with parallel policies, then some external depreciation of the dollar is to be expected and welcomed.

Professor Irving Fisher many years ago propounded a scheme for stabilizing the commodity value of the dollar by varying its gold content. This scheme has been held to be on right general lines in the past by many distinguished economists. But we do not think it would be effective in present circumstances. Two conditions are necessary for its effectiveness. (i) Action must be taken as soon as any tendency to deflation (or inflation) appears, so that the forces of slump or boom may be counteracted before they have gathered strength. (ii) The rest of the world, or most of it, must be on the gold standard.

If the rest of the world is not on the gold standard, raising the dollar price of gold is not likely to have much effect on the general level of dollar prices.

If a few other countries are on the gold standard, raising the dollar price of gold is tantamount to depreciating the dollar in terms of the currencies of these countries. The consequence of this is that the prices of commodities of a stable and internationally tradable character must be adjusted accordingly. This adjustment may consist of a rise of American prices or a fall of gold prices or partly of both. If the gold countries are of less economic importance than the U.S.A., the fall in them is likely to be greater than the rise in the U.S.A. Thus the rise in the price of gold has but a weak effect in raising dollar prices and a stronger effect in reducing gold prices. It plunges the gold countries into greater difficulties and is likely, if pursued *à l'outrance* to drive them off the gold standard. If this result is achieved, the gold policy becomes quite ineffective in raising American prices.

The consideration advanced in the last paragraph has a broader application. Any policy of dollar exchange depreciation has a weakening effect on the outer world unless accompanied by a vigorous internal inflation of American purchasing power. Now it is essential from the world and the American points of view that any revival of activity in the U.S.A. should be allowed to have a stimulating effect on the rest of the world.

External depreciation, unaccompanied by internal inflation, lowers the (foreign) prices at which Americans are prepared to offer their goods for export without directly increasing their demand for world goods. This must deepen foreign depression and may nullify, so far as the effect on America is concerned, the relative improvement of her position as an exporter directly caused by dollar devaluation.

Finally we should like to emphasize the positive policy outlined in paragraphs 2 and 3 as a matter of urgency and as the only effective method of reducing the commodity value of the dollar and increasing the level of activity in the country.

Among the economists signing this letter were Roy F. Harrod, D. H. MacGregor, J. E. Meade, L. M. Fraser, W. M. Allen, E. L. Hargreaves, R. F. Bretherton, many of whom were destined to be among the most influential of British economists.

Frankfurter's second enclosure to Roosevelt on November 23 was the letter from J. G. McDonald, League High Commissioner for German Refugees.

The Hague, November 20, 1933

Personal

My dear Professor Frankfurter:

I am very sorry that I was unable to see you when I was in London last week, because there is a matter of great urgency about which I wished to talk with you.

During the past ten days I have been engaged in intensive study in Geneva, Paris, London and The Hague, preparatory to the first meeting of the Governing Body of the new institution created by the League to integrate on an international basis the efforts on behalf of German refugees. There are many aspects of this task on which I later plan to ask your advice, but now I limit myself to one phase. It, however, is so fundamental and so pressing that I hope you may be able to help me on it at once.

I have learned, from unofficial but what I believe to be trustworthy sources, that the German Government is contemplating the issuance in the near future of a decree or decrees establishing formally a second-class citizenship for German Jews. Such action once taken would not only further humiliate and degrade hundreds of thousands of men and women; it would make much more difficult any softening in the German Government's attitude later. Such retrogression to the inhumane and unChristian practices of an earlier age should, I think, be forestalled if there is any conceivable way of doing so.

Moreover, I, in my official capacity as High Commissioner for German Refugees, have a special interest that this definitive action be averted. Under present circumstances the refugee problem is too large to be handled satisfactorily, but if conditions for the Jews become worse in Germany there is a grave danger that something like an exodus — panic in character and proportions — may be precipitated. This would create a situation in the bordering countries beyond the possibility of ordered control. You will at once sense the tragedy of such a situation.

In addition to all this, one can be quite sure that such an exodus would embitter further the relations between the Reich and many of its neighbors. It would tend to jeopardize every effort now being made to settle the more acute political questions such as disarmament — in which our own Government is so much interested.

Have you any possible suggestions as to what might be done to help avert such a blow? I should be most grateful for any help you may be able to give me.

Sincerely yours,
JAMES G. McDONALD

Governor Rolph was a weak and ineffective Governor of California who condoned a brutal display of mob violence. Before becoming Governor, he had served for many years as Mayor of San Francisco, where Frankfurter had met him years before in the labor disputes that had broken out in the First World War, and in the celebrated Tom Mooney case.

The director of the International Labour Office was Mr. Harold Butler, whose speeches and annual reports were among the most enlightened economic documents to be found anywhere in the depression years.

18, Norham Gardens, Oxford, England, December 10, 1933

Dear Mr. President:

1. Your impressive rebuke of Governor Rolph was greatly needed. Lynchings at best are dreadful. But when an outburst of the most primitive savagery receives the condonation of the Governor of a great state, what

else is to be expected than encouragement of like savagery elsewhere? Rolph's performance confirms an old judgment of mine that he has all the vices of Jimmie Walker without any of his talents. And so it is most necessary for you to drown the evil example by summoning the nation to civilized traditions.

2. When I left at the tail end of September it was already plain that, whatever may be the differences over details, the lines were fast being drawn between those to whom Recovery meant Return — return to the good old days — and those for whom Recovery was Reform — transformation by gradual process, but radical transformation no less, of our social and economic ways of thinking and therefore of our social and economic arrangements. What was happening was plain enough. Those powerful in finance under the old regime, who, between say January 1932 and your nomination and even till your election, exhausted the vocabulary of excoriation against you, after March exhausted the vocabulary of adulation, partly out of fear, partly out of hope that, after all, you were their kind of a fellow. When, after you enabled them to get their second wind and they came out of their storm cellars, they began to realize that the New Deal did not mean business at the old stand, they returned to all their old gods because, as a matter of fact, it was really a case of "the devil was sick." And so, the lines are being formed along true alignment of interests — which, as Hamilton and Madison so penetratingly made clear in *The Federalist*, is the essence of politics. But no one, I am sure, has been more fully alive than you from the very beginning that the lines would be formed along interests. I am equally certain that you welcome a true drawing of lines instead of a fictitious and unreliable maintenance of outward unity where there is no inner agreement.

3. During my two months' stay here I have, in order to gauge at first hand English opinion, rather avoided meeting Americans. And so I have seen all sorts and conditions of Englishmen — economists, financial writers, journalist, financiers, M.P.s and peers — Tory, Liberal and Labour. What emerges, on the whole, is that the reflex on this side represents, roughly speaking, the general line-up on our side. Tories and laissez-fairists prophesy failure and hope for it, while non-orthodox economists (which means most of the younger men), Labourites and people generally who realize that the old order is gone and that a new one must be fashioned, have the utmost eagerness for the success of what you are attempting and most anxiously invest in you their hope for reform and reorganization here. That is why they so touchingly ask for news from America and seek understanding. For, as I have indicated in an earlier letter to you, most of the news dished up for English readers has a Wall Street flavor. In this connection, I enclose a report of a recent speech by the Director of the International La-

bour Office, which will show you a more responsible effort towards interpreting sympathetically what is happening.

This letter will reach you near enough Christmas to bring you and your
household all the good wishes of the season.

Faithfully yours,

FELIX FRANKFURTER

*This letter proves that Frankfurter was in agreement with Roosevelt's
extremely controversial monetary experiments — while regarding them as
experiments rather than panaceas. He also supported the President's claim
that no constitutional barrier prevented him from applying his own gold
policy, a view not shared by the Supreme Court later; but the Court's opposition never shook Frankfurter's conviction that an unrestrictive reading of
the Constitution would have recognized the President's right to experiment
as a valid exercise of his powers.*

18, Norham Gardens, Oxford, England, December 12, 1933

Dear Mr. President:

Since writing you interesting American news has come, through newly
arrived American papers and cables, which leads me to make a few further
observations.

1. The election in the third district of West Virginia is extremely gratifying — quite different from the by-elections which the MacDonald Government has been getting. Not only is the result, in so fluctuating a constit-
uency, highly gratifying, but the size of the vote of confidence — for such
it was — shows how very actively engaged the public is in the work of the
Administration, and how thoroughly you have enlisted opinion.

2. Through the fog of the currency debate is the clear trend of business improvement. The reliable indices leave no room for doubt that the
downward trend from the high peak in July has been arrested and is health-
ily turning upward. As your report to the American Farm Bureau shows,
equally incontestable is improvement for agriculture.

All of which confirms me in my ignorant conviction that the currency
aspect of the situation has in fact — though not in feeling — been greatly
exaggerated. When I speak of my ignorance, it is not for lack of considerable effort, through reading and talk, to ascertain and understand the views
of the leading currency economists on both sides of the water.

3. As a result of our discussion about gold buying with Will Woodin,
that night in your study, I have felt quite clearly that you were giving that
policy a tentative trial to see what it could do without committing yourself
to that theory any more than to any other theory, as a solvent. I don't
understand why more people who are sympathetic to your efforts don't

understand that. And so for myself I hope you continue not to, what they call, "clarify" your monetary policy by declarations, but declare by action as and when action is called for. Monetary pronouncements are well enough for economists and journalists. *They* can afford the luxury of words, while you ought to be unembarrassed to be free to heed the flow of events. In the meantime, it will help and not hurt your objectives to have the extreme inflationist and deflationist wings murder each other and thereby enable you to mobilize general consent both in the country and in Congress.

4. Nor have I been unmindful of some of the plums you have been distributing. Who says you do not know how to pay honor to the ex-President of your University? It's more than a little funny to have Lawrence Lowell czar of Hollywood! I am sure *he* doesn't know how funny that is — and still more funny to have him share the triumvirate with Marie Dressler and Eddie Cantor.

5. When I last saw you, you told me that you almost got me a very good job, that of administrator for the Booze Industry. I never quite understood why you couldn't land it for me. If it was for lack of experience, I'm somewhat making up for my deficiencies. Recently I attended two perfectly swell dinners, at one of which — Grand Day at Inner Temple — they had nine courses of wine, and at the Founder's Day Feast at King's College, Cambridge, there were seven. Without having been truculent about it on either occasion, I thought it was my duty not to let Englishmen feel that an American did not have a capacity equal to theirs!

With warm regards,

Faithfully yours,
FELIX FRANKFURTER

Oxford, England, December 16, 1933

Dear Mr. President:

In response to the New York *Times*' request for his views on the American outlook, Keynes has written "An Open Letter to President Roosevelt," which is scheduled to appear in the Sunday issue of December 31st and is to be syndicated in other parts of the United States.

So that you may see what he has to say before it is published, Keynes this morning sent me the enclosed copy of his article, which I hasten to get off directly to you through Miss LeHand (without forwarding it through the pouch) in the hope that it may catch the Bremen which leaves tonight.

Yesterday's *Times* carried illuminating extracts from Wallace's Annual Report. What a good Secretary of Agriculture you have!

With warm regards,

Faithfully yours,
FELIX FRANKFURTER

An Open Letter to President Roosevelt
by John Maynard Keynes

Dear Mr. President,

You have made yourself the Trustee for those in every country who seek to mend the evils of our condition by reasoned experiment within the framework of the existing social system. If you fail, rational change will be gravely prejudiced throughout the world, leaving orthodoxy and revolution to fight it out. But if you succeed, new and bolder methods will be tried everywhere, and we may date the first chapter of a new economic era from your accession to office. This is a sufficient reason why I should venture to lay my reflections before you, though under the disadvantages of distance and partial knowledge.

At the moment your sympathisers in England are nervous and sometimes despondent. We wonder whether the order of different urgencies is rightly understood, whether there is a confusion of aim, and whether some of the advice you get is not crack-brained and queer. If we are disconcerted when we defend you, this may be partly due to the influence of our environment in London. For almost everyone here has a wildly distorted view of what is happening in the United States. The average City man believes that you are engaged on a hare-brained expedition in face of competent advice, that the best hope lies in your ridding yourself of your present advisers to return to the old ways, and that otherwise the United States is heading for some ghastly breakdown. That is what they say they smell. There is a recrudescence of wise head-wagging by those who believe that the nose is a nobler organ than the brain. London is convinced that we only have to sit back and wait in order to see what we shall see. May I crave your attention, whilst I put my own view?

You are engaged on a double task, Recovery and Reform; — recovery from the slump and the passage of those business and social reforms which are long overdue. For the first, speed and quick results are essential. The second may be urgent too; but haste will be injurious, and wisdom of long-range purpose is more necessary than immediate achievement. It will be through raising high the prestige of your administration by success in short-range Recovery, that you will have the driving force to accomplish long-range Reform. On the other hand, even wise and necessary Reform may, in some respects, impede and complicate Recovery. For it will upset the confidence of the business world and weaken their existing motives to action, before you have had time to put other motives in their place. It may overtask your bureaucratic machine, which the traditional individualism of the United States and the old "spoils system" have left none too strong. And it will confuse the thought and aim of yourself and your administration by giving you too much to think about all at once.

Now I am not clear, looking back over the last nine months, that the order of urgency between measures of Recovery and measures of Reform has been duly observed, or that the latter has not sometimes been mistaken for the former. In particular, I cannot detect any material aid to recovery in the National Industrial Recovery Act (NIRA), though its social gains have been large. The driving force which has been put behind the vast administrative task set by this Act has seemed to represent a wrong choice in the order of urgencies. The Act is on the Statute Book; a considerable amount has been done towards implementing it; but it might be better for the present to allow experience to accumulate before trying to force through all its details. That is my first reflection — that NIRA, which is essentially Reform and probably impedes Recovery, has been put across too hastily, in the false guise of being part of the technique of Recovery.

My second reflection relates to the technique of Recovery itself. The object of recovery is to increase the national output and put more men to work. In the economic system of the modern world, output is primarily produced *for sale*; and the volume of output depends on the amount of purchasing power, compared with the prime cost of production, which is expected to come on the market. Broadly speaking, therefore, an increase of output cannot occur unless by the operation of one or other of three factors. Individuals must be induced to spend more out of their existing incomes; or the business world must be induced, either by increased confidence in the prospects or by a lower rate of interest, to create additional current incomes in the hands of their employees, which is what happens when either the working or the fixed capital of the country is being increased; or public authority must be called in aid to create additional current incomes through the expenditure of borrowed or printed money. In bad times the first factor cannot be expected to work on a sufficient scale. The second factor will come in as the second wave of attack on the slump *after* the tide has been turned by the expenditures of public authority. It is, therefore, only from the third factor that we can expect the initial major impulse.

Now there are indications that two technical fallacies may have affected the policy of your administration. The first relates to the part played in recovery by rising prices. Rising prices are to be welcomed because they are usually a symptom of rising output and employment. When more purchasing power is spent, one expects rising output at rising prices. Since there cannot be rising output without rising prices, it is essential to ensure that the recovery shall not be held back by the insufficiency of the supply of money to support the increased monetary turn-over. But there is much less to be said in favour of rising prices, if they are brought about at the expense of rising output. Some debtors may be helped, but the national recovery as a whole will be retarded. Thus rising prices caused by deliberately increasing prime costs or by restricting output have a vastly inferior value to rising prices which are the natural result of an increase in the nation's purchasing power.

I do not mean to impugn the social justice and social expediency of the redistribution of incomes aimed at by NIRA and by the various schemes for agricultural restriction. The latter, in particular, I should strongly support in principle. But too much emphasis on the remedial value of a higher price-level as an object in itself may lead to serious misapprehension as to the part which prices can play in the technique of recovery. The stimulation of output by increasing aggregate purchasing power is the right way to get prices up; and not the other way round.

Thus as the prime mover in the first stage of the technique of recovery I lay overwhelming emphasis on the increase of national purchasing power resulting from governmental expenditure which is financed by Loans and not by taxing present incomes. Nothing else counts in comparison with this. In a boom, inflation can be caused by allowing unlimited credit to support the excited enthusiasm of business speculators. But in a slump, governmental Loan expenditure is the only sure means of securing quickly a rising output at rising prices. That is why a war has always caused intense industrial activity. In the past orthodox finance has regarded a war as the only legitimate excuse for creating employment by governmental expenditure. You, Mr. President, having cast off such fetters, are free to engage in the interests of peace and prosperity the technique which hitherto has only been allowed to serve the purposes of war and destruction.

The set-back which American recovery experienced this autumn was the predictable consequence of the failure of your administration to organise any material increase in new Loan expenditure during your first six months of office. The position six months hence will entirely depend on whether you have been laying the foundations for larger expenditures in the near future.

I am not surprised that so little has been spent up-to-date. Our own experience has shown how difficult it is to improvise useful Loan-expenditures at short notice. There are many obstacles to be patiently overcome, if waste, inefficiency and corruption are to be avoided. There are many factors, which I need not stop to enumerate, which render especially difficult in the United States the rapid improvisation of a vast programme of public works. I do not blame Mr. Ickes for being cautious and careful. But the risks of less speed must be weighed against those of more haste. He must get across the crevasses before it is dark.

The other set of fallacies, of which I fear the influence, arises out of a crude economic doctrine commonly known as the Quantity Theory of Money. Rising output and rising incomes will suffer a set-back sooner or later if the quantity of money is rigidly fixed. Some people seem to infer from this that output and income can be raised by increasing the quantity of money. But this is like trying to get fat by buying a larger belt. In the United States to-day your belt is plenty big enough for your belly. It is a most misleading thing to stress the quantity of money, which is only a limiting factor, rather than the volume of expenditure, which is the operative factor.

It is an even more foolish application of the same ideas to believe that there is a mathematical relation between the price of gold and the prices of other things. It is true that the value of the dollar in terms of foreign currencies will affect the prices of those goods which enter into international trade. In so far as an over-valuation of the dollar was impeding the freedom of domestic price-raising policies or disturbing the balance of payments with foreign countries, it was advisable to depreciate it. But exchange depreciation should follow the success of your domestic price-raising policy as its natural consequence, and should not be allowed to disturb the whole world by preceding its justification at an entirely arbitrary pace. This is another example of trying to put on flesh by letting out the belt.

These criticisms do not mean that I have weakened in my advocacy of a managed currency or in preferring stable prices to stable exchanges. The currency and exchange policy of a country should be entirely subservient to the aim of raising output and employment to the right level. But the recent gyrations of the dollar have looked to me more like a gold standard on the booze than the ideal managed currency of my dreams.

You may be feeling by now, Mr. President, that my criticism is more obvious than my sympathy. Yet truly that is not so. You remain for me the ruler whose general outlook and attitude to the tasks of government are the most sympathetic in the world. You are the only one who sees the necessity of a profound change of methods and is attempting it without intolerance, tyranny or destruction. You are feeling your way by trial and error, and are felt to be, as you should be, entirely uncommitted in your own person to the details of a particular technique. In my country, as in your own, your position remains singularly untouched by criticism of this or the other detail. Our hope and our faith are based on broader considerations.

If you were to ask me what I would suggest in concrete terms for the immediate future, I would reply thus.

In the field of gold-devaluation and exchange policy the time has come when uncertainty should be ended. This game of blind man's buff with exchange speculators serves no useful purpose and is extremely undignified. It upsets confidence, hinders business decisions, occupies the public attention in a measure far exceeding its real importance, and is responsible both for the irritation and for a certain lack of respect which exist abroad. You have three alternatives. You can devalue the dollar in terms of gold, returning to the gold standard at a new fixed ratio. This would be inconsistent with your declarations in favour of a long-range policy of stable prices, and I hope you will reject it. You can seek some common policy of exchange stabilisation with Great Britain aimed at stable price-levels. This would be the best ultimate solution; but it is not practical politics at the moment, unless you are prepared to talk in terms of an initial value of sterling well below $5 pending the realisation of a marked rise in your domestic price-level. Lastly you can announce that you will definitely control the dollar exchange by buying and selling gold and foreign currencies so as to avoid wide or meaningless fluctuations, with a right to shift the parities at any time but with a declared intention only so to do either to correct a serious want of balance in America's international receipts and payments or to meet a shift in your domestic price level relatively to price-levels abroad. This appears to me to be your best policy during the transitional period. In other respects you would regain your liberty to make your exchange policy subservient to the needs of your domestic policy — free to let out your belt in proportion as you put on flesh.

In the field of domestic policy, I put in the forefront, for the reasons given above, a large volume of Loan-expenditures under Government auspices. It is beyond my province to choose particular objects of expenditure. But preference should be given to those which can be made to mature quickly on a large scale, as for example, the rehabilitation of the physical condition of the railroads. The object is to start the ball rolling. The United States is ready to roll towards prosperity, if a good hard shove can be given in the next six months. Could not the energy and enthusiasm, which launched the NIRA in its early days, be put behind a campaign for accelerating capital expenditures, as wisely chosen as the pressure of circumstances permits? You can at least feel sure that the country will be better enriched by such projects than by the involuntary idleness of millions.

I put in the second place the maintenance of cheap and abundant credit and in particular the reduction of the long-term rate of interest. The turn of the tide in Great Britain is largely attributable to the reduction in the long-term rate of interest which ensued on the success of the conversion of the War Loan. This was deliberately engineered by means of the open-market policy of the Bank of England. I see no reason why you should not reduce the rate of interest on your long-term Government Bonds to 2½ per cent or less with favourable repercussions on the whole bond market, if only the Federal Reserve System would replace its present holdings of short-dated Treasury issues by purchasing long-dated issues in exchange. Such a policy might become effective in the course of a few months, and I attach great importance to it.

With these adaptations or enlargements of your existing policies, I should expect a successful outcome with great confidence. How much that would mean, not only to the material prosperity of the United States and the whole world, but in comfort to men's minds through a restoration of their faith in the wisdom and the power of Government!

With great respect,

Your obedient servant,
J. M. KEYNES

The White House, December 22, 1933

Dear Felix:

Your letters continue to delight and stimulate me. The memorandum from your economist colleagues was read by me to one of my little confidential gatherings — Morgenthau, Cummings, Governor Black, George Harrison, Warren, Rogers and Oliphant — and the comment was that the Oxonians are thinking much in our terms and that since their memorandum was written we had already put several suggestions into practical effect. Please extend to them my very warm thanks and ask them to send me another round-robin when they think the occasion merits.

You are right about the lines becoming more closely drawn — or rather you were until ten days ago. About December 10th the pack of Tories was in full cry, but for some strange, rather obscure, reason — possibly the advent of Christmas buying — the Tories have become extraordinarily silent for the moment. The true alignment will, of course, become more clear as the winter progresses, and I welcome it because so many predictions of the Spragues, Fesses, Mills, etc. have already hit the rocks.

I am honestly disturbed, however, about the news which England and the Continent, and indeed all the rest of the world, gets about the facts of our case. Even Sir Willmot Lewis sees things in his *Times* dispatches from the Mills-Mellon angle. For example, you have been reading of strikes and disturbances here. They are so extraordinarily few that I am almost worried by their scarcity. Bob Wagner's board has done a wonderful job.

The Christmas buying is beyond belief — streets jammed, stores sold out — more like the boom days than anything since 1928.

Even Congress looks almost lamblike. There will be speechmaking, of course, and probably two or three big rows on veterans, excessive public works, and possibly some currency development, but on the whole I really believe they will be businesslike (comparatively), and I am hoping that they will get away by May.

You can tell the professor (Keynes) that in regard to public works we shall spend in the next fiscal year nearly twice the amount we are spending in this fiscal year, but there is a practical limit to what the Government can borrow — especially because the banks are offering passive resistance in most of the large centers.

When you get a chance, send me a letter about British political prospects (via the Embassy mail bag). I am sending this to you by the same method, as I suppose it would be considered indiscreet if it should happen to be read by the British Postal Authorities.

Some day I will tell you all about Dean Acheson. I am sorry to say that after certain developments I did not feel that I could honestly send him the usual letter of appreciation and thanks after he retired.

All the good luck in the world, and the Happiest of New Years.

As ever yours,
F.D.R.

Henry Morgenthau, Jr., was Secretary of the Treasury; Homer Cummings was Attorney General; Eugene Black was a governor of the Federal Reserve; George Harrison served on the Federal Reserve Board in New York; George F. Warren, professor of farm management, was influencing Roosevelt at this time on the relationship between gold and economic recovery; James Harvey Rogers of Yale was another critic of orthodox monetary policy; Herman Oliphant was general counsel for the Treasury Department.

Senator Robert Wagner of New York was Chairman of the National Industrial Recovery Adjustment Board.

Dean Acheson had resigned as Undersecretary of the Treasury, at Roosevelt's request, because he disagreed with the gold-buying policy, with the price of gold being fixed from day to day, by the decisions of a few officials. Roosevelt believed that Acheson had leaked details of this controversy to the press. Later he changed his view of Acheson's conduct and praised him as an honorable official and gallant gentleman.

Professor O. M. W. Sprague of Harvard, Senator Simeon D. Fess of Ohio, and former Secretary on the Treasury Ogden Mills were all angry and determined critics of Roosevelt's monetary experiments.

London, England, January 8, 1934

Dear Mr. President:

How generous of your time, as well as of your thought, is your good long letter of December 22nd which has just reached me. Since your writing we've had your two messages — and a supporting response as encouraging as anything that has thus far happened in your Administration. Opposition seems to have evaporated — and conformed agreeable to your wish. I shall attempt an analysis of the English political situation as soon as I get back to Oxford. I've been here in London for about a week and have seen all sorts of people — leaders of all three parties, journalists — our own and English — financial writers and City men, labor leaders and businessmen, etc. etc. I shall reflect on all I have heard and read, and give you my summary of my three months' observations.

Now only a word about American news in the London press. All you say is so — or was so, until the last ten days or two weeks. You've had an admirable press since — the note has markedly changed. Ever since I came here I have noted the unfairness and especially the inadequacy of American news. As to *The Times* I have spoken to various friends about it, the Warden of All Souls (Geoffrey Dawson the editor is a Fellow of All Souls), Nancy Astor and Elizabeth Bibesco (Asquith's daughter) — for I did not want to complain to Geoffrey Dawson directly. But I believe that Lewis has been discreetly tipped off. But of course Lewis does play around with the Oggie Mills crowd — and his American family ties are what they are. But to show how the present wind is blowing I enclose the leader in today's *Times* and yesterday's leader in the *Observer.*

I also enclose a piece from this week's *Economist* on the Securities Act. Other comments I shall reserve until I get back to my secretary so that I do not further burden you with my wretched handwriting.

Waldorf Astor told me how fit he found you — I feel your vitality across the ocean.

Always faithfully yours,
Felix Frankfurter

Oxford, England, January 11, 1934

Dear Mr. President:

The inadequacy of the English news from America is strikingly revealed as I plough through the piles of American papers that have come during the holidays. They report a number of your acts and utterances about which I should like to cheer lustily. Of a few of them I must make mention:

1. The full text of your speech before the Federation of Churches. No wonder that, in writing me about it, L.D.B. called it a "noble utterance."

2. The full text of your Wilson Anniversary address, with your still further evolution of a civilized pan-American policy.

3. The restoration of civil rights to war-time offenders, coupled with the good sense, reported in this morning's cable, of letting a person like Emma Goldman enter the country. These timid souls have no confidence in the strength of our institutions! Justice Holmes once said the last word about tolerance. "The best thing for bad ideas, as for bad champagne, is exposure to the air."

4. The establishment of the Tennessee Farm and Home Equipment

Corporation. This may turn out to be a modest beginning of one of the most permeating of your social policies.

When one compares today with a year ago, one may well be stout of heart about the days that are ahead — and *you* have not been at it a year!

Always yours,

F.F.

The speech before the Federation of Churches was important because it gave Roosevelt the opportunity to define the moral purposes which influenced his conduct as President. The Wilson anniversary address was even more important since it enabled Roosevelt to put the pursuit of policies in the long perspective of history. Roosevelt once called Wilson "my President," and in this speech he expressed the hope that believers in the philosophy of Wilson, perhaps stronger in death than in life, would display the same tenacity of faith and idealism that had sustained the stricken and repudiated President in his campaign for the League of Nations. Emma Goldman, a controversial agitator of revolutionary upheaval, was admitted to the country because of Roosevelt's conviction that the United States was in a pretty fragile condition if it could not stand her presence.

Oxford, England, January 11, 1934

My dear Mr. President:

In response to your request for my views on the present English political situation, I shall endeavor to synthesize the diverse impressions that have come my way during the last three months. What follows is the off-spring of intensive and extensive reading of the English papers and weeklies, and much talk with all sorts of people. As you know, there is very close communication between Oxford and men of affairs in London; also I have been to London, off and on, and have just spent ten consecutive days there. I have talked with leaders of all three parties, with men in the Government, high officials, judges and barristers, American and English journalists and others whose business it is to watch closely the trend of politics. This is as I see things now:

1. The by-elections of the last six months show, broadly, two tendencies: (i) there has been a falling-off in the poll for the Government candidates of from 3 to 4%; (ii) the Labor figures are not far from the 1929 results. It should be added that while there is some talk of a Liberal revival, the remnants of the Liberal Party present internecine strife.

2. Enthusiasm for the National Government has worn off. It is plainly on the defensive. This is mainly due to two factors: (i) a feeling that the Government is drifting and has no aggressive, positive policy in the domes-

tic sphere, and (ii) the widespread belief, entertained even within the Government, that Sir John Simon has been a failure at the Foreign Office.

3. But it is most unlikely that there will be a general election for a considerable period. And for these reasons: (i) the eagerness of P.M. Ramsay MacDonald to retain office and the desire on the part of powerful forces within the Tory Party to have him as a façade; (ii) Baldwin's loyalty to the P.M.; (iii) the Tory Party's realization that it is certain to suffer the loss of a large number of seats at the polls; (iv) the unpopularity of an early election with business and finance, which believe (a) that recovery is under way and (b) that a Labor victory on the lines of 1929 — in other words, Labor as a predominant minority — is possible.

4. The Labor Party clearly has not yet recovered from 1931. (i) It is moving to the left, but its future leadership and direction are still uncertain. (ii) Its gains at by-elections are essentially due to dissatisfaction with the Government rather than to positive support for its own proposals. It seems to me highly unlikely that it will win over the electorate beyond its 1929 position until it has made up its own mind on crucial issues, can present a united front to the electorate, and give aggressive battle to the Tories.

5. Until that occurs, and it certainly will not be before autumn — until after the next Labor Conference at Glasgow — and I do not believe it will be then, the Government will proceed on its momentum of drift. Its position might be jolted by (a) a war either on the continent or in the East, or (b) by the forced resignation of Sir John Simon. If the latter occurred, the National Liberals could hardly stay, and their withdrawal from the Cabinet would make the P.M.'s position even more delicate and difficult in removing all pretense of a "national" Government. Before this letter reaches you, Geneva events may have already had an important bearing upon the British political situation. A breakdown of the Disarmament Conference might be disastrous for Sir John Simon. In this connection it must be remembered that there are excellent reasons for believing that Simon's policy is unpopular both with the P.M. and the advanced Tories in the Cabinet. From this angle the promotion of Mr. Eden (as Minister for League of Nations Affairs) was significant.

6. In the history of British governments the third year is usually the critical one. The weakness of the National Government seems to me to lie essentially in these factors: (i) it cannot satisfy the extreme die-hard Tories, *e.g.*, over the reform of the House of Lords; (ii) it cannot satisfy the advanced Tories, *e.g.*, over housing, industrial reorganization, disarmament; (iii) it has alienated the Liberals and manufacturers for export by its tariff policy. It lacks the necessary coherence to agree upon a policy of reconstruction and it survives fundamentally because its opponents have not yet learned sufficient integration to take the offensive. As soon as a clear alter-

native has been developed this will happen. The Tories will then — as with Lloyd George in 1922 — be anxious to dissociate themselves from coalition and resume their freedom of action.

7. While this Government continues, British foreign policy will remain predominantly as negative as it has been throughout Sir John Simon's period of office. There will be no powerful pressure for disarmament; there may even be pressure for re-armament in aviation. There will be continuing political difficulties about a trade agreement with Russia. A Russo-Japanese war would find Great Britain neutral — the feeling against war among the English people is very strong just now — but I know that the Russians are worryingly wondering whether Japan could float a loan in England. If I had to bet, I should bet they couldn't. As for the continent, Great Britain will try to steer a path between France and Germany, avoiding commitments to either.

8. In the domestic field the Government will rely on (i) better employment figures; (ii) slum clearance schemes, and (iii) a balanced budget with a surplus, making possible (a) some restoration of economy cuts and (b) perhaps some remission of taxation, to maintain its hold. The Government will argue that the return of Labor will arrest recovery, and that the P.M. will seek to go to the country as late as possible.

If there are any specific aspects of the British situation on which you would like to have light, please let me know and perhaps I can find it.

With warm regards and all good wishes,

Faithfully yours,
FELIX FRANKFURTER

Oxford, England, January 15, 1934

Dear Mr. President:

1. At Waldorf Astor's suggestion, Bob Brand, who, as you probably know, is one of the directors of *The Times*, asked me for a weekend to talk about *The Times'* American news. Having since October followed with great particularity the American news in the English papers, I was able to point out to Brand the failure of the English press to respond adequately to the news value of America these days and, more particularly, *The Times'* special responsibility. I drove home the intense interest of the British public in your effort and the growing feeling that the pessimistic accounts in the British press are unreliable. As a matter of fact, the New York cables to *The Times*, particularly the long weekly Monday cables, are even more misleading than Willmot Lewis' stuff. I told Brand that *The Times* can say what it pleases in its leaders, but that the news should be well-balanced and adequate. In the language of the late C.P. Scott of the Manchester *Guard-*

ian, "Opinion is free, but facts are sacred." He said what he could on behalf of their correspondence, but in essence agreed to its inadequacy. Brand was plainly impressed with the seriousness of the problem, and asked whether I would have a full talk, before very long, with Geoffrey Dawson, the editor-in-chief of *The Times,* and him. I agreed to do so, and he will arrange it as soon as I have an early opportunity for going to London.

2. The other night I dined with about a dozen young economists and financial writers, who invited me to be present when Sir William Beveridge, the head of the London School of Economics, was to make a report on his American visit. I had already had a bout with Beveridge some weeks ago at Nancy Astor's, and when he saw me at this dinner he realized he couldn't get away with the naive and doctrinaire *laissez-faire* views with which, on the most shallow inquiry, he judged the American situation. (Incidentally, it seems to me pretty outrageous and silly for the Rockefeller Foundation to pick a Tory like Sir Arthur Steel-Maitland and a doctrinaire Manchesterian like Sir William Beveridge to make a "scientific" report on the Recovery program.) Beveridge was most tentative and full of reservations — a very, very different story from his written report, which, although he does not know it, I have seen.

3. So far as the opinion of the general public is concerned, it reminds me strongly of the English attitude towards us at the time of the Civil War. Just as then, roughly speaking, the upper classes were for the South and the masses for Lincoln and the North, so now, in the main, the upper crust and the City are distrustful of what you are doing and are prophesying, if not hoping for, failure because of fear of the reactive influence of your success upon their situation, while the great masses are eager for your success in order that English reform efforts may be energized by our success.

4. I passed your acknowledgement for the Oxford economic memorandum discreetly on, and they were extremely grateful for your reception of it.

5. I assume you saw the two-page résumé of your Administration by James Morgan in the Boston *Sunday Globe* for Dec. 31. One paragraph in Morgan's piece especially pleased me:

> The President himself makes no bigger claim than that "we seem to be on our way, but we are not yet out of the woods." A leadership that makes no pretense to infallibility has communicated an unaccustomed patience and open-mindedness to a people given to dogma, doctrines, ancient fetishes and traditional catchwords. That change in national psychology is a large part of the battle.

As you know, it has been a very deep conviction of mine that not the least of the elements that have enlisted the public's great confidence in you is their realization that you don't pretend to be a miracle-worker. A lack of dogmatism and the spirit of true modesty, yoked to unceasing determination to get us out of the woods, are qualities that wear in season and out of season, that people can bank on as against those terrible promises, to be fulfilled by incantations, on which Hoover fed them for so long.

With warm regards,

Always faithfully yours,
FELIX FRANKFURTER

Oxford, England, January 29, 1934

Dear Mr. President:

1. This is a further word about the American news in the London *Times*.

Doubtless stimulated by Bob Brand, Geoffrey Dawson, the editor of *The Times*, came to Oxford for a talk with me, in the course of which he was rather frank about the temperamental limitations of Willmot Lewis, but there he is. Dawson invited frankness on my part, and I laid out to him with particularity the inadequacy of what his readers have been getting during the period of my close reading of *The Times*, since my arrival here. Out of a clear sky he said he wanted me to write a series of articles on the American situation. I was quite taken aback and made other suggestions. He was insistent, however, on his proposal, and I promised to take it under advisement. That's where the matter now rests.

If I am to do it at all, of course the articles must be most accurately informed by knowledge of the latest details. To be sure, I follow American events closely in four of our daily papers, and all that, but I don't feel that I would do the achievements and plans of the Administration justice unless, as a basis of my writing, I had memoranda from the various branches of the government about which one ought to write. I should like, therefore, to put to you the procedure that has occurred to me, by which I might be enabled to write such expository articles for *The Times*.

Even the best informed quarters here know next to nothing about (1) the Tennessee Valley Authority, (2) CCC, (3) the farm subsistence program, (4) the detailed accomplishments of AAA, (5) the PWA and (6) CWA. Most of the stuff that appears concerns currency matters and NRA. If you think well of this scheme, eliminating or adding what activities you think best, would it be feasible for you to ask the appropriate agencies respectively to prepare a memorandum, say of not more than five thousand words, summarizing (a) the legal authority under which they are operating, (b) their objectives, (c) the various means by which the objectives are being pursued, (d) the accomplishments to date and (e) the outlook for the future, both difficulties and hopes.

If this does seem both desirable and feasible to you, may I ask that the memoranda should come to me through you, so that not even the heads of the various agencies know for what purpose the memoranda are designed, inasmuch as Geoffrey Dawson put to me his proposal in strict confidence. Presumably he would want the articles to be anonymous and they are, as you know, terribly fussy about revealing the names of their anonymous authors.

That it is important to have adequate expository articles in *The Times* I have not the slightest doubt, and not merely because of the eagerness of the British public for news regarding your Administration and because of the amount of ignorance and misrepresentation that is now disseminated. *The Times* is also to a large degree a source of knowledge for the Continent. Walter Layton, just back from a trip all over the Continent, reports a predominant curiosity for news of what is happening in the United States.

2. I don't have to tell you how delighted I am with your drive against the political lawyers in Washington. They know not what they do. In that connection, I hope you will secure at this session of Congress legislation to put a crimp into one of the most corrupting influences of our profession, namely, the big fees for nursing claims against the Government. This is all the more essential legislation because the hope of large fees for tax refunds is one of the great leverages for raids on the Treasury. You will remember that I talked with you about this last spring, and somewhere in your files there is a bill which I drafted at your suggestion, putting a limit upon the fees that may be charged in cases of claims against the Government. Between ourselves, L.D.B. passed on that bill before I submitted it to you.

3. Indications that you are considering lifting some of the restrictions upon postal savings are also very cheering. There is no doubt that vast sums would be at your disposal if the bars were raised. I know it is argued that the banks would be prejudiced by having people put their money in postal savings. It seems to me the argument won't hold water. If people still withhold confidence from banks and are ready to put their money into the Government's keeping, the Government, with its knowledge of the conditions of banks (which the depositors cannot possibly have), can always redeposit in banks.

4. Your appointments of Blanton Winship and Dr. Splawn are very interesting. I haven't seen Winship for years, but I liked him so much when I saw a good deal of him in my early days in Washington. He is human and sympathetic, and ought to get on well with Latin people. I am sorry to see the opposition to Splawn, and I do hope it will be thoroughly cleared up, for he is a public-spirited and able man.

The best news from the United States is the assurance that you are in the best of health and spirits.

With warm regards,

Faithfully yours,
F.F.

CCC—*Civilian Conservation Corps*
PWA—*Public Works Administration*
AAA—*Agricultural Adjustment Administration*
NRA—*National Recovery Administration*
CWA—*Civil Works Administration*

Blanton Winship had been appointed Governor of Puerto Rico.

Dr. Walter M. Splawn became a member of the Interstate Commerce Commission.

The White House, February 3, 1934

Dear Felix:

I am delighted that you are discussing things with the London *Times*. It is my thought if we can get really correct news into the British papers, we can then start in to break down the vile situation in the French press. The Havas has got to the point where I am making unofficial representations to the French government. That agency, as you know, covers Latin America and they made deliberate efforts to sabotage our position at the Montevideo Conference.

All goes well, I will write you soon at more length.

Always sincerely yours,
F.D.R.

Oxford, England, February 14, 1934

Dear Mr. President:

1. The two most important recent items of American news are truly important — I mean, of course, your request for the regulations of the Exchange and your cancellation of the air mail contracts.

The restriction of the Exchange to its legitimate functions in our social economy has been long overdue. There has been more than ample time for self-regulation, and self-regulation they have shown is not in them. Your message and the proposed legislation ought to stop the naive talk that continues to go the rounds that the Administration should now concern itself only with "recovery" and postpone "reform" until later. What an unreal alternative that is! One is reminded of Macaulay's remark in answer to the objection that the British Reform Act of 1832 would undermine the British Constitution. "You must reform," said Macaulay, "in order to preserve." It is equally true that we must reform in order to recover an adequate way of life for the mass of our people. Of course such has been the basis of your whole program, and it is amusing how much idle chatter still goes on about "recovery" vs. "reform."

2. And the cancellation of those air mail contracts, following the drive against the political lawyers and the rigorous administration of the Civil Works Administration mark a very notable chapter in American history. The philosophy of it I thought you expressed with beautiful simplicity in your speech, on February 2, to the National Emergency Council. As a result of your insistence on the complete divorce of private motive from the conduct of public business, we ought by the time you get through with the Presidency, to have established those standards into national habits. It is amazing how such standards may be translated into settled practices. Everyone knows of the present purity of the British judiciary, yet one does not have to go back to Lord Bacon's days for examples of venal motives on the part of judges. Lord Westbury, one of the greatest of the Victorian Lord Chancellors, had to resign because of the dispensation of patronage to a relative. The way in which you cancelled those air mail contracts must again have greatly heartened our people in proving to them that the government *can* act with courage and with concern solely for the public interest.

3. Two other things have come out of Washington that cheer me. The lesser of the two is the inference I draw from the papers that you put the brakes on against prosecution in the Weirton steel case and have instead worked out the difficulties through negotiation and executive order. Naturally I followed the details of that case with great interest, and while I speak, of course, without having seen the official record and from the disadvantage of distance, I did get the strong impression from all the details I have read that that would not have been a good case on which to invite the first test of Section 7a.

4. Especially far-reaching is your pronouncement — here again I have not seen the full text — that interest rates will have to come down all along the line. I hope you'll get some sense into these creditors. Don't they know nuthin' — not even their self-interest?

5. On Monday I had lunch, privately, with Arthur Henderson and the chief officials of the League, who were here on disarmament matters. Since then, as you know, the meeting of the Bureau has been postponed to April 10. This is to give Anthony Eden a chance to drum up support at the various capitals for the Simon plan or something. Eden is a much more persuasive person than John Simon, but the outlook, as you know, is most unpromising. Both France and Germany are showing a cold shoulder to the English proposals, and the turn of events in Austria — inevitable from the

moment that Dollfuss surrendered to the Heimwehr — is not calculated to improve things. Henderson says that when the French prove to him, as they can conclusively, that the Germans have rearmed, he will ask, "What are you going to do about it — let it be a run-away rearmament rather than a controlled one?" He sums it all up by saying "it's convention or competition" in armaments.

6. The enclosed may interest you. I suspect you hardly foresaw that possibility when you established relations with the Russians.

With warm regards,

Faithfully yours,
FELIX FRANKFURTER

Despite repeated corrections, Frankfurter could never get the Macaulay quotation right. On March 2, 1831, in the debate on the First Reform Bill to broaden the franchise, Macaulay said: "Turn where we may, within, around, the voice of great events is proclaiming to us, Reform, that you may preserve."

The enclosure from the Morning Post, *a Tory paper, praises Roosevelt for having the courage to think afresh about relations with Russia.*

Section 7A of the National Industrial Recovery Act guaranteed the rights of collective bargaining to labor.

The White House, February 20, 1934

Dear Mr. Frankfurter:

The President has passed on to me your letter of January twenty-ninth. It is an extremely interesting communication.

All of us hope that you will comply with Dawson's request. We have been aware of the situation to which you refer and gladly send you, under separate cover, the data you wanted. If you find this inadequate and will let us know your wants, we will be glad to send additional information.

All luck to you. You have our blessings and gratitude.

Very sincerely,
STEPHEN EARLY

Telegram to Roosevelt

February 20, 1934

LONDON ADVICES FROM VIENNA INDICATE SERIOUS DANGER OF EXCESSES PARTICULARLY ANTIJEWISH. DEEPLY HOPE IT WILL COMMEND ITSELF TO YOU TO MAKE APPROPRIATE REPRESENTATIONS TO AUSTRIA IF INDEED YOU HAVE NOT ALREADY DONE SO. INTERNATIONAL USAGE AND OUR OWN PRECEDENTS AMPLY SUPPORT SUCH ACTION. WE JOINED IN PROTEST TO ROUMANIA IN 1872. IN 1891 PRESIDENT HARRISON DECLARED "SUGGESTIONS OF HUMANITY" WARRANTED

PROTEST TO RUSSIA. IN 1902 T.R. INVITED POWERS TO MAKE REPRESENTATIONS TO RUSSIA. NONE IN BETTER POSITION THAN YOU TO MAKE SUCH APPEAL. TIME OF ESSENCE. MAY BE TOO LATE TO AWAIT EARLE'S RETURN.

FRANKFURTER

George Earle, Roosevelt's first Minister to Austria, had returned home in late January 1934 from his post in Vienna.

Oxford, England, February 22, 1934

Dear Mr. President:

1. If the enclosed editorial from *The Times* has not already reached you, it may interest you because of the indication it furnishes that *The Times* has been made aware of the need of more accurate and sympathetic interpretation of American affairs.

2. The enclosed editorial from the Manchester *Guardian* regarding the Viennese situation puts in an English perspective some of the considerations which, in the light of some authentic information, led me to cable you about the Austrian situation. Things are not what they might seem from the Austrian Government's communiqués. That Dollfuss in his own feelings is trying to avoid and avert excesses, I believe. If he were a wholly free man he would go in for a policy of appeasement. But he ceased to be a free man from the time that he surrendered to the Heimwehr. The evidence is, I believe, conclusive that the advances made by the Socialists for an alliance with Dollfuss and his Party, on condition that the minimum requirements of a democratic state should be observed, were rejected by him. I need not tell you that Austria is really the football between the rivalries of Hitler and Mussolini. And that's where the matter now stands. The victimization which the Germans have made so familiar is proceeding and will continue to proceed in Austria in all sorts of ways, though much less fiercely — Austria being Austria.

3. I had a most interesting time the other night in speaking on the constitutional problems of your legislation before the Royal Institute of International Affairs. It would have amused you, I think, to have heard Sir William Beveridge and G. B. Shaw, who led the debate following my address, argue in the spirit of Jim Beck and Senator Fess. I had a really good time, the kind of good time one has in dealing with people who don't know what they are talking about.

4. The American papers have come, with the full details regarding air mail contract cancellation. I am glad to see Lindbergh's telegram dealt with as it deserves to be. He is plainly the dupe of others.

5. The New York papers also bring the full text of the Stock Exchange Bill. That is an astonishingly careful and acute piece of draftsmanship. The

Bill reveals real mastery of the intricacies of the Exchange and addresses itself with knowledge to them. A fine blend has been achieved between fixity and flexibility, between the things that specifically should be enumerated in legislation, in the light of the testimony before the Fletcher Committee, and the things as to which necessary discretionary power must be left to the Federal Trade Commission. Of course the Bill is a draft and not the final form. But I cannot help but be impressed with the fine press that the Bill has had, and especially with the essential meagreness of the Wall Street criticisms. Their game, plainly enough, is like unto that of the utilities in days gone by, namely, to have the "right" kind of regulatory body. They want, that is, a regulatory body devoid of the necessary courage and resourcefulness for making the legislation effective. They would like to have what might be called the Pendergast type of administration. Their game must add greatly to your amusement.

  With warm regards,

Faithfully yours,
F.F.

  The debate with Shaw is discussed in the Introduction.

  James M. Beck, a former Solicitor General, had become convinced that Roosevelt was determined to enlarge the scope of federal power to a point which would destroy all traditional states' rights. His eloquence made him a more formidable protagonist of this philosophy than Senator Simeon D. Fess of Ohio who shared the same views.

  Tom Pendergast of Kansas City ran the Democratic organization in Missouri and relied on having his friends occupy important administrative offices in the state.

  Senator Duncan Fletcher's Senate Committee on Banking and Currency had held hearings on the need for regulating the Stock Exchange.

  The Post Office Department in February 1934 canceled contracts with six airlines carrying airmail and then turned them over to the Army Air Corps on a temporary basis. The cancellation was caused by a Senate investigation which revealed payoffs in the form of stocks in airplane and engine manufacturer's concerns, and the awarding by President Hoover's Postmaster General of contracts to other than the lowest bidder.

Telegram to Roosevelt

New York, N.Y., February 11, 1934

YOUR ACTION OF YESTERDAY AFFECTS FUNDAMENTALLY THE INDUSTRY TO WHICH I HAVE DEVOTED THE LAST TWELVE YEARS OF MY LIFE. THEREFORE I RESPECTFULLY PRESENT TO YOU THE FOLLOWING CONSIDERATIONS. THE

PERSONAL AND BUSINESS LIVES OF AMERICAN CITIZENS HAVE BEEN BUILT UP AROUND THE RIGHT TO JUST TRIAL BEFORE CONVICTION. YOUR ORDER OF CANCELLATION OF ALL AIR MAIL CONTRACTS CONDEMNS THE LARGEST PORTION OF OUR COMMERCIAL AVIATION WITHOUT JUST TRIAL. THE OFFICERS OF A NUMBER OF THE ORGANIZATIONS AFFECTED HAVE NOT BEEN GIVEN THE OPPORTUNITY OF A HEARING AND IMPROPER ACTS BY MANY COMPANIES AFFECTED HAVE NOT BEEN ESTABLISHED. NO ONE CAN RIGHTFULLY OBJECT TO DRASTIC ACTION BEING TAKEN PROVIDED THE GUILT IMPLIED IS FIRST ESTABLISHED BUT IT IS THE RIGHT OF ANY AMERICAN INDIVIDUAL OR ORGANIZATION TO RECEIVE FAIR TRIAL. YOUR PRESENT ACTION DOES NOT DISCRIMINATE BETWEEN INNOCENCE AND GUILT AND PLACES NO PREMIUM ON HONEST BUSINESS. AMERICANS HAVE SPENT THEIR LIVES IN BUILDING IN THIS COUNTRY THE FINEST COMMERCIAL AIR LINES IN THE WORLD. THE UNITED STATES TODAY IS FAR IN THE LEAD IN ALMOST EVERY BRANCH OF COMMERCIAL AVIATION. IN AMERICA WE HAVE COMMERCIAL AIRCRAFT, ENGINES, EQUIPMENT AND AIR LINES SUPERIOR TO THOSE OF ANY OTHER COUNTRY. THE GREATEST PART OF THIS PROGRESS HAS BEEN BROUGHT ABOUT THROUGH THE AIR MAIL. CERTAINLY MOST INDIVIDUALS IN THE INDUSTRY BELIEVE THAT THIS DEVELOPMENT HAS BEEN CARRIED ON IN COOPERATION WITH EXISTING GOVERNMENT AND ACCORDING TO LAW. IF THIS IS NOT THE CASE IT SEEMS THE RIGHT OF THE INDUSTRY AND IN KEEPING WITH AMERICAN TRADITION THAT FACTS TO THE CONTRARY BE DEFINITELY ESTABLISHED. UNLESS THESE FACTS LEAVE NO ALTERNATIVE THE CONDEMNATION OF COMMERCIAL AVIATION BY CANCELLATION OF ALL MAIL CONTRACTS AND THE USE OF THE ARMY ON COMMERCIAL AIR LINES WILL UNNECESSARILY AND GREATLY DAMAGE ALL AMERICAN AVIATION.

CHARLES A. LINDBERGH

The White House, February 12, 1934

Except when the senders of telegrams or other communications act primarily for publicity purposes, the common practice is to allow the President, when he is addressed by them, the courtesy of receiving and reading their communications before they are read by others than the person addressed.

In this instance the giving out of a telegram, which bears the name of Colonel Charles A. Lindbergh, by his attorney and legal adviser, Colonel Henry Breckinridge, would indicate the message obviously was sent for publicity purposes — at least it was published before it was received by the President.

The President's Executive Order under date of February 9th was issued after the Postmaster General advised the President that "all domestic air mail contracts for carrying the mails have been annulled." The Postmaster General annulled these contracts. Colonel Lindbergh's telegram is in error in that it states the President ordered the cancellation of all air mail contracts.

Colonel Lindbergh's telegram will be referred to the Postmaster General and to the Secretary of Commerce for consideration and action.

STEPHEN EARLY

Oxford, England, March 6, 1934

Dear Mr. President:

1. You know of course the complexion of the *Morning Post*, but I believe one has to read it daily fully to appreciate how reactionary and anti-American it really is. In the light of this fact, its comment this morning on your first year is almost handsome.

You may also be interested in the editorial from this morning's *Daily Herald*, which, as you know, is the Labor organ, with a circulation of over a million.

2. I am sure you will want to see, if you have not already done so, an impressive letter which appeared in yesterday's *Times* from the Archbishop of York. It shows which way the wind is blowing here — and there is no doubt that the wind partly came from America.

3. Speaking of things English, the recent intrigues to effect the shift in the MacDonald Cabinet have doubtless been reported on the other side. There is the best of reasons for believing that MacDonald himself was trying gently to shift Simon from the Foreign Office. This is the second time the endeavor has been made. I know on excellent authority that it was all arranged to happen some time ago. Lord Sankey was to resign the Lord Chancellorship, Simon was to go to the Woolsack, and Lord Irwin (as Lord Halifax then was) was to go to the Foreign Office. But that nice plan was blocked by Lord Hailsham, who said if there was to be a new Lord Chancellor, he claimed the post. This time Simon himself blocked his removal, but the end is not yet.

4. I really don't see how you maintain your gaiety now that Dave Lawrence has sounded a call to arms for a New Constitution Party. For all I know, Dave's solemnity may make you even gayer. Isn't it all very wonderful: Oggie, the generalissimo of the new forces, Dave Lawrence and sombre Mark Sullivan the theoreticians (that lovely word so much used on the Continent) of the movement and Fess, Jim Beck, Bill Castle and Colonel Knox as corps commanders.

5. I am delighted to learn that you are supporting Hiram Johnson's bill for the withdrawal of state utility litigation from the federal courts. Such legislation has been long overdue. I notice also some talk of an Ad-

ministration measure for federal incorporation. That's a horse of a different color. Great difficulties are involved in such a measure, and I hope there won't be any urgency in pushing it. Of course many abuses have found shelter under our corporation laws. But the abuses that call for public protection and are essential to a healthy economic life can be dealt with by a number of specific improvements in federal legislation, especially through the use of the taxing power, without prematurely raising the many problems that are involved in a federal incorporation law.

6. In two days it will be just a year since I first saw you in the White House on that charming afternoon when you called on Justice Holmes. What a year it has been, and what a transformation you have wrought in the morale and faith of our people. And after all, morale and faith are the sources of wisdom and well-being.

With all good wishes,

Always faithfully yours,

Felix Frankfurter

David Lawrence and Mark Sullivan were prominent political columnists. Oggie is Ogden Mills.

Senator Fess of Ohio.

William R. Castle had been an Undersecretary of State in Hoover's Administration.

Colonel Knox was the publisher of the Chicago Daily News.

Senator Hiram Johnson of California, though a Republican isolationist, often supported Roosevelt on domestic legislation.

The Morning Post *wrote: "Looking back on the first year of Mr. Roosevelt's administration, one is at a loss to determine which is the more extraordinary, the voluntary surrender of almost absolute power to one man by a nation notorious for its critical individualism, or the energy with which the President has used the trust confided in him. The first may be taken as some measure of the despair which had caught hold of the nation. But despair is an emotion which does not long survive the adversity which induces it, and it hardly explains why, a year after the first flush, the authority of the President is not merely undiminished, but is perhaps greater than ever before."*

The Daily Herald *said: "Mr. Roosevelt's declaration that the basis of his policy is 'humanity first and profits after,' is not, indeed, Socialism. But, in the mouth of a President of the United States, it is subversive revolutionary doctrine. . . . Roosevelt has set himself to prove that democracy can be as dynamic, as decisive, as swift in action as any dictator; that the suggestion that it is necessarily lethargic and inert is nonsense."*

The Archbishop of York said in his letter to The Times: *"If the Chan-cellor of the Exchequer finds himself in a position to reduce taxation, the restoration of the cuts in the allowances for the unemployed shall have precedence over any other concessions, including remission of income tax."*

Oxford, England, March 19, 1934

Dear Mr. President:

1. The B.B.C. asked me to speak on the way England looked to an American, and I thought it would be a good chance to explain in general, uncontentious language, the forces of misunderstanding and misrepresentation of the United States in this country. You may be interested in reading what I said, particularly the marked portion dealing with the tainted centres of press despatches. I was hoping, of course, to reach not merely the editors of English papers but also opinion-making influences. Judging from letter comments, it hit some marks.

2. You will recall Sir A. Steel-Maitland, the Minister of Labour in Baldwin's Cabinet, who came to see you with Sir William Beveridge. Steel-Maitland, though a member of the Conservative Party, is a horse of a different color from Beveridge. He is keenly interested in what you are attempting and generally sympathetic. He has now been asked to write a book about us, to be published by Macmillan. He came here to see me a few days ago and spent a good part of the morning asking many detailed questions about the recovery program and particularly the background of some of the legislation. It gave me a good chance to educate an English statesman of considerable influence, whose book is likely to have wide attention here. I got down to details with him and immersed him as best I could in the details of the situation that confronted you when you took office and the mischievous financial and economic forces that had brought us to that pass. He is making another visit to the States a little later, and I shall then give him notes of introduction to some of the people he should have seen on his last trip and didn't.

3. My wife and I are making a flying visit to Palestine. I don't suppose that there is anything there that you would want me to look into, but if perchance a near-Eastern war breaks out while I am there and you would want me to be American military attaché with the Abyssinian or the Iraq army — please remember that I am a Major in the Reserve Corps — you can reach me c/o King David Hotel, Jerusalem.

4. The despatches carry ominous news about the threatened strike in the motor industry. I have some notion of the obstinacy of that situation, and my best good wishes go to you, for I suspect settlement will have to come through your personal intervention.

I had tea with Ambassador Bingham the other day, and he told me in what fit form he found you. But one did not need his testimony for that; proof of it breaks through all the despatches that come from America.

With warm regards,

Faithfully yours,

F.F.

THE LISTENER
Published by the British Broadcasting Corporation
Wednesday 21 February 1934
TRANS-ATLANTIC MISCONCEPTIONS
by Professor Felix Frankfurter

Professor Frankfurter, of the Harvard Law School, is now lecturing at Oxford under the Professorship established in 1929 by the Association of American Rhodes Scholars.

That the B.B.C. should invite the views of an American on the English character in itself reveals much, not only of English character but of English opinion about Americans. For one thing it bespeaks that confidence in the free expression of ideas which is so marked a characteristic of the English national temper. Perhaps this is due to the fact that Englishmen do not take ideas too heavily. On the other hand, to ask foreigners to tell you what they think of you may indicate a certain self-possession and indifference. Moreover, you naturally expect an American to undertake the extra-hazardous enterprise of telling you what we think of you, because Americans are known to be foolhardy enough to try anything — once. But that the B.B.C. should have asked an American to speak this night, February 12, reveals even subtler aspects of the English character. It is widely believed on our side that Englishmen have a talent for charming seduction; or if seduction be too harsh a word, let me say that we credit you with a most effective talent for undermining the independence of other people by your courtesy and by an almost unconscious graciousness in ministering to the pride and vanity of the rest of the world whom you deem less hardy than yourselves. Yet I daresay that the B.B.C. did not know the significance of February 12 to an American. It surely was some unconscious graciousness that made the B.B.C. pick the anniversary of Lincoln's birthday for an American speaker. But thus celebrating, as it were, Lincoln's birthday over your wireless, you predispose an American to note your thoughtfulness and to find in you that quality of imagination which you almost take pride in denying, partly in order to appear more stupid than you are, and partly because it belongs to good English tradition to distrust imagination as romantic and unsound. Moreover, on Lincoln's birthday one should try to catch something of his spirit towards his fellowmen, as exemplified in the phrase, "with charity to all and malice towards none," which was uttered in the midst of war.

Not that I have to suppress malice. Americans don't feel malice towards the English. And whatever be your defects or limitations, you certainly neither desire nor need charity. Indeed, the very attempt to analyse a whole people bespeaks on my part a certain humourlessness, unless it be done as a kind of conversational game. To presume to describe the characteristics of a great historic people is an arrogance exceeded only by presuming to explain how one people feels about another. For an American to tell you how the English look to the Americans implies not only an unwarranted authority to express the composite views of 130,000,000 people, but also to interpret the way 40,000,000 Britishers appear to 130,000,000 Americans. It would be sufficiently hard to talk about the English people if they were a solid unit — if every Englishman were like every other Englishman. But within the narrow confines of your English geography are great differences of class and region, of city and country, of lineage and language. Even a moderate acquaintance with English people makes one suspect that the typical Englishman really doesn't exist outside the pages of *Punch*, because England, in the words of Mr. Baldwin — and who should know better? — is "so rich in the variety of human character." One who dwells among you for any length of time soon comes to realise that. Yet you yourselves believe that you have some basic common characteristics. And from the distant and somewhat dim view across the Atlantic, the human scene naturally takes on a somewhat generalised aspect. As this little island is surveyed from Portland, Oregon, and Dallas, Texas, from Kalamazoo, Michigan, and Oshkosh, Wisconsin, from Painted Post, New York, and Athens, Georgia, you cease to be individual men and women, with all the differences that exist among you, and become a strange composite that never was on land or sea, called the English people.

Such composite views of peoples by one another in effect mean an interpretation of the whole history of the two peoples, for the way one people thinks about another largely depends upon the course of history between them. Our common speech — or as much of English speech as we have in common — deceives us into assuming a greater identity than really exists between us. The psychology generated by deep historic events long survives those events. It may seem far-fetched to find in the American Revolution, and the war of 1812, and England's attitude towards our Civil War, key explanations to the way the English appear to Americans today. But we fool ourselves in believing that the past is dead. I don't mean to suggest that there still is a lively sense of grievance against the England of George V because of the England of George III. But we do sometimes find in English behaviour the kind of attitude that leads some of your Dominions to say that the mother country doesn't quite realise that the children are grown up, that the Colonies have become Dominions. Our people occasionally suspect you are not wholly aware that we are no longer a young offshoot. It is a nice feeling on your part to look upon the gropings and growing pains of the American nation as the antics of a lively young child, interesting, at times even original, but nevertheless a child.

This feeling on our part hasn't anything to do with specific treatment or diplomatic relations or the way our statesmen talk to each other. It is something much more impalpable, but something real and permeating. The whole Civil War episode has left, I believe, very deep marks. That war was for us a kind of holy cause on behalf of freedom and democracy, and the hostility to it which we saw in the attitude of upper-class English opinion confirmed American belief that England was really hostile to the aims of the American Republic. Please remember that I am not suggesting this as the whole truth, or even a good part of it. The evolution of popular feeling is due as much to appearances as to reality, and when we try to convey your feeling about us or our feeling about you, we are dealing very largely with what seems and not what is. This series is a species of answer provided by the B.B.C. to Robert Burns' prayer: "O, wad some power the giftie gie us/To see oursels as ithers see us."

Unfortunately, others are apt to see only part of us, only the surface. The judgment of one nation by another is based on selected knowledge, and we are apt to take the bits of evidence, or even distortions of the bits, that are most congenial to our bias. We find, in other words, what we expect to find, and fasten on what confirms our previous opinion. Even when the medium of speech is the same, the opinion we form of another people is very far from a dispassionate judgment. So it has been in regard to the attitude of your people towards the American Civil War. I dwell on that, for while it is a long, long time ago and most Englishmen of today have only a dim notion that there was a civil war in 1861, what Americans then believed to have been your attitude continues to colour what we think about you today. Unfortunately the fun that *Punch* poked at Mr. Lincoln while he lived is much more widely remembered in the United States than *Punch*'s eloquent mourning at his bier. More Americans seem to remember that the government of England nearly came to the aid of the South against the North than cherish the moving eloquence and self-sacrifice of the Lancashire workmen in supporting Mr. Lincoln and the Northern cause. Even historians quote more glibly Lord Acton's partiality for the South than the powerful support of the North by men like John Bright and Goldwin Smith, and forget that Lord Acton also regarded the American example as the hope of the world.

To be sure, since the revolutionary farmers fought the British redcoats and British troops burned the White House and aristocratic England looked with sympathy upon the efforts of the Southern aristocracy to break up the American union, the American Doughboy has fought alongside the English Tommy. But just as childhood likes and dislikes, in strange and unexpected ways, crop up in maturity, so the feelings and prejudices of the childhood and youth of a nation become traditions handed down from generation to generation, absorbed in the air that is breathed. At bottom, our feelings about you result from our great self-consciousness about the English because of our intimate historical association with you.

We think you superior and at times even supercilious because somehow or other you have managed to make us feel that you think us inferior and crude. Nor have your great popular writers on America, like Charles Dickens, helped to dissipate such an impression. Caricature is a favourite medium in describing a people, and America lent itself, and still does all too readily, to caricature. The crudities, the hustle and bustle, the noise and energy, the excesses of violence and millionaires made overnight, offer obvious material for painting merely surfaces. It requires something more to see below the material conquest of a continent, the groping efforts, often stumbling and awkward, to create a more decent civilisation for the great mass of common people whom the Lord must have loved, as Lincoln said, because he made so many of them. And while in the process of building up the continent, Americans have been full of energy and optimism and self-confidence in grappling with the forces of nature; they lack that serenity and that inner self-confidence which are so largely the product of a settled and stable civilisation. Young nations are like young people; they don't take themselves for granted; they are sensitive and readily find disapproval and a sense of superiority in their elders. While the Frenchman may be indifferent to your criticism and indeed think worse of you for it, Americans may think worse of you but are not indifferent to it. Moreover, because we speak the same language you too readily assume we think the same thoughts. If our thoughts appear to you different, you have less indulgence for the difference than in the case of the French whom you expect to find different. Thus it sometimes comes to pass that you make us feel that you regard us as your spiritual poor relations.

You may think all this is as things were, not as they are. You will say that these misconceptions about one another — for such they are — belong to the bad old days when the governing historic facts were those of friction and not of substantial concord, when the Englishman's view of America was derived from the caricatures of *Punch* or of Dickens, before Marconi and the trans-Atlantic telephone, when, travel being slow and expensive, few Americans visited England and hardly any Englishmen visited America, except in course of duty or for profit. For although the English are the most travelled people in the world, for some reason or other, America was for a long time off their beat. This disregard of the United States as a place of mere interest or pleasure was to a certain extent justified. For we can no longer supply either the interest of the unexplored, uncivilised regions of the world or the attraction of the great centres of ancient civilisation. For you, therefore, we have neither epic nor historic nor aesthetic appeal. It is perhaps only very recently that Englishmen have begun to find in America something which genuinely excites their interest and curiosity, because there an attempt to meet the extraordinary challenge of these times is being made in a bold and dramatic manner.

It is because of a more constant and voluminous passing to and fro across the Atlantic — Americans coming in large numbers to England and English travelling more and more to the States — that the traditional view of the Englishman's "consciousness of effortless superiority" is becoming more and more a fiction that melts in the presence of fact. It must be confessed that the Englishman is not as a rule an expansive person, certainly not on a moment's notice. To Americans you seem rather thrifty of speech, and an American in your presence soon feels that the enthusiasm so natural to him is regarded as a form of bad manners. But Americans who see you on your own soil soon realise that behind apparent casualness there is an extraordinarily kind and civilised hospitality. Almost invariably this experience of the reality of English life accounts for the warmth of feeling aroused in Americans who come to know you intimately. The American beneficiary of English cordiality and friendliness sings the praises of England and thereby separates himself from his fellow Americans, who have not yet been subjected to your benign treatment. Particularly is this true if the new discoverers of English virtues happen to be men of affairs who, under the stimulus of a good dinner, give free rein to their eloquence in after-dinner speeches. Instead of helping understanding between the two peoples, the total effect often is an increase of suspicion on the part of the mass of Americans as to the subtle designing qualities of our British cousins. Ambassador Page affords a very interesting illustration of this. You took him so thoroughly to your hearts, and he so reciprocated, that unwittingly, quite unwittingly, he did, I believe, on our side on the water much more harm than good to Anglo-American relations by justifying the belief that the English air is inimical to American sturdiness and independence.

More than ever, in the present distracted state of the world, is Anglo-American amity an indispensable condition to civilised peace. However much for the time being we may be preoccupied with domestic questions, there are a few basic problems that are the common concern of mankind, which, unless they are happily resolved, will jeopardise the very national

well-being which is our immediate preoccupation. Accord in aim and attitude on these matters between the English-speaking peoples is, I am sure,
deeply desired by responsible people on both sides of the Atlantic. Such
accord, however, must come from harmony of aim and wise accomodation
of interests and not through the sophisticated construction of artificial diplomatic formulas. In a word, both peoples must be in substantial agreement
about the kind of sane and humane society towards which both of us should
move.

I am not at all sure that the promotion of this end is helped rather
than hindered by such specialized attempts at Anglo-American understanding as are most of the dinners of the Pilgrims. That their intentions are for
the best and with the best motives, I have no doubt. But often in this
world, alas! we defeat our intentions by the way in which we execute them,
and functions like the Pilgrim dinners are apt to fail of their purpose because they leave out of account the stuff out of which has grown the traditional feeling of America towards the English. It is important to realise that
that feeling continues to predominate because the opinions of most Americans about Englishmen and of most Englishmen about Americans are
largely derived at second-hand if not fourth-hand. Despite all the changes,
only a negligible percentage of English and Americans, and not always representative samples, see each other face to face and come to know each
other intimately. In this connection you must remember that regionalism
plays a part with us, as it does with you, only much more so. There have
always been lively currents of intercourse between a highly select class of
Englishmen and their friends on the American seaboard. Englishmen have
intimate connections with New York and Boston, Philadelphia and Washington, and they think they know the United States. Nothing could be
further from the truth. What happens is that members of the same limited
social classes in England and America thereby infect each other with their
social biases instead of serving as agents for the interchange of national
feeling. The story goes that when Mr. Balfour came to the United States in
1917, he asked Colonel House how he might best learn the feelings and
opinions of the great body of the American people. Colonel House is reported to have replied that the quickest way would be to spend a week-end
on fashionable Long Island, and the opposite of what he heard there would
be a good guess at what the American people thought. That is why the
Middle West is such an enigma to Englishmen, because they do not know
the Middle West and get their view about it from American friends in
Boston or New York or Philadelphia, or from the Eastern Press, which also
does not understand the Middle West. Hardly an Englishman ever goes to
Emporia, Kansas, to visit a man like William Allen White of the Emporia
Gazette, and yet that is a far better source of enlightenment on American

feeling than most of the eminent men in New York, who are made to speak for the United States.

The consequences are often very serious. When a leading English statesman, in a speech intended for America, says that even the Middle West ought to be able to understand his argument, is it any wonder that two-thirds of America should again be confirmed in its belief that the English are supercilious and superior? Suppose an American Cabinet officer should say that even Birmingham and Manchester ought to be able to understand. Such an attitude, of course, is born not at all of ill-will, but comes from ignorance about American life. It will bear reiteration that historic experiences leave impressions, biases if you will, and these biases flare up into renewed life when fresh experience seems to reveal a similar attitude.

Therefore it becomes most important to consider how we get the pictures in our minds of one another. Since our ideas about you are so largely formed from the impression you give us about ourselves, I should like to consider the sources of English opinion regarding America. I have already indicated that first-hand knowledge is very restricted, and even where possessed is apt to be fragmentary and unrepresentative. Perhaps that is the fault of our bigness and complexity. The complications of our government, the fact that we have a central government and forty-eight states with their separate governments, make the understanding of our political problems, for instance, very difficult. We cannot complain of that, because the Englishman takes comparatively little interest in the problems of federalism in the Dominions of Canada and Australia. But it does sometimes lead to an almost irritating detachment as to the way in which these queer people, the Americans, are governed. Why can't you have, we are frequently asked, a good cabinet form of government and be done with it? Here again, the Englishman illustrates his intellectual insularity, his lack of curiosity about our history and our difficulties, his failure to realise that to govern a continent is a very different thing from governing a tight little island. After all, the great educational centres are the fountainheads of knowledge, and perhaps it is not merely the vanity of Americans that is surprised to find the deep neglect of the study of American institutions in your universities. A beginning is being made, but only a mild beginning. In saying this, I am not forgetting that one of the best books ever written about the American government was by an Englishman, Lord Bryce, and only the other day another countryman of yours, Mr. D. W. Brogan of the London School of Economics, brought out a penetrating study of my country. Nevertheless, it is true that American history is still very much of a stepchild, and this, I think, largely accounts for the absence of natural centres of correction for wrong and inadequate notions about the United States.

As a result, the vast influence of sectionalism in the whole life of the

United States, cultural and economic as well as political, is something that is very remote from the knowledge of Englishmen. You think of the United States as all of a piece. In fact, however, apart from the great differences between the metropolitan areas and the countryside, the United States is a confederation of great regions. About the industrial and financial East there is a deal of knowledge among you, but very little, on the whole, of the feelings and sensibilities, the outlook and the interests of the South, the Middle West and the Pacific Coast. You learn about those places and those people largely through the distortions of the movies, and so romance and riot are your dominant impressions. While all of you know about Al Capone, probably not one in ten thousand has heard of Jane Addams. Yet Jane Addams is at least as significant of America as was Al Capone.

This is where the Press comes in. I am not criticising; I am reporting. It is a fact that your normal flow of news from the United States is through New York and Washington. Now, in many ways, New York is least representative of the currents of the United States. Washington is, of course, the political centre of the nation, but the currents of the country are only registered in Washington and not set up there. What the "folks back home" think and feel can hardly be known, therefore, through the clicking of a typewriter either in New York or Washington. When the Middle West or South breaks into print for you, it is usually because of some sensational murder or horrible lynching or some prison riot not unlike the one at Dartmoor. What is needed is that the exciting and violent and incomprehensible aspects of American life should be subjected against the background of the everyday, familiar, normal ways of life of 130,000,000 people in the setting of the varied circumstances of a continent. I know that the familiar is not news. A great American editor once said, "When a dog bites a man, that's not news; when a man bites a dog, that's news." But what is the everyday in the United States, so familiar that it is taken for granted, is quite unfamiliar to you, and so could be made news, but that means tapping the centres of life beyond the Atlantic seaboard. The surviving historical fictions and feelings on your side will gradually be displaced only if through the Press and over the wireless, through school histories and through personal contact, there is built up a sense and a feeling of what America — its vast, sprawling, groping civilisation — is like. Then, though you will find that the Americans have their oddities and eccentricities and enough of violence and intensity both to thrill and puzzle you, you will also come to see these excesses in the perspective of the whole, and you will find that the community between your people and ours is ever so much greater than our differences. Not that I should wish to minimise the differences. But you would understand our differences better and enjoy them more, and we should feel that you did enjoy them, or at least were pleasantly amused by them, and did not merely look at them with indifference or with chilly disapproval.

And now I must bring to a close what has been an uncongenial task. For implied in the invitation to tell you how you seem to Americans was the suggestion that I deal with only part of the truth, and the lesser part, namely, the faults that Americans see in you. It would have been so much easier, and more sympathetic to my feeling, to have enlarged upon your virtues. But it is not the least of your qualities that you would have been more displeased had I described to you the virtues you possess instead of attempting to indicate some of the faults that you do now know you have.

Radiogram to Roosevelt

Oxford, England, March 20, 1934

IF JUDGE COLEMAN'S SUCCESSOR BE REPUBLICAN HOPE YOU WILL PERSUADE TOM THACHER TO RETURN TO BENCH ON WHICH HE WAS SO GOOD.

FELIX FRANKFURTER

Thomas D. Thacher, a Republican, was appointed by Coolidge in 1925 as a federal judge in the Southern District of New York. He was Solicitor General in the latter years of the Hoover Administration. From 1943-1948, he was a judge of the New York State Court of Appeals.

Paris, enroute to Palestine, March 22, 1934

Dear Mr. President:

1. Today's papers bring me the first news of your appointment of George Messersmith to Vienna. Please accept my warm congratulations on this appointment. I do not know Messersmith personally, but everything one hears about him makes one confident that he will bring the good sense and courage so much needed at our Legation in Vienna in the days that are ahead.

2. I'm watching with the utmost concern, but also with sure confidence, your intervention in the threatened auto strikes. I assume that you will ask both sides to submit to an Australian ballot vote as to the men's desires. I do not see how the companies can refuse an uncoerced and even uncensored choice of the men as to the form of their collective association. I saw you handle the recalcitrant element in the coal strike situation — and that makes me sure you will triumph in this obstinate conflict, and thereby you will accomplish more, for the country's future, than merely avoid a bitter industrial struggle.

My best and prayerful good wishes.

Always yours,

FELIX FRANKFURTER

P.S.   I'm glad to see the railroad danger is averted. Good!

The White House, March 24, 1934

Dear Felix:

So many things have happened during the past month that I have not had a moment to write you, but I do appreciate everything that you send me.

On the District Court in New York in place of Judge Coleman I want to put a Democrat because Judge Knox is the only Democrat on that bench at the present time. There are great difficulties as you know on account of the thoroughly unsettled political conditions in that party in the city. The old leadership is gradually being eliminated, though I cannot say much for the new leadership. At least we have rid ourselves of Theopel in Queens, McCooey is dead, and Kings is under a triumvirate; and the Manhattan situation is crystallizing towards the removal of Curry.

The scattered forces of the opposition seized on the loss of life among the Army fliers to come together and make a concerted drive. For the last three weeks we have been under very heavy bombardment. The steel crowd have shown their teeth, the aviation companies have been shrieking to high heaven, using Chambers of Commerce and every small community with a flying field to demand the return of their contracts, the automobile companies are, at this writing, still trying to flout the provisions for collective bargaining, the bigger bankers are still withholding credits at every possible opportunity, the Republican politicians like Fess and Robinson and Fish are denouncing me as a murderer, and the old line press harps increasingly on state socialism and demands the return to the good old days.

As a matter of actual fact, however, I am inclined to think that most of our legislation will go through, that the agricultural and industrial and business situation still continues to improve and that this major offensive on the part of the enemy will fail just as the one last Autumn failed.

I will not burden you with details for I know that you can discriminate, even when you read the New York *Times*, between the true and the false. I am by no means discouraged, though the work during the past month has been just as difficult and the hours just as long as in the days of March and April, 1933.

Just to prove that I am not afraid of the big bad wolf, I hope to get off next Tuesday for a full week on the Nourmahal in the Bahamas.

As ever yours,
F.D.R.

John F. Curry was the boss of Tammany in New York.
Some army fliers, flying the mail shipments, crashed and were killed, thus reopening the controversy over the cancellation of the mail contracts.

Jerusalem, April 14, 1934

Dear Mr. President,

You may be interested in this bit of fiscal wisdom from the East.

This is a most exciting land — its beauty is magical and the achievements of the Jewish renaissance almost incredible. Someday I should like to tell you about it all, and when you are through with the White House, in 1941, you must journey to Palestine.

The news that trickles hither from the United States sounds good, above all that you had a decent vacation.

With warmest regards,

Ever yours,
F.F.

'ECONOMY CUT'
Indian Murders Too Expensive Wife

Allahabad — Because he regarded his wife as far too fashionable in dress and much too fond of cinemas, an employee of the Government Press at Allahabad chopped her head off.

He told the police that he had done this because he could no longer afford to keep her.

Oxford, England, April 23, 1934

Dear Mr. President:

1. On my return from Palestine, I find your letter of March 24th.

That you should find time to write me in the midst of all the burdens that rested on you during March is, indeed, very generous of you and a new confirmation of the buoyancy of your spirit. Of course I have been following home affairs as best one can by reading about five American dailies and therefore have some notion of the concerted drive that was made against you by all the old crowd, now that they have gained their second wind and are out of the storm cellar. There never was a more perfect illustration of "the devil is sick," etc. Those in the seats of ultimate financial and business power seem literally to have learned nothing. For, as you say, what they really want and expect, now that for them, as they think, the little storm has blown over, is "the return to the good old days."

Since early youth, I have wasted endless time as an inveterate newspaper reader. But one thing I think I have gained therefrom, and that is some talent for reading between the lines. Despite all the shrieking of the *Herald Tribune* and the subtler hostility of the New York *Times* and the echoes of Wall Street in the New York cables in the London press, one transcending fact emerges, namely, the permeating confidence of the American people in you and your capacity to mobilize it, on essential issues, whenever you choose to appeal to their good will and their good sense in support of effective measures towards the decent and humane society for which we are aiming. All the factitious supporters were bound to melt away: those who pretended support through fear or hoped to win your favor through blandishments. I ventured to say something about this in a letter I wrote you from the boat last September. It was then clear that the Ogden Millses and their journalistic allies and the unregenerate men in control of finance and industry and their Chamber of Commerce façades would come into the open as soon as they dared. No one, I suspect, knows better than you that reliance upon them was like reliance upon enemies of all the things that you really care about.

I am not the son of a prophet and certainly not a prophet. But it required no powers of clairvoyance for me to say, as I said to a number of people when they told me how big business and finance and the Republicans were all behind you, that at the very first sign of a real challenge by you of those vested interests and those abuses of power which really brought about the depression, you would be resisted and eventually personally assailed even more than was Theodore Roosevelt thirty years ago. And for the same reason as that which made all that crowd so bitterly and fiercely try to thwart your nomination at Chicago. From their point of view they know very well what they are doing. But there can be no doubt that your courage and your determination for a New Deal can confidently draw upon the support of the great body of the American people.

2. Judging from Willmot Lewis's cabled comments from American papers on the British budget you must have been seeing, without being impressed by it, a good deal of bunk regarding that budget. In some quarters a budget is wonderful if it reduces taxes, no matter how unwisely or unfairly. The first day's shouting over the budget is gradually subsiding even here and its true implications are becoming better understood. In this connection you may be interested in the enclosed analysis of the meaning of Chamberlain's budget, and I call your particular attention to the last paragraph.

3. I wrote you a line from Palestine indicating the magic that that country exercised over both my wife and me and the wonders that are being achieved there. When I'll see you I shall also want to talk to you about some of the neglect of American interests in Palestine. As an illustration, it will interest you to know that while America is the third largest exporter into Palestine (only Great Britain and neighboring Egypt excel us) at the very important Levant Fair now taking place at Tel-Aviv, which is really a fair for the whole Near East, there is no American building, although small countries with much smaller financial interest than ours, like Sweden and

Bulgaria and Czecho-Slovakia, have very nice exhibits. I had a good talk about this matter with our new Consul General in Jerusalem, Ely Palmer, and he is as mystified as I am by our absence at that Fair. And there are other aspects of this whole business which I shall venture to put to you when in good time I shall again see you.

　　With all good wishes,

Always faithfully yours,
F.F.

For two widely different reasons, this letter is significant as a pointer to future events. It shows that Frankfurter, at this formative stage of the New Deal, wanted Roosevelt to proceed vigorously with his policies of reform instead of seeking a truce with business leaders already hostile to his Administration. Secondly, the references to Palestine indicate that Roosevelt's own sympathies were not always reflected in the actions of the State Department. This conflict was to have serious results during the long and often unsuccessful campaign to apply a more generous policy on the admission of refugees to the United States, and to urge Britain as the Mandatory Power to open the gates in Palestine.

Oxford, England, May 7, 1934

Dear Mr. President:

　　1. Keynes is shortly leaving for America (confidentially, to receive an honorary degree from Columbia), and he is planning a week's visit to Washington. I am giving him a note to Miss LeHand in the hope that it may be possible for you to find time to see him. He is really devoted to your efforts and perhaps the single most powerful supporter of the New Deal in England. Not only does he wield a trenchant economic pen. As the head of an important insurance company, he exercises considerable influence in the City. Wall Street knows that and various Wall Street correspondents of his are seeking to reach his mind, with all the misrepresentations of which lower New York has such mastery. Therefore I believe it to be doubly important that he hear about the Administration's efforts and purposes at first hand, because during his stay in New York every effort will be made to fill him with poison. But he is no man's fool, and is on his guard.

　　Keynes is accompanied by his very charming wife, Lydia Lopokova, the famous dancer and actress. But I do not know whether she is to go to Washington with him.

　　2. Your extemporaneous speech at the Department of Commerce seemed to me especially felicitous, and more than that. It put in admirably forthright language the hopes and the purposes that you represent. No one knows better than you the need and the difficulties of political education.

To talk too often lessens the impact; not to talk enough creates a vacuum in the public mind, into which flow all too easily the kind of childish imbecilities and shrewdly promoted fears illustrated by the incredible Wirt-Rand statements. I venture to say, however, that particularly in these restless days, in which foolishness and fanaticism and self-interest are exploited by professional poisoners of the public mind, by the Ivy Lees and the Bernays, it becomes even more important than it was in the days of T.R. and Woodrow Wilson for the President to do what you are able to do with such extraordinary effectiveness, namely, to give guidance to the public in order to rally them to the general national interest. And I take it that's necessary not only for the public but also on behalf of the individual legislator, who is pounded so vigorously by the powerful resources at the disposal of selfish interests.

3. This morning's cable brings a good illustration of your power of speech, of saying the things that need to be said in order to sweep away all the miasma of nonsense and selfishness which tends to poison the public mind and to enfeeble its will. I mean your letter to the National Chamber of Commerce with its sharp challenge to business to "stop crying 'Wolf' and to cooperate in working for recovery and for the continued elimination of the evil conditions of the past."

4. There are a thousand things I would like to talk with you about, among others about the mischief that the Nazis are trying to promote all over the world. The Palestine Government found that the Nazis were pouring in "literature" to stir up the Arabs, and Sir Arthur Salter, who is just back from China, tells me astonishing experiences that he had there of Nazi tactics.

With warm regards and good wishes,

Faithfully yours,
F.F.

James H. Rand, Jr., of Remington-Rand, and Chairman of the Committee for the Nation, accused Roosevelt of trying to push the country "from democracy to communism." He supported this charge with a memorandum prepared by Dr. William A. Wirt, former Superintendent of Schools in Gary, Indiana, and an active monetary reformer of an eccentric kind.

Ivy Lee was the publicity agent for the House of Morgan, and Bernays was a public relations expert with clients hostile to Roosevelt.

Oxford, England, May 7, 1934

Dear Miss LeHand:

As you probably know, I wrote to the President of Mr. Keynes' forthcoming visit to the United States, and I have suggested to Mr. Keynes that he send this note to you, giving his available time in Washington, so that if possible for the President he may arrange to see him.

Very truly yours,

FELIX FRANKFURTER

The following was found attached to the above letter in F.D.R.'s files.

Missy:

I want to see him and get him in some time at tea alone. When you get ahold of Keynes, ask him to bring his wife.

F.D.R.

Radiogram to Roosevelt

Oxford, England, May 8, 1934

ARTHUR HENDERSON ASKED ME EXPRESS TO YOU QUITE INFORMALLY STRONG HOPE THAT NORMAN DAVIS WILL BE PRESENT AT OPENING FORTHCOMING DISARMAMENT CONFERENCE. HENDERSON BELIEVES OPENING DAYS VITAL MAKE OR BREAK CONFERENCE AND THEREFORE DAVIS PRESENCE MOST IMPORTANT.

FELIX FRANKFURTER

Arthur Henderson was the British Labour party's spokesman on foreign policy. Norman Davis was the President's representative in the disarmament negotiations.

Oxford, England, May 8, 1934

Dear Mr. President:

1. The Hon. Mrs. Phillimore, daughter-in-law of the late Lord Phillimore, is a common friend of Arthur Henderson's and mine. The other day she phoned me from London to say that Arthur Henderson was most anxious to see me on a matter of great public importance. As a result, I had dinner and a long evening with him last night, the upshot of which was my last night's cable to you. In view of Henderson's strong feeling on the subject, I felt that you would want me to be a conduit of his message, even though I was quite ignorant of the background of the situation in your mind regarding the Geneva Conference and America's relation to it.

Henderson is really one of the finest characters in English public life — completely disinterested, completely devoted to the things of ultimate worth in society. He is a simple, religious nature, but also a great organizer, the real architect of the Labour Party, and because of his character a man of the widest influence among the rank and file of the people. I cannot but think that it would have made a difference to the peace of the world if Henderson instead of Simon had been at the Foreign Office the last few years. Henderson has not been wholly well, as you know, and his doctor is urging him to go off before very long. There is a chance that he may be visiting America. You would, I am sure, like him much. May I tell him that you would be glad to see him if he comes to America?

2. Unless through your publishers or otherwise you have seen them, I think you may want to see the enclosed reviews of your book (which is receiving the widest attention here) from *The Times*, the *Post*, Lord Eustace Percy and Harold Laski. It is indeed astonishing to have the Tory *Post* say the things they are saying about the book and about you, but still more extraordinary to have the *Post* and Harold Laski say so much in common in admiration of your achievement.

3. You may be interested in the enclosed leader from *The Times* on "The Mind of Germany," which I suspect is by Ebbutt, their Berlin correspondent, an especially acute observer and interpreter of the Nazi regime.

4. The cables seem to indicate the passage of the Tariff Bill. It was really daring of you to ask Congress for such authority. It again proves the response that real leadership evokes. Incidentally, what a different thing democratic leadership is from *Führer Prinzip*. The cables also indicate that you are getting a stock exchange control act with a good set of teeth. Every bit of evidence that comes this way shows that in the totality, things are certainly on the mend.

Always faithfully yours,
F.F.

Arthur Henderson was one of the many leaders of the Labour party who refused to follow Ramsay MacDonald into Britain's national government. He thought the failure of the floundering Disarmament Conference in Geneva would deepen the depression by diverting scarce funds into a ruinous arms race. In addition, he predicted that the failure to achieve an agreement on disarmament would give frenzied nationalism in Germany its chance — a prophetic judgment on Nazi policies. Oblivious to these deeper trends in Europe, and quietly sabotaging the League of Nations, Sir John Simon at the Foreign Office used his matchless forensic gifts in finding the best arguments for a bad cause instead of seeking a fresh approach for the solution of festering evils.

The favorable book reviews were of Roosevelt's book On Our Way, *setting forth the principles of his Administration.*

Bloomsbury, England, May 15, 1934

Dear Miss LeHand,

On Prof. Felix Frankfurter's advice I venture to forward you this letter of his immediately on my arrival in New York. I expect to remain in the United States for about 3 weeks. I have it in mind to proceed to Washingtcn on May 23 for about a week; but I could arrange my visit equally well for any date up to about a week later.

Yours very truly,
J. M. KEYNES

Telegram to J. M. Keynes

The White House, May 21, 1934

PLEASE COMMUNICATE WITH ME OR MY OFFICE ON ARRIVAL WASHINGTON. WILL BE GLAD TO ARRANGE TEA APPOINTMENT FOR YOURSELF AND MRS. KEYNES AT WHITE HOUSE.

M. H. McINTYRE

Telegram to M. H. McIntyre

New York, New York, May 23, 1934

THANKS FOR YOUR WIRE. ARRIVING WASHINGTON THURSDAY EVENING. AT PRESIDENT'S DISPOSAL ANY TIME BUT FIRST HALF NEXT WEEK PARTICULARLY CONVENIENT. STAYING AT MAYFLOWER.

J. M. KEYNES

THE MAYFLOWER

Washington, D.C., May 25, 1934

Dear Mr. MacIntyre,

I have now arrived in Washington and am settled in this hotel. If you have any news for me from the President, I should be grateful if you would telephone it here (Ext. 437).

Yours truly,
J. M. KEYNES

Oxford, England, May 18, 1934

Dear Mr. President:

1. Lewis Einstein tells me that Homer Cummings is a friend of his and has been wanting to arrange, through Secretary Hull, who is also acquainted with Einstein, a talk for Einstein with you. Einstein, as you know, was for a number of years Minister to Czechoslovakia. He really is a scholarly gentleman and I believe is especially informed about central European affairs and the Nazi influences upon the general European disequilibrium of the moment. Einstein is a man of means and I believe quite disinterested. I merely write to say that while my acquaintance with him is not intimate, I know about him very intimately through Mr. Justice Holmes, and I do know that Holmes holds Einstein in very high esteem indeed. They have been friends for a very long time. I ought to add that Einstein is not seeking any position, cares for no post or title, but he may, because of

his background of knowledge and wide sources of information on the Continent, be of some use to the Administration as a source of knowledge.

2. I have heard both from Sir Stafford and Lady Cripps of the very generous effort you made to see them during their recent trip to the States. They were immensely touched by your manifestation of friendliness and the unusual resourcefulness on the part of the very busy head of a great state to try to see a couple of visitors without any official responsibility. I told them it was just like you.

3. I enclose herewith the full text of a leader from *The Times*, of which you doubtless have seen extracts. You will agree, I think, that it shows not a little understanding, on the part of the *editors* of *The Times* at least, of your problem. I have been seeing not a little of editors of some of the leading papers and other influential molders of opinion on this side, having reached the conclusion that it is much more important, because much more lasting, to educate their minds for a continuous understanding of your aims and methods and the problems of our country, so that right views and understanding will be generated by them, rather than attempt to write what would inevitably be regarded as partisan articles by a partisan of the Administration. To that end also I have been doing a good deal of informal talking in small clubs and groups and in the common rooms of the various colleges here, at Cambridge and in London.

4. You will be interested, I think, in the full text, if you have not already seen it, of the impressive letter which the Archbishop of Canterbury wrote to *The Times* the other day.

5. When I read some of the utterances of the so-called leaders of bar and business, I just wonder if the depression has taught them anything. A striking and representative sample is furnished by Silas Strawn's speech, of which I have just read the full text, before the Chamber of Commerce. The emergency is over, he announces, though he hasn't the decency to say that you pulled them out of their sloughs of despond; and since the emergency is over, let's go back to the good old days, for, as he says, "the temporary maladjustments" of the traditional system of the glorious Harding-Coolidge-Hoover era have been corrected, and now we can go back to those glorious days. Apparently our national economic system, as it was before the depression, was like a beautiful Bechstein or Steinway piano, which through excessive playing had two or three of its keys duller, and so the piano tuner, Roosevelt, was called in. But now that he has tuned the piano, that beautiful instrument is just as it was before. It really would be funny if it were not so sad. They really are Tories; they learn nothing and forget nothing. I wish I had time to dig out the utterances from the same and similar sources as those which are now expressing themselves so violently and so sanctimoni-

ously against your policies, uttered against T.R. when he proposed such bolshevist legislation as the Hepburn Act and the control of pipe lines, and later the attacks by leaders of the bar and finance against Hughes' proposals in New York for a Public Service Law, and still later, what you so well remember, the outcry against Wilson regarding the Federal Reserve Act. How the whole United States was going to the dogs because of that measure. I think I am right in remembering that the American Bankers Association, with only a single dissenting vote, passed resolutions against it. No doubt about it, the real trouble with capitalism is the capitalists.

I infer you've had your hands full with the silver people, but this morning's dispatches seem to indicate that you have worked out a *modus vivendi* to save us from financial foolishness.

With warmest regards and good wishes,

Always faithfully yours,
FELIX FRANKFURTER

At this time Sir Stafford Cripps, a leader at the British bar, had not yet fully emerged as an acknowledged leader of the left wing of the Labour party; but he was consolidating his political influence, and becoming steadily more active as the ominous drift toward dictatorships spread over Europe.

Henry I. Harriman, president of the Chamber of Commerce, became a shrill critic of the New Deal, and his standing in the business world rose as his shrillness increased.

Memorandum for Rex Tugwell, Assistant Secretary of Agriculture
May 28, 1934

I think you will be interested in this letter from Felix — especially paragraph five.

The last portion of that paragraph suggests an interesting thought. Do you think you could get someone to dig up the expressions and utterances made against T.R., Chas. E. Hughes, and Woodrow Wilson, when they were trying to get through their exceedingly mild type of legislation?

Will you let me have this letter back.

F.D.R.

Radiogram to Roosevelt
Oxford, England, May 15, 1934

WARMEST CONGRATULATIONS ON HOUSING MESSAGE. SURELY LARGE HOUSING PROGRAMME POWERFUL FACTOR FOR SECURING AND MAINTAINING RECOVERY.

FELIX FRANKFURTER

Oxford, England, May 23, 1934

Dear Mr. President:

What follows has relevance only if you have not yet filled the new commissionerships created by the final form in which the Stock Exchange Control Bills will come out of conference. Not that I shall tell you anything that you don't know. But it has been my business to study closely for more than twenty years the work of regulatory bodies both national and state, and perhaps you will forgive me some general observations.

No one knows better than you that in the last analysis legislation means predominantly administration. Pendergast is a good shorthand name for that truth, and a whole chapter could be written about the paralysis of the Federal Power Commission until your Presidency. The recent Supreme Court decision in the Chicago *Telephone* case is a dramatic illustration of what unaggressive and unresourceful regulation means, in dollars and cents and well-being, to the ordinary man and woman. More than $20,-000,000 would have been unjustly taken from the telephone users of Chicago through the hocus-pocus of corporate accountancy, but for the pertinacious and powerful fight, on behalf of the public, by one of the lawyers of the public, against whom were thrown all the obstacles that usually wear men down. The lack of moral zeal and intellectual capacity to meet the powerful resources on the other side on the part of public service commissioners throughout the country have, without a doubt, led not only to unfair charges to consumers but, what is worse, have been responsible for the grave abuses in the capitalization of public service enterprise and for the building up of concentrated financial power to thwart the public interest.

Now the administration of the Stock Exchange Act will, I am sure, be even more difficult and call for greater skill, resourcefulness, firmness as well as fairness of temper, a will not worn down by fatigue, than has been the work of the older regulatory commissions. The problems are more subtle, the abuses less obvious, the public more misleadable and the consequences of non-action more far-reaching. What will matter most to Wall Street indeed is what the Commission will refrain from doing, in view of what the law might enable a courageous and knowing commission to do. I don't know, of course, what the final terms of the Act will be, but I do know that the extent and effectiveness of the powers conferred by the legislation will depend largely upon the understanding of the possibilities under the statute by those charged with its administration.

And what is involved is not merely the Stock Exchange Control Act. Nothing less is involved than to keep Wall Street in its place, to furnish a counterpoise against its aggrandisement of power, by which the Street all along the line resists efforts by the government for the common interest. And so, plainly, you need administrators who are equipped to meet the best legal brains whom Wall Street always has at its disposal, who have stamina and do not weary of the fight, who are moved neither by blandishments nor fears, who, in a word, unite public zeal with unusual capacity.

To turn to a totally different matter — Sir John Simon's conduct of foreign relations. If you have not seen it, you may be interested in the enclosed account of a recent speech by Lord Lytton on the British Government's policy towards Japan.

Always with warm regards.

Faithfully yours,
FELIX FRANKFURTER

One of the stiffest fights waged by Roosevelt while Governor of New York had been against the Pendergast philosophy in the management of public power utilities. Under that philosophy the authority of the regulatory body was usually exercised in a supine fashion, as if the officials were more eager to avoid giving offense to the private utilities than they were to protect the public interest.

Lord Lytton, whose support of collective security contrasted sharply with Sir John Simon's lack of faith in the League system, had accused the British government of encouraging Japanese aggression against China.

Oxford, England, June 8, 1934

My dear Mr. President:

This is a brief note of commiseration and congratulation.

No American can fail to identify himself with the proportions of the tragedy that the drought is apparently assuming. Nature is still wilful and her blight beyond man's control, but not the consequences of nature's cruelties, and so it is a source of the utmost consolation to know that your courage and resourcefulness and, above all, your propelling humanity is at the helm to relieve the suffering from the disaster and stay as far as may be its course.

The passage of the Stock Exchange Control and Tariff Acts must be, as it should be, fraught with the greatest satisfaction to you. Oxford is a long way from Wall Street, but even at this distance one cannot escape knowledge of the powerful forces that were enlisted against you and your effort to domesticate abuses and excesses of financial power, which far too long have had full play. The Tariff Act is a fine vindication of your daring in a field which hitherto had been blotched by the most tenacious of selfish interests. It's a great thing to have achieved this grant of power, even though the misdeeds of Republican legislation and economic policy have made the exercise of this power, I suspect, extraordinarily difficult.

My time here is soon coming to an end. We are sailing back to Boston on June 30.

With warm regards,

Always faithfully yours,
F.F.

J. M. Keynes in a letter just received — writes me:

"I had an hour's tête-à-tête with the President which was fascinating and illuminating."

The White House, June 11, 1934

Dear Felix:

I had a grand talk with Keynes and liked him immensely.

The end of the Congressional grind is in sight and then I shall make a number of appointments to the new Commissions and set sail for the tropics.

I had a most satisfactory talk with Justice Brandeis before he left. He has and is a "great soul."

I hear you will get back about the seventeenth of July. When I return, about two weeks later, you and your better half must run down to Washington as soon as possible.

As ever yours,
F.D.R.

P.S.   If Henderson comes tell him I count on seeing him. Is there any chance of Morrison coming over too?

Arthur Henderson and Herbert Morrison were two recognized and respected leaders of the British Labour party.

As the next letter from Tom Corcoran and Ben Cohen reveals, serious differences on policy objectives had arisen in the inner circle of the President's advisers as early as the summer of 1934. These differences were not easily harmonized in the compromises of final policy, and they explain the shifts and turns in the President's thinking. As the depression and the drought showed no signs of going away, and as the early hopes of recovery by tinkering with the price of gold and using other monetary gadgets slowly faded into disenchantment, the New Deal lurched forward into a new phase. Roosevelt began to plan the outlines of a new program whose emphasis would fall on unemployment compensation and social security.

The group led by Rex Tugwell was in favor of social insurance but it was fearful that the new approach would divert attention from the task of purg-

ing the economic system of its deep-rooted inequities and inefficiencies. The group which followed Raymond Moley wanted the President to avoid a frontal assault on the prejudices and loyalties of the business community, to be flexible and pragmatic in his approach, and to remain aloof from special pleaders hawking their own brand of economic salvation. Brandeis thought the business leaders would accept neither economic reform nor social security unless they felt the constant goad of Presidential initiative on their reluctant backs. Frankfurter, agreeing with Brandeis, joined this controversy on his return from Oxford, finding resourceful and accomplished allies in Cohen and Corcoran.

Roosevelt in his first year in office had decided that there could be no recovery without reform. This decision had disappointed and angered his business critics, who thought he was slowing up the process of recovery by dividing the country with controversial measures of reform. Instead of retreating, Roosevelt attacked. The new watchwords were to be recovery, reform, security. The agenda of battle for the next ten years was ready.

This letter, one of many, is included to show the close working relationship between Frankfurter and Thomas G. Corcoran and Benjamin V. Cohen in the history of the New Deal. Frankfurter was preparing to return from his months at Oxford. The letter was written by Tom but signed by both Ben and Tom.

Washington, D.C., June 18, 1934

Dear F.F.:

(1) It's very difficult to map out just what you'd expect to do on getting home. The Skipper — knows when you're coming back — he will sail from Annapolis sometime late in June, probably the 26th, for a trip to Hawaii, back to the West Coast and then across country to Washington. He'll be gone "approximately thirty days," i.e. until at least August 1st, probably until August 15th. He might, of course, invite you to meet him in Seattle before he makes any speeches on the way home. Ray is writing the speeches. Or in the many other ways you know of making contact, you may be able to have an immediate influence on any planning made known to the public during the period before the return to Washington.

(2) The most important consideration, however, is that (no matter whether you are in touch during the vacation) before the Skipper's return you have adequate time and be sufficiently re-orientated in this peculiar atmosphere to be able to advise concretely. Much has gone over the dam since you went away and affairs have proceeded pretty far toward concrete forks in the road. The Tugwell crowd has been pushed by its enemies — and its own loose talk — away over to the left. Ray is vacillating consider-

ably toward the right. Isaiah is militant and impatient in the middle. You'll need, we should think, considerable detailed knowledge of what has gone on just to listen understandingly.

(3) A most important concrete way in which you can help tremendously prior to the return is as an adviser or possibly a member of an informal group being formed to work out the social insurance plan talked about in the last message. So far as we know, Ben and I are to be in that group — and possibly Paul Raushenbush. But there will also be Gerard Swope, Raskob and a lot more of that stripe, besides possibly some of the Epstein crowd who will be thoroughly and inpracticably wild. (They did their bit toward the shelving of Isaiah's unemployment insurance bill at this session as too tame.) So much turns on the performance of that group, now that the plan yet to be formulated is a political issue, that it's hard to overestimate its importance and the necessity that the Skipper be warned against making sweeping premature commitments in the course of his trip which may prejudice the working out of a sound scheme.

(4) With Ray's help we managed to have the President call in Isaiah on Isaiah's last day here, to discuss the social insurance message before it became public (although it had already been put in final form and had gone to Congress). They had an hour and a quarter of uninterrupted discussion during which they branched off into other things. Isaiah did not like the scheme in the Skipper's mind because it left administration completely in the Federal Government as opposed to the States. The Skipper gave the impression that there was nothing as yet cut and dried about the scheme and that it was all in the making. Our last information on the subject was from Ray Moley who told us that an informal committee was to be formed and that I would be secretary, "legman," and coordinator of the committee. I talked to him about your being on the committee and he thought it was a very good idea to take you in. (I don't yet know whether he did or what the Skipper's reaction was.)

I should say, therefore, that you would wisely plan to be able to participate on a really important scale in the formulation of the insurance program when you return and anticipate a couple of weeks of going over details of other programs with some of the crowd down here.

(5) You might also wisely begin a heavy campaign of picking up relations with Ray and Jerry Frank. The enclosed clipping about Ray is partly right and partly over-done. He is really important and you're going to find yourself strangely straddled between Isaiah on one side who wants to ride ahead hard with his full program, completely contemptuous of political obstacles — and Ray on the other side, who is afraid of Isaiah's belligerence, quite through with the agony and sweat of reforming, and wearily eager to settle down to a false security of sweet reasonableness. If you have

followed Ray's editorials lately, you have some feel of where he's going. He also made the mistake this month of becoming receiver of the Hotel St. Regis, representing Astor in a business way. And he's been possibly a little too close to Barney Baruch. He seems too willing to depend upon private contributions from Barney to finance this social insurance preliminary and to finance the continuance of the Pecora Investigation rather than fight Senator Jimmy Byrnes for an appropriation. He's also, for instance, taking a little to bawling us out for making things hard for him and pushing him to go to bat on matters connected with the Stock Exchange Commission and the Securities Act. Part of this I think is due to the fact that he's tired. Part is due to an over-concern with the politics of the fall elections. I do think you had better begin to contact him pretty assiduously ahead of your return to make sure that you'll be in the old position of being able to do a really good job on him when you return.

The personal relations of Ray and ourselves with the Jerry Frank group are also very unfortunate right now. Ray attacked Jerry in *Today*. Jerry blames us — particularly me — because we're so close to Ray. Gardner Jackson drunk hasn't helped. Jerry and ourselves have smoothed things over. Jerry and Ray haven't. If that can be smoothed out only you can do it. You'll have to assume that Jerry is still somewhat suspicious of us and will be suspicious of you, although very anxious to have you as an ally because he fully realizes the inherent weakness of his and Rex's position. Possibly you had better begin precontacting him also. There are many strained relationships under the surface of things not frankly admitted that only you have a sufficiently universal esteem to harmonize.

(6) Your Stock Exchange congratulations are premature — wait until we see the make-up of the Commission.

Our best to the Lady.

So, so glad you're coming home.

Yours,
TOM
BEN

Paul A. Raushenbush had helped to prepare Wisconsin's system of unemployment compensation. Gerard Swope and John J. Raskob were already moving slowly from their early support of Roosevelt to their later opposition. They were very energetic in organizing the opposition of big business to Roosevelt.

Abraham Epstein was executive secretary of the American Association for Old Age Security.

Jerome Frank, fired from the Agricultural Adjustment Agency by Henry Wallace in 1935, was able to turn with unabated conviction to the prob-

lems of social security on which he had a carefully thought-out liberal
philosophy. Gardner ("Pat") Jackson, a friend of Frankfurter's from Sacco-
Vanzetti days, was a generous-minded, humanitarian reformer; he too was a
casualty of the AAA "purge" of 1935.

In all these discussions, the influence of Brandeis and Frankfurter was
of central importance. Raushenbush was married to Brandeis's daughter
Elizabeth, and strategy meetings and drafting sessions were often held in
Brandeis's apartment, with Frankfurter present and very active.

Oxford, England, June 22, 1934

Dear Colonel Early:

First of all, let me ask your forgiveness in never having acknowledged
the materials you sent me regarding the various activities of some of the
leading agencies of this Administration. These came just as I started on a
trip to Palestine at Easter time. I should of course have acknowledged your
kindness in having got this material together.

But please be assured that the labor in collecting the material was not,
I believe, unprofitably invested. After considerable thought and consultation with those whose judgment I most value regarding English opinion, I
concluded that the most effective way of enlightening English opinion was
not for me to write articles but to educate the sources of English opinion
through intimate private talks in order that the current of comment on
American affairs by English editors be intelligent and friendly. This is what
I have done, and there has been ample opportunity for doing it. I have had
numerous talks with the editors of leading papers, as well as of the English
weeklies. Of course I do not mean to say that there has not been done
valuable educational work by others, but I have had the opportunities of
extensive and detailed exposition of the Administration's efforts both in its
separate parts and in their interrelations. And these talks have been reflected, as I know, in leading articles, and what is no less important in this
country, because of its size and homogeneity, through the medium of influential conversations by those whose opinions carry weight. It has seemed to
me most important to get Englishmen of authority to understand, to write
and to speak rather than to have the appearance of partisanship by a de
voted friend of the Administration.

I enclose the leading article in *The Times*, summarizing the President's relations with the 73d Congress, but in fact of course, serving as a
good résumé of the President's work to date. This, if you have not already
seen it, will serve as a good sample of the kind of steady educational work
whereby the most powerful English newspaper has come to be perceptive
of and friendly to the tasks that have confronted the President and the high
endeavor and achievement with which he has met those tasks. Similar un-

derstanding has been reflected in the editorials from time to time in the Manchester *Guardian*, the *Observer*, and even the *Morning Post* and in the various weeklies, the *New Statesman, Time and Tide*, the *Economist*, etc. And the speeches of public men, both in and out of Parliament, likewise prove the large and growing body of opinion in the country which both understands and is deeply sympathetic with the directions and accomplishments of the Administration. Barring a few public addresses before university audiences and the Royal Institute of International Affairs and suchlike learned bodies, it seemed to me that whatever I could do to bring understanding here, I could best do in the way in which I have tried to do it.

You must have all had a gruelling time during the last few months, and the vacation comes to you as an exceedingly well earned relief and reward and as refreshment for the heavy days that are still ahead.

Very cordially yours,
FELIX FRANKFURTER

Success and Frustration

July 1934 – December 1935

1934

July 25 — Assassination of Chancellor Dolfuss of Austria and abortive Nazi revolt against Austrian government.

October 9 — Assassination in Marseilles of King Alexander of Yugoslavia and Foreign Minister Barthou of France.

1935

January 7 — France and Italy adjust their conflicting aims in Africa.

February 1 — Anglo-French Conference on German problem begins.

April 11 — At the Stressa Conference, Britain, France and Italy establish a common front for dealing with Germany's claims.

May 2 — Franco-Russian alliance against unprovoked aggression.

May 6 —
May 9 — Silver jubilee in London of King George V.

June 7 — Stanley Baldwin, the Conservative leader, replaces Ramsay MacDonald as Prime Minister of Great Britain.

June 18 — Anglo-German naval agreement irritates France.

October 3 — Italy invades Ethiopia.

October 11 — Fifty-one members of the League of Nations vote economic sanctions against Italy.

December 13 — Resignation in Czechoslovakia of President Thomas Masaryk. His successor is Eduard Beneš.

The President left on July 1 for a cruise. On his way back home to Washington he planned to make several speeches, including a particularly important one at Green Bay, Wisconsin.

Radiogram to Roosevelt
Oxford, England, June 29, 1934

A VERY REFRESHING AND HAPPY TRIP TO YOU.

FELIX FRANKFURTER

Telegram to Roosevelt
Windsor, Vt., August 10, 1934

WELCOME HOME AND WARM CONGRATULATIONS ON YOUR WISCONSIN SPEECH.

FELIX FRANKFURTER

The White House, August 10, 1934

Dear Felix:

Thanks ever so much for that nice message of welcome which you were so good as to send me. I am grateful indeed for it and also for your congratulations on my Green Bay speech.

See you very soon.

Very sincerely yours,
F.D.R.

Telegram to Roosevelt
Boston, Mass., August 15, 1934

JUST SAW JUSTICE OLIVER WENDELL HOLMES. HE SPOKE OF YOUR SIGNIFICANCE TO THE COUNTRY WITH HIS OLD ELOQUENCE AND FIRE AND ASKED ME TO GIVE YOU HIS WARMEST GOOD WISHES.

FELIX FRANKFURTER

Telegram to Miss LeHand
Windsor, Vt., August 31, 1934

PLEASE TELL PRESIDENT ONE THAT ADDRESS OF CLARENCE AVILDSEN IS WHITMAN AND BARNES NOT WILLIAMS AND BARNES, DETROIT. TWO THAT GLENN FRANK WILL TRY TO HIDE BEHIND GARRISON'S UNWILLINGNESS, THEREFORE SUGGEST STRONG URGING ON GARRISON. THANK YOU AND GREETINGS.

FELIX FRANKFURTER

President Glenn Frank of the University of Wisconsin wanted Lloyd K.
Garrison, Chairman of the National Labor Relations Board, to resume his
duties as dean of the Wisconsin Law School. Frankfurter admired Garrison
and wanted him to remain with the government. He stayed on for a time
but then returned to Wisconsin.

Clarence Avildsen was suffering from a stomach ulcer and was in the
Battle Creek Sanitarium; he therefore asked to have his appointment with
the President postponed for a month. The President agreed.

Cambridge, Mass., September 11, 1934

Dear Mr. President:

1. And what a victory! I have talked with some of the Republican
editors in Boston, and they feel as a man does the day after a knockout.
Whatever they may say in their editorials, in their minds and hearts they
know that this is not to be explained on any local Maine grounds like the
popularity of Brann and the utter futility of Ames. They know that the
deepest issues of attitude towards your efforts and accomplishments underlay the Maine vote, and it was a verdict upon them.

If only a few hundred more votes had been cast against Freddie Hale.
What a joy it would have been to have him returned to private life. As for
the one Republican Congressman — Ralph Brewster — he is not likely to
give the G.O.P. much comfort. When Brewster was Governor, he had me
go up and address his Legislature on his power program, which in essentials
was quite in accord with your own.

2. A friend of mine has called my attention to the enclosed quotation
from Lincoln, which if you have not seen it, will interest you. The friend is
Larry Winship, managing editor of the Boston *Globe*, a very strong supporter of yours. He says that if one of these days you will use it, in any form,
the papers will simply have to print it, whereas if somebody else quotes it, it
goes in the wastebasket.

Always yours,
F.F.

The "victory" was the Democratic victory in the gubernatorial election
and general election in Maine then held in September before the national
elections.

Louis J. Brann, Governor of Maine, 1933–1937, had been elected to a
second term. He had defeated the Republican candidate, A. K. Ames. Sen-
ator Frederick Hale, a Republican, served four terms, from 1917–1941.
Frankfurter was wrong about Brewster, who ended up as a Senator belong-
ing to the right wing of the Republican party. The Lincoln quotation is his

famous statement on the rights of labor, rights inherent and fundamental, and superior to the claims of wealth.

Cambridge, Mass., September 18, 1934

Dear Miss LeHand:

This morning I had further word from another source about the Glenn Frank–Lloyd Garrison situation. C. C. Burlingham writes me about it, and he is intimately informed because he is a very close friend of Garrison's mother and writes from their common country place. The President will want to know, I think, the following from Mr. Burlingham's letter:

"Glenn Frank is acting badly about Lloyd Garrison, who would gladly open his Law School and then return for a few months. I have half a mind to get at the regents or La Follette on my own." I don't think Mr. Burlingham could be at all effective, and La Follette and Frank have for some time been at odds. I think the only thing to do is to act on Frank's public statement as though it were true, and hold him to it, and persuade Garrison, on the strength of that statement, to continue.

I enclose for you the N. Y. *Times* clipping.

Very cordially yours,
FELIX FRANKFURTER

The clipping stated that President Frank was applying no pressure to bring about Garrison's early return to Wisconsin.

Cambridge, Mass., September 20, 1934

Dear Mr. President:

1. Hugh Johnson's outburst about his alleged relations with Brandeis has created a very serious situation, about which I think we had better have talk.

2. Word has just come to me from a very close associate of Lloyd Garrison that sufficient pressure would make him stay.

3. My friend Frank Buxton of the Boston *Herald* (who, although he must obey his master's voice, is privately devoted to you) is a native of Woonsocket and a fascinating analyst of what he always calls "the corrupt state" of Rhode Island. He talked so illuminatingly about the riots in the Woonsocket situation that I asked him to put a short sketch of that and of Governor Green on paper. His letter may interest you, even though your own stout good sense saved Green, Rhode Island and the country from Green's funk.

4. And when I see you, I must also tell you of a visit I had from Ralph Brewster.

Always yours,
F.F.

General Hugh Johnson, the administrator for NRA, who had a vivid talent for melodramatic invective, had spoken with savage contempt of Brandeis's views on labor as senile and dangerous. Brandeis's friends heaved with indignation but Brandeis himself felt no poisoned arrows in his flesh. The controversy turned on vague Section 7A of the National Industry Recovery Act, which labor regarded as a charter for trade unionism and business used as an excuse for the company shop. Brandeis quietly observed that Section 7A was less than a masterpiece of legislative wisdom. Hence the General's outrage and explosion.

Roosevelt laughed uproariously over this letter from Frank Buxton, editor of the Boston Herald, *and had it copied for his permanent record and distribution among friends.*

Hyde Park, N.Y., September 14, 1934
Dear Felix, — I've never been able to get a quart out of a pint bottle or to insinuate my longshoreman's foot into a Vere de Vere pump several sizes smaller and ergo, as we Latin pundits say, I can't give the story of even the Social district of Woonsocket in the orthodox limits of a Christian letter.

Woonsocket is the most intensely French-Canadian section in New England, not excepting Lewiston or Manchester or Lowell or Lawrence. The Habitants began to come there seventy or eighty years ago, but often their allegiance remained Canadian. They worked for very low wages. When they were a step or two ahead of the sheriff, they would go back to Trois Rivières and the other Canadian sections continually — Senator Felix Hebert, for example, was born while his mother was temporarily on a visit to her Canadian home. They have never been thoroughly Americanized in the best sense of the term. Even when I was a lad in primary school, we used to sing the old French song, *C'est le mois de Marie, c'est le mois le plus beau,* etc. Cooking, dress, outlook on life, living standards, morality, pleasure, etc., were distinctly French-Canadian. They had very large families, usually brought up wretchedly, and French was their customary language. They lived largely to themselves, they made hardly any impress on the cultural life of the town — as it was then — they read regularly the French daily paper which began publication there in the nineties, the children of the more prosperous families went to Canada for schooling, and they merely hovered on the edge of the purely American life. They were employed mostly in the mills, mainly cotton, where hours were long, wages small, conditions none too good.

The Social section where the looting took place is named for a great mill, a woolen mill, I think, built by one Edward Harris, founder of the public library of the town, a friend, I think, of Daniel Webster, and an intimate of John Wanamaker. The town was made up of queerly named sections — the Globe, Bernon, the Privilege, Clinton, each named for a mill. The Social is peopled almost entirely by French-Canadians, with a few entrepreneurs of other races. It is an ugly, noisy, bustling, dirty place, rather remote, as Rhode Island distances go, from the commercial center of the city, and isolated from the Yankee and Irish sections — or what is left of them — socially and even religiously, the French having their own Catholic churches, with clergy who have given the hierarchy no end of trouble and have at times seceded. Standards of life are low there, sound leadership is lacking, thrift is not conspicuous, and all the outwards aspects of life are depressing.

These people have a native facility for graft which would make a Parisian, or, as the Canadians call a native of France, a France Frenchman, blush in mortification at his ineptness. The French-Canadian politicians are the slipperiest I have ever known. Most of their leaders are worse than the rank and file. They grafted in the days of prohibition and before, and the momentum is carrying them along smoothly now. Occasionally a good man has emerged — ex-Governor A. J. Pothier, Felix Hebert, Alphonse Gaulin, Jr., formerly mayor, later sent abroad on consular missions by Senator Aldrich, and incidentally a graduate of your Law School, a very brilliant chap now living in Paris and my host on a visit there last year. Mostly, however, they are Grade D minus. Like so many who are congenitally poor, . . . they regard a public treasury as something from which the private citizen should take treasure, and they have so little property of their own, except their houses, that the rights of property do not mean much to them. The youngsters are especially spirited, as we say when our lads try to burn down the house. They are ready for a lark or mischief at any time. They are not drys, but dry. They have the mercurial traits of the real French. They are easily led by persons of their own kind. I assume from what I read of the looters that they are similar to the crowd which I waved away with a gun the night of the Boston police strike — young, ardent, easily controlled by a show of force, not unwilling to get a pair of shoes or a bottle of liquor for nothing when the cops are looking in the other direction.

Perhaps I am unduly harsh on them. They have lived in miserable quarters as a rule. The town and city politicians of the last generation have not set good examples. The schools are poor; the health conditions are also poor, as I remember the last report I saw; the proprietor of the evening newspaper, *The Call*, was closely connected with the regnant Republicans for many years; the success of Boss Brayton and of the former state managers, Pelky and Peck, was an incentive to political skullduggery; and the whole environment of the Social district was perfect for the little outbreak of a night or two ago. The police department is anything but ideal, or was when I last made inquiries about it. The French dominate it, of course, just as they dominate the city in general, barring the banks and the larger aggregations of capital. An alert chief of police or head of the state militia might well have anticipated trouble of the kind that occurred and prevented it by a mere display of readiness.

As to Governor Green: he is a NICE man. You've heard the story of Leslie Howard. On two occasions he refused to go to dinner with some pals, explaining that he had engagements with the Prince of Wales. A bold fellow commented: "See here, Leslie, you needn't think that you're going to become Queen of England." Theodore is not slopping over with energy and resolution. He is unquestionably honest and can probably recite the Apostles' Creed without mistaking it for the Lord's Prayer. But he is wishy-washy, his testicles, if any, do not hang low, and certainly no expert in permanents could work on his chest hair. He's ornamental, possibly efficient in placid times, means well in the weak way of which T.R. spoke in relation to Taft. He'd be my first choice of the man not to do the vigorous and proper thing in a pinch. He'd also be my first choice if I were in the President's position and wanted to have my orders carried out. With a strong man behind him, and socially and officially above him, he should do very well. He'd not make a bad career diplomat.

As I've libelled the French-Canadian race and the Governor and several others in this indiscreet effusion, please be choice of it, as my mother-in-law used to say when she wanted folks to be careful of something fragile or precious. I go to Rhode Island periodically to see friends and relatives, and I'd be spitted upon if an echo of my comments ever got to them. So, beware.

FRANK

Governor Theodore Francis Green later became Senator Green and Chairman of the Senate Foreign Relations Committee.

Telegram to Miss LeHand for F.D.R.
Cambridge, Mass., September 21, 1934
HAVE JUST READ ADMIRABLE TEXT WINANT REPORT. IT WHOLLY CONFIRMS WISDOM YOUR APPOINTMENT OF THAT BOARD AND SHOULD LEAD TO EARLY CONSTRUCTIVE SETTLEMENT OF STRIKE. CONGRATULATIONS.

FELIX FRANKFURTER

The Winant report was the result of a presidential board of inquiry into the cotton textile industry. John G. Winant was chairman. The strike, with violence and kidnaping of union officers, began to spread. This report led to the settlement of the strike. Roosevelt then created the Textile Labor Relations Board.

The White House, October 1, 1934

Dear Felix:

Many, many thanks to you for your kind message. I am delighted to have it.

Very sincerely yours,
F.D.R.

Cambridge, Mass., October 1, 1934

In the matter of tactics he had the supreme gift of judging the crucial moment and the critical point in a battlefield. Two principles guided him. He never tied himself to a preconceived idea, but altered his plans to suit changing circumstances; also he never exhausted his resources, but kept always something in hand till it was certain that resistance was over.

Dear Mr. President:

The above is a quotation from John Buchan's *Life of Cromwell*, just published on the other side — and the quotation speaks for itself.

Yours always,
F.F.

The White House, October 4, 1934

Dear Felix: —

Your quotation is the worst blow of the year. I have been compared with Kerensky, Judas Iscariot, Cesare Borgia and Hitler but never Cromwell! Almost every day I wish to decapitate some new Charles I, but I restrain myself and I guarantee never to become as dour and sour as old Oliver. No modern biographer can ever persuade me that Cromwell never tied himself to a preconceived idea because he was just that kind of an idea himself!

As ever yours,
F.D.R.

Cambridge, Mass., October 3, 1934

Dear Mr. President:

You will recall my mention of Sam Zemurray of the United Fruit Co. At the time I spoke to you I only knew about him at second hand. Now that I have spent a whole evening with him, more than four hours, I venture to write that you simply must see him.

First and last, I've met many big business men during the Great War and since, but Zemurray is one of the very few statesmen among business men that I have encountered. He has the qualities that one usually finds in a great personality: simplicity as well as size. He has fine devotion to you and cares deeply about your aims and can, I am sure, be of real help.

For all practical purposes, he is at present the United Fruit Co. You will recall that United Fruit employs something like 60,000 people, in and out of the United States, and has cash deposits in Boston of something like $32,000,000. He owns, of course, a huge block of its stock, but he obtained control of the management not because of his holdings but because of his mastery of its business. How he obtained control is a fascinating story. But, as he said to me, it is important because, in his judgment, what he called the "disease" of the United Fruit Co. is characteristic of many American industries, and more particularly, the relation of industry to finance.

It is not merely because of his business significance and business wisdom that I think it is really important for you to have a talk with Zemurray. As one of the country's rich men, he has been invited to join what he calls the "organization" of powerful, rich interests against you, and I think you ought to hear from him at first hand the story of those efforts. He is a true friend of yours, and I know you will find him of real help. While he is of course subject to your call, Zemurray is a shyish man, and if you think there is any point in it, I shall be glad to come down with him. If by any chance you want me to come, I hope it will be possible for you to pick a day when I have no engagements in the School. Mondays, Wednesdays and Thursdays are such free days.

In any event, I urge you strongly to see Zemurray. You will find him a joy and a real helper.

Always yours,
F.F.

The White House, October 10, 1934

Dear Felix: —

I do want to see Zemurray and it would be fine if you could come down with him. Will you give him the enclosed? If the date does not suit — pick another.

Always sincerely,
F.D.R.

Cambridge, Mass., October 16, 1934

Dear Mr. President:

1. Many thanks for asking me to bring S. Zemurray, and we shall turn up for luncheon on Thursday the twenty-fifth.

2. There are two or three matters of major importance about which I hope much for an opportunity of further talk with you, following up the discussion at Hyde Park. These are subjects not for talk with Zemurray. I wonder, therefore, whether you can find time for these things during my coming stay in Washington. I can come a day ahead, be in Washington on Wednesday morning and stay over until it is time for the Federal Express on Thursday (for I must be back here Friday morning), and of course be at your disposal at any time during Wednesday or Thursday forenoon.

3. A friend of mine from Chicago has sent me the enclosed from the Chicago *Daily News* which, if you have not already seen it, will interest you. It strikes me as an unusually discerning piece.

4. I am very glad to infer that you are annexing Bob Hutchins. He has many admirable qualities, and not the least among them is that he pursues his social purposes with healthy humor.

With warm regards,

Always faithfully yours,
F.F.

The Chicago Daily News, *not always friendly to Roosevelt, had defended the President's program from the charges made by its extreme critics.*

Roosevelt wanted Robert M. Hutchins, then head of the University of Chicago, to become Chairman of the National Industrial Recovery Board. Hutchins withdrew his acceptance when various difficulties about the appointment arose in Washington.

The White House, October 18, 1934

Dear Felix: —

I speak before the Bankers on Wednesday evening at 9 P.M. and, of course, as usual I shall probably be working on the speech until the last moment. It will be very short and I expect to get back to the White House at 9:30 P.M. Why not show up at that time and we can have a good talk before bedtime. You will, of course, spend the night at the White House.

Always sincerely,
F.D.R.

P.S.   The next day we will have Zemurray to lunch.

Cambridge, Mass., October 20, 1934

Dear Mr. President:

Many, many thanks for asking me to spend Wednesday night at the White House, which of course I shall most gladly do.

I shall turn up, then, at 9:30 Wednesday next.

Always yours,
F.F.

Cambridge, Mass., October 27, 1934

Dear Mr. McIntyre,

I always knew that if he felt enough respect or enough fear, said Felix Frankfurter could get anywhere on time. And now that you have again given me the proof I intend to make the most of it. Many thanks!

Will you kindly bring this to the attention of the President.

Sincerely yours,
MARION FRANKFURTER

The White House, November 2, 1934

Dear Felix: —

I am enclosing a letter from Russell Leffingwell,[1] my reply to him[2] and his reply to me.[3] They are for your eyes only. Let me have them back. Somehow I feel strangely cold because I cannot see one constructive thought in either of his letters — do you?

As ever yours,
F.D.R.

[1]Dated October 13, 1934.
[2]Dated October 23, 1934.
[3]Dated October 30, 1934.

Russell Leffingwell, a partner of J. P. Morgan, had a national reputation as a business statesman. The President's letter and Frankfurter's answering analysis prove that both men thought the reputation was undeserved.

Cambridge, Mass., November 21, 1934

Dear Mr. President:

Many thanks for letting me see the correspondence between yourself and Russell Leffingwell. After reading and re-reading his letters, I am not at all surprised that they left you feeling "strangely cold." In neither of his letters is there the lift of life. The same old clichés, the same "old incantations" despite his disavowal of them. No more than you, can I see "one constructive thought in either of his letters," and for the same reason — there isn't a constructive thought in either of them.

1. The great remedy which Leffingwell offers you for the Country's salvation is "the reopening of the capital markets." And since, according to Leffingwell, the "Securities Act and the Banking Act have pretty much closed them" the removal of the controls over finance imposed by these Acts is his inevitable Q.E.D. It really is deeply disappointing that a man in Leffingwell's position has nothing more to offer after you invited his best thought. He never faces the crucial problem to which you directed central attention in your last "fireside talk," namely, how to provide employment for millions of men as soon as possible. He apparently sees the whole economic process of production and employment in terms of pieces of paper called securities. He regards finance as an end in itself rather than recognizing its essential function as that of an instrument of industry. Your problem is not to make finance easy, but to find economic activities to finance which will employ millions. And to the solution of that problem Leffingwell makes no contribution except to assume that you would create a healthy condition for industry were you to withdraw the controls you have established over finance, and thereby revert to the conditions in the securities market which prevailed prior to 1929.

2. I shall not waste your time by refuting in detail Leffingwell's assumptions and allegations. When even the New York *Herald Tribune* says editorially, as it did last Saturday, that the Securities Act "in its present form is not a serious deterrent to recovery, if it is a deterrent at all," it seems like flogging a dead horse to argue further against Leffingwell's untenable claim. With such a premise his conclusion is inevitably sterile.

3. In the present circumstances I am sure that you are right in your belief, which I was glad to see you again express in the admirable Tennessee Valley speeches, that a large public works program is the biggest possible stimulus to the capital goods industry. And with the tremendous credit reserve which we have built up in this country there is no basis for Leffingwell's argument that a five billion dollar government borrowing for a sound public works program will absorb all funds available for every sort of investment, and leave nothing to be tapped by investment bankers offering private issues. In the last decade expenditures of state and municipal works have averaged just a little less than three billion dollars a year. Five billion is about half the capital expenditures required to restore the normal balance between the capital goods and consumption goods industries. Public works will stimulate and not compete with private works; the two are complementary. And in this connection Leffingwell does not seem to remember that so far as their effect is concerned, private debts are just as much a

burden to service and retire as public debts. Indeed a good part of the public debt incurred in your Administration has been incurred to refund or bail out too burdensome private debts.

4. Leffingwell assumes, moreover, that a five billion dollar expenditure on public works means a public borrowing of five billion dollars. This is of course not true. The stimulation of business through such a program will, of course, increase the national income, and thereby greatly augment the yield of our present taxes, and make possible the payment of higher rates of taxation with less real hardship than the existing rates impose. Leffingwell apparently has not yet learned from your speech to the bankers that wealth is a dynamic force and not static. No wonder his two letters left you "strangely cold."

5. I should have told you before this how very basic seemed to me your reaffirmation, in your letter to the automobile industry, of your pronouncement on the annual wage. The implications of this desideratum have more significance for economic and moral health than most "principles" of classical economics and a good many of the new economic fantasies. I rejoice to infer that you will keep this aim before the country, the business community, and labor whenever opportunity offers.

6. The extempore, almost casual way, in which you said important things at Tupelo made them all the more important. Mr. Justice Holmes had a favorite remark, when, as a naughty boy, he used to put some stinger in an opinion. With a mischievous twinkle in his eye he would say such and such a phrase or sentence was "calculated to give the brethren pain." I think Holmes would have recognized a mischievous twinkle or so in your speech at Tupelo.

Have a good Georgian Thanksgiving time.

Faithfully yours,
F.F.

Cambridge, Mass., November 13, 1934

Dear Miss LeHand:

I must bother you about a trifle, but a trifle of importance to Harvard University, and, I think, to the literary and political history of the next generation.

The enclosed letter from Dr. Blake, the Librarian of Harvard, will tell the story. I am asking you to bring it to the President's attention, because I know how greatly this generation and succeeding generations of Harvard men will appreciate that he took a personal share in securing for the library of Harvard University what the Librarian regards as a great treasure. To that end, it is necessary that the seals of Romain Rolland's manuscripts, now on the high seas, be left intact upon arrival here. I am venturing to hope that the President will give the necessary order.

Always with warm regards,

Very sincerely yours,
F.F.

Cambridge, Mass., November 13, 1934

Dear Frankfurter:

The Harvard College Library is to become the recipient of one of the six copies of Romain Rolland's unpublished journal of the war years. This document, accompanied by a large amount of supporting correspondence, will unquestionably be one of the greatest historical and literary productions of this generation. It is to be sealed for 25 years, at the expiration of which time the Library received the rights to the English translation. The *sine qua non* of its being deposited here is that the packages should be brought to this country sealed. The packages are being transported to America by a special messenger who is arriving on the S. S. "Paris" of the French Line on Wednesday, November 21st. His name is Mr. Lewis Van Wezel. Is there any manner in which I can obtain either the freedom of the port for the messenger or in any case the passing of these packets in an unopened condition?

Very sincerely yours,
ROBERT P. BLAKE

Romain Rolland, the French novelist and musical authority, had opposed the First World War, which he regarded as a European civil war, and had gone into exile in Switzerland. He had corresponded during the war years with intellectuals in many countries in support of the peace movement.

Washington, D.C., November 16, 1934

Dear Mr. Frankfurter:

Referring to your letter of November 13 to Miss LeHand regarding the copy of Romain Rolland's unpublished journal, which, it is desired, should come in with the seals unbroken, arrangements have been made for Inspector Daniels to board the "Paris" from the revenue cutter, and inspect and examine the ship in such fashion as to allow the seals to remain intact.

Very truly yours,
HERMAN OLIPHANT

Cambridge, Mass., November 20, 1934

Dear Miss LeHand:

1. May I trouble you to give the enclosed letter to the President at your convenience?

2. I have never had before, and I don't ever again expect you to give me, a chance to tease you, and so I took advantage of it in my letter to the President.

3. Let me thank you, and through you him, for arranging so promptly and so effectively safe entry of the Romain Rolland Journal for the Widener Library.

Very cordially yours,
FELIX FRANKFURTER

Cambridge, Mass., November 20, 1934

Dear Mr. President:

1. These two sets of stamps are a meagre offering to you for extending the bounds of my geography. I now know, and I am not likely ever to forget, that Lithuania is Lithuania, and Besserabia is Besserabia, and never the twain shall meet. Lithuania is Lithuania; but the only philatelic recognition of Besserabia I have been able to find is a Roumanian issue of 1928 celebrating Besserabia's declaration of independence from Russia in 1918, and while Besserabia is no longer independent, the one leu and two lei stamps at least teach me that there is a Besserabian Parliament House.

2. Perhaps you will feel that I have learnt my lesson sufficiently well to relieve Miss LeHand of the burden of coming down my chimney this Christmas. I hope she won't mind my taking this indirect means of enlightening her.

3. Will you please tell a poor Law Professor how he can keep out of the papers. Don't tell me "by shutting up." The enclosed clipping will prove to you that mere silence is no proof against reportorial imagination. How this particular nonsense about Joe Ely as the "Fusion Candidate for President in 1936" got floated is beyond my own imagination. I happened to be with Ely at a party in the Harvard Club here the other day. Poor Ely is in a very disillusioned and almost bitter frame of mind because of Curley's election, and in order to cheer him up I drank — this was a very small party — to his successful law practice. One of Ely's friends was present, and he asked, "Why don't you drink to his Vice-presidential candidacy with Roosevelt in 1936?" I replied, "Because he needs a good law practice in 1935." That is as close as we got to the "Fusion Candidate for President," whatever that may be. I hope you have an enhanced respect as a result of this incident for the inventive powers of the Boston Press.

With warm regards,

Always yours,
F.F.

It is not without significance that the Administration in 1936 refused to support Mayor James M. Curley of Boston in the Senate race. In 1934

*Curley had been elected Governor of Massachusetts, and Governor Ely was
unhappy. The Boston clipping adds nothing to Frankfurter's version of
what happened.*

Warm Springs, Ga., November 27, 1934

Dear Felix: —

Many thanks for your letters. I wish you were here.

Perhaps you can run down for the night sometime between December
fifteenth and Christmas. I shall be working on the first draft of a Message
or Messages. From present indications the liberals will get more comfort
out of them than the Tories!

I am delighted that you have broken into print in the clipping which
looks as though it came from the *Transcript*. You ought to send an Ivy Lee
bill to Ely.

Yours for Besserabia! Down with Lithuania!

As ever yours,
F.D.R.

Cambridge, Mass., December 1, 1934

Dear Mr. President:

Many thanks for your letter of the twenty-seventh. I am obligated to
you for ruling that I have an "Ivy Lee" claim against Joe Ely!

Of course I shall be glad to "run down for the night after the fifteenth." I can come to suit your convenience, except that, if possible, I
ought not to disappoint the boys at the Christmas dinner of Lincoln's Inn,
our Law School students' society, on Tuesday the eighteenth, at which I am
scheduled to be the chief speaker. I have to be in New York on Sunday
morning, the sixteenth, and I wonder if it would be wholly convenient for
you to have me spend that Sunday night with you and stay over as much of
Monday as you want me. If not, I can turn up on Wednesday, December
19th, or any later day. Please let me know your wishes.

I enclose another leader from *The Times* which may interest you as an
indication of how the subsistence farm ideal is growing even in old England.

Always yours,
F.F.

P.S.   When I see you I must tell you about Zemurray's talk to his executive committee when they taunted him for being for the New Deal.

Warm Springs, Ga., December 3, 1934

Dear Felix: —

Sunday, the sixteenth, will be fine and I shall look for you sometime in the afternoon.

As ever yours,
F.D.R.

Cambridge, Mass., December 11, 1934

Dear Mr. President:

If agreeable to you I shall turn up at 4:30 next Sunday. Herewith are two enclosures:

1. If you have not seen the full text of General Smuts' speech on Freedom I think it is worth your reading.

2. And I am venturing to send you a letter from my friend Dr. Alfred E. Cohn, with an enclosure from Dr. Samuel Lambert. The latter you, of course, know. Cohn is one of the most distinguished medical scientists in the country, a great cardiac man, who happens now to be chairman of the Library Committee of the New York Academy of Medicine. Hence his deep concern for the upkeep of the special world-wide contributions which the Army Medical Library has long fulfilled.

I am venturing to trouble you with this item because I know your great interest in, and unusual knowledge of, the part that medical science plays in furthering civilization, and the part that medical learning plays in furthering medicine.

With warm regards,

Always yours,
F.F.

General Smuts, the South African statesman, delivered the Rectorial address on "Freedom" at St. Andrews University in Scotland. He said:

"The danger signals are up in many colors and in many lands. The new tyranny, disguised in attractive patriotic colors, is enticing youth everywhere into its horrid service. Freedom must make a great counter-stroke to save itself and our fair Western civilization.

"Perhaps I do not exaggerate when I say that of what we call liberty in its full meaning — freedom of thought, speech, action, self-expression — there is today less in Europe than there has been during the last 2000 years.

"In the long run only the spirit of international comradeship can solve the problems of freedom and of peace. But in the meantime the supreme cause has to be kept going and to be safeguarded from all danger until the coming of a new renascence of the European spirit."

New York, N.Y., November 23, 1934

My dear Cohn:

I am much pleased to read in your recent letter to Dr. Malloch that other efforts are to be made in addition to those of the Academy of Medicine to bring about a change in the policy of the Government toward the Library of the Surgeon General's Office.

It has been most disquieting to all physicians who are interested in the literary side of our profession to learn that the Government is gradually reducing its support of this most valuable addition to the equipment of the Medical Department of the Army.

The Medical Department of the Army has acquired an international reputation as a supporter of the best traditions of the schools for medical education and of their scholars. *The Index Catalogue of the Library of the Surgeon General's Office* is an instrument for reference to every scientific work in the profession.

It is unbelievable that the legislative authorities can't understand what is meant by decreasing the appropriation for the Army Medical Library. At present that Library has no money with which to purchase books after their subscriptions to medical magazines are met. If books are not purchased, obviously their titles cannot be entered in the *Index Catalogue* and so the usefulness of the *Catalogue* is much lessened.

I hope that our efforts, when added to those of others, will bring about a change in the policy of the Central Government at Washington.

Faithfully yours,

SAMUEL W. LAMBERT

New York, N.Y., December 1, 1934

Dear Felix:

This depression has affected corners of our life which should, I think, have been spared. We have spoken of many phases of the problem, but here is one which seems especially disturbing.

Through the scholarliness and interest of Doctor John S. Billings the profession of medicine came to possess not only one of the very good professional libraries (the Surgeon General's Library) but a Catalogue of that Library was published, universally regarded as one of the best, perhaps the best, of all bibliographic undertakings. For the want of a very few thousands of dollars, the labors of a generation seem likely now to be destroyed. If books are to be catalogued, books must be bought by the Library; there is no money to buy them. The appropriation has been cut so that it is no longer possible to do more than to maintain the periodical literature. First as a member and now as chairman of the Library Committee of the New York Academy of Medicine I have had more or less to do with efforts to wrestle with this catastrophe, but so far without success. The authorities of the Army Medical Library are eager to do what they can, but they are, or seem to be, powerless. Those who are interested in the medical sciences are much disturbed by this state of affairs. How unfortunate Doctor Lambert regards the current policy, and his opinion carries great weight, is clear from a letter, which I enclose, that he felt moved to write to me.

Tell me what to do. That national honor is in a way involved for we have taught everybody in the civilized world to rely upon the publication of the Catalogue and now seem unable to sustain a pace which costs incredibly little. Isn't it worth remembering that the British Museum, despite the depression, found it possible to acquire the Codex Sinaiticus to say nothing of publishing a new edition of their enormous catalogue of 133 volumes?

Sincerely yours,
ALFRED E. COHN

The President saw to it that the efficiency of the medical index was maintained.

Telegram to Miss LeHand

Cambridge, Mass., December 13, 1934

PLEASE CONVEY THE FOLLOWING MESSAGE. HOPE IT WILL NOT BE NECESSARY TO MAKE FINAL DECISION REGARDING FORM AND PROCEDURE FOR SYSTEMATIC PUBLICATION OF EXECUTIVE ORDERS UNTIL I HAVE HAD OPPORTUNITY FOR TALK WITH YOU. IT HAPPENS TO BE A PARTICULAR SUBJECT OF MINE AND I AM BRINGING A DETAILED SCHEME AND DRAFT FOR NECESSARY LEGISLATION.

FELIX FRANKFURTER

The President delayed his decision until he could review the whole problem of executive orders with Frankfurter, who argued that systematic and timely publication was a check on the abuse of executive power. Roosevelt agreed.

President Roosevelt at the beginning of 1935 did not foresee the shallows and miseries that would soon face him. The Congressional elections in November 1934 had weakened and demoralized the Republican party. In the House of Representatives there were 322 Democrats, 103 Republicans, and ten Progressives and Farmer-Laborites. Nine new Democratic Senators had been elected, including Harry Truman of Missouri, making a total of sixty-nine Democrats, or more than a two-thirds majority. The President thought he stood on the crest of the wave. But all omens were deceptive. Soon he would be swamped with troubles.

In one sense Roosevelt's victories in legislation, partial and limited as they were, had given his critics the chance to organize a counter-offensive. Business leaders were no longer numbed and paralyzed by the depression.

Roosevelt estimated that 85 per cent of the publishers and editors in the country — though not the Washington correspondents — were against him. Thunder growled on the left as angry and impatient reformers criticized Roosevelt for being a slick salesman of recovery instead of a resolute enemy of entrenched wrongs. Heywood Broun, most eloquent of the liberal columnists, derided Roosevelt as a politician who paraded generous promises and then retreated from battle. More than three hundred cases were in various courts across the land challenging essential legislation of the New Deal. His own advisers were divided and querulous, uncertain of the next turning, and struggling in open rivalry to sway the President's judgment in favor of their conflicting proposals. Soon the President found himself grappling with stubborn and skillful opposition in Congress, despite his huge majorities, and many observers thought the initiative was slipping sadly away from him. It was against this political background that his 1935 correspondence with Frankfurter began.

Telegram to Miss LeHand

Cambridge, Mass., January 4, 1935

PLEASE CONVEY FOLLOWING TO THE PRESIDENT. UNFORTUNATELY I HAD TO TEACH SOUND CONSTITUTIONAL VIEWS TO THE YOUNG BETWEEN TWELVE AND ONE BUT MARION HAS JUST TOLD ME THAT IT IS A PERFECTLY THRILLING MESSAGE: UNCOMPROMISING ON ESSENTIALS AND DELIVERED BEAUTIFULLY AND SHE, AS YOU MAY KNOW, IS NOT EASILY PLEASED.

FAITHFULLY YOURS
FELIX FRANKFURTER

The President had just delivered his message on the State of the Union.

Cambridge, Mass., Jaunary 6, 1935

Dear Mr. President:

On the very morning of your Message to Congress, I had a letter from one of the wisest, most level-headed of English students of politics, from which quote the following:

"We still look with hope and fear upon the American experiment. If it achieves something substantial, not in riches but in social peace, there will be little fear of fascism destroying Europe."

How deeply your message must have heartened my friend and all friends of "social peace" — for yours was precisely a formulation of directions for achieving substantial things "not in riches but in social peace."

All this silly twaddle of turning to the "right" or to the "left" is nothing compared with the unmistakable response of the country to your program for a true democratic society, uncorrupted and undeflected by the "appetite for great wealth and great power."

There can be no doubt that the country is ready for the same organizing energy in your effort for honest work and against relief as it showed in its response to the World War demands, and more recently, last year, to NRA. And there can be no doubt that lower costs — without lowering American standards or undue inroads upon private incentives — are essential, if successful public as well as private projects are not to be found prohibitive.

I'm sorry I did not hear your Message — but I was stirred even on reading it.

Faithfully yours,
F.F.

The English friend was R. H. Tawney, the most widely respected authority on the philosophy of the British Labour party.

The White House, January 15, 1935

Dear Felix: —

Homer Cummings and the other lawyers for the defense made only one mistake. I did not think of it until it was too late. They forgot to cite that very early case involving a solemn, signed, sealed and delivered contract. The Court held that under certain circumstances the terms of the payment were entirely unconscionable. You will find the case rather fully set forth in #14 Shakespeare #242! The case is known as *The Merchant of Venice.*

I am delighted to have the book from Harold Laski. Unfortunately, it is not very reliable either in its history or in its conclusions. All one has to do is to read the paragraphs that relate to the United States.

As ever yours,
F.D.R.

The jesting reference to the Merchant of Venice *concerns a "contract" which Frankfurter had persuaded the President to sign as a pledge that he would not lose his temper, in public, with his Democratic critics in Congress.*

Harold J. Laski, of the London School of Economics, had sent Frankfurter a copy of Admiral Sir Herbert Richmond's Sea Power in the Modern World. *Frankfurter gave the book to Roosevelt.*

Memorandum by the President for the Secretary of the Treasury
January 16, 1935

Sometime ago I asked Mr. Frankfurter to study the three subjects to which these proposed bills relate and to let me have a tentative draft of legislation. The enclosed represent much effort and careful study.

I am inclined to think that you should give serious consideration to their introduction. Will you have them checked and speak to me about them?

F.D.R.

Letter from Thomas G. Corcoran, dated Jan. 14, 1935, with accompanying drafts of and memoranda in support of three bills. Bills respectively:

(a) levy a discouraging Federal excise tax upon "tramp corporations" organized in states in which they do not do a substantial portion of their actual business.

(b) levy a discouraging Federal excise tax upon "insiders'" transactions with corporations — i.e. transactions between corporations and the officers, directors, dominant stockholders or affiliates of such corporations;

(c) limit the contingent fees which may be paid to lawyers in tax claims against the Government.

Cambridge, Mass., January 24, 1935

My dear Mr. President:

First as to the Harmsworth Professorship of American History. I am sorry to come empty-handed, but I have to start all over again. I was going to submit the names of four historians to you, all of whom combine distinguished historical scholarship with those qualities of a public personality which are ever so much more essential in the case of an American professor at Oxford than is required of any American professor at home. For good or for ill a visiting American professor at Oxford is the symbol of America. And so Ambassador Bingham is quite right in feeling that the new Harmsworth professor should be one who, in addition to scholarship, also understands and can adequately represent the new and best democratic forces in the United States. Unfortunately all four, when discreetly sounded, were compelled for financial reasons to decline to be considered. Professors do not expect large incomes, but really Oxford cannot ask the kind of scholar and semi-public man who ought to be sent on a salary of five thousand dollars. In addition to serious problems of transplantation for a few years, my men would have had to reconcile themselves to a reduction in salary from ten and twelve thousand to five thousand. The fact of the matter is that for such a salary Oxford is not likely to find any but some unknown young person, who would be very much of a gamble, or an old hack, or that rare person a distinguished scholar who has money. And the latter is likely to be either an Anglophilic snob or an American Tory.

I wonder whether Bingham does not know Lord Rothermere well enough to indicate to His Lordship that he ought to loosen up a bit if he really wants distinguished incumbents for his Chair. It is relevant to point out that the George Eastman Chair, the one that I had for a year, has a stipend of ten thousand dollars, as well as a very comfortable house. That the most distinguished English scholar of Harvard, perhaps the most honored American economist, and a Nobel Prize winner in Physics (and I understand that another Nobel Prize man is on the cards of the future) were glad to accept calls to the Eastman Chair, shows its attractions.

But I shall keep on in my quest for men to fill the bill for your submission. I assume, of course, that if you cannot submit a really first-class name you do not want to put your authority behind a second-rater, for in subtle kinds of ways he will appear to be your representative.

2. I just served as a conduit for Laski in sending on the Richmond book, and have not read it, but it would be more than surprising if any English admiral, however well-intentioned, could do justice to American naval history or American naval interests. You know how warm my feeling is about the English — I don't suppose it is any more warm than yours — and so I am more amused than disturbed by the fact that in their writings there always manages to be a surprising coincidence between their interpretation of history or their theories and British interest. This reflection has been aroused anew in me in reading Sir Henry Strakosch's supplement on Recovery in a recent number of the *Economist*, which will doubtless receive much comment also on this side. In a very quiet, almost statistical way Strakosch proposes remedies for international recovery, but strangely enough they have special advantages for Great Britain.

3. Your quotation of "14 Shakespeare 242" reminds me of one of those experiences which, while incredible, really happened. In telling a class a few years ago that at common law a public utility must serve everybody but only to the extent of its capacities, I added, "For the case of loaves and fishes has never been followed." I could hardly believe my ears when a student came up after class and asked me "to be good enough to give him a reference to the case of loaves and fishes."

4. I note with eager interest your conferences on holding companies. They really have no ultimate economic and social justification. That the national interest requires their elimination I have no doubt, and have had no doubt ever since I spent a few weeks of my young life in the old Hornblower, Byrne office on the intricacies of holding companies. Of course they cannot be eliminated over night, just as the Commodities Clause had to give carriers some time to cease being both shippers and carriers. The miserable holding company situation is even more complicated, and I suppose will take longer for complete liquidation. In the meantime drastic regulation and taxation are indispensable, both in themselves and also for insurance against the possibility of alleviating legislation by a future Congress, although I cannot imagine that the temper of this country will be more

favorable to holding companies say four years hence. Nevertheless the hazard cannot be taken and therefore the policy would seem to be temporary stiff regulation and taxation, with the defined objective of elimination.

5. Out of a clear sky yesterday came the following in a letter from Mr. Justice Holmes's secretary [*James Rowe, Jr.*]:

> From my month with the Justice I have gathered that he has relished more and more the President's call on him a year ago. He has told me about it several times, and the Christmas flowers from the President pleased him greatly. I hope it is not presumptuous to wonder whether there is any possibility of the President's being able to do it again this year, but the last call served so well to annul the Justice's feeling of being out of the battle, I felt it almost a duty to mention it to you.

Have I your permission to tip off the Justice's household that you do plan to visit him on March eighth next?

And now I had better stop and not make further inroads on your time. With warm regards,

Always faithfully yours,
F.F.

P.S.   And now I have read your National Resources Message. For the moment the Hauptmann case and the blizzard (fierce here) may be more dramatic — but I have no doubt that this message will remain as a memorable historic document and your appointment of the National Resources Committee as a great historic step. Why would it not be good education for the country for you to carry out your idea of giving that picture of the Associated Gas as a holding Co. Monster?

F.F.

The Hauptmann case filled the newspapers, for it concerned the kidnaping of Charles and Mrs. Lindbergh's child.

Frankfurter had sent Roosevelt some material showing the intricate financial structure of the Associated Gas Company in Boston.

Cambridge, Mass., February 5, 1935

Dear Mr. President:

1. If there is still time for a suggestion regarding the Harmsworth Professorship then I should like to make a proposal which, though novel, may have some sense to it. I propose Lewis Einstein, who, though not an academician, is a real historian. He has, I believe, written more important books on American history than have all but a handful of the most distinguished of American historians. Though a professional diplomat he has been all his life a gentleman scholar. His *Tudor Ideals, Roosevelt, His Mind in Action*

and *Divided Loyalties* — to mention only some of his writings — bear witness to his qualities. And I have heard Mr. Justice Holmes, during the last twenty-five years, frequently refer with the highest regard to Einstein's scholarship. And it is not uncommon in England to take a scholarly man from the world of affairs for academic posts. Recently Arthur Salter was made a professor of government at Oxford. I have no doubt that Einstein could amply fulfil the academic duties of his post.

And on the representative side he would admirably fill the bill. He is at home in the social and political life of England — he has a house in London — but unlike not a few of our countrymen he is totally devoid of snobbery, or that sense of inferiority which makes some people, whom you and I know, feel they are breathing better air when they are in Mayfair. In other words Einstein is civilized and tactful, and appreciative and understanding of the English, but he still remains a robust American. And I think he would be intelligent and sympathetic in his interpretation of the democratic forces of our country and of the social purposes that lie behind them. Einstein really has an uncommon combination of qualifications. He is a scholar, well versed in the affairs of the world, can write and speak admirably, has a liberal outlook, and has money. In the words of Heine, "*Mein Liebchen was willst Du noch mehr.*"

2. What do you say to the following from an opinion of the Supreme Court, written more than one hundred years ago, to be exact, on March 2, 1821?

> The science of government is the most abstruse of all the sciences; if, indeed, that can be called a science, which has but few fixed principles, and practically consists in little more than the exercise of a sound discretion, applied to the exigencies of the state as they arise. *It is the science of experiment.* [Italics mine]

The writer of that opinion was William Johnson of South Carolina, who was a very considerable fellow.

3. You might like to run your eye over the full text of the recent speech of Lloyd George's opening his campaign for an English New Deal. I have marked the passages which struck me as specially interesting.

4. The enclosed report on the United Fruit Company shows that our friend Zemurray satisfies the ultimate test of a good businessman — he knows how to make money for his company. I suspect that Zemurray's hardheaded good sense about social economic problems is not wholly unrelated to his successful conduct of business.

With warm regards,

Faithfully yours,
F.F.

Heine asked, "My dear, what more do you want?"

Cambridge, Mass., February 6, 1935

Dear Mr. President:

The enclosed leader, from the latest number of the *Economist*, affords interesting comparison between the attitude of the leading financial journal of England toward Lloyd's George's "general principle of a frontal attack upon unemployment, led and inspired by the Government," and the attitude of the financial and conservative press in this country toward your objectives and measures.

Faithfully yours,
F.F.

The White House, February 9, 1935

Dear Felix: —

Much that I could and would write about but these are truly hectic and somewhat disagreeable days. I have passed on the suggestion to Bingham.

I am working on the Holding Company Message.

Yes, do please tip off the Justice's household about the visit on March eighth.

Here is the latest. This afternoon twelve members of Congress, who said they represented one hundred others, moved in on me to find out whether I would go along with an Old Age Pension of fifty, eighty, one hundred or two hundred dollars a month. I explained the financial limitations, and that a sum greater than my recommendation might spell either failure to borrow or starting the presses. One of the spokesmen said — "Mr. President, is it not our sole duty to pass an ideal Old Age Pension bill and after this is done you can tell the Ways and Means Committee and the Treasury to find some way of raising the necessary money?" I thought (silently) of one of our mutual friends from the Hill who came in the other day, slumped into his chair and said to me — "What the hell is the use of education anyway? Let's reserve it for a select committee of one thousand and teach everybody else to speak but not to read, write or think."

Sometimes I feel that way at this period of the year — from which you may gather that this is dictated at 11 P.M., after a bad day. In the morning I shall feel better.

As ever yours,
F.D.R.

The White House, February 18, 1935

Dear Felix: —

That will be grand to have you and Marion. The Todhunter girls are coming down on the eighth to spend the weekend so I am wondering if you and Marion can arrange to come down and spend the night of the seventh.

I doubt if I shall see you in Cambridge, as I get there at 7 P.M. and leave at midnight — then to Hyde Park for, I hope, three full days with no telephone and no Senators!

As ever yours,
F.D.R.

Mrs. Roosevelt had taught at the Todhunter School in New York.

Telegram to Miss LeHand
New York, N.Y., February 18, 1935
PLEASE GIVE THE PRESIDENT MY CONGRATULATIONS.

FELIX FRANKFURTER

The Supreme Court had just decided the "gold clause" cases. The cases arose when John M. Perry tried to compel the government to pay his ten-thousand-dollar bond in gold or in money that had not been devalued. The Court held, in effect, that the government was not fully honoring its obligations and was tampering with the integrity of the dollar but nevertheless control of monetary policy was a clear prerogative of the federal government. It was in this case that Mr. Justice McReynolds, speaking for the four dissenters, exclaimed that "the Constitution as many of us have understood it, the Constitution that has meant so much to us, has gone." He added in the oral rendition of his opinion that Roosevelt was "Nero in his worst form.'

Telegram to Miss LeHand
Cambridge, Mass., February 19, 1935
I DO NOT WANT TO MAKE INROADS ON THE PRESIDENT'S LIMITED TIME HERE THOUGH OF COURSE I SHOULD VERY MUCH LIKE TO SEE HIM IF IT IS HIS PLEASURE TO HAVE ME DO SO AT ANY TIME WHATEVER DURING HIS STAY, AND IF I CAN BE OF ANY USE AT ALL IN ANY WAY IT WOULD GIVE ME MUCH SATISFACTION. MAY I TROUBLE YOU TO ADVISE ME? CORDIALLY YOURS.

FELIX FRANKFURTER

The President was coming to Boston to attend the Fly Club dinner. He saw Frankfurter during this crowded visit before leaving for a weekend at Hyde Park.

Mr. Justice Holmes, born March 8, 1841, had died on March 6, 1935, just two days before his ninety-fourth birthday. Mr. and Mrs. Frank-

furter had stayed with Roosevelt during the trying days that preceded the funeral. Holmes had called Roosevelt a "noble lad."

THE WHITE HOUSE
WASHINGTON

The White House, March 6, 1935

Dear Frank:

I don't know whether I'll have a chance to say *au revoir* — and it's easier to write than to speak what I want to say.

I wish the whole people might see you as I see you — your patience, your generosity, your unflagging zeal for the kind of a society for which this nation was avowedly established.

One of the most sophisticated friends of mine — who breathes the poisoning atmosphere of "upperclass" rich New Yorkers — said to me sometime ago, when I tried to explain what manner of person you are, "You make me feel as though he is the most magnanimous President we've ever had except Lincoln." Well, I leave with a renewed sense of the wisdom of your instincts and the great importance of having you act on your affirmative hunches rather than on the fears and timidities of those less wise or less capable of inspiring the faith of the American people. Continue to give them your leadership — and they will follow.

Devotedly,
F.F.

The White House, March 6, 1935

Dear Mr. President,

I don't know whether I shall see you again before we leave, and so I want to thank you for the sherry, and say how much it has meant to me to be here, where I feel so much the atmosphere of friendly, protecting warmth, during these trying days.

Gratefully yours,
MARION FRANKFURTER

The White House, March 7, 1935

Dear Mr. President.

I'm sorry to miss the glow of your farewell word, but I ought not to add to the burdens of your day so I send this note of affection and gratitude. It is a day of sorrow; and of transcending triumph, if the Grand Old Man's life have the significance that we know it has. And I shall always associate his meaning for me *with you*, at the most poignant and triumphant hours of life.

It was most generous of you to have had Marion and me here for these two days, and I leave with a renewed and intense sense of the kindly humanity and simple wisdom of the "noble lad" who guides the destiny of our beloved country.

Devotedly,

FELIX F.

Telegram to Miss LeHand

Cambridge, Mass., March 22, 1935

PLEASE CONVEY TO PRESIDENT FOLLOWING "PARTLY AT LEAST I THINK I UNDER-STAND YOUR PRESENT ANGUISH AND I FEEL FOR YOU DEEPLY."

FELIX FRANKFURTER

This refers to the passage by the House of Representatives of the Bonus Bill for Veterans. Roosevelt vetoed it and then Congress re-enacted it over his veto.

Cambridge, Mass., March 29, 1935

Dear Miss LeHand:

1. My friend, Professor Harold Laski is here for a short holiday from England, and is to be in Washington a little later. I think I am right in believing that the President would find Laski delightful and stimulating. He, of course, knows him. Laski is to be in Washington Wednesday April 24 and Thursday April 25, and I wonder if by any chance you can, despite the President's absence, arrange for Laski's visit. If I may suggest, if the President happens to be free on either of those evenings for a long, leisurely talk on the present European, and more particularly English situation, Laski would be most informing.

2. I am as gratified as you probably suspect at the arrangements made by the President for annexing for his immediate help the resourceful talents of Tom. I know this arrangement is essentially due to you, and I have no doubt that events will prove that in bringing it to pass you have rendered another great service to the President and the Administration.

3. What an almost miraculous turn Louis Howe has had. I am so glad that it enabled the President to have his holiday for I am a great believer in the public advantages of these intermittent periods of play for the President. The mind of the man who guides this Country should be constantly refreshed so as to be best fitted to make those subtle decisions of statesmanship which are not unlike a poet's intuitions and a philosopher's dreams. Unlike the philosopher and poet, he must also have a great deal of vitality

so as to energize the whole Government, and in these days invigorate the whole people.

Very sincerely yours,
FELIX FRANKFURTER

Tom Corcoran, from this point forward working closely with the President, becomes an increasingly important influence in the New Deal.

Louis Howe had been indispensable to Roosevelt after the attack of infantile paralysis and had done more than anyone else, except Eleanor Roosevelt, to sustain his spirit and his hopes for coming political battles. But when he became a Presidential assistant in the White House, he was misplaced and unhappy. His recovery from a severe illness at this time did not signify his return to complete health. Before many months had passed, he was dead.

Telegram to Frankfurter
The White House, April 20, 1935
PRESIDENT DELIGHTED TO HAVE LASKI LUNCH WITH HIM WEDNESDAY AND HAVE
YOU COME DOWN FOR DINNER AND THE NIGHT.

M. A. LeHAND

The Belcher case arose when a federal judge in Alabama held that W. E. Belcher, the owner of a lumber mill, did not have to observe the lumber code established by the National Industrial Recovery Act since that act was unconstitutional. Donald Richberg urged the President to appeal the case to the Supreme Court. The argument against such an appeal was presented by Stanley Reed, the new Solicitor General, powerfully supported by Frankfurter. Just two weeks before the Supreme Court was to hear arguments in the Belcher case, the government asked for the dismissal of its appeal.

This provoked a formidable outcry in the press that the government was continuing to demand compliance with NRA codes even while it shrank from testing the constitutionality of the Act in the Supreme Court.

To meet this criticism Attorney General Cummings had decided, to the alarm of Frankfurter, to rest the government's defense of NRA on the Schechter case. The Schechter brothers had been found guilty in a lower court of violating the Live Poultry Code and of selling kosher chickens that were unfit for human consumption — hence the popular nickname of the "sick chicken case." The Second Circuit Court of New York upheld the fair-trade provisions of the poultry code and other matters but ruled against the government on two important points. Frankfurter predicted that the Supreme Court would strike down NRA if the Schechter case came before it. On receiving this message from Corcoran about Frankfurter's views, Roo-

sevelt wired Cummings to delay the appeal. But the message did not reach Cummings in time to stop him. Frankfurter shared Corcoran's suspicions that people in the Administration eager for an appeal to the Supreme Court had delayed the transmission of the President's message.

Knowing that much of the New Deal legislation had been improvised in the emergency of the depression, Frankfurter was eager to have the government pick its test cases with care. He foresaw the government's defeat in the Schechter case, and predicted with gloomy conviction that the Supreme Court would now become the great antagonist of the New Deal and rule against many of its important measures. That is exactly what happened. He always blamed Attorney General Cummings for giving the President very bad advice in these cases, and in the events leading to the court-packing plan in 1937. It is not without interest that the legislation on which Frankfurter had worked with Landis, Cohen, and Corcoran escaped essential criticism and damage by the Supreme Court. The Schechter brothers would have appealed the case on the points they had lost, and so the case would have come before the Supreme Court regardless of the sudden and mistaken decisions by the Department of Justice. On May 27, 1935, The Court, 9-0, struck down NIRA as unconstitutional. The day of decision became known as the "Black Monday" of the New Deal.

Telegram to Roosevelt

Washington, D.C., April 4, 1935

F.F. CALLED. HAS LEARNED VERY VERY CONFIDENTIALLY CUMMINGS UNDER URGING OF RICHBERG TO SILENCE CRITICISM ON BELCHER DISMISSAL AND PURSUANT TO WIRE FROM YOU INTENDS ANNOUNCING TO PRESS THIS AFTERNOON THAT GOVERNMENT WILL IMMEDIATELY EXPEDITE TO SUPREME COURT A NEW NRA CASE FROM SECOND CIRCUIT IN NEW YORK INVOLVING POULTRY CODE. F.F. SUGGESTS MOST IMPOLITIC AND DANGEROUS TO YIELD TO ANTAGONISTIC PRESS CLAMOR NOW BECAUSE FUNDAMENTAL SITUATION ON COURT NOT CHANGED. FURTHER SUGGESTS YOU WIRE CUMMINGS NOT TO TAKE HASTY ACTION AND HOLD WHOLE SITUATION ON NRA APPEALS IN ABEYANCE UNTIL YOU RETURN. SUGGESTS AT THAT TIME THOROUGH DISCUSSION IN PRESENCE OF ALL CONCERNED. I AM SENDING THIS ALONE BECAUSE UNABLE REACH EARLY AND SEEMS VERY URGENT.

CORCORAN

Cambridge, Mass., April 22, 1935

Dear Miss LeHand:

The enclosed letter which has just come deserves, I believe, the President's special attention. For it is written by one of the most knowing, as well as one of the most devoted of his followers. I hope there is an opportunity for him to read it before I come down, for I should like to talk with him about it.

And the cartoon from the St. Louis *Post-Dispatch* if he has not yet seen it may amuse the President.

With cordial regards,

Very sincerely yours,
FELIX FRANKFURTER

FORD HALL FORUM

Boston, Mass., April 22, 1935

Dear F.F.:

You were away all last week apparently and so I am writing you what I wanted to tell you then. I am quite disturbed at the way our cock-eyed liberals are permitting themselves to be used in the campaign to discredit the Administration. I think it is only fair to assume that most of them are misled by their inability to grasp fully what it is the President is up against.

I am writing you now because before we know it next year will be upon us with the election and it will be up to us to try to line up the liberals in order to preserve the gains that we have already made. I think it is a mistake to wait until next year to line them up after the campaign has started. If possible I wish you could think up some way of getting them back in line immediately.

Some of our liberals are bellyaching because they are mentally constipated and others because they must have swallowed too big a chunk of hostile propaganda; but for the most part, I think it is due to their inability to recognize to the full what it is the President has to contend with. After all, trying to satisfy a hundred and twenty-five million people is a somewhat different problem from trying to please the relatively few thousand readers of the *Nation* and the *New Republic* and similar journals. By the way have you noticed how many new so-called liberal magazines and newspapers have been started this past year? However, these liberals and progressives are an important factor and will be needed, in my judgment, next year more than in any other campaign that we've been through. I wish, Felix, we could do something about it before they commit themselves too definitely to these different so-called progressive and liberal organizations that are cropping up all over the country. Once they have tied up with these groups it will be impossible to win them away.

It occurs to me that a frank talking-things-over between the President and these liberal and progressive leaders from all over the country should be of real help. It should be a kind of executive session from which all reporters are barred and during which these liberal and progressive leaders could tell the President what it is that disturbs them about his program and have him explain to them why it is so difficult to progress as rapidly as he and they would like.

Two years ago was the first time that the liberals and progressives participated in a victory and it is a new experience for them. They are naturally impatient and for the most part they are so emotionally constituted that it is easier to be anti-administration than pro; but I think at the bottom they are honest men and women and at a conference of this sort a common denominator can be found which will make them want to go out and fight those who would destroy the President's program once they understand better what the President's program is.

I for one believe, of course, that the President has a definite program, the carrying out of which depends on proper timing. If these people could be assured, and I think the President can assure them, that it *is* only a question of timing and that he is not going back on them, you will find that they are just as anxious to support him as they were when he first went into office.

We have got to remember that the so-called leaders of progressives throughout the country are being subjected to all kinds of pressure from individuals who perhaps are not getting all they hoped from the NRA or have been upset by the workings of the NRA, etc., etc.

I don't think it is important that I enumerate to you what it is that disturbs so many in this group. After all, what might disturb the liberal in the East might entirely satisfy the liberal in the West and so forth. Just between you and me, another advantage in getting these liberals together would be to let them see for themselves how divided they are in their criticism.

Cordially,
DAVID K. NILES

David K. Niles, the Director of Ford Hall Forum, later became an assistant to Harry Hopkins in WPA and to Roosevelt and Truman in the White House.

Telegram to Miss LeHand

Cambridge, Mass., April 29, 1935

PLEASE CONVEY FOLLOWING TO PRESIDENT: YOU AGAIN PUT WIND IN PEOPLE'S SAILS, YOUR SERENE AND WARMING VOICE, YOUR CONTAGIOUS RADIATION OF SELF-MASTERY, YOUR AUTHENTIC NOTE OF CONFIDENCE AND THE QUIET GOOD SENSE OF WHAT YOU SAID, INSTILLED, I AM SURE, THAT ENERGY OF FAITH IN OUR EFFORTS AND OUR OPPORTUNITIES WHICH THE PEOPLE FROM TIME TO TIME GREATLY NEED FROM YOU ALWAYS.

FELIX FRANKFURTER

Roosevelt, the previous evening, had reported to the nation on the Works Relief Program. "Never since my Inauguration in March 1933 have I felt so unmistakably the atmosphere of recovery."

Cambridge, Mass., May 1, 1935

Dear Miss LeHand:

Please hand this very important paper to the President and oblige.

Very cordially,

FELIX FRANKFURTER

Cambridge, Mass., May 1, 1935

Dear Mr. Ex-President of the *Crimson:*

Permit me to report to you the sequel of the story concerning the arrangements for the forthcoming annual dinner.

On my return I found the enclosed invitation on which Lewis William Douglas LL.D. '33, appears as the last speaker. This program was sent out before the talk young Ballantine agreed to have with me. I have now had my talk with Ballantine, Jr., and made it clear to him that while I care nothing about precedence and all that, I should think he and the *Crimson* would care about fair-play. It was a three to one program against the New Deal — Toastmaster Ballantine, Professor Baxter, and Lew Douglas — and the decencies of the situation required that I should have the opportunity of answering and not be followed by the chief speaker against the New Deal. I indicated, of course, that we weren't going to have a cock fight, that it will be a pleasant and gentlemenly occasion, but that I should have to insist on fair-play, even though I happened to be one of the speakers, because vital public issues were at stake. I cleared away all the nonsense about the courtesy that was due to an "outsider," etc. etc. Arthur, who is a nice lad, said he really thought I was right, and that he would make arrangements accordingly.

And so the matter stands. From my talk with young Arthur I was convinced more than ever that it was Arthur Sr. who was pulling the strings.

Always yours,

F.F.

THE EDITORS OF THE CRIMSON
*Request the Pleasure
of your company
at their*
SIXTY-SECOND ANNUAL DINNER
*in the sanctum
on
Wednesday evening, May the Eighth
at seven o'clock*

*The favor of a reply
is requested before
May first if you
plan to be present*

GRADUATE BOARD
Sherman H. Bowles '12
   Osborne F. Ingram '35
      Victor O. Jones '28
         Charles M. Storey '12
            Edward A. Whitney '17

DINNER COMMITTEE
Charles M. Storey, Jr. '37, Chairman
   Frederick P. Barrett '37
      George E. Enos '37
         Robert C. Hall '36
            Stephen V. N. Powelson '38
               William W. Waters '37
                  Hans H. Zinsser '38

TOASTMASTER
Arthur Atwood Ballantine '04

SPEAKERS
William John Bingham '16
Director of Athletics

James Phinney Baxter, 3D
Master of Adams House

Felix Frankfurter
Byrne Professor of Administrative Law

Lewis William Douglas LL.D. '33
Former Director of the Budget

Memorandum for Felix Frankfurter
The White House, May 4, 1935
If you are really hot under the collar at 11:55 P.M. on May eighth,
write me before you go to sleep. I appreciate my cakes hot off the griddle.
F.D.R.

Memorandum Regarding Crimson Dinner
May 8, 1935

1. About the third week in April Arthur Ballantine, Jr. phoned me to say that the Annual *Crimson* dinner would be held on Wednesday, May 8. That his Dad was to be Toastmaster, Professor Baxter and Lew Douglas were to be speakers, and they very much wanted me also to speak — perhaps on my Oxford experience. After a preliminary word of appreciation I told the boy that the *Crimson* dinner ought to be a gay affair, and that talk about educational matters is not apt to be exciting, at least in my mouth. And that in any event since three of their speakers were anti–New Dealers, and since his Dad would make not one but several anti–New Deal speeches during the course of the evening, of course I would not speak about Oxford were I to come, but would naturally take up the cudgels for the New Deal. The boy said they did not want to have a personal controversy, and I assured him that we were all gentlemen who were accustomed to handling differences of opinion in parliamentary ways, but that in any event I certainly would not go there to talk about education while Lew Douglas and his Dad lit into the New Deal. He then said they would be delighted to have me talk about the New Deal if I would, and I said that I would be delighted to come, but that inasmuch as there were three anti–New Dealers speaking, and his father would make a series of such speeches in his capacity as Toastmaster I should have to insist, in all fairness, on following Mr. Douglas, as it were, by way of rebuttal, particularly since his father would follow me and have a last word against the New Deal. The boy said that he thought that was entirely fair, and that he was perfectly delighted that I am ready to come and that the arrangements are entirely satisfactory to him, namely, that I should be the last speaker after Lew Douglas.

2. A few days thereafter, on April 22nd, I received a letter from young Arthur Ballantine, which bore every earmark of careful legal draftsmanship. In effect it stated that he had been reconsidering the arrangement that he had made with me, that he was troubled by it because Mr. Douglas is after all "not one of us," and therefore perhaps the proprieties required that he be the last speaker. He suggested that I might have a few minutes of rebuttal after Mr. Douglas spoke. In any event he wanted to have a full talk with me so that there should be no mistake, and the arrangements be all worked out before the dinner. I replied to him fixing a time to see him for a full talk, and assuring him that we certainly would not have a cock fight in the form of a public debate by having any such thing as a rebuttal after a main speech. I added that even before the talk I could not withhold the remark that Mr. Douglas would hardly like to be called "not one of us" since Alma Mater had conferred upon him her highest degree.

3. On April 29 Arthur Jr. came to see me at my house. We had about

an hour's talk, in which the whole matter was gone into with great detail for I resolved not to lay down any conditions — take it or leave it — but to address myself to Arthur's mind (he is a very intelligent fellow) and work things out so that he would see what the fair thing in the situation was. The upshot of the talk was an unqualified statement by Arthur (who in the meantime has been elected President of the *Crimson*) that under the circumstances it was fair that I should be the last speaker, in view of the political outlook of the other speakers, the general sympathy of the audience, and the fact that his father, after all, did have the final word. The boy said that the thing was now wholly clear, and that he would advise his father of the arrangements he had made. And so the matter was left.

4. I had no further communication whatever from anybody, and went to the dinner in complete reliance on the arrangement thus made, not having planned at all what I was going to say, expecting, of course, to get cues from what Arthur, Sr. and Lew Douglas were going to say.

5. The next stage of this affair is the night of the dinner. On arrival at the *Crimson* I had a very pleasant talk with young Arthur, and a little later on his father's arrival a very cordial few words with Arthur, Sr. The latter insisted that after the dinner I must come for a drink to his daughter's house (she lives in Cambridge) so that "you, Lew and I can have a long talk." I agreed to come provided I might take along two friends with whom I had tentatively arranged to go off, Lawrence Winship of the Boston *Globe* and Geoffrey Parsons of the New York *Herald Tribune*. The dinner proceeded as per schedule. As expected, cracks against the New Deal were the *leit-motiv* of all of Arthur, Sr.'s main and interlarding remarks. Arthur, Jr., Arthur, Sr., Bingham the Director of Athletics, Professor Baxter had spoken, and Lew Douglas, according to arrangements, was to be the next speaker. After two sentences or so Arthur Ballantine said something to the effect that "We shall now have some interesting glimpses into the impingement of the academic mind upon politics." Which was the first hint I had had that I was to be the next speaker. At that remark young Arthur, next to whom I sat, turned to me with his face as red as a beet, and said the following: "I made perfectly clear to Dad what my arrangement with you was, and for anything that may happen in not carrying out that arrangement I am not responsible. Dad thoroughly understood my arrangement with you." I said to the boy, I hope very quietly, "What your father is doing isn't cricket." And the boy repeated, "I made perfectly clear to him my arrangement with you. For whatever he does now I am not responsible." And I assured him that I had no doubt whatever that he was not responsible. And just about this moment Arthur Ballantine called on "Felix Frankfurter." I shall not soon forget the flushed face of that boy when he saw that his father had broken his son's word.

6. "Think fast, Captain, think fast." Well, never in my life did I have to think faster. When I got up my mind was like a completely empty bucket. I had, of course, quickly to decide whether to talk at all or whether to state the circumstances. Embarrassed as I was inside of me, it seemed to me that after all I ought to handle the situation as best I could without disappointing such expectations as the innocent audience had. Sparring for time I began by reading a fake telegram from "another distinguished former Editor of the *Crimson*" — such a telegram having been read previously from the absent President Conant. And so I began: "Mr. Toastmaster, before I proceed to my own remarks, may I read a telegram which has come to me, for some reason, from another distinguished former Editor of the *Crimson*:

"Please tell young Arthur Ballantine how much I rejoice that he is improving upon his father, among other things, for realizing that the road to the White House is not on the Oggy Mills special, but through the presidency of the *Crimson*. Give Lew my regards and tell him that by 1941 I shall have piled up so huge a deficit that even his appetite for balancing the budget will be satisfied when he follows me in the White House. And finally give my warm greetings to the *Crimson* gathering, and tell them that in my irrelevant way I recall what I once heard Uncle Theodore say: 'I love Harvard men as individuals, but I always feel more comfortable when most of them are against me, because then I am quite sure that then most of the country is for me.' "

It was needless to read the signature because the crowd broke into long and sustained laughter and applause.

I proceeded verbatim:

"Since this is an intimate family affair, and there are no reporters present, I will let you in to a little secret which thus far is shared only by Arthur, Sr. and Arthur, Jr. and myself. When I was asked to come here as a New Dealer, naturally it was expected that I would come empty-headed. I was to wait until I got my education from Arthur Ballantine and Lew Douglas, and then I was to say what I could in reply to them. I was to be told what the New Deal really was, and what its sins are, and then say what I could in mitigation of its sins. But here I am, as you can see, called out of turn, and as empty-headed as I was when I came here. I haven't been told what the New Deal is, but I now know what a Raw Deal is. In plain English it was very explicitly arranged by young Arthur, here, that Lew Douglas was to precede me, and I was to follow him, but for some strange reason Arthur over there has seen fit to break that arrangement, and so as you see,

I am sparring for time, and not at all informed about Lew Douglas's conception of the New Deal, but with a keener understanding, as I have said, of what a Raw Deal is, and also, if I may say so (looking hard at Arthur Ballantine, a few seats away) with a better insight into the mentality of the Republican party, and its best minds."

By that time I had internally resolved what to say, and spoke for a little over a half an hour on the history of the state of mind of, what might be called, the governing classes of America from the Interstate Commerce Act down to date, towards reform measures. Taking administration by administration, not sponsoring this or that specific legislation, but drawing a generalization, which I roughly documented, to the effect that our governing classes, and their lawyers and their editors — men like some of those who sit before me — have never realized with Macaulay, "that the way to conserve is to reform," and by violently resisting as destructive of reason, and fairness and of the Constitution, every effort to maintain our traditional system by adapting it to changing economic conditions, and making it fulfill the larger human needs of successive generations.

When I finished there was a really extraordinary outburst of applause, which I partly attributed to a resentment on the part of at least a good many of the audience against Arthur Ballantine's trickery. There was such applause that I had to "take a curtain."

Ballantine followed me with a seven to ten minutes' rebuttal of some of the things I had said, in a most appreciative way, but not a word of reference to my introductory disclosure of the violation of his son's agreement. He then introduced Douglas who in his opening words dissociated himself from Arthur's conduct as follows: 'Let me say at the outset that I think Professor Frankfurter should have been the last speaker, because the best should be last." Whereupon he proceeded to pour a whole barrel of molasses over me.

7. The dinner closed about midnight. I stood about a little while to talk to men who approached me, and finally took a cordial leave of Lew Douglas. Arthur Ballantine made no efforts to see me after the dinner, and I, of course, abstained from seeking him out. And I have had no word from him since, directly or indirectly, about the incident.

FELIX FRANKFURTER

Thereafter, Roosevelt, whenever anyone broke a gentleman's agreement, was in the habit of remarking that someone "was doing a Ballantine" on him. Arthur Ballantine had served with Roosevelt on the Crimson *at Harvard and had been Frankfurter's friend since before the First World War.*

Lake George, N.Y., May 13, 1935
Dear Professor Frankfurter,

That was a perfectly bully speech you gave us Wednesday evening. If it is possible, reflection makes it seem even better than its actual delivery.

Having had so much experience with Dad in the past, I hope that his performance as toastmaster strikes you as natural. As I said, I *can't* control him. That is the one aspect of the dinner that troubles me for we had talked over the whole matter beforehand. I do know that from everyone's point of view you gave such a fine speech that precedence could make no difference.

We were delighted to have you with us and would like to thank you very sincerely for your large part in making the evening such a success.

Sincerely yours,
ARTHUR BALLANTINE, JR.

Telegram to Frankfurter

The White House, May 2, 1935
DELIGHTED. TUESDAY EVENING, MAY FOURTEENTH. PLEASE SEND LIST OF NAMES.
FRANKLIN D. ROOSEVELT

The President had agreed to meet the liberal and progressive leaders in accordance with the suggestions made by Frankfurter and Niles.

Telegram to Miss LeHand

Cambridge, Mass., May 3, 1935
PLEASE CONVEY TO PRESIDENT FOLLOWING: WARM THANKS FOR FIXING TUESDAY THE FOURTEENTH AND WRITING ABOUT DETAILS.
FELIX FRANKFURTER

Cambridge, Mass., May 3, 1935
Dear Mr. President:

You were most kind to respond by wire fixing the evening of Tuesday the 14th for the meeting of the progressives. Do I correctly assume that the hour is 8:30?

Niles and I are trying to plan the thing with the utmost care so as to assure the greatest success. Niles, himself, is to be in Washington on Monday next to do the necessary preliminary work. Senator Norris was here yesterday — you will be interested in the enclosed interview with him — and Niles sounded him about the meeting. He was happy at the prospect, deemed it most important that free exchange should take place as soon as possible.

As to the participants there are the difficulties of keeping the meeting sufficiently small without offending sensibilities. Norris was particularly emphatic about the importance of a small gathering for an effective interchange. Niles has had the happy thought of including only those Senators who were members of the National Progressive League for Franklin D. Roosevelt in the 1932 campaign. This means, alphabetically, Costigan, Cutting, Johnson, La Follette, Norris and Wheeler. It draws, therefore, a relevant line against the inclusion of men like Bone, Nye, and Schwellenbach. What say you to this procedure?

Two members of your Cabinet, Wallace and Ickes, were also members of the Progressive League. What are your wishes in regard to their inclusion? If the visiting group is restricted to these six Senators, plus Niles and myself, it makes a party of nine. Wallace and Ickes would enlarge it to eleven.

May I trouble you to let me have your wishes so that Niles can have a specific mandate for going into action. Would it be at all possible to have word from you by wire or over the phone?

Always faithfully yours,
F.F.

Telegram to Frankfurter
The White House, May 6, 1935

IDEA OF THE ELEVEN YOU MENTION EXCELLENT. HAVE NILES LET ME KNOW SO THAT PROPER INVITATIONS CAN GO OUT FROM THE WHITE HOUSE.

FRANKLIN D. ROOSEVELT

Telegram to Miss LeHand
Cambridge, Mass., May 6, 1935

PLEASE GIVE THE PRESIDENT WARM THANKS FOR TELEGRAM ABOUT THE 11. NILES IN WASHINGTON AND I HAVE ASKED TOM TO TAKE HIM TO YOU TO CARRY OUT ARRANGEMENTS.

FELIX FRANKFURTER

Telegram to Miss LeHand
Cambridge, Mass., May 9, 1935

AM I EXPECTED ON TUESDAY NEXT? IF SO WHEN, PLEASE?

FELIX FRANKFURTER

Telegram to Frankfurter
The White House, May 10, 1935

YOU ARE EXPECTED FOR DINNER AND THE NIGHT ON NEXT TUESDAY.

M. A. LEHAND

Cambridge, Mass., May 16, 1935

Dear Mr. President:

1. There is no doubt about the high success of the Tuesday night session. I have heard from all the Senators, except Norris and Hiram Johnson, and they all were truly happy. According to Bob La Follette, "it was the best, the frankest, the most encouraging talk we have ever had with the President. I know Burt felt that way about it for I went home with him. I told Burt that hereafter if there is anything on his chest he should get it off to the President directly, that he no longer has any excuse for private grousing, now that the President has told him he could get in touch with him through Miss LeHand. The President was fair, and frank, and I felt greatly encouraged that he is going to go into the stride of his old aggressive leadership." There was real warmth and enthusiasm in Bob as I talked to him, and I know your assertion that "the time had come" heartened and invigorated them. Incidentally, it seems to me that Bob La Follette is steadily growing in stature, and I believe you have no more dependable friend and helper in Congress than Bob.

2. I wish you had seen Brandeis's face light up when I gave him your message about your tax policy and the forthcoming message about it. His eyes became glowing coals of fire, and shone with warm satisfaction. He asked me to tell you how deeply he rejoiced to have had the message from you, and with what eagerness he is looking forward to the enunciation of your policy. When I told him with what tender sadness you said to me that you had hoped the big leaders in finance and business would learn something, he very gravely shook his head and said, "I understand truly his feeling. We have all had that hope from time to time, but apparently they just can't."

3. Altogether I have come back greatly exhilarated and surer than ever that you can have full confidence in the country's response to the strength and serenity and courage of your leadership. It won't sound strange to you if I say that not least encouraging to me was to see you play with Sistie and Buzzie. I could make a little speech as to the implications of that scene and of the qualities that it revealed.

4. I am an obedient private and I delivered your message to Marion, with all its warmth and all its nuances, and told her if she has any doubts about it to come down and see for herself.

5. A friend of Arthur Sulzberger's and mine, who has good judgment, tells me it would be a wise thing if, before long, you were to ask Sulzberger and his Iphigene — *his* not mine — to the White House for a small quiet dinner, talking about nothing in particular. After all old Ochs was a friend of yours, and Arthur Sulzberger and his wife have succeeded to the respon-

sibility of Ochs in the conduct of our greatest newspaper. I am told that Sulzberger is capable of education.

My warmest thanks to you.

Always faithfully yours,

F.F.

P. S.   I'm glad to see the railroad danger is averted. Good!

Burt is Senator Burton K. Wheeler, an isolationist with a progressive record on domestic policy. Sistie and Buzzie are nicknames for Roosevelt's grandchildren, the daughter and son of Anna Roosevelt Dall.

Telegram to Grace Tully

Cambridge, Mass., May 27, 1935

PLEASE TELL PRESIDENT I AM LEAVING ON FEDERAL TONIGHT AND UNLESS OTHERWISE ADVISED WILL TURN UP AT THE WHITE HOUSE LATE TOMORROW AFTERNOON.

FELIX FRANKFURTER

Cambridge, Mass., May 29, 1935

Dear Mr. President:

In the interest of clarity may I put in a few words on paper the gist of my thoughts on the issue of the Supreme Court vs. The President.

1. Postponement of fighting out that issue at the present time does not rule the issue out as one on which you may later go to the country. I assume that a strategist like you will select time and circumstances most favorable for victory. I suspect that events may give you better conditions for battle than you have even now.

Decisions in other cases may accumulate popular grievances against the Court on issues so universally popular that the Borahs, the Clarks, the Nyes and all the currents of opinion they represent will be with you in addition to the support you have today. That is why I think it so fortunate that the Administration has pending before Congress measures like the Social Security bill, the Holding Company bill, the Wagner bill, the Guffey bill. Go on with these. Put *them* up to the Supreme Court. Let the Court strike down any or all of them next winter or spring, especially by a divided Court. *Then* propose a Constitutional amendment giving the national Government adequate power to cope with national economic and industrial problems. That will give you an overwhelming issue of a positive character arising at the psychological time for the '36 campaign, instead of mere negative issue of being "agin" the Court which, rising now, may not be able to sustain its freshness and dramatic appeal until election time.

2. That approach has these advantages:

(a) It defines a sharp issue — of the increase of Congressional power on industrial and economic problems — instead of attacking the Supreme Court's vague general powers. A general attack on the Court, unlimited in the changes it *may* cause, would give opponents a chance to play on vague fears of a leap in the dark and upon the traditionalist loyalties the Court is still able to inspire.

(b) It cuts across all technicalities of law and presents an issue which the common man can understand and which he can feel means something personally important to him.

I am, be assured, as anxious as you are that you should not try to fool the American people into believing that you can do more than the Supreme Court permits you to do. But I also know how much you still can do, how the Supreme Court can eat its words, and what a difference it makes in the Court's application of "the law" how statutes are drawn, how they are administered, how they are tested by the right selection of cases, how these cases are treated in lower courts by judges, district attorneys and government counsel, how they are handled and argued before the Supreme Court itself.

All of which is respectfully and affectionately submitted,

F.F.

Roosevelt, with sad and divisive consequences, chose to follow a different course; but he had Frankfurter's steady help, once the court-packing fight began in 1937, as will be seen later in this correspondence.

Senator William E. Borah, Senator Gerald Nye, and Senator Bennett Champ Clark all represented important groups of opinion throughout the Midwestern and Western states.

Cambridge, Mass., May 30, 1935

Dear Mr. President:

This is intended as a brief outline of a program for *immediate* action in dealing with the consequences of the Schechter decision.

(1) Promptly introduce a bill empowering the President to attach fair labor clauses to contracts for Government purchases and to contracts made with the proceeds of Government loans and grants. Stanley Reed is now perfecting such a bill and plans to have it in your hands by Friday night. The Bill will be short and ample in its discretionary powers.

Such a measure would directly affect extensive areas of industry. Indirectly, by the psychological force of the Government's authority, it would draw a much wider support to the standards promulgated by the Government.

To enforce such fair conditions, clauses will require ample and skilled administration.

(2) Therefore continue, by appropriate legislation or joint resolution, the administrative mechanism of NRA for a stated period, say to March 1937. This would also assure maintenance of the experience and technical information gained by NRA to be used

   (a) as a clearing house for voluntary formulation and observance
       of fair standards, and
   (b) as an aid and stimulant to appropriate action by the States.

Moreover, it would keep intact the mechanism for whatever ultimate policy will be evolved. Finally, the continuation of the mechanism will

   (a) prevent any lapse on June 16th through possibility of filibus-
       ter, etc., and
   (b) avoid any jerry-built lawmaking on the substantive constitu-
       tional problems.

By the continuance of the mechanism something really important will have been accomplished at the same time that the necessary period for maturing wise legislation is secured.

(3) As to labor's interest, the Wagner Bill has become the effective symbol and therefore that measure should be vigorously pushed to passage.

This, of course, implies an adequate appropriation to enable the proposed National Labor Board to do a real job.

Incidentally, it may be desirable to give an effective quietus, through one of those happy statements by the President at a press conference or otherwise, to the high-priced advice given by eminent New York lawyers that voluntary compliance with the labor provisions of the codes might be treated by the Government as a violation of the Anti-Trust Laws. An elementary lesson in law might be tendered — without charge — to the New York lawyers that while agreements to fix prices would offend the Sherman Law, agreements to maintain the decencies of life do not.

(4) The principle behind the Webb-Kenyon Act (liquor) and the Hawes-Cooper Act (convict goods) should be utilized by an appropriate bill to protect the decent labor policies of the several states by Federal legislation to the end that importation into any State of goods produced under conditions not conforming to the labor policy of that State would become unlawful. This device could be of real and dramatic value in meeting, certainly in part, the child labor problem. It should, of course, be drawn so as to cover as wide a range of decent State industrial standards as possible. Such an act would be one more assertion of Federal power under the Commerce Clause and at the same time it would help to effectuate State policies.

In this connection and as part of the whole program, the advantage of calling a conference of State Governors may well be seriously considered. Education and stimulation of the States in connection with the Social Security Bill will be necessary when the bill becomes Law. The two problems — complementary State legislation under the Social Security Act and the State NRA legislation — might be dealt with effectively at such a conference for they are interrelated. Such a conference would not at all imply an abandonment of Federal action, inasmuch as Federal methods are also being pursued and others definitely explored. It is significant that several telegrams addressed to you suggest the calling on such a conference.

Such a conference would be used as the occasion for a rounded presentation of the New Deal aims and the diverse methods by which they are being pursued. This is, I believe, essential, to take out of the public mind the false equation that NRA = New Deal instead of being simply one means of realizing some of its purposes.

(5) It has already been indicated that the Administration should vigorously proceed with legislation now pending, like the Social Security Bill, the Holding Company Bill and the Wagner Bill. These measures, as well as your proposals for taxes, are, of course, not at all an "answer" to the Supreme Court. But they will serve to the public mind as powerful symbols of the general popular direction of your purposes and prove that the momentum of your purposes and your leadership is unabated.

(6) The foregoing program, limited as it is, has, it is submitted, the following merits:

(a) it is intrinsically sound;
(b) it gives proof of prompt leadership and thereby satisfies the psychological needs of the situation;
(c) it affords evidence of effective adherence to the underlying purposes of NRA;
(d) it leaves ample time for maturing a permanent policy.

Faithfully yours,
F.F.

A large part of the "immediate" program advocated by Frankfurter was accepted by Roosevelt. But the time and the strategic advantages thus gained by the President were not used to develop a "permanent" program. Hence the clash with the Supreme Court could not be averted.

This letter led to repeated and prolonged conferences with Roosevelt and with Solicitor General Stanley Reed.

Telegram to Miss LeHand
Cambridge, Mass., June 2, 1935

PLEASE TELL PRESIDENT AM ARRANGING THINGS HERE TO BE DOWN WEDNESDAY AFTERNOON.

FELIX FRANKFURTER

Telegram to Frankfurter
The White House, June 4, 1935
VERY SORRY THE PRESIDENT IS TIED UP TOMORROW AFTERNOON AND EVENING.
CAN YOU COME THURSDAY INSTEAD?

M. A. LeHand

Telegram to Miss LeHand
Cambridge, Mass., June 4, 1935
SHALL OF COURSE BE THERE ON THURSDAY, LEAVING ON FEDERAL TOMORROW
NIGHT. WITH ALL GOOD WISHES.

Felix Frankfurter

Telegram to Miss LeHand
Cambridge, Mass., June 10, 1935
PLEASE CONVEY THE FOLLOWING: DO LET PAT HARRISON HAVE HIS KITTENS.
HE WILL FIND THEM AS DID BARON MUNSCHAUSEN THE LIONS IN HIS PATH
STUFFED AND HARMLESS WHILE OUR PEOPLE WILL FIND THROUGH YOU NEW
HOPE FOR THE TRADITIONAL DEMOCRATIC PROMISE OF AMERICAN LIFE BY
CURBING EXCESSIVE CONCENTRATION OF PLUTOCRATIC POWER. HAVE A GOOD
TIME.

Felix Frankfurter

*Senator Harrison had played a shuffling and equivocal role in the passage
of the rump NIRA bill after the Schechter case.*

*Roosevelt shared with Frankfurter a connoisseur's delight in good food
and good wine, but unfortunately his wife did not have these interests.
Frankfurter often was the recipient of the President's sad tales of unexciting
food in the White House. Judge Julian W. Mack touched Frankfurter's
life at many points far more important than an interest in food and wine.
They were united by their devotion to Zionism, their love of Harvard, and
their loyalty to high standards of legal scholarship. Frankfurter remembered
that the meeting with Judge Mack produced enough "wine taster" stories
from the President to satisfy even the greatest enthusiast. Roosevelt talked
about wine with the relish and excitement which he usually reserved for
stories of life at sea.*

*Roosevelt was in Hyde Park before going to the graduation ceremonies
at West Point.*

Hyde Park, N.Y., June 11, 1935
My dear Judge Mack:
Felix Frankfurter has been spending some time with me and I was
much interested to learn that aside from being one of our best jurists, you

are also a connoisseur of wines. I am hoping that as soon as things quiet down you will come to Washington to see me. I have some "wine taster" stories that I think will amuse you.

F.D.R.

The White House, June 19, 1935

I, Franklin D. Roosevelt, party of the first part, do hereby, solemnly agree to submit, in ample time for full discussion to Marguerite LeHand and Felix Frankfurter, parties of the second part, any and all proposed attacks, direct or indirect, upon the press or parts thereof, under any form or pretexts. So help me God.

In the presence of Grace G. Tully

FRANKLIN D. ROOSEVELT

The President wrote "Nerts" at the end of this memorandum.

In a letter to Sidney Shalett, who was working with Congressman James Roosevelt on a nonpolitical book on Roosevelt, Frankfurter did his best to recall what had happened. His letter, dated January 29, 1959, follows:

Cambridge, Mass., January 29, 1959

My dear Mr. Shalett:

Replying to your inquiry of January 21, I am afraid I cannot help you much. My recollection of the episode to which the document quoted by Arthur Schlesinger, Jr., on p. 566 of *The Coming of the New Deal*, refers is all too general. All that I can firmly derive from my memory is that I was staying at the White House at the time in question and one night at dinner with the President, at which beside myself there were present Misses Marguerite LeHand and Grace Tully, the President went on a gay rampage about some journalistic irresponsibility for which he was going to call the press to account at one of his press conferences. Both Miss LeHand and I expressed the hope that he would not get into a needless scrimmage with the press. Our attitude evidently intensified the President's shadow-boxing against the press. He simulated such seriousness that he took us in and we exacted a promise from him that he wouldn't waste his time on his planned attack on the press. The talk gradually gained hilarity and it took the form of a spurious formal agreement. That is the document that Schlesinger printed and I was greatly surprised to see it. That President Roosevelt should have put this among his files, however, is one more illustration of the completeness with which he kept all his records.

Sincerely yours,
FELIX FRANKFURTER

Memo for the President

Cambridge, Mass., June 17, 1935

Here is a stab at a draft of a message for legislation cutting off suits on the gold clauses.

A number of questions of tactics in the presentation of the issue are of course raised.

One problem is how much to argue or at least to refer to the merits of the suits that are going to be cut off. I do think it essential to take the line that the Perry case did settle and must be regarded as settling the whole matter. On the other hand, it is hard to avoid the implication that the proposed legislation is being urged precisely because it is feared that it did not wholly settle it. To keep silent about or to slur over the suits that are going to be hit may well give exaggerated importance to them. It seems to me, therefore, the part of wisdom to take the bull by the horns and state very briefly what the suits are likely to be and why they are not any good.

The draft states the problem as candidly as I believe the meaning of the Supreme Court decision to be. In other words, there is no likelihood that future suits will succeed. The one certain thing about them is that they will be a nuisance and the danger from that certainty far outweighs the possibility that cutting off access to the courts would be doing any substantial injustice. It seems to me good strategy to anticipate and frankly meet arguments against the proposed legislation rather than to be silent about them.

On the other hand, nothing is said about the foreign investor. The unfairness of allowing him suit might easily be stated but I am inclined not to bother about it.

F.F.

Gold Clause Message

Before the termination of this session of the Congress definite action should be taken to eliminate any uncertainty with respect to the right of holders of gold clause bonds of the Government to sue for payment in gold.

To this end, I urge the withdrawal by the United States of its consent to be so sued. The question of the effect of the so-called gold clause, in the light of the monetary legislation of the 73rd Congress, came before the Supreme Court at the Term just closed. After full argument and consideration, the Court decided that the clause was without effect and that the obligation of gold clause bonds was met by payment, dollar for dollar, precisely as tendered by the Treasury. Claims for additional payment under existing circumstances, the Court said, were claims for an "unjust enrichment" of those who made the claims. Plainly, the Nation should be protected against further claims of this character.

Litigation, however unreasonable, putting into question the amount of the national debt and the value of government securities is bound to be unsettling in its effects. The country should not bear this needless burden of insecurity. The United States refrained from exercising its prerogative to refuse suit until the Supreme Court had full opportunity to pass upon the question. The Court has now given its judgment and the highest considerations of public interest demand that other claimants should abide by it.

The asserted foundation for further suits upon the gold clause lies in some expressions of the prevailing opinion which apparently have been misunderstood. Whatever the exact import of those expressions, there can be no doubt as to the essence of the Court's decision; namely, that neither in justice nor in law does any basis exist for claims to payment in excess of the number of dollars promised and offered to be paid. Abstract speculation as to collateral questions ought not to be allowed to give intermittent uncertainty as to the status of holders of government securities. Ingenious attempts to circumvent the decision, even were they technically well-founded, would result only in the inequitable enrichment of a few investors shrewd enough to invent new objections.

I am advised by the law officers of the Government that these attempts are not well-founded. The Court's reference to the Joint Resolution of June 5, 1933, in no way weakens the force of its conclusion that other legislation, within the unquestionable constitutional powers of Congress, has taken away the right of United States bondholders, as of all persons, to demand payment in gold or to demand payment measured by weight of gold. Since the United States has properly refused the payment demanded, there is no warrant for a contention that there has been a breach of the obligation or that the right of the United States to call such bonds for payment is in any degree impaired. Nor does the Court's finding that the representative claimant in the case before it had failed to prove loss imply that some other claimant, upon a different hypothetical showing, might in the future be able to prove loss. Careful study of the opinion establishes that the ground of the Court's conclusion was that the dollars offered in payment were on a parity of value with the dollars promised. This conclusion will hold so long as the Congress adheres to its declared policy, now more than a third of a century old, to maintain the equal value of every dollar in the market.

Bonds of the United States issued with gold clauses have been continuously quoted on the exchanges at no higher prices than bonds not containing such clauses. But the continued possibility of litigation leaves open the continued possibility of speculation. There is no public interest under these conditions in permitting to a few private litigants opportunity for exploitation, to the potential injury of the public, of the supposed uncertainties of a judicial opinion in the hope of a wholly speculative private profit.

Cambridge, Mass., June 27, 1935

Dear Mr. President:

1. Some time ago you were good enough to ask me to think about the problems presented in safeguarding properly the papers you have collected before you came to the White House and since. It occurred to me that the best way to help was to consult the wisest man at Harvard on the subject, Samuel Eliot Morison, the historian (I assume you have read his delectable *Maritime History of Massachusetts*). He is at once very discreet and very knowing, and I put the matter to him in confidence. He undertook to think about it and I now have from him the enclosed letter. If I can be of further use of course I am at your disposal, as is, I know, Sam Morison who is a very warm supporter of yours.

2. My Boston newspaper friends who keep most track of the press of the country — Buxton of the *Herald* and Larry Winship of the *Globe* — tell me that your tax message has had the most favorable response possible from the press throughout the country, as well as among people whose views do not get into the press.

3. Naturally I have been following with the keenest interest the dispatches from Washington regarding the legislative strategy of the tax legislation. As I read between the lines you were up against another astute effort to put action on the message off until the Ides of March, and by very skillful manoeuvering you have placed the leaders in a situation where they had to promise action at this session. The whole game, of course, was to put it off until next year, and then next year have the forthcoming campaign put it off. In the meantime not only would there have been a new claim of business uncertainty due to unknown future taxes, but also the claim that your tax message was a "mere gesture" and not real business. Instead, as the dispatches make abundantly clear, you so guided matters that Doughton and Pat Harrison could not escape being committed to the promise of legislation now. That will clear the decks and give you the momentum of an accomplished program with which to enter the campaign. I suspect even the leaders on the Hill as professionals must appreciate the professional skill with which you steered things toward the result you desired.

With warmest regards,

Faithfully yours,
F.F.

Senator Pat Harrison and Representative Harry Doughton were the central Congressional figures involved in the consideration of this legislation.

Cambridge, Mass., June 25, 1935

Dear Felix,

It would not be wise for me to prescribe in the case of the President's papers, without knowing something of their bulk, scope, and complexity. The safe, general principle in archives is that of integrity, or as the French call it, *respect du fonds*, which means that the material should all be deposited in the same place, and that the order of it should not be disturbed. But there may be special conditions in the President's correspondence which would justify an exception being made. The obvious repository is the National Archives; and the President would earn the gratitude of historians as well as setting a proper precedent if he would make arrangements to deposit his material there, instead of, like his predecessors, taking it away with him from the White House.

The principal archival expert in the United States is Dr. Waldo G. Leland, Secretary of the Council of Learned Societies, 907 15th Street, Washington, D.C.; and a close second is Dr. R. D. W. Connor, head of the new National Archives Building in Washington. I would suggest that the President consult either, or both.

Faithfully yours,
SAM. E. MORISON

Samuel Eliot Morison, Professor of History, Harvard, author and editor. Frankfurter had been commuting from Harvard to the White House to plan future legislative strategy with the President to blunt the Supreme Court's opposition. The strategy was only partially successful.

The White House, June 20, 1935

Dear Frank:

These have been exhilarating and awing days for me. Exhilarating — for no one can be in your company without being exhilarated. Awing — for, after all, you are not merely yourself, but the symbol of the majesty of the most powerful nation. And it is indeed awing to have the head of our people so human, so simple, so unspoilably democratic, so gay, so purposeful.

Having spent so many hours in Lincoln's study, naturally Lincoln has been much in my mind. I'm sure he would have felt, had he had my experience during the last few weeks, as I feel about you. Seventy years after his death he would have found you dedicated to the noble purpose of the nation which he expressed in the Gettysburg address.

You surely know that if I can lighten ever so little your burdens you only have to say the word. Have a good brief holiday — and I hope affairs will soon permit you to have a long one.

Gratefully & affectionately,
F.F.

The following memorandum by Frankfurter, as Roosevelt recognized and indicated, was a historic document, for it showed that Roosevelt knew he would have trouble with the Congressional leaders of his party as early as the summer of 1935. The memorandum destroys the myth that the divisions in the Democratic party became serious only because of the court-packing fight and the attempt to purge uncooperative Democrats like Senators George and Tydings.

Memorandum
The White House, July 10, 1935

Last night, after a very delightful dinner on the South Porch, the President asked Ferdinand Pecora and me into his study in the Oval Room. He said he had a nasty little problem — a row between Senator Tydings, Chairman of the Senate Investigating Committee now examining conditions in the Virgin Islands, and Secretary Harold Ickes. The latter had sent an irate letter to Tydings charging him with unfairness in the conduct of the investigation. Tydings had replied with acerbity. There are involved several personalities — a constituent of Tydings, a Judge, a former Congressman, and Senator Pat Harrison who has taken up the cudgels for Tydings. Pat Harrison has enlisted the support of Senator Joe Robinson, and these Democratic leaders are asking for the scalp of Ickes. The President said Ickes is hot-tempered and impulsive and all that and treats Congressmen and Senators with brusqueness; but he is very valuable and the President refuses to let him go.

And then, the President, after ruminating on the situation, said, "Moreover, at bottom, the leaders like Joe Robinson, though he has been loyal, and Pat Harrison are troubled about the whole New Deal. They just wonder where the man in the White House is taking the old Democratic party. During their long public life, forty years or so, they knew it was the old Democratic party. They were safe and when the Republicans got into trouble, the old Democratic party won nationally. But in any event they, and in the South without opposition, were all right and old-fashioned. But now they just wonder where that fellow in the White House is taking the good old Democratic party. They are afraid there is going to be a new Democratic party which they will not like. That's the basic fact in all these controversies and that explains why I will have trouble with my own Democratic party from this time on in trying to carry out further programs of reform and recovery. I know the problem inside my party but I intend to appeal from it to the American people and to go steadily forward with all I have."

Frankfurter noted that he read his minutes of this conversation to the President, who asked Frankfurter to keep the memorandum because of its "historic value."

Memorandum for the President
SUBJECT: Chairmanship of Central Statistical Board.

The White House, August 15, 1935

Of the three men suggested — Frederick C. Mills, Wesley C. Mitchell, Stuart A. Rice, — I happen to know Mitchell well and know something of the work of Mills and Rice. Of course, I am not technically qualified to pass on the technical qualifications of these men, but I have tapped the judgment of men who know all three well and who are qualified to express an opinion not only as to the statistical ability and resourcefulness of Mills, Mitchell and Rice, but also as to their capacity for organization and administration. On all the evidence I am clear that Professor Mills holds the largest promise for the kind of work you would desire in the guidance of the Central Statistical Board, and for the following reasons:

1. Mitchell is, I suppose, barring only Taussig, the most distinguished living American economist. But he is, for your purposes, too old, too set in his ways and too "Hooverized."

2. Rice's experience has been predominantly along the line of vital statistics and not financial and economic statistics, and I take it that it is imaginative, illuminating work concerning social economic forces of the United States that the Central Statistical Board ought to make its major contribution. Moreover, I am informed that Mills has much more talent and adaptability for collaborative enterprise than has Rice and that is, of course, a most important faculty for the best work of a chairman of such a Statistical Board.

3. I am advised that Rice and Mills are warm friends and that Mills took himself out of consideration for the chairmanship when he heard that Rice was a candidate. If, therefore, Mills should be deemed the best choice, it will require the right kind of handling not to make him feel that he is doing his friend out of a job. I infer from Secretary Wallace's letter of the twelfth that he has personal relations with Mills or at least has means for diplomatic discussion with him.

F.F.

Frankfurter's advice was taken, and Ben Cohen remained as a general adviser to the President instead of becoming a member of the Securities and Exchange Commission. Robert Healy of Vermont, formerly Chief Counsel for the Federal Trade Commission, had not fulfilled expectations as a Commissioner on the SEC. The problems of the SEC now occupied a great deal of Frankfurter's time, and the President hoped that he would be able to get Frankfurter's advice on many other matters. Frankfurter twice came to Washington for these general discussions. The President also invited Frankfurter to accompany him on a forthcoming trip to the Western states. On September 5, Frankfurter ended a letter to Miss LeHand with these words: "Tell the President I did not 'hold out' on him about the abandonment of the Western trip. The time is too short — for I must soon be back training young lawyers for Wall Street!"

Memorandum for the President

The White House, August 21, 1935

Re: Securities and Exchange Commission Vacancy.

1. May I suggest that you tell Ben and Tom, when you have them in, that while Ben is doubtless the man best qualified to administer the three laws — looking forward to a Holding Company Act — which he largely drew, nevertheless, some men are needed for staff rather than line service and you will continue to need the team, Ben and Tom, for staff work. That is the reason Tom has not been utilized for other important posts.

2. If you think well of it, it would help to tell Ben that you have had a frank talk with me about the matter and that I felt very clearly that membership on the Commission was not the best use of Ben's abilities.

3. It would be well to ask the boys for names of people really qualified for the vacancy. I have tipped off Tom and he will propose Ross's name and give a number of powerful considerations that would make Ross a really ideal appointment.

4. The Commission ought to have a man with seasoned experience in utility affairs who is, at the same time, dependably liberal. Either at this session (as now seems likely) or next year a Holding Company Bill will become a law. Whether it does so at this season or not, a man with appropriate qualifications in this most vital field ought to be appointed because, in any event, utility issues constitute a large part of the business coming before the SEC.

5. Ross comes from the right section; he is liberal and has a record for fairness. Politically as well as intrinsically he would add enormous strength to the Commission. (Healy is very finicky and unimaginative and obstructive rather than constructive.)

6. Jim Landis is greatly concerned lest a mediocre new man really impair the work of the Commission. He says that their honeymoon period is over and, as a matter of fact, they have not yet touched some of the most

difficult problems before the Commission. He thinks it would be better to leave the place open until next year rather than have a mediocre man, a man who has had merely brokerage experience or is a second-rate lawyer.

7. I should think that since Ross is down here on PWA work, it should not be difficult to persuade him to go on the SEC certainly for a year or two, and thereby help see the Commission through the very critical year that lies ahead.

FELIX FRANKFURTER

Telegram to Frankfurter
The White House, September 10, 1935

HOPE YOU AND MARION WILL LUNCH WITH US ON TUESDAY SEVENTEENTH ONE O'CLOCK. MR. ZEMURRAY WILL BE HERE.

M. A. LeHAND

At the President's request, Frankfurter wrote the following unsigned editorial in Today, *the magazine edited by Raymond Moley:*

September, 1935

THE LIBERTY LEAGUE SUPREME COURT

For weeks the country has awaited with breathless suspense the fate of the various great measures recently passed by Congress. No, not awaiting the decisions of the Supreme Court of the United States — that obsolete tribunal which the Constitution of the United States set up and which has been functioning for a hundred and forty-six years as the authoritative voice of the Constitution. I mean, of course, the new super-supreme court — The Supreme Court of the Liberty League.

That august tribunal undertook a few weeks ago to review the legislation of Congress and voice the legal conscience for the guidance of the American people. And we have all been waiting, as I said, with breathless suspense, wondering whether the Liberty League Supreme Court would find the legislation of the New Deal constitutional or not. Here were able and distinguished jurists. Here was Mr. Raoul B. Desvernine, the partner of ex-Governor Miller, counsel for the Steel Trust and vigorous opponent of the Stock Exchange Act. Here was James M. Beck, the great self-constituted guardian of the Constitution, well-paid to declare the TVA legislation unconstitutional. Here was John W. Davis, Morgan lawyer, specially retained to contest the Holding Company Act. Here was former Governor Joseph B. Ely, who was professionally enlisted against the passage of the Guffey bill. Also Frank J. Hogan, one of Andrew Mellon's legal batteries. Also Forney Johnson, counsel in the suit to upset the TVA (which, incidentally, has thus far gone against him). Also Robert H. McCarter, brother of the head of the Edison Electric Institute. Also Joseph M. Proskauer, counsel of the Niagara Hudson and Consolidated Gas interests. Also ex Senator David A. Reed, another of Mr. Mellon's legal saviours. Also Earl F. Reed, counsel for the Weirton Steel Corporation and other interests who led the fight against the Wagner Labor Board. Also George Roberts, partner of Mr. Hoover's Secretary of State, who gave the leading professional opinion against the constitutionality of the Holding Company Bill. Also Ralph M. Shaw, a member of Silas Strawn's firm, (*res ipsa loquitur,* as the lawyers say). And also George W. Wickersham, who thought Theodore Roosevelt was a Communist. Would these grave and learned men of law find the TVA and the Stock Exchange Act and the Social Security Act and the Holding Company Act and the new Wagner Labor Act, constitutional?

Part of the suspense is over. The first of the pronouncements of the Liberty League Supreme Court is that the National Labor Relations Act is unconstitutional. We are promised similar death sentences against the other enactments.

Of course, one could not possibly tell what these lawyers would do simply because they had already, all of them, committed themselves against the New Deal legislation; one could not tell what this super-Supreme Court will do, simply because every lawyer who gives weight to this Committee is under heavy retainer to secure the invalidity of one or more of the enactments of the New Deal, or otherwise professionally lined up against the Administration.

The ordinary layman may be puzzled by all this. But it is the peculiar characteristic of the leaders of the bar that their minds are so detached, so impersonal, so disinterested, so serenely above the ordinary temptations and colorings of the mind, that while on Monday, Wednesday and Friday they are paid handsomely to prove that a law is unconstitutional, on Tuesday, Thursday and Saturday, they can sit in impartial judgment upon the same law.

The layman may be puzzled too, by the headline "Fifty-eight Lawyers Agree" because it is difficult for him to understand how fifty-eight lawyers can agree on anything. But the layman on reflection will not underestimate the unifying force of a gentle flow of fees proceeding from what is, in essence, a common source.

Alas, the most effective answer to Lawyers of the Liberty League can no longer be made, for Will Rogers is dead and he alone could have pierced their ludicrous sham with two or three conclusive shafts. But these Liberty Leaguers have over-reached themselves. They have assumed that when Will Rogers died the sense of humor of the American people died with him. Or perhaps these Liberty Leaguers with a diligent eye on their retainers, have assumed that the years of suffering of millions of homespun American men and women have taken the laugh out of the American people. Well, they haven't. It is the safest of prophecies that these solemn, selfish lucabrations on the Constitution by the heavily financed lawyers of one side of a law suit will be laughed out of the ultimate court of America, the court of public opinion.

Telegram to Raymond Moley

Cambridge, Mass., September 24, 1935

SINCE OUR INDEPENDENCE WE HAVE INSISTED ON WORKING OUT OUR DESTINY ACCORDING TO OUR OWN NOTION OF NATIONAL WELL BEING. TO BE SURE, WE HAVE BELIEF THAT THE PRINCIPLES ON WHICH WE HAVE STAKED OUR DESTINY OFFER THE BEST OPPORTUNITY FOR THE FULLEST REALIZATION OF THE QUALI- TIES WITH WHICH MEN ARE ENDOWED AND THE GREATEST ASSURANCE FOR THE PEACE AND SECURITY OF A PEOPLE. OTHER NATIONS HAVE THE SAME RIGHT AS WE CLAIM FOR OURSELVES TO DETERMINE THEIR DESTINY SO LONG AS SUCH NA- TIONAL SELF-ASSERTION DOES NOT UNJUSTLY IMPINGE UPON OUR OWN RIGHTS. IN OUR PUBLIC RELATIONS WE MUST RESPECT OTHER FORMS OF GOVERNMENT, HOWEVER REPUGNANT THEY MAY BE TO OUR OWN PRECIOUS TRADITIONS, BUT WHEN THE TRUTH OF THE ETERNAL PRINCIPLES UPON WHICH OUR NATION WAS FOUNDED IS SCOFFED AT AND THEIR EFFECTIVENESS IS SCORNED IT BECOMES OUR DUTY TO RENEW OUR DEVOTION TO THESE AMERICAN PRINCIPLES BY AVOWING THEM IN WORDS AND LIVING THEM IN DEEDS. WE ARE NOT A COM- MUNITY OF BLOOD; WE ARE A COMMUNITY OF COMMON IDEALS. WHAT BINDS US INTO A SINGLE PEOPLE AND INTO ONE NATION IS THE TRADITION OF FREE- DOM OF THE RIGHT TO PURSUE LIFE, LIBERTY AND HAPPINESS REGARDLESS OF RELIGIOUS ORIGIN. "THE CONSTITUTION OF THE UNITED STATES," SAID THE SUPREME COURT IN ONE OF ITS FAMOUS OPINIONS, "WAS ORDAINED, IT IS TRUE, BY DESCENDANTS OF ENGLISHMEN, WHO INHERITED THE TRADITIONS OF ENG- LISH LAW AND HISTORY. BUT IT WAS MADE FOR AN UNDEFINED AND EXPANDING FUTURE AND FOR A PEOPLE GATHERED AND TO BE GATHERED FROM MANY NA- TIONS AND OF MANY TONGUES." A NATION SO CONSTITUTED AND A PEOPLE SO DEDICATED TO LIBERTY WROTE INTO ITS CONSTITUTION THE RIGHT TO WORSHIP GOD UNTRAMMELLED AND THE RIGHT TO GIVE FREE UTTERANCE TO THE THOUGHTS OF MEN. WE SHOULD BE STULTIFYING OUR WHOLE HISTORY AND THE EXAMPLE OF THE NOBLEST AMERICANS IF WE DID NOT AVOW THESE PRINCIPLES WHENEVER THEY ARE CHALLENGED. WHATEVER BE THE RELIGION IN WHICH HE WAS REARED OR THE STOCK FROM WHICH HE DERIVED, THIS IS AT THE VERY HEART OF AMERICAN FAITH, AND THE WORLD'S EXPERIENCE REINFORCES RATHER THAN DIMINISHES THE STRENGTH OF OUR FAITH.

FRANKFURTER

This message is of central importance. He had been asked by Roosevelt to put on paper some essential principles of American freedom without at-

tacking, by name, either Nazi Germany or Fascist Italy. Here is the result.

Looking back years later on the different philosophies that struggled for supremacy in the New Deal, Mr. Rexford G. Tugwell wrote:

> *The progressive orthodoxy was simple. It was regarded as having been reinforced by the occurrence of the depression. Big business and big finance had been responsible. The admission of these very persons and interests to governmental partnership in the NRA had set up a kind of unnatural union. General Johnson became with the progressives a kind of bête noire, and their disapproval was made known in emphatic terms. Then, too, the many representatives around him [Roosevelt] of the Brandeis philosophy were annoyed, and in Franklin's Valhalla no figure loomed larger than the old Justice. His disciples, beginning with Frankfurter, had infiltrated the administrative organization to an almost incredible extent, and this was a movement that tended to enlarge. The partnership theory was one they refused to accept.*

This is a fair summary of a complicated situation, provided one makes allowances for the limitations that must inevitably occur in dealing with profound intellectual differences in a few compact sentences.

Following General Hugh Johnson's attack on him as the secret and malign power controlling the New Deal, Frankfurter decided to discuss his relations with General Johnson in candid detail. He wrote at length to his friend Dr. Alfred E. Cohn of the Rockefeller Institute, and then showed a copy to the President. This was the only effort by Frankfurter to reply to General Johnson's criticisms, insofar as the President was concerned. He was more interested in defending Brandeis against a campaign of vilification than he was in protecting himself.

Cambridge, Mass., October 30, 1935

Personal

Dear Alfred,

You ask me whether General Hugh Johnson has "a special grievance" against me. You must judge for yourself, in the light of the following recital of my entire relations with him so far as my recollection serves me.

(1) Johnson was, at least during part of the World War, on General Crowder's staff. Crowder was, as you will recall, Provost Marshal General as well as Judge Advocate General, and as the former, was charged with the formulation and administration of our draft laws. Crowder was a rather close friend of mine from my early days in the War Department, and through my association with Crowder, I saw something, but not very much, of Johnson in War days. Our relations were, however, uniformly pleasant.

(2) He completely dropped out of my life, I never saw him again,

until after NRA took the scene in the Roosevelt Administration. Prior thereto, I had had no communication with him, direct or indirect. After Johnson was placed in charge of NRA, he phoned me from Washington and in the course of a long talk asked me to become his counsel, the general counsel of NRA, and almost bludgeoned me to accept. The reasons which led me to decline the Solicitor Generalship were even more operative in connection with Johnson's offer. He would not take a no, and the vigor with which he insisted that I must accept was such that it would be inaccurate to describe it otherwise than as bludgeoning. He must have been on the phone certainly for half an hour, and it may have been longer. I was adamant in my declination, but in reply to his insistence that I was the only man to do the job, I told him there were others more competent, and in answer to his inquiry, I told him I thought Donald Richberg's experience amply equipped him for the work.

(3) In view of the emergency and Johnson's insistence, I did accede to his request to attend a meeting in New York at Bernard M. Baruch's house, at which Johnson was to have present leading industrialists and leading labor people for a discussion of NRA. You will remember my attendance at that meeting, for I came to you for breakfast before going to the Baruch meeting, and thanks to your kindness also had Richberg, Wollman and Sidney Hillman to breakfast, so that I might be duly apprised about matters that were to be discussed at the Baruch meeting. Present at the meeting, among others, were Baruch, Johnson, Gerard and Herbert Swope, Walter Teagle of the New Jersey Standard Oil, Alexander Legge, President of the International Harvester, William Green of the AF of L, John Lewis of the Miners, and the four others I have mentioned, Richberg, Wollman, Hillman and myself. There were a few others, but I do not recall their names at the moment. The talk was mainly as to the importance of devising ways and means for reaching a bottom to wages and prices, the means of achieving the necessary stability in industry through the maintenance of fair standards of wages and hours, whereby the whole economic process could again be started through absorption of the unemployed and through assurance of the conditions whereby employment was possible. This, subject to the incident I shall shortly relate, was the only connection I have had with NIRA, or NRA, at any time. I had nothing whatever to do with conceiving the legislation, with drafting its form, or with administering its provisions.

(4) Barring only the above attendance at the Baruch house, and a further talk in Washington following this meeting with Johnson (in which, in response to inquiry, I spoke to him of Leo Wollman's equipment as an economic advisor), I have had only two other contacts, direct or indirect, with Johnson while he was at the head of the NRA.

(a) On behalf of the General, Louis Kirstein phoned me during the summer of 1933 to say that Johnson was much troubled by some criticisms of Walter Lippmann's based, as Johnson believed, on misunderstanding of the facts. Through Kirstein, Johnson asked me if I could bring about a meeting between himself and Lippmann. I told Kirtsein I should be glad to communicate to Lippmann Johnson's desire for a talk, with a view solely to putting Lippmann in possession of the facts. I wired in this tenor to Lippmann, who phoned me to say that he would be glad to see the General, provided it was understood he had full freedom of inquiry. Through Kirstein, I communicated Lippmann's readiness, under the condition stated, to go to Washington and see the General. That is all I had to do with it — I do not know to this day whether the meeting between Lippmann and the General came off.

(b) Following the General's outburst last fall regarding his relations with Mr. Justice Brandeis, Baruch phoned me on behalf of the General to say how remorseful Johnson was, and how ready to make any public statement to correct the outrageously false impression which he had created concerning Mr. Justice Brandeis' observance of judicial propriety. I told Baruch that Johnson had created one of those messes that had best be left alone; the more he tried to explain, the more he would get into a hole. The damage that he had done to Brandeis in the minds of the uninformed and the malicious was simply one of the casualties of life, and that Brandeis' serenity would triumph over this new episode of unfairness against him.

(5) I saw Johnson again two or three days after the Schechter decision — it was either Wednesday May 29th or Thursday the 30th. I happened to be in Washington and the President called for me. When I came I found the General with him. Johnson greeted me very warmly. The President briefly indicated that Johnson had a scheme for a new NRA which in Johnson's opinion would meet the constitutional objections that the Supreme Court had found in the Schechter case, and asked me to talk the matter over with the General. The President left us, and Johnson and I talked about all sorts of things, including the Brandeis episode. He told me how terribly sorry he was, that he admired Brandeis beyond anyone in the country, and he was troubled never to have expressed to Brandeis his regret. I told him if he felt that way, the thing to do was to write Brandeis a straightforward letter. Whereupon he stated that someone quoted me as having said he ought not to write such a letter. I told him he was wholly misinformed, that to confess error and express regret could not possibly be objectionable under any circumstances. (I heard later from Mr. Justice Brandeis that the General did write him such a letter in the course of which he made a very friendly reference to me.) Johnson then talked about the

implications of the Schechter case and his formula for meeting the Schechter decision. He was sure that he could re-draft the statute in short order, which would do all that NRA was intended to do and yet not collide with the constitutional difficulties of the Schechter case. I did not want to enter into technical discussions with Johnson, for he revealed to me his whole incapacity to understand what the Supreme Court had really decided and the Supreme Court barriers to what he was trying to do. Later, the same day, we had another meeting with the President, in the course of which Johnson's general effort was to win the President to immediate new NRA legislation, while I emphasized the unwisdom and difficulty of sponsoring any jerry-built, over-night legislation in the face of the Schechter decision. Johnson stated that he would put his ideas into bill form and then get hold of me to go over his bill.

Johnson phoned me on Friday, May 31st to say that his draft was finished and that he was ready to go over it with me. In the meantime, the President had had his press conference on the Schechter case (about which, incidentally, I knew nothing whatever until the public at large knew about it, after the event). At that conference the President had stated that all suggestions for possible new NRA legislation and the legal questions arising thereon, would be cleared through the Attorney General and through the Solicitor General. Therefore, when Johnson asked me to consider his bill, I told him of this announcement of the President's — which was published in the afternoon papers — and suggested the unwisdom if not impropriety of my pretending to express a professional judgment on his bill. Johnson said all right and rang off. And that was the last time I have had any kind of communication, direct or indirect, with the General.

(6) This gives you, I believe, a complete account of my relations with the General.

Always yours,
F.F.

Cambridge, Mass., October 31, 1935

Dear Mr. President,

(1) Welcome home! No breathing spell was more important for the country than a stretch of sleep and relaxation for you. I hope you had ample of both — I infer you did from the general tone and *esprit* and vigor that have come out of Washington since your return. I suppose I should add that I hope you had successful fishing, but I am unsportsmanlike enough to care more about the sleep you had than the fishing you didn't.

(2) Perhaps the detonations of the legal saviours of their country reached you. Charlie Burlingham did move into action. Lest by any chance

you missed his letter, I am enclosing it, for it had wide currency, not only in New York (where it was printed in both the *Times* and the *Herald Tribune*), but also outside. Steps were taken to have it widely publicized.

I think it is fair to say that the outgiving of the Shouse Supreme Court was a boomerang. It is significant that even the Republican newspapers were largely silent instead of approving. There is not a little ruction as to the prudence of the business within the ranks of the enemy, for it has been brought home to them, I have reason to know, that the movement was rather resented in the quarter at which it was mostly aimed.

(3) I have a letter this morning from Laski dated October 18th in which he writes the following:

> Poor Uncle Arthur [Henderson] is dying. I had a touching farewell with him yesterday — too pitiful to narrate. I doubt whether he will last another week. Will you tell F.D.R. that nearly the last thing he said to me was that the certainty that the United States would not help any belligerent next time, was one of the few hopes of peace. He repeated that three times.

You would have liked Arthur Henderson — a simple, God-fearing, hard-headed fellow. And how anxious he was, when I saw him last, to meet you!

(4) Laski also writes me:

> There is altogether, a better atmosphere about America and about F.D.R. personally, now. Above all Vandenberg (unwittingly) left the impression of no possible alternative, and I hear our ambassador reported that, despite criticism, the President's success with Congress was remarkable. I feel that he is, with all the debits, one of the two or three beams of light in this bloody world.

Isn't "bloody" a naughty word for an English scholar to use?

Marion joins me in warm regards.

Always yours,
F.F.

P.S.   I had a good talk with John shortly after the beginning of the College year.

John Roosevelt was the President's youngest son.

C. C. Burlingham had protested against the conduct of the lawyers associated with the "Liberty League Supreme Court." Founded in August 1934 to fight the New Deal, the American Liberty League attracted the support not only of Republicans but of Democrats like Al Smith, Jewett Shouse, John W. Davis, and Bainbridge Colby.

Cambridge, Mass., November 11, 1935

Dear Frank:

1. I've just heard your Arlington address, and its admirable sentiments were admirably phrased and came beautifully over the air. Mussolini will get scant comfort from it, and the announcement of your agreement with MacKenzie King was most cheering and was neatly timed.

2. If you have not seen the enclosed rather charming review, in the *Times Literary Supplement,* of your mother's "Life," it will interest you.

3. And I also enclose an excellent editorial, from the St. Louis *Star-Times* on the "quack questionnaire" of the U.S. Chamber of Commerce. Now that the returns of this sham are coming in, as part of Republican propaganda, you might make good use of the St. Louis piece.

4. Zemurray is a generous giver to all causes that he deeply cares about. He will, I'm sure, want to help next year, as he becomes more and more familiar with the issues and needs of the coming campaign. To that end it might be well to have a talk with him, soon again, in the White House, say about Latin-American matters and trade with Russia — the latter being a new, important subject of interest to him.

5. The other night I had a long, good talk with the Arthur Sulzbergers. (Iphigene is intelligent and of good purpose — and yet, as I left, I said to myself, only partly ungallantly, "I haven't the *Times,* but I have Marion.") I think the evening was not wasted from the Administration's point of view. I wonder if you have had them, either at Hyde Park or at the White House. If not, it would really help — but wouldn't even mention Krock's name. And let them know how strongly you feel about Hitlerism.

With warmest regards,

Always devotedly,
F.F.

P.S.   There is just no doubt whatever that much of the recent Massachusetts Republican vote is sheer anti-Curleyism.

The President had referred to agreements on trade and security with Prime Minister Mackenzie King of Canada.

Arthur Krock, the political commentator for the New York Times, *had angered Roosevelt by some of his criticism.*

The Times Literary Supplement *had reviewed* Gracious Lady *by Rita Halle Kleeman.*

The White House, November 13, 1935

Dear Felix:

I am sorry you feel that way about Iphigene. Things never go just right in this life. It would have been so perfect if you could have married Marion and the *Times* too! We are having them down soon but when they come I shall tie a piece of string around my little (left) finger to remind me not to tell the truth about Arthur Sulzberger. I shall tie another string on my right little finger to be sure that the little devil, which you know is in me, does not cause me to remark that Hitler really is a pretty good sort after all! Also, when I get back from Warm Springs I shall have Zemurray to lunch and get Morgenthau and Welles to sit in and talk about Latin American finances.

Sincerely yours,
F.D.R.

Cambridge, Mass., November 15, 1935

Dear Mr. President,

(1) One of your most devoted well-wishers who is also a most knowing party, with unusual and little-known information about banking and financial matters, sends me the enclosed clipping with the following comment:

> The effective answer to this banker yapping would be an autopsy of the nearly 6,000 failed banks 1930-1933, showing the causes of the failures. I have been persistently trying for this since the summer of 1930. Couldn't F.D.R. give it a punch now and get it as a campaign weapon within the next seven months?

(2) You will want to see, if you have not already done so, the altogether admirable brief which Stanley Reed and his assistants are preparing for the appeal in the Butler — the AAA — case. You will relish it for its own sake. But it also contains the best marshalling that I have seen of the circumstances that led to the enactment of the Agricultural Adjustment Act, the important benefits that have flowed from it, and the relation of these benefits to the general welfare. I should think this portion of the brief would serve as admirable raw material for the speech which, by the papers, I see you are contemplating regarding the agricultural situation.

I hope you will make a full dress speech on the subject, going, that is, into great detail even if you speak from forty minutes to an hour. In the first place, people will of course listen to you at length, as they will listen to nobody who might attempt a reply. In the second place, I think it is extremely important to review with great particularity the extraordinarily powerful story of the terrible conditions that led to AAA and the equally extraordinary results of it. You are the last person to be reminded how very, very short is people's memory. Not only is it important to refresh the recollection, but it is also important to furnish detailed ammunition to those who are eager to put your case, all over the United States. And so I hope the facts which are so admirably put in the brief for the Supreme Court, will, through your art and the persuasiveness of your voice, be put to the whole country.

(3) One of these days I suppose you will also be speaking about relief and unemployment. In trying to allay the fears of big and little business, you will agree, I am sure, that it is important not to lose the allegiance of the millions who are still unemployed and on relief, not give even remotely the appearance that the Administration's interest in them is lessened. And nothing will so powerfully give the assurance of unabated sympathy with their hardships and deep sensitiveness to their needs, as your explicit identification of yourself with their difficulties and their needs by speaking about them and thereby proving how uninterruptedly they have been and are in your mind and heart. I know that ought to be taken for granted, but one whose business it is in life to teach people is constantly surprised by nothing so much as the realization that the things people ought to take for granted and know as a matter of course, they don't. In this respect at least men are not different from women — they have to be told with great frequency that you love them.

With warm regards,

Always faithfully yours,
F.F.

P.S.   C.C.B. was terribly pleased by your recent letter to him about his *magnum opus.*

Burlingham had again defended the President against charges that he was tearing up the Constitution.

Cambridge, Mass., November 23, 1935

Dear Frank:

Can you intimate any suggestions for me to make — very discreetly — to Alice Duer Miller. She is a real friend, and as you doubtless know, a persuasive conduit.

Ben Cardozo writes me: "yesterday we called on the President. He seemed strong and happy. To have a picture of him talking with McReynolds would be precious." Can we not have such a photograph!? It would be a superb campaign poster — or might McReynolds enjoin you from exhibiting it!

I hope the stuffin' and the turkey will be as delicious as I've heard Georgians boast they can be.

Marion joins me in warm good wishes — and some play as well as work.

Ever yours faithfully,
F.F.

Alice Duer Miller, who early in the Second World War wrote The White Cliffs of Dover *in tribute to the British people, was going to Ottawa as the guest of the Governor-General, Lord Tweedsmuir (John Buchan). She wanted some ideas on American policy so she could explain the President's program to Canadians.*

The members of the Supreme Court had called at the White House for their annual official visit. Mr. Justice McReynolds gloried in his opposition to the New Deal.

Warm Springs, Ga., December 1, 1935

Dear Felix:

Many thanks for your note and the memos.

At the annual reception to the Supreme Court, I think the Chief Justice pulled a fast one on me. After he had been talking with me himself for ten minutes he got up, said he thought some other members of the Court should have a talk with me, and went across the room and brought McReynolds and plumped him down. The Chief Justice has a sense of humor though few people realize it. Thank God no photographers were present.

Love to Marion. Hope to see you both soon.

As ever yours,

F.D.R.

P.S.   Alice Duer Miller can do a lot of good.

The White House, December 28, 1935

Dear Marion and Felix:

That nice message of holiday greetings which you sent me pleased me immensely. Thanks ever so much for your thought of me.

My best wishes to you both for the happiest of New Years. See you soon!

Very sincerely yours,

F.D.R.

Memorandum by Frankfurter

December 28, 1935

I.   *The situation before the administration took hold*

"Where we were and whither we were tending." Banks closed, railroads bankrupt, industry paralyzed, confidence completely gone. It is easy to say now that we should let nature take its course, which is the theme of complaining business men today; but this is not what the leaders of business and finance begged of me from the time of my election to inauguration. On the contrary, all begged that the government should intervene as much as possible.

There were three things the Administration might have done: (a) nothing, — a policy which in thirty days would have irretrievably wrecked our business and banking system; (b) gone to the extremes of the government's operation of the economic system, proposed by the radical extremists, or (c) used the facilities available only to the government to permit and aid private enterprise to reassume its normal functions.

With deliberate purpose every measure undertaken and every effort since March 4, 1933, has been the third course — that is, to aid private enterprise to reassume its normal function. As illustrations, discuss (a) the handling of the banking situation, (b) the handling of the railroad situation, (c) aid to industry and, as a specialty, NRA.

In passing, one cannot ignore the beneficial effect of the Securities and Securities Exchange Acts upon business, particularly for the long pull. Certainly nobody believes that we should have done nothing about conditions in the securities markets, and one of the most important influences in the restoration of business is the restoration of investment that comes with a restoration of confidence in the securities markets.

II.   NRA

Undertaken in response to the demands of industry obsessed with the idea that it was hobbled by the limitations of the Sherman Law and could not get on its feet without the removal of these limitations. As a matter of fact, business was mistaken in this assumption. Under the present interpretation of the Sherman Law, business men can do practically everything by way of cooperation which fair-minded business men feel that trade associations could be allowed to do. The NRA merely formalized the cooperative opportunities for trade associations which the Supreme Court has already permitted by its decisions in the Appalachian Coal Case, the Cement Association Case, and the Maple Flooring Case. The legal advisers to business who simply had not kept up with the development of the Supreme Court's interpretation of the Sherman Law had failed to advise business of this constant liberalization. (Brandeis has been the great leader of a philosophy of permitting business men to undertake anything decently fair through trade associations as a counter-balance to the necessity of avoiding Sherman Law restrictions by actual merger and monopoly.) The fact is that big business wanted to get out from under the Sherman Law, not knowing how light the burden of the Sherman Law really was. This year's experience with NRA has had the benefit of proving that after having the opportunity to try, we know we do not want business to be able to cut down competition to the degree for which business has previously been shouting.

But there are some things which no one would disagree with about the NRA. Certainly we should have some control to limit hours of labor, some government control over the cut-throating on minimum wages of labor, some government control over child labor.

End section with the quotation from Root on page 32 of F.F.'s book, *The Public and Its Government*.

III.   *Collective bargaining*

7A of the NIRA is merely a formalization of what the Supreme Court had already decided about the social necessity of trade unions in a modern economic system. (See Taft in the Tri-City Case, 257US, and Hughes affirming Hutcheson in the New Orleans Railroad Case. Shelter behind Taft and Hughes and the Supreme Court as much as possible, and avoid further discussion of the point.)

IV.   Inasmuch as all the matters above mentioned are concerned, certainly the whole government effort has been directed toward putting private industry on its feet again.

V.   *Government in industry:*

(1)   Relation of the Public Works program to private industry.

The Public Works program is no extension of the functions of government. It is simply stepping in to supplement with a government program fields not already occupied by private enterprise. Insofar as the objects of the Public Works program are concerned, no one can say the government is stepping out of its sphere. Roads, harbors and similar public improvements have never been considered, in our economy, private enterprise. The increase in the amount of government activity at the present time on objects traditionally of government concern is simply in accordance with the philosophy of all good economists for the last thirty years who have pointed out continually the advisability that public works should be expanded during slumps in private business to prime the pump of industry. Compare Hoover.

The drouth is a magnificent reminder of the need of being forehanded with public works in matters which affect the fundamental capital resources of the nation — flood control, reforestation, national parks and similar projects which simply cannot be undertaken as private enterprise. Expenditures on this type of project foster, rather than compete with, private enterprise. The orders for materials reach in to all kinds of private enterprise producing capital goods, create revenue for the railroads on freight tonnage, revenue for the government through taxes upon the profits of the supply companies. Analyze, for instance, the distribution of benefit to all kinds of suppliers and to all sections of the country out of the bridges in the San Francisco district.

Above all, the Public Works program ties up with a determination that we must arrange our economies on the assumption that we will not tolerate a permanent unemployment. "I stand or fall by my refusal to accept for this country as a necessary condition of its past or future that there should be a permanent army of unemployed." Common fatalistic suggestions that we must adjust ourselves to such an unemployed army are intolerable, economically untenable, morally indefensible, with all their implications of a necessary reduction in our social and economic standards to make it possible for the working portion of society to maintain the unemployed portion of society on permanent relief rolls.

The answer to this problem of employment is a continuation and expansion of the Public Works program which, at the same time that it takes men off relief rolls, adds permanent improvements to the underlying capital resources of the country.

(2) Water power.

No fundamental displacement of private power. An effort to add to the power facilities while, at the same time, developing a market for additional cheap power. Fill in with Tennessee Valley accomplishment — the actuality of far cheaper power already brought to Tupelo and the other towns already using Tennessee power. Get further story from David Lilienthal. Insofar as Muscle Shoals is concerned, point out that (a) the project was approved by two Congresses under Republican administrations, (b) it was a definite promise in the Democratic platform. "And I believe in keeping platform promises."

VI.   *Planning for security*

Meet the charges of our radicalism and the example of England's recovery with a recital of the daring and fundamental innovations of British policy in the last few years. Point out particularly the importance of (1) England's monetary policy — going off gold and the capital levy on English bond holders implicit in the so-called government bond "conversion" of last year, (2) reversal of traditional low tariff policy for Chamberlain's protectionism — the most important change in economic policy since the corn laws.

With respect to unemployment insurance, point out that Lloyd George's budget of 1909 contained more than the proposals the Administration is now making for social security. The English Tory papers are pointing out that America is not yet where England was ten years ago.

I will take my constitutional law not from counsel, however eminent, retained by private interests, nor from laymen, however important — but from the Supreme Court of the United States.

Throughout, try to point out that the entire direction of the Administration's program is to assist private industry to help itself — not to destroy private industry. Keep the speech completely a speech to business, leaving agriculture for another speech.

Frankfurter was asked by Roosevelt to give him some hints for an address to business executives. This request was turned by Frankfurter into an invitation for a general review of the Administration's record and philosophy.

The Great Mandate

1936

1936

March 7	Germany reoccupies the Rhineland by armed force.
March 16	Hitler proclaims policy of conscription.
May 5	Italian troops capture Addis Ababa to end the Ethiopian war.
May 9	Italian government proclaims the annexation of Ethiopia.
June 5	First Popular Front government under Léon Blum formed in France.
July 18	The civil war in Spain begins.
October 1	General Franco is appointed Chief of the Spanish State by the insurgents.
October 25	Italy and Germany establish the Berlin-Rome axis.
November 18	Germany and Italy recognize General Franco's government.
November 25	Anti-Comintern pact against Russia is announced by Germany, Japan, and Italy.
December 1	President Roosevelt attends Pan-American Conference in Buenos Aires.
December 10	Abdication in London of King Edward VIII.

IN JANUARY 1936, *partly at the prompting of Roosevelt, Frankfurter wrote an article for* Fortune *magazine entitled "The Young Men Go to Washington." Frankfurter did not bother to reply to the accusations that he had filled the Roosevelt Administration with bright young men to serve some hidden design of his own. He chose rather to outline his philosophy of government to explain why a democracy needs youth and brains. The editors of* Fortune *then ran their own article in comment on Frankfurter's influence in Washington. Both Roosevelt and Frankfurter regarded this* Fortune *article as the most accurate assessment of their relationship ever to appear anywhere in print. The article follows:*

Felix Frankfurter . . . is "the most influential single individual in the United States."

Or so at least opines General Hugh S. Johnson who has had considerable experience in the influencing business himself. The General's reasons are given. Mr. Frankfurter has "insinuated" his "boys" into "obscure but key positions in every vital department" of the present Administration and is presumably therefore boring at the Constitution of the United States and the American plan of government from within.

It is an interesting scenario and one which, in the absence of proof, will be accepted or rejected according to the preferences of the reader. But one thing the mere publication of the statement has already accomplished. It has made Mr. Felix Frankfurter a Mysterious Personality. "This Frankfurter—this silent man . . ." hoarsely whispers Mr. Hearst's New York *American*; adding impressively "the IAGO of this Administration." As a silent man, as an IAGO, Mr. Frankfurter becomes a legitimate object of the public curiosity. And as the most influential single individual in General Johnson's United States he becomes a proper subject of historical investigation. The country has an altogether understandable desire to know on what grounds it is possible, whether rightly *or* wrongly, to attribute such unusual significance to a professor in a private law school.

So far, and despite the fact that a considerable body of information relative to that question is easily available, very little information has been published. Newspaper readers are more or less aware that Mr. Frankfurter is a man in his early fifties who teaches law at Harvard. Some of them are even aware that he was born in Vienna of Jewish parents, that he came to this country without a word of English at the age of twelve, and that, ten years later, he was leading his class through the bitter competition of the Harvard Law School with nothing to show for his Vienna nativity but an eager spirit and a slight thickening of the letter s. But how he came to occupy a position in public affairs which makes possible in any man's mouth the allegation that he wields the greatest private influence exerted in America is a matter of complete mystification to the great majority of his fellow citizens.

The actual facts of the matter are in no way mysterious. Mr. Frankfurter's relation to the appointment of bright young men to fill Washington jobs remains today about what it has been for twenty-odd years. The only difference is that under Presidents Taft and Wilson and their successors bright young men in Washington were not an issue. The story begins roughly about 1906 when Felix Frankfurter, two months out of law school and safely tied to a clerk's desk in the top-flight New York law office of Hornblower, Byrne, Miller & Potter, was suddenly transferred to the public service. It begins with Henry Stimson. Mr. Henry L. Stimson, later to serve as Secretary of War under Taft and Secretary of State under Hoover, had in 1906 yielded to President Theodore Roosevelt's request that he dissolve his partnership with Elihu Root and accept the office of U.S. District Attorney for the Southern District of New York, in order there to attack the malefactors of great wealth and the wicked corporations with whom Mr. Roosevelt was engaged. Mr. Stimson had made only one condition — that his office handle all the legal business of the district instead of farming out important cases as had been the previous practice. And the result of that condition was the meeting of Henry Stimson and Felix Frankfurter — for only by hiring inexperienced young lawyers of high law school stand could the District Attorney, with his limited budget, build up the necessary staff. It was a meeting which had important consequences for both Mr. Stimson and Mr. Frankfurter. Mr. Stimson found an assistant who became an intimate friend and a source of considerable legal strength and Mr. Frankfurter found an urbane and able chief and a useful avocation. The avocation was the collecting of brains. Partly because he was the first Assistant U.S. Attorney selected, partly because he was fresh from the country's leading law school, and partly because he had by nature a large, exuberant, catholic, likable liking for human beings, he became the recruiting agent of the office. And becoming its recruiting agent he took the first steps in an activity which was eventually to acquire the curious significance of which General Johnson is now so sensitively aware. From 1906 until 1935, whatever his office and wherever his work, Mr. Frankfurter was never long out of touch with the problem of placing young men of brains in positions where they could use them.

He began with a fairly impressive list. Mr. Stimson's assistants, with the exception of his fellow Yaleman, Tom Thacher, later Solicitor General of the United States and Federal District Judge, were Frankfurter selections and Thacher was a close Frankfurter friend. They included Winfred T. Denison, later Philippine Secretary of the Interior, Goldthwaite H. Dorr, later President of the Cotton Textile Institute, Emory Buckner, now of the New York firm of Root, Clark, Buckner & Ballantine, and Wolcott Pitkin, now counsel for the International Telephone & Telegraph Corp. — having been Attorney General of Puerto Rico and adviser to the King of Siam in the interim. As individuals they were competent lawyers and as a team they were close to unbeatable. Mr. Roosevelt in his autobiography refers on two occasions to the work of Mr. Stimson's office and specifically to Mr. Frankfurter and on both occasions with praise. Mr. Stimson and his young associates handled successfully such matters as the rebate cases against the New York Central and the American Sugar Refining Co., the sugar weighing fraud cases against officers of the Sugar Trust, the prosecution of Charles W. Morse for his attempts to rig a steamship pool and to corner the ice market, and the Interstate Commerce Act proceedings against Edward H. Harriman. And in most of them Felix Frankfurter was active: in the sugar fraud cases for example, though then a youngster in his middle twenties, he carried alone the successful argument of the appeals.*

The fact is important because it bears upon Mr. Frankfurter's now famous radicalism. Mr. Frankfurter's radicalism was learned in the 1906, T.R. trust-busting era when a radical was a man who wanted to knock down the monopolies and restore the practice of private competition. It is still radicalism of that vintage. Like Mr. Justice Brandeis, who belongs intellectually to the same generation, Mr. Frankfurter continues to hanker nostalgically after the lost (and perhaps utopian) world of small business, free competition, and economic independence. The two New Deal measures with which he is known to have been associated are the Securities Act and the Public Utility Act which attempt, the one to establish free and fair competition on the stock exchanges, and the other to break down the huge holding companies in the utilities field. Both proposals Theodore Roosevelt would unquestionably have backed. Theodore Roosevelt's much publicized hostility to Mr. Frankfurter at a later period was not caused by a disagreement on principles. It was caused by a disagreement of facts. Mr. Frankfurter's report on the Tom Mooney case for the Wilson Mediation Commission struck the Colonel as subversive Trotskyism. And the same

* His success in appellate work was to continue. He had since won every case he has argued before the Supreme Court and the Circuit Courts of Appeal with a single exception. In that case he carried with him in leading dissent not Justice Brandeis but Chief Justice Taft.

Commission's report on the deportation by vigilantes of a thousand Bisbee, Arizona, miners and their marooning in a desert town struck the ex-President as a Bolshevik attack on his old friend Jack Greenway, late husband of Congresswoman Greenway, who had acted as one of the vigilantes. Today most historians of the period agree that the facts were pretty much as Mr. Frankfurter reported them. The Mooney findings in particular would now be accepted as mild even in California.

But it was not only T.R. radicalism that Mr. Frankfurter absorbed in the U.S. Attorney's office. He absorbed also a liking for the public service. An attempt in 1909 to retire with Mr. Stimson to Mr. Stimson's private practice failed in less than a year. In 1910 Mr. Frankfurter was back in the U.S. Attorney's office in charge of appellate work and in 1911, when Mr. Stimson became Taft's Secretary of War, Mr. Frankfurter followed him as Law Officer of the Bureau of Insular Affairs.

Theoretically the duties of that position were limited to the fairly broad field of legal advice and service touching the colonial administration of the U.S. In practice however Mr. Frankfurter remained what he had been in New York, the general legal assistant of his superior. Mr. Stimson scandalized the Judge Advocate's office by asking Mr. Frankfurter's advice even on army matters. And in the field of public works, directed by the Secretary of War in the exercise of his jurisdiction over rivers and harbors, Mr. Frankfurter was the Secretary's active counsel. It was a particularly interesting field at the moment because Theodore Roosevelt had made an issue of waterpower in connection with his conservation program and Taft had inaugurated a new policy of issuing no permits to build dams on navigable streams without a *quid pro quo* to the government. From this policy was to develop the Federal Power Commission and the present "yardstick" extension of federal activity into the public utility field. And from it also was to result an extension of Mr. Frankfurter's War Department career. When Wilson took office in 1913 his new Secretary of War, Garrison, asked the Law Officer of the Bureau of Insular Affairs to continue to serve in connection with waterpower litigation.

It was not only Mr. Frankfurter's War Department career however which was expanding. The "silent man" of the Hearst editorials (incidentally one of the least silent of God's creatures) was also expanding his avocational interest in bright young men. Since he was still in the early thirties himself, he knew the recent law school graduates. And since he continued, for professional reasons, to read the *Harvard Law Review* he knew something of the abler men still in the School. With the result that Attorney General Wickersham, who ran his office on the merit system, made frequent requests for Frankfurter suggestions as did others in the executive departments. And with the further result that a regular Washington practice of calling upon Mr. Frankfurter for able young lawyers was established.

The upshot of the whole thing was that when in the fall of 1914 Mr. Frankfurter left Washington to become Professor Frankfurter, he had had some eight years of experience in finding youngsters for legal jobs in New York and in Washington. From 1914 on, but from the Harvard Law School rather than from the bar, he continued the practice. He was asked regularly by the larger New York firms to suggest law clerks for them, such offices as Sullivan & Cromwell; Simpson, Thacher & Bartlett; Davis, Polk; Root, Clark, Buckner & Howland; Cravath & Henderson, and like concerns in Boston, Chicago, and Philadelphia made annual requests for his recommendations. And he became in consequence the regular and all but official channel by which bright young Harvard Law School men became bright young New York or Chicago or Cleveland or Atlanta law clerks. Not all able Harvard men found their first law clerk's jobs through Felix Frankfurter but more of them made use of his good offices than of those of any other man. He knew the needs of the offices, particularly the New York offices. He knew the tastes of the hiring partners, particularly the New York partners. And he knew the youngsters.

But if his relation to the annual recruiting for the New York offices was close, his relation to the rarer recruiting for the public services was even closer. There too Mr. Frankfurter, keeping in touch with Washington through his work as a professor of public law, knew the demand and knew the supply and was interested in the personalities of both. Very early in his teaching career he began supplying Justices Holmes and Brandeis and four judges of lower federal courts with one high-stand graduate a year apiece to act as legal secretary. These appointments, which often went to the top men in the graduating class, became honorable distinctions in the Law School. The Holmes and Brandeis posts have been held by such men as Dean Acheson, lately Under-secretary of the Treasury, James M. Nicely, lately of John W. Davis's firm and now a Vice President of the Guaranty Trust, Thomas G. Corcoran, now of the RFC, Alger Hiss, now Special Attorney in the office of the Attorney General, William McCurdy, W. Barton Leach, Calvert Magruder, and Henry Hart, now professors of law at Harvard, James M. Landis, now Chairman of the SEC, Robert Page, formerly of Root, Clark, Buckner & Ballantine, now with the SEC, Harry Shulman, associate professor of law at Yale, and William Gorham Rice Jr., of the International Labor Office in Geneva.

But the recruiting for public office did not stop there. In 1914 when the Federal Trade Commission was set up, Commissioner George Rublee naturally turned to Mr. Frankfurter for suggestions and so too did such bodies as the Interstate Commerce Commission. Harvard Law School infiltration in Washington, begun under Taft, reached a high point during the War, when the demand for good young lawyers was enormous, continued through the Republican administrations of the twenties (Mr. Wickersham for example asked Mr. Frankfurter to suggest technical personnel for his famous committee), and rose to a record peak with the legal demand created by the New Deal. And Harvard Law School, from the Washington point of view, meant *out of* Harvard Law School *by* Felix Frankfurter.

The War was largely responsible for this point of view, for the War considerably extended Mr. Frankfurter's acquaintance among officials. In April, 1917, he had packed his bag in Cambridge for a weekend with Secretary of War Newton D. Baker and had run his weekend into a two-year stay. He had served as Assistant Secretary of War, as counsel to the President's Mediation Commission above referred to, as assistant to the Secretary of Labor, and finally, as Chairman of the War Labor Policies Board, which attempted to deal with the problem created by the competition for skilled labor of the various purchasing departments of the government. And in all this work he had needed, and had been associated with men who needed expert assistance.

The War moreover had had another effect of some interest in this general connection. It had produced the physical conditions under which Mr. Frankfurter's genius for human relationships could develop, and the development of that genius had in turn produced a Washington coterie of considerable fame. The notion that Mr. Frankfurter is a conspirator by nature probably owes more to the fact that he lived with a group of his contemporaries in a modest dwelling on Nineteenth Street than to any other fact. Except perhaps the fact that Mr. Justice Holmes, with facetious intent, referred to that dwelling as the House of Truth. The House of Truth was nothing more extraordinary than the quarters which Mr. Frankfurter shared with Robert G. Valentine, who had been Indian Commissioner under Taft, Loring C. Christie, later legal adviser to the Canadian Prime Minister, and Lord Eustace Percy of the British Embassy, now a member of the Baldwin Cabinet. But the name gave it mystery. It was the scene of a good deal of talk, much of it good, most of it legal, and all of it fairly idealistic. Its breakfasts, luncheons, and dinners were attended by generals, judges, and lovely ladies. And it had, in consequence, that faint odor of the cabal which the salon always exudes. But even so it would hardly have been remembered but for Mr. Justice Holmes's too happy phrase.

That the end of the War did not mean the end of the demand for law clerks is of course obvious. With the return of business to the businessmen the demand if anything increased. The market was merely removed from Washington to New York and Chicago. Felix Frankfurter remained the key to the Harvard production. From 1919 on he was an institution in American law. There were some high-stand men from Cambridge who did not go after their jobs with a letter to Dear Jack or Dear Joe signed with the double F. And there were some metropolitan law offices which did not try to pick over the Harvard graduating class with the aid of F.F.'s experienced eye. But they were few in either category. By the time Franklin Delano Roosevelt was nominated at Chicago, Mr. Frankfurter was the most famous legal employment service in America — the more famous because his activities were unofficial, unpaid, and entirely disinterested. He was the man you went to if you wanted a good young Harvard lawyer. And Harvard Law School being what it is, it was quite often good young Harvard lawyers you wanted. Both in his capacity as member of the Federal Reserve Board and in his capacity as Hoover's Chairman of the RFC, Mr. Eugene Meyer, to take one example, asked for the Harvard brand of legal product. And it is worth noting in passing that one of the products he got was the now famous Tom Corcoran. Mr. Corcoran is not a Frankfurter appointee to the Roosevelt Administration. He is a Frankfurter nomination to Mr. Eugene Meyer. And his last address before Mr. Meyer hired him away to Washington was the New York corporation-law office of Cotton, Franklin, Wright & Gordon.

What happened *after* the nomination of Mr. Roosevelt was merely that Mr. Frankfurter, who had known the Democratic nominee intimately when they were young lawyers in Washington meeting weekly on the War Labor Policies Board, supported him. And what happened after Mr. Roosevelt was elected was merely that Mr. Frankfurter went on supplying the names of able young lawyers. The Harvard professor was no part of the Brain Trust, which had a strong Columbia flavor with noticeable anti-Harvard whiffs. He was a personal friend of the President's and as such he saw him on two or three occasions before the inauguration (largely to discuss matters within his experience as a professor of administrative and public law), and somewhat more frequently (save for a year spent in England) after the inauguration was over. Aside from his refusal of the Solicitor Generalship in March, 1933, most of these contacts were informal. Under Mr. Roosevelt as under previous Presidents he was asked to advise on certain appointments with the result that a score or so of younger graduates of the School went to Washington with his benediction and that his opinion was asked upon such friends or former pupils as Professor O. M. W. Sprague, John Dickinson, now Assistant Attorney General, Assistant Attorney General Harold Stephens, now a judge of the District of Columbia Court of

Appeals, Dr. Leo Wolman, Commissioner Raymond B. Stevens of the Tariff Commission, Lloyd Garrison, formerly Chairman of the Labor Board, and Chairman John G. Winant of the Social Security Board. Any complete list of the "boys" Mr. Frankfurter has "insinuated" into the Administration should contain these names as well as the names of his brilliant young friends, Messrs. Corcoran and Ben Cohen.

No one knows, perhaps not even the President himself and certainly not General Johnson, whether Mr. Frankfurter has more influence with Mr. Roosevelt than Mr. Roosevelt's other advisers. General Johnson, for example, is publicly proud of the fact that Mr. Frankfurter had nothing whatever to do with the establishment of his NRA; an emotion which Mr. Frankfurter may share. If Mr. Frankfurter had nothing to do with the New Deal's noisiest experiment it is open to the public to wonder whether Mr. Frankfurter's influence can be as ubiquitous as the General pretends. In any case the question is not one which can be answered with factual proofs. Only upon the charge that Mr. Frankfurter has packed the Administration with his "boys" can the light of fact be thrown. When so illuminated it appears that Mr. Frankfurter has done little more to place intelligent lawyers in contemporary Washington than he has been doing for the past twenty-five years.

Both parties knew that 1936 was a year of critical elections, and the Republicans refused to believe that they would not retrieve their 1934 losses in the Congressional races, though few believed they would defeat Roosevelt in the Presidential campaign. Henry P. Fletcher of Pennsylvania, Chairman of the Republican National Committee, who thought Roosevelt exercised powers "comparable to those possessed by Mussolini and Hitler," had objected to the radio broadcast of Roosevelt's annual message to Congress, and had made the usual demand for equal time.

Telegram to Roosevelt
New York, N.Y. January 3, 1936

THE PARTISAN INSTINCT OF FLETCHER WAS RIGHT IN NOT WANTING THE AMERICAN PEOPLE TO HEAR YOUR MESSAGE. THE OPPOSITION CANNOT WITHSTAND THE CANDOR, COURAGE AND CONSCIENCE OF YOUR HUMANE LEADERSHIP SO TRIUMPHANTLY AGAIN REVEALED TONIGHT. IT WAS REALLY A GREAT ADDRESS AND WILL A HUNDRED YEARS FROM NOW BE CHERISHED BY AMERICANS AS WE NOW CHERISH THE FIRST AND SECOND INAUGURAL OF LINCOLN.

AFFECTIONATELY YOURS,
FELIX FRANKFURTER

The White House, January 6, 1936

Dear Felix:

That was a particularly nice message you sent me about the address. I am delighted to have it.

Every good wish to you.

Very sincerely yours,
F.D.R.

Washington, D.C., January 7, 1936

My dear Mr. President:

Recently you requested me to obtain information from our Minister at Bucharest regarding a report which had reached you to the effect that the Rumanian Government was contemplating steps which might have a far-reaching effect upon the Jewish population. Mr. Harrison was instructed to report upon this matter and I submit herewith a copy of his reply for your consideration.

Faithfully yours,
CORDELL HULL

Frankfurter's information on this point was better than the State Department's. The situation in Rumania grew rapidly worse, as the Department soon discovered, and as the Minister in Bucharest accurately reported.

Washington, D.C., January 14, 1936

My dear Mr. President:

In my letter of January 7, 1936, I transmitted a copy of a telegram from our Minister at Bucharest relating to a report which had reached you that the Rumanian Government was contemplating steps which might have a far-reaching affect upon the Jewish population in Rumania. Our Minister has now telegraphed reporting an attempt on the life of the Grand Rabbi of Rumania. A copy of the Minister's telegram is submitted herewith for your information.

Faithfully yours,
CORDELL HULL

Bucharest, January 11, 1936

Secretary of State,

Referring to my telegram No. 34, Dec. 28, 9 P.M.

No anti-Semitic demonstrations have followed attempt to assassinate Grand Rabbi this morning. Ministry of Interior has issued communiqué describing assassin as mentally unbalanced religious fanatic. While this latter appears to be true, statement by Grand Rabbi and reported testimony of eye-witnesses allege presence accomplices who escaped, thus suggesting assassin was anti-Semitic tool. Other reported evidence tends to support this view, namely, assassin's statement that one thousand lei and revolver had been given him. Jewish community is apprehensive lest further acts of violence be committed.

HARRISON

Telegram to Frankfurter

The White House, January 9, 1936

I HAVE BEEN TRYING TO FIND A MOMENT TO HAVE A TALK WITH YOU IN THESE HISTORIC DAYS. CAN YOU COME TO SEE ME SUNDAY AFTERNOON ABOUT FOUR-THIRTY? AFFECTIONATE REGARDS TO YOU AND MARION.

FRANKLIN D. ROOSEVELT

Telegram to Roosevelt

Cambridge, Mass., January 10, 1936

YOUR TELEGRAM HAS JUST COME FOR WHICH MY THANKS. OF COURSE I SHALL TURN UP AT FOUR-THIRTY ON SUNDAY.

FELIX FRANKFURTER

The White House, January 13, 1936

Dear Felix:

It was indeed kind of you to send me that heartening telegram concerning the address on Jackson Day. I appreciate it indeed.

Very sincerely yours,
F.D.R.

Cambridge, Mass., January 17, 1936

Dear Mr. President:

(1) Herewith a draft of message, for your destructive and constructive blue pencil, in submitting new agricultural legislation to Congress. A number of factors seem to me important, however poorly I may have applied them. They involve impressions to be left in the mind of the general public as well as cautions to be exercised as a matter of legal strategy. To me it seems necessary (1) to launch the new legislation as a carefully considered mature effort and not as rabbit pulled out of a hat; (2) to build on the authority which the Supreme Court itself has furnished in the Hoosac Mills opinions; (3) to do so without any concession to the rightness of the majority opinion and yet (4) without making the message a vehicle of legal controversy with the majority; but instead (5) again quietly to educate the public mind to the significance of the two opinions; and finally (6) not to make any commitments which might conceivably be embarrassing to the

Government when this legislation will have to be defended before the Supreme Court.

(2) I have been mulling over in my mind ever since Sunday, the Bonus situation. The conviction becomes stronger and stronger that on the balance there would be clear loss in doing anything except to stand pat on your last year's veto, doing it as gently as possible, and also, promptly after the veto is over-ridden, to work out with the Legion leaders a cordial and vigorous cooperative method for carrying out the legislation.

Through two of my editorial friends here, I have had the feeling among the men in the composing rooms sounded. My friends report that, now that the men are convinced that the Bonus in some form will go through Congress, their feelings have greatly changed. They don't expect you to sign the bill, they understand your position, and will feel, once the fight is over, that there was an honest difference of conviction which grew not at all out of any unfriendliness on your part to them or their needs. And they will admire a fighter who has stuck by his guns in a friendly way. On the other hand, any retreat now will only stimulate new demands and continue to keep alive the issue which, so far as you are concerned, you can now bury.

I have talked also with important representative samples of your well-wishers who are not Legionnaires, and I think the effect upon them and their like throughout the country, of a disregard of the reasons that moved you last year, would be very unhappy. I think it is perfectly clear that whatever ill-feeling your message last year aroused cannot be wiped out by a reversal now, while, on the contrary, the great gain that came and comes from the kind of quiet determination and genially dogged adherence to purpose which the Jimmie Walker business manifested, and again the Bonus, will have enormous power in touching and winning the admiration and support of masses of American men and women.

Always faithfully yours,
F.F.

Cambridge, Mass., January 29, 1936
Dear Frank:

Tomorrow falls one of those rare occasions when the heart may speak with words. You know how I have felt about you as a symbol of manliness — of gallant grappling with life's vicissitudes, of noble ardor for Lincoln's "Common people," of unsullied devotion to the dream to which this country was dedicated. And that golden thread runs through your life — from Albany, in the days of the House of Mirth, through the war and then those days of spiritual triumph, after 1920, to the dark and devastating winter and the spring of '33, when you gave a whole people the restoration of their faith and the strength to triumph over chaos. And now, the power which you saved for those most privileged is being turned to unreason, to fear, to all the abuses that blind excesses of partisanship and self can generate.

But I think of that symbol of gallantry and unpoisoned humanity that you are to the anonymous millions — the symbol that is forever one of our great national possessions.

On this day, on the morrow, I send this word of personal affection — in which Marion, in her shy way joins.

FELIX F.

Frankfurter remembered the effortless gaiety of Roosevelt as a young man and the way he filled a room with his big laughter. Hence the reference to the House of Mirth. Frankfurter wrote Roosevelt a birthday message each year that plainly meant a great deal to both men.

Cambridge, Mass., January 29, 1936

Dear Miss LeHand,

When I was last down, the President asked me to get together some materials for him, and I am now sending these through to Tom to you. I hope it may be possible for the President to see Tom and go over these things with Tom, in the interest of time and because talk may suggest the most effective way of carrying out the President's wishes.

Very cordially,
F.F.

Cambridge, Mass., January 30, 1936

Dear Mr. President,

Herewith are materials bearing upon practices in pursuit of unconscionable lawyers' fees which directly affect the national Treasury and the Federal administration of justice. They concern (1) outrageous contingent fees in claims against the Government, and (2) illegitimate claims for lawyers' fees in the Federal courts.

(1) I need not recall to you the enormous role played by opportunities for indecently opulent contingent fees in drives against the Treasury. Very early in your Administration you saw the need for putting an end to these abuses. And you will recall that it was Lew Douglas who in his soft-spoken voice agreed with the principle but objected to its application. Few things are more needed in the interests of the Treasury, and not less to improve the morality of the bar. Of course there will be outcries from the beneficiaries. But I can hardly imagine a more popular response than would be received by publishing the amounts of some of the fees. And what a tribe of gentry it would take care of!

Senator Norris' bill introduced in the Second Session of the 73rd Congress (S. 2805) is the result of careful draftsmanship with every provision soundly based on precedents in federal and state legislation.

I enclose a copy of this bill with a memorandum in its support as well as notes on specific provisions.

(2) Judge Coxe's recent decision regarding fees in the Paramount reorganization is only one of a series of recent instances of disallowance of big lawyers' fees by Federal Courts in various parts of the country. I enclose a list of recent cases on fees. Surely the Senate Judiciary Committee ought to direct public attention to these abuses, as part of an educational effort for effective and enduring correction of these attempts to misuse other people's money.

Always with warm regards,

Faithfully yours,
F.F.

Cambridge, Mass., February 12, 1936
Dear Frank:

Your Stancourt letter appears appropriately on Lincoln's birthday. It is one of those bits of Presidential utterances — as rare as they are precious . . . that will live forever in the amber of history.

Ever faithfully yours,
F.F.

Roosevelt, L.I., N.Y., January 30, 1936
To His Excellency,
The President,
Franklin D. Roosevelt.
Sir:

Justice impels this clumsy effort at gratitude, sir; at the moment I try to be as my father, an honest man.

Tonight over the radio, a man spoke, a Republican, finding a stone for everything which your New Deal would do. I am too, perhaps, a Republican, a soldier; but as a Republican I long to thank you for the grip which you teach me in unemployment to hang to; as a soldier of the late war I can but salute the President, standing by his conviction, in a day when few profess any conviction but the shabby one of self-service.

The man on the radio tonight, sir, spoke of the American Guide, mixing what he considered a laugh with the picture of writers wasting public funds, at the rate of a dollar a word, for words that will be thrown into the waste basket.

If you will forgive this impulse, Mr. President, let me speak as one of these writers, wasting words at a dollar a word. Let me say, simply, that when the call to begin writing this Guide came, I found assigned to a district to report with me a quiet-spoken man, a radio lecturer turned out for daring to speak for you, a minister whose church failed in the economic storm. And he said wearily, "I love this work we are sent to do, please don't tell me that I overwork and am tired; we are doing the fact-book of our country."

Also in our district is a woman, a writer, who was left in the depression with house gone, head fractured in an accident, and a small daughter needing her; for her she has come through, fighting discouragement alone. The call to the writing post came in time, just in time. She too is working with all of herself in it, for the small glory of helping to do the country's Baedeker. A graying gentleman near us taught university class; he considers it not a jobless old man's chore but an American's trust, calling his sense of honor; and he too works past the hour. And so it goes in our small group. And I thought, sir, when I consider all these attacks upon a President from all sides, if you ever wonder, when alone, whether the unknowns for whom you bear the slurs of men from all directions, are aware of the burden you carry for us — so often with your own against you.

And I also thought of the food placed before my small family, which was bought with funds raised to give stranded men a lift in the fog.

Thinking these things after the radio man spoke, I thought of the honest Americans working with their hearts in the American Guide, and of men with whom we had worked in the ditch line with shovels before this, and of families whom I had been trusted to find and feed when they sent me as a relief investigator, and of another reporter who swept the streets with me after our newspaper jobs fell by our own fault, and of the police detective sweeping with us, all stilled people trying to find the way through again.

And I thought, if the intrusion be not considered too swiftly, that if the President who tries to lead us through the fog knew, in however small a degree, that we *do* understand the thankless thing which you do, and that you have the quiet blessing of unknown men whose voices seem never heard, and that among us many pray to our common God for the loan of his hand to the President of the Americans, that you might feel, sir, a little gladder for it.

Therefore I began this letter, and end it, simply,

Your humble servant,
Louis Stancourt

The federal government had given the opportunity to writers, many of them unemployed or finding it hard to find publishers for their books, to

*write a series of guide books for the various states. The project produced
some books that are read and admired to this day.*

The White House, February 8, 1936

My dear Mr. Stancourt: —

Though we have not met, your letter makes me believe that I can call
you a friend — an understanding friend.

It is not alone because you as a soldier of the late war have thought of
me as your Commander-in-Chief.

It is not alone because you, like me, feel a hurt when people who do
not know hold up to ridicule our efforts to do useful things with the public
monies.

It is not alone because you tell me that the American Guide is going to
be a useful fact-book for our whole country.

It is most of all because you give me the blessings of the unknown men
whose voices seem never to be heard — because you rightly believe that I
do try, as best I may, to understand the human and the spiritual problems
of the millions in our great land who are loyal to our common ideals and
who want to hold their heads high.

I am grateful to you. You have helped me.

Faithfully yours,
FRANKLIN D. ROOSEVELT

Cambridge, Mass., February 19, 1936

Dear Mr. President:

Tom tells me that he has checked with all the interested Departments
— Treasury, Justice and Agriculture — the provision for dealing with the
abuses of contingent fees in claims against the Government, and that the
proposal has been cast in legal form satisfactory to Stanley Reed and Oliphant.

I cannot tell you how happy this makes me and how much I rejoice at
the prospect of its early enactment. It will mean enormous saving to the
Treasury and withdrawal of the meritricious strengthening of evil forces. I
am not, as you know, much of an "if" man. But I think there can be no
doubt that if this legislation had not been blocked in the early days of your
Administration, by people wholly out of sympathy with your purposes,
whose hostility has since then been exposed, there would in all sorts of ways
be a different story to tell to-day. Powerful pecuniary motives for raids on
the Treasury and for assaults upon legislation would have been considerably
curtailed. And perhaps as important as anything, the real general staff of
the opposition, the lawyers, would not have been pork-fed by unconscionable fees. In the light of the present claims for the recovery of hundreds of

millions of dollars, resistance to this legislation on the part of a powerful legal lobby will not be very effective in and out of Congress, if a little truth be told and the light of publicity turned on them.

I am sure I do not overestimate the direct and indirect importance of this legislation to all that you are trying to do, and that is why I prayerfully hope that this much needed legislation will now secure prompt enactment.

Always faithfully yours,
F.F.

Roosevelt wrote to Burlingham to set at ease his fears that the Administration might begin to regard all the leaders of the American bar as the enemies of the President's program. The reference to John W. Davis and Max Steuer was given to Roosevelt by Frankfurter. Years later Frankfurter changed his mind about Davis but never about Steuer. He never wavered one inch from the contempt he expressed on October 18, 1932, in a letter to Walter Lippmann:

If there has been a corrupting influence to the succeeding generations of young men at the bar more powerful than Max Steuer, I am not aware of it. He has been the outstanding "success" of getting away with it. You will recall his outrageous behavior in the Daugherty trial, which provoked a public reprimand from Judge Mack; you will also recall his shabby attempt to deflect Seabury's tracing of a telephone message from Curry to Judge Sherman in the Doyle affair by asserting that he, Steuer, had put in the telephone call to his wife, a piece of trickery that was punctured by Seabury's proof that Loon Lake and Lake Placid (if I have the two places correctly) had different exchanges; and even his conduct of the Bank of the United States prosecution violated all the decencies of prosecution on which I was brought up by Stimson. Nothing that the best law schools can do in generating impalpable atmosphere and standards has weight against the example of those who are deemed the successful men at the bar. For one who has been hailed as the great regenerator of the Republican party of the state of New York (Kingman Macy) to acclaim as a great public servant the guiding brain of Curry (of Tammany Hall) and to reward him by giving a Supreme Court Justiceship to his son, is a piece of political immorality to which the Tom Platts and the Ben Odells would never have yielded. In speech at least they "pandered to the moral sentiments of the community." I speak with the deepest feeling about this because I know what the canonization of law and unworthy clever professional work — like Max Steuer's — does to the ambitions and purposes of the youth that pass through this Law School. I keep in touch with them by the scores after they leave here and enter practice. If leading Republican lawyers can keep silent in the face of Macy's letter (crowning Steuer), then they ought forever to have the decency to keep their mouths shut about legal ethics and professional standards and all their other hypocritical hot-air.

The White House, February 6, 1936

Confidential

Dear C.C.: —

You are right — and you are wrong! I know how you feel and I go along with you a long part of the way. On the other hand, for years — four years at Albany and then before that — I got rather fed up with the consistent and unimaginative type of Bar Association suggestions. They never, under any circumstances, suggested a "man of the people." Always someone from a big law firm, all of which did and do the same type of legal business. There is no use asking the Bar Association for suggestions — but I wish you would use that grand imagination of yours and dig me up fifteen or twenty youthful Abraham Lincolns from Manhattan and the Bronx to choose from. They must be liberal from belief and not by lip service. They must have an inherent contempt both for the John W. Davises and the Max Steuers. They must know what life in a tenement means. They must have no social ambitions. There is a job for you!

As ever yours,

F.D.R.

Honorable C. C. Burlingham, 27 William Street, New York, N.Y.

Cambridge, Mass., February 7, 1936

Dear Missy,

The enclosed, from Miss Helen Howe, speaks for itself. I thought that Mrs. Roosevelt and the President would want to know that Miss Howe is the daughter of Mark A. D. Howe, one of the best of Harvard men, who celebrated the President, not so long ago, in a charming poem before the Fly Club. Incidentally your Mark Howe was one of the most beloved of Justice Holmes' secretaries.

I envy you seeing Helen Howe's performance.

Very cordially,

FELIX FRANKFURTER

Frankfurter was sure Miss Howe would be a success with her recital at the White House. He was right. Her brother, "your Mark Howe," went on to be professor at the Harvard Law School and biographer of Holmes.

Boston, Mass., February 6, 1936

Dear Mr. Frankfurter,

Since you were kind enough to suggest telling Miss LeHand of my coming to the White House this is just to tell you that I am arriving at the

Mayflower Hotel on the morning of Tuesday the 11 (my recital is that evening).

I believe I am to be taken anyway in the afternoon to the East Room to look over the terrain before the evening, and of course if she were to know in advance that I had any link with you, I am sure all the doors, to the South, West, and North rooms, would fly open at my approach. Perhaps my connection with Father may mean something to them as I believe he and the President are fellow Fly Club members and Father stayed with them at Hyde Park some years ago on some literary business. But it is your banner I should be most honored to sail under, if you still feel kindly enough disposed to offer me one tiny fold as my buckler and strength for an onslaught which I find grows daily more terrifying in prospect!

In any case I shall hope to see you and your wife when I return to these parts in mid-March and report to you on how I fared. It was such a pleasure to see you both the other evening, and I do appreciate more than I can say your kind impulse, which I hope you may not already have regretted!

Very sincerely yours,
HELEN HOWE

The next three letters deal with the disposition of Mr. Justice Holmes's estate, which he bequeathed in its entirety to the nation. The Attorney General's letter asked for guidance.

Memorandum for Professor Frankfurter

The White House, February 10, 1936

What should the President say in reply to the enclosed letter from the Attorney General?

M. H. McINTYRE

Cambridge, Mass., February 10, 1936

Dear Miss LeHand,

The President last summer blocked an effort to have the Holmes bequest used in ways that would have, in the vernacular, left the Justice cold. The enclosed letter from the Justice's executor indicates that "concerted efforts" to do the unwise thing about that bequest are now on the way. The President may want to see this letter from Palfray.

Of course what ought to be done is to act on the recommendation in the President's message, namely, to appoint a commission that will thoroughly sift the possibilities, or, if there were additional funds available, to use the Holmes money for a lovely bridge across the Potomac or a public park in Washington. Something aesthetic and human is what the Justice would have liked.

Very sincerely yours,
F.F.

Cambridge, Mass., February 14, 1936

Dear Mr. President,

The Attorney General's letter and Lewis Einstein's views have led me to reconsider the bequest of Mr. Justice Holmes to the Government in its various aspects.

(1) About one thing there can be no doubt, and that is that the Justice left the money without any strings, so that could he be consulted now, he would say that he has no wishes. I think I can say this without qualification, not merely from one's knowledge of his temperament generally, but in the light of what he told me regarding his disposition.

(2) And so the responsibility clearly is the Government's but I do not think it follows from that, that in leaving his money to the Government, there was any implication that the money should drop into the general pool of the Government's funds. In other words, his bequest is really neutral and one cannot look to his will for guidance in disposing of it.

(3) The feeling behind your Holmes message, that the bequest serve as a permanent reminder of the special qualities of Holmes as a man and as a patriot, derives, I believe, naturally from one of Holmes' favorite ideas, "we live by symbols." Such a life as his, and so pointed an expression of attachment to his country and to his Government as the bequest implies, ought, if possible, to be turned into a concrete, abiding stimulus for successive generations of Americans. It is this, I believe, that makes it highly desirable that the money be put to some significant use and not absorbed in the general anonymity of the Treasury. Better that, of course, than to use the money for purposes that really would contradict the human, vivid, fructifying spirit of the Justice. But there is no hurry about fixing on the right purpose, and the suggestion of your message on this subject still seems to me the way out.

(4) In any event, I think a suggestion in the course of this campaign year to have the Holmes bequest go into the Treasury is likely to give rise to serious, even if insincere criticism. Would not there be a rather wide cry that the Administration, instead of using Holmes' bequest for some benevolent purpose, is employing it, relatively small as it is, for its own fiscal purposes? Of course the argument would be mean and silly. But we are living in days in which there are many people, in Holmes' phrase, "fired with a zeal to pervert." And they ought not to be given any superfluous

opportunities for making innocent, unsophisticated people the dupes of such misrepresentation.

Faithfully yours,
F.F.

P.S.   Since dictating the above I have made soundings with people whose judgment is not only good, but representative. One of my editorial friends said that to use the Holmes money for the Treasury would be "shocking" and would raise "a howl" about the deficit.

Years later part of the Holmes bequest, grown larger with the passage of time, was used to finance a history of the Supreme Court by a galaxy of legal scholars under the chairmanship of Professor Paul Freund of the Harvard Law School. The history, a project of which Holmes would certainly have approved, is being eagerly awaited. The bequest has also been used for the publication of learned lectures in the law by outstanding scholars.

Cambridge, Mass., February 29, 1936

The following is a line for line exact copy of the original, against which I compared it by having my wife read the original to me giving every line, punctuation, capitalization, etc., etc.

FELIX FRANKFURTER

He went to all this trouble because he regarded the following correspondence on Harvard's Tercentenary as "incredible among cultured men and without precedent in this country."

Boston, Mass., February 20, 1936

Dear Mr. President:

President Conant and the Directors of the Harvard Alumni Association have asked me to take charge of the tercentenary meeting of the alumni on the afternoon of September the eighteenth, and President Conant tells me that you have kindly consented to speak on this occasion. Now, it being a meeting for the mutual congratulation of the graduates at the three hundredth anniversary of their alma mater, we hope you will choose for your theme for a brief address something connected with Harvard and the tercentenary of higher education in this country, and feel that you would welcome this opportunity to divorce yourself from the arduous demands of politics and political speech-making. Do you not think it would be well to limit all the speeches that afternoon to about ten minutes? Does this express your idea?

Yours very sincerely,
A. LAWRENCE LOWELL

Mr. Franklin D. Roosevelt
President of the United States

Lowell was president emeritus of Harvard.

Hyde Park, N.Y., February 24, 1936

Dear Felix: —

Very confidentially, what do you think of this? I felt like replying — "if I am invited in my capacity as a Harvard graduate I shall, of course, speak as briefly as you suggest — two minutes if you say so — but if I am invited as President to speak for the Nation, I am unable to tell you at this time what my subject will be or whether it will take five minutes or an hour."

I suppose some people with insular minds really believe that I might make a purely political speech lasting one hour and a half. Give this your "ca'm jedgment" and suggest a soft answer "suitable to the occasion."

As ever yours,

FRANKLIN D. ROOSEVELT

Telegram to Roosevelt

Cambridge, Mass., February 26, 1936

WOULD MUCH LIKE TO SEE IF POSSIBLE TERMS OF ORIGINAL INVITATION. COULD YOU THEREFORE LET ME HAVE CONANT'S LETTER TO YOU AND YOUR ACCEPTANCE? IN THE MEANTIME I SHOULD NOT HAVE BEEN TERRIBLY SORRY IF YOU HAD TAUGHT THE GENTLEMAN A LESSON IN MANNERS AND WRITTEN TO HIM WHAT YOU FELT LIKE REPLYING. HOWEVER, YOU SHALL HAVE MY CALM JUDGMENT AFTER I HAVE HAD TWO DAYS TO COOL OFF.

FELIX FRANKFURTER

Memorandum

Cambridge, Mass.

On receipt of President's letter dated February 24th, I wired the President expressing the hope that he would let me see the whole file beginning with Conant's invitation, and that in the meantime I'd try to get cool.

Not having heard in reply I sent my letter of the 29th which crossed F.D.R.'s of the 29th.

F.F.

Memorandum for F.F.

The White House, February 29, 1936

On looking over the file there appears an interesting situation. On November 7, 1934, President Conant writes — "Dear Mr. Roosevelt (sic) I am now extending to you on behalf of the University a formal invitation to be present." Am I invited in my official capacity or just as a graduate? I wonder —?

On November 14, 1934, Jerome Greene says — "Dear Mr. President . . . I am . . . writing to you in support of President Conant's official letter . . . the preliminary arrangements for the great day would have to take very largely into account the welcoming of the President of the United States to his own College. . . ."

The plot thickens! It is developing into a detective story like that one that you and A. A. Ballantine were the principal actors in.

F.D.R.

Cambridge, Mass., February 29, 1936

Dear Mr. President,

When the other fellow's arrogance reaches such proportions as to become ludicrous, one's feelings become disengaged and the mind is left free to exercise a "ca'm jedgment." And so I am as clear and as sure as I can possibly be that the following are the ingredients for the right answer to Lowell: great brevity, impeccable courtesy, complete disregard of the impertinent inquiries and implied rebuke.

Words yield to your touch, but I offer as a scratch pad the enclosed draft, for which I only claim that it is the product of real calm and very considerable care.

With warmest regards,

Faithfully yours,
F.F.

This was the draft F.F. sent to F.D.R.

My dear Dr. Lowell,

I have your letter of the 20th.

In graciously asking me to attend Harvard's Tercentenary Celebration, President Conant of course invited me not as an alumnus but as the President of the United States. I took it for granted that he did not expect me to do otherwise than to be true to the requirements of the office which I shall represent on the occasion.

Sincerely yours,

Cambridge, Mass., March 4, 1936

Dear Mr. President:

My warm thanks for letting me see the file — herewith returned — on the Harvard Tercentenary invitation.

The controlling letter — that of November 7, 1934 — leaves no possible room for doubt that President Conant's invitation was addressed to the

President of the United States. I don't want to rely on the minor fact that the Conant letter went to:

Honorable Franklin D. Roosevelt
President of the United States

In contrast to Dr. Lowell's form, "Mr. Franklin D. Roosevelt." What is crucial is that President Conant extended to you "on behalf of the University a formal invitation to be present," so that the "celebration of the 300th Anniversary of the founding of Harvard College may be honored by your presence, as the celebration of the 250th Anniversary was honored by that of President Cleveland."

It is the Cleveland visit that I had in mind in sending you the scratch pad draft reply. Grover Cleveland was not an alumnus. He came as President of the United States. The whole tenor of President Conant's letter, with its explicit reference to the Cleveland visit, unequivocally proves that the invitation went to you not as alumnus but as President. Naturally enough, Jerome Greene, as director of the Tercentenary celebration, placed that interpretation upon "President Conant's official letter." No other construction is tenable.

In sum, of course you were invited in "Your official capacity" and not "just as a graduate." I'll bet you a St. Croix rum highball that even the Supreme Court would so rule, the Supreme Court, that is, ex McReynolds.

And so I stand pat on the form for a reply which I ventured to submit to you a few days ago. I have been sleeping on it for a good many days now and time only confirms the feeling of its appropriateness. Of course I don't mean the exact words, but that brief, courteous, conclusive kind of thing which, being what he is (in the light of his letter I would tell you one of these days a story which will shock even you), Dr. Lowell will fully understand.

Always faithfully yours,
F.F.

The following is the actual letter sent by FDR.

The White House, March 6, 1936

My dear Dr. Lowell: —

I have your letter of February twentieth.

In graciously asking me to attend Harvard's Tercentenary Celebration, President Conant of course invited me not as an alumnus but as the President of the United States. I am sure you will approve my thought that he did not expect me to do otherwise than to be true to the requirements of the office which I shall represent on that occasion.

Very sincerely yours,
FRANKLIN D. ROOSEVELT

Boston, Mass., April 14, 1936

To the President of the United States
Dear Mr. Roosevelt:

You are certainly right that you were invited to come to Harvard on the Alumni Day of the Tricentennial celebration as President of the United States. In that capacity I suppose you will want to say something about what Harvard has meant to the nation. In arranging the occasion there are about half a dozen other speakers — partly alumni, but mainly representatives of other institutions over the world, — who will naturally speak. I am thinking of asking each of them to take about ten, or at most fifteen minutes. Does not this strike you as appropriate?

Yours very sincerely,
A. LAWRENCE LOWELL

Memorandum for Felix Frankfurter
The White House, April 16, 1936

Before I get through I shall lose my temper completely and find it necessary to stay in Washington in September to attend the meeting of the International Power Conference instead of going to Cambridge!

Here is the latest. What is your slant on this one? Damn.

F.D.R.

Cambridge, Mass., April 19, 1936

Dear Mr. President:

If I said what I really thought of Emeritus, Jim Farley wouldn't allow it to go through the mail.

I submit the following as possible ways of returning his ball:

(1) You may assume that I shall speak, within appropriate limits, of the significance of Harvard in the context of our national history.

(2) You will have to assume that I understand the proprieties of an occasion like Harvard's Tercentenary.

(3) You will have to assume that I understand the proprieties.

Not having anything of the careful dullness of a John W. Davis, Marion says she hopes you will lose your "temper completely."

Very faithfully yours,
F.F.

The White House, April 29, 1936

Dear Felix: —

The enclosed has gone. Marion was right. Tell her, however, that I must be getting old because after two weeks of thinking things over I became a cooing dove. You will note that I have *completely ignored* the latter and more important half of A.L.L.'s epistle. Enough said!

As ever yours,
F.D.R.

The White House, April 29, 1936

Dear President Lowell: —

Thank you for your letter of April fourteenth. You are right in thinking that I will want to say something of the significance of Harvard in relation to our national history.

Very sincerely yours,
FRANKLIN D. ROOSEVELT

Frankfurter prepared this material for Roosevelt's address at the Harvard Tercentenary celebration. It expresses his own love of Harvard, of freedom, and of America.

Today we do not merely celebrate a great past to which we are all in heavy debt. We meet also to dedicate ourselves to a future we have to make worthy of that past. A university is something more than a society of scholars who seek knowledge for its own sake. For us, in America at least, it is an essential part of the living fabric of our civilization, expressing and thereby vindicating a faith that it amplifies and enriches. For all of us, I am sure, the greatness of Harvard has been its ability to function as a microcosm of the American ideal. There has been learning, but the glory of the learning has been its relation to that wisdom through which is handed down the torch of our civilized life.

To the enlargement of that wisdom the Harvard of the next age is committed. How can it do so in a manner befitting its past? Above all, it must be free to seek the truth. No creed, no dogma must impede its right relentlessly to search into the true foundations of enduring society. A university that is limited in its right of inquiry has lost the primary condition of wisdom. We, as Harvard men, must claim for the College we love that no man and no system jeopardize that right. It is the sole highroad to the truth; and by the truth alone can we continue to be free.

The right of inquiry presupposes the courage to inquire significantly. This epoch confronts a challenge as profound as any since the foundation of the College. Always, Harvard has been an integral part of that ideal which proclaims the right of man to search for the good in the pursuit of happiness. That happiness was the purpose which brought to these shores those pioneers who in the first years of this historic Commonwealth gave of their scanty means to make an institution which should be a worthy temple of the human spirit. That purpose also guided those of its sons who learned here in the critical years before the Revolution that without freedom to direct their own lives happiness was beyond attainment. It is, I am confident, of the inner essence of Harvard that its sons have fully participated in each great drama of our nation's history. They have met the challenge of the event; they have seen in the challenge opportunity to fulfill the end the university exists to serve. As the Chief Executive of the Nation I bring you the solicitation of our people. In the name of the American Nation I venture to ask you to cherish its traditions and to fulfill its highest opportunities.

Do not let us conceal from ourselves that this is a hazardous enterprise; the academic calling would not have won its place in the tradition of western civilization had it been otherwise. It is always a struggle with the unknown. Often it is an endeavor to build a track through the desert. Whether it be medicine or the law, whether it be economics or philosophy, the ultimate aim is to give men the means of mastery over their lives. It is hazardous, because it may involve scrutiny of ancient conventions from which in each age we can free ourselves only because the compulsion of the facts leaves us no alternative. Our standards of truth may not vary. But there is no meaning in our history unless we learn from it that each epoch requires its own application of abiding principles to an environment that is never stationary. I cherish for this University the high duty of making the meaning of our effort as a Nation known to those who live by its results. Here the clamor of the market-place is still. Here men may see with the clarity that learning should confer the larger horizon it is so difficult for others to decry. To promulgate his insights so that the voice of Reason may be heard; to do so with independence of the myriad interests that compete for his support; to be free and to be brave; to see through pretensions of class interest or prejudice or power; that surely is the vocation of the scholar whom Harvard is to create. I know no higher task in this Nation. For only through the interests and insights of its scholars can this Nation live amply. Their insights are the basis of effective statesmanship. There is no American without pride in Charles William Eliot. He is not only the founder of the modern Harvard in a special degree; his standard has become part of all that is best in academic education in America. There is no American without pride in William James. There, in the full sense of the word, was a free man. His love of America was a love of humanity. He made his philosophy, at least to a layman's understanding, an effort to add to the moral stature of man. There is no American who does not feel pride in Mr. Justice Holmes. He made of learning and the law a key to unlock the mysteries of society. By sheer love of truth he was able to transcend the prison of personal environment and make his method of analysis a sword in the service of American freedom. I mention these names only; I mention them because each in his own distinctive way turned fears into hopes and knew how to merge the historic beauty of the old with the solid contributions of a new time as a part of a continuing process of civilization. Each of them built a straight path from his special task to the central highroad of America. Each of them caught the significance of new needs demanding urgent attention. Most important, each of them by the relentless honesty of his mind made his insights a means of moral elevation for the age to which he belonged. Respect for them became part of the Nation's self-respect.

The University will never fail to produce its due proportion who are successful as judged by the common standard of success. Of such the world has need. But to produce that type is not, I am sure, the ultimate justification that you would make for Harvard. Rather do we here search for the atmosphere in which men are produced who have either the rare quality of vision or the ability to appreciate the significance of the man of vision when he appears. Where there is vision, there is tolerance; and where there is tolerance, there is peace. And I beg you to think of tolerance and peace not as indifferent and neutral virtues but as active and positive principles. It is the business of Harvard to inculcate these qualities with passion in her sons. Viewed in proper perspective, they are heroic qualities; for they imply in their holders the power of self-sacrifice, the ability to grapple with new difficulties, a temper of mind that is consistently generous, a mood of heart that sees in conflict the eternal enemy of truth.

I am not, you will observe, conceiving of the University as a mere spectator of the great national and international drama in which all of us, despite ourselves, are involved. A disinterested actor, if you will, but an actor called day by day to pledge afresh the claims of reason above all competing claims. Here are to be trained not lawyers and doctors merely, not teachers and businessmen merely; here are to be trained to the fullest sense — men. Those who pass from Harvard to the great world should go out servants of truth, and not of authority. They should be inspired by the belief that life is a noble calling, degraded always when it lacks right convictions stoutly held. Harvard should train men to be citizens in that high sense which compels a man to live his life unceasingly aware that its public context is its most significant context. For what above all this Republic demands of her citizens is loyalty to the creed it was created to fulfill.

It was Increase Mather who told the students of Harvard that they were "pledged to the word of no particular master," that they should "above all find a friend in truth." It was President Everett who insisted that "without any manner of doubt whatever, all humane matters must be tested by philosophy." It was President Hoar who sought "any advice or device by which we may become not only nominal but real scholars." It is the spirit which lies behind those words which we are here to reaffirm to-day. I am asking the sons of Harvard to dedicate themselves not only to the perpetuation, but also to the enlargement of that spirit. To refuse to con-found the conventional with the necessary; to pay ardent reverence to the past but to recognize no less the direction of the future; to be eager imagi-natively, to understand philosophies we do not accept and hopes we find it difficult to share; to account the service of mankind the highest ambition a man can follow, and to know that there is no calling so humble that it cannot be instinct with that ambition; never to be indifferent to what may affect our neighbors, always as Whately said, to put truth in the first place and not in the second; these I would affirm are the qualities by which the "real" is distinguished from the "nominal" scholar. It is as we bring this temper to our understanding of the universe that, in a creative way, our "humane matters" become transmuted into a philosophy that gives us con-trol of the Destiny we fulfill. It is only when we have attained this philoso-phy that we can "above all find a friend in truth." When America is dedi-cated to that end by the common will of all her citizens, then can she accomplish her highest ideals; and to the measure that Harvard participates in that dedication, she will be justified of her effort and her purpose.

Harvard's anniversary had a sad sequel. Long before 1936, for reasons which need not concern us now, the friendship between Frankfurter and Lippmann had lost its intimacy and had cooled to an ominous degree. As one of Harvard's most famous and most respected sons, Lippmann natu-rally wanted to honor his university on this great occasion. In writing of the preparations going forward to celebrate the three hundredth anniversary of the founding of Harvard College, Lippmann wrote that:

> *. . . the members of the university faculties have a particular obligation not to tie themselves to, nor to involve themselves in, the ambitions and purposes of the politicians, the parties and the movements which are con-tending for power.*
>
> *The choice has to be made. If there are to be universities which are not controlled by the Government, if there are to be universities free of the Government because they are privately endowed, if in accepting these en-dowments the universities are to be able to insist on their freedom from the promptings of private interest, then the universities themselves must also renounce the ambition to play a part in partisan political controversy.*
>
> *This does not mean that professors must not be consulted in matters where they are professionally competent. But it does mean that professors must not be office holders and political advisers to office holders. For once they engage themselves that way, they cease to be disinterested men, being committed by their ambitions and their sympathies. They cease to be scholars because they are no longer disinterested and having lost their own*

independence, they impair the independence of the university to which they belong.

Writing to Lessing Rosenthal on June 5, 1936, giving Frankfurter a copy, Judge Learned Hand said:

That article of Walter Lippmann's set me thinking. I rather think that he had in mind among others Felix, and whether it was or not, it will not improve the relations between the two distinguished gentlemen. I shall want to let the notion sink into my mind for a while before I express any opinion. It seems to me somewhat a large order to forbid professors in universities from taking any part in current politics, and that is what it comes to, as I understand its purport. Like everything else which Lippmann writes, it has its defensible side, and perhaps the danger outweighs the advantage. Just at first blush I am not disposed to take that point of view.

Judge Hand was grievously troubled because he was deeply devoted to both Frankfurter and Lippmann. But Frankfurter did not need Judge Hand's prompting to be convinced that Lippmann's criticism was aimed primarily at him. He never forgot and never forgave what Lippmann had written.

Cambridge, Mass., February 28, 1936

Dear Mr. President,

Herewith a miscellany of week-end reading to while away part of the large supply of leisure you must find heavy on your hands! Seriously speaking, there are a number of items that have come to me recently, some of which I think have real importance. In any event, they seem to me to be deserving of your attention. For brevity of comment, I will give the enclosures exhibit letters marked, of course, in red.

(1) The writer of "A" is a most devoted friend of the Administration, who has unusual opportunities for gauging opinion in various parts of the country and tested judgment in interpreting it. What he says bears interestingly on the observations of Professor Lasswell in "B" — regarding the ideas that are stirring among small business people, especially on the West Coast.

(2) You probably know Bishop William Scarlett of St. Louis. In any event, I hope you may find an early opportunity to see him. He is one of the finest characters I know or know anything about. I learned to know him during the war when he had the most important pulpit in Phoenix, and during the copper strike told the Lewis Douglasites of those days, in no uncertain terms of their duties to God and man rather than to Mammon. His moral and intellectual attainments make him a person of wide-spread influence.

(3) Lincoln — *not* E.A. — Filene's letter, "D," speaks for itself. I

shall only add what I am sure is unnecessary, that I know of no one who cares more disinterestedly for your reelection or feels more passionately that the national interest requires it.

(4) "E" gives a private picture of Landon by Bill Mullins, the chief political reporter of the Boston *Herald,* who has just returned from a visit to Landon. Mullins has a very good nose for such things. The *Herald* readers of Mullins' articles on Landon would get quite a shock if they heard his accounts of his real impressions of Landon.

(5) Finally, "F" is the editorial in the *Phillipian.* It came to me through Lawrence Winship, the managing editor of the Boston *Globe,* with a characteristic salty comment that the Andover editor "will be no good on the *Crimson.*" Winship tells me that the lad who wrote that editorial is Richard M. Weissman, the editor-in-chief of the *Phillipian.* By the way, I don't believe there are half a dozen newspaper men in the land as smart as Winship. And I suspect there are even fewer who are as wholeheartedly for your cause, and who think that one way to help you is not to take your time in seeing you, either on purpose or when he comes to Washington for the Gridiron Dinners.

Always faithfully yours,
F.F.

This letter opened up a new field of inquiry for Roosevelt. He had been seeking for some time to avoid any criticism of small businessmen in his public controversies with the giants of industry. But he had a sad conviction that his opponents were gaining ground by picturing him as a man who was simply "against business." The detailed analysis submitted by Professor Lasswell helped him to avoid any general attack on the business community.

Bishop Scarlett of St. Louis, the Bishop of Missouri, had urged Frankfurter to write an article "analyzing the accomplishments of the Roosevelt regime and unravelling the tangle in some of our minds." Having spent part of the summer in Berlin, he was able to report that conditions were "sickening" and more like "nightmare than reality."

Lincoln Filene asked Frankfurter to tell Roosevelt that it would be a great mistake to support Mayor Curley, now Governor of Massachusetts, in the Senate race. Roosevelt shunned any such support.

The last enclosure was from Frank Buxton, who reported that Governor Landon of Kansas refused to become excited over reports that he would be the Republican Presidential candidate later in the year. Landon said Roosevelt would be re-elected.

Memorandum for F.F.

The White House, March 2, 1936

(b)   I wish you and Lasswell would try to work up a list of these smaller, independent business men — say fifteen or twenty — whom I could invite to Washington. I know of no way of getting up such a list. Please let me have Professor Lasswell's letter back to read again.

(c)   Thank you for letting me see the Bishop's letter. I hope to see him sometime this Spring.

(d)   I hope to have a talk with Lincoln Filene. I saw him the other day for a minute but only with a group. Please ask him if he can come down a little later on.

(e)   I will try to see Buxton again this spring if he will let me know when he is coming to Washington.

F.D.R.

It is unknown why there was no paragraph (a) in the preceding memorandum.

Cambridge, Mass., March 4, 1936

Dear Mr. President:

1. First and foremost, let me congratulate you on your tax message. Wisdom and resourcefulness and determination are behind it, and I hope the legislation will embody the essentials of your outline. You will be glad to know that Oliver Sprague has come out warmly in this morning's Boston *Herald* in support of your tax program.

2. Speaking of the tax bill, I hear from lawyer friends of mine, not knowing of my interest in the subject, of the wind they had regarding the Administration's plan to curb lawyers' fees in claims against the Government and their confidence in being able to kill any such "outrageous attempts" to restrict the free pursuit of profit by the great leaders of the bar!

3. Many thanks for your memorandum of the 2nd:

(1) In accordance with your wish, I return herewith Lasswell's letter. I am communicating with him, and will do my utmost to get him to work up a list of these smaller, independent business men.

(2) In this connection, don't forget Clarence Avildsen, who continues to be a warm supporter of yours and ought to be able to help. Also, he absorbs a great deal of knowledge that is valuable through his business associations. Perhaps you can see him before very long.

(3) I am passing your message on to Lincoln Filene.

(4) I think it is just as well if you don't see Buxton until after your re-election. The poor fellow has to do the bidding of his masters, and he is now fiercely on paper on the other side.

(5) Instead of seeing Buxton, I wish you might, out of a clear sky, ask to see Lawrence Winship of the Boston *Globe*. He is true blue and a really wise New Englander.

Marion joins me in warmest regards.

Faithfully yours,
F.F.

Oliver Sprague, a Harvard professor, had a national reputation as an authority on taxation and on general economic policy as it affected American business.

The President saw Clarence Avildsen of Detroit several times to receive periodic reports on the state of mind among business leaders. Buxton and Winship always stood in the inner circle of Frankfurter's friendship. Frankfurter never wavered in his belief that Buxton belonged with the great letter-writers of history, and in time, Roosevelt grew to share this conviction.

Cambridge, Mass., March 10, 1936

Dear Mr. President,

You may be interested in the following telephonic conversation this morning:

Larry Winship — "Groves sent me word that McIntyre asked him whether I could come down and see the President on Friday. Is it imperative that I go?"

F.F. — "Why do you raise the question?"

L.W. — "Well because F.D.R. ought not to waste his time seeing me; instead he ought to see some of these Democratic sore-heads."

F.F. — "Don't you think the President of the United States ought to be allowed to waste his time in his own way?"

L.W. — "I guess that's right too, but why should he waste his time on me?"

F.F. — "I don't know why he should. But maybe by way of change he would like to talk with a sensible fellow who really doesn't want anything — doesn't even angle to see him."

L.W. — "Go to Hell."

Winship is really a shyish fellow and rather laconic — a poor boy who came to Harvard and never moved in the great world of the Arthur Ballantines — until he really gets going. And so I hope you will find enough of a free stretch on Friday to see him alone and for some little time. He is a real newspaperman, not one of these modern columnists or "interpretative" fellows. The *Globe*, as you know, is essentially a newspaper, having no editorial policy. And Winship has radiating connections with news sources all over the United States.

Faithfully yours,
F.F.

Groves was the Washington correspondent of the Boston Globe.

The White House, March 12, 1936

Personal
Dear Mr. Filene:

I am so glad that you agree with me that we should not mix hours, wages and labor relations with the other very different questions of competition, monopoly and unfair trade practices.

As you know, one of my particular difficulties with business leaders has been that while in talking with me personally they seem to be in complete agreement, as soon as they go out many of them rush to their friends and the Press and say, in effect, "We cannot and will not discuss, hours, etc., until and unless the Government eases up on the sword of the anti-trust laws which constantly hangs over our heads."

I greatly enjoyed that luncheon. The difficulty is, of course, that almost of necessity the President has to do most of the talking and, equally, individual members hesitate to express their views because of the size of the gathering. I sometimes think that honest discussion, where more than three or four people are present, is useless from the point of view of facts and policies and is only good for the dissemination of morale and a few ethical fundamentals.

To see each and every one of the membership of the Business Council alone or in small groups, is, of course, impossible for any President. Nevertheless, there are two or three of you whom I should like to talk with alone or in a very small gathering.

Perhaps when I get back from my fishing trip, about April fourth, you will be good enough to run down and lunch with me. I shall ask McIntyre to telephone to you and arrange a time. If you want to bring one or, at the most, two others with you, please make the suggestion.

Always sincerely,
FRANKLIN D. ROOSEVELT

A copy of this letter was sent by the President to Frankfurter. This again was part of the President's campaign to win friends in the business community.

Cambridge, Mass., March 13, 1936

Dear Mr. President,

(1) You will have seen items in connection with the conviction of three important business and financial people who were engaged in the pepper pool and in furtherance of it failed to make certain disclosures in a prospectus inviting popular subscriptions. When next you hear yapping about how much more room is left to rugged individualism in England, you might not only recall that instance, but also quote the following from the most substantial financial periodical in England. The *Economist* for February 29th asks precisely for those safeguards which the Securities Act furnishes.

> Many will think that the "pepper pool's" operations, legal as they are, have immeasurably fortified the demand for a strengthening of the 1929 Companies Act, especially in relation to the liabilities of promoters, the positive requirements of a prospectus, the compulsory publication of subsidiaries' results, consolidated balance sheets, and the disclosure of all the relevant current contracts to auditors.

(2) A friend of mine who sits on the Board of a financial concern with very large utility holdings reports, "in deepest confidence," the following comments made by their counsel, John Foster Dulles, on the utility situation.

1) The Baltimore suit he thought would be thrown out by the Supreme Court on jurisdictional grounds.

2) The Government's strategy in handling the utility cases had been remarkably astute. He referred to B. V. Cohen by name as chiefly responsible for the strategy, and called him a "very bright young man," but "a misguided idealist."

3) In selecting the Bond & Share case for a test case, the Government had selected the best possible case. And he doubted very much that Bond & Share could prove that the Act as applied to it was beyond Federal Power. The Government had also shown great strategy in refusing to do battle in any of the other cases which the utilities had so temptingly offered them.

He thought the litigation, however, might be very prolonged, and might never reach the Supreme Court on the basis of the present Act. He indicated that the Government was already making overtures to the utilities to see whether the Act couldn't be amended so as to make it more acceptable to the utilities and relieve the Government of some of the burdens placed upon it by the Act. The SEC, he also said, in other fields has shown a distinct inclination to be more merciful to the victims of misguided legislative zeal than the proponents of these measures.

4) In any event, the Act could not be carried out in its entirety for several years. The income of the utilities was increasing. He considered Utility stocks "cheap and a good buy."

If you don't look out, you will ruin these fellows into prosperity.

Ever faithfully yours,
F.F.

Telegram to Roosevelt

Cambridge, Mass., March 19, 1936

HERE'S HOPING FOR BITES WHILE SOME OF THE LAND LUBBERS CHEW ON WHAT YOU GAVE THEM YESTERDAY.

FELIX FRANKFURTER

Roosevelt was going on a fishing trip in Florida from March 22 to April 10. The day before this telegram, Roosevelt had delivered his message to Congress on unemployment.

Telegram to Frankfurter

The White House, April 18, 1936

PRESIDENT DELIGHTED TO HAVE YOU COME AND SWIM WITH HIM ON WEDNES-DAY, APRIL TWENTY-SECOND, AT FIVE-THIRTY. SORRY HAS EVENING TAKEN.

G. G. TULLY

Telegram to Frankfurter

The White House, April 20, 1936

IF YOU PLAN TO ATTEND FUNERAL TOMORROW COME AND SWIM AT FIVE-THIRTY.

M. A. LeHAND

This was the funeral of Louis Howe.

The White House, April 28, 1936

Dear Felix:

Many thanks for your kind message of sympathy in the passing of Louis. I am deeply grateful to you.

Very sincerely yours,
FRANKLIN D. ROOSEVELT

Louis Howe, who had never once wavered in his belief that Roosevelt would one day become President, even when he could not walk a yard because of infantile paralysis, had died.

Cambridge, Mass., April 13, 1936

Dear Missy,

The following paragraph comes to me from a wise English friend who knows this country rather intimately and who cares deeply about the success of the President:

> From the British Library of Information I learned that Mrs. Roosevelt is to speak on the same platform with George Lansbury. This, I should have thought, would be a dangerous enterprise. I should have expected F.D.R. to veto it. The Hearst Press and others will pervert it, on the score of a pacifist Labor leader butting in to hamper the American movement of defence, etc. If I were the Roosevelts, I should look hard at everything coming from the other side, with strict relevance to the re-election; and the more so as the present positions of England and the USA are so widely different.

As you know, I don't want to bother the President needlessly, and so I send it to you for your judgment as to its use. If it seems best, you will, of course, pass it on to the President. If you think I should write to him directly about it, please so advise me. If the wastebasket is the best place for this, put it there.

Very cordially,
F.F.

The English friend was Kingsley Martin, editor of the New Statesman and Nation.

The White House, April 18, 1936

Dear Mr. Frankfurter:

Miss LeHand has just given me your letter and I have spoken to the President about it.

I feel that, as far as I know, George Lansbury is a gentleman and not in any way a dangerous person. I do not happen to know whether I am speaking on any platform or on any program with him, but I have two speeches scheduled when I might be speaking, either at the same time or at some other time, to the same group.

The first is a broadcast on April 21st, for a peace group, and the other is a Labor Meeting in New Haven on the 28th. Many things will doubtless be said with which I do not agree, but I am responsible for my own opinions only, and they have accepted those.

What Mr. Hearst says or does not say seems to me to matter very little. Whatever he has to say has already been said, and so, though I appreciate your correspondent's concern, will you kindly tell him we will take our medicine and go on doing what things we want to do? The President will not be elected or defeated on anything I do!

> Cordially yours,
> ELEANOR ROOSEVELT

I've just discovered that George Lansbury speaks on the radio the 21st.

> Cambridge, Mass., April 21, 1936

Dear Mrs. Roosevelt,

What I ventured to say in my letter to you about the deep significance of your attitude toward the photograph of yourself and the two colored men, is equally applicable, if I may say so, to the views you express in regard to George Lansbury's visit in your gracious letter which has just come.

I wholly agree with you that fear of what "they will say" is the worst possible governing principle on which to run one's life, either in office or without. And yielding to such a sinister and systematic assassin of character as Hearst has been all his life is, in effect, to surrender to his own unworthiness. The correspondent whose concern I passed on not because I shared it but merely that it might be considered by those who have surer instinct for judgment — happens to be a man of singularly fine and courageous character who shares our view of Hearst and all his works, but also writes, I believe, more from consideration of the general state of mind of the great body of honest folk in this country, and speaking as one who is truly devoted to both of you. For you know him well and, I know, regard him very highly.

So far as George Lansbury is concerned, it becomes appropriate to say that he is an old and deeply valued friend of mine, one of the most lovable of men, and I know not a half-dozen people in public life on either side of the Atlantic who are as deeply interested and as Lincolnian in their humanity as is George Lansbury.

And so I am glad I passed on my correspondent's concern, because it gave rise to those superb and forthright expressions of yours which were not new to me, but nevertheless give one courage and a new confidence every time they are expressed.

> Faithfully yours,
> FELIX FRANKFURTER

> The White House, April 30, 1936

Dear Mr. Frankfurter:

Thank you very much for taking the trouble to write me again. I understood perfectly your reasons for sending on the comments concerning Mr. Lansbury and I appreciate all the kind things you say.

> Very cordially yours,
> ELEANOR ROOSEVELT

Cambridge, Mass., April 29, 1936

Dear Mr. President:

In raising for your consideration the suggestion I am about to make, I may well overlook a number of elements in an important situation. But I am confident that you will charge the suggestion to my great devotion to you and acquit me of intrusion into what is a very personal problem.

In brief, if you have not yet selected someone to take over some of the functions of the irreplaceable Louis, isn't Ray Stevens worth considering?

Of course, you know better than I all the circumstances of Ray's career, the qualities they reveal and their relevance to the manifold and personal functions for a member of the President's secretariat. But I don't think you have ever seen Ray as I have seen him — on his native heath of Landaff, N.H. — and had the revelation, on the spot from which they spring, of his Lincolnian shrewdness and simplicity, his genius for the common touch and his intuitive wisdom that seizes just the right way for putting straight all sorts of queer human quirks. What makes him so incredibly unique is that the same Yankee solitary who worked his milk farm all alone for years should have been equally at home in the palace of the last absolute monarch of the Orient.

Well I don't have to say more. But am I quite wrong in wondering whether there's anybody else who so epitomized the kind of hard-headed, practical political experience that enables him to find his way around on the main road as well as on the most obscure detours, who has such a sure instinct for knowing the difference between sense and nonsense, who can recognize cranks and fools without letting them be aware of it, who can placate dignity without subordination and subordinate with dignity important pretenders.

I am looking ahead, of course. I am thinking of all the domestic and international snarls that you will have to disentangle during the next four years, all the gallant fights that you will be reading. And I am thinking of the priceless value of a self-effacing, dedicated, palpitating background that understands without being talked to and never talks except with understanding.

That's my story and I stick to it — provided you think it's any good.

Devotedly yours,

F.F.

This time Ray Stevens was not appointed. But Frankfurter, taking even better aim, came forward with the inspired suggestion of Thomas Corcoran who, in time, being a man of ideas, would come to exert infinitely more influence in the White House than Louis Howe had ever done.

Cambridge, Mass., April 29, 1936

Dear Missy —

The President may be interested in the progress we are making to get into effective form, and effectively disseminated, proof that "The Interests" have for the last fifty years opposed all progressive legislation. And so I send the enclosed, which please return at your convenience.

Very cordially,
F.F.

The enclosed material, running to some twenty pages, was a primer on the way "The Interests" were able to invoke the highest sounding ideals in defense of their own economic privileges. Roosevelt marked several passages before returning the memorandum.

Telegram to Frankfurter

The White House, May 15, 1936

THE PRESIDENT HAS SEEN WILLERT ARTICLES. CONFERENCE ABOUT WHICH YOU TALKED IS SET FOR WEDNESDAY EVENING MAY TWENTIETH EIGHT THIRTY. LOOKING FORWARD TO SEEING YOU AGAIN.

MISSY

Sir Arthur Willert had written a series of articles for the London Times summing up his impressions of conditions in America. The conference with Frankfurter included a general review of the world situation.

Telegram to Roosevelt

Cambridge, Mass., May 19, 1936

KNOWING SOME OF THE DIFFICULTIES CONGRATULATE YOU ALL THE MORE WARMLY ON LILIENTHAL REAPPOINTMENT.

FELIX FRANKFURTER

David Lilienthal had been reappointed to the TVA Board of Directors.

Cambridge, Mass., May 22, 1936

Dear Mr. President,

Very few things seem to me more promising in their implication for the future than the settlement between the Railway Executives and the Railroad Unions which your gentle but firm pressure upon both sides, your far-sightedness and your tact alone made possible. It is a heartening example of constructive intelligence applied to modern technicological problems. But it also proves that without effective organization among the men, such collaborative solutions of the common problems of industry are not possible. That is why the Tory leaders of industry know not what they do in their obstinate resistance to the intelligence and character that unions in the long run foster by training men in organized responsibility.

And let me tell you again what a great thing it is for the country for you to have solved and resolved the trying TVA situation. I know what it meant in time and patience, in human understanding and incredible tact to save for the country continuity in the work of TVA.

You know how we all occasionally like to play at the children's game of what we would do if we were God. I would add four hours to your day.

Faithfully yours,
F.F.

London, England, May 26, 1936

My dear Felix,

So admirably does the machine work that to-night Messersmith is to dine to meet Clem Attlee, Stafford Cripps, Kingsley Martin and Ray Atherton. Crozier, being in Manchester, cannot come up here in time. Could your commands receive more adequate fulfillment?

Ever yours,
HAROLD J. LASKI

By this time Frankfurter, because of his interest in Austria, having been born in Vienna, had become a friend of George Messersmith, the American Minister in Austria, where reports on the growing Nazi danger were both accurate and prophetic.

Frankfurter loved Laski as if he were his son. Kingsley Martin was the leading Socialist editor in Britain, J. P. Crozier was the editor of the Manchester Guardian. *Attlee and Cripps were the leaders of the two wings of the Labour party. Ray Atherton then was with the American Embassy in London.*

Frankfurter wanted Messersmith to meet these British leaders so that his views on the German problem would have the greatest public impact.

London, England, May 27, 1936

Dear Frankfurter,

Thanks for letting me know that Messersmith was going to be in London. I met him in Berlin about three years ago and found him most interesting. As a matter of fact, I tried to see him when I was passing through Vienna three weeks ago but he was in the United States at the time.

I have arranged to see him to-morrow and am getting in touch with Geoffrey Dawson.

All best wishes,

Yours sincerely,
ASTOR

Lord Astor was the publisher of the London Times, *Geoffrey Dawson was its editor.*

The White House, May 27, 1936

Dear Felix:

You undoubtedly have seen the attached. I am, however, sending it along, merely for your information, on the chance it may have escaped your attention.

With kindest regards,

Very sincerely yours,
STEPHEN EARLY

Cambridge, Mass., May 29, 1936

Dear Steve,

It's a pleasure to hear from you, even if you are the innocent conduit of the Edmondson filth. Who do you suppose puts up the cash for the wide dissemination of his stuff?

These are days when folly, hate and lies have their day, which means that we on our side need serenity, a sense of humor, sagacity, and patience more than ever. It's a comfort to know that you are where you are.

With cordial regards,

Very sincerely,
F.F.

Between 1934–1940, Robert Edward Edmondson became a specialist in race hatred and published a number of anti-Semitic pamphlets and bulletins.

The struggle over the 1936 Democratic platform was, in essence, a struggle over fundamental principles of party doctrine. One group, reflecting the dominant sentiment of the party's Congressional leaders, wished the platform to emphasize the legislative record of the past four years. Implicit in this approach was the belief that enough had already been done to justify a more relaxed attitude to the need for additional progressive legislation — an approach directly in conflict with Roosevelt's "Forward March" strategy. In preparing a draft of the platform, Senator Wagner, as Chairman of the Resolutions Committee, in the interests of party harmony, had made many concessions to other committee members with the result that the cautious Congressional philosophy became obtrusive. Simon Rifkind had assisted Wagner in the draftsmanship.

Frankfurter, by contrast, having a much greater knowledge of Roosevelt's thinking, wanted the platform to be not a catalogue but a challenge, not a recital of past achievements but an incentive to new reforms. Tom Corco-

*ran was extremely active in all these discussions which shaped the 1936
campaign. It was Corcoran who gave Roosevelt the famous phrase for his
speech in accepting the Presidential nomination for a second term: "This
generation of Americans has a rendezvous with destiny." Samuel Rosenman and Stanley High worked on the Wagner committee draft to give it
resonance and eloquence. Roosevelt exemplified his own philosophy, and
reinforced Frankfurter's judgment, by declaring in the campaign that "we
have only just begun to fight."*

Cambridge, Mass., June 13, 1936

Dear Mr. President:

First, let me tell you what an absolutely ripping speech you made at
Arkansas. "Forward March" is precisely the right temper of command with
which to impregnate the campaign atmosphere. I know I am just a professor, but I eat the proverbial hat if I am wrong in believing that over and
beyond this and that detail of the campaign is the necessity of charging the
emotions of the American people anew with hope and confidence, and with
the conviction that you are the only dependable instrument for pushing
forward their hopes and justifying their confidence. And so as I take off, I
express the deep hope that the temper of the Arkansas speech is the one
that you will maintain throughout the campaign.

Feeling as I do, I cannot withhold my strong disappointment in the
preliminary draft of the platform that Tom has just brought, as it comes
from Rifkind's hands. I shall try to have my say, at least over the 'phone,
with Bob Wagner and Rifkind before I leave tomorrow but it may not be
possible to reach them. Therefore I am compelled briefly to say to you what
I am about to say. I understand that this is only a draft and that it certainly
does not satisfy Wagner and Rifkind but is the result of pleasing everybody
by omitting everything opposed by anybody. Since dictating this I've read
the Dallas speech and that's grand. Well, all-things-to-all-men produces
precisely this kind of a wishy-washy, uninspiring mush, worse than tame cat.
This draft has no inspiration, no generalized philosophy, no call to arms,
nothing to hearten anybody, nothing that anybody will remember the day
after it is published in the newspapers. In substance it hardly differs from
the Landon platform, and in tone it is even duller.

Of course, your acceptance speech will be the call to arms and will
furnish the philosophy. Nevertheless the platform ought to serve as your
auxiliary; the platform certainly should not be a handicap to you, at the
lowest the handicap of a collection of dead words without impact, without
lift and without courage. It ought not to leave any possible room for the
suggestion that the official party utterance does not fully express your own
outlook. For the life of me I don't see why the platform shouldn't express

the kind of general outlook that you expressed in the Commonwealth Club speech, that is reflected in the major policies of the Administration, and will serve as the general direction for the next four years.

Rifkind himself is aware of the flatness, the lack of cohesion and organic eloquence of this draft. I am not remotely suggesting that the draft which I placed in your hands should serve as anything more than as a draft for improvement and stiffening. But I do hope that you will find time to read that draft and compare the objectives in platform-making which underlay it with the present proposal.

I am asking Tom to put this letter in your hands. He will also give you in his own inadequate, un-Celtic way my affectionate greetings and my good wishes for everything, until I am gone — and way beyond.

Devotedly yours,
F.F.

Writing from London, Frankfurter begins his letter with praise of Roosevelt's acceptance speech at the Philadelphia Convention. It was apparent from the tone of this "rendezvous with destiny" speech that Roosevelt would carry his case to the nation in a challenging campaign. He had strengthened the Democratic party's prospects in New York by persuading Herbert Lehman to run for another term as Governor. Margot was the widow of former Prime Minister Herbert Asquith, and Elizabeth Bibesco was one of his daughters and an attractive memoirist. Charles Poletti continued to serve as one of Lehman's chief advisers, and became Lieutenant Governor of New York in 1939 and Governor in 1942. Robert Jackson had a larger destiny: after being the most brilliant Solicitor General of this century, he became Attorney General and still later an Associate Justice of the Supreme Court of the United States. Mussolini's successful assault on Abyssinia, in defiance of the League, had left an ugly legacy.

London, July 11, 1936

Dear Frank:

1. Unfortunately I could not hear your Philadelphia speech as conveyed by your own voice, but the vibrancy of your utterance triumphed over the cold type of the extracts which Wilmott Lewis conveyed and stirred feelings in me that have been aroused by not more than a dozen speeches in my life-time. And now that I have read the full text, I find in the speech (with all the insulation of feelings that time produces) that enduring quality which makes a classic. You have given us something not only to win with, but to win for.

2. Apart from all else, you have taken the aggressive, and again proven that the only effective defensive is an offensive. Political life, as all other

life, means affirmation and not negation, and the lead you have taken in Philadelphia has been the dominant political news from America since Philadelphia. Your persuasion of Herbert Lehman has of course had psychological effects much beyond the immediate New York contest. You must have handled him just right. The new drought is a terrible plight, but Lewis' cable indicates the bold and imaginative leadership with which you are meeting it.

3. In so-called upper class and even Tory circles here one moves in a wholly different mental climate from that which one finds on Park Avenue or Beacon Hill. In the first place, there is an immense amount of warm feeling for you personally on this side, not least for the gallantry with which you reversed the national morale in 1933. But in addition, there is a much calmer realisation that the general direction of your measures — never mind the details — is indispensable for the sake of capitalism itself, and that, in the language of Macaulay, in order to conserve we must reform. I have seen a number of your friends like Margot and Elizabeth Bibesco, who are passionately eager for the successful outcome of next November.

4. I have been importuned by some of those closest to Herbert Lehman to try to prevail upon Charlie Poletti to stay with Herbert after this year. I know that Charlie told H.H.L. some time ago that in any event he would not stay in his present post after January. I have been thinking about the business a good deal and I wonder if the whole problem could not be most effectively solved by running Charlie as Lieut.-Governor — this, of course, on the assumption that for one reason or another Bob Jackson is not to be named. Charlie would make a powerful appeal not only to his own people but also to the young, and thus enormously further the whole cause in New York. I am also assuming that Bennett will want to continue as Attorney General; otherwise Charlie could be named for that post, for he is in addition to all else a very good lawyer. Charlie's youth rules him out as a serious rival to the ambitions of others as Herbert's successor in 1938. At least, this is the way New York politics strike a mere professor across the ocean.

5. There will be much to say about the British situation when I return. For the present, suffice it to remark that it is my impression, with some knowledge of the history of the England of Chatham and Burke and Fox, that not even the defeat of the mother-country by the thirteen colonies left such a sense of national humiliation as has followed in the wake of the Abyssinian affair. Great Britain is now feverishly aroused to make herself strong, for whatever contingency may be in store. There is, as you know, not a little sentiment in the City and other high quarters looking towards "terms" with Germany — which means giving her a free hand in the East — but as soon as these tendencies reach proportions they are severely

checked by such Nazi performances as the recent conduct of Capt. Greiser before the Council of the League on the Danzig matter. By the way, has that delightful euphemism, "to cock a snook," reached you? It was the delightful way in which *The Times* described Capt. Greiser's thumbing his nose at the Council of the League.

I hope nothing will interfere for a real holiday for you before the strenuous months of the campaign begin. Marion joins me in affectionate greetings.

Ever yours,
F.F.

This is Frankfurter's draft of the 1936 Democratic platform. Carefully studied by the President, marked and annotated by him, it strengthened his own concept of the general philosophy he should advocate in the 1936 campaign. This is really the philosophy of liberalism in which both men believed.

Franklin D. Roosevelt and John N. Garner have led the American people out of panic and collapse onto the safe highway of courage and recovery. They have guided us through an internal crisis of disaster comparable to the dark days when the unity of the nation hung upon the patient wisdom and bold foresight of Washington and Lincoln. They have taken up the task of safeguarding our institutions where that task was laid down by Wilson. They have conceived the necessary adjustments of economic realities to the Jeffersonian ideal of political democracy. They have pursued these ends with the fearless determination of Jackson.

On March 4, 1933, as never before, this was a nation bereft of confidence, bewildered by failure, bankrupt of morale. The great majority of our citizens lived in poverty or insecurity absurdly, and tragically, out of relation to our natural resources and our means of production. Twelve years of virtual surrender by Government to the blind control of a dominant few had made our economic organization obsolete for distributing to the people as a whole the wealth they produce as a whole. In this fiercest test of moral leadership that ever faced America the present Administration has won an unchallengeable moral victory. It has stirred hope and constructive intelligence in a people who had lost hope. It has awakened faith that by intelligence our traditional system of individual enterprise can be reorganized to operate anew.

The Democratic Administration has saved that traditional system of individual enterprise and free competition. It has sought to vindicate it for its service to the common man and to enable it to operate for the children's children of today's free men and women by buttressing it against collapse in panic in another twelve years.

Through the Banking Acts, the Securities Act, the Securities and Exchange Act and the activities of the Reconstruction Finance Corporation, the Administration has given individual enterprise a truly sound financial system in which to operate by ensuring the stability of the banking system, whose credit creates our currency, and the integrity of the securities market whose trustworthiness makes it possible for capital to function.

By the revaluation of our currency in fair relation to our own debt structure and to the prevailing standard of international trade, the Administration has made possible a continuation and resumption of domestic and foreign trade and has supported the purchasing power of the nation against the vicissitudes of foreign disturbances and domestic maladjustments.

By the operations of the Farm Credit Administration, the Home Owners' Loan Corporation, the Reconstruction Finance Corporation and the Federal Reserve System, the Administration has refunded and reduced the fixed charges against the annual national income of vast aggregates of debt which endangered social order and the economic fabric.

By the enactment of the NRA at a critical juncture of the depression, the Administration broke the psychology of deflation, ostracized child labor and at the demand of industry itself conducted searching tests to ascertain the practical advantages and limitations of self-government in industry for capital, labor and the consuming public.

By its agricultural legislation, the Administration for the first time consciously helped to restore the lost balance of production and income between agricultural and industrial products which is essential to the functioning of the national economic exchange.

By its tax legislation policy and its utility legislation, the Administration has made a beginning of deliberate encouragement to moderate-sized, independent industry upon which the maintenance of our economic traditions of free enterprise and the continuance of our political democracy depend.

By its labor legislation the Administration has made a beginning of legal guarantee of an adequate bargaining status for our workers upon whose adequate sharing in the product of the nation the stability of our economic traditions of free enterprise and the continuance of our political democracy likewise and to no less degree depend.

By its Social Security legislation the Administration has made a beginning of ensuring employment stability for the worker during his years of reasonable efficiency, and a self-respecting pension when those years of efficiency are past.

By its continuing program of public works and the resolute conservation of natural resources, the Administration has aimed at constructive solutions of the problems of technological unemployment and made a beginning of linking together the conservation and development of the nation's fundamental material resources and its human resources. For a standing army of unemployed is inconsistent with the purposes for which our country was founded.

By its housing, resettlement and rural electrification projects, the Administration has aimed at the adoption of more healthy and intelligent ways of life and has definitely committed itself to the principle that higher standards of life for the great body of our men and women will not only be conducive to a higher social contentment but are indispensable to the fullest employment of our productive capital.

By its Public Utility Holding Company Act, its Tennessee Valley project, its Electric Home and Farm Authority program, its Rural Electrification program, the Administration has utilized constitutional powers of the nation to realize for the benefit of the country as a whole the possibilities of the Age of Electric Power already upon us.

By the repeal of the Eighteenth Amendment and the Volstead Acts, the Administration revived and restored our traditional faith in personal liberty. It recognized that it is the function of law to safeguard personal, political and economic liberty, but that neither enterprise nor temperance can be achieved by governmental regimentation.

Such policies have not only brought immediate relief; they have started the recuperative process of recovery; they promise the stability of an economy of individual enterprise designed to serve the enterprising many rather than the grasping few.

A common national purpose born of common suffering must not be lost as soon as national prosperity shows signs of returning. A return to the blind and selfish policies of the past would spell not recovery but relapse. There are grave and urgent economic problems confronting the nation, which cannot be shirked or avoided. The promise of American life has not yet been realized. If we would preserve our heritage of political freedom, men must again become economically free.

(1) Necessitous men are not free men. Freedom comes from a sense of security. Work for every able-bodied individual who wants to work has been an essential part of our American heritage. Its realization has made us a free, self-reliant nation. With the passing of the frontier of free land and the development of a mechanized civilization, that precious heritage can be maintained only if Government cooperates with private enterprise to create conditions which, barring temporary and inevitable vicissitudes, will ensure the opportunity of livelihood to all who are willing and able to work. Until

the average man has attained a standard of life far beyond that which he now enjoys, we cannot afford to require the employed portion of our people to support the unemployed in idleness or require the employed portion permanently to divide their work with the unemployed. Our aim must be not a lower but a higher standard of life for the average man. Our task is to find useful employment for all of our people by increasing the interchange of goods and services among them. Only thus can we utilize permanently the progressive advances in technology and not have the machine become our undoing. Work, not unemployment, creates wealth; without opportunity for free and normal work there can be no real political freedom.

(2) The pressure of unemployment and the terrible warning of the recent droughts and floods demand a well-formulated policy of action which will ensure the carrying out of works necessary to the conservation and prudent utilization of our natural resources when labor is idle and capital not productively employed. Such works are vitally essential to safeguard America's capital resources and to assure the future prosperity and contentment of our people both in the cities and on the farm. Such works the nation cannot afford to neglect.

(3) The fiscal and financial policies of the Government must be directed towards increasing not simply the Government's income but also the national income from which the Government's income is derived. The national wealth and the national income can be increased only by the wise employment of our human resources and the prudent utilization of our natural resources. So long as a nation which is not burdened with foreign indebtedness does not consume more than it produces, its national solvency and strength cannot be questioned. As recovery proceeds, the Government's expenditures must be carefully scrutinized to determine their effect upon employment and the national income. As the national income is restored, the reduction in relief expenditures and the increase in the tax revenues should make possible the balancing of the budget at the earliest moment consistent with the widest practical employment of our human resources and national capital. Balancing the budget through increased tax revenues or decreased expenditures, as the national income is restored, is an indispensable element in the eventual and complete success of a program of permanent recovery requiring Government intervention entailing deficit-financing when an economic recession is imminent and entailing debt-curtailment when inflation or excessive speculation threatens the stability of the national economy.

(4) Private enterprise is at the basis of our American system not because of the opportunity it affords a few to make fabulous or unearned fortunes, but because of the encouragement and freedom of action it gives to men to shape their own lives and to plan their own destinies. We have

believed in private enterprise not because it assures inherited wealth but because it has made men free to venture; because it has not forced the workingman's son to pursue the job of his father or the banker's son to pursue his father's calling, but because it has left men free to choose among many jobs and many callings. Considering the limitations of men, the social and economic interests of all of us are best served not by the minute orders of an all-directing state, governed by non-existent supermen, but through the multitudinous activities, experiments and strivings of all those whom Lincoln called the common people.

(5) Our American conception of the relation of Government to business and labor has always been to create conditions which would permit business to function and labor to find employment. The time has long since gone by when the best interests of all classes required that the Government should leave all business to its own devices. The whole postwar period has proved that private enterprise in the modern world is a far more complicated and fragile mechanism than in the early days of small-scale industry when the laws of supply and demand worked fairly automatically. It is doubtless difficult to devise controls which will be intelligently flexible. But we have no choice but to continue to apply ourselves to the task consciously and intelligently. The more farsighted business men, especially the younger generation, are agreed with all students of modern economics that left wholly to itself private enterprise will destroy itself — as it came perilously near doing in the dark days preceding the present administration.

(6) The new economic freedom must be a freedom not of theoretical absolutes but of concrete realities. Wholesome competition is the life of trade in a system of individual enterprise. To destroy effective competition is to destroy capitalism. The trend toward concentration is a very real threat against our traditional competitive system. If that trend is not reversed, there is a danger of a private socialism in this country as alien to traditional Americanism as state socialism. The backbone of that trend is the creed of greed — that no aggregation of property can be so large as to be beyond the control of concentrated and centralized managers, and that competition is an out-moded, discredited, useless feature of economic life. There is no practical way to regulate the economic oligarchy of autocratic, self-constituted and self-perpetuating groups. With all their resources of inter-locking directors, interlocking bankers and interlocking lawyers, with all their power to hire thousands of employees and service workers throughout the country, with all their power to give or withhold millions of dollars' worth of business, with all their power to contribute to the campaign funds of the acquiescent or to subsidize the champions of the obdurate, they are as dangerous a menace to political as they are to economic freedom. It is necessary to destroy the roots of economic fascism in this country, if we

wish to remove the dangers of political fascism, which engulfed freedom in other lands.

(7) The "merging out" of effective competition has brought neither economic freedom nor economic leadership to the modern world. As it has closed one by one the doors of independent enterprise, it has destroyed the only way men can work for themselves. In the words of the President, the process of concentration of power "has made most American citizens, once traditional owners of their own business, helplessly dependent for their daily bread upon the favor of a very few." Competitive freedom has undoubtedly been hampered by the inequitable distribution of wealth. But far more menacing to that freedom has been not mere inequality in individual fortunes but the undue concentration of economic power over other people's fortunes, other people's businesses, and other people's lives. The breaking down of that socially and economically unwarranted power over other people's property and destiny will best promote our traditional system of private property. Neither the ownership nor control of property can be pemitted to be the perquisites of a privileged few; in a truly democratic community the average citizen must have a stake worth preserving in the economic system.

(8) As fair competition is essential to the life of trade, so equality of bargaining power is essential to the dignity and security of labor. We cannot expect real industrial peace and sympathetic efforts on the part of labor to meet the problems of industry until we can expect cooperative responsibility on the part of labor with a frank recognition of a democratically chosen leadership. Without such cooperative responsibility on the part of labor, industry will be unable to protect itself from the unfair undercutting of labor costs by a recalcitrant minority of employers. No one can today justify child labor, chiseling workers' wages, stretching workers' hours as necessary methods of competition. We must safeguard and improve the standard of living of the average man and protect him against the vicissitudes of irregular employment. America must again become the land of opportunity, and those who give full measure of service must be enabled to obtain opportunities to render such service and obtain adequate recompense for their labor and their enterprise.

(9) America, if she does not waste her resources, has and may enjoy indefinitely advantages of relative economic self-sufficiency possessed by few other powers. Yet we do not and cannot live without the friendship and trade of other countries. A large percentage of our cotton and other crops have always gone abroad and we cannot wholly abandon these markets without radical disturbance of our domestic economy. If we sell abroad, we must buy abroad. True, we may grant foreign credits or make foreign investments to enable other countries to pay for our exports, but unless we

maintain a healthy interchange of trade we will again find our loans uncol-
lectible and our investments worthless. We must seek wholesome and reciprocal channels of trade with foreign nations which will not expose our
domestic markets to ruinous and unfair competition. The trade agreements
authorized by Congress and which already have been and are being carefully negotiated by our State Department give promise of providing for the
most intelligent handling of the tariff problem and for the wholesome extension of our foreign trade for the benefit, not of any special interests, but
for the nation as a whole.

(10) The United States has during the past four years been at peace
and has maintained friendly relations with all foreign powers. America cannot be unmindful of the wars which have broken out abroad and of the war
clouds that hang ruinously over other lands. Much as America deprecates
the strife and threatened strife abroad and the failure of some foreign countries to abjure war as an instrument of national policy, it is not America's
function to interfere in the quarrels of other nations. America, while prepared to defend its own interest in case of unwarranted aggression, must
faithfully observe not merely the forms but the actualities of neutrality. It
must not permit private trading or international banking to endanger public peace. It must guard against being drawn unawares into other people's
wars against the wishes and interests and conscience of the American people. America's task is not to fight abroad but to set an example at home of
the kind of constitutional government a peace-loving, liberty-loving people
can have if they will, — a democratic government without dictators, a government which recognizes the dignity and worth of the humblest of humanity and which values above material things freedom of thought and of
speech and the pursuit of happiness for all men regardless of race or religion.

(11) To the realization of such a program, the Democratic Party dedi-
cates itself and pledges its candidates. Modern government involves not
merely the enactment of wise and honest laws but effective, skilled and
unbiased administration. To perfect such administration the Democratic
Party pledges itself to the progressive improvement and extension of the
permanent civil service to the greatest degree compatible with maintenance
of free government. The purposes of a modern democracy must not be
thwarted or discredited by ineffective and unimaginative administration.

The Democratic Party pledges itself anew to the principles of constitutional government under our Federal System. The Fathers of the Constitution wisely contemplated that the States should have essential governmental powers in all matters of local concern and that the Federal Government
should have the necessary authority over all commerce among the States,
with wise guarantees against arbitrary use of such power by either the Fed-

eral Government or the States. In the words of the great Mr. Justice Holmes, who fought the war caused by the Dred Scott decision, "It is not lightly to be assumed that, in matters requiring national action, 'a power which must belong to and somewhere reside in every civilized government' is not to be found." The Tenth Amendment was expressly intended to leave to the States the sovereign power of legislation in all matters not delegated to the Federal Government. It is inconceivable that there is a No Man's Land where no government — not all the powers of the States and the Nation combined — can safeguard either liberty or property or protect the weak against exploitation and legitimate business against unfair competition.

To apply the platform of Lincoln of 1860 after the Dred Scott case, to "the new dogma" — that the Constitution is said to deny to both the Federal and State Governments power to deal with vital social and economic problems within their traditional spheres of action — "is a dangerous political heresy, at variance with the explicit provisions of that instrument itself, with contemporaneous exposition and with legislative and judicial precedents, is revolutionary in its tendency and subversive of the peace and harmony of the country."

In a fireside chat, Roosevelt had reported on the devastation he had seen in nine states stricken by the drought. The speech then broadened out into a restatement of his general program for recovery and reform.

Telegram to Roosevelt
Port Washington, N.Y., September 6, 1936

IT WAS A COMPLETELY AND PROFOUNDLY SATISFYING SPEECH. SERENITY, UNDERSTANDING AND PASSION WERE FUSED INTO AN APPEAL TO REASON WHICH TOUCHED THE CORDS OF DEVOTION TO ALL THAT MAKES US AMERICANS. THIS IS THE NOTE TO STRIKE AND THE ATMOSPHERE TO CREATE IN ALL YOUR FUTURE SPEECHES AND THEREBY NOT ONLY YOUR ELECTION BUT ALSO THE AMERICA WE LOVE WILL BE SECURE. MARION JOINS ME IN AFFECTIONATE GRATITUDE.

FELIX

The White House, September 8, 1936

My dear Felix:

The thoughtful message you sent me made me exceedingly happy. Thanks ever so much.

Best wishes to you and yours,

Always sincerely,
F.D.R.

Harvard's Tercentenary celebration was observed on September 18, 1936. Still angered by Lowell's coarse-grained rudeness, Roosevelt decided to strike back, courteously but vigorously. He deliberately omitted Lowell's name from his Salutation, and then, in his first sentence, emphasized that he was speaking as the President of the United States. It will be remembered that Lowell in his letters had never addressed him as "Mr. President" and had preferred instead to call him "Mr. Roosevelt," as if to emphasize that he would be taking part in the anniversary celebrations only as another Harvard alumnus. Believing that Lowell reflected the criticisms of important Republicans who wished that some Harvard graduate other than himself had been elected as President, Roosevelt decided to dispose of their objections at the very start. After his opening words — "President Conant, distinguished guests, my fellow alumni" — he said:

I am here today in a joint and several capacity, first, as the President of the United States; second, as Chairman of the United States Harvard Tercentenary Commission, which is composed of five members of the Senate, five members of the House of Representatives, a representative of the United States Army and one of the Navy, and two representatives of the Universities of the United States, the distinguished Presidents of the University of California and the University of North Carolina; finally, I am here as a Son of Harvard who gladly returns to this spot where men have sought truth for three hundred years.

The roots of Harvard are deep in the past. It is pleasant to remember today that this meeting is being held in pursuance of an adjournment expressly taken one hundred years ago on the motion of Josiah Quincy.

At that time many of the alumni of Harvard were sorely troubled concerning the state of the nation. Andrew Jackson was President. On the 250th anniversary of the founding of Harvard College, many alumni again were sorely troubled. Grover Cleveland was President. Now, on the three hundredth anniversary, I am President.

The audacity of this opening disarmed even Roosevelt's critics and the speech was off to a triumphant start.

At the morning session, held outdoors, Roosevelt sat on the platform. A light rain began to fall near the end of that session. The President spoke in the afternoon. By that time it was raining hard but the proceedings had been moved indoors to Sanders Theatre.

Telegram to Miss LeHand
Cambridge, Mass., September 18, 1936

IT CAME OFF BEAUTIFULLY. YOU SHOULD HAVE HEARD AND SEEN IT. HE TURNED A DIFFICULT SITUATION INTO A TRIUMPH. HE WAS AT HIS VERY BEST.

FELIX FRANKFURTER

Telegram to Roosevelt

Cambridge, Mass., September 19, 1936

HOPE MUCH YOU DID NOT CATCH COLD. IT WAS REALLY A GREAT TRIUMPH. YOU
FURNISHED A STRIKING EXAMPLE OF THE CIVILIZED GENTLEMAN AND ALSO OF
THE IMPORTANCE OF WISE SAUCINESS. CHARLIE BURLINGHAM, MARION AND
SOME OF THE REST OF US CELEBRATED YOUR PERFORMANCE WITH ENTHUSIASM
LAST NIGHT.

FELIX FRANKFURTER

*All through the 1936 campaign, Roosevelt kept up a taunting reminder
that his severest critics were the people whose fortunes he had saved when
the banks closed in the worst period of the depression. C. C. Burlingham,
who heard one of these informal campaign speeches, told the President
that "the blind Tory is the best friend of revolution because he is the
enemy of timely reform. We must make capitalism tolerable if it is to be
tolerated." Frankfurter agreed with Roosevelt's "sauciness" so long as it
was tempered by a sensitive awareness of the misery still being endured by
the unemployed and those fearful of losing their precarious jobs.*

The White House, September 22, 1936

Dear Felix: —

Did you really and truly like it — more important still, did Marion
really and truly like it? Your expression of the "importance of wise sauciness" is perhaps better than mine. I told the boys afterwards that I had
stuck my chin out and said "hit me" — and nobody dared!

I was awfully sorry not to see you both — I gave a wave to Charlie
Burlingham.

As ever yours,

F.D.R.

Cambridge, Mass., Sept. 27, 1936

Dear Mr. President:

Yes, I did really and truly like the speech you made at Harvard. I
paddled out in the rain to hear it, when I might have heard it at home,
because I wanted to be seen applauding. But the applause was so general
and prolonged that my nobility was unnoticed! Rather a blow for me.

Here's wishing you a good trip.

Sincerely,

MARION FRANKFURTER

Telegram to Roosevelt

Cambridge, Mass., September 30, 1936

A MAGNIFICENT CALL TO BATTLE. YOU TOOK THE OFFENSIVE BY GIVING THE

NATION YOUR ROUNDED GENERAL POLITICAL PHILOSOPHY, AND I BELIEVE YOU NEVER CONVEYED MORE EFFECTIVELY OVER THE AIR YOUR PERSONALITY AND PURPOSES.

FELIX FRANKFURTER

Hyde Park, N.Y., October 2, 1936

Dear Felix:

Many thanks for your telegram about the Syracuse speech. As always, you say things that hearten.

Very sincerely yours,
F.D.R.

On September 29, in his first major formal speech in the campaign, Roosevelt delivered a comprehensive and challenging speech at the Democratic State Convention in Syracuse, New York.

As the 1936 Presidential campaign went on, Frankfurter became increasingly irritated by Governor Landon. It seemed to him that Landon was being used by the most negative and discredited leaders of the Republican party in a campaign of blind opposition to the New Deal. He discussed these issues in a letter written to a friend on September 25, 1936, a copy of which was shown to Roosevelt.

Frankfurter in this letter was concerned with keeping the liberal and progressive forces as the vigorous allies of Roosevelt. He recalled that in 1928 Professor Holcombe of Harvard had voted for Hoover because Al Smith did not go far enough to suit him on the power issue. He hoped "mental quirks" of this kind would not influence liberal voters now. They should concentrate on the main issues and remember that if Roosevelt had not pleased them in everything he had done, they would in all probability find very little in Landon's record to satisfy them. Then, in the central passage of the letter, Frankfurter discussed the familiar defense that Landon was not "the tool of the interests." Frankfurter wrote:

I don't think he is, in any naïve or sinister sense. But if American history means anything it means that Presidents, on the whole, are the expression of the convergence and conflict of dominant forces, except in so far as a very great personality imposes his own view of society upon a considerable body of public opinion. Whatever else one may feel about Landon, I suppose no one will contend that he is one of these rare personalities, who does impose himself upon the forces of his time. Indeed, Lippmann finds comfort and hope in Landon just because he is not a powerful personality. And so, whatever may be the nice rationalization of simple generalities that are uttered on the stump, Landon, like Taft and Harding and Coolidge, and

Hoover — very different men, yet subdued by the same forces — will be bound to express the predominant forces that are now enlisted in his cause. The most powerful forces behind him are those of laissez-faire, of xenophobia, of spiritual standpatism. These will be triumphant. And they will indubitably register their power as when they were triumphant in the past, indeed more so, since the triumph will mean a rejection, not only of this or that legislation or this or that administrative inadequacy, but of the aspirations that lie behind them. I hold fast to the proposition that what matters in politics is the direction to which impetus is given, and what determines impetus is very largely the direction of the powerful forces that are enlisted on one side and on the other. That doesn't mean that very nice and well intentioned people are not going to vote for Landon. But I'm talking about those powerful interests that Madison talked about as a determinative of politics. It is because for me the division of the determining forces is so clear that I deem this such a critical election.

From all of which you will infer, what I am sure you need hardly to be told, that the impingements of personalities or judgment upon their motives, are not in my mind. We are at one of those periods in American history where really fundamental issues are at stake. Of course, the air is charged with all kinds of nonsense, with all kinds of calculated exploitation, with fears, with a shrewd attempt on the part of the Landon strategy to be not for the New Deal, and yet not against it, carrying emphasis and the accent according to group and locality. But what matters, as I see it, is what kind of hopes will be furthered and what kind of hopes will be thwarted by the outcome of the election. What forces will be encouraged and what forces will be discouraged. Those are the decisive things in politics. It seems almost childish to me to assume that an ordinary fellow like Landon, with his limited experience both in action and thought, can be coached overnight to ride the great storm of the next four years and guide his country's destiny in what may well be a world war. An English friend of mine, of seasoned judgment, who had an hour's talk with Landon very recently told me that Landon asked more simple-minded questions than would be asked by a fellow who read no more than *Time.* But the theory is again the old theory of the "best minds," that because Landon is a smallish man, he would draw big men into counsel, and the big men would give him the right answers. What touching naivete — and what a complete disregard of experience.

After consulting Roosevelt on various issues in the campaign, Frankfurter wrote to Mr. Arthur Hays Sulzberger of the New York Times *to emphasize the underlying issues of the election and to thank the* Times *for supporting Roosevelt. The letter read:*

October 1, 1936

Dear Mr. Sulzberger:

It is not a partisan or perfunctory word of appreciation that I venture to send you on the "reasoned choice" announced by the *Times* this morning. I am not a party man; I'm an old-fashioned mugwump, who has voted for, and served under, Republican administrations. And this campaign has significance for me because of its relation to the outcome of the transcending issue of our time, namely, the conflict between democracy and authoritarianism.

The maintenance of democracy, as English history so unequivocally demonstrates, cannot be secured either by narrow nationalism or a mere philosophy of negation toward the great social and economic changes which science and technology have generated. How to make the necessary adjustments within the framework of a democratic society, is the great task of statesmanship. With the quiet impressiveness of reason the editorial in this morning's *Times* gives solid justification for believing that the greatest encouragement to the rational, democratic forces of the nation will come through the reelection of President Roosevelt.

Sincerely yours,
FELIX FRANKFURTER

Frankfurter's assessment of the real but hidden forces behind Landon's campaign was confirmed by a letter from William Allen White, a friend of the Kansas Governor and an enlightened Republican. When he saw this letter, Roosevelt told Frankfurter that he was "lucky the Republican party did not have enough brains to take White's advice." White's letter follows:

Emporia, Kans., October 31, 1936

Dear Mr. Frankfurter:

I am sending you today a little batch of cold potatoes in the shape of a little book. It is what I wrote about the campaign and its inception. My idea of the campaign as it should have been and was not. I am sending it to you, hoping you will look it over after the election and understand how I should like to have seen this campaign go if I had been on Landon's board of strategy.

As I think I told you, I have not been in Landon's entourage. He has invited me to go on every trip and I have refused each time. I have written none of his speeches. The only paragraph I contributed was his denunciation of the teachers' oath.

I was not on his board of strategy. I would have conducted a different kind of a campaign. And the reason why I have not visited him in Topeka since his nomination is that I did not want to go in and fight for my ideas with a bunch of conservatives and take the responsibility for what looked like an inevitable defeat. That on the one hand. On the other hand, I did not want to stay and be a part of a compromise which would get nowhere, stultify me, and at the same time leave me with no liberty of action which would not be misconstrued as involving Landon.

For instance, I have supported George Norris in this campaign heartily. I supported Jim Couzens in Michigan before the primaries with editorials and letters. If I had been next to the throne, my support would have involved Landon. So I have kept away. But I do respect him. He is forthright, courageous, honest. He is new at the game of economics. If he had won, perhaps I should have been happy to help him if he had let me. I don't know whether he would or not. This is all confidential between two American citizens who, if they had been nearer each other during the years, would have been dear friends, I think.

Always most cordially yours,
W. A. WHITE

Telegram to Roosevelt
Care Presidential Special, Grand Rapids, Mich.
Washington, D.C., October 15, 1936
FELIX HAS ASKED ME TO WIRE YOU AS FOLLOWS: "HEARD YOUR CHICAGO SPEECH WITH HIGH REPUBLICAN AUTHORITY WHO AT END OF IT SAID, MORE IN ANGER THAN IN CONTENTMENT, 'THIS IS THE DAMNEDEST BEST SPEECH HE HAS MADE. IT LEAVES US VERY LITTLE.' THEY HAVE BEEN A SUCCESSION OF VIBRANT, HEARTENING, TAKE-THE-OFFENSIVE SPEECHES. ALL GOOD WISHES. FAITHFULLY YOURS."

THOMAS CORCORAN

In the Chicago speech Roosevelt said he was not attacking all the great bankers, nor all the great corporation executives, nor all multimillionaires — just as Theodore Roosevelt, in speaking of "malefactors of great wealth," had never meant to imply that all men of great wealth were "malefactors."

Then, later in the speech came a passage which Frankfurter memorized, and spouted for years, with or without invitation, so ardent and overflowing was his admiration of its political skill. Roosevelt said:

Some of these people really forget how sick they were. But I know how sick they were. I have their fever charts. I know how the knees of all our rugged individualists were trembling four years ago and how their hearts fluttered. They came to Washington in great numbers. Washington did not look like a dangerous bureaucracy to them. Oh no! It looked like an emergency hospital. All of the distinguished patients wanted two things — a quick hypodermic to end the pain and a course of treatment to cure the disease. They wanted them in a hurry; we gave them both. And now most of the patients seem to be doing very nicely. Some of them are even well enough to throw their crutches at the doctor.

Telegram to Miss LeHand

Cambridge, Mass., October 20, 1936

GREETINGS TO YOU AND PLEASE CONVEY THE FOLLOWING: BELOVED SIR: I AM BOUND TO REPORT THAT JAMES MORGAN WHO HAS WATCHED THE POLITICAL RINGSIDE FOR FIFTY YEARS TELLS ME "THAT CHICAGO SPEECH WAS THE MOST EFFECTIVE CAMPAIGN SPEECH THAT I HEARD OR READ IN FIFTY YEARS. HE WENT AT THE OPPOSITION THE WAY JOHN L. SULLIVAN DID AT THE HEIGHT OF HIS POWER." CONTINUING GOOD LUCK.

RESPECTFULLY SUBMITTED,
FELIX

James Morgan wrote scholarly and trenchant political articles for the Boston *Globe.*

The White House, October 20, 1936

Dear Felix:

Tom Corcoran sent me your nice message about the Chicago address and it did my heart good.

I think the whole trip went very well. I am looking forward to seeing you.

Faithfully yours,
F.D.R.

Cambridge, Mass., Sunday before Election, 1936

And now, Dear Frank, you have fought your fight — and ours — and the Nation will crown it with victory. But the enduring victory is always within. As you pause, before you go on with the terrific tasks that lie ahead, surely you must feel, as you are entitled to feel, securely serene.

When, a good many years ago, I read all of Lincoln's speeches and writings, what struck me most, apart from his felicity, was the temper of what he said, that in the midst of war he said nothing which fifty years later he would want to change. I've heard or read all that you publicly spoke during this campaign, and I do not recall a single word that the understanding historian of the future would want unsaid.

I have no doubt that in your second Administration you will prove

yourself the master of the dark and ignorant forces of our country. Nor
have they! But what is no less true, and what is indispensable to the realization of your objectives, you have proved anew in this campaign that in a
democracy the essence of true politics is popular education. And so, you
will enter your second term not only with the confidence of our people but
with that informed intelligence, for you have informed it, which is indispensable for bringing nearer the dream of brotherhood to which America
was dedicated.

May your strength and contagious spirit remain unabated.

Devotedly yours,
F.F.

*In the letter that follows, Frankfurter complains of the personal cam-
paign waged against Roosevelt.*

John D. M. Hamilton was Landon's campaign manager.

*Agnes Meyer, the wife of Eugene Meyer, later to be the publisher of the
Washington* Post, *was an intellectual force and public-spirited citizen in
her own right.*

Cambridge, Mass., November 6, 1936

Dear Frank:

Some things need to be killed not merely scotched. That was especially
true of the mean and meretricious conception of "the American way of
life" with which the Hearsts and the Hamiltons and the minor fry of the
Arthur Ballantines and the Agnes Meyers tried to fool and frighten the
American people. For the country's welfare and for the fate of western
democracy, it was essential to destroy the synthetic concoction which was
offered by a poisonous press and a blind plutocracy to a people whom the
hard school of experience and the greatest national educator since Jefferson
taught to discriminate between fraud and fact, between fear and reason.
Nothing short of so decisive a rejection of the perversion of the aims and
ideals to which this country was dedicated would have cleansed the air and
given the bracing atmosphere indispensable to healthy action.

Shabby motives and bigoted ignorance were clothed in all sorts of high-
sounding phrases of which the need for "national unity" was one of the
loftiest. Yes, in the perplexities and travail of the modern world we do need
national unity — the unity of aiming at a gracious, humane society which
only a true democracy can secure. And, Lord be praised, the election has
demonstrated such a national unity to a greater degree, I believe, than at
any time in the history of this country.

Of your personal achievement I had my say before the election, and I

shall not offend your true modesty by saying more than that my heart is full
of gratitude and devotion.

Ever yours,
F.F.

Cambridge, Mass., November 9, 1936

Dear Mr. President,

Felix let me see his letter to you, with some idea that I might share in
it. But it seemed far too much an essay or a speech for me to have anything
to do with it! All I want is to say how happy I am about it all. This is more
than victory. It creates, for the moment at least, and I hope a long moment,
a new world in which hate and violence are discredited.

With all my good wishes and affectionate regard,

Sincerely,
Marion Frankfurter

The White House, November 14, 1936

Dear Marion: —

This is a very short note to tell you how much I appreciate your writing
me — I am glad you do not let Felix write all the letters.

It was an exciting election and I am sure no one but Jim Farley could
have believed that it was going to happen.

I hope I shall have a chance to see you both very soon.

Always sincerely,
F.D.R.

*As James Farley said, "as Maine goes, so goes Vermont." Those were the
only two states carried by Governor Landon and the Republican party.*

The White House, November 14, 1936

Dear Felix: —

Although I am not writing any acknowledgments to letters of congratulation, I must send you this line to thank you for your various letters and
for all the generous things you have said.

I do hope I shall have a chance to see you soon after I return. I am
looking forward to a really grand rest and Buenos Aires should be interesting.

As ever yours,
F.D.R.

*Rabbi Stephen S. Wise of New York was the most famous and eloquent
rabbi in America, and a leader of the Zionist Movement, a cause which*

always commanded the greatest support from both Brandeis and Frank-furter.

Cambridge, Mass., November 8, 1936

Dear Missy:

The President called Rabbi Wise for a draft of a letter on Mr. Justice Brandeis' 80th birthday, November 13 — Friday next — and Dr. Wise asked me to draw such a letter. Here it is — and I'm availing myself of Tom's presence here to send it by him. I don't believe that the President will want to say anything about the big contribution and the little men but that and everything else he can strike out. This draft may help him a little.

Yours very sincerely,
F.F.

Draft enclosure

Almost from the time when, as a young man, I entered the public service it has been my privilege to know you as a friend. Today, in common with thousands who share this privilege, I salute your eightieth birthday with affectionate gratitude, rejoicing that it finds you still in the full exercise of your great powers.

But the occasion permits me to go beyond the expression of friendship. I am sure I can speak for the nation in saluting you as a great American.

The greater part of your life, most of it without holding office, has been spent in being a great citizen. For you indeed the law has been a public profession. From the beginning you have shown that popular faith in law can be secured only through the public-spirited work of its ministers.

Not content with mere lip service to noble causes, you have pierced through phrases to reality, conscious that the watchwords of liberty and democracy must be vindicated in the quality of the opportunities which wise statesmanship provides for the men and women of our society. Though you have welcomed science as the medium for enlarging man's freedom, you have not blinked at new difficulties which increasing facilities for production have created. The necessity for disciplined, patient inquiry and resolute will in seeking the solution of these difficulties has had in you its most illustrious example. You have been a great teacher and prophet, always recognizing that right solutions, founded on a sound ethical basis, are the product of hard thinking and not of incantation.

Five years ago the late Mr. Justice Holmes publicly bestowed upon you the accolade "a great judge." And great judges, as he himself illustrated, are those whose vision of the Constitution is not obscured by the littleness of men.

May you long continue to be, as you have been for fifty years, the servant of the nation.

The White House, December 5, 1936

My dear Mr. Frankfurter:

How very kind of you to write about Gus. We are all deeply grieved and, of course, shocked by his sudden passing. He was such a loyal and devoted friend to all of us we will miss him more than I can say. He was a grand person — cheerful, willing, honest, and straightforward. It is particularly sad because he was really beginning to enjoy life after a long period of family responsibility and had so much joy out of his farm.

With many thanks, I am

Very sincerely yours,
ELEANOR ROOSEVELT

August "Gus" Gennerich, the President's personal bodyguard and friend, died of a heart attack on December 1, 1936, while with the President in Buenos Aires for the Inter-American Conference for the Maintenance of Peace.

Cambridge, Mass., December 17, 1936

Dear Mr. President:

1. Welcome home after your trip that evidently so admirably combined relaxation and the abiding historic promotion of effective neighborliness among the peoples of the Americas. How great was your achievement through your South American trip is indicated by the profound importance which the reports in the London *Times* attached to it. But how clouds chase even the most effulgent sun. It is hard to think of Gus' going. He seemed such a permanent jet of life, so strong, so devoted, so joy-exuding. How much bigger Gus was in his simple station than so many so-called "big men." I feel for you deeply in your loss of him.

2. As a professional student of British Constitutional Law and as an amateur student of the human heart, I have naturally followed the King and Wally Simpson affair with the closest interest. After the things I learned in London last summer, the explosion did not come as a surprise. In view of the King's temperament and desires, I don't think there was a real alternative. I deem it a great good fortune for the democratic forces of the world that the situation eventuated as it did. An enormous amount of Hollywood slush has been poured out about the business, but of all the reams of writing that I have read, the two most illuminating comments were a piece by Wickham Steed and another by Harold Laski. On the chance that during your trip you may have missed them, I venture to enclose them.

3. The other day I had a talk with a warm friend of mine, who happens to be counsel for very important interests (no, sir, not John W. Davis). I asked him if there was really to be another "era of good feeling." He replied, "Yes — provided that man in the White House becomes sensible." Aren't they amusing?

With warm regards,

Faithfully yours,
F.F.

P.S.   I was shocked to read this morning how serious Franklin's sinus was — and greatly relieved by the good news.

F.D.R., Jr., was in the hospital with a serious sinus infection, from which he was recovering rapidly.

Both Steed and Laski went to the root of the Constitutional problem in the abdication crisis — there was no room for a King's party, or for special moral privileges for the King, or for any arrangement which outraged the feelings of most citizens of the British Commonwealth of Nations. Expressed most memorably by The Times of London, these came to be the overpowering convictions of the British people, with Churchill and Beaverbrook as forlorn defenders of the King's position before his abdication to marry Mrs. Simpson.

The White House, December 23, 1936

Dear Felix: —

A hasty note to thank you for your letter of the seventeenth, and to wish for you and Marion a Very Merry Christmas and the Happiest of New Years.

As ever,
F.D.R.

Frankfurter had sent Roosevelt a copy of his book The Commerce Clause under Marshall, Taney and White, *the text of his lectures at the University of North Carolina. James Bradley Thayer, of the Harvard Law School, was the greatest single influence on Frankfurter's legal and judicial outlook, greater even than Holmes or Brandeis. The Thayer quotation expounded a doctrine of judicial review in which the courts allowed wide latitude for bold experiments in legislation, and did not restrict the scope of the Constitution by narrow interpretation. With the court-packing fight just ahead, Frankfurter inscribed the book: "To F.D.R., who is a better friend of the Supreme Court than its present majority. F.F. Christmas 1936."*

Dear Frank —

This is not the most exciting of tales, but there are in it things, "calculated" — in the language of Mr. Justice Holmes — "to give the Brethren pain." Do look at the quotation from James Bradley Thayer, beginning page 112.

With my deepest good wishes,
F.F.

Telegram to Roosevelt

Sea Island Beach, Ga., December 23, 1936

GAY HOLIDAYS FOR YOU AND NEXT YEAR THE PEOPLE'S VINDICATION OUR AFFECTIONATE GREETINGS.

MARION AND FELIX FRANKFURTER

The Court-Packing Fight

1937

*Some of the important Supreme Court cases leading up to
Roosevelt's decision to pack the Court are listed below.*

1935 *In* U.S. v. Bankers Trust Company, Norman v. Baltimore and Ohio
Railroad Company, *and* Nortz v. U.S., *the constitutionality of the
Congressional Joint Resolution of June 5, 1933 (nullifying the
gold clause in private and public contracts) was questioned, but
upheld. However, in* Perry v. U.S. *it was held that government
bonds were contractual obligations of the federal government and
that therefore the Joint Resolution was unconstitutional.*

In Schechter v. U.S. *the Court held unanimously that the NIRA
was unconstitutional.*

In Railroad Retirement Board v. Alton Railroad Company, *the
Court invalidated the Railroad Retirement Act by a vote of five
to four.*

1936 *In* U.S. v. Butler *the AAA was declared unconstitutional.*

*During 1937, the following cases upheld various pieces of
New Deal legislation by a vote in each case of five to four:*

West Coast Hotel Company v. Parrish *upheld a Washington
minimum wage law.* National Labor Relations Board v. Jones and
Laughlin Steel Corporation *and* National Labor Relations Board
v. Friedman–Harry Marks Clothing Company *upheld the National
Labor Relations Act.*

Stewart Machine Company v. Davis *and* Helvering v. Davis *upheld the Social Security laws.*

ON January 20, 1937, in his second Inaugural Address, President Roosevelt spoke of "one-third of a Nation ill-housed, ill-clad, ill-nourished." It seemed as if he were summoning the people to a renewed war against poverty and injustice. But the trumpet, when it sounded, was directed against a different foe and it found the President enlisted under a strange banner. For the President laid rough hands on the Supreme Court. He had decided to break the Court's opposition to his program and pack the Court, as the general public saw the issue.

On February 5, 1937, Roosevelt sent Congress a plan to reorganize the federal judiciary. The declared purpose of the plan was to make the administration of justice swifter and more efficient; but its sting was turned against the Supreme Court, in virulent fashion. The President sought the power to increase the membership of the Court from nine to fifteen, and to add one new Justice to the Court for every Justice who failed to retire at full pay within six months after reaching the age of seventy.

Smarting from judicial rebukes and reversals, Roosevelt had long meditated some reprisals against the Supreme Court which had so grievously wounded the New Deal. Attorney General Cummings was the evil genius. He proposed the plan, and after the most meager consultation with other advisers, the President accepted it. The advice and help of wiser men than Cummings were sought only after the plan had already landed the President in the most complicated trouble.

Four members of the Supreme Court — Justices McReynolds, seventy-five, Sutherland, seventy-five, Van Devanter, seventy-eight, and Butler, seventy-one — were usually ranged in formidable and almost instinctive opposition to the New Deal. They were widely accused of reading their own notions of economic and political policy into the Constitution. All this meant that they had to pick up only one vote from another Justice to decide a case by one of those 5–4 verdicts that so irritated the President. He felt that the scales of justice were unfairly weighted against him and he resolved to redress the balance. What was the Supreme Court, to dare stand against him, when he had just been re-elected President by the triumphant choice of every state in the Union except Maine and Vermont? Chief Justice Hughes was seventy-five and Justice Brandeis was eighty-one — but they stood on a different footing from the "relentless four."

The plan split the Democratic party and left a squalid legacy of bitter-

*ness and estrangement that never disappeared. To the surprise of the Presi-
dent, the Court suddenly endorsed legislation which he expected it to reject. Justice Roberts had changed sides, and a cheap gibe described the
change as the switch in time that saved nine. Actually, Justice Roberts had
rendered judgment before the court-packing plan had even been given to
Congress. The Court's decision had been delayed for reasons having nothing to do with the President's plan.*

*For weary and embattled months, the controversy dragged on, amid al-
most hysterical bitterness. Finally a patched-up compromise brought truce
to an exhausted field, with the President picking up a tattered banner and
pretending that it was a talisman of victory. Yet everyone knew that he had
suffered the worst defeat of his career. The Court remained unpacked.*

What of Frankfurter's role in this whole affair?

*He always claimed, even to his closest friends, that he had never had any
role at all. When he was nominated by Roosevelt at the beginning of 1939
to go on the Supreme Court, and appeared before the Senate Judiciary
Committee, he prepared a brief statement pointing out that he had always
remained silent and neutral during this entire controversy and had refused
every opportunity to say whether he approved or disapproved of the court-
packing plan.*

*What he failed to explain, to the committee or to anyone else, was that
he had given the most solemn oath of silence and public neutrality to the
President. After the plan was announced, Roosevelt phoned Frankfurter at
Cambridge and exacted this pledge. He told Frankfurter that he intended
one day to put him on the Supreme Court, and he did not want him entangled in this particular controversy. Would Frankfurter help him to get out
of this mess even though he strenuously disliked many parts of the court-
packing plan? Frankfurter agreed, out of friendship, out of a profound conviction that the Supreme Court had provoked reprisals by its abuse of judicial power, and out of the justified belief that his legal scholarship would
save the President from more flagrant blunders.*

*What Frankfurter never told anyone was that, while remaining officially
neutral, he had been a central and constant adviser of the President, and, a
few days before joining the Supreme Court himself, had actually helped to
edit the official version of the court-packing controversy for the Public Papers of President Roosevelt.*

*One final word. These revelations are now being made public not only
with Frankfurter's approval but on his direct instructions. I discussed this
matter with him in careful detail before his death. He wanted the full story
told as part of his obligation to history, so that the American people could
reach their own independent judgment on the evidence of the real facts,
and not be swayed by misleading rumor and hearsay.*

Telegram to Miss LeHand

Cambridge, Mass., January 6, 1937

PLEASE CONVEY THE FOLLOWING: MOST HEARTENING ADDRESS. SUPERB EXPOSI-
TION OF DEMOCRATIC PROGRESSIVE PHILOSOPHY WITH EFFECTIVE INTIMATION
TO ALL WHOM IT MAY CONCERN WHAT THIS MEANS CONCRETELY FOR THE
NEEDS OF OUR DAY. WITH WARMEST REGARDS.

FELIX FRANKFURTER

*Roosevelt had closed his annual message to Congress with an obscure
and veiled warning to the Supreme Court to adjust its thinking. But the
bulk of the address was an appeal for support of his reform legislation and
the social security program.*

The White House, January 7, 1937

Dear Felix:

Thank you indeed for your kind message of the sixth. I am truly grateful to you for it.

Very sincerely yours,
F.D.R.

When do I see you both?

*The next few letters, though they deal primarily with TVA problems and
with young men in the government, belong here because they lead directly
to Roosevelt's veiled announcement that he is planning to give Frankfurter
an "awful shock" — by the court-packing plan.*

William Nichols later became editor, and then publisher, of This Week
magazine.

Cambridge, Mass., January 9, 1937

Dear Mr. President:

The Lord, I hope, will forgive me for breaking the confidence imposed
by a trusting young man in letting another than myself see the enclosures.
And your eyes were the very last for whom they were intended. But occasionally a single wisp of cloud shows the shifting of the wind into a bad
quarter.

Bill Nichols, the writer of these letters, is not a lawyer, but he has
crossed my path up here. He is the nicest kind of a Harvard man — he has
ability, character, public zeal, and the common touch. He entered the government as did so many youngsters — he graduated from Harvard in 1926
— under the inspiration of your leadership. From all accounts, he has
served the government with a fidelity and usefulness for which private enterprise usually pays many times what his salary is.

TVA has, of course, its own peculiar problems. But Nichols faces what, I am sure, agitates scores of able men in other branches of the government. I know that the realization of your purposes predominantly depends on your own leadership, but I am sure you will agree that your ability to achieve your purpose depends in no small measure on a successful contest between you and private interests for the command of brains. Now I see too many able young men every year and keep in too close contact with many of them after they leave here, not to be justifiably confident of the ability of the Government to attract the best brains. You can have them, provided certain conditions of security and *élan* in serving the country are satisfied in the breasts of youth. Napoleon's wisdom of the ribbon on the coat and the baton in the knapsack still wins great battles. And the young Assistant Secretary of the Navy who directed naval operations overseas need not be reminded that, although imaginative captains of thirty may never be seen at G.H.Q., they are the ones who too often have to take the objectives which grand strategy needs.

You will forgive me for saying things of which no one has had more experience than you. But you also know how passionately I care about the still greater triumphs for your second Administration. Not even you can do it all yourself. And I am greatly troubled about brains leaving you. Indeed, the strange paradox is that the more recovery you bring the more good men you are in danger of losing. Every good man you lose unsettles ten other good men, and debilitates their enthusiasm. The great civil service of England gets down to about a thousand really commanding brains. The same is true of the kind of government to which you are summoning the nation. Like Gideon, you may wisely say to the Lord, as you fight his battles, "By the three hundred that lapped I shall save thee."

I am not suggesting anything or recommending anything. This letter has no specific purpose. It conveys a general concern which I venture to believe has more concrete applications and is more immediately practical than any specific thing I might put to you.

With warmest regards.

Always faithfully yours,
F.F.

Chattanooga, Tenn., December 28, 1936

Dear Mr. Frankfurter:

I hope I am not making a nuisance of myself, sending you "pieces" for editorial review. But recently, while our directors have been in their tents, I have had several occasions to pinch-hit on fairly important talks. I have taken it pretty seriously, both because of the TVA and because it offers a good form of personal training and experience. The Springfield, Illinois, talk I sent you some time ago was one. More recently, a 36-hour notice came through to substitute for Dr. Arthur Morgan at a talk he was supposed to give before a lot of high school debaters in Purdue, Indiana. It meant sitting up all night on the Pullman and trying to write something without any references at hand, but anyhow I am sending you a copy of the result. I am doing so because I genuinely want some frank, and if necessary, brutal criticism, as that is the only way to make the next one better. You will note that I attempted no discussion of TVA: that was because I had no opportunity to check with the directors, so I thought it best to avoid any statement that might involve them.

More than advice on speech-making, however, I need advice on Things-in-General. I am attaching a copy of a letter I have just written to Mr. Lilienthal. Naturally I hope you will treat it as confidential. The job in this case is the editorship of a prosperous West Coast magazine with a chance for development of editorial policies, and a participation in its growth. I think you can appreciate the difficulty of making a decision in the face of all the present confusion, but a number of those in the TVA who, I feel, have the best minds and imaginations, are now facing the same problem. If they all go, there won't be much left of the TVA except a lot of concrete and some pretty hopeless office-holders. My own inclination is to stay on, because I enjoy life here, because I still feel the TVA is a magnificent conception, and because the latest 19-company injunction has made me mad and I'd like to stand by and help "larn 'em." On the other hand, however pleasant the immediate job, people in my circumstances just simply can't afford to get lost in the shuffle and wake up in middle age to find themselves on a siding. I think you realize that I am talking not about money alone, but about the opportunity for growth and personal fulfillment.

Well, it's an old story, and probably a boring one to anyone like yourself who has been *in loco parentis* to so many people. But anyhow, I am mentioning it to you, for, from the beginning of my stay down here, I have been conscious of your friendly interest and grateful for it.

With all best wishes,

> Faithfully,
> BILL NICHOLS

December 28, 1936

Dear Mr. Lilienthal:

At a time when you undoubtedly have a great many bothers of your own, I hesitate to write you a bothersome, personal letter.

My reason for doing so is that I am trying to use this vacation season for a year-end "stock-taking" about my present work and future plans.

Within the past few weeks a reasonably attractive opportunity for private employment has turned up, and I feel confident that others could be discovered with a little effort.

In trying to determine what to do, the principal "unknown," of course, is the future course of events at TVA. I don't need to tell you how much I have enjoyed life in Chattanooga, and the opportunity to do what I felt was interesting and fairly constructive work for the TVA. On the other hand, the questions now arises as to how long it is wise or desirable to continue, and on that I badly need advice. The injunction and the power pool are, of course, disturbing factors, but only superficially so, I feel. More serious to me is the feeling that TVA has lost some of its sense of direction, that morale is rapidly going to hell, and that bureaucracy is beginning to creep in to the exact extent that the personal leadership of the directors is being withdrawn.

Through your personal knowledge of Mary and me, I think you are familiar with our dilemma. We are entirely dependent on our own efforts for survival and success. There are no incomes or endowments or rich relations in the offing, and so we have got to keep moving and growing. Under these circumstances, can we afford to sit still here and wait on the chance that things will get straightened out, or should we strike out for ourselves? I know that is a hard question. Perhaps I am wrong to ask it. But I hoped that you might be able to help us with some advice, sent not as a Director, but as a friend.

Mary joins me in best holiday wishes.

Faithfully,
BILL NICHOLS

The White House, January 15, 1937

Dear Felix: —

The enclosed letters are, of course, typical — but is it not true that many of the youngsters get tired and lose enthusiasm when the novelty of the job wears off? What should be everlastingly inculcated into these boys is that a thing like TVA is a twenty year goal (at least) and that in the process of succeeding months there will be of necessity many temporary discouragements, such as the present injunction and the strange problem of Dr. Arthur Morgan. The injunction must wait on courts and the Morgan-Lilienthal head-on collision will probably be solved in the next few months by the adoption of the national power policy which I am in the midst of here in Washington, and which is going to make definite progress whether I get the legislation or not.

If I were writing to this youngster I would tell him that if he is looking for (a) a new thrill; (b) a higher salary; (c) an immediate assured and permanent future, he had better leave — but that on the other hand, if he is willing to go through with a great ideal, remain on Government pay and hope that the Government will some day set up adequate pensions, etc., he had better stick.

The other day Ed McGrady came in to see me to tell me of an offer of three times his present salary; that he is sixty-two years old and that he ought to think of his declining years. I told him he was right in doing the thinking but to weigh against that thought the fact that he is an important part of a great human movement, doing a splendid job and almost impossible to replace. I said "Ed, I want you to stay." He said "Right, Boss, you have given the word and I will stay."

Very confidentially, I may give you an awful shock in about two weeks. Even if you do not agree, suspend final judgment and I will tell you the story.

As ever yours,
F.D.R.

Cambridge, Mass., January 18, 1937

Dear Mr. President:

Many, many thanks for your letter of the fifteenth, especially because it sounded as though I heard you actually talking.

1. I did not deal with the case of the particular youngster except as a straw in the wind, else I would have told you that I promptly replied to him in terms that you would have found strikingly like your own. I have been singing that song for a great many years and particularly during the last few years, summarizing it all in the phrase that the kingdom of heaven cannot be stormed by a single sortie.

2. You know that there is no single aspect of public affairs with which I have been more deeply concerned than the promotion of public service as a permanent career for the nation's best abilities. That, in a way, has been my predominant interest in the School here. Nothing brought home to me more poignantly the post-war materialism and the debasing influence of the so-called leaders of the bar than the standards of worldly success by which youngsters of generous impulse were so often deflected from public service. After all, we live by symbols, as Holmes was fond of saying, and, if the symbols of leadership and distinction are high monetary returns in the service of so-called big interests, the youngsters naturally will follow such lodestars. Relatively very few people can be expected to be either heroes or saints. That is why the force of example and right standards is so important.

But you and your leadership during the last few years have made an enormous difference. In many ways, perhaps the single most far-reaching achievement — because everything else, I believe, is dependent upon it —

is the extent to which you have stirred the imagination of younger people to the adventure of, and the durable satisfactions to be derived from, public service, and have made them realize its indispensability in maintaining the best traditions of the past and bending them to a civilization worthy of our times. And the youngsters, I think do respond and will respond in ample measure. I haven't any doubt, as I have indicated to you, that you can get in sufficient numbers as good brains for the sake of service, as those on the outside buy with money.

3. But that means that somehow or other the vibrant stimulus, which you so frequently impart to the Ed McGradys, must by some galvanic rays be sent down the line. I know that you cannot see hundreds or thousands of the juniors — it is a source of constant surprise to me how, in the brief hours of each day, you manage to hold as many hands as you do — but it does mean that this stimulus or inspiration must, somehow or other, be conveyed by the sub-chiefs, the atmosphere must somehow or other be impregnated with at least a part of the exhilaration that you radiate in the immediate precincts of the White House.

4. Perhaps one of these days before very long you will give me a chance to talk to you about all this in some detail. How to build up a passionate, devoted, capable, fighting personnel for national administration has been the one subject about which I have been continuously thinking for thirty years. I hope, therefore, there will be a chance of talking with you about all this in your good time. I hope to see you shortly — I mean literally to *see* you, for Marion and I will be among the many thousands who will see you on Wednesday.

5. Are you trying to find out how well I can sit on top of a Vesuvius by giving me notice that "an awful shock" is in store for me "in about two weeks"? Well, I shall try to hold my patience and fortify my capacity to withstand "an awful shock," but you certainly tease my curiosity when you threaten me with something with which I may not agree. That, certainly, would be a great surprise.

Ever faithfully yours,
F.F.

P.S.   If you have not seen the enclosed it will interest you — coming as it does from a hide-bound Republican paper, but from an editor who has secretly always been for you.

Edward McGrady was the Assistant Secretary of Labor.

The "awful shock" referred to by Roosevelt must be considered in the light of his own commitments and those of the Democratic party. At the Democratic National Convention in Philadelphia in June 1936 the platform committee was informed that President Roosevelt would tolerate no "short cuts of any kind" in dealing with the constitutional problem. Senator Walter F. George, a member of that committee, said the President had given assurances that "if the social and economic program of the party could not be solved by legislation within the Constitution, we would seek such clarifying amendment as would assure to the legislatures of the several states and to the Congress, each within its proper jurisdiction, the power to enact those laws. An increase in the number of Justices of the Supreme Court had been suggested before the convention met in June. We declared that we would go back to the people who alone have the power to make or change the Constitution if we could not carry out the program within the letter and spirit of the Constitution."

Without notice to the public, without consultation with the Congressional leaders of his own party, Roosevelt decided to reject the method of seeking constitutional reform by a constitutional amendment. He defended his action by saying that he had as much right to depart from the 1936 platform as from the 1932 platform. But this argument was unconvincing for two decisive reasons. In the first place, the economic crisis in Roosevelt's first year in office conferred its own mandate; and secondly, the advanced age of the "relentless four" on the Supreme Court meant that he would soon be able to appoint new and younger men without forcing an unprecedented constitutional crisis on the nation. Besides, his absence for weeks from the country after the 1936 election — he had gone by ship to Buenos Aires for a Latin American conference — had given him no opportunity to prepare public opinion or opinion in the Senate for the favorable reception of his unexpected proposals.

Felix and Marion Frankfurter were going to Washington on Wednesday for the Inaugural ceremonies. Frank Buxton, in the Boston Herald, had given Roosevelt an encouraging send-off for the second term.

Cambridge, Mass., January 21, 1937

Dear Frank:

Had Providence vouchsafed us children and had a grandchild of mine asked me in my old age, what manner of man was this President Franklin Delano Roosevelt, I think I should have replied by telling the child a story, something like this:

Very often, the wisest experience of life is compressed in one of those pithy, homely proverbs that have come down the ages. Such a one is the saying "like master, like man." For what matters about people is not their noble sentiments, but the extent to which they live up to them, and nothing proves that better than the habits that they unconsciously generate in those about them, the "moral climate" that they create in their immediate environment. And so, the quickest way to tell you what manner of man this

F.D.R. was is to tell you the experience I had with one of his closest, colored servants, on that memorable day of January 20, 1937 — on the occasion of his Second Inaugural, when the skies opened their floodgates.

And then I'd tell how McDuffie somehow found out that I was drenched inside and shivered, and sent word that he could help me out if I came upstairs, and here he was, a joyous, efficient "first-aid" to the shiverer, and when I protested, and asked whether it was all right for him "to help me out of the President's own closet," he said in looks and accents that left no doubt, "Shu-ah, yess-sah. The President would want me to do this — he sure will be tickled when he hears what I've done." There, I'd say to that grandchild, that little episode tells more than most of the "source materials" that historians pore over.

And now I shall say no more, except that one can be as sure as one can be of anything in the future, that the kids of 2036 (on the occasion of the two hundredth anniversary of McGuffey's *Reader*) will be reading and reciting your Second Inaugural.

With warmest good wishes,

Ever faithfully yours,
F.F.

The following is Frankfurter's first letter to Roosevelt after the President had announced his plan for the reorganization of the federal judiciary. Frankfurter recalled, years later, that it had taken him only a few moments to dash off the first paragraph, for he had long been convinced that the Supreme Court had violated the proper canons of judicial interpretation. But he also remembered that it had taken him more than an hour to compose the meager troubled sentences of the second paragraph in which he dealt with the President's plan for removing this judicial obstruction. He became the President's adviser during the entire court-packing controversy when the President earnestly and repeatedly sought his help.

Cambridge, Mass., Sunday [February 7, 1937]
Dear Frank:

And now you have blown me off the top of Vesuvius where you sat me some weeks ago. Yes, you "shocked" me by the deftness of the general scheme for dealing with the mandate for national action which you received three times, in '32 and '34 and '36, and each time with increasing emphasis. You "shocked" me no less by the dramatic, untarnished secrecy with which you kept your scheme until you took the whole nation into your confidence. Dramatically and artistically you did "shock" me. But beyond that — well, the momentum of a long series of decisions not defensible in the realm of reason nor justified by settled principles of Constitutional interpretation had convinced me, as they had convinced you, that means had to be found to save the Constitution from the Court, and the Court from itself. No disinterested student of our Constitutional system and of the needs of our society could view with complacency the impasse created by a blind and stubborn majority of the Court. There was no perfect easy way out. Risks had to be taken — for you had to consider the costs and limitations of possible choices of action, as well as the risks of non-action.

And so it was clear that some major operation was necessary. Any major action to the body politic, no less than to the body physical, involves some shock. But I have, as you know, deep faith in your instinct to make the wise choice — the choice that will carry intact the motley aggregation that constitutes the progressive army toward the goal of present-day needs, and that will, at the same time, maintain all that is good in the traditional democratic process.

With all good wishes,

Ever faithfully yours,
F.F.

The White House, February 9, 1937

Privatissimo.
Dear Felix:

I am awfully glad to have your Sunday letter and to know that although shocked you have survived; but most important of all that you understand the causes and the motives.

As a matter of fact, the decision was arrived at by a process of elimination. The amendment process, as you will remember, was fought bitterly by the conservative element through the past four years — the only concession being a few words from Landon which meant absolutely nothing. It is interesting to note that these same people this week are demanding the amendment method in place of any other.

The reason for the elimination of the amendment process was to me entirely sufficient: to get two-thirds of both Houses of this session to agree on the language of an amendment which would cover all of the social and economic legislation, but at the same time not go too far, would have been most difficult. In fact, the chance of a two-thirds vote in this session was about fifty-fifty.

Supposing such an amendment had passed at the close of this session, every state legislature would have adjourned for the year. In 1938, only about one-third of the legislatures meet and because of the Congressional elections in 1938 the issue would, in all probability, be delayed in enough states to make ratification in 1938 impossible.

That brings us to 1939. The chances are that quite aside from this issue an unwieldy Democratic majority in both Houses will be slightly reduced as a result of the 1938 elections. Any such reduction would be used as an argument against ratification thus, in all probability, leaving the amendment unratified up to and through the 1940 national election.

If I were in private practice and without a conscience, I would gladly undertake for a drawing account of fifteen or twenty million dollars (easy enough to raise) to guarantee that an amendment would not be ratified prior to the 1940 elections. In other words, I think I could withhold ratification in thirteen states and I think you will agree with my judgment on this.

It is my honest belief that the Nation cannot wait until 1941 or 1942 to obtain effective social and economic national legislation to bring it abreast of the times, avoid serious labor troubles, maintain farm prices, raise the purchasing power of the "one-third of the population that is ill-housed, ill-clad and ill-nourished."

The return of prosperity, at this moment, may blunt our senses but under it all I am very certain that the maintenance of constitutional government in this Nation still depends on action — but it is the same old story of the failure of those who have property to realize that I am the best friend the profit system ever had, even though I add my denunciation of unconscionable profits.

After this elimination, I searched through all the other proposals for legislative action and almost at once came face to face with the problem not of the Supreme Court but of the whole Federal Judiciary. From this it was a logical step to build up a program covering the whole of the judiciary impartially. You will realize that in this process I eliminated the suggestions of compulsory retirement, seven-to-two decisions, etc. as being, in all probability, unconstitutional per se.

Do you want to help me? Probably, I shall in the course of a normal fireside chat, in a few weeks, dwell on the reorganization of the judiciary, at the same time that I speak of the reorganization of the executive and of flood relief, etc. Do you want to send me a little elaboration of what you have mentioned in your letter and anything else you think I could use in a talk to the people themselves?

As ever yours,
F.D.R.

Cambridge, Mass., February 15, 1937

Dear Mr. President:

You are extremely generous of your time and thought to write me as fully as you do in your letter dated the ninth. I deeply appreciate the analysis you make of the "process of elimination" by which you reached your present major proposal.

Of course if any "elaboration" of the central remarks I made in my letter will be of help to you, I want to see if I can helpfully elaborate them. Let me mull over the thoughts that I tried to express and see what I can put on paper in the course of the next few days, and write you again.

The issues raised are, of course, very complicated and rather subtle because of the great mystery with which the work of the Court is enveloped, and the uncritical assumptions that are made as to what the Court does when it decides constitutional controversies. The situation presents a very difficult problem in public education because, I believe, the easy, emotional slogans are mostly the other way. If you have no objection I plan to go over the situation very thoroughly with Tom and then have him convey to you the way the matter lies in my mind.

You will hear from me in a few days. Again let me thank you very warmly for your full, generous letter.

With warmest regards,

Very faithfully yours,
F.F.

February 18, 1937

Dear Mr. President:

Here are some notes dealing with what is the heart of the difficulty about the Supreme Court. These observations, in elaboration of what I wrote you, may or may not be of use to you. But I have a deep conviction that the problem is essentially an educational one — to make the country understand what the real function of the Supreme Court is and how, for a long stretch of years, it has been exercising it.

It is a creditable aspect of human nature that it wants some object of veneration, and veneration to no small degree thrives on mystery and mysticism. A majority of the Court have, as it were, been exploiting the public's devotion because they have been exploiting the mystery which so largely envelops the Court. People have been taught to believe that when the Supreme Court speaks it is not they who speak but the Constitution, whereas, of course, in so many vital cases, it is *they* who speak and *not* the Constitution. And I verily believe that that is what the country needs most to understand.

T.R. did it in his Eighth Annual Message. You will recall these sentences which go to the root of the business:

"The chief lawmakers in our country may be, and often are, the judges, because they are the final seat of authority. Every time they inter-

pret contract, property, vested rights, due process of law, liberty, they necessarily enact into law parts of a system of social philosophy; and as such
interpretation is fundamental, they give direction to all law-making. The
decisions of the courts on economic and social questions depend upon their
economic and social philosophy; and for the peaceful progress of our people
during the twentieth century we shall owe most to those judges who hold
to a twentieth century economic and social philosophy and not to a long
outgrown philosophy, which was itself the product of primitive economic
conditions."

Ever faithfully yours,
F.F.

Dissatisfaction with a few isolated judicial decisions would never have
given rise to deep and widespread disquietude concerning the relation of
the Supreme Court to the national welfare. With accumulating disregard of
its own settled canons of constitutional construction, the Supreme Court
for about a quarter of a century has distorted the power of judicial review
into a revision of legislative policy, thereby usurping powers belonging to
the Congress and to the legislatures of the several states, always by a divided court and always over the protest of its most distinguished members.
With increasing frequency a majority of the Court have not hesitated to
exercise a negative power on any legislation, state or federal, which does not
conform to their own economic notions. In 1923, Mr. Chief Justice Taft
protested against the Court's invalidation of the Congressional minimum
wage regulation for the District of Columbia because, as he said, "it is not
the function of this court to hold congressional acts invalid simply because
they are passed to carry out economic views which the Court believes to be
unwise or unsound." (*Adkins* v. *Children's Hospital*, 261 U.S. 525, 562.) In
1924, Mr. Justice Brandeis was obliged to note that the Court was assuming
the "exercise of the powers of a super-legislature — not the performance of
the constitutional function of judicial review." (*Burns Baking Co.* v. *Bryan*,
264 U.S. 504, 534.) And by 1930, Mr. Justice Holmes was compelled to
exclaim, "As the decisions now stand, I see hardly any limit but the sky to
the invalidating of those rights (the constitutional rights of state legislatures) if they happen to strike a majority of this court as for any reason
undesirable. I cannot believe that the (due process) Amendment was intended to give us *carte blanche* to embody our economic or moral beliefs in
its prohibitions." (*Baldwin* v. *Missouri*, 281 U.S. 586, 595.) Such was the
condition created for the law-making bodies of the country — for both the
Congress and for the state legislatures — before the depression came and
before the Congress, by three successive and increasingly emphatic popular

mandates, was called upon to deal with the depression, both in achieving recovery and in avoiding the recurrence of future disasters.

The unfortunate situation thus created by the judiciary long before the depression has been intensified by the events of the depression. In 1935, Mr. Chief Justice Hughes had to protest a decision of a majority of the Court who refused to confine their decision to the statute actually before the Court, in accordance with the traditional limits of judicial review, but, disregarding all judicial restraint, declared by judicial fiat that the Congress was without power by any form of legislation under the Commerce Clause to devise any pension system for railroad workers. The Chief Justice described the action of the Court as "a departure from sound principles" and "an unwarranted limitation upon the Commerce Clause of the Constitution." (*Railroad Retirement Board* v. *Alton R. Co.*, 295 U.S. 330, 375.) In protesting the decision of the majority of the Court invalidating the Agricultural Adjustment Act, Mr. Justice Stone, who had been President Coolidge's Attorney General, felt impelled to remind the Court that while legislative power may be unwisely used, "So may judicial power be abused," and that "A tortured construction of the Constitution is not to be justified." (*United States* v. *Butler*, 297 U.S. 1, 87.) The climax of a generation of experience with judicial disregard of the proper distribution of governmental powers under the Constitution was reached when a majority of the Court decided that a "State is without power *by any form of legislation* to prohibit, change or nullify contracts between employers and adult women workers as to the amount of wages to be paid." (*Morehead* v. *New York ex rel Tipaldo*, 298 U.S. 587, 611.) That decision arbitrarily brushed aside as unconstitutional the New York Minimum Wage Act which had been most carefully drafted to meet the objections theretofore raised by the Court to that type of legislation, objections which, according to Mr. Chief Justice Taft, Mr. Justice Holmes and Mr. Justice Sanford (Mr. Justice Brandeis was not sitting in that case), could not be found in the Constitution. In vain did the minority of the Court protest that "it is difficult to imagine any grounds, other than *our own personal, economic predilections,* for saying that the contract of employment is any the less an appropriate subject of legislation than are scores of others, in dealing with which this court has held that legislatures may curtail individual freedom in the public interest." (298 U.S. at 633.)

The Minimum Wage decision exposed the extent to which personal economic views were attributed to the impersonal Constitution. If we should allow this situation to continue, we shall have abandoned a constitutional government of law for a government of men. Thus, the Supreme Court has twice declared minimum wage legislation invalid, once in 1923 and again in

1936. Thirteen Justices have recorded their views on such legislation: seven Justices have sustained such legislation while six have found it unconstitutional. Yet the legislation has been thrown out simply because a bare majority of a particular set of Justices who happened to sit on the Court on each occasion did not like that kind of legislation.

I am not expressing a personal or party view. Ten days after the Court had thrown out the New York Minimum Wage Act on the ground that the state was "without power by any form of legislation" to establish minimum wages for women, the Republican party, in convention assembled, expressed its belief that such legislation *could* be enacted "within the Constitution as it now stands."

By reason not of a few erratic decisions but of a long course of adjudications, it has become evident that an inflexible majority of the Court has frustrated and will continue to frustrate legislative action by the states as well as by the nation, and not because anything in the Constitution so requires.

The states have properly been allowed by the Court to protect the good will of manufacturers from unauthorized price-cutting, but the states have been denied the right to protect labor by minimum wage legislation. The states have been denied the right to protect union workers from discrimination and to protect the unemployed from exploitation by private agencies. The states have been denied the right to encourage local investments and local industries by a rational tax policy. The Congress has very properly been allowed to use the Commerce Clause to protect the children of the rich from kidnappers, but the Congress has been denied the right to use the same power to protect the children of the poor from the terrible exploitation of child labor.

These decisions, and many more that I could cite, cannot be justified by anything in the Constitution. They are explained by the fact that some of the Justices have identified the Constitution with their private social philosophy.

It is the duty of the Chief Executive and of the Congress, no less than that of the Court, to protect and defend the Constitution. "Interpretation of our great charter of government which proceeds on any assumption that the responsibility for the preservation of our institutions is the exclusive concern of any one of the three branches of government, or that it alone can save them from destruction is far more likely, in the long run, 'to obliterate the constituent members' of 'an indestructible union of indestructible states' than the frank recognition that language, even of a Constitution, may mean what it says." These are not my words. They are the characterization by Mr. Justice Stone of the decision of a majority of his Court. (*United States* v. *Butler*, 297 U.S. 51, 87-88.)

And so, the aim is not to impair the authority of the Constitution or the independence of the Court, but to protect the Constitution which, as John Marshall told us, was "intended to endure for ages to come, and consequently, to be adapted to the various *crises* of human affairs." (*McCulloch v. Maryland*, 4 Wheat. 316, 415.) Once we acquiesce in spurious and arbitrary constructions of the Constitution never intended by its makers, once we degrade the Constitution to a body of rules unadaptable, except by specific and constant amendments, to the changing conditions of a dynamic society, the Constitution loses its strength and its meaning as the symbol of the orderly continuity of our national life. Nor is it admissible that we should yield our constitutional destiny to the personal judgment of a few men, however sincere.

It is necessary not only to protect the Constitution but to protect the judiciary itself from losing its essential safeguards. For its security depends ultimately upon the confidence of the people. Only thus will the necessary independence of the judiciary be assured. But the first requirement of an independent judiciary is that judges should be intellectually free to make impartial judgments. Judges who cannot rise above their private views are not free judges. A Court which wields the delicate and enormous power of reviewing the legislative acts of a nation must not justly be deemed to have its judgments determined by its own economic predilections. In the famous language of Mr. Justice Holmes, "A Constitution is not intended to embody a particular economic theory. . . . It is made for people of fundamentally differing views." (*Lochner* v. *New York*, 198 U.S. 45, 75-76.)

Memorandum for F.F.

The White House, February 18, 1937

In case you have not seen this, it is worth reading. What would happen, for example, if I were to go on the air and talk to America along the lines of Chase's article to the *Times?*

F.D.R.

Stuart Chase's letter, which the New York Times *did not run, read as follows:*

February 15, 1937

To the Editor
New York *Times*
Sir:

In the hullabaloo which has followed the President's proposal to ease the pressure of the courts on social legislation, the real point at issue is in danger of being submerged. The point might be phrased in the form of a question: What would you do if you were President of the United States, following a mandate such as that delivered in the last election? Hysterical appeals to Imperishable Traditions would not help you much, particularly if the traditions were constantly perishing in the face of concrete situations. Learned studies of what Jefferson, Jackson and Grant did in the past would not help much. There are certain grave problems demanding solution in 1937. Your task is to find a way to attack them which is at once legal and effective. Looking over the frothing rhetoric to the real land and the real people of America, you find that:

Six million farmers were left in a legal vacuum by the AAA decision. The overwhelming majority of them are frightened, sore and determined to secure legislation which will rescue agriculture from the curve of progressive degeneration in evidence since 1920.

Fifteen million industrial and clerical workers, more or less, were stripped of wage and hour protection by the NRA decision. They are baffled, alarmed and determined to secure this protection in some form. An unfavorable decision in the Wagner Act will increase their resentment. An unfavorable decision in the Social Security Act will increase it again.

Half a million coal miners and many operators are disgruntled and angry about the Guffey Coal Bill decision.

A million railway workers are thoroughly aroused over the Railway Retirement Act decision.

Eight million unemployed want work and will continue to be bitter and resentful until they get it.

A land-less tenant class turns to the government to save them from peasantry or worse.

Here are stock markets, banks, investment trusts likely to go on the loose again as they did in 1929, cleaning out millions of small depositors and investors without some form of orderly control, which will not be thrown out of court.

Finally, and perhaps most important of all in the long run, here is the continent of North America sliding to the sea at the rate of three billion tons of top soil a year, and increasingly stricken with flood, drought and dust storm. Only vigorous action, inaugurated by the federal government on a regional rather than a state basis, can cope with this appalling situation. The Ohio River is not conversant with the interstate commerce clause.

In brief here are a series of acute problems in 1937 which somehow somebody must meet. Failing energetic action, we are faced with a serious lowering of the survival value of the American community. It is not a case of Eternal Verities, the Principles of the Founding Fathers, or Hallowed Traditions, it is a case of maintaining a functioning community. The first duty of a government is not to preserve traditions, its first duty is to govern.

The President I take it has heard from the farmers, heard from the workers, share croppers, coal miners, railway men, the unemployed, the small depositor, and heard in no uncertain terms from the Ohio River and the Dust Bowl. As a result, he sees the situation in practical terms, unclouded with Imperishable Principles and other absolutes. His guiding principle is to make this country more viable and a less hazardous place in which to live and work. He is on the spot. He is responsible, together with Congress, for doing something. He has the tough job of devising ways and means to give millions of distressed people definite hope for a better and more secure existence.

When he devises such measures, what does he hit? A stone wall. Five old gentlemen say: No, you can't do it. Four old gentlemen say: Yes, you can. So he can't do it. The urgent needs, desires and demands of the majority of the people are thus rendered irrelevant and immaterial.

What is the President to do? What would you do? Tell the 27 million citizens who voted for the New Deal to forget their difficulties because five old gentlemen consider them insoluable, or to warn the five gentlemen that the people demand action? Perhaps you prefer a constitutional amendment as a more dignified way out of the impasse. I do. But what if you and I knew that to get an amendment at all would take a long time — the Child Labor Amendment has been kicking around State Legislatures for thirteen years; and knew further that by concentrating their still formidable powers in thirteen States, those who are quite satisfied with things as they are, stand an excellent chance of heading off any amendment indefinitely? And here are all these farmers and workers. Now. Here are women laboring 48 hours a week in New Bedford mills for $5. Now. Here is the Dust Bowl beginning to blow again. Now. Here are millions of land-less tenants progressively sliding to economic perdition.

If we really cared about America, I think we should act. Now.

Yours very truly,
STUART CHASE

Cambridge, Mass., February 23, 1937

Dear Frank:

Many thanks for sending me the Stuart Chase letter, otherwise I should not have seen it, for it was not published in the *Times* that comes to Cambridge.

What would happen if you were to say over the radio what Chase wrote in his letter? The American people would get some enlightenment. Why shouldn't you explain these things — saying them pitched, of course, in your key. And you should enlarge upon Chase's recital — pointing out the long course of judicial abuse in preventing not only national but also state action — denying Maryland the right and duty to regulate telephone rates reasonably, and Vermont the right to devise its own local tax policy, and so also North Dakota, and denying Nebraska the means of preventing short-weighing of bread, and New York the means of preventing exploitation of the economic necessities of working women and protecting the bulk of fair-minded employers, etc., etc., etc. — and always over the powerful protest of the great men of the Court against putting private social views into the Constitution.

And then, why not tell the American people of the various remedies that were open to you for dealing with this major problem of democracy — what the costs and difficulties of each were, why you discarded them and why you chose what you did.

I believe that you should take the country to school — give them a free dress exposition and analysis such as you can give them.

Ever yours,
F.F.

Charles Culp Burlingham, one of the enduring giants of the American bar, lived to be nearly 101 years old, and during that long span of time no lawyer was more vigilant in maintaining the highest traditions of the legal profession. No one exceeded his influence with the New York bar or indeed with the entire company of lawyers and judges across the country. It was thus a matter of anxious concern to Roosevelt and Frankfurter when Burlingham turned against the President's Supreme Court plan and denounced it, for Burlingham to both of them, was an old and cherished friend and mentor. Frankfurter passed on Burlingham's letters to the President, and Roosevelt in turn showed Frankfurter his own correspondence with Burlingham.

These exchanges provide essential information on Frankfurter's views during the court-packing controversy. They also give us additional and emphatic proof of the zeal with which he applauded Mr. Justice Black's appointment to the Supreme Court. With prophetic wisdom, Frankfurter remained undisturbed by Justice Black's nominal membership in the Ku Klux Klan, and by charges that Black had transgressed the principles of due process during some of his Senate investigations.

On January 2, 1937, Frankfurter wrote Burlingham a light letter in which he said "maybe Jim Farley is the fellow to get us four judges! !" But even in that jesting letter Frankfurter had a suspicion that great decisions were in the making, for he remarked that "F.D.R. is shrewd in his silences these days."

The next month, as the controversy began, Frankfurter told Burlingham

*that "F.D.R. is confounding those foolish notions of the people who (a)
don't like him, (b) don't realize that government needs power, especially
democratic government, (c) will soon have all the 'opposition' they want."*

*But Burlingham did not like the opposition being offered by the Presi-
dent. He told the President that his message on the Supreme Court was
"specious." He brought evidence to show that the Supreme Court was
"abreast of all its work." Much the same evidence was later used by Chief
Justice Charles Evans Hughes in his letter to Senator Wheeler — the letter
which placed the President's plan at a crucial disadvantage in the Senate. As
these letters show, Frankfurter thought Hughes had violated the traditions
of the Supreme Court in consulting only Brandeis among his brethren on
the Court. Frankfurter always believed that Hughes behaved like a politician rather than like a Chief Justice in this particular controversy.*

*Burlingham also told the President that there is "no congestion" in the
Court's business, and that all the justices are "in full mental vigor."*

*When Frankfurter heard these views, he dared Burlingham to present
them to the students at the Harvard Law School. "Come up here," he
wrote, "and persuade these informed and generous lads that the Court is
not playing politics!"*

Cambridge, Mass., March 13, 1937

Dear C.C.:

The chief trouble with these "discussion" groups is that they are not
groups for discussion. I hate crowds of all sorts and I don't think one really
comes to grips with problems when there are fifty or sixty people. And,
therefore, I am the more troubled by Mr. Willcox's suggestion to you that
"it may be advisable for members to bring guests." I do not want a full
attendance — honestly I don't. I would rather sit down with about ten or a
dozen men who are really anxious to find out what they think and why they
think it about an important issue than to talk to fifty. And still less do I
want people to come and look at me as though I were a stuffed exhibit in
Bob Moses' menagerie. Believe it or not, I don't give a damn about persuading even nice people that I am not a monster — much as I am deeply
grateful for the affection and devotion which moves you to disabuse people
of their funny views about me.

I am tempted strongly to talk about the Court — mind you, the Court
as an institution and not about the President's proposal in regard to it. I am
tempted to tell with particularity and with thorough-going analysis what
the functions of the Court are and how it has been exercising them during
the thirty years of which I have, I think, very intimate knowledge. For that
is all I care about, that people should know what the problem is, and then I
do not care what they think about remedies. For this is not a new prob-

lem — it is just one phase of an old problem which, I suspect, will recur in the lives of your great grandchildren, assuming that we will be wise enough to maintain the essentials of our democratic society, and that, therefore, the Court will survive. But I will let it simmer in my mind and see what may profitably be discussed with such a group. And so, now, I'm not committed to any subject.

F.F.

Frankfurter did come to New York to address a private meeting of lawyers. It was his usual performance — very explicit on the background to the crisis, very vague on the President's plan.

Cambridge, Mass., March 30, 1937

Dear Frank:

And now, with the shift by Roberts, even a blind man ought to see that the Court is in politics, and understand how the Constitution is "judicially" construed. It is a deep object lesson — a lurid demonstration — of the relation of men to the "meaning" of the Constitution. This behavior (in the light of the outrageous misrepresentation by Butler of the scope of the issues in the Tipaldo case, confirmed as late as October 12, in denying the petition for rehearing) comes on top of the Hughes letter. *That* was a characteristic Hughes performance — part and parcel of that pretended withdrawal from considerations of policy, while trying to shape them, which is the core of the mischief of which the majority have so long been guilty. That Brandeis should have been persuaded to allow the Chief to use his name is a source of sadness to me that I need hardly dwell on to you.

I have absolutely dependable editorial friends on the other side who tell me that some foolish folks (enemies of yours) are doing their damndest to make me attack the court so as to start a new line of attack against your proposal. They miss their guess. I shan't help them to divert the issue from the misbehavior of the Court. There are various ways of fighting a fight!

I infer that you had a refreshing Warm Springs time.

My fondest good wishes to you.

Ever yours,
F.F.

Frankfurter deeply regretted this letter in after years. He is shown here as joining in the vulgar cry that Mr. Justice Roberts had changed sides for political rather than judicial reasons. When Frankfurter wrote an article for the December 1955 number of the University of Pennsylvania Law Review, dedicated to the memory of Mr. Justice Roberts, he corrected this mistake. Frankfurter wrote that "it is one of the most ludicrous illustrations of the power of lazy repetition of uncritical talk that a judge with the character of Roberts should have attributed to him a change of judicial views out of deference to political considerations. One is more saddened than shocked that a high-minded and thoughtful United States Senator should assume it to be an established fact that it was by reason of 'the famous switch of Mr. Justice Roberts' that legislation was constitutionally sustained after President Roosevelt's proposal for reconstructing the Court and because of it."

The accusation about "Roberts' Switch" arose from his conduct in two cases, conduct that was gravely misunderstood not only by the public but by the legal profession. In June 1936, in the Tipaldo case, Roberts had voted with the majority in reaffirming the decision in the Adkins case and thereby invalidating the New York Minimum Wage Law. But in March 1937, in the Parrish case, he was again with the majority in overruling the Adkins case and sustaining minimum wage legislation. All the public saw in these two cases was that Mr. Justice Roberts had voted on both sides of the same issue in less than a year. Hence the cry that he had switched his vote. In reality, the situation which faced the Court was vastly more complicated. Believing that Mr. Justice Roberts had an obligation to set the record straight, Frankfurter, after "not a little persuasion," convinced Roberts to lift the curtain on the Court's deliberations. Roberts, after he had resigned from the bench, gave Frankfurter a memorandum on November 9, 1945, to be used at his discretion. Ten years later Frankfurter decided that the time had come to have Roberts explain what had really happened. The Roberts memorandum follows:

A petition for certiorari was filed in Morehead v. Tipaldo, 298 U.S. 587, on March 16, 1936. When the petition came to be acted upon, the Chief Justice spoke in favor of a grant, but several others spoke against it on the ground that the case was ruled by Adkins v. Children's Hospital, 261 U.S. 525. Justices Brandeis, Cardozo and Stone were in favor of a grant. They, with the Chief Justice, made up four votes for a grant.

When my turn came to speak I said I saw no reason to grant the writ unless the Court were prepared to re-examine and overrule the Adkins case. To this remark there was no response around the table, and the case was marked granted.

Both in the petition for certiorari, in the brief on the merits, and in oral argument, counsel for the State of New York took the position that it was unnecessary to overrule the Adkins case in order to sustain the position of the State of New York. It was urged that further data and experience and additional facts distinguished the case at bar from the Adkins case. The argument seemed to me to be disingenuous and born of timidity. I could find nothing in the record to substantiate the alleged distinction. At conference I so stated, and stated further that I was for taking the State of New York at its word. The State had not asked that the *Adkins* case be overruled but that it be distinguished. I said I was unwilling to put a decision on any such ground. The vote was five to four for affirmance, and the case was assigned to Justice Butler.

I stated to him that I would concur in any opinion which was based on the fact that the State had not asked us to re-examine or overrule *Adkins* and that, as we found no material difference in the facts of the two cases, we should therefore follow the *Adkins* case. The case was originally so written by Justice Butler, but after a dissent had been circulated he added matter to his opinion, seeking to sustain the *Adkins* case in principle. My proper course would have been to concur specially on the narrow ground I had taken. I did not do so. But at conference in the Court I said that I did not propose to review and re-examine the *Adkins* case until a case should come to the Court requiring that this should be done.

August 17, 1936, an appeal was filed in *West Coast Hotel Company* v. *Parrish*, 300 U.S. 379. The Court as usual met to consider applications in the week of Monday, October 5, 1936, and concluded its work by Saturday, October 10. During the conferences the jurisdictional statement in the *Parrish* case was considered and the question arose whether the appeal should be dismissed on the authority of *Adkins* and *Morehead*. [*Evidently he meant "should be reversed summarily," since the Washington Supreme Court had sustained the statute.*] Four of those who had voted in the majority in the *Morehead* case voted to dismiss the appeal in the *Parrish* case. I stated that I would vote for the notation of probable jursidiction. I am not sure that I gave my reason, but it was that in the appeal in the *Parrish* case the authority of *Adkins* was definitely assailed and the Court was asked to reconsider and overrule it. Thus, for the first time, I was confronted with the necessity of facing the soundness of the *Adkins* case. Those who were in the majority in the *Morehead* case expressed some surprise at my vote, and I heard one of the brethren ask another, "What is the matter with Roberts?"

Justice Stone was taken ill about October 14. The case was argued December 16 and 17, 1936, in the absence of Justice Stone, who at that time was lying in a comatose condition at his home. It came on for consideration at the conference on December 19. I voted for an affirmance. There were three other such votes, those of the Chief Justice, Justice Brandeis, and Justice Cardozo. The other four voted for a reversal.

If a decision had then been announced, the case would have been affirmed by a divided Court. It was thought that this would be an unfortunate outcome, as everyone on the Court knew Justice Stone's views. The case was, therefore, laid over for further consideration when Justice Stone should be able to participate. Justice Stone was convalescent during January and returned to the sessions of the Court on February 1, 1937. I believe that the *Parrish* case was taken up at the conference on February 6, 1937, and Justice Stone then voted for an affirmance. This made it possible to assign the case for an opinion, which was done. The decision affirming the lower court was announced March 29, 1937.

These facts make it evident that no action taken by the President in the interim had any causal relation to my action in the *Parrish* case.

After quoting this memorandum, Frankfurter added:

More needs to be said for Roberts than he cared to say for himself. As a matter of history it is regrettable that Roberts's unconcern for his own record led him to abstain from stating his position. The occasions are not infrequent when the disfavor of the separate opinions, on the part of the bar and to the extent that it prevails within the Court, should not be heeded. Such a situation was certainly presented when special circumstances made Roberts agree with a result but basically disagree with the opinion which announced it.

The crucial factor in the whole episode was the absence of Mr. Justice Stone from the bench, on account of illness, from October 14, 1936, to February 1, 1937.

The Supreme Court had ruled in 1923 in the Adkins *case that there was no federal power to enact legislation for minimum wages in the District of Columbia. A powerful dissent had been written by Chief Justice Taft. During these Roosevelt years, Frankfurter, assisted by Mr. Benjamin V. Cohen, had drafted a model bill to improve the working conditions of women and to protect them with a minimum wage. That bill formed the basis for legislation in various states, including the New York legislature. Thus in the course of time the* Tipaldo *case involving minimum wages for women came before the Supreme Court. With the exception of Brandeis, no one had been more concerned than Frankfurter with the history of litigation to end child labor and to establish a minimum wage for women, and thereby for men also. He had prepared the briefs in several of the most important cases and had appeared as counsel before the Supreme Court to argue in defense of these reforms.*

When Roosevelt had sent his plan to Congress for the reorganization of the federal judiciary, on February 5, 1937, he had recalled the various changes in the composition of the Supreme Court. In 1789 the Supreme Court had six members; it was reduced to five members in 1801; it was increased to seven in 1807; it was increased to nine in 1837; it was increased to ten in 1863; it was reduced to seven in 1866; it was increased to nine in 1869.

*Roosevelt rested his case for an enlargement of the Court, barring resigna-
tions to permit the appointment of younger Justices, on the claim that "the
simple fact is that today a new need for legislative action arises because the
personnel of the Federal judiciary is insufficient to meet the business before
them." As far as the Supreme Court was concerned, that was no "simple
fact"; it was a factual error. Attorney General Cummings had brought Roosevelt into this fight without finding out the true nature of the Supreme
Court's current business. There was no congestion of cases to justify the
President's indictment.*

*When he discovered these facts, Senator Wheeler, an ardent and re-
sourceful opponent of the President's plan, decided to make the best possible use of the Administration's mistakes. He read a letter to the Senate
Judiciary Committee from Chief Justice Hughes giving an impressive and
reassuring account of the Court's disposition of cases and current business.
That letter bore only one other signature — the honored name of Brandeis.
The great Justice had signed Hughes's letter because he was certain that the
President's plan was so unnecessary, so provocative, and so destructive of
the division of powers that sustained the American system that it deserved
to be discredited and repudiated.*

*Brandeis's willingness to sign the letter provoked a stern disagreement
with Frankfurter. It was the closest the two men ever came to a quarrel, and,
once tempers had cooled, they agreed not to discuss the Supreme Court
crisis for a time to avoid placing such a strain on their friendship again.*

*Hughes said there was no time, in replying to Senator Wheeler's request,
to gather all the signatures of the nine Justices but he claimed to speak for
the entire Court. It now is known that Hughes, in fact, could not have
obtained all these names for his letter. Mr. Justice Stone, for one, would
have refused to sign it. It was this kind of performance, which amounted in
Frankfurter's eyes to trickery, which made him so critical of Chief Justice
Hughes during this controversy, despite his admiration for the Chief Justice's immense powers of logical analysis and profound scholarship.*

The White House, April 5, 1937

Dear Felix: —

It is good to get your letter of the thirtieth. I wish I could see you and
have a good long talk. Is there no way in which you can slip into town and
to the White House unobserved — any time after April twelfth? You are
dead right in keeping — for the moment — wholly out of the hearings. As
you know, we are carrying out the dignified process of keeping still and
watching each new witness damn the proposal and offer a new remedy. My
last count runs to over two hundred amendment proposals and over one
hundred legislative proposals.

It is quite clear that the utter confusion of our opponents among themselves means success for us even though it may be deferred until June or July. The opposition has daily epilepsy because we are keeping "our shirts on."

As ever yours,
F.D.R.

On this letter Frankfurter wrote: "April 23, 1937. Was at White House on Tuesday April 20, 1937, from 5 P.M. to ten minutes of 10 o'clock Wednesday morning. Alone with F.D.R. except at dinner when Mrs. Roosevelt and her Secretary joined us."

F.F.

Cambridge, Mass., April 8, 1937
Dear Frank:

Many thanks for your letter. I'm delighted to have your authoritative estimate of what one inferred were happy prospects.

Of course I'm eager to come down for a talk. I can manage to be there Wednesday next, the 14th — but I have to be in New York on the 15th, to speak at the annual dinner of the Harvard Law School Alumni, and to be back here on the following Saturday, to be toastmaster at the 50th anniversary of the Harvard *Law Review*. And so, if Wednesday is not inconvenient for you, I can come, any time after Monday in the week of the 19th. Please let me know your wishes and I shall act accordingly. As for managing the visit — I shouldn't think that would be very difficult. I might stay either with Mr. Justice Butler or Mr. Justice McReynolds — that would make my visit wholly Constitutional!

Yes — You're "keeping your shirt on beautifully."

Marion joins me in warm regards.

Faithfully yours,
F.F.

Telegram to Roosevelt
Cambridge, Mass., April 12, 1937
AFTER TODAY I FEEL LIKE FINDING SOME HONEST PROFESSION TO ENTER. AFFECTIONATELY YOURS.

FELIX FRANKFURTER

This telegram was sent after the Supreme Court had found the Wagner Act constitutional. Frankfurter had never doubted the validity of this Act; he wondered, however, how the majority on the Supreme Court could rec-

oncile this verdict with their previous decision outlawing essential parts of the New Deal. He thought Chief Justice Hughes had decided to support the Wagner Act in order to weaken the President's case for changing the composition of the Supreme Court. Though Frankfurter agreed with the decision in the Wagner Act to establish a National Labor Relations Board, he objected to the motives which, he was convinced, had inspired the ruling. Hence his sardonic telegram to the President.

In obedience to the President's instructions, Frankfurter had slipped into the White House, unobserved, for a long and secret discussion of the next moves in the court-packing fight.

Cambridge, Mass., April 21, 1937

Dear Frank:

In the glare of the white light of Pennsylvania Avenue and under the eagle eyes of three Secret Service operatives I "slipped" out of the White House. But, in any event, "slipped out" is a very inaccurate expression. If anything, I flew out. For, after my long happy exhilarating hours with you I was, as it were on wings and you put more spirit into me than possibly could any Bacardi rum — or any that you will have put in wood, even for forty years in the Virgin Islands!

What you did to me, and what you do to all who have the good fortune of your personal impress, winds into sails, air into flat tires — is the reason why I so much hope that you will be able to meet on a familiar family basis the junior administrative officials once a year. It will give them a tonic the effect of which you yourself can hardly appreciate.

And it was such a comfort and reassurance to find you so fit in every way — so unabated in your vitality and understanding as the great democratic leader of our time — fully aware of the qualities and difficulties of the motley progressive forces whom you are leading and who look to you for hope and fulfillment, but no less aware of the forces, pleasant and otherwise, who are arrayed against you. The Good Lord keep you strong and fit — and may the principle of Luck continue to mark you as its own.

My very fondest,

Faithfully ever yours,
F.F.

Henry M. Hart, Jr., now one of the most distinguished professors at the Harvard Law School, had written an article for the Harvard Alumni Bulletin *taking the President's side in the quarrel with the Supreme Court. A copy of this article was sent to Roosevelt by Frankfurter.*

Justice Oliver Wendell Holmes with Justice Louis D. Brandeis

With the affectionate regards of his old friend Franklin DRoosevelt

President Roosevelt

To Franklin D. Roosevelt,
in affectionate friendship,
20. October 1939   Felix Frankfurter

Justice Frankfurter

Governor Roosevelt with his son James at the 1932 Democratic Convention in Chicago

Professor Frankfurter walking to the Harvard Law School from 192 Brattle Street

Roosevelt's nomination of Frankfurter to the Supreme Court

WASHINGTON EVENING STAR

Ajax!

A cartoon which appeared in the Washington
Evening Star, February 5, 1941

Frankfurter with
Dean Acheson in Washington

President Roosevelt with Prime Minister Winston Churchill and
Premier Josef Stalin at Yalta, February 5, 1945

SYLVIA SALMI

Marion Denman Frankfurter

Frankfurter, Eleanor Roosevelt and Franklin D. Roosevelt, Jr. during the
Memorial Day Services at Hyde Park, May 30, 1956

Cambridge, Mass., April 27, 1937

Dear Frank —

This is from one of my pet products here — and now among my junior colleagues. Grand person, of whom some "distinguished Harvard men" do not approve. Strange — isn't it?

I hope the fish will bite for you, heartily and well — both on land and sea. A gay good time.

Ever yours devotedly,
F.F.

Roosevelt sent Frankfurter a copy of this exchange of letters with C. C. Burlingham.

New York, N.Y., May 25, 1937

Dear Governor:

Now that the Chief Justice and Roberts have crossed the line and Van Devanter has retired, you have accomplished your real purpose by bringing about a reasonable interpretation and application of the Constitution by the Court.

I wish it were in my power to persuade you now to drop so much of the bill as relates to the Supreme Court, with a statement in your own inimitable style that one of your main objectives was to direct attention to the fact that in some of its decisions the Court had failed to recognize the changed conditions of our economic and social life by its narrow and legalistic interpretations; that during the last two months the majority had adopted a more reasonable interpretation; that many of your supporters strongly opposed the bill as the wrong method; that while you had not altered your own view as to the bill, which you could state was in no sense an attack on the independence of the Judiciary nor an attempt to coerce the Court to make particular decisions, you have no pride of opinion on the subject, and now that things were going along reasonably, you had no objection to the withdrawal of those portions of the bill which affect the Supreme Court; that the other recommendations embodied in the bill should, of course, be fully discussed and decided on their merits.

This is probably one of the most audacious and effronterous letters ever written to the *Pater Patriae*.

As always,

Yours,
C.C.

The White House, May 27, 1937

Personal

Dear Charles:

I do not in the least object to what you have written but may I put it this way: I think you are looking a day or a week or a year ahead, while I am trying to look a generation ahead.

For exactly thirty years I have been watching, as a lawyer, the processes of American justice. I have attended Bar Association meetings of many kinds. I have read Law Journals and Reviews. I have met, liked and given honor to many great lawyers and many great judges. But the net result is this — neither the American Bar nor the American Bench in that whole period have been responsible for any major improvement in the processes of justice. And on the other side of the picture, the American Bar and the American Bench have encouraged bad morals and bad ethics on the part of American non-lawyer citizens. It is, therefore, not to be wondered that a large majority of the lawyers and judges of the country would prefer to see nothing done in regard to reforming the Federal Courts — to say nothing of state and local courts.

It is perhaps amusing that while I dictate this I see a paragraph in the local Washington paper "D.C. Bar Association opposes Juvenile Court Bill."

Under your hat — within a few weeks quite a storm is going to break over the heads of a large number of individuals who have been cheating their own Government. Watch and see how many lawyers condemn them and how many lawyers condone them!

As ever yours,

FRANKLIN D. ROOSEVELT

Honorable C. C. Burlingham

This last paragraph refers to income tax evasions by a number of prominent Americans.

Using the intimacy of a very old friend, Burlingham often addressed the President by the more familiar title of Governor. It is crucial to an understanding of Frankfurter's hidden role in this prolonged constitutional crisis that when he saw this letter, he advised the President to accept no compromise.

Yet several things had already happened, or were about to happen, that made a compromise altogether feasible.

On April 12 the Supreme Court found the Wagner Labor Relations Act to be constitutional.

On May 18 Mr. Justice Van Devanter resigned. He was to be succeeded by Mr. Justice Hugo L. Black.

Chief Justice Hughes informed Senator Wheeler that "more judges to hear, more judges to confer, more judges to discuss, more judges to be convinced and to decide" would retard rather than facilitate the discharge of judicial business.

On May 24 the Supreme Court upheld the constitutionality of the Social Security Act.

The Senate Judiciary Committee, in its majority report, condemned the President's plan because it sought "a change in the decisions of the Court — a subordination of the views of the judges to the views of the executive and legislative." The Committee voted, 10-8, with six Democrats in the majority, that the President's bill "not pass."

On July 14, while the protracted debate on the committee report was still continuing, Senator Joseph Robinson, the majority leader in charge of the President's bill, was suddenly stricken in his hotel room and dropped dead.

On August 24 the President signed the Judicial Procedure Reform Act. This act gave him important procedural reforms but it contained not one word granting him the power to enlarge the Supreme Court or to appoint additional judges to other federal courts.

It is clear that on these terms it had always been possible to arrange a compromise settlement, and indeed to avoid the Supreme Court controversy completely.

Cambridge, Mass., June 9, 1937

Dear C.C.:

1. Bob, to my knowledge, has been working sedulously. He is in the thick of exams. Don't worry.

2. No, I don't see ghosts about Charles Evans Hughes. I merely know intimately the history of the Court, and especially during the last few years. Apparently it's alright to know the facts about the President, but not alright to know the facts about the Chief Justice. I have just been refreshing my memory of the Dreyfus Case by reading Pierre Dreyfus' volume, just issued by the Yale Press. It confirms me in my conviction that no institution — neither the French army nor the Supreme Court of the United States — can ultimately survive by not facing the truth about it. When I think that so candid and so sensitive a person as you should have allowed yourself to say the things that you said about the Court's attitude towards civil liberties, including McReynolds, and to have signed the statement that you did about the Supreme Court not nullifying legislation — I should think *that* old wheeze would be dead, at least, ever since Birkenhead's devastating reply to Davis in the 1924 American Bar Association meeting — I realize how even for the best of men at times a film of loyalty may obscure the truth. My kick against the Chief Justice, in a single word, is that he has

been just as political as the President. And the less you say about his letter to Senator Wheeler the better, because it is indefensible on several scores: it was disingenuous in saying there wasn't time to consult other colleagues, and it grossly violated the settled practice of the Court against giving advisory opinions in so far as it expressed views regarding Article 3 (I talked pretty plainly to Brandeis about this).

But I suppose T. R. Powell is right when he says, "it serves you right. You have done more than any one person to build up respect for the Supreme Court," and now I am hoist by my own petard, having built up a myth of infallible respectability behind which all sorts of shenanigans are allowed to go unchallenged.

You see I take the law very seriously.

3. All of which has nothing to do with the merits or demerits of the President's Court bill. But it has a great deal to do with intellectual rectitude and living up to judicial professions. For I speak as one who has a teacher's sacred duty of trying to answer as honestly as he can the honest questions of youth. I tell you, it has gone hard with me in recent months to be both truthful with students and build up in them respect for the Supreme Court as an institution. Come up here and try it. These bright minds, you know, aren't fools — or rather C.E.H. ought to be subjected to their questioning.

4. By the way, I meant to write a word about your reference to the *Humphrey* Case. I haven't the slightest notion whether F.D.R. felt that deeply: I never heard a peep from him about it. But of all the silly things, one of the silliest is to charge F.D.R.'s dismissal of Humphrey as an act of lawlessness. No lawyer with proper respect for the Supreme Court would have advised the President otherwise than he was advised — not by me. I had no hand in it whatever — that in view of the Myers Case he was free to terminate Humphrey's services without charges. (There were ample grounds for charges against Humphrey, but the President was too kind to subject Humphrey to such a proceeding.) Considering the circumstances of the *Myers* decision it was almost indecent, and certainly not judicial-minded, the way in which the Court swallowed the weighty and deliberate scope of Taft's opinion in the *Myers* Case. I wish you would look at what I said about that at the time, though very mildly, in the *Harvard Law Review* for November, 1935 (49 *Harv. L. Rev.* pp. 105-106).

Affectionately and ever yours,
F.F.

Bob is Burlingham's son. Thomas Reed Powell, an authority on constitutional law, was a famous colleague and beloved friend of Frankfurter at the Harvard Law School.

Roosevelt had been opposed by the Supreme Court in removing William E. Humphrey from the Federal Trade Commission after twice asking for his resignation. The Myers case dealt with the Presidential power to remove appointed officials.

The next two letters refer to Governor Lehman's public statement in opposition to the President's plan for reorganizing the Supreme Court. The profound political importance of Lehman's letter came from the fact that it was signed by a man known to have a long-standing friendship with the President. It seemed as if the President's own camp was in disarray as the struggle continued.

Cambridge, Mass., July 20, 1937

Dear Frank:

Last night I tried to reach you by phone, and, on the whole, I am glad that I did not succeed. For I'm afraid I would have used language hardly decorous over the wire. I was — and am — hot all over regarding Herbert Lehman's letter. Some things just aren't done — they violate the decencies of human relations and offend the good taste and the decorum of friendship. And so I was — and am — "hot" — but less with anger than with sadness.

I wanted to tell you this — at least inadequately to hint at my feelings, and to wish for you your own powers of serenity and generosity and good humor and pertinacity in the good fight and the long, patient resourceful persistence in vindicating the democratic ideals to which this country is dedicated.

Devotedly yours,
F.F.

Frankfurter wrote at the bottom of this next letter in his scribble: "Letter to 'My dear Senator Wagner' asking him to vote against Supreme Court proposals." This scribble referred to a letter which changed American history, for Governor Herbert L. Lehman's unexpected and staggering letter to Senator Robert Wagner showed that Roosevelt no longer could control even his most devoted friends on this controversial issue, and persuaded Roosevelt that the time had come to accept a reluctant compromise, dressing it up for public consumption as a qualified victory.

The White House, July 22, 1937

Dear Felix: —

If you had got me on the telephone your language would have been just like Bernie Baruch's when he heard of the Lehman episode. Like you, I have no anger but only sadness. If I were British I would say only one thing — "it isn't cricket" — and you know all the implications of that remark.

As you know, you and I will continue to think in terms of the ultimate objective and, where occasionally we run into barbed-wire in front and people who take pot-shots at us from the rear, we still do not lose sight of the goal.

As ever yours,
F.D.R.

This was sent by Frankfurter with a covering letter to F.D.R. on August 10, 1937.

Notes for an Address on the State of the Union

I.   Foreign Relations:

The precariousness of the European situation and dangers of entanglement and threats in Asia. Our constant alertness to take steps to avoid entanglement and to do what we can to assure peace. The passage of the Neutrality Bill during the present session of Congress. Conferences with British, French and Belgians in an effort to express to them the sentiments and desires of the American people for peace, and the readiness of the American people to make their contribution to peace and prosperity through the removal of unnecessarily harsh economic restrictions and trade barriers.

The harmonious cooperation of the neighboring powers of North and South America in the interest of peace has been our special concern. The importance of this cooperation has been signalized by the President's visit to South America and his participation in the Pan-American Conference at Buenos Aires.

II.   Home Affairs:

In November, 1936, there was an overwhelming popular approval of that general direction of affairs, which is colloquially known as the New Deal. That approval meant nothing unless it meant a desire for continuing efforts on the part of Government to satisfy more adequately and more securely the economic needs of the great body of our people. But the continuation of these efforts of Government depend upon the constitutional ability of Government to function in the economic sphere. Government cannot choose among, or effectively shape measures of, economic reform when there is no assurance that any economic reform is within the Constitutional sphere of Government. Before we can determine how to use, we must determine whether we *can* constitutionally use, the taxing power to stimulate purchasing power which is indispensable to the maintenance of modern large scale industry. Before we can determine how to promote, we must determine whether we can constitutionally promote, peaceful relations between capital and labor vital alike to the progress of industry and to the moral and physical well-being of our people. Before we can determine how to safeguard, we must determine whether we *can* constitutionally safeguard, the country against the devastation of another depression by scientifically recognized measures of social insurance, and public works. The Supreme Court by a series of decisions over the protest of its most distinguished members had interposed its veto, as some of its most distinguished members have charged, by giving tortured constructions to the Constitution and by acting as a super-legislature.

Something had to be done. If nothing was done, the mandate which the people of the United States had given to carry on would have become a nullity.

Something was done. The Supreme Court reversed itself. But the Supreme Court reversed itself only after it had become the duty of the President to protest the want of cooperation between the judicial and legislative branches of Government and to insist that what was needed was not a change in the Constitution but a proper interpretation of our fundamental law. Thereafter the Court rendered three memorable decisions this year, the result of which a year ago could have only been obtained by drastic amendments to the Constitution. Everyone knows that such amendments could have been obtained, if at all, only after long years of agitation. (Here insert summary of Court's action during period preceding February 5, 1937 giving Court record not only on New Deal legislation but also voluminous nullifications of *State Laws*.)

[*F.F. inserted by hand on margin the following notes: "Here give in detail Supreme Court's obstructions to dealing with Child Labor, Exploiting Labor, Collective Bargaining. And period subsequent to February 5, 1937 — a somewhat more detailed summary than that given by the President at his press conference on July 23."*]

The President has merely asked that the Constitution be viewed as Marshall and Holmes viewed it, so that it would be possible for the Constitution to survive periods of economic strain and political stress. His concern is to fulfill the mandate of the American people, to obtain those social and economic objectives within the framework of the Constitution which the American people are determined to obtain. His concern is with those objectives: the method and manner of their attainment, though important, are secondary.

For the present at least we have recognition by a majority, even though a precarious majority, of the Supreme Court that the Constitution as framed by the wise founders, if construed with a judicial mind and not made the instrument of narrow economic views, contains within itself powers adequate for the national government to deal with national problems. No one has ever wanted the Supreme Court to register political decisions. On the contrary, the nation could not continue to allow a majority of the Court to register its political and economic views and call them constitutional decisions.

For the present at least there appears to be a majority of the Court which realizes that the function of legislation belongs to the Congress and not to the Court. But in every period of economic change, there is danger of the Court assuming legislative power under the guise of exercising judicial power. Unceasing vigilance is required to preserve the constitutional rights of a free and democratic people. At the very beginning of the century, President Theodore Roosevelt warned us: "The decisions of the Courts on economic and social questions depend upon their economic and social philosophy; and for the peaceful progress of our people during the twentieth century we shall owe most to those judges who hold to a twentieth century economic and social philosophy and not to a long outgrown philosophy, which was itself the product of primitive economic conditions. . . . Judges, like executives and legislators, should hold sound views on the questions of public policy which are of vital importance to the nation" (Messages and Papers of the President, Vol. VI, p. 7214).

Being authorized, through the reversal by the Supreme Court this year of its prior obstructive position, the President and the Congress are now in a position to honor their election promises to the American people.

Here insert brief statement regarding such proposals (Guffey Coal Act, Railroad Retirement Act) as have been and as may be enacted at the present session of Congress.

Those promises were clear and definite. There should be no doubt as to what our promises were and what our aims are. I enumerated them very specifically in my closing address of the campaign in Madison Square Garden.

Here insert quotations from Madison Square Garden address.

These remain my aims.

The White House, August 12, 1937

Dear Felix: —

Just a line in haste to tell you that I am very grateful for that grand letter of yours and for the notes. You are absolutely right about the radio. I feel like saying to the country — "You will hear from me soon and often. This is not a threat but a promise."

Also, I may take a trip but don't tell anyone.

Just now I have a thoroughly dis-combobulated Congress, running around in circles between wages and hours and crop control, with reorganization, sugar, etc., thrown in for good measure. And to all and sundry who come to me for help, I shake my head, smile and say — "I told you so."

I hope to go to Hyde Park about five days after Congress adjourns (God knows when that will be) — and I hope then that you and Marion will motor over and spend the night. I want to talk with you both of many things.

As ever yours,
F.D.R.

Cohasset, Mass., September 1, 1937

Dear C.C.:

1. I wish we could make as much headway into the problems we so arrogantly call the social sciences as the M.D.'s have been making in their study of that strange bag of tricks called the human body. But think of being told, after fifty years, that my posture is all wrong — that I don't know how to sit or walk or exercise. So they are really hopeful of being able to teach me, now that this diabolical mechanism of a harness in which my jaw has been encased for all these days, has, by means of the pressure of weights, gradually been working to bring my misplaced cervicals into alignment. It really is wonderful what they can do with their x-rays and their intravenous dye tests and what not. Anyhow, after having been told for twenty-five years that these intermittent pains in the back are functions of fatigue, I am now assured — and the x-rays seem to prove it — that it is all mechanical, the miserable disharmony of two bones.

I hope to be back in Cohasset by tomorrow, and there will have to undergo some more humorless and unpleasant orthopedic regimentation, but all to the end that I may ultimately continue to have a good time.

2. That Bob got an A with Manuel — or was it A— — delights but doesn't surprise me. I have never had any doubt about Bob's intrinsic stuff. The difficulty, as you well know, has been that he has not been educated in the strict sense of the word — the stuff in him has not been led out of him. Of course he has temperament and all that, which simply means that good teachers can do things with him that bad teachers can't. I am eager to hear what Friedrich gave him.

3. And, of course, we are very glad to have encouraging news about Mrs. B. Give her our best wishes and fondest regards.

4. The New York mayoralty campaign is at once a scream and an interesting mirror of the fluidity of American politics. That the New York *Herald Tribune* and the Communist party should both be supporting the

Little Flower must make the gods on Olympus rock. I thought La Guardia's comment on the declaration by the C.P. was just right.

5. Is it true that Pecora is supporting La Guardia?

6. Did you read the full debate on Black's confirmation in the *Cong. Rec.* for Tuesday, August 17, 1937? Be sure to read Senator Schwellenbach's speech which authoritatively disposes of all the charges of illegality in the seizure of telegrams in Black's conduct of the Lobby investigation. Then there is Borah's statement saying that the Senate knows that Black has several times, long before the present matter came up, denied that he was a member of the Klan. Incidentally, I have seen the private letter from Borah in which he speaks very warmly of Black's character and ability, says he isn't a "yes" man at all, and doesn't share any of the feelings about Black's prosecutorial tendencies. Of all the asinine things that I have seen about the Black appointment, Ozzy Villard in the *Nation* takes the prize. I wish some of my patriotic friends would know a little American history. It would do most lawyers and editors good to read the sewage that was poured on Taney's head when Jackson appointed him. Which doesn't prove that any charges ever made against anybody are unfounded. But it should generate a little humility in assuming that because the good and the great say them they are necessarily so. From this talk about great legal experience and fine judicial qualities one would suppose that McReynolds and Sanford and Sutherland and Butler and Roberts were men of wide culture and juristic detachment when they got on the Supreme Court. The fundamental fact that is too widely forgotten is that the Supreme Court of the United States is, in everything that matters about it, not like unto other courts. If you want proof of this, see the last chapter of my *The Business of the Supreme Court*.

Yours,

F.F.

The medical treatment, painful and irksome, which Frankfurter received for his back effectively removed his sense of recurrent fatigue.

Professor Carl Friedrich is one of the most distinguished professors at Harvard, with exacting standards of research in history and the problems of government.

Instead of being embarrassed by the offer of Communist support, Mayor La Guardia ridiculed it and managed to preserve his own independence untarnished.

The Congressional debate on Senator Hugo Black's nomination to the Supreme Court became a rather pitiless inquiry into his record as a Senate investigator — it was charged that he abused the procedures of due process

— and into his Ku Klux Klan involvement. Frankfurter defended Black with Roosevelt — where it mattered most — and also wrote scores of letters across the country in praise of Black's liberalism.

This is the draft of the Constitution Day speech September 17, 1937, as prepared for President Roosevelt by Felix Frankfurter with some contributions by Thomas Corcoran. The first seven pages, omitted here, are plainly the work of Mr. Corcoran but the rest of the twenty-four-page memorandum, given here, is Frankfurter's work with an occasional flashing phrase contributed by Corcoran. The President followed this draft in abridged form for his Constitution Day speech. More important still, he used Frankfurter's arguments about the place of the Supreme Court in the American system of government in defending his own campaign on this issue. It is therefore a revealing and important document in the entire controversy over the court-packing plan.

The framers of the Constitution were men of destiny. They purposely created a governmental scheme intended for the illimitable future, to be extended over a continent still to be wrested from Nature. Whenever we have applied this statesman's attitude to the language of the Constitution, it has yielded us powers of government adequate to deal successively with the new worlds created by the steamboat, the railroad, the telegraph, the pipeline, the radio and the airplane. But the statesman's spirit has had constantly to beat off the ingenious obstructions of the lawyers who for the purposes of their individual clients from time to time have tried to read into both the affirmative powers and the negative denials of the instrument, limitations and qualifications which the Founding Fathers wisely refused to write into the original instrument.

The history of the last 150 years of the Constitution has been an unending struggle between those who would shrivel the Constitution into a lawyer's document and a lawyer's opportunity for private obstruction, and those true to its conception as a means of founding, maintaining and promoting a great nation in the public good. Lawyers' cries of unconstitutionality are nothing to be alarmed at — they have been the normal accompaniments of every period of growth in our history.

Important lawyers tried to write into the Constitution a provision giving the Supreme Court a lawyer's veto over Acts of Congress. And the Convention overruled them.

Important lawyers insisted that the Constitution itself was unconstitutional under the Articles of Confederation. And the ratifying conventions overruled them.

Important lawyers warned Washington and Hamilton that the protective tariff was unconstitutional — warned Jefferson that the Louisiana Purchase was unconstitutional — warned Monroe that to open roads to the West was unconstitutional. And Congress overruled them.

Important lawyers persuaded a divided Supreme Court that Congress had no power to govern slavery in the territories, that the long-standing Missouri Compromise was unconstitutional. And the nation fought the War between the States to overrule them.

Important lawyers persuaded the Odd Man on the Court that the methods of financing the Civil War were unconstitutional. And a new Odd Man overruled them.

Important lawyers persuaded the Odd Man on the Court that democracy in taxation based on ability to pay, i.e. the commonplace Federal income tax of today, was unconstitutional — as well as Jacobinism and Communism. After twenty years of struggle with a constitutional amendment, the people overruled them. And last year the Supreme Court itself, in effect, decided that its original decision had been wrong and the struggle for the amendment unnecessary.

The great constitutional authority of the United States Senate of his day, Senator Evarts, warned that body that it was unconstitutional to pass the Interstate Commerce Act and establish Federal regulation of railroad rates from the farm to the seaboard. And he turned out to be wrong.

Less than two years ago the fifty highest paid lawyers in the country solemnly agreed that the Wagner Labor Relations Act was unconstitutional, and a few months later, they were wrong.

For twenty years the Supreme Court Odd Man insisted that state minimum wage laws for women were unconstitutional. Six months ago he admitted that for all twenty years he had been wrong.

This constant struggle between the great mass of the plain people of the United States who want national unity and justice against the lawyers who professionally complicate things in the service of those who want neither unity nor justice has not been a struggle in which any political party — mine or any other — has an unblemished record.

But ultimately every effort to read a charter for the unfolding of our national life as if it were the fine type on the back of an insurance policy has failed. When the people and the lawyers have clashed on great questions of national legislative policy, ultimately the people have had their way. When Congress and the Supreme Court have clashed on questions of national legislative policy, Congress has ultimately triumphed. That triumph has come once by war, once by unnecessary resort to an unnecessary process of amendment, and otherwise by reversal of decisions. And tonight on the 150th anniversary of the signing of the Constitution, that triumph is temporarily complete.

But the triumph is never permanently assured. And in these days when the undemocratic concentration of economic power has brought with it a corresponding concentration of legal ability against the democratic purposes of the Constitution, only the utmost vigilance and the utmost willingness to fight for our Constitutional heritage will guarantee its continuance.

Furthermore, a democracy cannot help counting, and seeking ways and means to avoid for the future, the terrible cost at which its ultimate triumphs have had to be achieved. We did not need to have a Civil War to recognize the constitutional power of Congress to levy taxes upon those most able to pay. We did not need twenty years of exploitation of women's labor to recognize the constitutional power of the states to pass minimum wage laws for the protection of women. Those were unwarrantable costs in restoring to the governments of both the nation and the states powers for action which the Constitution itself had not denied them. Nothing that possibly could have been gained by delay can justify such a price. We know that it takes time to adjust government to the needs of society and that deliberation upon the remedy is indispensable to wise reform. We also know that government must keep pace with changes in circumstances substantially as the changes occur. If wise reform is delayed too long, resentments, grievances and injustices accumulate to such a degree that orderly, wise reforms are rendered impossible and unreasonable and forcible measures in one form or another come to prevail. Time is vital in statesmanship, and orderly reforms, too long delayed or denied, have too often in modern history jeopardized peace, undermined democracy, and swept away civil and religious liberties.

These unwarranted delays in the accommodation of the government of today to the needs of today have not been due, I cannot too often repeat, to any language that the Fathers used in the Constitution to bind their successors. I ask you laymen for whom George Washington and Benjamin Franklin spoke at Philadelphia 150 years ago — look into the simply worded Constitution which I hope is in your hands tonight. Read it in the light of our history and in the light of its expressed purpose — to form a more perfect union and provide for the general welfare.

Then see if you can find anything in it which says that the government of the nation cannot help the one-third of its population engaged in national agriculture to stabilize their national market.

See if you can find there anything which says that the government of the nation cannot require a system of pensions for the vast army of railway employees on whose vigilance and well-being rests the safety of everything and everyone moving on the great railway systems.

See if you find anything that says the government of the nation cannot help to reorganize the sick coal industry which operates in so many states of the Union and provides the motive power for national industry and transportation.

See if you can find there anything which forbids the government of the nation to regulate the unholy practices of the great network of public utility holding companies which, admittedly, have proved too powerful for State regulation.

See if you can find there anything which forbids the government of the Nation to apply every resource of science to the development of a great river basin, to improve its water transportation, to end its floods, to conserve its natural resources, to demonstrate the potentialities of electricity, that greatest servant of democracy.

I know and every lawyer knows that you will find nothing in our Constitution which forbids the national government to do any of these things.

They have been forbidden or jeopardized, not because of anything the Constitution says but because men with axes to grind have chosen to put their lawyers' own notions of policy upon the silence or the vagueness of the Constitution. When the framers wanted to be specific, they could be specific. They forbade titles of nobility and attainder of blood, for instance, in no uncertain terms. But when they came to the great areas of governmental action, they used vagueness and silence as conscious instruments for the flexible statesmanship of the future, as they had used explicit denial as a guarantee of the observance of what to them were eternal verities unaffected by time and circumstance.

To a profession trained in the exact use of words, the categories of denial in the Constitution have always been congenial and the broad and purposely vague grants of power to government have always been uncongenial. That is not a criticism of the legal profession, either as men or as citizens. It merely takes note of the fact that professional habits bend their minds in a certain direction. It was a great conservative statesman who noted the dangers that flow from the fact that "the law sharpens the mind by narrowing it."

It is the limited business of most lawyers to protect the interests of the individuals by whom they are retained, not the interests of the larger society of which those individuals are a part. In more recent years, the business of lawyers has become more concerned with corporate interests than with individual interests. Therefore, the preoccupation of the legal mind of today is with these private and corporate interests against all the rest of society.

Furthermore, it is a well-known saying that men are subdued by the medium in which they work. And men whose daily work is the nice use of language in conveyances and contracts and legal instruments of every variety, where the rules of the game provide that nothing is included in the scope of the document unless expressly mentioned, instinctively forget what the statesmen of 150 years ago at Philadelphia and the statesmen of their own profession did not forget — that a Constitution is a great instrument of government — not a conveyance, not a contract, not even a statute. That is why when a great lawyer does triumph over his absorption with words and with the limited outlook of individual interests — when he adds vision to his technical skill, then he is a statesman indeed.

The most important sentence ever written by Chief Justice Marshall is a part of the opinion in which over one hundred years ago that great Chief Justice established the constitutionality of the legislation which saved the banking system of this country in 1933 and insured the safety of your deposits for the future. In that opinion Marshall, who had fought through the Revolutionary War and had experienced all the difficulties of his generation in the founding of a nation, admonished those who would narrowly limit the great document to remember *"that it is a Constitution we are expounding."*

And the modern Marshall — Mr. Justice Holmes — who like Marshall had seen the price paid on the battlefield to establish a nation, elaborated the thought of Marshall in these memorable words: "the provisions of the Constitution are not mathematical formulas having their essence in their form; they are organic living institutions transplanted from English soil. Their significance is vital not formal; it is to be gathered not simply by taking the words and a dictionary, but by considering their origin and the line of their growth." *Gompers* v. *United States,* 233 U.S. 604, 610 (1914).
. . . "When we are dealing with words that also are a constituent act, like the Constitution of the United States, we must realize that they have called into life a being the development of which could not have been foreseen completely by the most gifted of its begetters. It was enough for them to realize or to hope that they had created an organism; it has taken a century and has cost their successors much sweat and blood to prove that they created a nation. The case before us must be considered in the light of our whole experience and not merely in that of what was said a hundred years ago." *Missouri* v. *Holland,* 252 U.S. 416, 433 (1920).

Whether the Constitution is treated primarily as a text for interpretation or as an instrument of government makes all the difference in the world.

In the last 25 years government, State and Federal, has struggled particularly hard to utilize the powers given them under the Constitution to create economic conditions under which the great mass of people would feel convinced of justice and security. Those efforts have included attempts at establishment of minimum wages and maximum hours, prohibition of child labor, encouragement of the unionization of labor, reasonable stabilization of farm and industrial markets, conservation and development of natural resources, regulation of utilities and of other public businesses in private hands. Consistently the lawyers representing those interests wishing to block such efforts have invoked the Bill of Rights to protect their clients. Until last spring, for instance, they had argued successfully that it interferes with the freedom of a charwoman to work if an employer is not permitted to underpay her. And until last spring they had argued successfully that it interferes with the property of an employer to refuse him the right to discriminate against an employee who joins a union, while at the same time large corporations were indulging in espionage to root out union workers, as outrageous in essence as any search and seize prohibited to government.

I have often wondered whether those interested in the realistic protection of the individual and of minorities against intolerance and arbitrary power appreciate the danger to minorities of such perverted applications of great constitutional provisions. For unless government can succeed in creating conditions under which the great mass of people do feel convinced of justice, economic security and ample scope for human dignity, that tolerance of differences and that general concern for fair play which are the real protection of the individual and minorities will disappear. As a practical matter that tolerance and that concern rest only in small part upon legal formulas. Far more importantly they are the natural reflection of magnanimity of spirit in the masses which in turn depends upon generally distributed well-being.

No one cherishes more deeply than I the civil liberties achieved by much blood and anguish through many centuries of Anglo-American history. No one is more zealous that the safeguards they write into the Constitution be scrupulously and undeviatingly observed in spirit as well as in letter not only by government but by all those who wield a private power comparable to that of government.

But we should be deaf to the teachings of history and the admonitions of other lands if we do not recognize that civil liberties and non-discrimination against minorities can long be maintained only in a contented society.

No true student of the agony of our Southern States in the period after the War between the States can overlook the fact that courts discredited by the victorious and callous majority were able to give the South the protection of only paper and sporadic enforcement of the Bill of Rights, while hundreds of injustices which the courts could not reach were daily being done to the Southern people. And not even those of us who are most zealous for the protection of minority rights and most happy at the effectiveness of that protection today can have any illusions that if the economic crisis of '33 had not been surmounted by the responsible use of affirmative powers available to the national government through the Constitution, the practical position of minority groups today would be as unhappy as it is in some other lands.

More and more the guarantees of civil liberties to which minorities have looked in this country for protection available in no other land depend for real effectiveness upon the full usefulness of the affirmative powers given to government to safeguard the life of the nation.

The men who signed the Constitution 150 years ago were fundamentally much more realistic about these things than we are today. . . . To them the protection of civil rights was not a platform for politicians nor a breastwork for corporation lawyers. For those rights these men or their fathers had come to the new country when it was not a comfortable country to come to. And to vindicate those rights these men themselves had written the Declaration of Independence and had fought a war. Freedom of speech, freedom of religion, freedom from unreasonable searches and seizures, and a fair trial for the humblest accused — sacred from attack not simply from tyrannies and oppressions which they had known and experienced but from whatever forms of tyranny and oppression the evil ingenuity of intolerant men might devise — were at the very top of their thoughts.

And yet when in the midst of such economic chaos as we faced in 1933, they came to write the Constitution, their first concern was not with written guarantees of these civil rights but with the formation of a government strong enough to bring economic order and economic security to the land. There was no Bill of Rights at all in the Constitution as it was first signed 150 years ago tonight. The Bill of Rights was added a year later by the first Congress as the first ten amendments.

We profited by the spelling out of those rights which for them were so fundamental as to require no literal spelling out. But it is significant that in their judgment the first thing they felt they needed, to preserve the liberties for which they had fought, was a central government, strong enough to avert economic chaos. They knew that guarantees of tolerance written on parchment were nowhere near as important as guarantees written in the hearts and the character of the American people so long as those hearts and that character were not embittered by economic distress.

Tolerance and concern for fair play are virtues which do not flourish in the stony soil of economic want and social distress. They are flowers that grow only when nurtured by a fertile soil and a warm sun. And none of us to whom the protection of minorities is a daily concern can have any illusions that in a world of aggression and of sudden and imperfectly understood economic disruptions no minority has any assurance of tolerance and fair play unless by the affirmative use of governmental power we succeed in this generation in collaborating with the private processes of economic enterprise so as to enable every class of our society to live at least on a level of civilized decency. Those of us whose circumstances have been cast in fortunate lots are too prone to bear with fortitude the hardships of a goodly portion of our fellow countrymen and women.

There is a group which — either in secret despair that inevitable calamity can be averted or in reckless ignorance of the day-to-day problems of those who are not lost to fear — would deny the government powers it needs to protect us and ask it to make bricks without straw. To such people, misinterpreters of the Constitution seem fortunate allies indeed.

Happily the great mass of the American people have lost neither their courage nor their common sense. And the framers of the Constitution, who had the greatest courage and common sense in history, have left us instruments with which we can use both. Their handiwork did not shackle us. They left us free if we will use all of the Constitution they bequeathed to us. Their legacy was the wisdom which they embodied in the Constitution and that included the opportunity and the right to draw upon such wisdom as each generation can summon to the problems each generation has.

The Bill of Rights is precious to all of us. The reserved powers of the States to deal with matters of purely local concern are also precious. But the great affirmative grants of power to a strong national government democratically responsible to all of the people, is no less precious — for without such a national government, civil liberty and states' rights would have scant chance of survival in the modern world. Let us give our allegiance not to a part but to the whole Constitution. The exercise of the whole Constitution is the real way to guarantee the effectiveness of every part of it.

The perennial conflict of American history and the conflict of today centers around the way you look at the Constitution, whether you look at it through the narrow eyes of the partisan lawyer, whether you invoke the whole of the Constitution or only that part of it which seems to serve the purposes of certain limited interests in the nation which from time to time seek to appropriate the Constitution as their special shelter. This is the controversy that has cut athwart every effort of American society to adjust itself to new circumstances. For this is the question which concerns not the expedience of legislation, not the application of the method of trial and error in solving new difficulties; this is the problem that challenges the power of statesmen to find solutions. It touches the very existence of government. The misinterpretation of the Constitution is a fortress which democracy on the march simply cannot afford to leave untaken on its flank or in its rear.

We shall hold to this true course; we shall be most loyal to our history and most reverent to the framers of the Constitution if we view it as the great interpreters have always viewed it, as Marshall viewed it, as Holmes viewed it.

Thus only will we be true to the avowed purposes of the Constitution itself — "to form a more perfect Union, establish Justice, insure domestic tranquility, provide for the common defence, promote the general Welfare, and secure the Blessings of Liberty to ourselves and our Posterity. . . ."

Telegram to Roosevelt

Cambridge, Mass., September 17, 1937

MY FRIEND FRANK BUXTON, EDITOR BOSTON HERALD, JUST 'PHONED ME AND YOU MUST PROTECT ME IF I QUOTE WHAT HE SAID, "HAVE JUST READ COPY OF PRESIDENT'S SPEECH TONIGHT. OH, IT'S ONE HELLOVAH SPEECH. IT'S ABOUT TOPS. US REPUBLICANS MUST GET RID OF THAT FELLOW IF WE ARE EVER GO-ING TO GET ANYWHERE. REALLY, FELIX, IT'S AN AWFULLY SWELL SPEECH. ABOUT THE BEST EVER AS YOU WILL HEAR BEFORE VERY LONG."

FELIX

Telegram to Roosevelt

Cambridge, Mass., September 17, 1937

BUXTON WAS RIGHT. GRAND AND GRANDLY DELIVERED. AS HOLMES WOULD SAY, THERE WAS THE RIGHT POISON IN IT.

FELIX

Roosevelt had spoken at the battlefield of Antietam on Constitution Day and had observed, with great emphasis, that "the Constitution of the United States was a layman's document, not a lawyer's contract."

Hyde Park, N.Y., September 21, 1937

Dear Felix:

Thanks ever so much for those three messages you sent me. The comment by Frank Buxton is interesting, and of course you know that I am pleased to have your word of approval of the address.

My kindest regards and best wishes to you and Marion.

Always sincerely,
F.D.R.

Taxes and Millionaires

1937

1937

I N his annual message to Congress, on January 6, 1937, Roosevelt had
emphasized that every branch of government, the judicial no less than
the legislative and the executive, "must continue the task of making
democracy succeed."

In the history of the New Deal, 1937 was to be known as the year of
strikes.

There were 4,740 strikes involving 1,860,000 workers, resulting in
28,425,000 man-days of idleness. This was the greatest number of strikes in
the country's history up to this time.

The contrast between workers striking for better wages and working conditions, and the ease with which some millionaires slipped through legal
loopholes to escape their taxes, was always a shameful reality to Roosevelt
and Frankfurter, and sharpened their zeal to close the loopholes.

The White House, January 7, 1937

Dear Felix:

Thank you ever so much for that delightful little book which sits beside my bed. I am glad to have it.

I am glad you liked the speech yesterday — I enjoyed delivering it!

A very happy New Year to you and Marion. I hope to see you soon.

As ever,
F.D.R.

The book was Frankfurter's famous book on The Commerce Clause.

Telegram to Roosevelt

Washington, D.C., January 20, 1937

YOU DID EVER SO MUCH BETTER THAN GOD TODAY. YOUR INAUGURAL HIT ME
WHERE I LIVED. I GO BACK TO COLD BOSTON WITH FAITH, CONFIDENCE AND
HOPES STRENGTHENED.

FELIX

The weather was very bad for the Second Inaugural, which explains the
facetious note at the beginning of the telegram. Frankfurter had come to
Washington for the ceremonies.

In his Inaugural Address, Roosevelt said: "I see one-third of a nation ill-

housed, ill-clad, ill-nourished." He pledged his second Administration to
continued policies of reform and recovery.

The White House, February 16, 1937

Dear Felix: —

A very short and very late note to thank you and Marion for that nice
birthday telegram. I hope to see you both soon.

As ever yours,
F.D.R.

Telegram to Roosevelt

Cambridge, Mass., May 24, 1937

T.R. WOULD HAVE SAID "BULLY" TO YOUR MESSAGE. MAY I? WITH WARM RE-
GARDS.

FELIX FRANKFURTER

Roosevelt had sent a message to Congress recommending legislation on
minimum wages and maximum hours. "A self-supporting and self-respect-
ing democracy," he said, "can plead no justification for the existence of
child labor, no economic reason for chiselling workers' wages or stretching
workers' hours."

To draw a contrast between his campaign for a minimum wage and the
privileged positions of a wealthy minority, Roosevelt so timed matters that
he kept both issues before the country at the same time. Perhaps he was
too clever in his methods, for many business executives felt they were being
condemned by public opinion before they had the chance to defend them-
selves. Roosevelt's message was deliberately sharp and aggressive. He de-
scribed it as a message for the prevention of income-tax evasion. He quoted
Justice Holmes's remark that "taxes are what we pay for civilized society."
Then he added with deliberate and caustic emphasis: "Too many individu-
als, however, want the civilization at a discount." He said the Treasury
Department's study for 1936 revealed efforts at "avoidance and evasion of
tax liability so widespread and so amazing, both in their boldness and their
ingenuity, that further action without delay seems imperative."
He added:

Very definitely, the issue immediately before us is the single one relating
to the evasion or unethical avoidance of existing laws. That should be kept
clearly in mind by the Congress and the public. Already efforts to befog this
issue appear. Already certain newspaper publishers are seeking to make it
appear — first, that if an individual can devise unanticipated methods to
avoid taxes which the Congress intended him to pay, he is doing nothing

unpatriotic or unethical; and, second, that because certain individuals do not approve of high income tax brackets, or the undistributed earnings tax, or the capital gains tax, the first duty of the Congress should be the repeal or reduction of those taxes. In other words, not one but many red herrings are in preparation.

But it seems to me that the first duty of the Congress is to empower the Government to stop these evil practices, and that legislation to this end should not be confused with legislation to revise tax schedules. That is a wholly different subject.

In regard to that subject, I have already suggested to the Congress that at this session there should be no new taxes and no changes of rates. And I have indicated to the Congress that the Treasury will be prepared by next November to present to the appropriate committees information on the basis of which the Congress may, if it chooses, undertake revisions of the tax structure.

The long-term problem of tax policy is wholly separate from the immediate problem of glaring evasion and avoidance of existing law.

In this immediate problem the decency of American morals is involved.

The example of successful tax dodging by a minority of very rich individuals breeds efforts by other people to dodge other laws as well as tax laws.

It is also a matter of deep regret to know that lawyers of high standing at the bar not only have advised and are advising their clients to utilize tax avoidance devices, but are actively using these devices in their own personal affairs. We hear too often from lawyers, as well as from their clients, the sentiment, "It is all right to do it if you can get away with it."

I am confident that the Congress will wish to enact legislation at this session specifically and exclusively aimed at making the present tax structure evasion-proof.

I am confident also that the Congress will give to the Treasury all authority necessary to expand and complete the present preliminary investigation, including, of course, full authority to summon witnesses and compel their testimony. The ramifications and the geographical scope of a complete investigation make it necessary to utilize every power of government which can contribute to the end desired.

Roosevelt emphasized the "ethics" which inspired his message. His opponents called it "revenge." Nothing did more than this tax message to widen the gulf, at this time, between Roosevelt and the business community. He found it harder, because of this controversy, to have effective public support for new initiatives in foreign policy; and business leaders said Roosevelt was attacking the Supreme Court because it refused to accept the President's "arbitrary proposals" without full examination. But Frankfurter

*was with Roosevelt all the way. In fact, he had been advising the President
to adopt such measures almost from the day he first entered the White
House. Once more J. P. Morgan became the symbol of the "business conscience" Frankfurter so deeply abhorred.*

Cambridge, Mass., June 3, 1937

Dear Frank:

How could anyone not morally obtuse fail to read your account of the
shabby devices for getting civilization at a discount without a feeling of
deep indignation? To forecast the future is a rather irresponsible sport, but
I should lay the heaviest kind of odds that your tax message of Tuesday will
find a place fifty years, and a hundred years after that, in even the slender-
est volume of American state papers. How can they behave that way? And
these be the "leaders" of finance and industry, and, to our shame, even
"leaders" of the profession in whose special keeping is the law. With all the
unedifying aspects of a social caste system, the English aristocracy are in the
main at least under the sway of *noblesse oblige*. While our "economic roy-
alists," and their auxiliaries, haven't even the morality of prudence — the
prudence of not undermining the very system to which they profess devotion.

I can't help recalling a story of T. R. Powell's. He found himself with a
bunch of important financial and legal people who were ranting about my
alleged radicalism until his patience gave way, and then Powell said, "Felix
a radical? Hell!! The damn fool is wearing out his heart trying to make
capitalism live up to its pretensions."

And the pathos of it all is that it is the same old story — their lack of
enlightened self-interest. Of course their response to T.R.'s efforts to prune
away the excrescences and abuses of our economic society are fresh in your
mind, but it is funny to go back, as I have done recently, and re-read the
ferocity of the terms in which T.R. was assailed for such rudimentary reforms as the *Hepburn Act*, the *Pure Food and Drugs Act*, and his proposal
for an inheritance tax. "They know not what they do." And so, I look
forward to the investigation which you proposed as another indispensable
process of national education.

F.F.

*Roosevelt asked for a memorandum to be prepared by his staff giving the
details of the opposition to President Theodore Roosevelt's reforms.*

Cambridge, Mass., June 8, 1937

Dear Frank:

This is a belated word of warm appreciation for your Conservation
message. T.R. more than thirty years ago stirred even my understanding (I,

who don't know what "winter wheat" is! so you say!!) of the fundamental
significance of the soil, and you have now given classic expression to the
many phases of the organic problem by pointing out that "prudent husbandry of our vital estate requires far-sighted management." It was a beautiful piece of exposition — for it so admirably related the aspects of nature
to the needs and duties of man.

What a temper of mind J. P. Morgan revealed in this morning's press.
I nearly exploded — so I had to write this mild letter to Charlie Burlingham. I thought I'd touch one or two tenderspots of CCB.

Keep on keeping very fit,

Ever yours,
F.F.

Cambridge, Mass., June 8, 1937

Dear C.C.:

Evidently J. P. Morgan confounds Christianity with the ethic of "getting away with it." Before he again gives his moral sanction to the incorporation of a yacht, as a means of "avoiding" taxes, some one should suggest
to him that he ask his good friend, the Archbishop of Canterbury, or his
other good friend, the late Prime Minister, Lord Baldwin, whether an English gentleman would think of doing such a thing, or, having done it, continue to enjoy the esteem of his class. And while he is about it, he might ask
some of his eminent legal friends in England how long such decisions in tax
cases, as that in the *Stock Dividend Case* and *Heiner v. Donnan,* and
others which the Supreme Court rested on the Constitution, would survive
in England.

The mentality revealed by Morgan furnishes a striking commentary on
the claims of Walter Lippmann that F.D.R.'s tax message was merely
wealth-baiting. When the most esteemed of financiers discloses such a morally obtuse, anti-social attitude, one realises anew that the real enemy of
capitalism is not Communism but capitalists and their retinue of scribes
and lawyers.

Ever yours,
F.F.

*The "little Steel Strike" had broken out on May 26. Alarmed by the
violence which marked successive strikes, Frankfurter, while visiting the
White House, had learned that the President shared this concern. He sent
Roosevelt, on June 23, a detailed technical memorandum, omitted here, on
the law of peaceful picketing and on the scope of collective bargaining,
with the obligations imposed on the employer no less than the worker.*

Paul van Zeeland, the Belgian statesman, was a most useful influence in world affairs at this time, particularly in matters affecting the liberalization of trade.

The White House, June 25, 1937

Dear Felix:

I have not time for more than to dictate this brief note before I leave for three days at Jefferson Island. It is good to have yours of June twenty-third.

Things are all right except for the strike situation. That is a real headache.

Van Zeeland is a grand fellow — wish you knew him.

What about your plans for the summer?

As ever yours,
F.D.R.

Telegram to White House

Hyde Park, N.Y., August 27, 1937

HAVE BOX OF FLOWERS SENT TO FELIX FRANKFURTER, BETH ISRAEL HOSPITAL BOSTON MASS., WITH PRESIDENT'S CARD.

M.H.M.

This telegram is from Marven McIntyre, the President's assistant. The next letter explains why Frankfurter was in the hospital. Tom Corcoran was also in the hospital, and he had told the President about Frankfurter's troubles.

Boston, Mass., September 1, 1937

Dear Mr. President:

How characteristic of you to cheer me in my imprisonment in this very pleasant hospital — in so far as any hospital can be pleasant — by the warm color and fragrance of your roses. Tommy shouldn't have "spilled" — but that is the only time he does "spill," when his warm heart sees a chance for kindness and a new proof of devotion. Your roses gave me really very great delight, and, while they were still fresh, I did with them what I know you would want me to do. I extended their power for delight by sharing them with the children's ward of the hospital. My deep thanks to you.

Isn't it fun to be told at my age that for decades I've been sitting and walking wrongly. And so the fifth and sixth cervicals have been getting out of the happy harmony that nature intended for them and pressing inhumanly upon the nerve which passes through them, with the result that that nerve has been hollering like fury down the line. And so for days and days I've been lying here flat, with my jaw in a harness to enable weights to pull the cervicals back into alignment. That's one way of getting a fellow's mouth shut, isn't it?

This accounts for my delay in responding to your kind invitation to have Marion and me come to Hyde Park. Of course we want to do so very much, but this business of mine will have to put it off for a little while. I expect to be back in Cohasset in a day or two to be subjected to some more orthopedic cruelties. And so, perhaps, you will let me write you later when we shall be free to come, subject, of course, to your pleasure.

As a matter of fact, for three days I have been having a perfectly swell time here with Tommy across the hall. It was a good chance for him to undergo his long-postponed thorough examination. Like most people with terrific vitality, he has been operating on the assumption that the laws of physiology don't apply to him. But he has got his marching orders now, and, if he obeys them, they won't curb exuberance of mind and spirit at all, but will enable him to avoid future troubles. I don't know what the hospital authorities think of us, but Marion and Tom and I turned my room for three days into an uncommonly gay gathering place.

I am terribly glad to read that you are going off to fish and to watch the races, for I know how greatly relaxing these diversions are for you. For there are days ahead that will make demands even upon your vitality.

With warmest regards, in which Marion joins,

Faithfully yours,
F.F.

On October 5, in what might otherwise have been a routine ceremony dedicating a bridge across the Chicago River, Roosevelt spoke of a "quarantine" of aggressor nations. He closed his speech with words often quoted over the next few years: "America hates war. America hopes for peace. Therefore America actively engages in the search for peace." On October 12 Roosevelt issued a proclamation calling Congress into Special Session on October 15. The evening of the same day Roosevelt gave a fireside chat.

Telegram to Roosevelt

Boston, Mass., October 12, 1937

YOU COULD NOT HAVE TAKEN THE COUNTRY TO SCHOOL BETTER. JUST RIGHT IN DIRECTION AND DETAIL. VERY SATISFYING. AFFECTIONATELY.

FELIX

Hyde Park, N.Y., October 15, 1937

Dear Felix:

Thank you ever so much for that grand message. I am so glad you liked the speech and do appreciate the nice things you say.

My best wishes to you.

Very sincerely yours,
FRANKLIN D. ROOSEVELT

Telegram to Mr. and Mrs. Frankfurter

Hyde Park, N.Y., October 26, 1937

THE PRESIDENT HOPES YOU BOTH CAN SPEND THURSDAY NIGHT HYDE PARK, AR-
RIVING THAT AFTERNOON ABOUT TWO-THIRTY.

MISSY

Cambridge, Mass., October 31, 1937

Dear Mr. President:

1. Ben Cohen and I have been working on the three phases of tax legislation about which you and I talked, and I enclose the results of our labors. These are three memoranda dealing with proposals regarding (1) relief from the undivided profits tax through the exemption of stock dividends and the necessary subjection of such dividends to taxation in the hands of the stockholder; (2) restriction of tax-exempt abuses by (a) imposing surtax upon non-exempt income with due regard to total income, and (b) declaration of policy by Congress for reciprocal non-discriminatory taxation by state and nation of income from governmental obligations hereafter to be issued; (3) modification of capital gains tax to encourage (a) building construction and (b) other productive enterprises.

The memoranda speak for themselves, and, to make the proposals concrete, draft provisions embodying them are annexed. I need hardly say that, in view of the terrific pressure under which we worked, these are, in the truest sense of the word, really drafts, and, particularly with reference to the capital gains problems, they are of the most tentative nature — merely something for your critical eye. In addition to the proposal to modify the capital gain tax, so as to encourage housing, you will find an enlargement of the general idea so as to cover productive enterprise generally. I am venturing to put this to you because there may be the germ of a real idea there, though I need hardly add that, in opening this door to a modification of the capital gain tax, we must be on our guard lest the whole army of greed try to push through.

2. You were good enough to ask me to submit drafts on two other topics that we discussed — (1) the actual gains in recovery as a way of

easing into the ground that still must be won, and (2) what broadly may be called the monopoly problem, so as to put to the country your sympathetic realization of the economic consequences of the results of the Sherman Law to date, as reflected in the high cost of living and in the curtailment of competitive opportunities. I understood that the tax matters were the more exigent, and so Ben and I concentrated on those. The drafts on these two other topics will come to you in due time.

Ever faithfully yours,
F.F.

Frankfurter Memorandum on Tax Policy

A government can no more function without taxes than a business without profits. The Government cannot perform the duties with which the American people have charged it with less revenues than it now obtains. We cannot be reminded too often that taxes are the price we pay for civilized society.

The American people rightly do not heed irresponsible complaints about taxes from those who are unprepared to show in a very concrete way how we can raise more equitably and more productively the revenues which we must have. Mere imperfections in the working of fundamentally equitable tax laws should not be seized upon to discredit the principles of such laws. Such imperfections where they exist can and should be rectified.

UNDISTRIBUTED PROFITS TAX

There have been complaints against the undistributed profits tax. Like all sound principles of taxation, the undistributed profits tax should, of course, accommodate itself from time to time to the lessons of practical experience. Whatever difficulties or disharmonies may have revealed themselves in the working of this tax should, of course, be adjusted. One of the greatest of English statesmen once said that the wit of men has not yet devised a tax which will be popular with those who must pay it. And so we must not allow any imperfection in the undistributed profits tax to serve as an excuse for scuttling the first serious efforts of the American people to make the graduated individual income tax applicable to the undistributed income accruing to individuals of great wealth through corporate enterprises and investments.

Until the enactment of the tax on undistributed corporate profits, the equitable purposes of the graduated income tax systems were in large measure defeated. Persons of great wealth could readily avoid the individual surtaxes by the accumulation of corporate profits in corporate enterprises. So long as undistributed corporate profits were subject only to the normal corporate income tax, not only did men and women whose income came

from their wealth, as distinguished from their services, escape the incidence
of surtaxes on individual incomes, but corporations were encouraged to accumulate surpluses far beyond their economic needs. The evils of concentrated economic power were accentuated, and the growth of giant holding
companies controlling an ever greater proportion of business enterprise was
encouraged.

The tax on undistributed corporate profits was designed to encourage
the distribution of such profits so that they would be taxable as part of the
stockholder's individual income. It was not the purpose of the tax to impose burdens upon corporate enterprise, but to prevent the stockholder
from using the corporate form to avoid the individual income tax.

The undistributed corporate profits tax has been criticised on the
ground that it prevents corporate enterprise from accumulating funds for
legitimate expansion or for reserves against adversity. Such criticism usually
ignores the fact that the law does not require distribution of profit in cash,
but recognizes distributions not only of property but of a corporation's own
obligations or securities, provided only that the distributions be in such
form as to be taxable in the hands of the stockholder. For example, a corporation may distribute its profits and be free of the tax on undistributed
profits by declaring a dividend to its common stockholders in the form of
long-term bonds or preferred stock. The only reason that a dividend in
common stock to the common stockholders has not served the same purpose is the decision of the Supreme Court in *Eisner* v. *Macomber*.

But it is true that a common stock dividend may be the most appropriate and the most convenient form for the distribution of corporate profits
to take and that the decision in *Eisner* v. *Macomber* has caused unnecessary
difficulty for a number of corporate enterprises. If a corporation is to be
allowed to satisfy the purposes of the undistributed profits tax by making
other than cash distributions, there is serious objection to compelling a
corporation to increase the amount of its senior securities when a common
stock dividend might be more advantageous to its credit and would not
complicate its corporate structure. Government tax policy ought to encourage the simplest form of corporate structure. But obviously common stock
dividends cannot be recognized as a distribution of profits under the undistributed profits tax, unless such common stock dividends are taxable in the
hands of the stockholders.

It is important, therefore, from the point of view of wise tax and corporate policy that common stock dividends should be taxable in the hands
of the stockholders.

Thus far, however, uncritical submission to the decision of *Eisner* v.
Macomber has prevented recognition of this wise tax and corporate policy.
But *Eisner* v. *Macomber* was decided more than eighteen years ago by a

bare majority of the Court before the principles of the graduated income tax and their effect upon corporate enterprise were adequately understood. The case was decided over the vigorous protests of a distinguished minority, including Mr. Justice Holmes, as well as Mr. Justice Brandeis, who today is recognized as the great judicial authority on economic and financial matters. Nor has the Court itself treated *Eisner* v. *Macomber* as though it embodied a salutary principle. The decision is difficult to reconcile with many of the Court's later adjudications. Legitimate corporate enterprise and a wise revenue system alike require a frank reconsideration of *Eisner* v. *Macomber* in the light of what the Chief Justice has recently called "supervening economic conditions." The annexed amendment to the Revenue Act of 1936 (Appendix I) is a way of effectuating such reconsideration.

Appendix I is omitted here.

TAX-EXEMPTS

In earlier days, when conditions were much simpler and the tax load much lighter, and before the income tax was universally recognized as the most just means for distributing the costs of government, it was a common practice for government to issue its own obligations freed from the burden of taxation. It was in the mental climate of these earlier days that there grew up the rather uncritical assumption, translated into Court decisions, that our federal system of government impliedly required, though the Constitution did not say so, a reciprocal immunity from taxation on the income of obligations issued by the Federal and State governments respectively. The increasing amount of wealth that has been withdrawn from the taxing power of the nation and the states and the dislocation that this has wrought to public finance, as well as the unfair consequences of these immunities when judged by present standards of social justice, have led our statesmen and economists with practical unanimity to insist on the necessity of calling a halt to a practice no longer justified either by economics or good morals. For more than twenty years an unbroken line of Secretaries of the Treasury has reported to the Congress the growing evils of tax-exempt securities.

But giving the fullest legal status to outstanding tax-exempt securities, neither law nor economics nor morality can possibly justify ignoring, as our present Revenue Acts do, the existence of income free from tax-exempt securities in fixing the rate of the surtax on all additional income.

Take a concrete illustration: Smith and Jones each has an annual income of $100,000. Smith has $50,000 income from corporate dividends; Jones has $50,000 income derived from tax-exempt securities. In addition each of them as a corporate executive receives a salary of $50,000. Smith must pay not only normal surtaxes on the $50,000 he receives from corporate dividends, but surtaxes on his corporate salary at the rates applicable to incomes between fifty and one hundred thousand dollars. Jones pays no tax on the $50,000 income derived from tax-exempt securities and pays a surtax on his $50,000, not at the rates applicable to incomes between fifty and one hundred thousand but at the rates applicable to incomes which do not exceed $50,000. In other words, in taxing the income of a taxpayer over and above his income from tax exempt securities, the present law assumes not only that income from tax-exempt securities is not taxable, but that such income does not exist. I wholly adopt the views expressed by Senator Glass in his report as Secretary of the Treasury for 1919:

> It is intolerable that taxpayers have been allowed, by purchase of exempt securities, not only to obtain exemption with respect to the income derived therefrom, but to reduce the supertaxes upon their other income, and to have the supertaxes upon their other income determined upon the assumption, contrary to fact, that they are not in possession of income derived from state and municipal bonds.

There cannot be any constitutional difficulties in a matter so clear in reason and ethics.

We ought not, however, to rest content merely with subjecting to the surtaxes wealth which now enjoys a wholly unjustifiable immunity. We ought now to make a declaration of policy whereby the unwarrantable shelter, which tax-exempts now afford a large proportion of the wealth of the country, shall cease. This is the more necessary because the approved efforts of the Government to stop the inequalities of our present tax burdens by plugging up the holes in our graduated income tax system may be self-defeating through the increasing flight of taxable income into tax-exempts.

We do not have to wait upon the realization of the cumbersome and doubtful remedy usually proposed for this evil, namely, a constitutional amendment. The present unfortunate situation is the product of adjudication and adjudication can undo its mischief. For we must remember that the immunity from state taxation enjoyed by federal obligations and the reciprocal immunity from federal taxation enjoyed by state and municipal obligations are not requirements of the Constitution, but are merely the creations of Supreme Court decisions. More than one hundred years ago doubts and difficulties attending these absolute immunities were expressed by members of the Court, and in recent years the underlying assumptions of the doctrine have been impressively questioned by some of the most eminent of the Justices. The doctrine was originally evolved out of a totally different set of economic circumstances than those which are now dominant. It is a familiar principle of law that rules of law lose their binding force when the reasons which gave rise to the rules no longer exist.

Inasmuch as the Court's doctrine is avowedly an expression of policy, the Congress itself should define the scope and limits of this policy. The Court undoubtedly would be guided by Congressional formulation of fiscal policy which protects all existing individual rights and adequately safeguards the sovereign interests both of the nation and of the states against discriminatory taxation one by the other.

I, therefore, suggest that the Congress should authorize the states to tax income from future federal obligations, so long as there is no discrimination against the federal borrowing power, and that, by the same token, the federal government should assume authority to tax without discrimination income from state and municipal obligations.

The annexed draft (Appendix II) indicates ways for effectuating these recommendations [here omitted].

CAPITAL GAINS TAX

Attacks have also been levelled against the capital gains tax. There are those who apparently believe that it is equitable to apply surtaxes to large income from professional services and to large income from dividends when they happen to be paid in cash, but that the surtax should not be imposed upon speculative gains realized from the sale of securities, real estate or other capital assets.

On the whole there is no tax which can so readily and equitably be borne as the capital gains tax. It is difficult to justify surtaxes on large incomes received for personal services if we are not to tax large gains realized upon the sale of stock and other investments. A removal of substantial modification of the capital gains whereby speculation for a market rise would be encouraged rather than investment for the prospect of increased income has little to commend it on the score of sound public finance and healthy development of productive enterprise.

There is, however, urgent need for encouraging investment in housing. This is so in order to avert a possible housing shortage in the near future, as well as to further our campaign against unemployment. Without running the risks of encouraging speculation generally, we might well consider the exemption from the capital gains tax of any investment actually made to construct new dwelling houses and apartments. Such investment at this time should encourage the revival of the building industry and may well help to retard the excesses of a building boom some years hence.

It is also urged that the capital gains tax has in some instances deterred business men from selling their interests in established businesses in order to risk some of their profits in new enterprises. It is claimed that it is much more difficult to obtain money for new enterprises than it used to be. I am not at all persuaded by these claims, and Mr. Justice Brandeis in his book, *Other People's Money*, showed that new enterprises have never found it very easy to obtain money through ordinary investment banking channels. But about these matters we ought not to be dogmatic. In so far as we can make financing easier for new productive enterprises we might experiment with some relaxation in the capital gains tax. While there are serious objections to the adoption of a tax policy which would encourage constant shifting of investments for trading profits, a proposal to permit persons of means who can afford to take risks to shift funds, free of the capital gains tax, from investments which have succeeded and become seasoned into new enterprises deserves exploration.

The annexed amendment to the Revenue Act of 1936 (Appendix III) is a way of effectuating these proposals [*here omitted*].

This Tax Message was prepared by Frankfurter at the President's request in cooperation with officials of the Treasury. Frankfurter's memorandum became the basis for the final Treasury Draft of the President's Statement.

I.

As the fiscal year draws to its close it becomes our duty to consider the broad question of tax methods and policies. I wish to acknowledge the timely efforts of the Congress to lay the basis through its committees for administrative improvements by careful study of the revenue systems of our own and of other countries. These studies have made it very clear that we need to simplify and clarify our revenue laws.

The Joint Legislative Committee, established by the Revenue Act of 1926, has been particularly helpful to the Treasury Department. The members of that Committee have generously consulted with administrative officials, not only on broad questions of policy but on important and difficult tax cases.

On the basis of these studies and of other studies conducted by officials of the Treasury, I am able to make a number of suggestions of important changes in our policy of taxation. These are based on the broad principle that if a government is to be prudent its taxes must produce ample revenues without discouraging enterprise and if it is to be just, it must distribute the burden of these taxes equitably. I do not believe that our present system of taxation completely meets this test. Our revenue laws have operated in many ways to the unfair advantage of the few and they have done little to prevent an unjust concentration of wealth and economic power.

With the enactment of the Income Tax Law of 1913 the Federal Government began to apply effectively the widely accepted principle that taxes should be levied in proportion to ability to pay and in proportion to the benefits received. Income was wisely used as the measure of benefits and of ability to pay. This was and still is a wholesome guide for national policy. It should be retained as the governing principle of federal taxation. The use of other forms of taxes is often justifiable, particularly for temporary periods; but taxation according to income is the most effective instrument yet devised to obtain a just contribution from those best able to bear it and to avoid placing onerous burdens upon the mass of our people.

The movement towards progressive taxation of wealth and of income has accompanied the growing diversification and interrelation of effort which mark our industrial society. Wealth in the modern world does not come merely from individual effort; it results from a combination of individual effort and of the manifold uses to which the community puts that effort. The individual does not create the product of his industry with his own hands; he utilizes the many processes and forces of mass production to meet the demands of a national and international market. Therefore, in spite of the great importance in our national life of the efforts and ingenuity of unusual individuals, the people in the mass have inevitably helped to make large fortunes possible. Without mass cooperation great accumulations of wealth would be impossible save by unhealthy speculation. As Andrew Carnegie put it, "Where wealth accrues honorably, the people are always silent partners." Whether it be wealth achieved through the cooperation of the entire community or riches gained by speculation — in either case the ownership of such wealth or riches represents a great public interest and a great ability to pay.

My first proposal, in line with this broad policy, has to do with inheritances and gifts. The transmission from generation to generation of vast fortunes by will, inheritance, or gift is not consistent with the ideals and sentiments of the American people.

The desire to provide security for one's self and one's family is natural and wholesome but it is adequately served by a reasonable inheritance. Great accumulations of wealth cannot be justified on the basis of personal and family security. In the last analysis such accumulations amount to the perpetuation of great and undesirable concentration of control in a relatively few individuals over the employment and welfare of many others. Such inherited economic power is as inconsistent with the ideals of this generation as inherited political power was inconsistent with the ideals of the generation which established our government.

Creative enterprise is not stimulated by vast inheritances. They bless neither those who bequeath nor those who receive. As long ago as 1907, in a message to Congress, President Theodore Roosevelt urged this wise social policy:

A heavy progressive tax upon a very large fortune is in no way such a tax upon thrift or industry as a like tax would be on a small fortune. No advantage comes either to the country as a whole or to the individuals inheriting the money by permitting the transmission in their entirety of the enormous fortunes which would be affected by such a tax; and as an incident to its function of revenue raising, such a tax would help to preserve a measurable equality of opportunity for the people of the generations growing to manhood.

A tax upon inherited economic power is a tax upon static wealth, not upon that dynamic wealth which makes for the healthy diffusion of economic good. Those who argue for the benefits secured to society by great fortunes invested in great businesses should note that such a tax does not affect the essential benefits that remain after the death of the creator of such a business. The mechanism of production that he created remains. The benefits of corporate organization remain. The advantage of pooling many investments in one enterprise remains. Governmental privileges such as patents remain. All that is gone is the initiative, energy and genius of the creator — and death has taken them.

I recommend, therefore, that in addition to the present estate taxes, there should be levied on inheritance, succession, and legacy a tax in respect to all very large amounts received by any one legatee or beneficiary; and to prevent, so far as possible, evasions of this tax, I recommend further the imposition of gift taxes suited to this end.

Because of the basis on which this proposed tax is to be levied and also because of the very sound public policy of encouraging a wider distribution of wealth, I strongly urge that the proceeds of this tax should be specifically segregated and applied, as they accrue, to the reduction of the national debt. By so doing, we shall progressively lighten the tax burden of the average tax payer.

II.

The disturbing effects upon our national life that come from great inheritances of wealth and power can in the future be reduced, not only through the method I have just described, but through a definite increase in the taxes now levied upon very great individual net incomes.

To illustrate: The application of the principle of a graduated tax has always stopped at $1,000,000 of annual income. In other words, while the rate for a man with a $6,000 income is double the rate for one with a $4,000 income, a man having a $10,000,000 annual income pays at the same rate as one whose income is $1,000,000.

Social unrest and a deepening sense of unfairness are dangers to our national life which we must minimize by rigorous methods. When such unrest is justified by a generally recognized fact that such great incomes come not only as the result of the efforts or ability of those who receive them, but because of the opportunities in the creation of which advantages created by government play no small part, the duty rests upon the government to restrict such incomes by very high taxes.

III.

In the modern world scientific invention and mass production have brought many things within the reach of the average man which in an earlier age were available to few. With large scale enterprise has come the large corporation drawing its resources from a widely diversified and numerous group of investors. And the community has profited when large scale production has resulted in substantial economics and lower prices.

The advantages and the protections conferred upon corporations by government increase in value as the size of the corporation increases. Some of these advantages are granted by the State which conferred a charter upon the corporation, others are granted by other States which, as a matter of grace, allow the corporation to do local business within their borders. But perhaps the most important advantages, such as the carrying on of business between two or more States are derived through the Federal Government. Great corporations are protected in a considerable measure from the taxing power and the regulatory power of the States by virtue of the interstate character of their businesses. As the returns to such a corporation increase, so the value of its advantages and protections likewise increases.

Furthermore, the drain of a depression upon the reserves of business puts a disproportionate strain upon the modestly capitalized small enterprise. Without such small enterprises our competitive economic society would cease. Size begets monopoly. Moreover, in the aggregate these little businesses furnish the indispensable local basis for those nation-wide markets which alone can ensure the success of our mass production industries. Today our smaller corporations are fighting not only for their own local wellbeing but for that fairly distributed national prosperity which makes large-scale enterprise possible. It seems only equitable, therefore, to adjust our tax system in accordance with economic capacities and advantages. The smaller corporations should not carry burdens beyond their powers; the vast concentrations of capital should be ready to carry burdens commensurate with their powers and their advantages.

We have established the principle of graduated taxation in respect to personal income, gifts and estates. We should apply the same principle to corporations. Today the smallest corporation pays the same rate on its net profits as the corporation which is a thousand times its size.

I, therefore, recommend, for the consideration of the Congress the substitution of a corporation income tax graduated according to the size of corporation income in place of the present uniform corporation income tax of 13¾ per cent. The rate for smaller corporations might well be reduced to 10¾ per cent, and the rates graduated upward to a rate of 16¾ per cent on net income, in the case of the largest corporations.

In addition to these three specific recommendations of changes in our national tax policies, I commend to your study and consideration a number of others. Ultimately we should seek through taxation the simplification of our corporate structures through the elimination of unnecessary holding companies in all lines of business. We should likewise discourage unwieldy and unnecessary corporate surpluses. These complicated and difficult questions cannot adequately be debated in the time remaining in the present session of this Congress.

I renew, however, at this time the recommendations made by my predecessors for the submission and ratification of a Constitutional Amendment whereby the Federal Government will be permitted to tax the income on subsequently issued state and local securities and likewise for the taxation by state and local governments of future issues of Federal securities.

In my Budget Message of January seventh I recommended that the Congress extend the miscellaneous Internal Revenue taxes which are about to expire and also to maintain the current rates of those taxes which, under the present law, would be reduced. I said then that I considered such taxes necessary to the financing of the Budget for 1936. I am gratified that the Congress is taking action on this recommendation.

Frankfurter Memorandum for the President
Cambridge, Mass., November 10, 1937

At Hyde Park you asked me to consider the comparative wisdom of giving your forthcoming message to Congress in person or by writing. Offhand I ventured the opinion that it depended on the kind of message. You were good enough to ask me to think over the question, and since my visit, it has been much on my mind. I am still of the opinion that it depends on the nature of the message; but I am now clear that the temper of the public mind makes it most desirable that it should be the kind of a message that you ought to deliver orally.

Whenever, since March 4, 1933, the public mind has been confused, you alone had the power to give it composure and coherence. We are again in one of those phases where the so-called leaders of business and finance, with their journalistic and legalistic echoes, are trying to infect the general public with their own panicky and short-sighted disquietude. As in the past, the great body of the nation will be ready for reassurance from you by making them realize the hopeful directions which you are pursuing as well as the difficulties that confront us. The people don't expect you to pull rabbits out of your hat. To say the kind of homely things that you said on your western trip, but to the whole nation and in the perspective of the best estimate of the present situation, would, I am sure, again stiffen the muscles of hope and confidence of the millions of men and women on farm and in factory, in little shops and in mines throughout the land. They would again hear, as they were so glad to hear in the past, at firsthand and from your own lips, that *you* are not panicky, that you know better than any of the croakers that there are difficulties and what they are, that nobody is more concerned to do what can be done towards remedying difficulties, that you have a well-defined direction toward objectives to which you will adhere because they are the objectives of national well-being, but that you are open-minded in pursuing these objectives by whatever methods carry the greatest promise for realizing them. It would do no harm to indicate that you have sought to avail yourself of all the wisdom in the minds of industrial and financial leaders and economists, but that anybody who implies that there are nice, sure-fire little answers to these terrifically difficult problems — or that any slogans like "individualism," "collectivism," "confidence," etc., etc., will solve problems that baffle the wit of statesmanship in the Western world — is simply seeking to play with the lives of men and women whose only ultimate security is a society of good-will and devoted effort, for which the cordial and confident cooperation between the people and its government is indispensable.

I say all this because I feel very strongly that our business and financial leaders are again showing that they do not know even their own self-interest, and that they are trying to create a negative and poisonous public atmosphere. Therefore, it becomes essential for you to fill the atmosphere, through the air, with your own robust energy and good sense and contagious confidence in the working out of our difficulties through sensible effort in the general direction in which you have been going.

Cambridge, Mass., November 15, 1937

Dear Missy,

In a day or so, some cheese will come to you — brandied cheddar — which, if you will find it as probably pleasing to the President's taste as I did, please see to it that he is allowed to have it!! Don't have it cut up as though it were avocado.

My fondest regards to you,

Most cordially,
F.F.

The White House, November 17, 1937

Dear F.F.: —

The cheese has just arrived and is delicious. We were terribly suspicious when we saw "Harvard Club, Boston" and found food inside, but we all took a chance! The President asks me to thank you ever so much for your thought of him.

My best to you and Mrs. Frankfurter.

Always sincerely,
M. A. LeHand

Telegram to Roosevelt

Cambridge, Mass., Thanksgiving Day, 1937

THIS IS JUST TO TELL YOU THAT WE HAD A NEW DEAL THANKSGIVING DINNER AND GAILY DRANK YOUR HEALTH. WITH EVERY GOOD WISH FOR THE DAY AND ALL THE DAYS BEYOND. AFFECTIONATELY.

Marion and Felix

Cambridge, Mass., December 14, 1937

Dear Frank:

1. It was a great relief to me to hear from so shrewd an observer as my friend, Larry Winship, of the Boston *Globe*, that you appeared so fit at the Gridiron dinner. Frankly, I have been really troubled because the wisest medical man I know, Dr. Alfred E. Cohn, told me that the kind of a tooth infection that you have had that touches the bone is nothing to trifle with. And so your buoyancy and force at the Gridiron were greatly reassuring. You would need all the reserves of strength and freshness if these were ordinary days, and, what with things popping all over the world, I should suppose the job is not less exacting than it was in the early days of '33. So intermit, for a little while, holding the hands of too many people, and just remember that there are laws of physiology which are much more authoritative than the law of the Supreme Court.

2. Under separate cover I am sending you a book which, if you have not yet read it, may delight and even excite you. It is Borgese's *Goliath*. The author is one of the few gifts which Mussolini has made to us for which I am grateful. Borgese is one of those old-fashioned, capacious, versatile, continental fellows in the tradition of Goethe — at once critic, novelist, poet, historian and marvelous talker. I suppose, Croce apart, Borgese is the most gifted Italian intellectual. He refused to take the Fascist oath, resigned his professorship in Italy, and is one of those men who, like the precursors in 1848, will greatly add to the cultural heritage of this country. He is now a professor at the University of Chicago, and, if you will only

sniff at his book, you will agree that it is an extraordinary achievement for a man whose first book in the English language it is.

3. I've been having a little fun at sundry parties in reading some of the things that were said about President Roosevelt just thirty years ago. I know this is an old game, but I do think my extracts are particularly choice, and so I enclose them. What really saddens me is that there should have been so little development in originality of attack in the course of a whole generation.

Do take the best care of yourself.

F.F.

"Criminal" is the "Roosevelt doctrine of Federal power to enter within State lines and regulate and manage private business of all sorts. . . . This theory of Federal control over the corporation within State lines, extending to matters of its organization, its operation, its finances, its policies . . . its own employees, opened before Mr. Roosevelt's eyes a boundless prospect of benevolent activity along untrodden pathways . . . what will come next in the fantastic procession."

(New York *Sun,* July 16, 1907)

"Those anxious and confiding Republican business men and editors who expected the President to utter a 'reassuring' word did not know their man. His way of calming a nervous patient is to give another shock . . . A prudent consideration of the strain under which the whole financial world is now laboring would have kept him from saying anything which might add to it . . . none of the qualifications and protests which he characteristically introduces, will prevent the general public from thinking that . . . he contemplates still more radical and disturbing action. . . .

"What we fear is that the President does not admit into his reckoning the nature of credit, the world wide assaults that are now made upon its maintenance unimpaired, and the disastrous results which are certain to follow its overstrain or breakdown."

(New York *Evening Post,* August 20, 1907)

"Always more law, more law — when will the President's clamor for legislation end? When will he give the legitimate business interests of the country a breathing spell? . . . he has no policy. Mr. Roosevelt advances one new scheme after another until the business mind is bewildered in the mazes of Presidential experimentation. . . . More legislation has been passed in a single year than the courts can dispose of in the next three years. . . . It is double folly to invent new schemes of regulation and excite new unrest when acts already passed are yet to be worked out in prac-

tice and tested by the courts. Nothing is settled. Nothing is certain. . . .
Confidence is shaken, and confidence is the mother of credit."

(New York *World*, August 20, 1907)

"It will take millions of idle machines and miles of hungry bread lines
to pay the price of atonement if President Roosevelt's destructive policies
are permitted to continue; his policies threaten to paralyze every line of
legitimate business . . . and this in a country where without the interference of the President, the Square Deal would be a mechanical, an auto-
matic fact!"

(*American Business Man* for December, 1907)

The White House, December 16, 1937

Dear Felix: —

I am glad you dug up those excerpts about T.R. I may use them in the
next fireside.

Tooth nearly well. It did not touch the bone but was deep in the gum.
Taking very good care of myself.

I shall be delighted to have Borgese's book. I have heard much of him
and I hope he will raise a dozen American-Italian children, all good citizens.

In case I do not write again, Merry Christmas to you and Marion. Do
both of you come down soon.

As ever yours,
F.D.R.

Telegram to Roosevelt

Cambridge, Mass., December 31, 1937

MAY THE NEW YEAR BLESS YOU AND THROUGH YOU THE NATION.

MARION AND FELIX FRANKFURTER

Munich and Isolationism

1938

1938

February 18
Anthony Eden resigns as Foreign Secretary from the Chamberlain government in protest against Britain's continued appeasement of Italy.

March 12-13
German invasion and annexation of Austria.

April 16
Anglo-Italian pact is signed without adequate notice to the United States by the British government.

May 3-9
Hitler visits Mussolini in Rome.

September 15
Chamberlain and Hitler confer at Berchtesgaden on the Czech crisis.

September 22-23
Chamberlain meets Hitler at Godesberg.

September 29
Munich Agreement, with Czechoslovakia excluded from conference as demanded by Hitler and Mussolini. Prime Minister Chamberlain signs for Britain and Premier Daladier for France. In the House of Commons the Munich Agreement is denounced by Winston Churchill as a total and unmitigated defeat. His speech destroys Chamberlain's claim that the Munich Agreement represents "peace with honor" and ensures "peace for our time."

September 30
Czechoslovakia reluctantly bows to imperious circumstances and accepts the Munich Agreement.

October 5
Eduard Beneš resigns as President of Czechoslovakia.

November 26
Russia and Poland renew their non-aggression pact.

December 24
Twenty-one American Republics sign the Declaration of Lima pledging themselves to oppose foreign intervention and to protect themselves by collective action against aggression.

Telegram to Roosevelt
Cambridge, Mass., January 3, 1938
YOU ROSE TO THE HEIGHT OF YOUR GREAT ARGUMENT. THE COUNTRY NEEDED
TO FEEL THE MUSCLE OF YOUR MIND AND TO BE LED BY THE COURAGE OF YOUR
CANDOR. YOU ARE CONTINUING WHERE JACKSON AND WILSON LEFT OFF.
FELIX FRANKFURTER

*The President's annual message to Congress, at the beginning of 1938,
recounted his progress on the home front against a world scene growing
steadily more anxious and somber. Far ahead of public opinion, Roosevelt
had to limit himself to warnings and exhortations, while Britain and France
slithered and stumbled into appeasement and the Munich Agreement.*

The White House, January 4, 1938
Dear Felix:
Miss LeHand has brought to my attention that nice telegram about
my Message to the Congress. Of course you know I am delighted to have
your expression of approval. My grateful thanks to you.
Very sincerely yours,
F.D.R.

The White House, January 11, 1938
Dear Felix: —
Thank you ever so much for the delicious cheese which you sent on
from the Harvard Club. I understand that several of the people in the
kitchen were asphyxiated in the process of serving it, but once it arrived on
my desk all was well!
I do hope to see you soon.
As ever yours,
F.D.R.

Telegram to Roosevelt
Cambridge, Mass., January 30, 1938
FOR OLD AND YOUNG THIS DAY BRINGS NEW STRENGTH AND FRESH COURAGE.
OUR AFFECTIONATE GOOD WISHES.
MARION AND FELIX FRANKFURTER

Birthday greetings to Roosevelt.

Cambridge, Mass., February 5, 1938

Dear Mr. President:

I have just learned that Hamilton Fish Armstrong's name is under consideration for the Vienna post, and venture to trouble you, for the first time since March 4, 1933, with an uninvited suggestion for one of your appointments. I break my rule because of my special interest in Austrian affairs, and my deep conviction that Armstrong would bring to your aid unique qualifications as a source of information and comment on the delicate complexities of the Continental problems, hardly eased by yesterday's news from Berlin.

My own relations with Armstrong over a course of years have been almost exclusively restricted to discussions of problems raised by European totalitarianism. You probably know him more intimately than I do. But I have had overwhelming evidence of the depth and breadth of his understanding as well as of his knowledge, his balanced judgment, his completely impersonal temper of mind. He has, of course, a background of acquaintances with European events and men that it would be difficult to match, joined to the gift of lucid and luminous exposition.

In view of the inter-relation between foreign and domestic issues these days, and the importance of complete dependability in our diplomatic representatives, a vital point about Armstrong is the fact that he has been devoted to the causes which you represent, in an environment bitterly hostile. When one considers that he has actively espoused the democratic faith at home as well as abroad, as represented concretely by you, among powerful people who are the sponsors of his professional enterprise, *Foreign Affairs*, it shows his courage and character as well as his discernment and disinterestedness. I count it nothing but a high good fortune that he should be ready to serve you at Vienna.

I am writing this neither at the suggestion nor with the knowledge of Armstrong.

Faithfully yours,
FELIX FRANKFURTER

Two days before this letter was written, Mussolini, as a further token of his growing dependence on Nazi Germany, had ordered the Italian army to adopt the German goose-step. The morning papers on February 5 had carried the news of Hitler's dismissal of Field Marshal von Blomburg and General von Fritsch, together with the appointment of Herr von Ribbentrop as Foreign Minister and the elevation of General Goering to the rank

of Field Marshal. These events portended a new Nazi campaign to humili-
ate and annex Austria, with the final act coming on March 13.

Mr. Herbert Feis, economic adviser to the State Department, shared
Frankfurter's convictions that Austria would provide the classic test of Nazi
Germany's intentions. He thought it was imperative to have a man of the
stature and eminence of Mr. Hamilton Fish Armstrong, editor of Foreign
Affairs magazine, as the Ambassador in Vienna where he could keep a
watching brief on the Nazi program. Mr. Sumner Welles, Undersecretary
of State, welcomed the suggestion but doubted that it would be possible
to name one outside the Foreign Service to a post of this importance.
Throughout the Nazi years Mr. Armstrong remained an unofficial but re-
spected adviser to Roosevelt on European problems.

Cambridge, Mass., March 14, 1938

Dear Mr. President:

1. Now that I have read the stenographic minutes of your TVA Hearing last Friday I can hardly express in words of moderation my admiration
for the extraordinary, Lincoln-like patience which you showed to Arthur
Morgan's contumacy, as well as for the skill with which you developed
complicated issues under the most trying circumstances. I do not know
when I have read the full text of a proceeding of inquiry which left me with
anything like as much admiration for its conduct. If these minutes were
fairly disseminated throughout the country and widely read, there would be
nothing left of the matter, and people generally would feel as Frank Buxton
of the Boston *Herald* felt after he and I talked about it at length, when he
said, "After that hearing it's all over with Arthur Morgan."

2. But it's not all over because, in their present form, the Hearings will
not be widely read, and a great deal of confusion and misrepresentation will
remain in the air. Therefore the business raises very practical problems for
the future. It would be very surprising indeed if the Chairman should
change his attitude. The minutes make abundantly clear that Arthur Morgan is fanatically self-righteous and is altogether a pathological case. He
will, therefore, be obstinate in his recalcitrancy, counting on vindication
from Congress.

3. Bob La Follette was here yesterday and we had a long talk canvass-
ing the situation, the result of which he hopes to put before you in person.
On the assumption that Bob is right in his conviction that a Congressional
investigation is inevitable, I am sure you agree to the importance of maintaining the initiative which you now have, of having any further investigation come through you and not against your seeming wishes, and of having
the issues framed by you so clearly that there can be no possibility of mis-

understanding. In other words, the present situation can all be turned to your account.

4. This can easily be accomplished by a message from you to Congress, which in simple, lucid, and inescapable language will convey the substance of the facts and the atmosphere, which so clearly emanate from the stenographic minutes, together with the full text of the Hearing. If the record will substantially remain as it is now, as I assume it will be, it is easily susceptible of formulation to Congress by enumerating the specific issues that cut across all questions of TVA policy — the "factual matters" that relate to elementary standards of honesty and honor — together with your conclusion that, on the record, the charges by the Chairman affecting the honor and honesty of his colleagues are wholly without foundation. That much vindication of the other two members of the Board is, of course, essential in order to enable them to carry on the work of TVA. In such a summary of the record I think it would be particularly well to emphasize the charge, in effect, of attempting to suborn perjury and John Lord O'Brian's letter to the Chairman regarding that Charge.

5. I am sure such a message would so impregnate the atmosphere with the true situation that it would dominate opinion. Neither any hostile members of Congress nor Arthur Morgan would be able to change the atmosphere except by dealing specifically with those "factual matters" to which you so effectively kept the Hearing last Friday.

I am venturing to write as I have because I have thought a great deal about the matter.

With warm regards,

Faithfully yours,
FELIX FRANKFURTER

Arthur E. Morgan, Chairman of the Tennessee Valley Authority, was less interested in the development of TVA as a public power utility than as a model of social and economic planning on a regional basis. As early as 1933 Frankfurter had warned David E. Lilienthal, then a TVA director and later its famous chairman, that Morgan's approach was "fraught with every kind of danger." For some troubled months, with Roosevelt's wavering support, Morgan seemed to emerge as the victor in this internal dispute, savagely fought out of public view. But Morgan could not end the controversy, for he had, with high-minded fuzziness, given a fatally wrong twist to TVA's philosophy and development. Exasperated and nervous, he launched an angry attack on Mr. Lilienthal and on Harcourt A. Morgan, another director. An inquiry followed, in which Arthur Morgan's fluent but repetitive answers showed that he had departed from Roosevelt's hopes for

TVA as primarily a generator of cheap public power. Morgan was dismissed. At every stage of this prolonged controversy Frankfurter was against Morgan and with Lilienthal.

John Lord O'Brian is one of the acknowledged leaders of the American bar.

Cambridge, Mass., March 26, 1938

Dear Frank:

Let me break in on your vacation just long enough to thank you from the bottom of my heart and head for the hope that your actions and your words must be bringing to literally hundreds of thousands of victims of brute unreason. Most of them won't find a haven of refuge, either here or elsewhere. But what you have done will help sustain their souls in their material enslavement. And your noble leadership is no less important for the spiritual well-being of this country.

Darkness is descending over so much of the earth's surface, that it becomes all the more essential to keep our own sacred light burning brightly. You have given a practical confession of the faith in which the United States was founded in a way that would make Franklin and Emerson and Lincoln feel that the authentic, traditional American spirit still flourishes vigorously.

Marion and I wish for you the best possible refreshment at Warm Springs.

Ever devotedly yours,
F.F.

Cambridge, Mass., March 31, 1938

Dear Mr. President:

The following, which has just come to me from one of the most distinguished Republican editors in the land, will interest you:

"What has happened in Austria has distressed me profoundly and I am overjoyed that President Roosevelt has the imagination and courage to pledge this country to help in the one way that is possible. One point that I feel should be stressed by those who desire to help the President is the fact that the refugees from Austria are inevitably bound to be of a high type intellectually and regardless of financial status, highly unlikely to become a charge upon this country. I am thinking of people like the Stolpers from Berlin, for example. Such recruits to Americanism are precious, I feel. It would be an extraordinarily effective move, for example, if Freud could be persuaded to come to this country, assuming that he is strong enough to travel and can escape. Some sacrifice is involved in accepting immigration of any kind at the present time of national unemployment on a wide scale.

I think it important, therefore, as a practical matter, to stress the riches of mind and imagination which must ultimately far outweigh any economic cost in the present."

Faithfully yours,
FELIX FRANKFURTER

The Republican editor was Mr. Geoffrey Parsons of the New York Herald Tribune. Freud ultimately went to England instead of America, but Frankfurter showed unremitting zeal in helping to get him out of Austria and in pleading his cause with English friends.

The White House, April 4, 1938

Dear Felix: —

It is good to get your cheery note in the middle of all kinds of weird doings by the boys in Washington while I was away. The trouble with the people in the country who keep crying "wolf, wolf" is that some day a wolf might appear from the opposite direction when they least expect it.

I do hope to see you and Marion soon. Is there any chance of your coming to Washington during the Easter vacation?

As ever yours,
F.D.R.

Cambridge, Mass., April 8, 1938

Dear Mr. President,

Alas, our Easter vacation has had to be devoted to Harvard, but we are hoping to be able to go to Washington for a few days in early May. Would the latter part of either the first or second week be a good time to have a glimpse of you?

I have been wanting to write you a note to say how wonderful I think your stand in regard to refugees. I dare say it will be enormously difficult to do, but it's so important to express the right feelings, and for us, as a nation, to take this position at this time, makes me proud.

With affectionate greetings from us both, and looking forward to seeing you in May, I am, as always,

Devotedly yours,
MARION FRANKFURTER

Frankfurter, who knew how outraged Roosevelt was by the Nazi persecutions, also respected the political caution imposed on the President by a divided Congress and a troubled country. The year before, after urging in his famous "quarantine" speech that the dictator states should be quarantined by economic and moral and political techniques, and treated as ene-

mies to the health and peace of the international community, Roosevelt had found it necessary to beat a retreat and use all his skill to avoid dangerous losses in public support. A farsighted minority applauded his proposal as the one essential measure which could avert a cataract of disasters from sweeping over civilization. But the prevailing view was that Roosevelt had blundered too close to the edge of Europe's quarrels. For many Americans, though not for Roosevelt or Frankfurter, American policy at this time meant peace without sacrifice, or even worse, peace at the expense of other people's sacrifices.

The suffering of the refugees complicated this general problem, for most of the refugees were Jewish, and this was a disturbed period when anti-Semitism was showing an alarming increase. During the agitation to help the refugees it became clear that Roosevelt, despite all his goodwill, could bring only a small portion of the refugees to this country or find a haven for some other victims of Nazi intolerance, through his influence, in friendly countries of Latin America. The great mass of the refugees would have to remain in Europe.

Roosevelt was not without advisers who told him it was unwise to keep discussing a problem which was so clearly beyond his control. Out of these discussions, tragic and inconclusive, slowly came the conviction that Palestine offered the only hope to the refugees and that England must be persuaded to open the gates to them as the mandatory power for Palestine.

Proud of his Zionist faith, and equally devoted to the greatness of England, Frankfurter at first thought that he would see two of his great intellectual allegiances united in a happy reconciliation. Then, with a mixture of anger, indignation and revulsion, he watched with dismay as England, in his judgment, violated and betrayed her obligations as the mandatory power. The Zionist leaders of this country, in the controversy that spread over the next few years and ended only with the establishment of Israel, never had Frankfurter with them when they saw the President or the Secretary of State. But except for Mr. Benjamin V. Cohen, no one could match Frankfurter's constant influence in the highest reaches of the Roosevelt Administration in pleading the cause of Zionism or in helping the refugees.

Boston, Mass., April 11, 1938

My dear Professor Frankfurter:

I am enclosing herewith a copy of the letter which I received from Dr. Hans J. Loewi, the son of Otto Loewi, Professor of Pharmacology at the University of Graz. There is no doubt that Otto Loewi is one of the most fruitful and eminent investigators in biology. His simple experiments performed in 1921 opened a new field of scientific investigation. The facts which have sprung from these experiments have already revolutionized our ideas of activities in the nervous system and the relations of the nervous system to muscles, and they promise to give us deep insight into the complex functioning of the brain. It was because of his classical and fundamental discoveries that Loewi was made a Nobel Laureate in 1936.

When I heard that Loewi had been arrested I was appalled because I knew of his extreme sensitiveness. Some years ago, as Chairman of the Dunham Lectureship Committee, I had the pleasure of inviting him here to give the Dunham Lectures. He told me that on his way to Graz he intended to spend two weeks visiting relatives in Frankfurt. On reaching home he wrote to me that he found conditions in Frankfurt so depressing that he was not able to stay more than a few days. I can imagine the distress which he experiences now while in prison.

Here you have presented the plight of a great scholar, a man who has done to humanity an immeasurably great service. Surely some action ought to be taken to relieve his present indignity and humiliation. If there is any influence which you can bring to bear that may have that effect, I most sincerely trust that you will use it.

Yours sincerely,

WALTER B. CANNON

P.S.   I am sending a copy of these two letters to Alfred Cohn.

P.P.S.   I have just been talking with one of my advanced students, Dr. Colman Lissak, of Hungary. He worked in Loewi's laboratory in 1936-37. Dr. Lissak testifies that Loewi expressed stern disapproval of the sending of Nazi professors away from Austrian universities into Germany and declared that scientific men should not suffer disturbance of their labors because of differences of political opinions. Furthermore, Dr. Loewi advised Dr. Lissak to go to Berlin for extension of his experience in learning physiological technique, which indicates an absence of animosity toward Germany under the Hitler regime.

Cambridge, Mass., April 12, 1938

Dear Mr. President:

The enclosed letter from Dr. Walter Cannon has just come. I don't have to tell you that Cannon is perhaps the most distinguished member of the Harvard Medical School Faculty and a physiologist of world-wide reputation. His account of the plight of Professor Loewi, a Nobel prize winner — "the plight of a great scholar, a man who has done to humanity an immeasurably great service" — is just a striking illustration of the hundreds of men and women who are among the finest flowers of our contemporary civilization, in whose behalf you are trying to lead the noblest traditions of this country and the civilized sentiment of the world. From numerous letters that I have had from non-Jews I have every confidence that our own people will respond to your noble efforts. More strength to your powers.

Faithfully yours,

F.F.

Zagreb, Jugoslavia, March 29, 1938

Prof. W. B. Cannon
Harvard Medical School
Boston, Mass., U.S.A.

Dear Sir:

I am the eldest son of Otto Loewi, Graz, and just by chance outside of the country, called Austria before. I remember that my father very often has spoken about you. I hope this will authorize me to call on you in this very moment of my father being in distress.

My father has been arrested the 12th March. The authorities give as reason that they found communist material in a Jewish commonwealth society. I am sure that this can't be true and even if it would be, my father had no responsibility about it, as he was a simple member of this society. Nevertheless I remember that jealous people tried to blame him for having taken part in the International Congress of Physiology in Russia, where you have been also, if I am right. My father was never interested in politics. An honest judge would be unable to find any fault with him. Although I hear now, that it is intended to keep him in prison for three months at least. There are the facts.

Being myself in a very bad situation at this moment I cannot do more in favor of my father, than to inform you and Sir Henry Dale. Therefore I would ask you, if you could do something for him. I only see one way. A carefully prepared action of the American Government, any attack by newspapers would surely be most dangerous and I think the only effective way to speak to the German authorities might be the American Embassy.

I thank you in advance for your kindness.

Yours very sincerely,

(Dr.) HANS J. LOEWI

Memorandum for the President

Dear Missy,

Please bring this item about Dr. Loewi to the President's attention.

It was the President's intercession, as he will recall, that saved Loewi's life at least from torture and, probably, death.

F.F.

Excerpt from periodical

Franklin C. McLean, professor of pathological physiology at the University of Chicago, writes: "Professor Otto Loewi has been released from Germany. He may be addressed in care of Club de la Fondation Universitaire, Rue d'Egmont, Brussels. Before being released he was stripped of all his property, both inside of and outside of Germany, including his Nobel prize money, which had never been in either Austria or Germany. Mrs. Loewi is still detained in Germany."

In a fireside chat, Roosevelt discussed economic conditions, before issuing a grave and measured warning on the danger of dictatorships. "History," he said, "proves that dictatorships do not grow out of strong and successful governments but out of weak and helpless ones. If by democratic methods people get a government strong enough to protect them from fear and starvation, their democracy succeeds, but if they do not, they grow impatient. Therefore, the only sure bulwark of continuing liberty is a government strong enough to protect the interests of the people, and a people strong enough and well enough informed to maintain its sovereign control over its government."

Telegram to Roosevelt

Cambridge, Mass., April 14, 1938

MARION WITH HER ACUTE EAR SAYS IT WAS BEAUTIFULLY DONE. IT WAS A RELAXED, MUCH NEEDED EXPOSITION AND YOUR FINAL INTIMATE TALK SURELY MUST HAVE GONE STRAIGHT TO THE HEART OF LINCOLN'S COMMON PEOPLE.

FELIX FRANKFURTER

The White House, April 16, 1938

Dear Felix:

Many thanks for that fine telegram. You have sensed exactly the message which I sought to convey. You know I have great respect for Marion's judgment and I want to believe she is right this time. Anyway, your message made me very happy.

Very sincerely yours,

F.D.R.

Memorandum for F.F.

The White House, April 21, 1938

FOR YOUR INFORMATION.

F.D.R.

Washington, D.C., April 19, 1938

My dear Mr. President:

With reference to your memorandum to me of April 18 concerning the arrest of Professor Loewi, it would seem to me that there was little that we could do of a specific character.

I have, however, as a result of the facts contained in the correspondence you sent me with your memorandum under reference, sent a telegram to Hugh Wilson in Berlin asking him to seize an appropriate occasion to explain to the proper officials of the German Government the interest which is felt in this country with regard to distinguished scientists like Professor Loewi and to indicate his belief that the release with permission to leave German territory of such distinguished men would undoubtedly create a favorable impression on public opinion everywhere. Direct intercession on our part on behalf of persons like Professor Loewi would probably have the opposite effect from that desired.

If you think there is anything further that should properly be done, please let me know.

Believe me

Faithfully yours,
SUMNER WELLES

Cambridge, Mass., April 21, 1938

Dear Miss LeHand;

Thank you very much for your note. Please tell the President that we shall be in Washington from Thursday morning, May 12th till Sunday night, and should love to stay at the White House but don't want to be a nuisance. (I don't that is, Felix doesn't mind!) So then we could spend part of that time — any part that is convenient — at the White House, and the rest with friends.

And please thank him a great deal for both of us.

With warm regards,

Sincerely,
MARION FRANKFURTER

Cambridge, Mass., April 27, 1938

Dear Frank:

1. The ultimate deposit in history, I suspect, of the work of a statesmen, derives from the sheer humanness of his simple, unostentatious daily deeds. His letter to Mrs. Bixby reveals the true Lincoln, and history, I am sure, will see you in the same light through such spontaneous, compassionate responses as that which you made to Dr. Cannon's appeal on behalf of Professor Loewi. I sent it on to you merely because it furnished a striking

glimpse of what Nazi rule means to the heritage of civilization. But, characteristically, you read it as a human appeal, and sought to help with the full reach of your powers. I am deeply grateful and you will, I hope, not disapprove the discretion that I exercised in letting your interest be known to a few dependable people like Dr. Cannon. Such interest as yours in these dark days, in matters dear to men like Dr. Cannon, means much.

2. Your remarks to the D.A.R. the other day did not constitute one of those half-hour speeches which it takes ten hours to prepare. What you said was much better than that — it was one of those deep summaries behind which was the preparation of a lifetime. For your "text" to the ladies put in one pithy sentence that which sets this nation apart from all others. It may have jolted them a little to have been reminded that you and they are descendants of "immigrants and revolutionists." But the implications of these few words go to the heart of American history. In this connection, don't you think that the enclosed card from G. A. Borgese announcing his American Citizenship is touching?

3. And your message on governmental tax immunities was an admirably quiet but effective lesson in your continuous educational process on the proper place of the Supreme Court in our national life. It was all so deftly done, but its meaning will not have been lost to the priests in the Temple of Karnak. Aren't you a bit afraid though, that you are making some of the "lads," as Holmes used to call them, jittery! ? I certainly didn't expect to live to see the day when the Court would announce, as they did on Monday, that it itself has usurped power for nearly a hundred years. And think of not a single New York paper — at least none that I saw — having a nose for the significance of such a decision. How fluid it all makes the Constitution!

4. Speaking of the Constitution, you will be interested in the enclosure regarding your dismissal of Arthur Morgan. At least the Harvard *Law Review* in its forthcoming number will announce to the world the clear legality of your act. The note was written by two pet students of mine. I think they've done a fine job.

I am very glad you are going off for a few days. Have a good time!

With warmest regards

Ever devotedly yours,
F.F.

Telegram to Frankfurter
The White House, May 11, 1938

YOU BOTH ARE CERTAINLY EXPECTED AT THE WHITE HOUSE TOMORROW MORNING. SEE YOU THEN. WIRE TIME OF ARRIVAL.

MISSY

Cambridge, Mass., May 18, 1938

Dear Frank,

1. First and foremost, I want to tell you what deep joy Marion and I carried away in finding you so fit. I wish I could put into adequate words the sense of serenity that everything about you conveyed. With some knowledge of American history, I had the feeling that not since Lincoln has the White House had an occupant with such imperturbability of soul. It cannot be mere accident that not since Lincoln has there been a President who possessed in equal measure such a combination of the democratic faith, antiseptic humor, and largeness of view. Somehow or other, those qualities manage to convey themselves to the common understanding of ordinary folk, if they are given frequent enough opportunities through sight and speech to feel the radiations of those qualities.

2. I saw four of the Justices and not a little of both the Blacks. She is an altogether grand person, with a keen realization of the psychological aspects of the situation, and with unusual talents for mitigating difficulties and softening hard feelings. Various experiences of his life have been calculated to make him a bit of an Ishmaelite — to expect every hand to be raised against him, and therefore, at times to be unwarrantedly suspicious when nothing but friendliness is intended. Certainly Isaiah, Stone and Reed have the friendliest disposition toward him. I know, because I talked with all three rather intimately. I took the bull by the horn and told Stanley Reed that he must not allow Black to interpose the barrier of formality between them, and that, as a matter of fact, Black will gradually soften to influences of friendliness and affection. Marion and I had tea with the Blacks out at Alexandria, and later dined with them at the Reeds. Altogether a very good time was had, and I have high hopes for the future.

3. You asked me to remind you of a few things about which we talked:

(a) Monte Lemann is just past fifty-four, and I do not believe any informed person would gainsay Stanley Reed's opinion that "Lemann is about the best lawyer south of the Mason and Dixon line." He has independent means (though not very rich), and I am confident that he would go on the Circuit Court of Appeals. He is that very rare thing at the contemporary American bar, a lawyer highly equipped technically, but not made narrow or unprogressive by his professional and business associations. He has, as you know, really cared about the social reforms of the New Deal, and has been not a little influential in securing the effective sympathy of his client, Zemurray, for your Administration.

It would really be a great thing to put Lemann on the Circuit Court of Appeals. By a few such appointments you would not only prevent judicial obstructions but perpetuate your social outlook in the administration of law for the next twenty years. With men like Monte Lemann in the Fifth Circuit, Stuart Guthrie in the District, Francis Biddle in the Third, and Charlie Wyzanski here, you would be creating judges mindful of the basic function of law as the body of arrangements for realizing social needs. Such men have not only a progressive outlook now, but they would be open-minded to needful changes ten and fifteen years hence.

(b) You also wanted me to put on paper the suggestion of a really able committee to inquire thoroughly into technological unemployment. This would fit into your so-called monopoly studies, and could be launched so as to expose the present baffling ignorance of the critics of the New Deal on what are really fundamental economic issues. Not only the statement in which the purposes of such a committee would be explained, but also its personnel, would carry great assurance to the country and give further indication of your long-range planning. The committee ought to be a real directing body, even though the technical work would be done by technicians. The kind of people that suggest themselves — and it should be a smallish committee — are Zemurray for industry, Averell Harriman for the railroads, Sidney Hillman for the CIO, and some very good man for the AF of L, Wesley Mitchell as a professional economist, and Dr. Alice Hamilton who would be a distinguished representative of the scientific and social aspects of women in industry.

(c) Finally, you asked me to give you Julius Rosenwald's remark about money-making. I don't know whether he ever put it on paper, but I myself heard him say: "Money-making is a special knack. The fact that a man has made a lot of money doesn't mean that his opinions on any other subject are worth anything."

We had an altogether delightful time. It wasn't until we got back that Marion confessed to me, what she had already confessed to you, namely, that when the guard tried to stop her from entering the White House, she said, "Why, I am living here." That's the way you made her feel. Incidentally, she says it was perfectly wonderful the way you roared with enjoyment when she told you about it.

F.F.

Frankfurter's references to Mr. Justice Black may surprise many people by their cordiality, for Black and Frankfurter have often been put in opposition to one another as antagonists on the Supreme Court. In actual fact, their judicial differences never hampered their mutual respect and long friendship. Both knew that they had left an enduring mark on the traditions and principles of the Supreme Court, and were content to await the assessment of their work in the patient perspectives of time and experience. Few things moved Frankfurter more profoundly, in his last lingering illness, than the kindness and respect invariably shown him by Mr. Justice Black.

The first man appointed to the Supreme Court after Roosevelt's court-packing fight, Mr. Justice Black was attacked as an unrepentant New Dealer and as a brief and routine member of the Ku Klux Klan (at that time membership in the Klan was almost a necessity for many Southern politicians). The subsequent career of Mr. Justice Black is, of course, a magnificent and unanswerable vindication of his allegiance to the noblest principles of racial justice and civil liberty.

But Mr. Justice Brandeis (Isaiah) could not have foreseen these developments and he chafed at the appointment. On this one important point Frankfurter was not completely candid with Roosevelt. He minimized the extent of Brandeis's doubts, and glossed over his long and passionate plea to Brandeis to cast aside his misgivings and make earnest overtures to Black. In the spacious contours of legal history it is not without fascination to find Frankfurter acting as the friendly mediator between Black and Brandeis.

Roosevelt offered Monte M. Lemann a seat on the Court of Appeals for the Fifth Circuit, but Lemann declined it for personal reasons. Apart from his renown as a most accomplished lawyer, Lemann deserves to be remembered for his dissenting minority report of one, as a member of the Wickersham Commission investigating the problems of prohibition, when he declared there was "no alternative but repeal of the Eighteenth Amendment."

Julius Rosenwald, the merchant prince, was head of Sears, Roebuck and widely honored for his philanthropies, including help for Negro education.

Cambridge, Mass., May 25, 1938

Dear Frank,

This must have been a breath-holding weekend for you, for I suspect it was pregnant with more real cause for alarm than any period since 1914. Happily the Czechs were true to the will and wisdom symbolized by their two great statesmen, Masaryk and Beneš — one of my profoundest post-War memories was a two hour talk with Thomas Masaryk at Prague — and thereby they proved anew that the way to deal with a bully is not to yield to him. It is at once mortifying and inspiring that this small nation should teach a lesson to both Great Britain and France in not feeding the bully's strength by showing weakness. But, of course, all the elements of the difficulty remain, and, I suspect, the price that will inevitably be asked of the Czechs will be ultimate separation. I should be more than surprised if they yielded.

But I started to write this letter about two matters not touching world affairs.

In response to the interest you expressed when I was down, I have made further inquiries about the Boston *Transcript*. People who ought to know tell me it could be bought for $100,000. It has an A.P. franchise.

Since writing you about Monte Lemann I have very good reasons for believing that Claude Pepper would be agreeable to the appointment of Monte Lemann. He recognizes, as I think everyone in the south would, the rare combination of qualities of Lemann.

The tide generally seems to be running the right way. I hope you get out of Congress during the rest of the session all you want and prevent from being done what should not be done.

F.F.

Frankfurter refers in the first part of this letter to the beginning of the crisis over Czechoslovakia which brought the world in September within sight of war. Hitler began the crisis by demanding the incorporation of the Sudetenland in the German Reich. Beneš and Jan Masaryk, the son of Thomas Masaryk, resisted this demand for the mutilation of their country. The crisis exploded with great fury, leading Britain and France on September 29 to sign the Munich Pact with Hitler, giving Germany all it then wanted of Czechoslovakia and opening the way to the seizure of the rest of Czechoslovakia the next spring. These are among the fateful landmarks on the road to world war.

This was one of the recurrent speeches in which Roosevelt began to sound the alarm about conditions in Europe. He was not yet ready to propose any specific policies. His task at this stage was to awaken the American people to dangers which seemed to most of them very remote and improbable.

Telegram to Roosevelt

Cambridge, Mass., June 24, 1938

UNFORTUNATELY WHEN YOU SPEAK I SHALL BE ON TRAIN TO ROCHESTER TO ENLIGHTEN WESTERN NEW YORK BAR ASSOCIATION ON CONSTITUTION. BUT THANKS TO FRIENDLY REPUBLICAN EDITOR HAVE HAD PREHEARING. NO WONDER HE SAYS IT'S A DAMN GOOD SPEECH. IT IS ALL THAT ALTHOUGH HE WOULD ONLY ADMIT THAT PRIVATELY. IT REALLY IS AND MY WARMEST CONGRATULATIONS.

FELIX FRANKFURTER

Hyde Park, N.Y., June 28, 1938

Dear Felix:

Just a little note to tell you how interested and pleased I was to receive your telegram of congratulations. Ever so many thanks for your thoughtfulness in letting me know of your approval of the radio address.

As ever yours,
F.D.R.

Frankfurter had sent the President a list of scientists who had been dismissed in Nazi purges or in some cases sent to concentration camps. It proved impossible to save all of them or to prevent the Nazi persecutions from becoming steadily worse. But a few were helped.

The home of Mr. Justice Holmes did not become the headquarters of the American Historical Association.

The White House, July 5, 1938

Dear Felix! —

Many thanks for letting me see these letters. That list of scientists is amazing and I fear the dismissals have not ended yet.

Is there some way in which the mental feelings of a large group of people can be divorced from stock market fluctuations? I might almost say physical feelings as well, because when the market goes up these people actually feel physically better, as well as mentally.

I hate to have to admit it but the market of the past two weeks seems to have brought an enormous psychological change in the political situation — and, as you have perceived, I am capitalizing on it and intend to do so on the trip across the country.

If there is no war in Europe before July sixteenth, I hope to leave San Diego on the U.S.S. "Houston," visit lower California, Clipperton Island, the Galapagos, Cocos Island, the Panama Canal, Old Providence Island and land at Pensacola on August ninth.

Meanwhile, I hope Marion will see to it that you behave yourself and that she will bring you to Hyde Park sometime in August, after I get back.

By the way, Dr. Connor, the Archivist, made an interesting suggestion yesterday — that Justice Holmes' house be loaned or given to the American Historical Association, which, as you know, has a national charter and is, on the whole, a pretty decent and useful body. His idea is that they would use it as a national headquarters — a rendezvous for their many members who visit Washington or do research work here. What is your slant on this?

As ever yours,
F.D.R.

The next letter is, in a sense, Frankfurter's comment on the Munich Agreement, signed a few days before, and on the Czech crisis that had threatened a European war. Frankfurter's attitude to the Munich Agreement resembled Léon Blum's famous judgment: he had heard of the Agreement with gratitude and with shame, gratitude that war had been postponed, but shame that the reprieve had been won by the betrayal of an ally. Like Roosevelt, who had defended the Munich Agreement as an act of necessity, Frankfurter had no confidence that England, with Churchill still an exile from power, would use these precious months to strengthen Europe's defenses against Nazi Germany. He saw the Munich Agreement as a humiliating truce between recurrent threats to peace, with the democracies in the end being forced to fight for sheer survival because they had been so blind to the moral challenge inherent in the doctrine of Nazi Germany and Fascist Italy.

It is one measure of Frankfurter's anxiety during this prolonged Czech crisis that he had put in a transatlantic call to Mr. Ferdinand Kuhn, the courageous and greatly respected London correspondent of the New York Times. When so much of the British press was bemused by Chamberlain's policy of appeasement, Mr. Kuhn correctly saw Chamberlain's leadership as leading directly to the war which it was powerless to avert, a war which would be fought under conditions of maximum danger to the democracies.

In April 1938 Frankfurter had delivered three lectures to the general public, on the invitation of the Committee on Extracurricular Reading in American History of Harvard University, on "Mr. Justice Holmes and the Supreme Court." Roosevelt showed his discernment as a reader by recognizing at once that the little book was marked by a grace of exposition and a power of argument not often surpassed by Frankfurter.

James Roosevelt had just recovered from an illness: hence the reference to the President's "anxiety over Jimmy."

The reference to the defeat of O'Connor recalls Roosevelt's intervention in local Democratic primaries to remove or "purge" some Democrats who had fought his program in Congress, while professing loyalty to his leadership. He was particularly anxious to defeat Senator Walter George, Senator Millard Tydings, and Representative John J. O'Connor of New York City. Congressman O'Connor was the only one who suffered defeat. Roosevelt never tried these "purging" tactics again.

Cambridge, Mass., October 3, 1938

Dear Frank:

These lectures delivered to the laity last Spring, at the request of the University, will tell you nothing that you do not already know, if, perchance, you were to page this little volume. I wrote it as an application of Holmes' admonition that "we need education in the obvious, more than investigation of the obscure."

For these past three weeks you have been especially in our minds. We have been hanging on radio and telephonic news — I even phoned to Ferdie Kuhn in London, who warned me of the direction of Chamberlain's mind weeks ago — all these days, Marion and I, like a mother over a life-and-death struggle at a sick bed. And so I can imagine what your days and nights have been. I'll say no more — except what I already wired you, that your intervention and the way you did it all was just right.

Of course, we thought of your personal anxiety over Jimmy and were greatly relieved when that anxiety was removed.

I don't know when I rejoiced over a man's defeat as much as I did over O'Connor — one of those really bad men in politics.

I rejoice to infer that you are keeping very fit.

With devoted regards,

Faithfully yours,
F.F.

Washington, D.C., October 13, 1938

Dear Miss LeHand:

Last night Felix spoke to the President over the telephone about the Palestine situation. The President suggested that Felix dictate to me a draft of a note which the President might send to Mr. Neville Chamberlain. The following is the draft which Felix dictated to me:

"With increased pressure on the Jews in Central Europe the tasks of sheer humanity we set for ourselves at the Evian Conferences have become even more difficult of fulfillment. Apart from mere numbers Palestine is a significant symbol of hope to Jewry. Therefore I earnestly urge that no decision may be made which would close the gates of Palestine to the Jews. Shutting the gates of Palestine to Jews would greatly embarrass efforts towards genuine appeasement because it would be interpreted as a disturbing symbol of anti-Semitism."

Sincerely yours,
Benjamin V. Cohen

The Munich Crisis. Roosevelt had appealed to Hitler to stop short of war. It is usually forgotten that Roosevelt praised Neville Chamberlain's role in arranging the Munich Pact. Both Roosevelt and Frankfurter loathed the Munich Agreement but they thought the alternative of war was even worse, and they did not see why the United States should assume military risks from which Britain and France shrank. Meanwhile Britain and France insisted they could not be more resolute while the United States remained aloof. It was a vicious circle, and in the process civilization was almost strangled.

Cambridge, Mass., October 27, 1938

Dear Mr. President:

Thank God for your Forum speech! It would, under any circumstances, have been profoundly significant for you to speak as you did speak, but the events since Munich — including Joe Kennedy's Trafalgar speech — make your forthright, eloquent, concrete reformulation of our American ideals one of those utterances that amount to action. For action ultimately depends on the mental climate of a society, and a speech like yours confirms the forces of reason as against the power of force, reinvigorates the faith of democracy as against the rule of the mailed fist.

I wonder if Joe Kennedy understands the implications of public talk by an American ambassador, and realizes the discouragement to right things and the encouragement to wrong things that he may, however unwittingly, give. Take his latest remarks. Yesterday, in speaking before the Worcestershire Association on the difficulties that confront an ambassador, Joe said, "If you see anything good in dictatorships, you alienate the democracies." Joe seems to be unmindful of the fact that, since the days of Washington, it is the traditional function of American representatives abroad *not* to "see anything good in dictatorships" — at least not in public. Such public approval of dictatorships, in part even, plays precisely into their hands in that it helps to debilitate confidence in the democratic way of life, and emphasizes those weaknesses upon which the agents of the dictatorships are constantly playing.

And so I am sure those who care for the democratic way of life the world over will be heartened by your uncompromising and eloquent espousal of that way of life because it is the way of reason and of humanity.

I recur again and again in my mind to that little scene between you and Peter Rowan, a few weeks ago. For me, in its homely way, it symbolizes our democracy in action.

F.F.

Roosevelt had spoken to the New York Herald Tribune *Forum. He looked at Europe, and warned the dictators that "you cannot organize civilization around the core of militarism and at the same time expect reason to control human destinies."*

Ambassador Joseph P. Kennedy was out of sympathy with Roosevelt's European policy, and in his speeches in England, he spoke about the challenge of the dictator states with far less alarm and determination than was now being consistently expressed by the President he was supposed to represent.

Peter Rowan, a neighbor at Hyde Park, had bargained frankly and honorably about the price of a bit of land with the President, and then had ended the negotiation by remarking that they were both busy men. Frankfurter never forgot this episode, and described it in detail in his tribute to Roosevelt in 1956, reprinted in the epilogue of this book.

Speaking as a New Yorker, Roosevelt had sent a message explaining why

he supported the Democratic candidates in the state elections. His rule
against interference in local contests could be set aside in this instance be-
cause he was speaking as an individual voter about his own state, and not as
President.

Telegram to Roosevelt
Cambridge, Mass., November 5, 1938

AS A TEACHER I FEEL ENVIOUS ADMIRATION FOR YOUR PELLUCID EXPOSITION
OF THE MEANING OF THE GOVERNMENT OF NEW YORK. AS A DEVOTEE OF DE-
MOCRACY I FEEL GRATITUDE FOR YOUR POWERFUL INSISTENCE ON CONTINUITY
OF LIBERAL ACTION AS INDISPENSABLE TO THE MAINTENANCE OF DEMOCRACY.
WARMEST REGARDS.

FELIX FRANKFURTER

Hyde Park, N.Y., November 8, 1938
Dear Felix:

It was indeed good of you to send me that very nice telegram. I am
happy to know that you think so well of the speech.

My best wishes to you,

Always sincerely,
FRANKLIN D. ROOSEVELT

In the President's handwriting:

This is a "form" reply! I really mean lots more than these words. I
wonder whom you and Marion are voting for!

F.D.R.

James Michael Curley, the gifted but controversial Boston politician, had
served as Mayor of that city three times before becoming Governor of Mas-
sachusetts from 1935-1937. He was defeated in 1938 in his race for the
United States Senate. Forsaking his wife's example, Frankfurter voted
against Curley.

Cambridge, Mass., November 15, 1938
Dear Miss LeHand,

May I entrust this note to you? Its contents are so startling I would
hate to have it get into the wrong hands. Many thanks, and warm regards.

MARION FRANKFURTER

Cambridge, Mass., November 15, 1938
Dear Mr. President,

It gives me great pleasure to announce that I voted for Mr. Curley. I
won't say the choice was easy, but I'm clear and unashamed. Being both, I

take great pains to tell all my friends. The odor of sanctity is so strong they need a shock or two.

Felix — the coward — won't tell me what he did. He too says the ballot is secret!

We both send you our love.

MARION FRANKFURTER

Cambridge, Mass., November 25, 1938

Dear Frank:

Let me break in on your holiday just long enough to thank you on the courageous resourcefulness with which you are making the Chamberlain Government do its duty in utilizing Palestine as the obvious first line of relief for the victims of the latest and largest Nazi barbarities. So much of recent British policy reminds one of Artemus Ward's eagerness, in his patriotic devotion, to offer up his wife's relations on the altar of patriotism. Palestine is here and now — that and Trans-Jordan — as an obligation of action by Gt. Britain, instead of merely pious words. And you have driven home your whole effort with Downing Street beautifully, with your statement of hope at Warm Springs, I admired it immensely — merely as a piece of art.

Your homely Thanksgiving Day remarks were the best possible way of vindicating and re-invigorating our traditional democratic faith. I've been reading *Hansard* — and the speeches of Chamberlain and Simon and even of Halifax are sickening. How Gladstone and Bryce and Dizzy and Balfour must wince in the other world! Thank God, say I, with millions upon millions of Americans, for the way in which you keep the flame of civilization aloft and burning brightly.

Ever faithfully yours,
F.F.

Warm Springs, Ga., December 1, 1938

My dear Felix:

It would give me great pleasure if you could come to luncheon with us at the White House on Saturday, December tenth. I am asking a small group of people from different parts of the country to come together to discuss with me a matter which lies very close to my heart and on which I should like to take some definite action in the very near future.

Because I would greatly value your advice on the right way to work out the plan I have in mind and because I know of your deep interest, not only in the preservation of historical source material but also your current interest in current affairs of government, I hope very much that you will be able to lunch with me that day at one o'clock at the White House.

I am enclosing a short and very sketchy memorandum which I hope you will be thinking over.

This necessarily must remain a matter to be kept in the strictest confidence, because I think it would be a pity if there were intimations relating to the general plan before I have something definite to go on.

My sincere regards,

Faithfully yours,
FRANKLIN D. ROOSEVELT

Memorandum

Personal and Confidential

Since 1910 — or in other words for a period of twenty-eight years — I have carefully preserved all of my correspondence, public papers, pamphlets, books, etc. This includes all incoming material and copies of practically all outgoing material. These years cover my service of nearly three years in the New York State Senate; seven and one-half years as Assistant Secretary of the Navy, including the World War period and two trips to Europe; my business and legal correspondence; much political material between 1920 and 1928, including the campaign for the Vice Presidency, the 1924 Convention, and the 1928 Convention; my campaigns for Governor in 1928 and 1930; all of my personal papers as Governor of New York, 1929-1933; the campaigns for the Presidency, 1932 and 1936; and all of my Presidential papers from March 4, 1933 to date.

Because these papers relate to so many periods and activities which are not connected with my service in the Federal Government, I do not wish to break them up, leaving a portion of them to the National Archives and dividing the rest between the State of New York Archives, the New York State Historical Society, the Dutchess County Historical Society, the Harvard College Library, etc., etc.

In other words, it is my desire that they be kept as a whole and intact in their original condition, available to scholars of the future in one definite locality.

I have carefully considered the choice of locality and for many reasons have decided that it would be best that they remain permanently on the grounds of my home at Hyde Park, Dutchess County, New York.

I realize that the Library of Congress, the National Archives, the New York State Library, Harvard University and the New York State Historical Society would probably be glad to have the whole collection intact. It is my thought, however, that an opportunity exists to set up for the first time in this country what might be called a source material collection relating to a specific period in our history.

My own country place at Hyde Park will, without doubt, eventually go to the Federal Government to be maintained for the benefit of the public by the Federal Government.

It is, therefore, my thought that funds can be raised for the erection of a separate, modern, fireproof building to be built near my house at Hyde Park, so designed that it would hold all of my own collections and also such other source material relating to this period in our history as might be donated to the collection in the future by other members of the present Administration.

I forgot to mention that in addition to the very voluminous correspondence, I have also two rather specialized collections which are of some definite historic value; a collection of paintings, drawings, prints, manuscript letters and documents, log-books, pamphlets and books relating to the American Navy from 1775 to date; and a smaller collection of similar material relating to the Hudson River, and especially Dutchess County and the town of Hyde Park. These collections would be placed in the proposed building, together with the public papers, etc.

I have also a very large number of books and pamphlets — far more than my children could possibly use, many of them inscribed by their authors to me. The bulk of these books would also be added to the contents of the building and, incidentally, they form the nucleus of a library relating to this period which would be available to students in the future.

It is my thought that if a building such as I suggest is erected and the material — not only my own but that of others who would contribute their own material — is placed there, the title to the building and all the material would be vested in the United States Government and placed under the primary responsibility of the Archivist of the United States. This would insure permanent care and the provision of adequate facilities for its use. At the same time, being somewhat familiar with historical material, its preservation and its availability for students and scholars, I should much like to have the assistance of recognized scholars in American History and Government, past and present. That is why I believe that a collection of this kind should be under the supervision of a committee of historians working in cooperation with the Archivist and the Librarian of Congress.

It is my hope that during my lifetime I will continue to live at Hyde Park, and if a period collection of this kind is permanently domiciled on what is my own place, I will be able to give assistance to the maintenance of the collection during my lifetime; as I have said before, it is my expectation that while the title to the collections would vest immediately in the Government, my house and that portion of the place on which I live would revert to the Government on my death.

I may mention that the place at Hyde Park is located on the New York–Albany Post Road two hours from New York City by train or motor, and four and one-half miles from the City of Poughkeepsie, which has good hotel and other accommodations.

FRANKLIN D. ROOSEVELT

Memorandum for Professor Felix Frankfurter
The White House, December 8, 1938

I am delighted that you are coming to lunch on Saturday. Could you join three or four others whom I am asking to come to the White House at 12:15 P.M., in order that we may have a little personal chat before the others join us at the luncheon at one o'clock?

F.D.R.

Cambridge, Mass., December 12, 1938

Dear Frank:

Wasn't that a fine affair on Saturday! It seemed to me that it was as edifying a gathering as I ever experienced. The talk was good, because free, at lunch, and your plan was persuasive because intrinsically patriotic and imaginative. Such minor suggestion, complementary to your proposals, merely confirmed and strengthened what you planned. I did appreciate your letting me join that interesting if not wholly scholarly group. Frank Walker and I saved it from being completely academic.

Have you the enclosed thoughts, sent me by a friend, who says that Hitler did not like his face and so recalled this issue.

It was grand seeing you so fit and I had a good time — even though I heard that Marion sent you a dirty dig against me.

Our affectionate regards to you.

Ever devotedly,
F.F.

Frank Walker, who had a gift for conciliating differences, was often used by Roosevelt to smooth away personal differences in the New Deal. He began to work on early plans for the Roosevelt Library.

Frankfurter sent Roosevelt an unattractive German stamp with Hitler's face on it, together with a mocking and derisive comment on the Nazi leader.

Mrs. Frankfurter had complained that her husband was finding it increasingly more difficult to arrive anywhere on time.

The White House, December 15, 1938

Dear Felix:

It was grand of you to come down to Washington, and as you suggest, we leavened the loaf of professionalism. I hope much that Frank Walker's end of the job will go ahead successfully and in the meantime, I am working on the legislation and the architectural drawings.

Many thanks for those stamps even though I do not think it is the least bit humorous to send me that face!

My best to you both,
F.D.R.

Tell Marion she is an honest person, and unlike a few other persons she and I know, does not refuse to testify on grounds of incrimination.

The White House, December 20, 1938

My dear Professor Frankfurter:

Inclosed is an unrevised galley of a proposed introduction by the President to one of the volumes of the President's Public Papers. It is highly confidential for the present. He would like very much to have your criticisms and suggestions in the form of a memorandum or of marginal notes on the galleys themselves.

He would appreciate it if you could let him have such a memorandum within a week as the publication date makes early action necessary.

Very sincerely yours,
M. A. LeHand

Telegram to Miss LeHand

Cambridge, Mass., December 21, 1938

YOUR SPECIAL HAS JUST COME. YOU WILL HAVE MY COMMENTS WITHIN TIME LIMIT. ALL GOOD WISHES FROM US BOTH.

F.F.

Cambridge, Mass., December 27, 1938

Dear Frank —

1) The Introduction to Volume Four is just right in its direction and substance. Apart from a few minor suggestions to conform with more meticulous accuracy to the cases that are canvassed and other factual items of American history, the governing consideration of the suggestions that I have to make is a desire to retain all the "poison" as Holmes would have called it, and at the same time not to give commentators, friendly and particularly unfriendly, any opportunity to write it off with criticism or correction of irrelevant details or contentious language.

In other words no room should be left for diverting the attention from the powerful argument and its detailed proof, by legitimate discussion of doubtful points or points that at least plausibly enable dust to be raised.

2) To this general end I have indicated a few excisions and modifica-

tions particularly with reference to the dead issue of whether or not the Supreme Court usurped power in exercising judicial review over legislation. What the hell!

Since as you rightly say this issue is now "academic" it seems clearly best not to open the door to its discussion again. That kind of discussion is a favorite red herring to divert attention from abuses of the exercise of judicial power.

3) I have also made two additions, as indicated in Inserts A and B.

Insert A has a powerful quotation from Holmes uttering his protest against the long series of abuses by the Court which seems to me important to quote not only because it puts Holmes and his language behind your indictment but also because it shows that the real grievance against the Court culminated rather than began during your Administration.

Insert B is an effort to weave the Humphrey case into the web of your argument. And I believe that the vindication of your action in the Humphrey case and the criticism to be made of the Court for that case are extremely important for the record — for the present and for history. It is the favorite instance to which resort is made whenever the argument of your "arbitrary" and "dictatorial" behavior is asserted, and it gives a very good concrete chance to show up the Court's own capricious conduct.

4) I have indicated but not written out another insertion that I believe to be greatly called for. There is a third case decided twenty five years before your Administration, the evils of which you inherited, to the great mischief of the country. That is *Adair* v. *United States*, 208 U.S. 161 (1908). The "shadow" of that "narrow limiting decision" hung like a heavy cloud over the effective utilization of the commerce clause and more particularly over every effort to deal in statesman-like fashion with the various aspects of industrial relations, collective bargaining, pension systems, etc., etc. I suggest that it is most important to take note of that case and have it precede your paragraph beginning "Fifteen years before my Administration."

5) The other suggestions speak for themselves, as indicated on the margins in my illegible handwriting (for which I deeply apologize). Be good enough to consider them in the light of their aim — to say everything you have said to educate the laity and (in the words of my great master, Holmes) "calculated to give the brethren pain," but at the same time give the scavenger profession nothing to feed on. Therefore, I suggest that even the citations follow fastidiously the Supreme Court model for citing cases (you can afford to retain the form of its citation when you overrule a case); I also suggest, as several rephrasings will indicate, that throughout you should appear as the real guardian of the Constitution adequate to all the

needs of the nation if only judges would be obedient to the majestic powers of the Constitution.

> Ever faithfully yours,
> F.F.

Cambridge, Mass., December 27, 1938

Dear Frank:

When I left the other day, after your archival luncheon, you said that you would like to see me, in two or three weeks, to talk about lower court appointments. This is just a word to say that I am at your disposal at any time — and shall be free from any engagements here until January 9th.

I had a most intimate talk with Lothian, fresh from London, who is *now* as hot against Hitler as any of us, and said that Chamberlain now knows his "appeasement" policy is a complete flop as to Hitler, but that he — Chamberlain — hopes to wean Mussolini from Hitler! Old Joe Chamberlain would never have been as naive as all that.

I hope that you are having some joyous days. At least on one thing Marion and I speak with one voice — in wishing you our warmest good wishes.

> Devotedly yours,
> F.F.

Lord Lothian, later British Ambassador to the United States, had been an assistant to David Lloyd George at the Paris Peace Conference and always felt a measure of personal guilt for the Versailles settlement. He persisted in the view, for several blundering years, that Hitler was a mere protest against the evils of the Versailles system and should not be treated as a dictator who wanted to push the world into war. He acknowledged his mistake later. Cut off early by an untimely death, he rendered heroic and indispensable service as Ambassador in Washington during the early struggles of the Second World War.

Frankfurter gave the President this exchange of letters with Lady Nancy Astor. His uncle, a famous scholar and librarian, in Vienna, had been arrested and placed in a concentration camp after the Nazi seizure of Austria. His uncle's "unguarded remarks" had actually been a brave and defiant protest against Nazi intolerance, especially as it destroyed the independence of free scholarship. His suffering while under confinement had been much greater than Lady Astor knew. Roosevelt was unaware of this episode until years later. On principle Frankfurter refused to seek a favor from the President in an intimate personal matter of this kind. He had already thanked Lady Astor for her help in an earlier message.

Throughout the appeasement years, the spacious estate of Waldorf and Nancy Astor at Cliveden was the frequent meeting place of people eager to promote a settlement with Hitler and Mussolini. Some, like Lothian, had noble but misguided motives. Others, like George Bernard Shaw, were seized with the infatuation that Mussolini was a modern Caesar. Still others, like Geoffrey Dawson, thought the mutilation of Czechoslovakia was a small price to pay for the preservation of peace. Holding great positions in the intellectual and social life of Britain, the members of the Cliveden Set exercised an influence on national policy far greater than one would have thought possible. Frankfurter knew too much about these men and women to question their patriotism; he doubted their wisdom and their knowledge of what was happening in Europe. He had argued with them at Cliveden, as had Churchill, and had seen for himself their dangerous assumptions and limited vision. Even his gratitude to Lady Astor for saving his uncle's life could not blind him to the folly and peril of the Cliveden philosophy, or wipe out his contempt for the advocates of appeasement in weakening the democracies in the face of the growing German and Italian danger.

London, England, May 1938

Dear Friend:

The minute I received your wire I spoke to the German Ambassador in London, and gave him, in no uncertain terms, our views on arresting aged scholars. He promised to do what he could. Three days afterwards, having heard no more, I talked to him again and warned him that unless I received good news of Herr Frankfurter, I should go myself to Vienna! He assured me that it would be alright. As you know, your uncle was released on the 28th March. The Ambassador tells me that he was only imprisoned a few days as a result of some unguarded remarks.

With regard to the "Cliveden Set," I am feeling as strongly about this as you are. There is not one word of truth in all this propaganda. It started in a Communist sheet. I send you a copy of a recent pamphlet. It is an attempt to create suspicion and a class war. Waldorf and I were in America and Lord Lothian in India when the fateful weekend was alleged to have been held at Cliveden in January!! It is now being used by the Communist, Socialist and Liberal oppositions in their effort to bring down the Government. Unfortunately a lot of journalists have seized it as "good copy." As you know, Philip Lothian and Waldorf have believed for about fifteen years that something should have been done in the re-organization of Europe, so as to rectify some of the mistakes of the Peace Treaties and remedy some of Germany's grievances. It was plainly impossible to keep Germany permanently down. You know this as well as I do. Unfortunately by not making voluntarily certain concessions to Germany, we have made them feel that they can only get redress by force. A dangerous lesson or belief.

I loathe all dictatorships whether of the Russian or German type. They are all equally cruel.

Some years ago I fought for a Trade Pact with Russia and recognition of the Soviet and I was then called a Communist.

Today I have supported those who wanted to improve the relations between Britain and Germany and between Britain and Italy, and now I am called a Fascist.

I am neither a Fascist nor a Communist, and I am very much surprised that you, knowing me and having visited Cliveden, should have swallowed this propaganda against us! [*In handwriting, Lady Astor added*] — ! That really is surprising. I know where most of this hatred comes from so don't you be caught up by it. Love to your wife. & be grateful that we are good in England but not if we listen to Extremists on right or left. I meant to go to France but hadn't to.

NANCY ASTOR

Cambridge, Mass., June 2, 1938

Dear Nancy Astor:

Unfortunately my letter must have reached you just about the time that the papers were full of the silly chatter regarding plots and conspiracies hatched at Cliveden. I am sorry about that, for not only was I not referring to such gossip-mongering, but when I wrote there wasn't even any publicity about it. Heavens! After all, have I not partaken of your ample and democratic hospitality at Cliveden all these years, beginning with my first visit in those grim days of March, 1918, when you had me speak to your invalided soldiers at Cliveden together with Jimmie Thomas and Alfred Zimmern. I have known you ever since those early days when the beloved and much lamented Phyllis first sent me to you, and knowing you, I know that there's nothing conspiratorial about you — that you are one of the most forthright, above-board people I know.

When I was referring to the attitude of you and your friends, I was thinking not of plotting but of political philosophy. I had in mind the views expressed in the summer of 1935 by Montagu Norman when he said that Hitler saved Europe from Bolshevism, a point of view that I often encountered during my year in England and again in the summer of 1936; the point of view of "appeasement" by acquiescence in the series of violent measures taken by Hitler and the general undermining of international law and order and the decencies of civilization. I had this out in part with

Lothian in 1936. The general point of view is expressed in two enclosures which put the matter not as I would put it, but at least will indicate the general direction of thought of those who think that the policy pursued toward Hitler and the Spanish adventure of Mussolini is neither conducive to the peace of the world nor likely to conserve those precious aspects of civilization which coincide with the best interests of the British Commonwealth of Nations. Please don't bristle at what Norman Angell and Dorothy Thompson have written. I send them as an indication of an outlook differing from yours, but very different from the silly newspaper talk about Cliveden.

And since we are talking with the candor of friendship let me suggest to you that you must not be too surprised if you are widely misunderstood regarding the anti-Semitic aspect — an essential aspect — of Nazism. When you make the kind of statements that you made at Dartmouth House, earlier in the year, about the control of advertisements in the American Press by Jews, and offer that as an explanation of what is the instinctive, traditional liberalism of American opinion against Hitler's brutality and cruelty, which make the old Russian pogroms seem kind by comparison, you not unnaturally make people who do not know your warm human qualities infer a sympathy on your part with Hitler's anti-Semitism which people like me, of course, know to be untrue. I wish we could talk all this out.

With warm regards,

Very sincerely,
FELIX FRANKFURTER

James H. Thomas, who owed his early success to his skill in trade union negotiations, rose to become a leading member of Ramsay MacDonald's Labour government. Sir Alfred E. Zimmern, an influential supporter of the League of Nations, had written The Greek Commonwealth, *which Frankfurter, like Brandeis, reread once a year. Montague Norman was the Governor of the Bank of England. Sir Norman Angell was a respected student of world affairs, as was Dorothy Thompson.*

New York, New York, December 29, 1938
Dear Felix:

This is the revised Introduction to Vol. Four with your suggestions and some others. He did not want to use the Humphrey case.

Would you please look over the enclosed and return it directly to me, with any further suggestions or criticisms, at the above address.

We are in quite a rush now, so I'd appreciate it if you could get at it as soon as possible. Thanks.

Yours,
SAM I. ROSENMAN

About a week later, on January 5, 1939, Roosevelt nominated Frankfurter to be an Associate Justice of the Supreme Court of the United States.

The Struggle Against Neutrality

1939

1939

February 27   Britain and France recognize Franco government in Spain.

March 15   Annihilation of Czechoslovakia when Germany, despite the Munich Agreement, occupies Bohemia and Moravia.

March 21-23   German annexation of Memel.

March 28   End of civil war in Spain.

March 31   Britain and France give Poland a pledge of assistance against aggression. David Lloyd George issues a warning in the British parliament that the pledge is meaningless without Russia's cooperation.

April 7   Italy invades Albania.
Franco government in Spain joins Germany, Italy, and Japan in the Anti-Comintern Pact.

April 13   France and Britain pledge their assistance to Greece.

April 15   President Roosevelt asks Hitler and Mussolini for assurances against any military attack on thirty-one nations in Europe and the Near East. The Dictators continue their plans for aggression.

May 3   Maxim Litvinov, Soviet Foreign Minister for eighteen years, is dismissed by Stalin and is replaced by Vyacheslav Molotov.

May 12   Britain and Turkey sign a mutual assistance pact.

May 17   Sweden, Norway, Finland announce that they will remain firmly neutral.

May 22   Germany and Italy proclaim their full military alliance.

August 20 —
September 1   Danzig crisis between Germany and Poland.

August 23   Molotov-Ribbentrop pact binds Germany and Russia to refrain from attacking each other and to remain neutral if the one is attacked by a third country. Japan leaves the Anti-Comintern Pact.

August 24   President Roosevelt appeals for settlement of the Danzig crisis by mediation. Poland agrees. Called into special session, the British House of Commons grants emergency

*powers to the Chamberlain government. Britain and Po-
land sign a pact of mutual assistance.*

August 25   *Hitler demands a settlement in Poland on his own terms.*

August 30   *Poland enforces partial mobilization.*

September 1   *Germany invades Poland.*

September 3   *Britain and France declare war on Germany.*

September 5   *United States proclaims neutrality in European war.*

FRANKFURTER *never expected to be appointed to the vacancy on the Supreme Court created by the death of Mr. Justice Cardozo in July 1938. In fact, the President had told him, with regret, that the appointment had to go elsewhere and Frankfurter began to submit various names for the President's consideration. Frankfurter at this stage found himself excluded from consideration because a group of powerful Senators and Governors wanted the appointment to go to someone from the Midwest or the Far West. In addition, Attorney General Cummings was against the Frankfurter appointment because he feared the Senate would make trouble before it confirmed him.*

Months passed, however, without a successor to Cardozo being found. While Frankfurter, privately but actively, was looking for the best man, the sentiment in the country began slowly to gather behind him as the ideal appointee, despite his repeated efforts to discourage these expressions of public support. The letters and memoranda written by Frankfurter during this waiting period show that he would have been happy to remain at the Harvard Law School. Beyond all question Mrs. Frankfurter would have preferred Cambridge to Washington. There was never any suggestion of Frankfurter thrusting himself forward to grasp the great prize. His friendship with Roosevelt made it a point of sensitive honor to avoid the advancement of his own claims. But events were generating their own momentum and forcing a Presidential decision.

National polls among leading members of the American bar made Frankfurter the overwhelming favorite for the appointment. Important legal authorities pointed out that the vacant seat on the Supreme Court was the scholar's seat; it had been filled by Story, Holmes, Cardozo. They thought the seat now belonged to Frankfurter by right of personal distinction and by reason of his legal scholarship. This theme was accepted and amplified by editorial writers and columnists.

A more sensitive point must now be explained. One day a group of wealthy and important Jews called on Roosevelt to beg him to make no effort at all to get Frankfurter appointed. They were afraid that Frankfurter's appointment would cause a dangerous growth in anti-Semitism. They made no impact on the President, except to give him a feeling of revulsion. He had no intention of turning their squalid fears and ignoble prejudices into acts of national policy.

Frankfurter learned with disgust of this interview, and with regret that Mr. Arthur Hays Sulzberger of the New York Times *had taken part in it. For years he had the mistaken notion that Mr. Sulzberger had opposed his nomination. Mr. Sulzberger in fact never changed his conviction that Frankfurter was incomparably the best qualified man in the United States to fill the Supreme Court vacancy. He joined the delegation reluctantly and after repeated entreaties from friends only because of his belief that in 1939 anti-Semitism was no imaginary danger. Frankfurter was glad at long last to get the true facts, for he respected Mr. Sulzberger and always referred to the New York* Times *as "my paper."*

Meanwhile, the presumed political opposition began to evaporate. Senator George Norris of Nebraska, the most respected liberal leader in the Senate, wrote a long and persuasive letter to the President urging that Frankfurter be appointed. Not content with this private endorsement, Senator Norris let his views be widely known, and later issued a public statement in support of Frankfurter. The President was delighted by Senator Norris's campaign since he knew it would silence the agitation for a Western appointment and would make Frankfurter the rallying point for liberal and progressive support. It gradually became clear to Roosevelt that Frankfurter was the preeminent and almost inevitable choice for the Supreme Court. There is strong reason to believe that Roosevelt had made his decision long before Frankfurter, at the President's request, began working with Judge Samuel Rosenman on the official account of the court-packing plan. Savoring his secret pleasure to the last drop, Roosevelt waited until he had delivered his annual message to Congress on January 4 and then phoned Frankfurter to tell him that he would be named to the Supreme Court the next morning. For once reduced to silence by the magnitude of the honor and the responsibility — it is not too strong to say that Frankfurter venerated the Supreme Court — he could only murmur to a pleased and sympathetic President that he wished his mother had been alive to see this day.

Incidentally, Attorney General Cummings was completely wrong. The Senate confirmed Frankfurter without a single dissenting vote.

Telegram to Roosevelt

Cambridge, Mass., January 4, 1939

THE PREREQUISITE TO AN EFFECTIVE TECHNICAL PREPAREDNESS IS THE ENLISTMENT OF THE UNDERSTANDING AND WILL OF OUR PEOPLE FOR THE PURPOSES OF DEMOCRACY AND THE MEANS TOWARD ACHIEVING THEM. TO THAT END YOUR ADDRESS WAS ADMIRABLY CALCULATED AND MUST GO A LONG WAY IN SECURING THAT SPIRIT OF UNITY WHICH UNDERLAY IT.

FELIX FRANKFURTER

With the memory of the 1938 crisis and the Munich Agreement still fresh in all minds, Roosevelt told Congress that "a war which threatened to envelop the world in flames has been averted; but it has become increasingly clear that world peace is not assured." Foreshadowing his later system of Lend-Lease to Britain and France, Roosevelt followed the advice of Frankfurter and others in calling for a revision of the neutrality laws. He said that "we have learned that when we deliberately try to legislate neutrality, our neutrality laws may operate unevenly and unfairly — may actually give aid to an aggressor and deny it to the victim. The instinct of self-preservation should warn us that we ought not to let that happen any more."

The White House, January 9, 1939

My dear Professor:

The President deeply appreciated your congratulatory message on his address at the opening of Congress. He asked me to be sure and thank you for him.

With all good wishes,

Sincerely yours,
M. H. McIntyre

Cambridge, Mass., January 4, 1939

Dear Frank:

And now I have the highest authority in the land to prove that those much malign me to say that I'm a talker. You will testify that you found me tongue-tied. How could I have responded to your gracious phone message otherwise than to be moved to mumbling silence. When so much is involved of past and future it would shrivel great things into small to speak of "honor" and "confidence" and all that. Believe me that I am humbly aware of the consecrated task that you have laid upon me. And to have it at your hands — with all that you signify for my most precious devotion to the country — is to sanctify Law with its humanest significance.

With the affectionate devotion of old friendship,

Ever yours,
F.F.

Telegram to Roosevelt

Cambridge, Mass., January 6, 1939

SAYS MARION "I HOPE YOU'LL BE ON THE STAND FOR DAYS SO THAT I CAN LEARN SOMETHING ABOUT YOU."

FELIX FRANKFURTER

Anticipating events soon to come, Mrs. Frankfurter expected Frankfurter to testify before the Senate Judiciary Committee, if asked to do so on his nomination to the Supreme Court, and to answer questions with candid detail. The President's reply to Frankfurter's jesting telegram was deliberately formal: he too expected the hearings to take place and to result in a Frankfurter triumph, thus vindicating his judgment in making the appointment, but at this point he was merely awaiting events.

The White House, January 7, 1939

Dear Felix:

Thank you indeed for your kind message of the sixth. I am truly grateful to you for it.

Very sincerely yours,
FRANKLIN D. ROOSEVELT

Telegram to Roosevelt
Cambridge, Mass., January 7, 1939

OUR NEW MR. DOOLEY WENT OVER BIG AND BEING STILL A FREE MAN I GLORY IN YOUNG HICKORY.

FELIX FRANKFURTER

In his Jackson Day speech, Roosevelt began by identifying himself as a "young fellow" having a conversation with "Old Hickory." The imaginary General Jackson reminded him that he was the only President who had two full terms with a majority of his own party in both the House and the Senate in all the time since James Monroe 114 years ago. Roosevelt then went on to a detailed and derisive analysis of the Republican party, with a humor sometimes reminiscent of Mr. Dooley. Since Frankfurter had not yet taken his seat on the Supreme Court, he felt free to call Roosevelt "Young Hickory," our new Andrew Jackson.

Telegram to Miss LeHand
Cambridge, Mass., January 17, 1939

WE ARE TAKING THE FEDERAL TOMORROW NIGHT, ARRIVING IN WASHINGTON THURSDAY MORNING. WARMEST REGARDS.

FELIX FRANKFURTER

Mr. and Mrs. Frankfurter were en route to Washington, where he was to appear before the Senate Committee. Instead of a sedate judicial atmosphere, Frankfurter found the committee room swarming with photographers and reporters, and several hundred people lined up in the corridor waiting for a chance to enter the crowded room. Mr. Dean Acheson sat

beside Frankfurter as his counsel but Frankfurter did all the talking. It was
Frankfurter talk all the way — crisp, sparkling, learned, overwhelming —
and it moved the audience, in defiance of the rules, to periodic applause.
More important, it persuaded the committee to recommend him unani-
mously for confirmation.

Cambridge, Mass., January 16, 1939

My dear Mr. President:

You and I have at least one strong prejudice in common, namely a
fastidious regard for hallowed precedents, even when their observance entails inability to enjoy a pleasure which was gaily and deeply anticipated.
That's the nature of this hard world.

And so I am bound to report the sad findings of a meticulous and
arduous research on my part. With every desire to discover the contrary, I
must report that I find no exception to the rule that no Associate Justice-
Designate, before he became a full-fledged member of the Court, has ever
attended the dinner given by the Chief Executive to members of the Supreme Court. The records are not clear whether this practice carries out a
"theory" or a "principle" of the American constitutional system. Certain it
is that there is no deviation in practice. Such hallowed customs should not
suddenly be broken in upon.

I will not add to the poignancy of our grief by dwelling further, at least
in words, over our sad inability to attend the dinner to which we were so
graciously bidden.

God, the President and the Senate willing, perhaps our opportunity to
attend such a dinner is not forever barred.

Respectfully yours,
F.F.

The following letter, the first written by Frankfurter on his Supreme
Court stationery, was one of which he was deeply proud and to which he
often referred. He thought it revealed more of himself than could be found
in a formal biographic memoir.

Washington, D.C., January 30, 1939

Dear Frank:

In the mysterious ways of Fate, the Dutchess County American and
the Viennese American have for decades pursued the same directions of
devotion to our beloved country. And now, on your blessed birthday I am
given the gift of opportunity for service to the Nation which, in any circumstances would be owing, but which I would rather have had at your
hands than at those of any other President barring Lincoln.

This is my first writing as an Associate Justice and it brings you my affectionate good wishes.

> Ever yours,
> F.F.

Frankfurter, continuing his campaign against the neutrality laws, sent on to Roosevelt the following letter from Mr. John H. Walker, of the Illinois Commerce Commission. The President asked both the State Department and the Treasury Department to intensify their study of the neutrality problem.

Springfield, Ill., February 2, 1939

Dear Felix: —

I suppose I should not be pestering you as I do, but you know, having been engaged in pretty active, strenuous, and sometimes important work all my life, I get restless at times now. By comparison, it almost seems complete idleness, although the work is interesting and also important; but what I wanted to bother you about is this: I heard both in the broadcast over the radio and saw in the newspapers this morning that the Republicans in the Senate — the Senate Military Committee — had taken the position that we should be absolutely neutral in the sale of military equipment and supplies for war purposes; that we should not only sell to the democracies, but that we should also sell to the dictator nations as well — The Fascists and Nazis. They did not mention the Communists, with which I am not finding fault. I understand that former President Hoover, who is the recognized spokesman for the Republican Party in the United States, has also taken the same position. In my opinion this is nothing more or less than a bid on their part to the sources of wealth that are supplying the Fascist and Nazi governments with finances and supporting them in every other way, for the Republican Party now, and later. It puts us in the position of making no distinctions between the robber, murderer, dictatorial, primitive, savagely-ruled nations and the peaceful law-abiding civilized nations ruled by democratic methods and who want, perhaps, more than anything else in the world, all differences arising between nations, settled by peaceful methods on the basis of justice.

They should be charged with not only being willing for sordidly selfish reasons, for cash, with being willing to support the beast nations against the Christian, peace-loving, civilized nations; but they should be charged by coming out in their real colors on this issue now, as suggesting and encouraging those influences in our own country, *now*, and that that means they are encouraging and supporting the overthrow of our government by force, now.

I believe that if the powers that be, in the Democratic political organization, will wait until the Republicans get out so far on that issue that they can't get back, and then make that the principal issue in the coming election, that we can beat them in every village and hamlet in the United States.

With every good wish, I am,

Yours,
JOHN H. WALKER

Washington, D.C., February 8, 1939

Dear Missy:

I know the President keeps a watchful eye on events in Seattle, and so he may already have seen this item. Harold J. Laski writes me that the main effect of all this bubbling is that his public lectures have been crowded "as nothing in the history of this place." Do you suppose he has arranged this with the D.A.R. on a fee basis?

Ever yours,
F.F.

Professor Harold J. Laski of the London School of Economics was lecturing at the University of Washington in Seattle, holding seminars and addressing large meetings. Since he loathed both appeasement and reaction, and thought Roosevelt one of the supreme leaders in world history, it is not surprising that he was denounced by the local members of the Daughters of the American Revolution. Their praise would have killed him.

Washington, D.C., February 16, 1939

Dear Mr. President,

I'm so sorry you've had to be laid up by this dreadful bug. This is only wishing you a grand trip and lots of sunshine and laughter.

Affectionately,
MARION

The President, recovering from the grippe, was going to the Caribbean to watch the naval games and to recuperate.

Washington, D.C., March 7, 1939

Dear Missy:

Justice Brandeis has, in effect, made his beloved University of Louisville the depositary of his papers, and his wishes are being carried out through his intimate friend, Mr. Bernard Flexner. The enclosed letter brings a request for the original of the Justice's letter of resignation to the

President, and, since all the other letters regarding the Justice's retirement have now been made available as part of the Brandeis collection at Louisville, the President may like to present, as his gift to the University of Louisville, the original of the Justice's letter of resignation.

Faithfully yours,
F.F.

The White House, March 11, 1939

Dear Felix: —

Personally, of course, I would most gladly give to the University of Louisville the original of Justice Brandeis' letter of resignation — but I do not think that the original ought to be separated from the official Presidential files which contain all similar original letters.

However, it will, of course, give me great pleasure to have the original photostated for the University. Also it occurs to me that possibly a better form of facsimile could be obtained. I will look into it. Will you let Mr. Flexner know?

As ever yours,
F.D.R.

The following letters concern Frankfurter's status as a reserve major in the Judge Advocate General's branch dating back to the First World War. A minor official in the War Department had sent Mr. Justice Frankfurter a routine letter advising him that his name was being taken off the reserve list. It seemed hilarious to Frankfurter that the army should be worrying about a matter of this kind when the world was rushing to war. Later, the army had second thoughts and believed Frankfurter should be kept in the reserve with some honorary status. Roosevelt laughed over this episode as a classic example of bureaucratic muddle and futility. Echoes of this rough handling of an obvious affair kept reappearing in their talk and letters whenever they were seeking examples of how public business should not be transacted.

Senator Nye, an isolationist spokesman, was convinced Roosevelt was dragging the country into war and wanted him shorn of his powers as Commander-in-Chief.

Washington, D.C., March 8, 1939

Dear C-i-C:

Inter leges arma silent was not a maxim of the hard-headed Romans. Nevertheless, under the circumstances, it is, I suppose, sensible for me to lay down my paper arms by resigning my commission as a Major in the Reserve Corps.

There is probably some official in the War Department to whom I might appropriately make this martial communication, but I should like to salute once more my Commander-in-Chief before Senator Nye takes away his constitutional powers!

With great respect, I am, Sir,

> Faithfully yours,
> FELIX FRANKFURTER
> Major, J.A.G.-Res.

The White House, March 14, 1939

My dear Major Frankfurter: —

Your effort to retire from the United States Army at this time of crisis has been rejected.

If instead of consulting the words of Cicero (a mere talker) to find the motto "inter leges arma silent," you had consulted the famous phrase of Major General Caesar (a doer), "leges impellent arma," i.e., laws make for war — you would see that it is more essential than ever that you remain in the Army.

I am enclosing a memorandum from the Chief of Staff, which I take it results from a three day consideration of your case by the whole general staff.

I regret that it is impossible at this moment to consider you for promotion to the rank of Lieutenant Colonel. I am informed that this will depend somewhat on your conduct during the next few years.

If shortly before January 20, 1941, you will re-submit your request for promotion, I shall be glad to act on it one way or the other before I retire as Commander-in-Chief of the Army and Navy in favor of Senator Nye.

> With great respect, I am, Sir,
> FRANKLIN D. ROOSEVELT
> Commander-in-Chief

Washington, D.C., March 14, 1939

The Honorable, Franklin D. Roosevelt,
Commander-in-Chief of the Armed Forces
of the United States.

Sir:

Even though it be couched in the unlaconic language appropriate for the judicial mind, I recognize a military order when issued, and so

I remain, Sir,

> Obediently and martially yours,
> FELIX FRANKFURTER
> Lieutenant Colonel *in spe*, J.A.G.-Res.

The White House, March 23, 1939

Dear Felix:

The President has asked me to forward to you, for transmission to the University of Louisville, the enclosed copy of Justice Brandeis' resignation.

This copy is an etching of the original and I think it should be labeled as such when it is placed with the other Brandeis papers at the University of Louisville.

With kindest regards,

Very sincerely yours,
STEPHEN EARLY

Bloomington, Ind., March 27, 1939

Dear Miss LeHand:

Would you please give this to the President? I should take it as a great personal favour if you could find your way to support the proposals and warnings it contains.

Very sincerely yours,
HAROLD J. LASKI

Bloomington, Ind., March 27, 1939

Dear Mr. President,

1. I threw up my hat with joy over Bill Douglas' nomination. He is second only to Felix in the list of those I want to see there. One more good resignation (by death or art is indifferent to me) and it really will be "our" Supreme Court.

2. I read with dismay some correspondence between you and Mr. Justice Frankfurter in which the latter practically asks to be nominated to a lieutenant-colonelcy in the U. S. Reserve. I ought, as a friend, to warn you of two things. First, it is quite certain that the Justice has not for many years given any adequate study to military science, especially on the side of physical drill; and second, you will remember the awful effect on the eminent jurist, Professor S. H. Wigmore, when he was made a Lt. Colonel in 1917. Ver.sap.sat.

3. But if F.F. is to be promoted, I hereby apply to be made an honorary corporal (note my modesty) on the Staff of the Commander-in-Chief of the U.S. Army (or equivalent naval position would do)!! I may point out that members of our Royal family are colonels, admirals etc. in many foreign armies, and that my knowledge of the duties involved is probably about on par with theirs. I should, however, expect to be presented with the necessary uniforms, including mess kit. Such an appointment, I may

add, would in my opinion spur Mr. Justice Frankfurter to those studies he has so shamefully neglected in recent times.

> With affection and respect,
> I am, Sir,
> Your humble, obedient servant
> LASKI

The following memorandum was attached to Laski's letter:

MEMORANDUM FOR JUSTICE FRANKFURTER

The White House, March 29, 1939

For preparation of reply.

F.D.R.

William O. Douglas, a graduate of Columbia Law School, had been Commissioner and Chairman of the Securities and Exchange Commission from 1934 until his appointment to the Supreme Court.

Calvert Magruder was appointed federal judge in 1939 and retired in 1959 as chief judge of the Court of Appeals for the First Circuit. Seven of Frankfurter's law clerks came to him after their postgraduate judicial year with Judge Magruder. Frankfurter used to recall with relish that he had chosen Magruder to be Brandeis's first law clerk even though Magruder had shunned all the three courses offered by Frankfurter at the Harvard Law School. Between him and Magruder there was an easy and affectionate relationship notable even in Frankfurter's gallery of friendships.

Washington, D.C., April 6, 1939

Dear Frank,

You've done three swell things — the Magruder and Levinson nominations and your Reorganization order, with its message to Congress. These are things that continue to give proof that democracy can function.

I'm glad that Lothian has at last discovered that Hitler wants to dominate. Who denies that the British are bright!

> Ever yours,
> F.F.

The day before, Roosevelt sent an appeal for peace to Hitler and Mussolini which the two dictators never bothered to answer. Roosevelt said that "an atmosphere of peace cannot exist if negotiations are overshadowed by the threat of force or by the fear of war. I think you will not misunderstand the spirit of frankness in which I send you this message. Heads of great governments in this hour are literally responsible for the fate of humanity in the coming years. They cannot fail to hear the prayers of their peoples to

*be protected from the foreseeable chaos of war. History will hold them
accountable for the lives and the happiness of all — even unto the least. I
hope that your answer will make it possible for humanity to lose fear and
regain security for many years to come."*

Washington, D.C., April 15, 1939

Dear Frank —

Your messages to Hitler and Mussolini were not words but acts — the
most potent of acts, the mobilization of the moral forces of the world. Profound prayers must be going up for your success in this endeavor to save the
world from considerable self-destruction.

And you were cunningly delicious last night.

"F.F.: Isn't it a joy and satisfaction to have a cultivated gentleman in
the White House? Justice Roberts (with Emphasis): 'By God it *is*.'"

Ever yours,
F.F.

Memorandum for F.F.

The White House, May 3, 1939

I have had a bad time picking a Librarian to succeed Putnam. What
would you think of Archie MacLeish? He is not a professional Librarian
nor is he a special student of incunabula or ancient manuscripts. Nevertheless, he has lots of qualifications that said specialists have not.

What do you think? You might consult with Sam Morison and any
other Twentieth Century minds you think useful. I assume you will not
revert to the Nineteenth Century in making your recommendation!

F.D.R.

Washington, D.C., May 11, 1939

Dear Mr. President:

By your kind inquiry of me regarding Archie MacLeish as a possible
successor to Herbert Putnam you touch a subject of very special interest to
me. Not only have I had to think about the nature of a great library during
my twenty-five years at Harvard, but I have been ancestrally concerned, as
it were, with the problem, for since my early boyhood an uncle of mine was
the Director of the great library of the University of Vienna. Ever since
1911, I have had more than casual acquaintance with the Congressional
Library, and Archie MacLeish I have known in his various manifestations
from the time that he first swam into my ken as a law student in 1915. I say
all this by way of indicating the point of view and experience from which I
have derived the observations that follow.

(1) According to the best American and European tradition, the li-

brarians that have left the most enduring marks have not been technical librarians. Every eminent librarian of the last fifty years in Oxford or Cambridge or the British Museum has been a scholar or man of letters. Dr. Richard Garnett and Sir Frederick Kenyon of the British Museum, Dr. Edmund Gosse of the Library of the House of Lords, and Sir E. W. B. Nicholson at the Bodleian Library immediately come to mind. The librarian of the Widener Library in its greatest formative days was, as you know, Archie Coolidge, who wasn't a scholar and not a librarian. This is also true of the great library of the Harvard Law School. I should also mention John S. Billings, of the Army Medical Library. It has been true of similar institutions that the necessary technique for the technical running of a library can be supplied by subordinates. What is wanted in the directing head of a great library are imaginative energy and vision. He should be a man who knows books, loves books and makes books. If he has these three qualities the craftsmanship of the librarian's calling is an easily acquired quality. But only a scholarly man of letters can make a great national library a general place of habitation for scholars, because he alone ready understands the wants of scholars.

The danger of the technical librarian is that he over-emphasizes the collection and classification of books — the merely mechanical side of the library — and fails to see the library as the gateway to the development of culture. I believe it to be true that the failures in the British Museum and elsewhere have been largely promotions from within the staff of people who have grown up with the job, and who were rewarded for the obvious fidelity which, happily, is rather characteristic of those in the Government service.

(2) The need for qualities other than those which are trained in a professional librarian are accentuated in the case of the head of the Congressional Library. That Library is not merely a library, and in the immediate future even more so than in the past it will be concerned with problems quite outside the traditional tasks associated with collecting, housing and circulating books. For one thing the Library of Congress is a museum as well as a library. It has a distinguished collection of etchings and engravings — an aspect of the library which was of the greatest importance and edification to a person like Mr. Justice Holmes. It has a great collection of music — especially manuscript music — and its general manuscript materials, especially recent acquisitions like the Taft papers and the Roosevelt papers, present delicate questions which can be adequately dealt with only by a person of sympathetic and imaginative insight.

(3) But we are at the threshold of deeper problems than any that the foregoing present. Of course, the culture of books in the old-fashioned sense is still and will continue to be dominantly important. But in the educational influence of our democracy two new media are already compet-

ing for primacy with the printed page — the radio and the movie. In both of these educative forms Archie has been a pioneer. He was the first to experiment with a literary form constructed especially for its effectiveness through the unseen voice of the radio — he is the father of the so-called radio play. In the field of the motion picture he was the moving spirit in a series of "Contemporary History" which released two pictures that received widest acclaim — one a picture of the civil war in Spain with Hemingway commentary, and another on China done by Ivens, the famous Dutch picture photographer. With television entering the phase of practicality, the Government, through the Federal Communications Commission, will be presented with the most subtle and difficult problems pertaining to the movie industry.

(4) Another factor is likewise not to be lost sight of — Latin America. If the various attempts at cultural exchange with Latin America are to be wisely pursued by the Government, the Library of Congress should play a very important part. Archie has a wide and sympathetic understanding of our cultural relations with Latin America. Indeed, this is only one phase of the whole gamut of culture over which Archie's experience and human associations extend.

(5) It must be remembered that Archie was one of the leaders of his class at the Law School, proved his metal as a very able lawyer, was invited to join the Harvard Law School Faculty, then pursued his poetic career, was the most effective editor of *Fortune*, and this year showed astonishing personal and organizing faculties in connection with the Nieman Fellowships at Harvard. He unites in himself qualities seldom found in combination — those of the hardheaded lawyer with the sympathetic imagination of the poet, the independent thinker and the charming "mixer." He would bring to the Librarianship intellectual distinction, cultural recognition the world over, a persuasive personality and a delicacy of touch in dealing with others, and creative energy in making the Library of Congress the great center of the cultural resources of the Nation in the technological setting of our time.

Faithfully yours,

F.F.

Mr. MacLeish was appointed Librarian of Congress.

Roosevelt had made yet another effort, in deliberately simple terms, to explain that America's safety was closely linked with Europe's problems — and that the connection was growing closer all the time. Frankfurter had praised the statement as an admirable example of the way a complicated subject should be explained to a national audience.

The White House, May 24, 1939

Dear Felix:

Many thanks for your note. On Monday night I felt a little like a cross between a First Grade Primer and a Congressman — but anyway the vaccination seemed to take and I may try another shot soon.

My best to you both,

As ever yours,
F.D.R.

Frankfurter had sent the President three memoranda on the European situation. They were all designed to strengthen the President's conviction that he must always stress the threat of Nazi Germany to freedom and peace, even when he was urging Congress to take some specific action to increase the capacity of the United States to defend itself. It was this ability to see the problem of security in the largest international context that made Roosevelt, even more than Churchill, the destined spokesman of the United Nations.

Memorandum for Missy
The White House, June 3, 1939

Send back to Felix and say that the President remarked that Felix was at least headed down the right road.

F.D.R.

Telegram to Frankfurter
The White House, June 13, 1939

PRESIDENT DELIGHTED TO TALK WITH YOU 8:30 DAYLIGHT TIME THIS EVENING.

GRACE G. TULLY

Frankfurter wanted to talk with Roosevelt about two subjects — refugees, and the revision or repeal of the neutrality laws so that the United States would not be forced to remain a helpless neutral spectator while the dictators attacked the democracies.

On June 8, Roosevelt had warned that the refugee problem "may at any time be greatly aggravated by a new wave of persecution in Germany." He also, in a passage foreshadowing the crucial place of Palestine in the later debate, said "the problem in its larger aspects appears almost insoluble except through a basic solution such as the development of a suitable area to which refugees could be admitted in almost unlimited numbers." This passage made almost no impact on European statesmen, but Frankfurter knew why Roosevelt had said it and what it meant about the drift of American policy. During this period Frankfurter was in touch with both Dr. Chaim Weizmann and Mr. David Ben-Gurion, the two most important Zionist leaders, and he wished to give their views to the President.

On June 12, the day before Frankfurter's telegram, Roosevelt had emphasized that America's devotion to peace should never be mistaken for weakness. Speaking at West Point, he said that "we seek peace by honorable and pacific conduct but that must never be mistaken for weakness on the part of the United States." Frankfurter regarded this statement as a negative and inadequate formulation of America's purposes.

He thought the dictator states in Europe and Asia would be impressed only when they saw America's strength being actively used to bar the march of aggression. To awaken public opinion to the growing danger, Frankfurter wanted a committee formed of distinguished Americans to conduct a national campaign whose theme would be that the United States could survive only as a beleaguered and improverished fortress if the democracies in Europe were struck down and devoured by the dictatorships. Months later, in the early phase of the European war, this idea took shape in the committee under the chairmanship of William Allen White to bring all aid to our allies short of war.

It was Frankfurter's unswerving purpose to enforce the lesson that the democracies of endangered Europe were our inevitable allies no matter what our statute books said about neutrality.

During the accumulating anxieties of this spring and summer, before the thunder of war broke on the world, Frankfurter sent nearly three hundred notes to the President on the international peril that faced America. Most of these notes, as Frankfurter remembered it, were scribbled on the small memorandum pads of the Supreme Court. They were usually delivered by hand to the White House by Frankfurter's messenger or else were phoned to the White House when Frankfurter was away from Washington on a summer holiday. Sometimes a reply was written on the back by the President; at other times he asked a question; sometimes he told Frankfurter to await a phone call from someone in the White House or the State Department. Then the brisk exchange of notes, running on occasion to five a day, continued.

Most of these notes were only a few lines in length and were intended to keep the two men in constant touch on what was to both of them by now the supreme reality in world affairs — the menace of war and America's duty to defend herself by defending freedom.

For some reason never clear even to himself, Frankfurter destroyed all the notes with the President's comments on the back; and Roosevelt did not keep Frankfurter's notes in his papers at Hyde Park. From time to time Frankfurter did dictate a brief memorandum to himself to summarize the course of his dialogue with the President. This is the only important part of the Roosevelt-Frankfurter correspondence of which the documentary record has been destroyed. But that is not as serious a loss as it seems, for enough material is available to reveal the direction of the President's planning and the nature of Frankfurter's advice.

With the start of the Second World War only a few days away, Frankfurter sent this telegram to Roosevelt. Despite his efforts to gain another uneasy truce, Roosevelt agreed with Frankfurter that the time had come for Britain and France to end their retreats and to accept the ordeal of war.

Telegram to Roosevelt

August 25, 1939

YOU AT LEAST ARE DOING ALL THAT ANY MORTAL CAN DO. OUR AFFECTIONATE GOOD WISHES.

FELIX FRANKFURTER

Washington, D.C., August 30, 1939

Dear Missy:

Be good enough to pass this on.

Now that "the crisis" has worked out as by the clock you will remember that I told you, when I came back, that in London they had definite word it was to begin about the 21st.

I hope you had some refreshing fun and no heat.

Our best,
F.F.

New Milford, Conn., August 30, 1939

Dear Frank:

As Marion and I sit glued to the radio during the day and for a good part of the night, I reflect not only on those enduring values of man we call civilization and the fate of friends and relatives in Vienna and Paris and London, but also think of what burdens these anxious days are casting on you. All your communications seem to me to have been just right — rightly conceived and admirably phrased — and you have given the right leads for this country and for all those to whom brute rule is intolerable.

As wise a man as I saw in London was the Chinese Ambassador, and I thought this letter from him, about the effect of your abrogation of the Japanese Treaty, would interest you.

Take good care of yourself — for in any event we are in for a heavy sea. . . . Marion joins in warmest regards.

Ever yours,
F.F.

Chinese Embassy, 49 Portland Place, London W. 1.

August 13, 1939

Dear Justice Frankfurter,

I think I should write you this note not only to thank you for your letter from the ship and posted at Cambridge, but also to comment how promptly prophetic your conviction proved to be that the long run need not be too long, if only the will and understanding of even a few men are determined enough to insist on the decent ends. President Roosevelt's courageous act of abrogation fulfilled your convictions only two days after I had received your letter. It literally transformed the whole international situation, and I can only wish that equal will and understanding over here may sustain that transformation.

I had no opportunity to get in touch with Mr. Morgenthau, glad as I should have been to do so, as he was in town for only three hours on his way to Holland. Currency remains China's central vital problem in the present situation.

I trust that you and Mrs. Frankfurter may be fortified by plenty of the good Massachusetts and Maine air before you face Washington again.

Sincerely yours,

Quo Tai-chi

On September 1, Nazi Germany invaded Poland. Two days later Britain and France were at war with Germany. That night Roosevelt delivered a fireside chat to the American people. "This Nation," he said, "will remain a neutral nation, but I cannot ask that every American remain neutral in thought as well. Even a neutral has a right to take account of facts. Even a neutral cannot be asked to close his mind or his conscience."

In taking this stand, Roosevelt was deliberately repudiating the example of President Wilson, who had urged Americans from 1914-1917 to be neutral not only in their deeds but in their thoughts. Nothing could have pleased Frankfurter more than this bold repudiation.

On September 21, Roosevelt asked Congress to repeal the embargo provision of the neutrality law. The effect of such a repeal would be that Britain and France, with their command of the sea, would be able to buy arms from the United States and carry them in their own ships. Nazi Germany could make their purchases only by risking a decisive battle with the British fleet.

As it actually operated, the neutrality law placed all the combatant nations on the same level, regardless of their ability to carry supplies at their own risk. Frankfurter had persistently argued that the neutrality law violated the traditional principles of international law. Fully agreeing with him, Roosevelt told Congress that the Neutrality Act must go. "I regret," he said, "that the Congress passed that Act. I regret equally that I signed that Act." On November 3, after weeks of harsh and violent debate, Congress repealed the embargo on arms.

Telegram to Roosevelt

New Milford, Conn., September 3, 1939
MANY THANKS AND ESPECIALLY FOR NOT REQUIRING US TO BE NEUTRAL IN THOUGHT.

FELIX FRANKFURTER

The White House, September 5, 1939

Dear Felix:

It was very thoughtful and kind of you to send me that message of September third, and I want you to know that I appreciate it.

Very sincerely yours,
F.D.R.

Heath, Mass., September 13, 1939

Dear Frank:

1. Only if you knew how deeply I feel the dependence of the well-being of this country and of the world on *your* well-being, could you realize with what happiness I found you as fit as I did. Your Lincolnian calm — compounded of sagacity and good-humor — is precisely what is most needed for the long pull ahead, and as an infectious example for the country.

2. The enclosed from Buxton shows how the wind is blowing up here.

3. I hope that the proprieties and prudence will justify some such sentiment as the following in your message to Congress:

"A so-called neutrality law which in practical operation favors the forces of aggression must be fundamentally wrong in conception. It runs counter to American traditions and ideals, and is in conflict with international law."

All good luck to you — and your unabated good health — and good spirits!

Ever faithfully yours,
F.F.

Frank Buxton had reported to Frankfurter that opinion in Boston and throughout New England was veering strongly in the direction of American help for Britain and France. It was recognized that it was impossible for the United States to help Poland, bombed and overrun by the Nazi armies.

Roosevelt marked Frankfurter's statement on neutrality with a heavy

*pencil, had it copied out as a separate memorandum to himself, and used it
in preparing his case against the Neutrality Act.*

*Roosevelt attached this memorandum written in longhand, to Frank-
furter's letter of September 13:*

"Miscalled Neutrality Act." In every case puts us on the side of the
offenders.

1. Return to international law.
2. (a) Repeal
   (b) Citizens not to go to War Zones. Vessels.
   (c) Credits
   (d) Title
   (e) American vessels with contraband to go to European ports of
       belligerents.

Memorandum by Roosevelt

September 28, 1939

From F.F.

"A so-called Neutrality Law which in practical operation favors the
forces of aggression must be fundamentally wrong in conception. It runs
counter to American traditions and ideals and is in conflict with international law."

Memorandum for F.F.

The White House, October 5, 1939

Here is my latest. I send it to you for correction or editing.

A radical is a man with both feet firmly planted — in the air.

A conservative is a man with two good legs who has never learned to
walk.

A reactionary is a somnambulist walking backwards.

A liberal is a man who uses his legs and hands at the command of his
intelligence.

F.D.R.

Washington, D.C., October 8, 1939

Dear Frank:

This spells out what I thought might be good for Henry M. to consider. You will know best whether it *is* any good.

Please do look at the Asquith quotation on page 2. That is so pertinent
for your situation.

Isn't it a scream that word has gone out over the radio that "Mr. Justice Frankfurter has remained in the Army"! I suppose that is for foreign consumption to affect the European war situation.

Ever faithfully yours,
F.F.

Henry M. Morgenthau, Secretary of the Treasury, made this Frankfurter memorandum the basis for his own recommendations to the President on wartime taxation. During the drafting of this legislation, the Treasury experts on several occasions sought Frankfurter's advice on questions of legal draftsmanship.

Some Observations Regarding Taxes

1. This Problem of Confidence.

No earthly government is free from error, but the people of the United States have a confidence in government today which they did not have in 1933. Nor can there be serious doubt that confidence in government today is much more deserved, much more justified, than it was in 1928 and 1929 when government abdicated its responsibility to the rulers of business and finance.

It is unfortunate from the viewpoint of true conservatism that business and finance do not more fully recognize that in a changing world a truly liberal government is a very real assurance that the orderly processes of government will not break down because of stubborn resistance to change or unreasoning insistence on change. Liberal government cannot afford to lose the confidence of the mass of the people in its willingness to concern itself with their needs. In their *Life of Lord Oxford and Asquith* (Vol. 1, p. 103), by J. A. Spender and Cyril Asquith, Asquith wisely observes:

> It is of course a much easier thing to lead their (the Tory) party than ours, as you and I will find if we ever have a share in the work. The function of the Tories in these days is neither to originate nor to resist *à outrance*, but to forestall inevitable changes by judicious compromises in the interest of threatened classes and institutions. They have, just as much as the old Tories had and even more, wealth, property and the *vis inertiae* on their side, and as their game is a difficult one and full of intellectual interest, they admit a vast deal more than they used to do of the higher intelligence of the country. But they need neither intuition, initiative, constructive power (except of a low kind), nor (what is rarest of all) the ability to organise and concentrate the scattered discontent and diffuse enthusiasm of a half-educated society.

2. In a modern industrial state, the problems of taxation are difficult and complicated. And there is no one simple key to their solution.

It has sometimes been urged that taxes should be levied for revenue only. But nearly all taxes affect revenues in some way. Even a prohibitive protective tariff may be justified on the ground that protected industries may yield more tax revenues to the government than unprotected industries. One cannot be indifferent to the fact that some taxes for revenues may fall upon those least able to bear them and other taxes for revenues may fall upon those best able to bear them. Some taxes for revenues may have a more adverse effect upon consumers' purchasing power than other taxes for revenue. And some taxes for revenue may have a more adverse effect on industry than other taxes for revenue. Tax measures cannot be judged simply by the amount of revenue they produce, but must be appraised in light of their effect on the economic system.

Generally speaking, a modern industrial society must increasingly rely upon progressive taxation which is graduated according to ability to pay and must avoid regressive taxation which curtails the purchasing power of the great mass of consumers. There is respectable economic authority for the view that purchasing power and employment could be increased by shifting some of the tax burden, particularly the burden of indirect taxes from those least able to pay to those whose surplus savings are not fully absorbed in new investments. In rehauling our tax system we cannot be unmindful of the fact that there is inadequate purchasing power among the lower income groups and that there is oversaving, i.e., savings which do not find their way into new investment among the higher income groups. Government must be concerned with obtaining a permanently higher standard of life for all the people as the only sure way of securing recovery, in any abiding sense, for business.

The need for increased government revenues during a period of business recession and faltering recovery has retarded a comprehensive revision of our revenue laws in conformity with progressive standards of taxation. In fact the need for increased revenues has to some extent made necessary further indirect consumption of taxes.

The Government has not been unmindful of the inequities of our tax system. The undistributed profits tax, while imperfect and faulty in operation, was intended to turn surplus corporate savings into purchasing power and to prevent the avoidance of the individual surtaxes. The proposed elimination of tax-exempt securities is also intended to prevent the avoidance of the individual surtaxes and to make it possible for private enterprise to compete for the funds of those who have sufficient means to be able to afford to take business risks.

Only a beginning, and not a wholly successful beginning, has been made in rehauling a system of taxation which is much more regressive than might be supposed because of the nominally high individual surtax rates which are in theory prescribed by the statutes, but which are in practice avoided through the corporate accumulation of undistributed profits and the holding of tax-exempt securities.

Unquestionably there are other inequities in our tax system which should be attacked. And in attacking these inequities, the advice and counsel of really disinterested experts not under retainer, within and without the government, should be obtained.

3. Much can be said in favor of a frank lowering of the nominally and deceptively high surtaxes on high-bracket incomes. It is quite possible that these surtaxes are too high to yield their maximum productivity, and their very severity in a sense puts a premium on evasion. The retention of high individual surtaxes and the virtual repeal of the undistributed profits tax suggests that there is a political school which favors high surtaxes only because they can be evaded.

But if the deceptively high surtaxes are to be reduced, wholehearted cooperation ought to be ensured in advance to ensure that the reduced surtaxes are really to be effective in practice. That means the elimination of all future tax-exempt securities and the application of the so-called Glass plan so that even the income from existing tax-exempt securities will not be ignored in assessing the surtaxes against income from other sources. That means a genuine undistributed profits tax, made workable by treating all stock-dividends as distributed profits taxable in the hands of the stockholder. That means a strengthening rather than a weakening of the capital gains taxes. That means plugging up every other device which may be used to evade the surtaxes. That means limiting the contingent fees which lawyers take in order to discover new devices of evasion.

4. The capital gains tax is inherently not an unjust tax. It is a tax which falls on those best able to bear the burden of taxation and at a time when they are best able to bear that burden. A great amount of the proceeds of the tax comes from dealings in securities, and the tax may to a very considerable degree be regarded as a windfall tax. The present rates are in many instances much lower than they should be. It is difficult to avoid some cases of individual hardship under almost any tax law. A few cases of individual hardship do not justify tax-immunities for rich speculators. Last year much of the taxes on capital gains was given away under claims that modifications would help business. The small capital gains tax now in force on securities held for more than 18 months may some time lead to stock market liquidations which will imperil rather than help recovery. The mere encouragement of speculation in old existing securities is of very doubtful help to a program of sustained recovery.

Generally speaking, the capital gains tax should be strengthened, not weakened. Capital gains on assets held for a long or short period ought not to be taxed at a rate lower than the highest surtax rate the taxpayer pays on his income, exclusive of capital gains. Greater liberality might, however, be allowed in carrying over capital losses to be applied against capital gains in subsequent years.

5. It is claimed that the capital gains tax makes it more difficult for new enterprise to get capital. The validity of this contention is open to grave question. The present rates on capital gains are not in fact substantially higher than those prevailing under the Mellon-Mills-Hoover regime. But if we want to help new enterprise, the way to do it is modify the tax as it relates to the assumption of equity risks in new enterprise and not to put a further premium on speculation in old securities which may make it harder for new enterprise to get risk-assuming capital.

If we want to encourage the assumption of risks in new enterprise we might permit capital gains to be invested within a given period in unsecured equities in new enterprises (as defined under Treasury regulations) without those gains being taxed until after the new investment in the new enterprise is liquidated. This privilege could be continued indefinitely so that there would be in effect no tax collected on capital gains as long as those gains continued to be promptly invested in new enterprise. Such a law would create a reservoir of funds specifically seeking outlet in new enterprises. Of course there are administrative difficulties in the application of such a tax, but certainly it is better to face those difficulties than to consider dropping the tax entirely. It would be an unhappy paradox if the present Congress should eliminate taxes on capital gains which not even Mellon, Mills and Hoover could get even their Congress to eliminate.

6. The health of the economic system depends upon the smooth functioning of its interrelated parts. Intimate knowledge and understanding of the working of a small segment of the economic system does not necessarily connote knowledge or understanding of the delicate interrelations upon which the smooth functioning of the system as a whole depends. One part of a machine may fail to function not because of any defect of its own but because some other part of the machine is clogged or broken. A business man caught with excessive inventories for which he cannot find a ready market, may think that he needs bank credit and in a sense he does, but he and everyone else would be better off if he had ready customers for his wares.

The problem of government in relation to economic recovery is not an ordinary business problem. Economic recovery requires the full employment of labor as well as capital. To understand the forces which will make or break economic recovery requires an understanding of something more than how to meet a payroll.

The sustainment of economic recovery may depend much more upon the predicability of the federal spending policy to which the economic system has become accustomed than upon any so-called appeasement policy. There may be much more ground to fear an interruption of recovery from the sterilization of the increased social security payroll taxes which become effective in January 1940, than from any of the taxes against which complaint is made.

The following letter to Frankfurter was written by a complete stranger.

Reno, Nevada, October 14, 1939

Dear Sir: —

In *Life*'s magazine, October 16th, I noticed your smiling face, also noticed that the bottom button on your vest was not buttoned. I wonder if your vest is too tight, or your waist line is expanding.

Being one of your many admirers, though from Senator Pat McCarran's home town, and being of your age, I would suggest that you walk as much as your valuable time will permit, and eat and drink sparingly. Not only that you will be able to button up and tighten up, but you will enjoy a more pleasant and longer life.

Very respectfully yours,
FRED PHILLIPS

Memorandum for F.F.

The White House, October 19, 1939

You got off mighty easy. All your friend Fred Phillips says is that your bottom button was unbuttoned. A few years ago I got a letter from an admirer complaining that my bottom button was not only unbuttoned but was off. Marion is hereby appointed "button-upper" to little Felix before he goes to school every morning.

F.D.R.

The White House, November 7, 1939

My dear Justice Frankfurter:

Thank you so much for sending me your speech. It is beautiful and I am very glad to have it.

The speech I made at the *Herald Tribune* Forum grew out of a rising indignation against some speakers who seemed to me to know so little of their own country and their own people.

Very sincerely yours,
ELEANOR ROOSEVELT

Frankfurter sent Mrs. Roosevelt a copy of his speech at Radcliffe in which he had spoken with the greatest solemnity about America's stake in a victory for the democratic forces in the European war.

At the New York Herald Tribune Forum, Mrs. Roosevelt had spoken out in protest against those who thought America's conduct in the war would be governed by material considerations alone.

Memorandum for Mr. Justice Frankfurter
The White House, November 21, 1939

I am secretly disturbed to find that one so young as Mr. Justice William O. Douglas has so soon taken advantage of the old subterfuge of quoting from obiter dicta of his colleagues and law school professors, expressed through letters, editorials in the *New Republic*, and 1937 speeches by a recent Harvard Law School don.

Because of your seniority, I suggest that you hold a seminar for Bill, asking him to apply the vivid rules of life in place of the musty rules of law and get him to answer in language which even the President can understand the simple query "Do Baptists play poker?"

In the utmost confidence, in view of your recent assertion to me that you are about to take a freshman course in that ancient and honorable game, you will perhaps be good enough, again in the utmost confidence, to tell me whether we can muster five votes for the game as the Court is now constituted. I am deeply interested because, as you know, there is a vacancy in your honorable body.

F.D.R.

Washington, D.C., November 20, 1939

Dear Missy:

One never can tell — therefore I wish to put into your safekeeping this letter as an expression of my wish that all my correspondence, books, pamphlets, memoranda and papers of every sort, pertaining to the period which will be known to history as the New Deal should permanently be deposited in the Franklin D. Roosevelt Library at Hyde Park. An original duplicate of this letter will be found in the file of my papers marked "F.F. Private," in a sealed envelope bearing the following: "Instructions regarding disposition of all my papers, books, etc. pertaining to the New Deal."

Faithfully yours,
FELIX FRANKFURTER

Frankfurter later changed his plans. He gave many of his books to the New York City College, which he had attended as an undergraduate. His material on Zionism and Judaica went to the Hebrew University in Israel. The Harvard Law School was the repository for his legal and judicial papers. All the general papers and documents, including the material on the New Deal, went to the Library of Congress. Never quite sure why he had made the change, Frankfurter decided on reflection that it was because of his immense and long-continued admiration of Mr. David Mearns, the famous Lincoln scholar who is the director for the Library of Congress of its Manuscript Division.

Washington, D.C., November 21, 1939

Dear Felix:

I am perfectly thrilled by your memorandum to Missy and I cannot tell you how happy I am in the thought that your correspondence and papers will be resting for all time beside mine. Incidentally, they will give a far better picture of our day than mine because you, in your work, have had so much greater opportunity to analyze and suggest on paper, whereas, I have been compelled to work, in great part, by word of mouth or through the medium of stodgy orders, proclamations and political speeches.

It is really a marvelous thing that you propose to do and I am made very happy by it.

Archie MacLeish was perfect. I lived up to the agreement but while he was speaking I was watching like a hawk for that sixteen word sentence. It was well worth waiting for.

As ever yours,
F.D.R.

The White House, December 20, 1939

Dear Felix:

I am perfectly delighted to have that photograph of you. To me it is a wonderful picture of a very old friend.

My best wishes to you and Marion for a very Merry Christmas.

Always sincerely yours,
F.D.R.

December 27, 1939

Dear Marion:

I have heard with deep sorrow of the great loss you have sustained in the death of your dear mother. Eleanor and I want you to know we are thinking of you and wish it were in our power to do something to soften the pangs of a grief so overwhelming. Our hearts sorrow with you.

Ever affectionately yours,
FRANKLIN

The Arsenal of Democracy

1940

March 30	*Japan establishes a puppet Chinese government in Nanking.*
April 4	*Winston Churchill becomes responsible for direction of Britain's military program in the Chamberlain government.*
April 9	*Germany occupies Denmark and invades Norway.*
May 10	*Germany invades Belgium, Netherlands and Luxemburg. Chamberlain resigns and Churchill becomes Prime Minister as head of a coalition government.*
June 3-4	*Last Allied troops leave Dunkirk.*
June 10	*Italy declares war on Britain and France.*
June 13	*Germany occupies Paris.*
June 22	*France and Germany sign an armistice agreement, thus breaking France's pledge to Britain not to conclude a separate peace. Air raids on Britain next few days mark the beginning of what develops into the Battle of Britain.*
July 5	*Vichy government in France severs relations with England in retaliation for British naval attack on French ships at Oran.*
July 14	*Colonel Batista elected President of Cuba.*
September 22	*Japan begins occupation of French Indo-China.*
September 26	*President Roosevelt embargoes export of scrap iron and steel.*
September 27	*Germany, Italy and Japan sign three-power pact pledging complete mutual assistance to each other for the next ten years.*
October 28	*Italy attacks Greece.*
November 5	*President Roosevelt is re-elected President for an unprecedented third term.*

Washington, D.C., January 1, 1940

Dear Frank:

Will you let me say something very personal on this New Year's Day? Not even you can quite feel what this country means to a man like me, who was brought here as an eager sensitive lad of twelve — for America has been in your blood, as it were, for generation upon generation. My father — who was a small businessman — came here in 1893, on a business trip, and fell in love with the country, and particularly with the spirit of freedom that was in the air. And so he persuaded my mother to uproot the family, and from the moment we landed on Manhattan I knew, with the sure instinct of a child, that this was my native spiritual home. I began to read English avidly, and very soon Lincoln became my hero.

Such he has remained, except that the years have transformed him into a companion. I have read those ponderous volumes of Nicolay and Hay, and all of Lincoln's State papers, and I do not feel closer to any living friend than I do to Lincoln.

Knowing him this intimately — I say so in deep humility — I feel I know to a considerable measure what the load of the Presidency must be for one who has difficulties not less grave and heavy than those that weighed on Lincoln's soul, and carries them as gallantly as he did and with the inevitable solitude of Lincoln's compassion and wise private humor.

And so I think of you as the New Year begins, with its unrevealed new task, not as President but as man and friend, and I wish you personal solace and happiness and strength, drawn from your deep sources, to continue to live with fortitude and gaiety and wisdom.

Affectionately yours,
FELIX FRANKFURTER

This letter is probably the frankest and most emotional avowal of Frankfurter's devotion to Roosevelt, as friend and President, to be found in the entire body of this correspondence. Frankfurter explained that he wrote in these personal terms, and with a lack of reticence, because they were living in a time of the breaking of nations, when it became more important than ever to honor courageous leadership and cherish personal ties. For neither Frankfurter nor Roosevelt had any illusions that the absence of stern fighting on the Western front, the period of the "phony war" following the

Nazi conquest of Poland, was anything but a deceptive and dangerous calm. They knew the Nazi storm would burst on Europe, though neither man anticipated its devouring fury.

All through this waiting period Roosevelt pursued three related aims. He tried, gallantly, but never with any hope of success, to use every diplomatic and economic weapon at the disposal of the United States to limit the scale and devastation of the conflict. At the same time he was trying to organize the home front so that it would be ready for any emergency that might suddenly be thrust on the American people. Finally, he was trying to teach America to think of the Atlantic not as a moat separating us from Europe but as a bridge connecting us with the deepest sources of Western civilization.

In none of these aims was he completely successful. The war slowly broadened its scope and increased its destruction with every succeeding month. The strident and passionate debate with the Isolationists and the America Firsters continued to divide the country and confuse national policy. The aid to Britain came when the British people stood all alone, at their last gasp, ready to spend all their blood and treasure, determined to save themselves by their exertions and hopeful of saving the world by their example.

In retrospect, however, a more generous and wiser verdict is possible, and it is one in which Frankfurter certainly believed. He thought it was the President's leadership, on all these fronts, during these two tragic and terrible years, which alone made it possible for the American people after Pearl Harbor to spring into action with such instinctive and indomitable unity. Pearl Harbor silenced all doubts, but the nation fought better and stood the strain of war better because, as Frankfurter said, the country "had been taken to school" so often by the President.

Frankfurter himself was in torment as he watched his beloved British people endure the Battle of Britain. Cruel jokes and barbed sarcasms were circulated in Washington about him, but he treated them all with contempt. For he knew, with Santayana, that a world without a free and generous Britain was a world in which it was not worth living. So he rejoiced as he saw Chamberlain fall from power and watched Churchill and Roosevelt form their invincible alliance. To him it was the triumphant omen of victory, even in the most desperate days.

Frankfurter would have approved of an assessment of Roosevelt as President, especially as a war leader, given by Professor Frank Freidel of Harvard. Mr. Freidel recalled that Roosevelt used to refer to a visit, as a boy, to the White House where his father had taken him to meet President Grover Cleveland. The President said wearily, "My boy, I hope when you grow up you'll never have the misfortune to become President." Years later a group

*of young people gathered around President Theodore Roosevelt asked him
how he liked being President and "Teddy" replied, "Bully, simply bully."
No one, surely, will challenge Mr. Freidel's judgment that there was never
any doubt during "F.D.R.'s years in the White House which view he took
of the President." This gay courage in adversity, this determination that the
forces of freedom would march through terror to triumph, steadied him in
sustaining the burdens and agonies of war, and made him serve even unto
death. Thus Frankfurter saw his friend and leader in these tremendous
years, and followed him steadfastly with affectionate devotion.*

*As the year opens, we move gently from these tremendous themes to
more familiar intimacies.*

The White House, January 3, 1940

Dear Marion:

The cheese is delicious. Many thanks to you and Felix for keeping me
so well supplied.

I hear you saw the New Year in very pleasantly and this carries to you
both my affectionate good wishes.

As ever,
F.D.R.

The White House, January 9, 1940

Dear Felix:

That was an extraordinarily touching note which you sent me on New
Year's Day and I am grateful to you for it and for the fine loyalty which you
have shown me always. It is things of this kind and there are not too many
— which have helped lighten the task of this office.

A happy New Year to you and Marion.

Faithfully and affectionately,
F.D.R.

The White House, January 9, 1940

Dear Marion:

Please excuse me for dictating this letter but I know that otherwise you
would be greeting that new President before I have a chance to tell you of
my appreciation of your sending me that book in which Felix wrote such a
pleasant inscription.

Your note was sweet and I am very glad that you did say all those
things.

As ever yours,
F.D.R.

Mrs. Frankfurter, at the President's request, had sent him a copy of the letters of Sacco and Vanzetti, which she had edited. In the inscription Frankfurter said Sacco and Vanzetti would have received fairer treatment if the officials and judges of Massachusetts had been endowed with some of Roosevelt's passion for justice. In her note Mrs. Frankfurter said she would "leave the speeches to Felix." She simply wanted to tell him why the President meant so much to her as a man and as a great American.

Memorandum for F.F.

The White House, January 17, 1940

For Heaven's sake! Surely you did not let your Trott friend get trotted out of the country without having him searched by Edgar Hoover. Think of the battleship plans and other secrets he may be carrying back. This is the height of indiscretion and carelessness on your part.

F.D.R.

The jesting tone of this letter should not confuse the grave issues with which it deals. Dr. Adam von Trott was a brave German who thought the Nazi leaders were abominations who should be removed from office, and preferably from the earth. He and his friends were ready to risk their lives in this challenge to Hitlerism.

He came to the neutral United States to attend a conference in Virginia, making that his excuse to travel across the country. While here, he saw several important Americans, including Frankfurter, and with the greatest discretion informed them of his plans. The FBI, which kept Dr. Trott under constant watch with admirable vigilance, did not clearly grasp the purpose of his mission. It thought he wanted to enlist the aid of Americans in the dangerous enterprise of overthrowing the Nazi government, and so reported to the President in a voluminous document. In reality, Dr. Trott was anxious to find out what peace terms would be offered Germany if a new government spoke for the German people.

Roosevelt was kept informed of all these secret discussions, which by their nature could not be properly assessed by the FBI, and shared Frankfurter's amazement over the FBI's efficiency even when it really did not know what it was doing.

At no time did Frankfurter turn his hatred of the Nazis into a vendetta against the German people. He despised Henry Morgenthau's plan to strip Germany of her industrial strength, reducing her to a pastoral third-rate power. He was always opposed to a vindictive peace, and remembering the Versailles settlement, urged Roosevelt to resist a policy of reprisals. He believed there were millions of decent and compassionate Germans who would agree with Dr. Trott, but he knew they felt themselves powerless to stop the organized despotism which supported the Nazi war machine.

The White House, January 24, 1940

Dear Felix:

Thanks for letting me see those two letters. They are most interesting and I am returning them herewith.

I wish you and Marion would come in Saturday afternoon about five for a little gossip — I think this should be done before you return to the Black Robe!

As ever yours,
F.D.R.

The enclosed two letters dealt with widely different subjects. The first was from the Chief Justice of India and gave a detailed report on the political ferment visible not only in New Delhi but in the villages. The sympathy and support of the United States were described as essential elements in India's struggle for complete freedom and independence.

The other letter was from Lord Wright, one of England's most respected judges. Lord Wright described how popular prejudice, from fear of a "Fifth Column," was eager for harsh measures against refugees and aliens. He predicted that it would be hard to reconcile the traditional principles of British justice with the demands for security. In coming months Lord Wright became the foremost judicial authority in reminding the British people during the Battle of Britain that they were fighting not only for their own lives but for British justice.

From time to time Frankfurter sent opinions by the Supreme Court to the President because he thought it important that Roosevelt should read the full text of the more significant decisions. The attached first pages of three decisions show how Frankfurter applied this principle in actual practice. Quite often, as indicated in the note to the third opinion, Frankfurter discussed a particular decision with the President in person.

In all such discussions Frankfurter made it a point of scrupulous honor to expound the public issues which had been settled or left unresolved by the Supreme Court. He never tried to use these sessions to prejudice the President against any other member of the Court, no matter how strenuously he and Frankfurter may have disagreed in a particular case. It is significant that Frankfurter often sent dull technical cases to the President, as well as dramatic civil liberties cases, because all questions considered by the Supreme Court have far-reaching national consequences.

Supreme Court of the United States

Nos. 110, 111, 112, 183 and 399. — October Term, 1939.

Guy T. Helvering, Commissioner of
Internal Revenue, Petitioner,
110   vs.
Mary Z. Hallock and Central United
National Bank of Cleveland, Trustees.

Guy T. Helvering, Commissioner of
Internal Revenue, Petitioner,   On Writs of Certiorari to
111   vs.   the United States Cir-
Mary Q. Hallock, Executrix, Estate of   cuit Court of Appeals
Henry Hallock, Deceased.   for the Sixth Circuit.

Guy T. Helvering, Commissioner of
Internal Revenue, Petitioner,
112   vs.
S. H. Squire, Superintendent of Banks
of the State of Ohio, etc.

This is guaranteed to induce deeper and quicker sleep than even nature can produce.

But — beginning on the bottom of p. 8 things are said that may not
be without interest to you.

F.F.

Supreme Court of the United States

No. 195. — October Term, 1939.

Isiah (Izell) Chambers, Jack Williamson,
Charlie Davis and Walter Woodward   On Writ of Certiorari to
(Woodard), Petitioners,   The Supreme Court of
                  vs.   the State of Florida.
The State of Florida.
(February 12, 1940.)
Mr. Justice Black delivered the opinion of the Court.

The grave question presented by the petition for certiorari, granted in
forma pauperis, is whether proceedings in which confessions were utilized,
and which culminated in sentences of death upon four young negro men

in the State of Florida, failed to afford the safeguard of that due process of law guaranteed by the Fourteenth Amendment.

Dear Missy:
    The President may care to see the full text of this opinion.

                                                        Yours,
                                                        F.F.

Supreme Court of the United States

No. 265. — October Term, 1939.

Federal Communications Commission, Petitioner, vs. The Pottsville Broadcasting Company. (January 29, 1940.)	On Writ of Certiorari to the United States Court of Appeals for the District of Columbia.

This reveals a situation about which I should like to have talk with you one of these days.

                                                        F.F.

                                    Washington, D.C., January 26, 1940
Dear Missy:
    The President might perhaps be interested to read this letter of Mr. Justice Stone written to educate Jim Farley into the very important work that Ed Bruce is doing for the things that are enduring in American civilization.
    We hope to see you tomorrow.

                                                        Ever yours,
                                                        F.F.

                                                        December 13, 1939
Dear Mr. Postmaster General:
    The enclosures in this letter will indicate to you a little more fully, than I was then able to, what I had in mind when I spoke to you the other evening at the Gridiron Club dinner.
    The enclosures are a black and white photograph of the mural recently painted and installed by Peter Hurd in the post office at Big Spring, a small city in Texas, and a letter of the postmaster giving his impressions of it.
    The photograph, notwithstanding the absence of color, indicates that the mural, in its decorative quality, its beauty and its symbolism, meets to a

high degree the demands of good mural painting. It is a fair example of paintings which have been placed in many public buildings in this country as the result of the highly intelligent and competent service of the Section of Fine Arts, headed by Mr. Edward Bruce. The postmaster's letter is typical of the response which these works of art have provoked throughout the country, and particularly in small communities.

In just a word I would like to indicate to you what I think has been accomplished by this government activity through the expenditure of a comparatively small amount of money:

1. Public buildings with which the great mass of the population come most in contact have become focal points of beauty for the eye of literally hundreds of thousands of people. The walls of post office corridors, usually drab and uninteresting, have stirred the interest and aesthetic emotions of great masses of people who have had all too little of that kind of experience in the past.

2. The artists have been given the kind of opportunity, without which there can be no real American art. The interesting thing about it is that under the inspiration of the Section of Fine Arts the artists of America are, for the first time, painting the American scene, something they know and understand, instead of the weak imitations of the work of foreign artists, chiefly Parisian, of which we have seen so much in the past. They are painting the genuine instead of the imitative or the cheap and tawdry, which is the beginning of all art.

3. Aside from all other considerations, and what perhaps is most important of all is that great numbers of the people of this country are, for the first time in the lives of many of them, being impressed with the fact that the artist finds beauty and dignity in their lives. And one of the many things we need to be taught is that our lives, however simple or humble, may be both beautiful and dignified. What could be more impressive in this respect than the mural, photograph of which I enclose? And this is only one of many.

I congratulate you on having had a hand in so important an achievement. I wish that when I come to lay down my work I could think I had had a hand in something as worth while, and which would live as long.

With kind regards, I am,

Yours sincerely,
HARLAN F. STONE

Roosevelt's birthday had become the focal point in the "March of Dimes" campaign to help children stricken by infantile paralysis.

Washington, D.C., January 30, 1940

Dear Frank:

The compassionate purpose to which our national tradition has now dedicated your birthday has a profound symbolism. For, in a way, we are all crippled children. And we are the more poignant in our disabilities than the immediate beneficiaries of your tender statesmanship, just because we think we are grown-up and big and strong, and yet are so often unhumorously immature and unequal to the tasks our times impose on us.

This is to greet you with our affectionate good wishes, and to tell you how fitting it is that this day has become, and will forever remain, a national holiday.

Devotedly yours,

F.F.

Memorandum for Felix Frankfurter

Enroute to Pensacola, Fla., February 14, 1940

That is a nice letter from Bishop Sheil. He is a grand fellow.

Your old flame is right about the need for coordinating foreign relief agencies — and she is right about Dr. Frank Kingdon. If you get a chance, will you speak to Adolf Berle about this? He is working on the subject.

I have your two sets of Obiter dicta — the Helvering case and the FCC case and will read them on the way south and then use them as a bait for sail fish. That is the highest compliment I can pay them because sail fish are notoriously discriminatory in what they swallow.

I wish to goodness you were on the trip with me. I hope your next door neighbor on the Court will rejoin you before Easter but I doubt it for I think he is doing Lenten penance.

As ever,

F.D.R.

Bishop Sheil of the Archdiocese of Chicago had written to Frankfurter giving precise and documented examples of efforts being made, not altogether without success, to stir up tensions between Catholics and Jews. He suspected that people who wished to divide the country were secretly behind this campaign. The President in a memorable utterance later in the year denounced efforts to pit "race against race and religion against religion." Bishop Sheil was both astonished and delighted to learn from Frankfurter that his letter had reached the President.

The "old flame" — too vivid a phrase for an old friendship — was Ernesta Bullitt, now Mrs. Samuel Barlow, a quick and compassionate spirit stung into action by human suffering. Adolf Berle was carrying great responsibilities throughout this period in the State Department.

Washington, D.C., March 4, 1940

Dear Frank:

It is still true that "the only thing we have to fear is fear itself" — and no less true is it that our people respond to your "leadership of frankness and vigor." That's the ultimate meaning of democracy — faith that Lincoln's common people will so respond. And through you it's been consistently and superbly vindicated for all the world that can be reached by reason to know — and to take pride in, for humanity's sake.

This is — and will remain as long as we remain a civilized nation — an historic day. God bless you. So say Marion and

FELIX

On this day Roosevelt began his eighth year as President. The exact origin of the reverberating sentence about fear is unknown. The most probable explanation is that a sentence from Thoreau, whom he had been reading, provided the President with the first impulse. Thoreau wrote: "Nothing is so much to be feared as fear." The President may have changed and sharpened this sentence to suit his own purposes. At all events, it is the sentence by which Roosevelt's First Inaugural is remembered.

The White House, March 8, 1940

Dear Marion and Felix:

Thank you both so much for your thought of me on March fourth. It is very like you both to have done this.

Always affectionately,
F.D.R.

Washington, D.C., April 13, 1940

Dear Frank:

Fear is the child of ignorance and the parent of intolerance. Therefore your first task was to bring calm and confidence to our people. And *that* your fireside-talk undoubtedly will accomplish, with its blend of concrete facts and the high mood of a firm, common humanity with which you began and closed. And your own warming, confirming voice must, unconsciously, have greatly helped to quicken the firm, vigorous and serene forces among all our people. The ground work for action — the right atmosphere — has thus been laid by you. Keep fit — and give the country your continuing self.

Ever yours,
F.F.

Roosevelt was speaking soon after Nazi Germany had invaded Denmark and Norway. He said that if civilization is to survive, the rights of the smaller nations to independence, to their territorial integrity, and to their unimpeded opportunity for self-government, must be respected by their more powerful neighbors.

Washington, D.C., May 3, 1940

Dear Frank:

It was very sweet of you to have Harry Stimson for lunch. He is a fine old Roman — he is, you know, close to 73 — and wants to feel he is still of use to the Republic. And he is — though his party for narrow, partisan reasons professes departure from its traditional foreign policy. You made Stimson feel he *is* of use — and gave him fresh impulse to go on. Many thanks for taking me out of my marble prison.

I was most happy to see you so fit.

Ever yours,
F.F.

P.S.   Will you please tell your mother that Marion knows some fine brands of canned peaches!

This marks the beginning of Frankfurter's successful efforts to have Colonel Stimson appointed to the cabinet. He wanted Roosevelt to see for himself that Stimson was able to discharge great responsibilities even though he was more than seventy years of age.

Telegram to Roosevelt
Washington, D.C., May 10, 1940

TO PARAPHRASE NELSON THE BOLDEST SPEECH IS THE SAFEST. OUR GRATITUDE FOR PROVING THE TRUTH OF THAT ONCE MORE AND AT YOUR BEST.

FELIX FRANKFURTER

On May 10 Roosevelt delivered one of the greatest speeches of his career. Germany had invaded Belgium, Luxemburg, and the Netherlands. Soon the Battle of France would begin. He said the dictator states seek to dominate hundreds of millions of human beings in vast continental areas — and, if they are successful in that aim, "they will, we know down in our hearts, enlarge their wild dream to encompass every human being and every mile of the earth's surface."

The White House, May 13, 1940

Dear Felix:

I just want to tell you how much I appreciate that kind message you sent me. I am truly grateful for what you say about the address.

Always sincerely,

FRANKLIN D. ROOSEVELT

Roosevelt had told Congress that neither the Atlantic nor the Pacific granted the United States any immunity from the dangers of war. He fixed the production of planes at fifty thousand a year — the actual production in 1943 reached ninety thousand planes. And he promised the European Allies — and this now meant Britain above all — the military supplies they had ordered. "For the permanent record," said Roosevelt, "I ask the Congress not to take any action which would in any way hamper or delay the delivery of American-made planes to foreign nations which have ordered them, or seek to purchase new planes. That, from the point of view of our own national defense, would be extremely short-sighted."

Washington, D.C., May 16, 1940

Dear Frank:

These are days when one realizes the importance of things unseen, and is sure of things not susceptible of ordinary proof. As I listened to you, an hour ago, in the chamber of the House, how could I not become absorbed by the mysterious good fortune which has you where you are — the embodiment of hope and of faith of all the peoples of the earth who care for the good life as against mere existence, the inspiration of all who are determined that the precious achievements of man's spiritual nature shall not perish from the earth.

And I also thought that you, who are truly the world's reservoir of hope, must try to conserve and replenish your own energy, and so maintain your strength and serenity so as to be able to impart it, and in even more exacting measure, to our own people, and to the languishing fellow beings in other lands. The conservation and fruitful husbandry of your abounding resources constitute the very first line of national defense.

Your message was just right. You can count on Lincoln's "common people."

Bless you,

F.F.

Washington, D.C., May 17, 1940

Dear Missy:

Despite, or perhaps because of, these anxious days, this report on the Holmes bequest, which carries out the President's original thought, might divert him for a few minutes, and so you might want to put it among his bedside reading matter.

F.F.

Frankfurter enclosed the "Report of the Oliver Wendell Holmes Devise Committee" which submitted "recommendations concerning the use of the bequest and devise made to the United States by the late Justice Oliver Wendell Holmes."

Washington, D.C. May 26, 1940

Dear Frank —

This is Sunday morning and I humbly believe that not the most pious church attendant has his thought more outside himself and on the ultimate destiny of mankind than I have this forenoon here in my study. It is in that mood that I am venturing to break in on you. My one excuse is that I cannot resist doing so.

You don't have to be told what thoughts you stirred in me yesterday morning about our country and your relation to it at this juncture. And these thoughts have been with me for all these weeks — hardly anything else has been. I have one very deep conviction which I want to urge on you with all my devotion.

Nothing would so clear the air, invigorate the mind and will of our people, give that impulse to patriotic endeavor and shame all lesser motives which only eloquent action can give, if you could say something like the following to our people tonight:

"Appreciating as they do to the fullest that a crisis not of our making is confronting the world, but one that has also swept our beloved country into its dangers, the patriotic citizens who compose my Cabinet have placed their resignations in my hand so that I may be free to deal with this new situation unembarrassed by the past and wholly regardful of present needs."

Not only am I confident that the nation would receive such an announcement with an abiding feeling of confidence. I am sure that the members of your Cabinet would have a deeper sense of pride tomorrow than they ever had. Do give them this chance to show themselves worthy of their country and their President.

Devotedly yours,
F.F.

Roosevelt agreed that a reorganization of his cabinet was necessary but he proceeded to make his own preparations for the changes he had in mind. The key appointment concerned the Secretary of War. When he requested

Harry Woodring's resignation, Louis Johnson, then Assistant Secretary of War, thought the appointment would go to him and sought it actively. But the Johnson appointment was repugnant to Roosevelt. He therefore accepted with enthusiasm Frankfurter's suggestion that Stimson be named as Secretary of War, with Robert Patterson as his assistant.

Washington, D.C., June 4, 1940

Dear Mr. President:

I have been doing some hard thinking since our very happy party yesterday, and the more I think the more sense Stimson and Patterson make. In the present circumstances the important thing, of course, is to forecast how an appointment will be received, not what theoretical objections may be made in anticipation of the appointment. I am sure that geographical objections would not interest the country as they would in ordinary times, and the real thing to do is to fire the imagination of the country with what a particular appointment may represent because of the assurance that the War Department would really be in effective and dependable hands. Stimson and Patterson surely are such a combination.

Stimson has been for so long associated in the public mind as a supporter of your foreign policy and he has been so completely out of sorts with his own party that no one would deem it a manifestation of the "coalition" idea. On the contrary, it would be realized that here is a man who had had outstanding experience as Secretary of War; he had himself served with distinction in the World War; and because of his work in the Philippines and as Secretary of State is particularly conversant with the relation between force and diplomacy; and as a firm supporter of your foreign policy since 1933, he could be counted on to carry the responsibility of the War Department in strict conformity with your general policy. Of his complete freedom from partisan motives or partisan ambitions, there would be not the slightest doubt in anybody's mind. And, as I said last evening, you couldn't possibly have a more devoted aide in your Administration than he would be. The only doubt about him, of course, is his age. But his mind is alert and vigorous and, freed from details, you would have an extraordinarily equipped man for this vital post.

To enable him to give attention to major things, he would have to have a first-rate assistant on whom he, as well as you, could intimately rely. And Bob Patterson is really made to order. He is young, he is vigorous, he is able. He is the kind of person who combines qualities that made him the first man in his class at the Harvard Law School and also enabled him to have a distinguished war record. He is, I suppose, as able a judge as there is in the land off the Supreme Court who, because of his years and his ability would have a right to look forward to an eventual seat on the Supreme

Court. It would be a stirring thing that such a man is ready to forego every-thing to become an Assistant Secretary of War. It is the kind of thing that also would fire the imagination of public opinion and particularly of our younger people.

He has, I believe, four children and no means, but I know of no man whose devotion to country is greater. Therefore I am confident that he would do anything you would ask him to do. In other words, I am confi-dent that, with all his prospects, he would resign as a Circuit Judge. Stim-son knows him, has confidence in him, he admires Stimson, and as a team it would have that interplay of understanding and trust which is so vital, particularly for a war administration.

Bob Patterson is not a New York City man. He lives somewhere up the Hudson and in his outlook and in antecedents he is as different from down-town New York as though he came from Iowa. Marion does not often express an opinion about public matters, but she has an uncommonly wise judgment of men. Recently after Bob Patterson was with us for an after-noon, she said, after he left, "Why isn't he the man to be Secretary of War?" He has all the brains and productive capacity that are needed for the job, but in addition he has that very rare quality of leadership that he is able to evoke not only the devotion of men but capacities that ordinarily slumber unused.

Some things click — they seem just right — and I cannot help but feel that the combination of Stimson and Patterson would take off your shoul-ders a very great burden and would put the War Department in charge of men on whom you could rely completely for their understanding and exe-cution of your policies.

It was grand to see you so fit and I only pray that the heat be merciful during the Washington days and that you maintain strength and peace that seem almost impossible to achieve.

Very faithfully yours,

FELIX FRANKFURTER

P.S.   I had to dictate this just as I was leaving town. Forgive, therefore, that I was not able to read the letter, shorten it and sign it.

New York, N.Y., June 5, 1940

Dear Felix —

Thanks a lot for your kind message written during the "blitzkrieg of verbal, incendiary bombs" coming up from the counsel table to the bench.

I am glad that the message did not turn out to be a great letdown after the fireside chat of Sunday.

I am also glad I had a chance to talk with you about it and get your advice — to say nothing of the help later on.

I am still hoping to get some time off when I am down there to call on you and Marion and have a real chat.

I hope you appreciate how difficult it is to get away while these things are being born. Those who do the conceiving have an easier and more pleasant job than the obstetrician who has to stay on during all the labor pains.

With kindest regards,

Yours,

SAM

Judge Samuel Rosenman, who shares with Mr. Theodore Sorensen the distinction of being the best Presidential speech-writer in our century, was always very generous in acknowledging any suggestions from Frankfurter. The opening phrase concerns a brief scribbled note expressing Frankfurter's appreciation of three Presidential utterances. On May 16 Roosevelt went to Congress to ask that no action be taken that "would in any way hamper or delay" the delivery of American planes to foreign nations which have ordered them. It was in this speech that Roosevelt set the goal for the production of 50,000 planes a year. In 1943 no less than 90,000 planes were produced.

Departing from custom, and broadcasting on Sunday night to emphasize the gravity of his message, Roosevelt on May 26 spoke from the White House to appeal for a much greater defense effort. He said he had never had the illusion that the United States could live in security in remote isolation, and now, despite the disasters in Europe, he had no fear that democracy in America would be wiped out by retreat and defeat.

At the end of May, Roosevelt sent still another message to Congress asking for a larger defense appropriation.

Frankfurter thanked Rosenman for his indispensable part in the preparation of these three Presidential statements of policy.

Washington, D.C., June 5, 1940

Dear Mr. President:

Ideas are like men. One gets to know them after one lives with them for some time. The more I have lived with the idea of the Stimson-Patterson combination, the more right it seems — meaning by right that it fits the immediate situation. It would relieve you of a pressing problem and would arouse in the country a surge of confidence with reference to this particular situation.

About Stimson, there is nothing I can tell you, but it occurred to me that it might not be wholly useless to put on paper with more particularity what I know and believe to be the truth about Patterson. I have therefore dictated the enclosed memorandum to my secretary over the phone.

Faithfully yours,

FELIX FRANKFURTER

Robert P. Patterson was born in Glens Falls, New York, in 1891. He graduated from Union College in 1912 and later from the Harvard Law School where he had a distinguished record and was President of the Harvard *Law Review*. He started practice in New York City with Root, Clark, Buckner and Ballantine, and his work in that office was of outstanding excellence.

He very early joined the 7th Regiment of the New York National Guard and went with that Regiment to the Mexican border in 1916. When the Guard was released from border duty he returned to New York and resumed practice until the entry of the United States into the World War. He served during the War first as captain and later as major in the 306th Infantry with the 77th Division.

The War Department record would show the details of his war service, and so it would suffice to say that it was distinguished both for competence and for courage. He was awarded the Distinguished Service Medal for extraordinary heroism in action. After the War he returned to practice in the Root, Clark office which he left in 1922 with Vanderbilt Webb to form the firm of Webb and Patterson. Later Morris Hadley joined them and the firm became Webb, Patterson and Hadley. In 1929 it was associated with the Milbank firm, now known as Milbank, Tweed and Hope.

In 1930 Patterson became a judge of the United States District Court for the Southern District of New York, and on 1939 he was elevated to the bench of the Circuit Court of Appeals for the Second Circuit, which office he now holds.

He married Margaret Winchester in 1920 and has four children.

So much for the dry facts. Let me now say something about his personal qualities.

On its face the record shows that Patterson is a man of unusual intelligence, but the facts go beyond the record. He has a most extraordinary clarity and rapidity of mind. It is the common testimony of lawyers that in the courtroom he is always a step ahead of counsel. He catches all the implications of what is going on before anyone else in the courtroom. He has always been extraordinarily sound in his judgment of the law and has unflagging industry and great capacity in mastering complicated facts.

With all this his mind has the uncommon quality of simplicity and directness. In spite of his outstanding scholarship, he has never shown the slightest trace of pedantry or love of mental thrill. He is never confused, baffled or tired when working overtime or when dealing with difficult or rapidly developing situations. This is partly an intellectual trait, but partly it is due to a trait of character which makes him free from the hampering doubts and inhibitions which afflict even many good men to some extent in matters carrying responsibility and calling for decision which would recoil upon the actor in case of error.

Patterson is one of those rare men to whom other men become easily attached. His colleagues on the bench, without exception, not only respect him but are personally fond of him. It is a well known fact that his troops were fond of him. They made him, even in that period just after the War when one of the popular sports was "panning" officers, the head of their regimental association. It is impossible to know him at all without getting to like him and to respect him. This is true of all manner and conditions of people.

He has another outstanding quality at which the record hints but does not fully disclose, and that is that it is hard to imagine a more unselfish person — one who is more interested in the job to be done or more oblivious of the effect on himself. In his early practice he never seemed to have the slightest concern about what is called "getting credit." Although a man without means, he left an extremely strong and prosperous law firm at great financial sacrifice to go on the bench because he liked the idea of public service.

Brilliant and effective as his career has been, his private life has always been modest and quiet in the extreme. He lives at Garrison-on-the-Hudson on a farm which he farms himself. He takes the most whole-souled delight in the land and in the homely farming operations. All this seems part of his clear-headed, simply brave and determined character.

There is a sort of personal power about the man which has always given those who know him a conviction that whatever he put his hand to would be well done.

Telegram to Roosevelt

Dover, Mass., June 10, 1940

HAVE JUST HEARD YOUR ADDRESS IN A NEST OF FRIENDS MOST OF WHOM UNTIL THE OTHER DAY WERE PRIMARILY REPUBLICANS BUT ALL OF WHOM TODAY ARE ONLY AMERICANS. THEY HAVE THE ENTHUSIASM OF DEEP SILENCE AND WHOLE-HEARTED GRATITUDE FOR WHAT YOU SAID. IT COULD NOT HAVE BEEN BETTER, NOR MORE EFFECTIVELY SUMMONED OUR PEOPLE TO OUR DUTY. AFFECTION-ATELY.

FELIX FRANKFURTER

The White House, June 11, 1940

Dear Felix,

I can only say thank you from the bottom of my heart for that kind message you sent me. Such expressions of approbation are indeed encouraging.

As ever yours,
FRANKLIN D. ROOSEVELT

Italy went to war with Britain and France on June 10. That same day, speaking with cold contempt of Mussolini, the President said "the hand that held the dagger has struck it into the back of its neighbor." In an important declaration, Roosevelt added that "we will extend to the opponents of force the material resources of this Nation; and, at the same time, we will speed up the use of those resources so that we ourselves may have equipment and training equal to any emergency." The signs and signals "call for speed — full speed ahead."

Cambridge, Mass., June 13, 1940

Dear Frank:

If your mind is not settled as to War and Labor, the following may not be useless information:

(1) You asked me whether Lloyd Garrison was a good administrator. Since talking with you I have made discreet but dependable soundings which convince me that he is a smooth and very effective dispatcher of business and would without a doubt quickly attain mastery of a Department like Labor.

(2) I've had it somewhat on my conscience to throw out the names of Stimson and Patterson without reasonable assurance that they would be available. Here again I've assured myself that they both regard themselves as soldiers and you as their Commander in Chief.

If this part of the country is an index to the rest of it, our people are ready for any call that you may make of them.

The "stab-in-the-back" was a grand tonic. We need that kind of moral summons.

I hope that Washington is not too unbearable, and that, despite all, you are keeping very fit.

Marion joins me in affectionate messages.

Faithfully yours,
F.F.

Telegram to Miss LeHand
Cambridge, Mass., June 19, 1940
HOPE PRESIDENT CAN FIND TIME TO READ FULL TEXT OF STIMSON SPEECH PAGE
17 TODAY'S TIMES. WARMEST REGARDS.

FELIX FRANKFURTER

*On June 18, Henry L. Stimson delivered a radio address emphasizing the
necessity to adopt compulsory universal military training without delay and
urging immediate increases in our aid to Britain and France.*

Telegram to Roosevelt
Cambridge, Mass., June 20, 1940
SIMPLY GRAND. YOU HAVE AGAIN SHOWN HOW TO SUMMON THE COUNTRY'S
SERVICE AND PLACE THE NATION'S NEED ON THE LEVEL WHERE IT BELONGS.
LET ME EXPRESS MY GRATITUDE OF THIS NEW MANIFESTATION OF LEADERSHIP
FOR A FREE PEOPLE.

FELIX FRANKFURTER

*This refers to Roosevelt's appointment that day of Henry L. Stimson as
Secretary of War and Colonel Frank Knox as Secretary of the Navy. Both
were Republicans. Frankfurter had urged Roosevelt to bring Stimson into
the cabinet, and had advised Stimson to accept the appointment despite
his advanced age. He was sure that Colonel Knox would give valiant service to the navy and the nation. As Frankfurter once told Roosevelt — to
the President's approval — the war was being fought for democracy, not
for the Democratic party.*

Washington, D.C., June 26, 1940
My Dear Mr. President:
    You don't have to be told that Harold Laski's passionate patriotism
will make him share whatever fate befalls his country. But it occurs to me
that he might want to put what you probably know to be his rare collection
of books, pamphlets and manuscripts, including several hundreds of letters
from Mr. Justice Holmes in the latter's fine hand, beyond the reach of
senseless destruction. I wonder, therefore, whether you would not want to
send word to Joe Kennedy asking him to put at Harold's disposal the facilities of our Embassy for these rare treasures of the mind. They might either
be put in safekeeping, in whatever way our own documents are protected,
or in part at least — as for instance, the Holmes letters — actually shipped
to this country, either in Archie MacLeish's or my custody.

Faithfully yours,
FELIX FRANKFURTER

At the height of the speculation as to whether President Roosevelt should run for a third term in 1940, Justice Frankfurter saw the President to discuss this problem. The President was plainly inclining toward a third term but he wished to have his judgment reinforced by the opinions of trusted friends. Frankfurter said he would draft a memorandum explaining why normal rules did not apply in a period of war when the basic values of Western civilization were under attack. He thought it would also be useful to have the views of Mr. Archibald MacLeish, who was a sensitive interpreter of the deeper tides of public opinion. The President urged Frankfurter to make haste in the preparation of these two memoranda. Frankfurter wrote out his statement in his own hand and took it himself to the White House together with Mr. MacLeish's typewritten letter. The President returned both documents to Frankfurter after studying them very carefully and explaining that they had greatly assisted in clarifying his final decision to be a candidate for an unprecedented third term. In his acceptance speech the President incorporated a large section of Mr. MacLeish's letter, together with other phrases, and Frankfurter's analysis of the meaning of the war influenced the structure of the whole speech.

Frankfurter's Memorandum

The task of safeguarding our institutions is two-fold. One must be accomplished, if necessary by guns and bombs and tanks, by ships and planes, on land and sea and in the air, by the Armed Forces of the nation. The other, by the united but diversified efforts of the many men and women of the country, individually and banded together in trade unions and farm granges, trade associations and cooperatives, and in that common effort of all of the people which is the Government. For we must continue to pursue our two great actions at the same time: we must be ready to defend the right of our democracy to continue to exist; we must have a democratic society worthy of survival.

Whatever its new trappings and new slogans, tyranny is the oldest and most discredited rule known to history. And whenever tyranny has supplanted a more humane form of government it has been due more to internal causes than external. Democracy can thrive only when it enlists the devotion of those whom Lincoln called the common people. And it can hold their devotion only when it adequately respects their dignity by so ordering society as to assure to the mass of men reasonable security and to stir in them confident hope for themselves and for their children.

If democracy becomes merely a set of negations, or degenerates into empty political forms in which insecurity and hopelessness become the lot of many, the road is open for the so-called "strong-man" with all his meretricious promises. We know only too well what happens to these promises once the "strong-man" comes into power. Trade Unions are banned; the cooperative movement is taken over; freedom of the press is at an end — and, indeed, so is every freedom that gives dignity to man.

In the last eight years under your leadership much has been done to make effective, in the lives of the mass of our people, the hopes and principles to which this country is dedicated — a life of dignity, of liberty not in the abstract or on paper, but the liberty of a free man who is able to serve his nation and engage in the pursuit of happiness. Under your leadership we have moved towards a life of economic as well as of political independence for our people who felt the bludgeonings of misfortune and adversity when you first were summoned to the headship of our nation. In view of this record you would not be open to the charge of trying to seize power as a "strong-man." You would in fact be protecting the nation from the convulsions, dangers and upheavals in a period of acute national anxiety and world strain that could indeed lead to the establishment of arbitrary power in Washington by men no longer responsible to the values of democracy and the wishes of Lincoln's common people.

I now turn to foreign policy and suggest these thoughts for your consideration: You would not undo, if you could, the efforts you made to prevent war from the moment it was threatened, and to restrict the area of carnage down to the last minute before Italy entered the struggle. Nor do you now soften the condemnation expressed from time to time by Secretary Hull and yourself for the acts of aggression that have wiped out ancient, peace-preserving, liberty-loving countries which had scrupulously maintained their neutrality and independence. Nor do you recant the sentiments of sympathy with all free peoples who are resisting such aggression. Nor do you regret your consistent endeavor to awaken this country to the menace for us and for all we hold dear in this new attempt to conquer the world, to establish the despotic rule of an aggressive tyranny, and to extinguish the lights of the human spirit. In all these efforts you have tried to follow the inspiration of the great men who laid down the principles which must guard this Republic if it is to remain a sanctuary of freedom. You now look beyond a world war to the years of peace and you want to play your part in making sure that these tragedies will never again fall on civilization, that we will do better than our fathers did when they tried to organize a system of collective security to restrain or punish aggression, and that we will succeed in replacing the law of force by the force of law. That is the great aim, the great hope and sustaining purpose, by which you now chart your course.

You know, and you must hope none has yet forgotten, that in these last few months and years you pursued your campaign against the aggressors, and pursued your campaign to preserve the world's endangered peace, against the opposition of powerful newspapers and leading public men who charged you with being guilty of hysteria and war-mongering. But you have no apologies to offer, no excuses to make. History will judge your actions, and every day your motives are becoming clearer for all to see and understand.

You felt it your duty to arouse your countrymen with a great sense of urgency to the new and dangerous forces loose in the world and to emphasize the hazards which they presented for us in this beloved land. In this conduct of our foreign relations you were guided by the principles which have brought our country to its present greatness. You knew how vast a prize we were for the pride and greed of the dictators, and you were resolved that they would never lay their evil and brutal hands on America, if all of us, recognizing the danger and standing together, could stop them from carrying out their wicked design of conquest and enslavement. For we have no deeper tradition in our history than resistance to tyranny and devotion to freedom. In your warnings, you were aware that the Constitution makes the President that originating impulse and guardian of our national safety. In all that you have attempted, in your efforts to maintain the peace of the world, in all that you have done to maintain the peace of this country and to prepare it morally as well as physically for whatever dangers yet may come, you can gladly submit your purpose, your achievements, and your record to the judgment of your countrymen for a third term in the midst of unprecedented conditions that impose their own duties and obligations. A President must continue in office when the voice of the people calls him to the continuing task.

Mr. Archibald MacLeish's Memorandum

Dear Felix:

It's a dangerous thing to ask a man for his two cents' worth because he may throw in a couple of bushels of orts. But you have and you'll have to take it.

The more I turn it over on my tongue the more certain I am that the President should not "accept a call." Undoubtedly the actual truth is that he will be doing precisely that. But to put it that way is to lead with the chin. I can see the cartoons from here.

What I should like him to say would be something like this: that like most men of his age — most men who have occupied positions of great responsibility — he had made plans for himself; plans for a private life of his own to begin in January 1941. That these plans, like the plans of so many others, like so many other plans, had been made in a world which now seems as distant as a different planet. That today all private plans, all private lives, have been repealed by a public danger. That in the face of the public danger all those who can be of service to the Republic have no choice but to offer themselves for service in those capacities for which they may be fitted. That if a majority of the members of his party believe he can serve his country best in the capacity in which they have nominated him he has no choice but to accept the nomination. That if a majority of the voters believe as a majority of his party have believed he will have no choice but to accept their judgment.

I should like, also, to hear a statement in explanation of the President's failure to declare himself sooner. I think the people are entitled to such a statement and will surely demand it. Obviously I am not in a position to supply such a statement myself but I should suppose that the development of the line suggested above might supply the words. Obviously a man who believes his country faces a crisis so severe that it overrides every other consideration and who believes therefore that every citizen must hold himself ready to serve where he best can, will not declare himself in advance to be unwilling to serve in any capacity whatever. Neither, by the same sign, will he offer himself until the necessity appears.

However — for the main point. You ask me for a couple of paragraphs. Here are a few sentences for whatever they may be worth. . . .

In times like these — in times of great tension, of great crisis, the compass of the world narrows to a single fact. The fact which dominates our world is the fact of armed aggression, the fact of successful armed aggression, the fact of successful armed aggression aimed at the form of government, the kind of society we in the United States have chosen and established for ourselves. It is a fact which no one any longer doubts — which no one is any longer able to ignore. In the early days of Fascist aggression it was said and it was believed that the struggle was a war of rival imperialism. Later and after the first Fascist successes by force of arms in Europe, it was still said and it was still sometimes believed that the war was an imperialistic war, the end and aim of which was land and goods. But with the unambiguous successes of Fascism in Europe in the spring of this year, and above all with the conquest of France, it was no longer possible to say this or to believe it. For the purpose of this aggression is now declared in the irrefutable and unarguable terms of the results which it has itself accomplished. Now that successful Fascism has imposed upon defeated France not only its will but its image, it is no longer possible for any man to doubt what the consequences of successful Fascism will be. It is not a war of imperialism which threatens all men everywhere; it is a revolution imposed by force of arms not from within but from without. It is a revolution which proposes not to set men free but to reduce them to slavery — and to reduce them to slavery in the interest and to the advantage of a dictator who has already demonstrated the nature and the extent of the advantage which he hopes to obtain.

This is the fact which dominates our world and which dominates as well the lives of all those who live in it. In the face of the danger which confronts our time no individual retains or can hope to retain the rights of personal choice which free men can enjoy in times of peace. He has a first obligation to serve in the defense of our institutions of freedom — a first obligation to serve his country in whatever capacity his country finds him useful — which must override all personal preferences — whether the preferences he would establish for himself or the preferences custom and tradition would establish for him. . . .

But you see, Felix, how impossible it is to go on with this. For if ever there was a personal document it is this document of which we are thinking. It can be, if it is deeply derived from the emotions and convictions of the man who speaks it, one of the most moving and convincing utterances of which history has record. It can also be something very different.

Yours,
ARCHIE

New Milford, Conn., July 1, 1940
Dear Frank:

A letter from Harold Laski, which has just reached me, is so poignant in its almost farewell tone, that I'm sending you the whole of it — or, rather, a copy to facilitate its reading.

I see by the "papers" that you are to be at Hyde Park over the Fourth. I hope that means over the week-end, so as to give you a few days away from Washington.

I shall be at New Milford by the second, and now particularly I hope very much that Marion and I can run over at some time convenient for you. I shall phone — or a message will reach me at New Milford (phone New Milford 917). There are many things to talk about, including the gentleman from Indiana. I once had him under observation for hours — some two or three years ago. I debated with him, at a closed meeting in the N.Y. Harvard Club.

It will be a joy to see you again. In the meantime, as always,

Faithfully yours,
F.F.

The gentleman from Indiana is Wendell Willkie, the Republican candidate in 1940, but derisively called by Frankfurter "the wonder boy." His recollection of that debate at the Harvard Club in New York differed from

his feelings at the time. Following that debate, there was a courteous and generous exchange of letters between Frankfurter and Willkie, in which they spoke of each other with respect and admiration. But that admiration was transformed into contempt as Frankfurter listened incredulously to Willkie's promises to keep the war away from America's shores. A third phase of their relationship opened when Frankfurter made it clear to Willkie, after the election, that he greatly admired the gallant way in which Willkie supported every effort to strengthen national unity. He mourned Willkie's premature death as an impoverishment of the civilized forces available to American public life.

Laski's letter, which moved Frankfurter to tears, is a poignant description of the heroic mood that sustained the British people during the Battle of Britain which began after the fall of France.

Ruth and Alfred are Dr. and Mrs. Alfred E. Cohn, two of the closest friends of the Frankfurters and the Laskis.

Addison Bridge Place, England, June 10, 1940

Dearest Felix,

The French are fighting magnificently, in the face of overwhelming odds, both of machines and men. We pray that they may hold. Every available man and gun and plane is going from Britain to their aid. But now that the weight of Italy is added to the powers of darkness, it looks as though the next phase may well be the defeat of France. Then, I suppose, the full weight of the German attack will fall on us. I don't pretend to guess even what it will be like. I know only that there is not one person among my friends or colleagues who contemplates any alternative but to fight on. Who of us lives if England dies?

But I do beg you to stimulate every American you can to realize fully the measure of the evil things we are fighting. Make them see the need to organize in time. Make them settle all internal quarrels and find the resources that alone give victory. Make them learn the lesson a million of us are going to die for, because Chamberlain would not learn it. There is little you should not be ready to sacrifice to kill this thing. That was what America was founded for; that is the chance you still have. Unless you learn the lesson, your fate will be no different from that which threatens us. Tell the President to explain to his people that Fascism is so literally the enemy of mankind that there is no price you can pay for its destruction that is too high. I wish I had a pen of flame to tell you in America these things as I have heard them from the men of Dunkirk. But if you do not get ready now, you will have your Dunkirk too; and were that to come, there would be no prospect for the sons of men. He must burn it into Americans now that we relied on our strength, we were confident in our resources, we thought right was certain to triumph. And now we stand on the edge of the abyss, thinking of the things we have left undone that might have stopped this Armageddon before it was unleashed. Either you or Hitler makes the future. You will have to fight for the right to make it. I beg you realize the need to be ready for the conflict.

All personal things seem so little and shrunken in the grave hour. We are well; somehow, somewhere in us, there is a gleam of light which refuses to go out. Somehow, however heavy be the tidings, we shall find the strength and the courage to struggle on. I think the darkest days still be ahead, and I do not yet see the prospect of dawn. But I want you and Marion to know that, whatever befall, you have given us golden hours that have made us understand things which only so rich a friendship could make understood. My America has been a great America. I hope all of you who love it, will do all in your power to keep it a great America. Then, one day, the world's great age may indeed begin anew.

We send you both our love as always; and, please, to Ruth and Alfred, too. And tell F.D.R. that we know how stoutly he strove for us and our cause.

Devotedly,
H.

Washington, D.C., July 5, 1940

My dear Mr. President:

With reference to your memorandum of June 29, 1940 enclosing a letter from Mr. Justice Frankfurter, I attach a draft reply which you may wish to send to Mr. Justice Frankfurter.

Faithfully yours,
CORDELL HULL

Washington, D.C., July 9, 1940

My dear Felix:

I have received your letter of June 26 and have given careful consideration to your suggestion that Joe Kennedy be asked to assist in the safekeeping of the invaluable collection of books, pamphlets and manuscripts belonging to Harold Laski.

I should of course like to be of all possible assistance in this matter. There are, however, as you know, a number of Americans living abroad who have extremely fine libraries or other art collections. Since the outbreak of the war we have had to adopt the policy of refusing to authorize our Ambassadors or Ministers to comply with requests in all instances that they take over custody of these collections. This action was necessitated by the fact that it would be impossible to comply with all such requests and it was felt that it would be inappropriate to take action in connection with one American's property and not with another's. In view of this precedent which has been established with respect to our own citizens, I feel sure that you will appreciate that I am not in a position to ask Ambassador Kennedy to take the action which you suggest with respect to the collection of Mr. Laski. It is, of course, always open to Mr. Laski to send his collection, or a part of it, to this country, should he so desire.

Very sincerely yours,

F.D.R.

Telegram to Miss LeHand

New Milford, Conn., July 10, 1940

PLEASE TELL THE PRESIDENT THAT COL. KNOX PHONED LAST NIGHT TO ASK ME TO SWEAR HIM IN. I SHALL TURN UP TOMORROW MORNING TO DO SO.

REGARDS.

FELIX FRANKFURTER

Following this ceremony, Frankfurter spent some time working with Mr. Rosenman on Roosevelt's acceptance speech for the Democratic National Convention. Mr. James Farley and others were preparing to contest the convention to deny him a third term; but their strength, which looked impressive, faded when the votes were counted. The President had a much harder struggle in persuading the convention to nominate Mr. Henry A. Wallace as the Vice-Presidential candidate. The vote on the Presidential nomination for the third term was Roosevelt 946 votes, Farley 72 votes, Garner 61 votes.

Telegram to Roosevelt

Heath, Mass., July 19, 1940

THE MOST DIFFICULT TASK IN OUR POLITICAL HISTORY COULD NOT HAVE BEEN MORE BEAUTIFULLY DISCHARGED. THE EXPLANATION WAS WORTHY OF THE MAGNITUDE OF YOUR DECISION AND YOU HAVE ENDURINGLY EXPRESSED THE LIBERTY-LOVING ASPIRATIONS OF MANKIND. MARION CALLED IT NOBLE AND HER THREE CHILDREN WILL SOON ECHO HER SENTIMENTS.

FELIX

Roosevelt's acceptance speech explaining why he was running for a third term provoked this immediate telegram of praise. The closing sentence has a reference to the three young British children to whom the Frankfurters were gladly offering their home while Britain was being bombed by night and day.

Heath, Mass., July 23, 1940

Dear Frank:

You may have transcended the limitations of distance better than you did last Friday and brought yourself more persuasively into the presence of your listeners, though out of their sight, but if so I never before experienced it, nor did Marion, as we did in your address to Chicago. *That* was a triumph — in every way, persuasive and deeply moving, giving the tone and direction to the months that are immediately ahead for us, and confirming the hopes of all freedom-loving people throughout the world. I had better not say more — for never before were my feelings as engaged in hearing you, as they were during those thirty odd minutes of last Friday, and beyond.

The enclosed, from the Springfield *Republican*, speaks for itself.

I assume that you know of the skilful plan that's afoot — shared in by some of your supporters — to have you and Willkie come to an agreement on "foreign policy" between now and November! The scheme is even more ensnaring than the similar proposal in '32, and calls for even more deft handling. It's a pretty snare — to have it appear (1) that there is no difference between you two and (2) that Willkie is already sharing the responsibilities of Government and that you have to draw on him for wisdom in guiding our affairs. I hope that you will often return to Hyde Park for a few days at least, as intermissions from your confinement at your White House desk and your tours of inspection in your personal oversight of the execution of the defense program.

We shall be at New Milford next week. Will be there into September.

With affectionate regards from us both

Ever yours,
F.F.

Roosevelt spoke by radio to the Chicago Convention in accepting his nomination for a third term.

The Springfield Republican *had praised Roosevelt's concept of public service in the national emergency.*

The White House, July 26, 1940

Dear Felix:

My sincerest thanks and deep gratitude for that generous message you sent me. I cannot tell you how much I appreciate it.

Always sincerely,
FRANKLIN D. ROOSEVELT

The White House, July 27, 1940

Dear Felix: —

Thank you for letting me know about that pretty little scheme for Willkie and myself to share the foreign policy 50-50 between now and November. I had heard a similar rumor here.

I had three days of real rest at Hyde Park and hope to go back about August third and get a week. I am most anxious to have you and Marion come over for the night and will let you know.

As ever yours,
F.D.R.

Frankfurter, through Mr. John McCloy, had heard of Mr. Willkie's plan to give himself higher status in the 1940 campaign by being consulted by the President on foreign policy in return for keeping that policy out of the campaign as a divisive election issue. This plan seemed absurd to the Democrats at the time, and was offered clumsily by Willkie, but it helped to shape the bipartisan tradition in foreign policy. Roosevelt was understandably reluctant to trust Willkie in 1940 when the Republican party was still overwhelmingly isolationist and bitterly hostile to the President's foreign policy.

New Milford, Conn., August 12, 1940

Dear Missy:

(1) The President wanted me to send him by Tuesday hints as to line of speech next Saturday by the gentleman from Indiana. Here they are. Please have them copied, so that the President's eyes may be spared — not to say his temper in trying to read my scribble.

(2) That's how good you are — that I don't care how "bad" you are! But don't you dare go off on a spree when we are asked to come over with "our" children after Labor Day.

It was an altogether joyous visit.

Affectionately yours,
F.F.

Frankfurter's Notes Anticipating Willkie's Speeches

I. Country's prosperity depends on business prosperity — business including farmers. Social progress can only come through business prosperity.

II. Excessive concentration of power is evil — evils of excessive economic concentration cannot be cured by evils of excessive concentration of power in government.

Therefore

I. Need business-like approach to government, and so

(1) must not have attitude of defeatism about business development.

(2) must not have "hate business" attitude, treating business as
an inferior category in U.S.

(3) tax policy must not discourage business incentive.

(4) spending program must aim *primarily* to generate opportunities for private enterprises.

(5) long-term policy of budget-balancing like Swedish system.

II. Government must be a *limited* federal system, respecting local–
state powers and avoiding personal government, through excessive, capricious grant of power to agencies.

As to foreign policies

I. U.S. should be strong, but President should not be provocative.

II. Administration that "hates" business and has no business approach
to govt. is not competent to assure defenses.

There will also be attacks on

(1) "indispensability" and (2) city "bosses"

New Milford, Conn., Labor Day, 1940

Dear Frank:

They were admirable speeches and admirably non-political. It was
good to have them dove-tail, and on this day and for these times. I shan't
particularize the grounds of my appreciation — they gave such a harmonious sense of sentiment and sound, of historic appeal and spur to future
effort — but I cannot forbear rejoicing over your rebuke of those who invoke "the mean and petty spirit that mocks at ideals . . ." Since when
have selfishness and materialism been synonymous with Americanism?
Since when have we refused to sympathize with efforts anywhere on behalf
of liberty, and regarded the gains of tyranny anywhere as immaterial to us?
Certainly the great names in our history never pursued such low views.

Since I'm now a prisoner on the bench, I've taken to ancient history,
present politics being *verboten*. And so I've been reading in Sandburg
about the "Fierce Fall Campaign of '64." It's surprisingly interesting!
Sometimes I wonder if Sandburg is slyly slipping in something immediately
current. For instance, John Bright wrote Greeley that English liberals
wanted Lincoln re-elected because "throughout the world" it would deepen
men's faith in republican institutions. He went on to say:

"It is not because they believe Mr. Lincoln to be wise or better than all
other men on your continent, but they think they have observed in his
career a grand simplicity of purpose . . . regarding his Presidential path
with the calm judgment which belongs rather to history than to the present
time." The chapter is full of good things.

I suppose at the U. of Pennsylvania you will remind them of some strange things B. Franklin said, long, long ago!

Our affectionate regards,
F.F.

New Milford, Conn., September 4, 1940

Dear Frank:

My wire yesterday went to you immediately after I heard the flash over the radio announcing the bases-destroyers agreement and *before* I had heard or seen the text of your message to Congress. Now that I have read the message I write this note with pride and humility — humility that I should have made the comparison of your performance with that of Jefferson's in securing the Louisiana domain when it was contained in your message; pride that I should have had the same thought independently.

And the morning after, the achievement assumes even and ever bigger significance. The imponderable effects on Latin America, the doubtful and oscillating opinion of other countries, Spain and Greece and Turkey and Egypt and even Russia, apart from the practical and moral influence for the English-speaking world — are found to be enormous.

Fred Dumaine phoned me today because he "had to share his enthusiasm with someone who could really understand how he felt." He was simply dithyrambic. He spoke of "that feller Willkie" — to my great surprise, coming from that grand pirate — with scorn. I told him to let you know how he felt — he said he didn't want "to behave like a senile old man." I assured him that expressing the right kind of enthusiasm was a sign of youth.

Do make Bob Jackson deal with the falsehoods in that *Saturday Evening Post* article — especially since W.W. left it out of his book!

Ever yours,
F.F.

The White House, September 6, 1940

Dear Felix: —

Ever so many thanks. I like that John Bright letter and will use it through somebody, who, regardless of Hatch, can still talk.

Incidentally, great minds still think alike about the Louisiana Purchase, the Monroe Doctrine announcement, and the Emancipation Proclamation. Probably legalists held all three unconstitutional — but the combination of the three of them has helped to build and maintain America.

As ever yours,
F.D.R.

Frankfurter took particular delight in sending the John Bright letter to Roosevelt because the renowned British liberal statesman and orator was a special favorite with Lincoln, his other hero. Frankfurter had marked a passage in which Bright spoke contemptuously of people who are ready to crawl through dirt to dignity. He thought this passage aptly characterized the Republican charge that Roosevelt, with his belief in strong government, was really trying to establish a personal dictatorship in Washington, based on the cult of the indispensable man.

The Hatch Act was designed to keep members of the Civil Service from taking any public part in election campaigns.

New Milford, Conn., September 12, 1940

Dear Frank:

You got out of your "quandary" very well, by throwing yourself on the "indulgence" of the radio companies and on that of the American public. But where does that leave me with my poor quandary? For history is judicial meat, but politics is — or are — judicial poison, and so, while I am entitled to praise a disquisition on history, I must hold my tongue and pen even about the most Lincolnian-Gladstonian political utterance. But how am I to know which is what or what is which? There is only one way out — to follow the path I always pursue when I encounter a new problem, and that is, to follow precedent. My very distinguished precedent is, happily, furnished generously by yourself — I shall throw myself on *your* indulgence! Please consider this a word of hearty approval of your views and sentiments, in your Teamster speech, and admiration for the deftness with which you inserted a good deal of poison into it, *provided*, it was an historical address and not a political speech. If, by chance, you decide that it was a political speech then, of course, you will treat the above as though it had not been written.

This business of being a prisoner on the bench presents all sorts of difficult problems. It is, I assume laudable even for a judge to be interested in education but not in political journalism. And so, I hope that you will agree with my conclusion that in having helped *P.M.* to keep going by counselling from time to time with Ralph Ingersoll, I have been merely showing an active interest in proper educational agencies!

Before long, the judicial halter will be upon me.

I hope you are keeping fresh and re-freshed. I am told that even Long Island is troubled down to its Ballantine grass roots.

Ever yours,
F.F.

Washington, D. C., September 21, 1940

Dear Frank:

Marion and I rode Friday morning through the rich farming country of Chester County, Pa., with its white houses glistening in the sunshine, and our spirits greatly cheered by the Gallup figures in the morning papers. But in the afternoon we were even more cheered as the radio transported us to the University of Pennsylvania exercises in Philadelphia. The extraordinary enthusiasm with which you were welcomed, and which was sustained throughout your speech and reached a crescendo at its close, was even more significant and revealing than the cold statistics of Gallup.

And your speech came off as did your Harvard Tercentenary address, I cannot say more — except that your good humor and saucy thrusts were even more infectious than they were in the sterilized atmosphere of Cambridge. You ought to make addresses at University celebrations one of your professional side-lines — you are so skilful and felicitous at them. Yes — everything you said at Philadelphia on September 20, 1940 would have been just as appropriate, just as effective had the bi-centennial fallen on September 20, 1939. But what you said — and you remember the old, old line "it wasn't what he said, but the nasty way he said it!" — was astonishingly pat, "appropriate and felicitous," in the historical setting of Sept. 20, 1940!! Evidently a good time was had by all — or almost all. Certainly your enjoyment clearly crackled over the radio.

Here I am, soon to begin again my judicial servitude — to be lightened this year, by the diverting sounds of children's voices happily away from the scene of carnage.

Marion joins me in affectionate regards.

Yours ever,
F.F.

Washington, D.C., October 7, 1940

Dear Sam:

Herewith notes which may be of some help. I do believe that both quotations from Monroe — and certainly the formulation of the Monroe Doctrine — are very timely and put history behind immediate policy. It is always helpful when stiff language speaks, as it were, impersonally and with the power of the past. Also, Latin peoples care more than we do for texts, particularly texts that minister to their pride. Therefore T.R.'s quotation of Root deserves to be recalled.

Above all, I hope you agree to the suggestion that I made over the phone regarding the importance of emphasizing that the indispensable defenses — those without which tanks and planes even are of no avail — are the defenses of the mind. In other words, the clear realization of spiritual ends — the ideals of life — which alone give dignity to man, and passionate determination to maintain them, are the possessions which alone give that quality to a society which deserves the name of civilization; they alone are the possessions for which men will fight longest and best, if their dispossession is threatened. To be sure, tanks and planes are indispensable, and in adequate volume. But if recent history teaches anything, it is that those who are hostile to the democratic way of life count most on disorganizing the moral forces of a democracy, which means allegiance to the democratic purposes and determination to defend them at all hazards. From every point of view, this general thought cannot be emphasized too strongly in addressing the Americas.

Ever yours,
FELIX

Frankfurter Memorandum

The destiny that fate had in store for the Americas was symbolized by the enterprise which founded the Continent. It was led by an Italian of vision and will. It was made possible by the imagination and faith of Spain. And it was achieved by the hardihood and devotion of a crew which at various times was composed of Spaniards, an Irishman, an Englishman, and a Jew. The cooperative nature of the discovery of the New World has been reflected in its development. And so when nearly three hundred years after Columbus first landed, the union of North American states was formed, the Constitution by which it was established could authoritatively be characterized by our Supreme Court as one ordained "by descendants of Englishmen, who inherited the traditions of English law and history" but "made for an undefined and expanding future, and for a people gathered and to be gathered from many nations and of many tongues."

Inevitably, when the ferment of freedom asserted itself in South America, the United States was prompt to make fraternal response. In his message to Congress, on March 8, 1822, President Monroe told the world that "The revolutionary movement in the Spanish provinces in this hemisphere attracted the attention and excited the sympathy of our fellow-citizens from its commencement. This feeling was natural and honorable to them, from causes which need not be communicated to you." This expression of fraternity was a prelude to President Monroe's famous declaration in his message of December 2, 1823, which is as timely now to recall as it was for him to promulgate:

"With the existing colonies or dependencies of any European power we have not interfered and shall not interfere. But with the Governments who have declared their independence and maintained it, and whose independence we have, on great consideration and on just principles, acknowledged, we could not view any interposition for the purpose of oppressing them, or controlling in any other manner their destiny, by any European power in any other light than as the manifestation of an unfriendly disposition toward the United States."

The Monroe doctrine has served as an instrument of peace by being, in effect, a veto on war between Europe and the Americas. The underlying conception has been that of a fraternity of the American peoples. Our relations with our fellow American peoples received classic expression in the administration of President Theodore Roosevelt when he sent Secretary of State Root on his famous mission to South America. "We wish," said Mr. Root in language which President Theodore Roosevelt communicated to Congress in his message of December 3, 1906, "for no victories but those of peace; for no territory except our own; for no sovereignty except the sovereignty over ourselves. We deem the independence and equal rights of the smallest and weakest member of the family of nations entitled to as much respect as those of the great empire, and we deem the observance of that respect the chief guaranty of the weak against the oppression of the strong. We neither claim nor desire any rights or privileges or powers that we do not freely concede to every American republic."

The new world which Columbus and his companions opened up to man was not merely the American Continent. It was that world of the spirit — that source of new hopes — which the discovery of the Continent has ever since stirred in the minds of men. For this new continent gave the fullest opportunities for a gracious civilization of peoples of every variety of origin and culture. The new world was indeed the new home for the free and intrepid spirit of man.

This letter by Frankfurter to Judge Sam Rosenman offered some ideas for a forthcoming speech by Roosevelt on the defense of the Western hemisphere.

The White House, October 7, 1940

My dear Mr. Justice:

Thank you for your letter and for the enclosure. I like it and I pray the Statue of Liberty may continue to represent a country which means liberty.

Very sincerely yours,

ELEANOR ROOSEVELT

Mrs. Roosevelt was thanking Frankfurter for a speech which he had made on what the Statue of Liberty signified to people who came here with the hope of freedom in their hearts. Though brief, this was a deeply felt utterance, for Frankfurter was reflecting the experience and dreams of his own family.

Washington, D.C., October 10, 1940

Dear Missy —

Here are two documents which I'll trouble you to pass on to the President.

(1) The telegram is very important — for his diversion.

(2) The President will understand the obligation he is to sign in the enclosed note intended for his signature.

Thank you!

Ever yours,

F.F.

Telegram to Frankfurter

Canton, Mass., October 10, 1940

NO PORTUGUESE ON COLUMBUS'S VOYAGES.

SAMUEL E. MORISON

Cambridge, Mass., October 10, 1940

Dear Felix:

Your inquiry about the Portuguese with Columbus came when I was away at Concord, New Hampshire. This morning I wired you that there were none. The authority is the exhaustive article on Columbus's crew by Miss Alice Gould in the *Boletín de la Real Academia de la Historia,* volumes 84-92 (1924-28). She finds that there were no foreigners with Columbus on the First Voyage. I remember there being a few Portuguese with him on the Third Voyage, but only as common sailors.

If the President wishes to give the Portuguese credit on Columbus Day, there are two legitimate ways of doing it.

(1) Columbus married Felippa Moniz, daughter of Perestrello, one of the captains trained under Prince Henry the Navigator, and that gave him the inside track with the Portuguese.

(2) All his maritime experience and nautical science were derived from voyages that he sailed on Portuguese ships to Madeira, the coast of Africa, etc.

I am sending the President today a copy of my new book on Portuguese Voyages to America.

I am very much worried about the Portuguese now. From the best information I have Hitler is going to jump Portugal shortly, and Salazar will hand it over to him on a platter. Last November we saw German merchantmen at Horta and Ponta Delgada with plenty of crew to seize those islands, and I wish that our navy might grab them first to protect our communications. Corvo, outermost of the Azores, is only 1024 miles from Newfoundland. Ponta Delgada is only 1250 miles from Newfoundland. There you have it! I have written to the State Department and had the usual formal reply. Is there anyone there like Berle whom I might approach personally with any chance of success?

Always affectionately,
SAM E. MORISON

Memo for the files

Washington, D.C., October 10, 1940

Following was sent to Felix Frankfurter 10/10/40

"Washington, D.C., October 10, 1940

"Thirty days after date I promise to pay to Felix Frankfurter, in the legal tender of Conversational Currency, an account of Latin B.

(signed)   F. D. Sucker   in the President's
U. S. N."   handwriting.

(*Above "note" prepared by F.F.*)

The President, who wanted material in praise of the Portuguese for a little speech, hoped that he could satisfy national pride by showing that Portuguese sailors had gone with Christopher Columbus on his voyages. Samuel Eliot Morison, the historian and biographer of Columbus, disappointed him on that score, but his letter must have brought joy to Roosevelt, with his love of naval lore. It is interesting that several times during the war Roosevelt adopted Mr. Morison's technique of giving stark statistics to show America's proximity to points of danger by sea and air.

The Presidential memorandum recorded a rash promise to Frankfurter that Roosevelt could recover his ability to speak a few consecutive Latin phrases. No forfeiture ever was exacted. As the signature shows, Roosevelt knew he had made a mistake.

Washington, D.C., November 3, 1940

Dear Frank:

This brings you our affectionate non-political and political good wishes. Both of us — Marion and I — have had full-time jobs these past few weeks, and hers, to make three children happy, has been fuller and better. And both of us have been having a hard time to attend to our jobs so absorbed have our thoughts and feelings been in the effort to make our beloved country continue to be effective and aggressive on the side of civilization. For *that's* the ultimate meaning of your role in history — *that's* the real issue of Tuesday's election. All the rest is cooked-up stuff — copy-writers' *Ersatz*.

To us two, who for seven years have been, as it were, outside insiders, it has been given, perhaps, as well as to anyone, to understand the sweet, human, basically human, purposes to which all your energies and measures, your plans and experiments have been devoted. And *that's* the decisive thing — the goal toward which your weight and works, your faith and fervor, have been directed. For the silent, inarticulate, common folk the world over, your re-election will bring new hopes and confirmation of old faiths.

We invoke for the world's sake, for the sake of the common lot of mankind, our fervent prayers and our deepest wishes.

To you personally we say — God bless you.

Faithfully yours,
F.F.

Telegram to Roosevelt

Washington, D.C., November 5, 1940

PLEASE CONSIDER REPEATING THAT WONDERFUL PRAYER IN ANY REMARK YOU MAY MAKE HERE TOMORROW. WHAT IS THE OPPOSITE OF KATZENJAMMER? THAT IS WHAT WE HAD THIS MORNING.

FELIX FRANKFURTER

Roosevelt closed his final radio speech of the 1940 campaign, delivered from Hyde Park, with a stately and moving prayer. The following letter gives its history — and gives us one small glimpse of Frankfurter's consuming interest in the most recondite matters.

Roosevelt in his last campaign speech said "democracy is not just a word to be shouted at political rallies and then put back into the dictionary after election day."

The Thanksgiving Day proclamation had a resonant passage — "defend our liberties, and fashion into one united people the multitudes brought hither out of many kindreds and tongues."

New York, N.Y., November 26, 1940

My dear Mr. Burlingham:

Both Howard Robbins and your Rector have asked me to send you whatever information I can as to the source of the now-famous prayer used by the President in a speech and in the Thanksgiving proclamation.

The author is the late Rev. George Lyman Locke, who was Rector of the Episcopal Church in Bristol, Rhode Island. He was a great friend of Huntington of Grace Church. During the 1880-1892 revision of the Prayer Book, while Locke was visiting Huntington, the latter said to him. "We

must have a prayer for our country and you are just the man to write it."
Locke complied and the prayer was included in *The Book Annexed*. On
what ground General Convention vetoed it so that it failed to get into the
1892 Prayer Book no one living today seems to remember. The 1913-1928
revisers rescued it from oblivion so that it now appears in our Prayer Book
in virtually its original form.

It has always been in my Father's *A Book of Offices and Prayers* published by Gorham, which came out originally in 1896, and it has been
widely used ever since then. My father greatly regrets that the 1928 revisers,
against his wishes, changed "Fashion into one happy people" to "Fashion
into one united people" — not only because the latter is redundant but also
because it abandons the reference to the beautiful fifteenth verse of psalm
144.

With best wishes, I am

Very sincerely yours,
JOHN W. SUTER, JR.
Church of the Epiphany

Washington, D.C., November 7, 1940

Dear Frank:

Ever since Dunkirk, we have seen growth in the stature of Man
through the behavior of our fellow-men in Britain. And now the common
people of our country have demonstrated the same essential qualities of
manliness. Confronted by the masked power of fear and obfuscation, they
responded with clarity and courage. Thereby they not only averted a real
menace to the nation. They have given one new and strong confidence in
human nature.

I know enough to know how much of literal truth there was in your
remark that you "will have to bear the cross" of a third nomination. And
the people have insisted that you must "bear the cross" of another term.
For partly, indeed, it is a cross — but, thank God, the people won't be on
that cross!

And so I wish you the strength and serenity of yourself for ourselves.
Terrible days are ahead — and the world is fortunate to have you where you
have been. The quiet, conclusive faith of the people in you will give you
solace and refreshment to enable you to give strength and wisdom to the
people.

To you, personally, the fullness of your powers and the peace of your
dedicated life.

With affectionate regards from us both,

Ever yours,
F.F.

Frankfurter's letter of congratulations on Roosevelt's election to a third term.

The White House, November 8, 1940

Dear Felix:

A very brief note to thank you and Marion for that grand letter of congratulations.

I want to thank you for all you personally have done during these months and for all the help you have given me and those who are working with me, who always felt that they could call on you at any time for advice and help.

I want to see you both and also the three children some time very soon — as soon as I get caught up on some sleep!

As ever yours,
F.D.R.

P.S.   I am returning that extraordinarily nice letter which you sent me.
F.D.R.

The enclosed letter was from Mrs. Frankfurter's sister, and described what Roosevelt's leadership meant to parents in this war.

Washington, D.C., November 8, 1940

Dear Frank:

A kind of Nemesis is pursuing Willkie in his persistence to challenge comparison with you. But it is good for the country. For he is a bad man — being a man with appetites and without convictions — who needs not only to be defeated but to be destroyed. And he will destroy himself.

Armistice Day will help. I hope that you will speak more than a minute or two — speak for ten or fifteen minutes in the tone and temper of your Hyde Park Monday night talk, with Arlington, where are buried men who "gave their very names to their country," as the background for your appeal to our common humanity and our common free men's devotion to country. And then let W.W.'s raucous appeal to faction shriek itself hoarse that night.

Ever yours,
F.F.

Willkie, still smarting from defeat, had not yet recovered the breadth of vision which made him later a symbol of unity instead of a partisan figure.

Washington, D.C., November 10, 1940

Dear Felix:

I want you to know that I deeply appreciate your kind message. Many, many thanks.

As ever yours,
FRANKLIN D. ROOSEVELT

Washington, D.C., November 10, 1940

Missy, you will find this a very interestin' item — that is, if you ain't heard it before!

F.F.

Item from "Alumni Notes" in the HARVARD ALUMNI BULLETIN, p. 236:

"On November 5 Franklin D. Roosevelt, LL.D. (Hon.) '29 was elected President of the United States for a third successive term."

By this time it has become evident that there is scarcely one friendly or generous word about Ambassador Joseph P. Kennedy in all these letters. In one important sense they do him a severe and undeserved injustice: they judge him on a single issue alone. Appeasement, isolation, neutrality, the challenge of Hitlerism — all this was of supreme importance, but concerned only one set of values. Place Ambassador Kennedy in a different context, judge him on other issues, and the verdict of Roosevelt and Frankfurter would have been seasoned with admiration.

Roosevelt would never have forgotten Mr. Kennedy's valiant service in the early years of the New Deal. It took courage for a man to tame Wall Street, by scorpions if necessary, and teach the financial community no longer to behave like the money-changers denounced by Roosevelt in his First Inaugural. As Chairman of the Securities and Exchange Commission, Mr. Kennedy provided that courage and that leadership. It took courage for Mr. Kennedy to disturb the prejudices of powerful business leaders by writing a little book with the proud and challenging title Why I Am for Roosevelt. *Before his rupture with the President, he gave abundantly of his ideas, his energy, and his wealth to the advancement of Roosevelt's program. These things, too, deserve to be remembered.*

Frankfurter knew the entire Kennedy family very well. He always had the greatest respect for Mr. Kennedy's intellectual power. He called him "a formidable fellow." He admired Mr. Kennedy's identification with the Irish people and respected his pride in the Catholic faith. He shared Mr. Kennedy's rough impatience with the Boston Brahmins. After all, he had gone through his own experiences with them. Above everything else, he knew from personal observation something of Mr. Kennedy's genius as a father. He watched with amazement and with delight as Mr. Kennedy trained his independent and courageous children to have a passion for public service — often in service to causes which did not command the father's loyalty. And these things, also, deserve not to be forgotten.

Mr. Kennedy wanted to be the American Ambassador in London; he had earned an important appointment by his years of service to the Democratic party; his great ability was never in dispute; and the London appointment had traditionally gone to a man of vast wealth. So he became the Ambassador to the Court of St. James's in London.

With all our present knowledge, there is no risk that Mr. Kennedy's service as Ambassador will be judged as either wise or successful. It is more useful to remind ourselves of certain facts which Roosevelt and Frankfurter ignored. Mr. Kennedy was right in his estimate of the terrible power of Nazi Germany. He was right in thinking that Poland would be conquered. He was right in predicting that France would quit. He was right in foreseeing that England would be bled white by a long-continued struggle against Germany. But he was wrong in his judgment of the British people, and being wrong on that essential point, he marred everything.

Roosevelt dismissed Mr. Kennedy as Ambassador to Great Britain without warning. Every political leader, said Gladstone, must be somewhat of a butcher: the art consists in never letting the blood show. Mr. Kennedy can be pardoned for ignoring the artistry and remembering only the sudden and imperious brutality. He never forgave Roosevelt — or Frankfurter for his discussions with the President leading to his dismissal. But the President knew Ambassador Kennedy wanted to come to terms with Hitler; he himself regarded Hitler as the most dangerous menace to peace. They had to part.

Washington, D.C., November 11, 1940

Dear Frank —

If you have not seen the full text of the Joe Kennedy interview in yesterday's Boston *Globe* you will want to. But what is printed watered down some of the things Joe said. They were so raw the *Globe* did not want to print them. More of this when I see you.

Ever yours,
F.F.

BOSTON *SUNDAY* GLOBE, NOVEMBER 10, 1940
KENNEDY SAYS DEMOCRACY ALL DONE IN BRITAIN,
MAYBE HERE
PINCH COMING IN U.S. TRADE LOSS
Ambassador Asks Aid To England Be Viewed As

"Insurance"; Begs America Wake Up, Give
More Power to Mobilize Industry
By Louis M. Lyons (Copyright 1940, By Boston Globe)

Joseph P. Kennedy was sitting in his shirtsleeves eating apple pie and American cheese in his room at the Ritz-Carlton. His suspenders hung around his hips.

It was the setting for an interview that every American reporter has known 1000 times in interviewing the visiting head of the Elks, or the Rotarians, or the Lions Club — as American as apple pie.

Mr. Kennedy's own words cut sharply across this picture when he lifted the telephone to say, "This is the Ambassador." But his next words brought us back where we were. "O hello Bob, how are y'?"

HE AND EDITOR SEE EYE-TO-EYE

A journalistic colleague from St. Louis who shared the interview — Ralph Coglan, editor of the St. Louis *Post Dispatch* — liked Joe Kennedy from the first look at him. He liked him more every minute and every sentence of the hour and a half that Joe Kennedy poured out to us his views about America and the war in a torrent that flowed with the free, full power and flood of the Mississippi River.

My Missouri friend's eyes flashed in response to Kennedy. He was seeing eye to eye with the American ambassador as he hadn't been able to do with any of the intellectual leaders of Boston and Cambridge he'd seen in his crowded visit. As these two glowed together in the discussion, it struck me that Joe Kennedy of Boston birth probably comes closer to representing the Mississippi Valley, the great heart of America, than any ambassador the Court of St. James's has had the luck to meet in modern times.

WOULD SPEND ALL TO KEEP OUT

"I'm willing to spend all I've got left to keep us out of the war," Kennedy flashed toward the end of his talk.

"There's no sense in our getting in. We'd just be holding the bag."

KEEP U.S. OUT OF WAR

He's started already on a quiet but determined and fighting crusade, to "keep us out." He's just gone to California to see one of America's influential publishers. He's already seen others and he means to see more and let them have it straight and tough, as he sees it. He's talked to Congressmen and Senators and means to see more. "They've got to understand it," he says, with passion. He's been amazed at how little — so it seems to him —

the Congressmen who've visited with him so far do understand the war and America's relation to it.

"I know more about the European situation than anybody else, and it's up to me to see that the country gets it," he says in explanation of the role of carrying the torch that he has cut out for himself.

U.S. CHANCES OF PEACE BETTER

Coglan asks what he thinks are the chances of our keeping out.

"Better than they were three months ago," says Kennedy.

"I'm happy to see that you aren't another Walter Hines Page," says the St. Louis editor as we leave. (Page was our Ambassador in the crucial 1916-17 period who made it his crusade to see that President Wilson appreciated the British side of the war.)

Kennedy laughed. "Americans find it hard to understand that a man can be in that atmosphere and not succumb to it," he said.

"A couple of years ago I told my friend Joe Patterson," a reference to the New York publisher, "that the Queen was one of the most intelligent women I ever met."

"He said, 'O, now I know you've succumbed to their blandishments, Joe. If you'd said most gracious, or most charming, but most intelligent —'. Well, he saw her on her American tour which presented her a tremendously difficult problem that she handled magnificently. After that he told me he was half willing to admit her intelligence. This time I saw him, he said, after following her conduct in the war, he'd go all the way with me.

QUEEN CALLED GREAT WOMAN

"Now I tell you that when this thing is finally settled," Kennedy declared, "and it comes to a question of saving what's left for England, it will be the Queen and not any of the politicians who will do it. She's got more brains than the Cabinet.

"It's partly because she wasn't born into the Royal Family. Her background is of the people. She's an omnivorous reader. Daladier told me, after he'd first met her, that she knew more about French history than almost any Frenchman."

"What do you say about Eleanor Roosevelt?"

"She's another wonderful woman. And marvelously helpful and full of sympathy. Jim will tell you," as he turned to Dean James M. Landis of the Harvard Law School, coming in as we were going out, "that she bothered us more on our jobs in Washington to take care of the poor little nobodies who hadn't any influence, than all the rest of the people down there together. She's always sending me a note to have some little Susie Glotz to tea at the embassy."

REPORTER'S DILEMMA

Coglan and I rushed for a cab to get to an office where we could compare notes and save every crumb we could of Kennedy's talk. Coglan, an editorial writer, wanted it only for background. He didn't have a story to write.

"I wouldn't be in your shoes," said Coglan. "How do you know what you can write? He just puts it up to you to follow your own conscience and judgment and protect him in his diplomatic capacity."

"Well, last time I interviewed him, in 1936, he poured himself out just like this, without laying any restriction on me, and I wrote every bit of it, and it went all over the country — the interview in which he said why he was for Roosevelt. And he said it was the best interview he'd ever had. But he wasn't an Ambassador then."

"It all depends on how you handle it," advised Coglan. "Any story can be told if it's told right."

RUNNING OVER THE NOTES

Well then, with all care, but without losing the color and force and pungency that makes Joe Kennedy one of the leading figures on the world stage today, we'll run over the notes. Charles Edmondson, Nieman fellow from Coglan's editorial staff, who arranged the interview for his visiting boss while I was arranging it for myself, comes in and checks my notes again.

"Don't forget," he said, "Lindbergh's not so crazy either," he reminds me. Edmondson has been carrying on a running debate, from the Mississippi Valley point of view, with his interventionist friends in Cambridge all Fall.

The Ambassador had just finished his physical checkup at the Lahey clinic when we saw him. "They say I'm in better shape than I was last time," he told us.

"It's a funny thing. I slept through the anti-aircraft guns in London. But when I got out to Lisbon the auto horns kept me awake."

CAN'T GET USED TO BOMBING

"But don't let anybody tell you you can get used to incessant bombing. There's nowhere in England they aren't getting it. The people are standing up to it. They go to work the next day. They have to let them off two hours early to get to shelters. Of course transportation is interrupted. I could tell you it takes seven hours to deliver a telegram and often two hours to get downtown. Plenty of that. But it doesn't help to emphasize that.

"Their shipping losses are greater this time because they haven't so many destroyers and what they have they have to divide, in the Mediterranean and for defending England, besides convoys. Our fifty destroyers filled a great need. And the German submarine bases are nearer the traffic lanes this time.

"Hitler has all the ports in Europe, you see. Never forget that. The only reason the English haven't taken over the Irish ports is because of American public opinion.

IF WE GET IN, DEMOCRACY ENDS

"People call me a pessimist. I say, 'What is there to be gay about? Democracy is all done.'"

"You mean in England or this country, too?"

"Well, I don't know. If we get into war it will be in this country, too. A bureaucracy would take over right off. Everything we hold dear would be gone. They tell me that after 1918 we got it all back again. But this is different. There's a different pattern in the world."

"What about British democracy?" Edmonson asked. "Is there real opportunity there, or does the aristocracy keep a rigid class structure that keeps the common man down?"

"When there's a strong upsurge from beneath you can't stop it," Kennedy replies. "You can't blame the aristocracy for keeping it down if it doesn't come up."

"Well, what does it mean to have labor men now at the center of government?" I ask.

NATIONAL SOCIALISM FOR ENGLAND

"It means national socialism is coming out of it," says Kennedy flatly.

"You don't see much then in the picture H. G. Wells and Harold Laski give us of a developing democracy as a new permanent basis of British society?"

"You've picked the two worst examples to take. Laski is greatly overrated over here. He doesn't represent anything.

"Democracy is finished in England. It may be here. Because it comes to a question of feeding people. It's all an economic question. I told the President in the White House last Sunday, 'Don't send me fifty admirals and generals. Send me a dozen real economists.'

"It's the loss of our foreign trade that's going to threaten to change our form of government. We haven't felt the pinch of it yet. It's ahead of us."

WHY HE SUPPORTED ROOSEVELT

"Did you support Roosevelt with some misgivings?" Coglan asked.

"No. I supported Roosevelt because I feel he's the only man who can control the groups who have got to be brought along in what's ahead of us."

"You mean the men who control industry?"

"No. They have a stake that they've got to defend. I mean the have nots. They haven't any stake of ownership. They've got to take it in whatever faces us.

"It's all a question of what we do in the next six months. The whole reason for aiding England is to give us time. Whatever we give England, we shouldn't think of getting it back. It's insurance. We can pull the teeth of the William Allen White Committee, and of the anti-English groups, too, by just not arguing at all. We can just accept whatever they say, and our answer is 'It's just one question, self-preservation for us. England is doing everything we could ask. As long as she is in there, we have time to prepare. It isn't that she's fighting for democracy. That's the bunk. She's fighting for self-preservation, just as we will if it comes to us.'

"I don't draw any line on how much aid. It is a practical question of judgement, how much to send. It is a question of how long England can hold out. If she collapses soon, then stop.

ANY MORE LOANS — INSURANCE

"If we went in we'd just be holding the bag. I tell everyone, 'Don't expect to get the World War debts paid. We'll never get that back. But we must see that they don't wind up this time holding all our securities and we with a long debt. We'll take it from them while they can pay for what they need. But when they get through, give it to them. Mark it off as insurance.' "

He wouldn't venture a judgement on how the war was coming out. But he felt the months just ahead would tell.

"The Blitzkrieg won't beat the British," he said positively. "Their danger is from movement. A march on Gibraltar through Spain. The march for Iraq and for Cairo . . ."

"Then what about Canada if the worst comes to England?"

"Well, we're sucked in on that, and the Monroe Doctrine and all.

"The thing is, what we do with the next six months. It would be fatal to let it go by without making the most of every working day for defense. We aren't doing the maximum now. We've got to. We've got to realize it. Nobody could handle industrial mobilization but Jesus Christ with any legislative power we're willing to give him now. We've got to educate America to the need for defense. Fast too."

WHEELER AND KENNEDY BUDDIES

Coglan asked what senators Kennedy had in mind seeing. He asked about Burton K. Wheeler, who has been rated a strong isolationist.

"Burt Wheeler and I are buddies," Kennedy said. "Why, I financed his campaign with La Follette."

We must have gaped at that. The La Follette-Wheeler third party contested the Presidential election of 1924 against Calvin Coolidge, Republican, and John W. Davis, Democrat. That was on the crest of the "Coolidge Boom" and Joseph P. Kennedy was riding in with others in Wall Street.

Wasn't aid to England likely to draw us in as in 1917, asked Edmondson, mentioning Walter Millis' "Road to War."

"No," said Kennedy positively. "Not if we know the answer. Not if we are coldly realistic and for America all the time. If they ask me to get in more than is safe for us, we ask them, 'What do you want us to do? How can we send troops over when Hitler has the ports? Why do you ask for men when you haven't called up all your eligible men?' If they want us to patrol the Atlantic by taking our Navy out of the Pacific, we answer that that would bring a howl clear across America to California. If they want aviators, what ships are they going to fly in? As to ships, we haven't got any. I know about ships. We couldn't send an army anywhere now. It would be senseless to go in. What would we be fighting for?"

AID ENGLAND AS FAR AS WE CAN

"If Hitler wins the war," Coglan asks, "do you believe we wouldn't trade with Europe?"

"That's nonsensical," Kennedy replied. "But the thing now, is: aid England as far as we can; that's our game. As long as she can hold out, give her what it takes, whatever we don't have to have, and don't expect anything back."

As to the cost, and the increase in the tax limit, he laughed at our questions.

"Nobody knows how far you can add to the debt limit. It isn't a yardstick question. All you'll know is if it goes so far that it goes sour and people won't have any part of it.

"Nobody knows what inflation is. If you mean in terms of currency, how can we inflate our currency when we can base it on nearly all the gold in the world? You could issue any amount of currency on it. You can't have inflation in this country under present conditions. Hitler's kicked all the economic theories out the window. The two greatest bankers in the world are Montagu Norman and Schaacht."

"And Schaacht is the greater," puts in Edmondson.

"Yes. Norman admits it," Kennedy says.

WHAT IS INFLATION?

"I said inflation to Norman one day and he challenged me, 'What is inflation? Define it.' Try it sometime.

"But if you're talking about debt limit, suppose we got into the war. I've surveyed every aspect of the British war economy. The first year of the War cost them half their national income. At that rate in the first year we'd spend $35,000,000,000 (35 billions). What would we get out of it? Lindbergh isn't crazy either, you know.

"I say we aren't going in. Only over my dead body. I'll spend everything I've got left to keep us out."

He stopped and laughed.

"Everybody is always asking if Joe Kennedy is going back home when I'm over there, and if he's going back over when I'm home. Nobody wants to know his ideas or to find out if he's got any. I know more about Europe than anybody else in this country because I've been closer to it longer. I'm going to make it a point to educate America to the situation.

"Well, I'm afraid you didn't get much of a story."

Washington, D.C., November 17, 1940

Dear Frank:

Knowing your generous thoughtfulness about your friends, I should have picked a birthday that would not have interfered even for a brief moment with your quest for fish and sleep. I do hope that you get a good installment of both.

It was very sweet of you to remember my day — or, rather my mother's — and you greatly cheered me with your message and your flowers.

Devotedly yours,
F.F.

Frankfurter's birthday was on November 15.

Radiogram to Frankfurter

Oxford, England, November 20, 1940

OXFORD PRESS IS PUBLISHING BOTH IN ENGLAND AND AMERICA THE AMERICAN SPEECHES OF LORD LOTHIAN. SHALL BE MORE THAN GRATEFUL IF YOU CAN SEE YOUR WAY TO ASKING PRESIDENT ROOSEVELT IF HE WILL HONOUR WITH AN INTRODUCTION A BOOK SO IMPORTANT TO OUR TWO COUNTRIES.

HUMPHREY MILFORD

Lord Lothian was the British Ambassador to the United States and had been absolutely invaluable in smoothing away points of friction during the critical months of 1940. Without his aid it would not have been so easy to move American Aid to Britain, including the provision of the overage destroyers to fight the Battle of the Atlantic. Only premature death robbed him of the distinction of being the most successful British ambassador in Washington of this century since Bryce.

Washington, D.C., November 21, 1940

Dear Missy:

This cable is from Sir Humphrey Milford, the head of the Oxford University Press. I shall be glad to convey whatever reply the President may indicate.

Yours,
F.F.

The White House, November 23, 1940

Dear Felix:

I am returning Humphrey Milford's cable which you sent to Missy. I wish I could do as he suggests but it is against the rule. I am really sorry.

The happiest of Holiday Seasons to you.

Very sincerely yours,
FRANKLIN D. ROOSEVELT

Washington, D.C., November 29, 1940

Dear Mr. President:

The special circumstances of Finland's needs and their relation to the blockade will doubtless still further be urged upon you. It may not, therefore, be a waste of your time — however much I feel like a culprit to draw upon any of it — for you to see a copy of my letter to Lothian as well as the enclosures to which my letter refers.

Faithfully yours,
F.F.

Russia invaded Finland on November 30, 1939. For months afterward Finland surprised the world by its resistance. The Western world concluded that Russian military power was a hollow shell. It had reason to be grateful for this mistake when Germany in 1941 invaded Russia, and the Soviet armies bent but did not break under the terrible weight of the Nazi assault.

November 27, 1940

Dear Philip:

You know what I think about the uncompromisable importance of maintaining the blockade, and therefore you know what I think about various efforts to allow food to go to the occupied territories. On the other hand, I know you will agree that because of the surface humane appeal of proposals like those of the Friends and of Mr. Hoover, and the lack of adequate appreciation of the role of the blockade in the present conflict, the denial of such appeals is more and more likely to be mischievously misunderstood on this side of the ocean. Therefore, nothing should be left undone to minimize the danger of a situation which I think will increasingly develop as the winter comes on.

The enclosed documents and some explorations of my own have led me to believe that the case that can be made for putting Finland in a class by itself is very impressive. The writer of one of the letters is an old friend of mine, Mrs. Samuel Barlow, the former wife of Bullitt.

I know the stupendous burdens that rest on you these days and the almost supernatural effort that is called from you. Nevertheless, I hope you can make an independent study of the facts underlying these documents. You will know best how to pursue the matter effectively and quickly if they warrant the conclusion that at least experimental action should be taken which would inevitably be on so small a scale that, should the experiment turn out to be unfeasible, no harm really will have been done and Britain will be able to put her case so far as Finland is concerned on the basis of proof instead of that of abstract assumption. It has thus far been possible to postpone public appeal of Finland's cause by a very influential group.

From the point of view of American public opinion, I deem this matter very important.

Ever yours,
F.F.

His Excellency
The Most Hon. The Marquess of Lothian, C.H.

The enclosed documents have been omitted, except for Mrs. Barlow's letter.

11 Gramercy Park

Dear Felix:

I do not know if you are aware that the Finns are in dire need this winter. If they were not as heroic as we believed them to be last year they would have cried aloud from the housetops for all the world to hear. They lack grain, cotton, fats — the greatest need of all in this arctic country —

warm clothing and blankets. Without immediate supplies of these things many thousand of these gallant folk will not survive. The first three things are our greatest surpluses.

I believe in the British blockade of occupied countries. But Finland to date is not occupied. She is still, to her own astonishment, under her own management. Until the situation changes it seems an unnecessary cruelty to withhold the navicerts which will enable the Finns to carry to Petsamo, unescorted in their own twenty-seven available small tankers, these vital supplies. The Germans let the Finnish boats go unmolested from New York to Petsamo. We can, through Red Cross representatives or anyone else the British ask for, keep a check on all distribution. The British have their own inspector in Petsamo now. The moment there is any evidence that either Russia or Germany are benefitting either directly or indirectly by the entry of these supplies, the supply can and should stop. The Finnish tankers are so small, the port facilities of Petsamo so meager, distribution so difficult owing to gasoline and truck shortage that they can only take care of very small quantities at a time. There is no possibility of laying up great stores for capture. Finland would be fed through an eyedropper, but fed she could be and saved from misery.

I think public opinion is awakening here to the plight of their last year's hero. There are plans for petitions to the President of names that will make news, campaigns for editorials in the newspapers, hot words from the columnists. I would, for the sake of the British, avoid this publicity. I don't think the distinction between occupied and unoccupied territory is an obvious one for the general public. If the Finns are fed there will be no outcry and people will accept what is already done. Couldn't this be done by quietly letting the Finnish slip out from the U.S.? I feel it would be a useful blockade weapon in British hands to say "We are not just pig-headed ornery mules who make a rule and then stick to it no matter what. When we have proof that supplies are not strengthening our enemies we allow them to pass." Incidentally they may find it expedient to allow token shipments to reach Norway in order to keep the Norwegian fleet sailing for Great Britain, but I'm not arguing that point. I am too wholeheartedly pro-British to want to hamper their great fight in any way but I do not think we need humor their distress so far as to refuse to ask their reasonable consideration of a matter such as this. They are, to their eternal credit, humane as well as stubborn. Might not a more liberal navicert policy for unoccupied Finland also be a weapon against the Hoover campaign?

The Finns need 3,500,000 bushels of grain and 17,000 tons of fats. These are subsistance rations for themselves only and include no provisions for saving their livestock and poultry. Finland is pleading for raw cotton as another vital necessity, but if the British balk on that we know one can't eat it for breakfast anyway. The estimated cost of grain, fats and clothing is six to eight millions. Only the President has access to the $50,000,000 appropriated by Congress, only he can instruct the Red Cross to spend so large a sum, only the President can send for Lord Lothian and say such a policy would further popularize the British cause here.

With much affection to you always,

ERNESTA

Washington, D.C., November 29, 1940

Dear Frank:

Just a word to express deep joy over the way you solved the thorny problem of Defense reorganization. It was, of course, essential to symbolize the equal status of Labor with Management as the partners and co-responsibles for Production. The way you did it — by putting Sidney on the directing board — was best.

As you know, since the election a vacuum was created — and I partly suspect by your wise design — and some poisonous vapors (the Gen. Woods and the Joe Kennedys and the Roy Howards and their retainers) have tried to fill it with their poison. And now *your* decisive actions and controlling and encompassing voice will be filling the minds and purposes of our people to the realization of the objectives which *you* represent, and for which they summoned you for four more, albeit very hard, years.

It was grand to see you look so refreshed on Tuesday.

Ever yours,
F.F.

General Wood was a leader of the America First Movement, and Ambassador Kennedy and publisher Roy Howard were alarmed by what Roosevelt was doing in foreign affairs.
Sidney is Sidney Hillman, the labor leader.

Telegram to Roosevelt
Washington, D.C., December 2, 1940

HERE'S HOPING THAT AT LEAST FOR A FORTNIGHT YOU WILL HAVE COMPLETE SURCEASE FROM HOLDING THE WHOLE WORLD'S HANDS AND ENJOY REAL REFRESHMENT. AFFECTIONATELY.

FELIX FRANKFURTER

Memorandum for General Watson
The White House, December 2, 1940

The President wants to see Justice Frankfurter and Professor Samuel Eliot Morison of Harvard at five o'clock at the House some afternoon soon after he returns from his cruise.

M.A.LEH.

Archibald Coolidge had been a famous librarian at Harvard and an authority on history. Roosevelt was so moved by Gaetano Salvemini's letter that he asked Frankfurter to convey his "grateful thanks" to the new citizen.

Washington, D.C., December 17, 1940

Dear Frank:

I cannot think of a better way to greet you on your return and to send you cheer for your accumulating tasks than to let you see this letter, which has just come to me.

Salvemini, according to the late Archie Coolidge, is as distinguished a European historian as lived when the Fascists came to power. After hairbreadth escapes from Mussolini's designs on his life — because of Salvemini's uncompromising opposition to Fascism — Salvemini came here, and through Ruth Draper's generosity found a scholar's haven at Harvard. He is a truly great soul. The other day he became an American citizen and I sent him a word of pride in having him as a fellow-citizen. And this is his reply.

With affectionate devotion,
F.F.

Cambridge, Mass., December 15, 1940

Dear Felix:

Your telegram moved me deeply. There is in this country a wider area of generosity than in any other country — at least in Europe. It is this feeling that one is at home here that conquers you little by little. And one fine day you feel that you are no longer an exile but a citizen in your own country. When I took my oath I felt that really I was performing a grand function. I was throwing away not my intellectual and moral but my juristic past. I threw it away without any regret. The Ethiopian war, the rape of Albania, the Spanish crime, and this last idiotic crime, had really broken my connection with sovereigns, potentates and all those ugly things which are enumerated in the formula of the oath. It is a wonderful formula. Your pledges are only juridical and political. You are asked to sever your connection with the government of your former country, not with the people and the civilization of your former country. And you are asked to give allegiance to the Constitution of your adopted country, that is, to an ideal of life.

Thus I took my oath with a joyous heart, and I am sure I will keep it with the whole of my heart as long as I am alive. I only was sorry that I am sixty-seven years old. I can give my adopted country only my love! My blood has been already sucked by the other one.

A good Christmas and — well, I do not dare to say — a Happy New Year to you and Marion.

Ever yours,
G.S.

Washington, D.C., December 19, 1940

Dear Mr. President:

The considerations advanced in the enclosed memorandum seem to me very important. While doubtless not new to you, their source may lend desirable confirmation to your own thinking. They come to me from a "free" Frenchman of proved sagacity, extraordinarily well-informed about French currents of opinion, and with reliable recent information regarding the special situation in Northern Africa. He is a man in whose understanding and discretion I have complete confidence.

It is because of my special relations with him that he sent me these notes, of which he has said not a word to another soul.

Faithfully yours,
F.F.

This is Jean Monnet's memorandum on the need of a Presidential message on Hitler's "New Order" in Europe. The President accepted the advice that the United States should make it clear to all the world that it would not accept any arrangements made by Hitler as part of the "New Order," since these arrangements were based on fraud and force.

Jean Monnet Memorandum

December 18, 1940

I.   In his last statement to the Press the President gave practical expression to what has so far been the "help to Britain policy." He declared that the U.S.A. would see that the weapons necessary to England would be supplied to her and that no financial difficulties would be allowed to stand in the way. But what is as important as this decision itself is the reason on which the President bases it: he linked definitely the security of the U.S.A. to the capacity of England to continue the fight and eventually win.

II.   This very important announcement will likely be implemented in a further statement by the President, this time speaking to the American people and to the world.

The occasion of this statement is of very great moment at this time and may greatly influence the course of the war: indeed, the whole world had been awaiting with anxiety the result of the Presidential election. To the democracies outside of the U.S.A., the name of President Roosevelt has become a symbol. His election has consolidated the hope that the sentiments of the people of the U.S.A. are those for which President Roosevelt's name is the symbol. Since the election they have been anxiously waiting to hear from him. So far he has not spoken. When he next speaks one cannot exaggerate the importance of his statements and the repercussion that they will have not only in this country, but in England, in the countries of the Axis, and especially in France.

III.   France is now subjected to the greatest possible pressure by the Germans, who are relentlessly pursuing their settled policy — namely, obtaining from France her willing adherence to the new "European Order"; her giving up of the Northern African bases, and of the remainder of her Fleet. So far the Germans have failed to obtain these results essential to them. Pétain has refused, supported and probably guided by two forces of resistance in France — French public opinion which is more and more opposed to "co-operation" with Germany, and Weygand and other authorities in Northern Africa who have stated they will resist any foreign intrusion into any part of the French African Empire.

These two forces are of course encouraged by the British resistance, but in the last analysis they *look to the U.S.A. for final hope and guidance*.

What is the attitude of the U.S.A. and of President Roosevelt, not only towards helping England but towards *Europe as a whole* and, therefore, towards France, that vital part of Europe? This is the question that French men and women and General Weygand are surely asking themselves.

If the President's next statement was made without providing the reply, a great harm would be done. If he gives that reply, a great hope will be created and the power of France and Northern Africa to resist the German pressure greatly strengthened.

IV.   The answer is partly given by the statement that the security of the U.S.A. is now linked to Great Britain's resistance and survival and that the U.S.A. will provide Great Britain with weapons. But it should be completed by a statement of the U.S.A.'s position towards what Hitler is now trying to force on Europe — "the new totalitarian order"; the "New Order" intended to present to the world a "United Europe," brought about by coercion, fear and terror.

Without French acquiescence no "new" European order can be created. The French people are now resisting this pressure. How long, however, will the French Government still resist? — only so long as French public opinion and Northern Africa possibly compel it to do so. Therefore, if, on the occasion of his statement, the President linked together the security of the U.S.A., the providing of weapons to Great Britain, and the refusal of the U.S.A. to recognise any "New Order" forced on Europe, he would very likely galvanise the forces of resistance which in France and in

Europe are now making it impossible for Hitler to achieve the first part of his goal.

Washington, D.C., December 24, 1940

Dear Frank:

After talking with the author of this memorandum, I thought that the best way to get this very important story to you is to have the facts put on paper for your perusal. I need only add that I have seen the originals of the documents referred to, and the principal in this amazing story is subject to your wishes.

Ever yours,
F.F.

The President sent the memorandum to the State Department, where it was examined in detail, opening new fields of inquiry into events in Vichy France. The author of the following memorandum is identified by a private Frankfurter note in his own files but it need not be revealed now. Roosevelt was pleased to find that Churchill also had his troubles with Vichy France. In fact, Churchill emerges very badly from this memorandum.

Memorandum for Sumner Welles
The White House, December 31, 1940

To speak to me about.

F.D.R.

THE STORY OF A SECRET NEGOTIATION
(*absolutely confidential*)

I.   *The State of Mind at Vichy around July 10*

On my arrival at Vichy about July 10, I was struck by the "wishful thinking" which prevailed there. The military men explained that England would be beaten before the end of the month, and that Reynaud's plan for an uprising in the Empire had therefore no point. The men of the world and the industrialists wanted England to be defeated as quickly as possible, because they regarded it as inevitable and because the end of hostilities would mean the end of the blockade, and the return to normal life and to business. Pétain and Baudouin developed a mystic theory about the armistice: Frenchmen had given way to the spirit of pleasure; the defeat was a just punishment for easy going politics and lax morals; they could only hope for salvation through their own moral regeneration. The people felt that they had been betrayed by their leaders, morally abandoned by England, whose military effort had been too late, and by the great American democracy, which had severely criticised the Munich peace, but had given them no help or support beyond the "cash and carry" clause. There was therefore no other course but to come to an understanding with Germany in order to put an end to continual invasions which made the French people the perpetual defenders of democracies which were always too late to help them. The German peace was painted by the friends of Laval and Bonnet in the most laughable colors: a United States of Europe; a France aggrandized by the annexation of Walloon Belgium and Latin Switzerland; on September 1, with magnificent celebrations, Hitler would proclaim the unity of Europe and the "Pax Germanica" in Paris.

II. Laval's First Maneuver: the "parti unique français"

In order to assure France of an "honorable" place in the reconstruction of Europe under German hegemony, Laval thought that the best plan would be to align France on the side of the Axis in the war against England so that she would be treated as an ally and not as a defeated nation. The affair of Mers-el-Kebir had aroused French opinion because the government had consented to tremendous sacrifices at Wiesbaden in order not to give up the fleet. To succeed in his plans, Laval launched the idea of the "parti unique," which was presented as the French national party.

The leaders of the party were to be Déat, Bergery, Doriot, Tixier-Vignancourt, Montigny, and Chateau under the titular presidency of Pétain and the real presidency of Laval. They held their secret conferences at the Queen's Hotel where I was staying. Their secret plans were, once powerfully endowed and organized, to take power with the aid of the occupying power, on the pretext that the government of the "old man" was definitely not revolutionary enough, and immediately to declare war on England. They were waiting during the course of the week for the decree-law which would establish the "parti unique."

III. My Intervention with Weygand

I decided to intervene with Weygand. I showed him the parallel between the Nazi party and the French party. The former was founded on the stubborn rejection of the "Diktat" of Versailles; the latter would be founded on the unconditional acceptance of the defeat and its consequences. The Nazi party, on the myth of Germany's innocence in the war of 1914; the French party on the myth of the unilateral responsibility of France and England in the war of 1939. The former, on a racist theory which it forgot every time it was to its interest to do so, when organizing the betrayal of the white man in the Far East; the latter, on an authentic racial theory, forgetting that France was an imperial nation including colored inhabitants who had shed their blood for the French flag. . . . The

General asked me brusquely to put all this in writing, in order that he might read it the next day to the Council of Ministers. Two days later Pétain sent for Doriot, Déat, and Bergery and gave them missions in the occupied zone and told Laval that he rejected the "parti unique."

IV.   The British Blockade and My First Journey to Geneva

On July 30, Churchill had announced in the House of Commons the blockade of France and her colonies. Baudouin, whose secretly anglophile feelings were wounded each time England did something impolitic in giving good reasons to the partisans of war against England, felt obliged to deliver a sensational speech in which he announced to the French people that, if they must suffer from famine, it was the fault of the British.

I obtained the authorization to go to Switzerland from Weygand. I asked the British Consul to allow me to send a coded telegram to Robbins, Professor of Political Economy at the London School of Economics, who was working on the blockade. I explained to him that the food blockade had ceased to be an effectual military weapon after so many countries were being exploited by Germany; that it should be used as a psychological and political weapon; that, for the moment, it was necessary to conciliate French opinion toward England by showing liberality and allowing the colonial produce from French West Africa, Morocco and North Africa to come by sea to Marseilles. The psychological benefits gained by lifting the blockade would largely compensate for the breach in the blockade.

I received a reply from Robbins in the form of a telegram: "Suggestions extremely interesting; but in order to discuss them properly, it would be necessary for you to come to London."

V.   My Return to Vichy and My Mission to London

Armed with my telegram, I went back to Vichy. I could say to Baudouin: "The British are not intransigeant, look at their telegram. Let me go to London to negotiate with them." Baudouin, wishing to pass himself off to me as an anglophile, told me that he could see nothing but advantages to the plan. I went to see Weygand again, and he said to me, "Explain to the British that they must not try to arouse North Africa, because we could not defend our possessions against the Spanish divisions full of Germans, which are massed in Spanish Morocco." Finally I saw Pétain who said my idea was excellent, assured me that he did not wish the British ill, and gave me a note accrediting me with "une mission officieuse."

VI. *Negotiations with the British Ministers before the Laval-Hitler and Pétain-Hitler Meetings*

Arriving in London on October 21, I negotiated with Churchill and Lord Halifax on three points:

1. *The Blockade.* In reply to the arguments I had already given Robbins, the British ministers agreed to regard the transfer of colonial produce from French ports to French ports as coastal trade which would not come under the blockade, that is to say the transfer of produce from Dakar, Casablanca, Oran, Algiers and Tunis to Marseilles. I had been assured by Admiral Moreau, Commander in Chief of the Navy and Merchant Marine at Marseilles. The British agreed to authorize Spain to pay for her purchase of Moroccan phosphates in sugar and green tea, the basic food of the inhabitants, and to allow pharmaceutical and para-medical products through.

2. *Radio.* I persuaded the British government not to treat the Vichy government as a bloc. I persuaded them to hold the person of Pétain above criticism, since he had become an emblem to the French people, and to reserve their denunciations for the Germans and for Laval.

3. *Colonies.* I told the British ministers the news of Laval's attempt to involve France in the war. Laval had persuaded Darlan to send the fleet to recapture French Equatorial Africa. This would have provoked a naval battle which would have established a state of war between France and England. I proposed the following "modus vivendi" to the British: "they should keep French Equatorial Africa until the end of hostilities, since it is indispensable for attacking Italian Libya from the south; but, in return, they should abstain in the future from all attempts to arouse the North African colonies." They accepted my proposal.

VII. *Negotiations after the Laval, Pétain–Hitler Meetings*

The British ministers recalled me to the Foreign Office after these meetings. They were extremely upset, believing that the bases would be ceded. Churchill wanted nothing less than to send the British Air Force to bomb the Vichy Government. I reassured them to the best of my ability: "A new agreement with Germany could only improve the armistice if it was to be a success with the Vichy Government. To cede the bases would mean ceding the Empire, that is to say losing the last diplomatic and military card." The ministers told me that there would be no confidence until the day they saw Laval go. Churchill suggested to me in addition that a meeting be arranged in Tangier between a French officer and a British officer to discuss immediate assistance in materials to Weygand if, after the bases were ceded, he would think the time had come to arouse the Empire.

VIII.   *Return via North Africa: Conversation with Weygand*

I returned via North Africa in order to meet Weygand. At the very moment I began my talk with him, an officer brought him a letter from Churchill, which Churchill had written without telling me after I had left. Churchill was inciting Weygand to raise the standard of revolt, assuring him of immediate aid from the Empire and renewing his proposal of a meeting of officers in Tangier. Weygand was annoyed. Such a meeting would not escape the German spies, and Hitler would demand his recall. He only knew one set of instructions: that of defending the Empire against *everybody*. For this he was endeavoring to rebuild a little army in Africa. If the bases were to be ceded, he would not be able to prevent the uprising of the Empire, but he did not believe they would be ceded. His civilian associates, and his son, a captain, who was serving as his secretary, seemed to me to be much more decided: "the French Empire should participate in the British victory at the opportune moment, but that moment has not yet arrived." In particular, that is the opinion of Monick, General Secretary of the Residence in Morocco, and of Chatel, General Secretary of Weygand's mission.

IX.   *Return to Vichy: Understanding with Pétain*

On my return to Vichy, in the second week of November, I found public opinion completely transformed. Nobody believed any longer in the constructive German peace. Everybody hoped that Britain would win. France was becoming anglophile again as fast as she was again becoming germanophobe.

I learned that Pétain had not ceded a single base and that "the principle of collaboration" with Germany was a formal principle empty of content. Unfortunately Hitler had convinced Pétain during the course of the conversation that England would be defeated.

It was at this time that three influences changed Pétain's opinion. On *November* 9 a report from a Frenchman in Dublin who had gone to London came through Lisbon into Baudouin's hands: it drew a picture of the effects of bombardment and of the British morale which my account was to confirm. On *the 10th*, Colonel Fonk, the hero of aviation during the war of 1914-19, made an analysis to Pétain, using purely theoretical and technical reasoning, in which he showed him that it was impossible for Germany to crush British resistance by aerial attack. Finally, having seen Baudouin on the 10th, I had a two hour conversation with Pétain on November 11th.

I convinced him of three things:

1) the decision of the British people to fight to the death and not to make a peace through compromise.

2) the necessity of accepting the "modus vivendi" on the question of the colonies which I had proposed to the British ministers: French Equatorial Africa remaining for the duration of the war under the rule of General de Gaulle, French West Africa, Morocco and North Africa remaining under Weygand's rule.

3) the necessity of "liquidating" Laval.

I learned through Fonk, and later through Admiral Fernet who had been present at my conversation with Pétain, that on the afternoon of Monday, November 11, Pétain had telegraphed to Samuel Hoare that he would *never* abandon the fleet or cede any of the bases; that, in return, he demanded that the British cease their attempts at promoting an uprising in North Africa. In addition, I learned that he had decided to "liquidate" Laval as soon as his "Garde de Protection" was strong enough.

Thus, the danger of war between France and England was definitely eliminated. About November 25th, I found a telegram in Geneva from the Foreign Office which summarized the whole negotiation and confirmed the results.

X. *The Policy America Should Follow*

The naming of an American ambassador to Vichy, and the return of the ambassador from Rome give the State Department a chance to inaugurate a great diplomatic maneuver.

I should like the opportunity to explain orally to the State Department how it will now be best to proceed: 1) as regards Weygand and Nogués; 2) as regards Pétain; 3) as regards the Vatican, the Italian monarchist, military and industrial circles. For all that is too complicated to be put in writing.

Washington, D.C., December 25, 1940

This is Christmas morning and I am moved to say, Dear Frank, "May the Good Lord keep you — and for all the world."

Before announcement was made of your fireside talk next Sunday, I jotted down some notes (with Ben's help) for a possible message to the new Congress. Such as they are, I am volunteering to send them to you.

Ever devotedly and affectionately yours, and Marion joins me,

FELIX FRANKFURTER

The notes, prepared with Ben Cohen's help, are omitted here because, with all their vivid phrasing, they duplicate points made in earlier speeches. What is vastly more important is the use of the phrase "Arsenal of Democracy" to describe America's present role in the war. That phrase was used by Jean Monnet at lunch one day with Frankfurter. Pledging Monnet not to use that phrase again, Frankfurter promised to pass it on to Roosevelt who said he "loved" it. The fireside speech of December 29 is known as the "Arsenal of Democracy" speech.

Washington, D.C., December 31, 1940

Dear Missy,

    This thick package looks like delicious candy for you, but is really smelly cheese for the President. You know how F. gets fixed ideas about things — his F.I., about cheese, is that all cheese for the President should be sent directly to you. I know you won't keep it long. It brings him our love as always.

    We don't like a bit what we hear about your being laid up. Be well soon.

Ever affectionately,
MARION

The Abyss of War

1941

1941

March 11	Congress passes Lend-Lease Act.
April 13	Russia and Japan sign neutrality treaty.
May 27	Russia proclaims national emergency.
June 22	Germany invades Russia.
July 13	Britain and Russia conclude mutual aid treaty. Russia also prepares to receive Lend-Lease assistance.
August 14	The Atlantic Charter is signed by Churchill and Roosevelt. On September 24, the Charter is endorsed by fifteen governments, nine in exile.
October 17	General Tojo becomes Japanese premier and Minister of War.
November 25	Bulgaria joins the Rome-Berlin-Tokyo Axis.
December 7	Pearl Harbor Day. Japan attacks Hawaii, the Philippines, Guam, Midway Island, Hong Kong and Malaya.
December 8	Congress declares a state of war with Japan.
December 11	Germany and Italy declare war on the United States.

Telegram to Roosevelt
Washington, D.C., January 6, 1941

YOU HAVE RAISED THE STANDARD OF THE MORAL ORDER AND THE PEOPLES OF
THE WORLD WILL RESPOND.

FELIX FRANKFURTER

This telegram is in praise of Roosevelt's annual message to Congress on the State of the Nation. The speech is remembered for its definition of the "Four Freedoms" — freedom of speech and expression, freedom of every person to worship God in his own way, freedom from want, and freedom from fear, for all men and women everywhere in the world. But the speech might equally be remembered for the prophetic remark that "when the dictators are ready to make war upon us, they will not wait for an act of war on our part." For this was to be the year of Pearl Harbor.

The White House, January 7, 1941

Dear Felix:

Thanks ever so much for your telegram of January sixth. Your conclusive statement, after listening to the message to the Congress, is indeed heartening, and I hope you are right.

As ever yours,
F.D.R.

Frankfurter Memorandum for the President
January 8, 1941

For a combination of reasons Tom lacks mental health just now. He is, therefore, in great danger of making a wrong turning, with possibilities of vast harm to himself and of undoubted serious damage to the present national effort.

For, were Tom to leave Ben would also go. That is the last thing that Ben wants to do — leave here — but Tom's leaving would operate as a coercion of Ben because of the latter's devotion to Tom.

The answer is absorption of Tom in a defined, adequate task, intimately related to the program for national defense. His energies and resourcefulness would therein have ample outlet and could produce material results of which few people are capable. Ben, on the other hand, is almost

indispensable in a variety of ways, because of his extraordinary resourcefulness and imagination and his rare gifts of character. A dozen or more of the
leading and best talents in the administration give this estimate of Ben's
present usefulness.

The key to the situation is to gain time by finding the square hole for
Tom's square peg. That can be attained if he were to receive a letter, constituting an appropriate blend of affection and direction, from the Commander-in-Chief ordering him to stay here until the right outlet is found
for him. In the meantime, however, Tom must be employed. But it ought
not to be difficult to have him temporarily made a Special Assistant to the
Attorney General. A command, showing affection that would compose his
troubled soul, is the practical, constructive solution.

*To Frankfurter's regret, the gifted Thomas Corcoran and the President
had come to the parting of the ways by the beginning of 1941. As so often
happens in Washington, there was growing jealousy of Corcoran's influence
and power. Corcoran mistakenly blamed Frankfurter for joining in this criticism. He knew nothing of this memorandum, nor of Frankfurter's repeated praise of the unique gifts brought to the service of the President
by the Tommy Corcoran–Ben Cohen team. Unfortunately, Frankfurter's
advice was not heeded by Roosevelt. During the 1940 campaign Roosevelt
had displeased Corcoran by suggesting that he leave Washington and go to
New York to work with Mayor La Guardia on the Citizens' Committee for
Roosevelt. In 1941 Corcoran quit the Administration altogether. Ben
Cohen was persuaded to stay on, but he had lost his interest for the time
being in domestic affairs, partly out of loyalty to Corcoran and resentment
at the treatment suffered by him. Cohen's interest shifted to foreign policy,
where he rendered increasingly distinguished service over the next few
years.*

Washington, D.C., January 20, 1941

Dear Frank:

The sun has set upon Inauguration Day, and the last echoes of pomp
and circumstance have died upon the night's stillness. Your words have
passed into history, to join the utterances of Washington and Lincoln who
alone, of all our Presidents, represent the destinies and fate of our country
comparable to those which you symbolize.

And in the quietness of my study I see your grave and kindly countenance, as you stood there shortly after noon, the response to our needs and
the hope of their fulfillment. There must be literally millions upon millions
who share my thoughts and prayers — those unuttered thoughts and
prayers in the deepest recesses of the heart, that strength may be vouch-

safed you, strength of body and mind and spirit, to carry the awful burden
the people have put upon you, strength, also, to endow the people with the
strength they need for the great enterprise.

Affectionately and devotedly yours,
FELIX FRANKFURTER

*Judge Rosenman has told us that Roosevelt's Third Inaugural was based
largely on the President's own words and a draft from Mr. Archibald Mac-
Leish. "The next morning," Rosenman wrote, "I asked Justice Frankfurter
to come over for breakfast and we discussed the speech at length before
taking it into the President's bedroom."*

Washington, D.C., January 30, 1941

Dear Frank:

This day you are to Marion and me stripped of all your public character — you cease to be a quasi-institution. We greet you as a beloved friend
and send you the whole-hearted affection of a happy friendship. Just as a
human being you have done so much for so many. That's a gift of yours
which, by the strange alchemy of the human spirit, must continue to feed
the springs of energy and life within you. We wish this deeply for your own
dear family — we wish it for all the countless men and women and children
for whom you are a life-bringer — by giving hope and strength and broad-
ening opportunities to their being.

Affectionately yours,
F.F.

The White House, February 4, 1941

Dear Felix:

I want you and Marion to know how deeply touched I was by your
extremely nice note sent on my birthday. Your good wishes are always appreciated and this takes to you both my affectionate regards.

As ever,
F.D.R.

Washington, D.C., January 28, 1941

Dear Missy:

Madame Monnet has a daughter about nine years old who fell violently in love with the President on Inauguration Day. As is true of other
ladies under similar circumstances, she poured out her heart, and, as is
equally true, was hesitant to communicate her outpour. Her mother told

me the story and I craved the privilege to be the conduit of the child's wise and generous feelings. So here's the result.

Ever yours,
F.F.

January 27, 1941

Dear Mr. President,

I was at the Inaugural parade, and heard everything over the radio in the morning, it was very nice, I liked it so much, didn't you?

In this letter are ten dimes, for infantile paralysis, it is very little, but it is all I have, and I hope they will help.

Happy birthday Mr. President, and lots of luck

your friend, respectfully
ANNA MONNET

The President wrote to Anna as follows, on February 7

Dear Anna,

I want to thank you for that nice little note you sent me through the courtesy of Justice Frankfurter. Your thought of my birthday is deeply appreciated and I am grateful too for your generous contribution to the Infantile Paralysis Fund.

My best wishes to you.
Very sincerely yours,
FRANKLIN D. ROOSEVELT

Washington, D.C., February 4, 1941

Dear Missy:

1. A little while ago the President asked me to give him a memorandum on the more recent judicial work of Judge J. J. Parker. Here it is. A page and a third summarize the general impressions that his opinions have made on me.

2. The other day over the phone I told the President that there were two or three matters of real importance on which I am very anxious to have talk with him as soon as he has a stretch of free time, preferably on some unhurried evening. I appreciate, of course, what days these are for him, but I want to see him in the hope of relieving and not adding to his burdens. Therefore I am keeping free every evening this week (except Saturday) in the hope that he may be able to find time to see me. The Court is now sitting, and that makes the daytime pretty impossible for me.

Ever yours,
F.F.

P.S.   By Missy to the Appointments Secretary:
     I called the Justice's Secretary and explained that the President was jammed this week but we would let him know about an evening next week. Will you arrange?

Frankfurter's ten-page analysis of the judicial opinions of Chief Judge Parker are omitted here since that analysis merely sustains his conclusion that "the opinions cannot fail to give an impression of a high degree of competence." He added that they "regularly contain a clear statement and painstaking discussion of the issues, and a careful survey of the authorities. They are more noteworthy for these qualities than for freshness or resourcefulness or creativeness. There is a recurrent search for the case directly in point — not an objectionable undertaking on the part of a judge of an inferior court."

The episode is important for two reasons:

President Hoover had named Chief Judge Parker to the Supreme Court but the Senate had denied confirmation. Roosevelt was considering Judge Parker for a possible appointment to the Supreme Court, a magnanimous act in the circumstances. In the moments of decision, however, the appointment went elsewhere.

To prepare his report for the President, Frankfurter read all Judge Parker's opinions in the law reports, volumes 89 through 114, together with a less systematic search in earlier volumes. He found time for this research, despite his duties on the Supreme Court, because the President had asked him to do it.

Washington, D.C., February 12, 1941
Dear Frank:
     Besides letting you see these appreciations of two recent sojourners in London, you will want to know the following:
     Yesterday, in the midst of a most technical and difficult argument of a complicated case, my baby Brother turned to me on the Bench, and said: "I wonder if the President knows how bad things are in the Philippines. I hear from my friends out there constantly. No one in the United States knows that problem as well as I do, and I know how to handle it." F.F. "Would you be willing to go out there?" F.M. "Not permanently. But, while I love the work of the Court, I do want to serve my country, and I'd be glad to go out there for a few months, and then on the way back to Mexico, which also needs attention."
     Here endeth *that* day's lesson!

That was a really grand talk with you, the other morning, and I've been thinking about it much.

Ever devotedly yours,
F.F.

The "baby brother" is Justice Frank Murphy, whose judicial attainments Frankfurter could describe in something less than the language of eulogy.

The enclosures satirized the work of Mr. Joseph P. Kennedy as Ambassador in London.

Washington, D.C., February 26, 1941

Dear Frank:

This morning's papers report three items which rejoice my heart because all three serve still further to "implement" (how I loathe that word!) your spirit with actions, to wit:

1. Your admirable letter on wire-tapping — limiting its uses to the strictest possible area, and then only under utmost safeguards.

2. Your declaration of the "war aims" to be winning the war!

3. Your uncompromising insistence on the powers of the Lease-Loan Bill adequate to the needs of the emergency.

Grand — all three performances for their own sakes, and the drive and energy, that they reveal you brought back from Hyde Park.

Devotedly yours,
F.F.

This is the first reference to the Lend-Lease bill on which Roosevelt and Frankfurter worked as closely together as they ever did on any large matter of public policy. The practical effect of Lend-Lease was to help England, quickly and generously, without regard to her immediate ability to pay.

Both men justified Lend-Lease by the most urgent considerations of self-interest. But they were stalwart advocates too of the importance of saving Britain from Nazi domination, a domination which would be "a crime against civilization," in Frankfurter's impassioned words.

It was Frankfurter who had first suggested that the House resolution on Lend-Lease should be entitled H.R. 1776. Once America had gained her independence by fighting England, now she could protect her independence by helping England. For we had "to seek independence through interdependence," a Frankfurter phrase which the President relished and repeated to visitors.

Congress passed the Lend-Lease bill on March 11, 1941, some two months after the President asked for this legislation. The President signed the bill thirty minutes after Congress passed it. Five minutes later, he approved a list of goods for immediate shipment. He also recommended an appropriation for new material to the extent of seven billion dollars. The United States had moved from neutrality and embargoes first to cash-and-carry and now to Lend-Lease.

Frankfurter Memorandum to Roosevelt February 27, 1941

I

It is today clear that the number of weapons available for Great Britain in 1941, while sufficient to enable her to resist, will not enable her to conquer.

The number of weapons which Great Britain will have to carry on the war during 1941 is known and though their production can be accelerated, it cannot be greatly increased because it is the result of the capacity of production laid down in England and the United States during 1939 and 1940. The major part of the planes that the United States will produce during the first half of 1941 is the result of the productive capacity laid down in the spring of 1940.

For England to conquer Germany in 1942 it is essential that she maintain her control of the seas, that she maintain her mercantile fleet strength, that she establish her domination in the air, and that she obtain a striking force of air, sea and land at home, and striking power through the air abroad. Dominance of the air is England's only protection against the ultimate destruction of her essential industries by enemy bombing over a prolonged period of time.

Since British production is already geared to its maximum, she must obtain from the United States the balance of the supplies that will enable her to top the German strength in 1942. To achieve this, an immense effort is necessary here. To result in effective supplies in 1942, this effort must be decided, planned and made now, and made on a scale that will permit supremacy and victory in 1942. Indeed, neither human will nor genius can change during 1942 the process of production based on decisions taken now.

Such an effort will mean serious modifications of our conventional business habits and assumptions. It means appropriate transfer of labor, intensive working on a three shift system, utilization of machine tool capacity wherever it can be found, and diversion of material supplies from civil use. But such a program of action, duly pursued, will prevent the long period of agony which would be involved in a prolonged diversion of civil life to military production without such a supreme effort decided upon and undertaken *now*.

II

The present scale of the present plans of production in the United States do not meet these vital requirements. This is emphasized particularly by the airplane situation.

(1) Air power today is measured and obtained by productive capacity, not merely by the number of planes at a given moment. Productive capacity means ability to turn out new models quickly, and a relatively smaller number of new high performance, heavy striking power planes can ground for a time a force superior in numbers but inferior in essential qualities. Research and experimentation are the backbone of any air program, for we need not only greater capacity but greater capacity for building better planes.

(2) By whatever yardstick we measure our effort against Germany's we are vastly inferior now and are likely to remain so through 1942. Our present actual production, for both U.S. and British needs, is less than a third of Germany's exclusive of recently occupied countries. Even our future maximum production now planned for the middle of 1942 (about 2800 monthly) is less than Greater Germany's *present* full capacity (about 3000/3500). By the middle of 1942 Germany may well add the capacity of the conquered countries to her own.

Measured by number of personnel or numbers of first line combat ships the comparison is even more unfavorable to us.

(3) In addition to the advantages of greater plant capacity, German operational conditions enable them to achieve greater results with a much smaller force than can be obtained by a British air offensive over Germany having regard to the differences in distances. Germany bombs England from northern France and Belgium.

(4) To equalize the great disparity between German and British aircraft stocks, to be caught up and to start towards building up a supremacy in numbers that will counteract the geographical operational obstacles, there is no doubt that the United States must be able to produce by June, 1942, between 4000 and 5000 tactical planes per month, of which a much larger number than now should be four-engined heavy bombers; the importance of the heavy bomber for an effective air offensive over Germany cannot be over-emphasized.

(5) Since the bringing of new capacity into full production takes eighteen months, it is essential that these new plans should be decided upon and put in hand forthwith. Only in this way can it be established that we are planning on a scale adequate for victory.

III

While no genius or super-human effort can change in 1942 the course of production that is now effectively planned, it takes neither genius nor super-human will to take the effective steps now to secure the fighting fruits necessary in 1942.

All that is needed is that now, in the days immediately ahead, the program above summarized be authoritatively decided upon in concrete terms as the objective to be accomplished by full exercise of all governmental powers.

The accomplishment of the above objective is, of course, dependent on the grant of powers asked from Congress in the Loan-Lease Bill but the whole defense administration must today proceed on the assumption that the powers will be granted. In other words, all steps of planning and organization must at once be begun and pursued so that the very day the bill is signed the powers granted by the bill will be capable of being translated into action.

Specific measures for translating the central policy here indicated into action will readily suggest themselves. But to give concreteness, the following items emerge as pressing needs:

a) Double the existing air program of the Army — from about 50 groups to about 100 groups. Even then the Air Corps, apparently, would still have only about half the first line combat plane strength now reported as attained by Germany.

b) Increase plant production capacity to around 4000 to 5000 monthly.

c) Take the necessary steps to bring this about. Without proper organization the job will hardly get done.

To postpone decisions on the indispensable 1942 program and to postpone preparation for the necessary steps to carry this program into effect is to throw away the one irreplaceable element — time. Such postponement would contradict the whole aim of the program, namely, that it is to be accomplished in 1942.

Unlike Roosevelt, Frankfurter each year allowed himself to hope that the war would end in twelve or eighteen months. He indulged these hopes not out of a low estimate of Germany's striking power but for precisely the opposite reason. He was fearful that Germany would wreck Western Europe in a prolonged war and exhaust England's strength. For that reason he wanted a maximum production effort to shorten the war. Roosevelt was in full agreement with the objective but was far more aware of the practical hazards and difficulties which first had to be overcome. They were pulling at the same harness but with different intensity.

Washington, D.C., March 4, 1941

Dear Frank:

Not even a Norris Amendment can make 8 less than 4 + 4. And so today will live in history as the eighth birthday of your Presidency, and, through that, of the birth of the renewed Republic. For there is not any doubt that history will see even more clearly than contemporary historians already recognize that because you came to the headship of the nation, March 4, 1933 brought new courage and new hope to our people. And you achieved such an ultimate accomplishment of statesmanship not by any magic or miracle, but by proving anew what Pericles told the people of Athens 2500 years ago — that the secret of happiness is freedom, and the secret of freedom is a stout heart. To apply the principles of freedom to the complexities of modern society is the awful task of your leadership, and it is because you are pursuing it, as you have been pursuing it for eight years, that there is hope and courage not only among the people of our own country, but the world over — in China and Canada, in Palestine and Peru, and not least among the millions temporarily writhing under the tyrant's heels.

I greet you with affection and gratitude, and may the Mercies of the world give you continued strength.

Ever yours,
FELIX FRANKFURTER

Senator Norris had begun the campaign to limit the Presidency in the future for any one man to no more than two consecutive terms, even though he was an ardent and unrepentant supporter of President Roosevelt.

The White House, March 10, 1941

Dear Felix: —

That was certainly a grand letter you sent to me on March fourth. I was deeply touched by it and, as always, I am grateful for your friendship and counsel.

My best to you,

As ever yours,
F.D.R.

This letter from Mr. Hamilton Fish Armstrong, which Frankfurter sent on to Roosevelt, was a salutory warning from the editor of Foreign Affairs *magazine that the United States should not forget the importance of the*

Danubian states even while concentrating on events in Western Europe. His advice was followed but only in part and this half-policy produced later troubles in Yugoslavia.

Count Sforza consulted Frankfurter on occasion about the possibilities that would be open to a democratic Italy once Mussolini had disappeared from the scene. The Italian diplomat appealed to Frankfurter as an exponent of the virtues of a cultured and dexterous diplomacy which he associated with such traditional European figures as Jules Cambon of France and Stresemann of Germany.

Washington, D.C., March 6, 1941

Dear Missy:

The President will want to see this letter because Ham Armstrong speaks on matters affecting Jugoslavia with a knowledge that is seasoned and mature, and not acquired over night.

Ever yours,
F.F.

New York, N.Y., March 4, 1941

Private
Dear F.F.:

I knew you would take to Sforza. I'll see what I can do in connection with the matter he mentioned in his telegram to you.

But this letter is about Jugoslavia, the European country which I probably know best, having been Military Attaché there just after the last war, and having kept up my personal friendships there by almost annual visits in the intervening twenty years. Fotitch, the Jugoslav Minister, has just been up in New York to see me about the crisis developing there. He is one of the very best of the foreign diplomats now in Washington.

Hitler is bringing all possible pressure to bear on Paul to take Jugoslavia into the "new order" by signing up with the Axis. I know Paul pretty well. Though he is nothing like so strong as Alexander was, he is honest, pro-English, and anxious to turn over his trusteeship to the little King without any diminution of the Karageorgevitch patrimony. He is resisting Hitler as best he can, supported by the very general anti-German and anti-Italian sentiment of the Jugoslav people.

The best Paul can hope for is to avoid actually signing up with the Axis — e.g. to persuade Hitler to leave Jugoslavia in the position of Sweden rather than in the position accepted by Hungary, Rumania and now Bulgaria. Paul has just gone to his country place up in Slovenia, where I have often visited him, either to receive Ribbentrop there or en route himself to Berchtesgaden. Thus a showdown is coming.

Fotitch is convinced that Paul is sincere in telling us and the British he will do everything possible to avoid joining the Axis, but he realizes, as I do, that the Nazi menace may become too great and that Paul may be forced to give in. If that happens, it is Fotitch's intention to resign as Minister in Washington. He will hope to join with other Jugoslavs in this country, and with various Jugoslav-Americans, in keeping alive the ideal of Jugoslav independence and working for the restoration of the country after the war is over. He has no intention of attacking Paul or the present Jugoslav Government. He feels, however, that if Jugoslavia joins the Axis, the country will soon be disintegrated by Nazi and Fascist agents, and that puppet governments will be set up in Belgrade and Zagreb under bandits chosen by Hitler and Mussolini respectively.

I am writing to urge that if the worst happens, if Jugoslavia does join the Axis, and if Fotitch does resign, our Government shall express a disinclination to accept a new Minister in Fotitch's place. Fotitch's present assistant could continue to act as Chargé. A request by the present Rumanian Government that we accept a new Rumanian Minister is now pending. I hope it is not going to be accepted. In any event, I urge very strongly that if Jugoslavia joins the Axis under the menace of invasion, we indicate our disapproval of that act, and our hope for the reassertion of full Jugoslav independence at a later date, by leaving the Jugoslav Legation in Washington in the hands of the Chargé.

I also believe that in this event we would be wise to freeze the Jugoslav balances here. We might well have taken such a course with the Hungarian balances when Hungary joined the Axis. If Jugoslavia joins the Axis, I think it would be a kindness to her to freeze her assets here immediately.

I am writing you thus at length because I am extremely anxious that the implications of the decision in foreign policy which is about to be made should be brought to the President's attention at once. As I hope you know, I don't set myself up as an authority on many matters. But I do believe that no other American has been a more continuous student of Balkan affairs than I have in the last twenty years. Can't you find an opportunity to make my views on this matter known to the President before the Jugoslav crisis actually arrives?

I am pretty well tired out, and also have been having sinus trouble again, so when Mrs. Dwight Morrow asked me to go with her and one or two other friends to Mexico the end of this week, I jumped at the chance. I am starting Saturday night and will be gone about two weeks. If you have any advice after I am gone won't you telephone Fotitch and ask him to come and see you?

Yours ever sincerely,
HAMILTON FISH ARMSTRONG

(*Note in margin:* "*Wilson's policy toward the Danubian and Balkan peoples was an important weapon in winning the last war. Roosevelt's can be in this one.*")

Telegram to Roosevelt

Washington, D.C., March 8, 1941

THANK GOD THAT'S OVER.

FELIX FRANKFURTER

On March 8, Roosevelt made a somber speech on the European war, uttering the stern warning that "we cannot be an island." The same day, as a mark of his own respect and in tribute to his friendship with Frankfurter, the President issued a statement to commemorate the one hundredth anniversary of the late Mr. Justice Holmes's birth. Frankfurter drafted the original tribute. Roosevelt said Holmes "believed passionately in the moral worth of the individual regardless of race or religion or the accidents of antecedents. He therefore believed in the unfettered spirit without which man cannot live a civilized life." Frankfurter was momentarily depressed because the Holmes tribute had fallen on a day when the civilized values cherished by Holmes were under such desperate siege.

Washington, D.C., March 14, 1941

Dear Missy:

(1) This correspondence may shed some light on Joe's statement about Laski.

(2) The enclosed on the Italian vote may interest the President. It is from *Il Mondo*, an Italian monthly published by American Italians in whom I have much confidence.

(3) It was a grand party and I only hope you didn't curse me for staying too late.

Ever yours,
F.F.

London, England, August 20, 1940

Dear Harold,

I have just received two copies of Jack's book by air mail from the States. I thought you would be interested in reading it. I gave one to the Prime Minister and as this is the only one I have, I should appreciate your sending it back to me as soon as you have finished it. When a further supply arrives, I shall see that you have one. The reviews have been swell. I am tickled to death for Jack. If you feel like writing him a line, I know he would be delighted to hear from you.

With all best wishes,

Sincerely,
JOE KENNEDY

Addison Bridge Place, England

Dear Joe:

The easy thing for me to do would be to repeat the eulogies that Krock and Harry Luce have showered on your boy's work.

In fact, I choose the more difficult way of regretting deeply that you let him publish it. For while it is the book of a lad with brains, it is very immature, it has no real structure, and it dwells almost wholly on the surface of things. In a good university, half a hundred seniors do books like this as part of their normal work in their final year. But they don't publish them for the good reason that their importance lies solely in what they get out of doing them and not in what they have to say. I don't honestly think any publisher would have looked at that book of Jack's if he had not been your son, and if you had not been Ambassador. And those are not the right grounds for publication.

I care a lot about your boys. I don't want them to be spoilt as rich men's sons are so easily spoilt. Thinking is a hard business, and you have to pay the price for admission to it. Do believe that these hard sayings from me represent much more real friendship than the easy price of 'yes men' like Arthur Krock.

Yours very sincerely,
HAROLD J. LASKI

The article from Il Mondo *had analyzed the way Italian Americans had voted in the 1940 election. Districts with a large Italian population had given Roosevelt huge majorities. This was a fact of some consequence to Roosevelt in view of Mussolini's partnership with Hitler.*

More important for our present purposes is the correspondence between Ambassador Joseph P. Kennedy and Professor Harold J. Laski. It took place nearly a year before Frankfurter's covering note. The "statement" by Ambassador Kennedy was that Laski was "an unfaithful friend."

Laski's letter was written in reply to a letter asking him to endorse the book written by the youthful John F. Kennedy analyzing the forces which had brought England to follow a policy of appeasement. Even as a young man John Kennedy had never been able to reconcile the doctrines of appeasement with his conscience or his judgment. But he wanted to examine the interplay between government and public opinion, and explain how national policy could be warped and fettered by popular misconceptions. Those were the themes of his book which had a deserved success in the United States.

It is a measure of Ambassador Kennedy's immense regard for Laski that, having only two advance copies, he sent one copy of the book to him and the only other available copy to Churchill.

Laski was a man of almost incredible generosity and sensitivity. For once these qualities deserted him. He failed to realize what such a letter of cruel criticism would mean to any father, whether Ambassador or not, whose son had written his first book. Besides, his letter had nothing but candor to commend it. His independence of judgment exceeded his discernment. For the book gave the American people their first rewarding glimpse of the qualities later to blossom and develop in their future President.

Washington, D.C., March 15, 1941

Dear Mr. President:

It is a pity you do not know Arthur D. Hill of the Boston bar. Thanks to T.R., who sent me to him (Hill was one of his most devoted Bull Mooses) when I joined the Harvard Law School faculty, he became the closest and most delicious of my friends in Boston. The following, from a letter of his that has just come, will give you a sample of his quality:

> The old Yankees are working themselves up to a considerable state of zeal. The amount of knitting is large, substantial funds are being raised and sent, and there is a reasonable amount of talk. I think they are even getting a kick out of being loyal to F.D.R., it is so very disagreeable to them. On the other hand, your Irish Democratic friends are many of them in a state that with a less gifted and superior race one would describe as the sulks. I enclose herewith a clipping giving an account of a meeting of the Ancient Order of Hibernians. . . . I have written Mr. Murphy for a full copy of his speech and if I get it I will send it to you. I am all against Judges being allowed to live on Olympian heights without knowledge of what is going on in their constituencies.
>
> By the way, I hope you are as pleased as I am with Woodbury's selection as the new Circuit Judge in your circuit. He is a first-rate fellow, and incidentally a friend of Sherman's as well as mine. He and Sherman are on the Board of an Episcopalian Church School which Sherman usually describes as his meeting of bishops and sons of bishops.
>
> Apropos of New Hampshire I wish I had time to write you a full description of the center of war feeling, Portsmouth, New Hampshire. That city has not been as prosperous since the war of 1812 and its inhabitants are confidently looking forward to getting a large proportion of the new $7,000,000 asked for this morning. But I have got to get to work on several

tangled matters, none of importance — but all taking time. However, as
the white king said — important — unimportant.

Faithfully yours,
F.F.

*Arthur D. Hill (1869-1947) become counsel for Sacco-Vanzetti in the
last stages of that long controversy. A leader of the Boston bar, he accepted
this assignment on Frankfurter's plea and took the case without a fee. He
did so because he could not refrain from exhausting all legal remedies on
behalf of Sacco and Vanzetti "simply because they are poor devils against
whom the feeling of the community is strong and they have no money with
which to hire me."*

The enclosure from the Boston Herald *contained a report of a speech by
Mr. Murphy who expressed his "shame" at the thought of any Irishman in
America wanting to aid Britain in this war.*

Washington, D.C., March 16, 1941

Dear Frank:

I did not need the wireless to tell me that all England and Scotland
and Wales would be listening in — even though your voice would not
come to them till the early morn and in the caves, that are now the homes
of so many of their people. Still less did anyone who knew them at all need
to be told that your voice and words were to them as fresh water to parched
throats, as food to the hungry. For them, as for all of us, the power of your
speech derived from our own inner needs and from the fact that you voiced
the depth of humanity's aspirations, and the assurance that your prophecy
of victory was the expression of our determination to attain it.

But that you voiced our national purpose is true because you educated
our people to make *your* purpose theirs, and by your almost uncanny wisdom imparted your insight to our conglomorate population so as to unify
them to the point of making the present effort possible. It was a noble
speech — but more than that, an enduring act of leadership for a free
world.

Yours ever,
F.F.

Washington, D.C., March 18, 1941

Dear Frank:

1. My Brother continues to show uninterrupted preoccupation with
affairs outside the narrow confines of the law. He asked me how things, I
thought, were going, and I replied, on a chit, that from all I heard I was
cheered by the way supplies were moving to Britain. He replied, "Yes, but

now it's necessary to work on every front — Central America, the Orient, and the salient labor situation at home." I've never known such restlessness — and I have ample opportunity for hearing and seeing and reading his notes to me.

2. Yes — the dedication of the National Gallery was a most relevant way of proving what this world struggle is about, and your address conveyed the significance of the struggle for preserving and advancing the things of the spirit that alone raise man above the level of animals, however well-fed or secure or useful and even kind.

3. I'm so glad you're going off to the refreshment of the sea — to sleep and to invite your soul. Have a good trip!

Ever yours,
F.F.

Once again Justice Frank Murphy was irritating Frankfurter by his restless conduct on the Supreme Court.

Washington, D.C., April 3, 1941

Dear Frank:

You may want to see this letter from Ham Armstrong.

Welcome home! — glad as I was that you went away. Your Jackson Day speech had, I hope, an important by-product in making all sorts of people realize the importance for everyone to go, at least figuratively, down to the sea in order to go down into one's soul, and not be atomized by the daily grind of details. That speech had a fine simplicity and directness — the simplicity and eloquent directness of ultimate issues. And that quotation from Lincoln goes to the very heart of civilized society.

With fondest regards,

Always devotedly,
F.F.

New York, N.Y., March 28, 1941

Dear F.F.:

The Jugoslavs have come through handsomely, as well as we dared hope. I have been in constant touch with Fotitch, to whom a generous amount of the credit for what has happened must go. He has had splendid cooperation from the State Department, in particular from Sumner Welles. Indeed, I think the influence both of the Department and of the Jugoslav Legation has been about as intelligently directed vis-à-vis Belgrade as possible.

I have one specific suggestion, namely that when the President gets back to Washington, he should send for Fotitch for a personal talk. In the

first place, it would be a natural way for the President to show his appreciation of Fotitch's intelligence and character. Secondly, it would not only
reward Fotitch, who is definitely on our side, but would also further
strengthen his influence at home, which is highly desirable. Thirdly, it
would give the President a chance of sending a friendly word of encouragement and advice to the young King and his new ministers. This would have
the advantage of keeping up the President's own influence in Belgrade and
throughout the Balkans, which can be of continuing value both in this
crisis and in the future. I have already spoken to you about the similarity
between the role that the President is playing and Wilson's role in Eastern
Europe and the Balkans in helping win the last war. I can't over-emphasize
the importance of this consideration.

Yours ever sincerely,
Hamilton Fish Armstrong

P.S.   If we could give Jugoslavia concrete help now under the lend-lease
bill even in token amounts, the effect not in Jugoslavia alone, but in Turkey
also, would be electric. Can't it be done at once, while the iron is hot?
Jugoslav ships to carry planes, anti-tank guns, etc., are already in U. S. ports.

*Roosevelt had gone sailing off Florida for a brief holiday. He insisted that
the Jackson Day speech on March 29 should celebrate national unity instead of being the usual robust call to partisan loyalties. As part of that
purpose, he praised Willkie for rallying Republican support to ensure the
passage of the Lend-Lease bill without tedious and dangerous delay. He
said Willkie was showing in word and in action "what patriotic Americans
mean by rising above partisanship and rallying to the common cause." He
pointed out that dictators destroy all party differences and give despotic
power to their own ruling group. In America the differences between the
parties were important, but they vanished when the country faced a foreign
danger. He warned the industrialists who wanted to do business with Hitler
that Nazi Germany had no room for freedom in business. Equally emphatic was his warning to the few Communist-controlled unions that Russia had no room for the freedom of labor. He ended with the reminder that
Lincoln, in his first message to Congress, had asked this question:*

*"Must a government, of necessity, be too strong for the liberties of its
own people, or too weak to maintain its own existence?"*

*Roosevelt went on to say that Lincoln answered that question as Jackson
had answered it — not by words, but by deeds. "And America still marches
on. We of today have been presented with that same question. We too are
answering it by deeds. Our well-considered philosophy for the attainment
of peace comes not from weakness but — everlastingly — from the courage
of America."*

Washington, D.C., April 8, 1941

Dear Frank:

Loring Christie was one of my oldest and closest friends. His personal life was very tragic. Now that he is gone, I would like you to know that your warm friendliness toward him and the comfort your generous messages to him during his earlier illness brought him, were, as he told me not once but many times, among the few, deep personal satisfactions of his life. Dr. Alfred Cohn, who had charge of him at the Rockefeller, told me that in all his long medical career he had never had a more gallant patient than Loring. It's a sad day for me.

Gratefully, ever yours,
F.F.

Frankfurter's friendship with Loring Christie, Canadian Minister to the United States, went back to the early days of the First World War. Among other common intellectual interests, they shared a profound concern with the history and problems of federalism as a system of government. Frankfurter kept among his papers a long appreciation of Loring Christie written by John W. Dafoe, the famous editor of the Winnipeg Free Press. Why Frankfurter should have been reading a newspaper from western Canada is a mystery known only to himself. Christie, during his years of service with the Canadian government, became one of the recognized architects of the British Commonwealth.

Washington, D.C., April 15, 1941

Dear Missy

This, from the chief of CBS in Europe, may interest the President.

Ever yours,
F.F.

Radiogram to Frankfurter

London, England, April 14, 1941

MANY THANKS FOR SENDING ME THE BATTLE OF 1776. YOUR FRIENDS WINANT AND COHEN ARE DOING EVEN BETTER THAN YOU SUSPECT. REGARDS.

ED MURROW

The final text of the Lend-Lease bill, H.R. 1776, had been sent to Ed Murrow in London by Frankfurter. Mr. John G. Winant, former Governor of New Hampshire and former Chairman of the Social Security Board, was the new Ambassador to Great Britain. A leading member of the Embassy staff was Mr. Benjamin V. Cohen. On Winant's death in 1947, Frankfurter said that the British people had found in Winant "strength and succor at

*a time when they were called upon to summon all their spiritual resources
against overwhelming material power."*

Washington, D.C., April 25, 1941

Dear Frank:

Quite spontaneously there bubbled up in me a phrase that, coming
from you, might hit the right spot — your saying "The American people
expect me to deliver the goods" has a colloquialism that might stick.

Need I tell you how constantly and deeply I think of you these days!
As you sit in your oval room and look out toward the Washington monu-
ment, your thoughts, I am sure, most often turn toward Lincoln and his
fateful days. That you draw strength from his stout and serene heart, I have
no doubt. But you must also, I'm sure, draw refreshment and strength, as did
he, from his and your common people — the unknown and silent men and
women, who understand the compelling issue now facing us, as they did
the issue of 1861. And the issue *is* fundamentally the same — touching as it
does, the ultimate significance of human life. For man is without dignity
unless he has freedom — freedom of body and mind and soul.

Affectionately and faithfully yours,
F.F.

*Roosevelt made a note in his speech file to use the suggested colloquial-
ism.*

Washington, D.C., May 5, 1941

Dear Frank:

Your Wilson speech was a gem of a Greek Chorus — or, shall I say, an
admirable curtain-raiser. It was more like the finest example of the Greek
chorus, in that it told in pointed but general terms the plot of the play to
follow. For, from what you said at Staunton, I infer that you will speak soon
and tell the plot so that not even the saber-rattler in fustian (whether German or Italian or Japanese) will possibly misunderstand. "And the nations
of the world shall call him blessed."

It was heart-filling to have talked with you the other morning.

Ever devotedly yours,
F.F.

*On May 4, Roosevelt went to Staunton, Virginia, to dedicate Woodrow
Wilson's birthplace as a National Shrine. "He taught — and let's never
forget it — he taught that democracy could not survive in isolation. We
applaud his judgment and we applaud his faith." Roosevelt, who once described Wilson as "my President," converted the occasion from an exercise*

*in national piety to a confession of his own hopes for America in a turbu-
lent world.*

*Once again the army could not get things straight in dealing with Frank-
furter's presumed military status. The letter was addressed wrongly and
quite plainly the army had lost its way. By this time Frankfurter had been
on the Supreme Court for more than two years and was approaching his
fifty-ninth birthday. He sent the army document to General "Pa" Watson
in the White House. An amused President wrote at the bottom of the
note: "Is this zero Fahrenheit or Centigrade or the absolute zero? If the
latter, there is no hope. If one of the first two, I will take his temperature
myself. F.D.R."*

Washington, D.C., May 16, 1941

My Dear General:

When you get around to it, please show our Commander-in-Chief the
perfect military record in reverse which the enclosed document establishes.

Where do I go from here?

Faithfully yours,
FELIX FRANKFURTER

Major General Edwin M. Watson

HEADQUARTERS SECOND MILITARY AREA, U. S. ARMY
1304 U. S. POSTOFFICE AND COURT HOUSE
Boston, Mass., May 9, 1941

Subject: Credit Hours for Reappointment.
To: Major Felix Frankfurter, JA-Res.
37 River Street,
Boston, Mass.

1. Records of this headquarters indicate that your present appointment expires on *January 7, 1942* and that you have not at time of dispatch
of this letter, secured a certificate of capacity for your present or the next
higher grade, possession of which would qualify you for reappointment
with full privileges.

2. Existing regulations provide that in such cases where officers fail to
secure a certificate of capacity as indicated above, they may qualify for reappointment with full privileges by earning during their current appointment
a minimum of 200 hours of credit, at least 100 of which must be earned by
inactive-status training.

3. The records show that you have earned to date in your current appointment a total of 0 hours of credit; 0 hours of such credits were earned

by reason of active status; o hours of such credits were earned by reason of inactive-status training.

4. It will be seen from the preceding paragraph that you lack 200 hours of credit, including 100 hours for inactive-status training, to qualify for reappointment with full privileges. You may earn the required inactive-status hours of credit by means of pursuit of Extension School courses, attendance at classes, administrative duties in connection with the unit to which you are now assigned, or inactive-status training with troops.

5. *It is desired that you inform this headquarters without delay as to whether or not you propose to qualify yourself for reappointment with full privileges.* In this connection, you are advised that failure thus to qualify will mean that it will be necessary, at the proper time, for this headquarters to recommend to the War Department that you be reappointed without eligibility for active duty, promotion or assignment.

By order of the Executive:
CHARLES E. COATES,
Colonel, Infantry,
Adjutant

Washington, D.C., May 21, 1941

Dear Missy:

The President sees so many cry-babies, he may be relieved for a passing minute to look at our three little English children.

Yours ever,
F.F.

Please return photos.

This picture shows Frankfurter with Ann, Venitia, and Oliver Gates — the three children of Mr. and Mrs. Sylvester Gates of London — to whom the Frankfurters were American parents during the London blitz. Childless themselves, the Frankfurters took great joy in the children, who swiftly became favorites with everyone. The President often asked about them and sent them his greetings. They returned home when their mother no longer could bear the separation. When Frankfurter died, Mr. Gates and Oliver, now grown into an attractive young man, flew to Washington to console Mrs. Frankfurter.

Memorandum for F.F.

Washington, D.C., May 26, 1941

I am delighted to see these pictures and for Heaven's sake bring the children in to see me, week after next, before you go away.

F.D.R.

Roosevelt had let it be known in advance that a forthcoming speech would deal with American policy toward the war in Europe. The White House in the next few days received twelve thousand letters and telegrams offering various suggestions. Here is Frankfurter's letter to the President.

Washington, D.C., May 24, 1941

Dear Frank:

Lincoln's notation on one of the letters found in his desk "From a young man on how to win the War" ought to be a standing admonition against writing to Presidents in time of stress. I haven't even the excuse of being a young man in joining the many who are taking it upon themselves to tell you what to say next Tuesday. But that is not the purpose of this letter.

One would have to be a polyp not to be preoccupied with the thought of your forthcoming address to the people. But my main thought has been not on what you should say but what is to be accomplished by it. I have been thinking this to myself: What state of mind and will does one desire from the American people — that is, the overwhelming number of them, say about 70%, — on Wednesday morning after they have slept on what they have heard?

Since leading people is essentially a task of education done on a vast scale, I venture to draw on the experience of twenty-five years of teaching. Even for one dealing with as good brains as the country produced, the dominant conclusion I drew from my teaching experience is that one reaches minds, to a large extent, by repetition and concreteness. If our people grasped with clarity and conviction that this struggle is their struggle because it is an immediate menace to everything that we cherish in our institutions, all the rest will follow. For we must start with the unshakable faith that they want their own cherished country to survive. Therefore, they must have their convictions renewed and incontestably established — that what all this is about is not aid to Britain but preservation of America.

You have told them that during the last few years. But it seems to me important not merely to repeat it with new impressiveness, but to refresh their memories and to strengthen their convictions by quoting what you said in your address to Congress when you gave the distances between points in Africa and this hemisphere in order to prove that we are not engaged upon an altruistic enterprise, that Uncle Sam is not Lady Bountiful. He is concerned with his own skin and his own soul. They should also be made to feel on Wednesday morning that the nature of the threat and our readiness to resist it had been decided. The enlistment of American youth, the Lease and Loan Bill, the imposition of burdensome taxes, mean the reality of that threat and our active resistance to it, or they mean nothing.

And so the real issue is whether the American people, in the language of T.R., mean these things or merely mean them feebly.

He who wills the end wills the means. If we mean to resist the danger that is upon us, then we must resist it, unaggressively of course, but effectively. We must not be deterred by fear of the very danger which we are resisting. That, I take it, is our policy and we must not withhold execution of it by waiting on what is called an "incident."

A powerful and self-reliant nation will not determine its policy by the accident of an incident.

There is need of concreteness in putting all this. The tension that characterizes our people needs concrete direction. Backed-up energy is very bad. What the people want is a "let's go." They want to know why, where and how. The rest will be clear sailing — that is, there will be the clarity of a nation conscious of its own purposes and those of its traditions, and ready for the fate destiny may have in store for it. You will forgive me, an affectionate and devoted friend, for saying this.

Faithfully yours,
F.F.

Washington, D.C., May 25, 1941

Dear Frank:

Yesterday I ventured to express my deep conviction that the backed-up energy of our people's will and feeling can be effectively released and directed only by your concrete guidance. I now have seen the paragraphs that Stimson has sent to you today, and you will let me say how strongly I hope that some such concrete statement in your address will commend itself to you.

It is the kind of thing that would give the country the awaited "let's go!" It would do so with complete regard to the susceptibilities of Congress, being an announcement of your execution of the decision that Congress and the country made when the Lease-Loan Act was passed — a carrying out of the mandate of Congress.

If there is one thing that the last eight years have established beyond doubt it is that our people always respond when you invoke their approval for a policy that combines candor with courage in the cause of America. And this time it is also the cause of the Americans and of humanity. I know in my bones that on Wednesday morning you would have behind you the energy and devotion of the American people with a fulness paralleled only by the Hundred Days.

Faithfully yours,
F.F.

Realizing that American aid had become indispensable in the defense of Britain, Hitler had begun to attack and destroy American ships in the Atlantic. The President's advisers were divided. Mr. Stimson wanted the danger to be met by armed American convoys. Mr. Cordell Hull opposed this measure as a provocative act; but other officials in the State Department, notably Mr. Sumner Welles and Mr. Adolf Berle, were less cautious. Even at the risk of giving comfort to Japan, Mr. Stimson wanted the President to announce that some American ships and planes had been moved from the Pacific to the Atlantic. A compromise was reached when Roosevelt agreed to announce that the forces in the Atlantic had grown and would increase even more. Frankfurter was with Stimson all the way. In his speech on May 27, with its theme "We choose human freedom," the President proclaimed a state of unlimited national emergency, thus arming himself with vast executive powers. Roosevelt said: "When your enemy comes at you in a tank or a bombing plane, if you hold your fire until you see the whites of his eyes, you will never know what hit you. Our Bunker Hill of tomorrow may be several thousands miles from Boston."

Telegram to Roosevelt

Washington, D.C., May 27, 1941

THE DRESS REHEARSAL LEFT ME DEEPLY AND GRATEFULLY HAPPY. IT WILL BE AN EVENT THAT THE GIBBON OF 1976 WILL RECORD AS OF DECISIVE SIGNIFICANCE.

FELIX FRANKFURTER

The "dress rehearsal" has two meanings. Frankfurter had heard the National Emergency speech in the White House before it was given its public delivery. But Frankfurter, like the President, intended the phrase to carry a deeper meaning. They both knew that sterner decisions awaited America. The country had to move from proclamations to deeds.

Washington, D.C., May 28, 1941

Dear Frank:

Even history has accelerated its tempo and projected itself into the present. The Gibbon of the future will confirm the judgement on last night's speech and not render it. I have not known greater unanimity in our life-time. Straws have been blown my way by the winds gathered from all over the country, and the response was everywhere the same. That sense of elation and hush when great deeds have been resolved and the purpose to pursue them uttered with an impressiveness worthy of the awfulness of the theme — its awfulness, but also, its majesty. For it is not less than man's endeavor to fulfil his dream of Freedom: the only conception of himself that makes man nobler than an animal, capable of moral stature but not possessing it.

Keep on being yourself — that's my only and all-sufficient wish.

> Devotedly yours,
> F.F.

The White House, May 29, 1941

Dear Felix:

Your grand message of approval went straight to my heart. Your generous prophecy makes me feel humble indeed but I am more grateful than I can say.

> Very sincerely yours,
> F.D.R.

Washington, D.C., June 3, 1941

Dear Missy:

These enclosures speak for themselves. The President told me sometime ago that early June would be a good time for taking up the detailed arrangements for the Cambridge visit.

I assume these arrangements will be made directly but of course I shall be glad to act as intermediary if that will be more convenient.

> Ever yours,
> FELIX FRANKFURTER

Memorandum for F.F.

The White House, June 6, 1941

Thanks for the Leverett Saltonstall letter. I had to write him that if I go to Cambridge I should have to leave immediately after the Commencement exercises and before lunch.

For that reason I fear I must also forego the little gathering for photographs at the President's house. I will, however, make my appearance at the exercises themselves, floating through a window (with wings flapping) at the proper moment. My lunch must, I fear, be solitary and on the train. Colonel Starling will go to Cambridge shortly to make the final arrangements.

Early in the morning I will go straight from the train to Robinson Hall.

See you next week, I hope.

> F.D.R.

Copy for Colonel Starling

The President planned to attend the Harvard Commencement Exercises on June 19 and invited Frankfurter to take a hand in making the arrangements. This led to a mixture of letters, some official, others purely personal. Frankfurter sent the President a letter from Governor Saltonstall of Massachusetts, a letter from Jerome Greene giving the details of the Cambridge ceremony, and a friendly note from Fred Dumaine. The President on June 16 was still planning to go to Harvard but he canceled his trip at the last moment. Frankfurter had discussed this visit with the President as long ago as May 1, and the last-minute cancellation disappointed both of them. Colonel Starling is the celebrated "Starling of the White House," whose care and foresight in making security arrangements for the President have become legendary.

The date affixed to the following memorandum is June 1941, where it belongs, but it really was written in early 1935, when Senator Wagner and Representative Connery were pressing for the enactment of the National Labor Relations Board. This was the one major achievement of the New Deal where the initiative did not come from the President himself. Throughout the long struggle in Congress, dragging out over many months, Frankfurter was Senator Wagner's close adviser. Before the 1936 election, Frankfurter wrote a very long memorandum for the President, summarizing the legislative record of Roosevelt's first term. The memorandum had been returned to Frankfurter to assist him in the work he would do for the President in the 1936 campaign. Included in this memorandum, as a separate section, was a statement incorporating the arguments which Frankfurter had used in support of the Wagner-Connery bill.

By the summer of 1941 Roosevelt was worried about labor problems that would interfere with production and alienate the business community. He suddenly remembered Frankfurter's old memorandum on the Wagner-Connery bill and asked him if he had kept a copy. Frankfurter had destroyed the 1936 memorandum, since it had served his purposes as a campaign document, but he had kept the section on the National Labor Relations Board because of his absorbing interest in labor problems.

He sent it to the President, whose enthusiastic reply shows that he found it very helpful.

Frankfurter Memorandum for the President June 8, 1941

Another constructive achievement of the 74th Congress was the passage of the Wagner-Connery Bill, establishing the National Labor Relations Board upon a permanent statutory basis. Opposition to the Bill, based in large measure on misunderstanding, will gradually disappear, I believe, as the text of the statute is calmly studied. There is nothing of novelty either in the principles underlying its substantive requirements, or in its procedural provisions.

The facilitation of collective bargaining by freely chosen representatives of the employees was a governmental policy of the War Labor Board during the World War. The Congress has been engaged for many years in an elaboration of this policy as applied to the railroads, culminating in the Railway Labor Act of 1934. Section 7 (a) of the National Industrial Recovery Act reaffirmed the same policy by requiring the inclusion in every code of fair competition of a provision that: "Employees shall have the right to organize and bargain collectively through representatives of their own choosing, and shall be free from the interference, restraint, or coercion of employers of labor, or their agents, in the designation of such representatives or in self-organization or in other concerted activities for the purpose of collective bargaining or other mutual aid or protection." At the time of the passage of the National Industrial Recovery Act in 1933, employers generally announced their acceptance of these principles as the basis of their labor relations. This being so, they have no reason to be apprehensive of the new National Labor Relations Act, which, first, prohibits certain unfair labor practices by employers constituting an interference with these rights of employees to organize themselves and to bargain collectively through representatives of their own choosing, and, second, provides an improved administrative machinery for enforcement. Under the specific requirements of the statute, every essential of due process of law must be observed by the National Labor Relations Board in its investigations and hearings preliminary to the issuance of order; and careful provisions for court review of the Board's orders — patterned after the Federal Trade Commission Act — constitute a safeguard against arbitrary administrative action.

The day of industrial absolutism is done. All our experience since the industrial revolution demonstrates that employers as a class cannot be relied upon, voluntarily and out of the goodness of their hearts, to give a square deal to unorganized labor; this has been precluded by the pressure of immediate self-interest and the inexorable workings of the competitive system. We hear much of the thesis that sound labor relations must be founded upon mutual understanding and good will between capital and labor whose interests are common, not diverse. The truth is, however, that while labor and capital have a community of interest in the prosperity of the industry upon which both wages and dividends depend, there is at the same time, in the words of Mr. Chief Justice Taft, in *American Steel Foundries* v. *Tri-*

City Central Trades Council (257 U.S. 184) "an economic struggle or competition between employer and employee as to the share or division between them of the joint product of labor and capital." The efforts which employers at various times have made to prevent effective organization of their employees is, in itself, a recognition of this obvious conflict of interest.

Ideas which are unacceptable to one generation often become habitual modes of thought in the next generation. Thus, I believe, employers who have not already done so will eventually accommodate themselves, easily and as a matter of course, to the conception which underlies the National Labor Relations Act; namely, that employers have no business to meddle with or impede the self-organization of their employees; and that when the employees have chosen their form of organization and designated their representatives, the employer must accept them as such and negotiate with them in an effort to arrive at collective agreements covering wages and other conditions of employment. If a genuine question arises as to whom the employees want as their representative, the National Labor Relations Board is authorized to conduct a secret ballot among the employees to determine their choice. Employees may sometimes choose their leaders unwisely; but they stand to gain in the long run by making their own mistakes and profiting thereby, rather than by relying on the supposed paternal interest of their employers in the matter of organization. Once the employer has ungrudgingly accepted the process of collective bargaining with the freely chosen representatives of his employees, differences as to wages and hours are more readily reconciled by negotiation or arbitration. Reasonableness begets reasonableness. On the other hand, stubborn refusal to deal with the representatives chosen by the employees, the irresponsible use of force or economic power, the maintenance of elaborate systems of espionage, black lists, and other familiar devices, to thwart efforts of employees to organize in their own way, only result in an accumulation of bitterness that sooner or later will break out in the most serious manifestations of industrial disturbance. The employers, and especially the leaders in the big association of employers, have a grave responsibility at this juncture. Mock heroics about preferring to go to jail rather than submit to this iniquitous statute, incitements to mass disobedience of its provisions, will tend to produce dangerous frustrations of labor's reasonable human aspirations and play into the hands of extremists who insist that nothing is to be gained by peaceful processes. Acceptance by employers, wholeheartedly and in good faith, of the principles of the National Labor Relations Act, would remove a fighting issue that jeopardizes our industrial peace at many points, and would thereby contribute mightily to our match toward recovery from the depression.

Memorandum for F.F.

The White House, June 10, 1941

This really is excellent. Thank you for letting me see it.

F.D.R.

Washington, D.C., June 11, 1941

Dear Frank:

Says Marion "what a lot he sees where other people are blind, what a lot he feels where other people are without what they call 'evidence.'" And so you must have seen and felt how you made me feel regarding your views last Monday. Now, your phone confirms it all and I am deeply happy.

I wish you could have been the fly on the wall during my talks with Isaiah, Stone and Bob Jackson, who told me all since your phone this morning. It makes me know that your decision is everlastingly right, and history will vindicate you as will the morrow.

Like the best things in the world, the by-products will be most important.

I am as sure as I am of anything that you will enormously advance the mobilization of the moral resources of the nation — and, after all, the great conflict of civilization now raging will be resolved in favor of our side precisely because behind our material resources will be the eternal strength and power of right and spiritual authority and steadfastness of spirit.

Faithfully yours,

F.F.

The day on which Roosevelt submitted his first annual report on the Lend-Lease Act, June 10, also marked the beginning of the fighting in the Battle of Britain with deadly intensity. Roosevelt expected Germany to increase her submarine raids on all shipping as an added pressure to the air raids on Britain. He had foreseen what this would mean to America's own security by declaring on May 27 that "our patrols are helping now to insure delivery of the needed supplies to Britain" and "any and all further methods or combinations of methods," needed to achieve this purpose, would be put into effect.

At the conference in the White House on Monday, referred to in Frankfurter's letter, Roosevelt had outlined some additional measures he had in mind and had announced very firmly that he would go ahead with these measures no matter what the outcry in Congress or the country might be. In order to rouse the American people to the magnitude of the impending danger, Roosevelt, with the knowledge and consent of the British government, had already announced that the present rate of Nazi sinkings of merchant ships was more than three times as high as the capacity of British shipyards to replace them, and was more than the combined British and American output of merchant ships. But the outcry against Roosevelt continued and he was accused of being a warmonger, sometimes by responsible and prominent Americans who would blush to have their names recalled now.

It is easy to talk in the abstract about public opinion. One stark statistic will show the mood of the nation as reflected in Congress. Less than four months before the attack on Pearl Harbor, the House of Representatives, on August 12, endorsed the extension for one more year of the Selective Service Law — the "draft" — by a majority of only one vote. The vote was 203 in favor of the limited extension and 202 in opposition. The lines were being fiercely drawn between those who wanted stronger measures and those who were afraid of war.

The phone call that morning was, of course, weeks before this crucial vote on the draft, but these bitter cleavages in the country were already growing. Roosevelt had phoned Frankfurter to tell him that in his judgment the country would slowly but steadily come to accept the full implications of the unlimited national emergency. He also assured Frankfurter that he was going ahead with the other measures discussed at their White House conference. Some of these matters are revealed in later letters.

At Frankfurter's request, Attorney General Robert H. Jackson had given him a complete report on what the proclamation of a national emergency portended in terms of new legislation and executive orders. With Jackson's permission, Frankfurter had then given this information to Chief Justice Stone and Justice Brandeis (Isaiah).

Washington, D.C., June 14, 1941

Dear Frank:

After leaving you I felt as though I had champagne, and damn good champagne, for lunch. It was a great joy to see you so fit — your energy of mind and spirit, and above all, the serenity of your soul. Only a man who has come to terms with himself, and faced Destiny for himself and his people, ever achieves such serenity. And so, a deep inner peace and confidence came also to me.

Grim days are here, and grimmer ahead. You, I know, are ready for them — and how fortunate the country that you were called to its guidance.

Devotedly yours,
F.F.

Washington, D.C., June 15, 1941

Dear Frank:

Of course my mind these days is absorbed with only one subject — the world situation and our dear country. And some of my thinking insists on getting on paper — and getting to you. I cannot help, therefore, sending you what I have written in the enclosed memorandum, not because it says anything that you have not thought of, and probably long ago. I venture to bother you with it, because it sometimes is not without value to see one's own thoughts on paper through another man's language.

Anyhow — here it is, without further apology.

And may the good Lord keep you for His special own!

Affectionately,
FELIX F.

Frankfurter Memorandum for the President

1. The assumption of this memorandum is that action affecting any of the Atlantic islands fits much more into the conception of defense made explicit in the speech of May 27th than action on any European or African mainland. Public opinion has been educated readily to understand protective action affecting such non-belligerent island territories.

2. The occupation of Iceland and its development as an American base for transit purposes both by sea and by air is the ideal first move. It is ostentatious yet innocent in that it does not involve any immediate risk of hostilities.

3. The Azores and Cape Verde islands would be a natural next step. But this requires an invitation from Portugal and perhaps an active movement into Spain. Thus it is problematical how soon such a move can become effective.

4. Meanwhile there is another Atlantic island of the greatest possible importance from every aspect, military, psychological and political, namely, Ireland. The safeguarding of Ireland as a defensive measure against Nazi aggression by collaborative arrangement between Ireland and the United States would be appealing to the needs of De Valera, be responsive to our political climate and afford these signal practical advantages:

(a) It would be a case not of relieving the British but of providing a vitally necessary safeguard which they are precluded from providing themselves.

(b) The chances of a German invasion of Ireland in the first instance are surely greater than that of a direct invasion of England. It is not easy to see what effective opposition Ireland could now put up. The protection of Ireland is thus an overwhelmingly urgent need.

(c) Not only would the protection of Ireland carry with it the use of bases denied to the British navy but it would provide an ideal depot for the American navy and air force for any subsequent deployment. As in the case of Iceland, except more so, it would advance enormously the effective defense of the Atlantic and its approaches without implying the risk of hostility.

5. That such a coincident protection both of Ireland and of this country, would touch the imagination and bring comfort to some American groups otherwise troubled, cannot be doubted. And for these somewhat kindred reasons it would surely appeal to De Valera:

(a) There can be no doubt that he is anxious about the risks that Ireland is running and its inadequacy in defense. In no other direction is it politically possible for him to look for help. What is proposed would be collaboration of one non-belligerent with another non-belligerent for purely defensive purposes, and mutually defensive.

(b) It is common knowledge that Ireland is facing acute and increasing economic difficulties which would be greatly eased by the execution of the present proposal. For it would involve a flow of necessary supplies and also provide a local demand for Ireland's own surplus produce.

(c) The United States by such active collaboration would be placed in a peculiarly effective position for a final and satisfactory solution of partition and of the whole Irish problem.

A few weeks later, on July 7, Roosevelt reached an agreement with Iceland to establish a base in that island for American forces and to protect it against all attacks.

He also prepared all the necessary plans to seize the Azores as an "island output" if Hitler began to carry out his threat to move into Africa through Spain.

The State Department and the British government had misgivings about the plan for Ireland. But De Valera was made aware that Roosevelt's benevolent eye was cast on Ireland's safety, and he was grateful.

Telegram to Roosevelt
Cambridge, Mass., June 19, 1941

OF COURSE YOUR ABSENCE WAS A SORROW. OTHERWISE IT WENT OFF ADMIR-ABLY. PA FACED THE HARVARD CROWD ALMOST AS CALMLY AS HE WOULD HAVE THE ENEMY. BUT I AM UNDER PAINFUL DUTY TO REPORT THAT HE DISOBEYED HIS COMMANDER IN CHIEF'S ORDER REGARDING OLD VIRGINNY. AFFECTIONATELY.

FELIX FRANKFURTER

This is a report to the President on the Harvard Commencement Exercises which Roosevelt was unable to attend. He had ordered General "Pa" Watson, who had gone to Harvard for the White House, to restrain his usual bragging about the glories of Virginia. Apparently this was one order he had no intention of honoring, especially when confronted with the counter-glories of Harvard and Massachusetts.

New Milford, Conn., July 19, 1941

Dear Frank:

I want to add to my pleasures at Campobello by telling you a few words about them.

And my pleasures were many — gayly introduced by that wonderful scow ferry-boat. That might be called an Elegant Commencer!

In the appropriate vernacular of your students' colony, your mother gave me the biggest "kick." She had improved so enormously from the time I last saw her, a short stretch, at Hyde Park. What extraordinary resilience for *her* years. We really had a gay time — at least she gave me one. I wish I had known her fifty years ago, or rather sixty years ago. In her twenties she must have been a real menace to men!

Your Missus will have told you what a grand lot those boys and girls are. It was a most imaginative thing to turn your house over to this experiment. It's just the right setting for them — and as an old hand with young men (though not, of course, with young women!) I can assure you that they are a truly exciting group of kids, and much good must come of it.

That is an enterprise of which you and the country should feel deeply proud. It is a stirring achievement. I know enough about facts to feel sure that those lads, — some 700 of them — are happy because they are effectively functioning.

It was a joy to see Jimmie and his wife. He has grown with big strides. He spoke exceedingly well — just the right proportion and emphasis. He was admirable, as I told Marion, in substance and form. That lad has real stuff in him.

Iceland turned out as you had a right to expect it would — real, pervasive support and approval from the country, and discomfiture for the enemy, at home and abroad. I feel it deep, deep in my bones that we have entered a new phase of the struggle — the phase of not too remote triumph, if you will continue to give the direction to things you have been giving, *including* the persistent bombing of the widest area of German cities. Shirer's book shows what a taste of that did to the Germans, even in 1940. If Russian civil morale is maintained — as it looks as though it would be — and we employ the skill and the will, and therefore the weight of which we are capable, we may not have a war in the winter of '42-'43. The most important thing is for you to remain fit and fresh. Marion and I send you our affectionate regards and always our devoted good wishes.

Ever yours,
F.F.

Washington, D.C., July 25, 1941

Dear Felix:

Just a line dictated before I leave for Hyde Park. I am delighted you approved of the Campobello conference. A little bird told me that you had remarked you never had such hard work on such a skimpy diet in your life! Don't forget the range in the kitchen was built for a family of eight and not a family of forty. Come and see us very soon and I will give you some caviar and cocktails to make up for it.

If somebody kidnaps Wheeler and shanghais him on board an outgoing steamer for the Congo, can a habeas corpus follow him thither? You need not answer, if you don't want to because it would never get as far as the Supreme Court. Wheeler or I would be dead, first!

As ever,
F.D.R.

Senator Burton K. Wheeler was becoming increasingly violent and vituperative in his opposition to Roosevelt.

New Milford, Conn., August 1, 1941

Dear Frank:

On my return from Campobello I was greeted by Marion with "Heavens! how many pounds have you put on. Did you do nothing up there except eat — I thought you went to feed *their* minds not *your* stomach!" I shall not say your anonymous little birdie was wholly imaginative — but I did count on that bird also having a gay sense of humor. They not only had plenty of food — it must be a very flexible range — they even had a dietician! And you and I are not addicted to merely wholesome food!!

Did you also hear from your little bird that Dr. Cohn and I took up two bottles of Bellow's Club Special — of course for medicinal purposes — which, with Jimmy's able help, your mother served us at lunch. So you see I wasn't starving!

The tide seems to be running all in the right current. What a good batch of items the last two days — your inflation message, Harry's visit to Moscow, the Czecho-Slovak recognition, the Russo-Polish Pact, Tom Connally's succession to Foreign Relations Chairmanship, the MacVeagh Iceland appointment, the Wallace Board!! Yes — I feel it in my bones that the vast effort is moving powerfully and right.

As for Burt Wheeler — he needs the medicine you used to administer to poor Charlie Tuttle and Oggie Mills et al, intelligent neglect plus good, long rope.

I dare to think that the Nazis may be "done in" before the winter of '42-'43 will be over.

Marion joins me in affectionate regards,

Ever yours,

F.F.

Mrs. Eleanor Roosevelt had taken the initiative in organizing a leadership institute for young people at Campobello, the summer retreat where Roosevelt years before had contracted infantile paralysis. The conference, from June 29 to August 2, was attended by 29 students, 16 boys and 13 girls, from 23 colleges, and never were students more fortunate in their speakers. Among the speakers were Mr. Archibald MacLeish, Dr. Alfred E. Cohn of the Rockefeller Institute, James Roosevelt, and Frankfurter. Before speaking on the lawn to the assembled students on the subject of "The Law," Frankfurter had asked them to consider two questions. "Why does a civilized society need an organized body of law? How is the law actually made and enforced?"

Then Frankfurter, in effect, behaved as if he were back in a seminar class at the Harvard Law School. He made his own statements a spur to searching out the ideas of the students and enlisting them in a cooperative exploration of a complicated subject. No wonder Mrs. Roosevelt said afterwards that she understood at last why Frankfurter had for so long held the reputation of being one of the most gifted and inspiring teachers ever to appear in the classroom of any American university.

Frankfurter kept returning to his hopes for an early end of the war, though Roosevelt twice phoned him during these exchanges to advise him sadly that he must lower his expectations.

Harry Hopkins had been sent by Roosevelt to see Stalin in Moscow.

Henry A. Wallace had assumed new duties as Chairman of the Board of Economic Warfare.

New Milford, Conn., August 18, 1941

Dear Frank:

Not even constant misuse can rob some phrases of their noble meaning. Therefore regard for truth compels me to say that somewhere in the Atlantic you *did* make history for the world. And like all truly great historic events, it wasn't what was said or done that defined the scope of the achievement. It's always the forces — the impalpable, the spiritual forces, the hopes, the purposes, the dreams and the endeavors — that are released that matter.

And so, all that is implied in the fact that you and Churchill met, in the circumstances under which, and the aims for which you met, that is the vital achievement from which all else will flow. "We will live by symbols," as we cannot too often recall. And you two in that ocean, freed from all the tawdry accompaniments of cheap journalism, in the setting of that Sunday service, give meaning to the conflict between civilization and arrogant brute challenge, and give promise, more powerful and binding than any formal treaty could, that civilization has claims and resources that tyranny will not be able to overcome, because it will find that force and will and the free spirit of man are more powerful than force and will alone.

It was all grandly conceived and finely executed. All this talk of press and pictures and "releases" and what not, are the merest trivia. The deed and the spirit and the invigoration of a common human fraternity in the hearts of men will endure — and steel our will and kindle actions toward the goal of ridding the world of this horror.

Affectionately yours,
F.F.

The great transformation in the war had come with Hitler's invasion of Russia on June 22 but it took some time for that fact to be understood in all its dimensions. Churchill, discarding his lifelong horror of Bolshevism, at once pledged British help to Russia on the principle that any nation engaged in the task of killing Nazis fully deserved any assistance which Britain could spare from her own grim defense. In Washington the great events taking shape on the Eastern front were misunderstood.

The invasion of Russia produced gloom, not jubilation. The overwhelming view was that Hitler would crack Russia like an eggshell, would have his armies in Moscow in a few weeks, and then would be able to turn at his leisure, and with Russian resources added to the Nazi war machine, to break the British people. The first brutal surge of the Nazi armies deep into Russian territory did nothing to expose the triviality and falsehood of these estimates. Then the Russian grip hardened, the Russian people roused themselves to a heroic defense of their homeland, they fought for every city and village with desperate courage that never knew despair, and slowly it dawned on the Washington experts that Hitler was not taking part in a triumphal march but had committed a military blunder which exceeded the gigantic folly of Napoleon's attack on Russia.

From the start Frankfurter belonged to the very small group of Roosevelt's advisers who believed Russia would not sink into swift collapse and therefore should receive military and economic aid from the United States. He told Roosevelt that there was no natural affinity between Hitler and Stalin, though both were brutal dictators. Indeed, he boldly told the President that Russia had decided to work with Germany in the Molotov-Ribbentrop pact of 1939 only after Chamberlain and Daladier had snubbed

Russia and excluded her from their diplomacy while Britain and France followed their disastrous experiments with appeasement. He predicted that the ancestral hatred of a foreign foe would animate the Russian people to a stern resistance. Roosevelt listened without agreement, perplexed by contrary advice, but at least he listened.

Then it became evident even to those soaked in the most virulent prejudices about Russian Communism that Hitler was not going to walk over Russia the way he had promenaded over Poland. There was a chance, if one made it a fighting chance, that Russia might hold.

It became imperative for Churchill to meet with Roosevelt and decide on common policies in the light of a totally new situation. They met early in August "somewhere in the Atlantic," actually on the British warship the Prince of Wales, somewhere off the Newfoundland coast. The result of their conference was the Atlantic Charter. Frankfurter's letter was written three days before Roosevelt sent his message to Congress on this Atlantic Conference.

In essence, the Atlantic Charter bound Britain and France to fight Nazi Germany to a finish, to accept no compromises, to honor no truce, since Germany would break any treaty and once she had caught her breath — "her armed breath" — she would again lunge savagely against the world. Churchill and Roosevelt also spoke of their hopes for the world after the war, a world with freedom from fear and freedom from want.

But they spoke too, plainly and firmly, about Russia — at that particular moment the most important point in the entire war. They agreed to conferences with Russia "to aid it" in its defense against Germany, described by Churchill and Roosevelt as "the principal aggressor of the modern world." They agreed also that Lord Beaverbrook, the Minister of Supply in the British government, would go to Washington to discuss not only the joint needs of Britain and America but "the supply problems of the Soviet Union." From these discussions came the huge aid program for Russia, an indispensable source of strength in her long-continued resistance.

Roosevelt was eager to meet Stalin without delay but Stalin was evasive, slipped out of apparent commitments, and displayed a genius for the vague answer that signified nothing. They were not to meet until the Teheran Conference in 1943. But trusted advisers like Harry Hopkins and other senior officials did of course visit Russia on various missions during this interval.

On a visit to the White House during these fateful days in the summer of 1941 Frankfurter was asked by Roosevelt to explain why he was so sure of Russia's staying power when most of the President's advisers were predicting an early and ignominious collapse. Frankfurter gave three reasons in a long and carefully reasoned reply.

He said, in the first place, that he had never shared the violent prejudices felt by so many people against Soviet Russia, though he profoundly deplored its extinction of personal freedom. All his violent feelings were reserved for Czarist Russia, which he described as "the most shameful government in the chronicles of human servitude, with the solitary exception of Nazi Germany." Secondly, he believed that Hitler had exemplified the truth of Sir Walter Scott's saying that men sometimes reserve all their folly for one prodigal expenditure. In defiance of his own published teachings, Hitler had doomed himself to fight on two fronts. The urgent need now was not to question Russia's capacity but to apply relentless pressure against Germany. Finally, he said he had learned from his reading of Russian history and literature that Russian patriotism — fierce, implacable, avenging — always became a shield and sword against the invader. Churchill, with all his genius, had never understood that sovereign fact. That is why he had talked of strangling Bolshevism at its birth or in its cradle. On Russian affairs David Lloyd George was much wiser. He feared not Bolshevik power but the avenging strength of Russian patriotism. So Lloyd George had opposed the mischievous folly of trying to pull down the Soviet government with Western troops. Now we had come to one of the really decisive tests of the whole war. Frankfurter thought Roosevelt would never forgive himself if he gave help on an inadequate scale to the Russian people in throwing back the common Nazi enemy — help that would be timid, tiny, tentative, and tardy, to use words once employed by Churchill in a totally different context.

Frankfurter remembered with a smile that Roosevelt listened to this long exposition without a single question or interruption. Then the President said he wished his other advisers could state the reasons for the faith within them so clearly.

New Milford, Conn., August 29, 1941

Dear Frank;

I am very glad that you will speak on Labor Day. The country needs your voice again.

The enclosed few sentences welled up within me. I am venturing to send them because you have a waste-basket handy.

Ever devotedly,
F.F.

For anyone, whether in private industry or in government, to take advantage of this grave national emergency in order to lower the standards of living of any portion of our people or to make inroads on those rights of free association that have so largely made possible such civilized standards, is to play, however unwittingly but powerfully, into the hands of the ene-mies of democracy. And for those who toil with their hands, or for those who lead them, to jeopardize national security by failing to utilize orderly and effective means for asserting their claims or pressing their grievances without interruption of the processes of defense production, is to put in peril all those free institutions on which rest the very existence of our Bill of Rights, including the right of free association, and the means for achieving progressive betterment. Hitler has said the present conflict is one between "two worlds" — his and ours. He is absolutely right. Shall it be his world or ours, is the awful issue. Consciously or unconsciously to help his victory or to hinder its defeat, is to promote a world of human slavery.

Roosevelt gave emphatic affirmation to Frankfurter's theme in his Labor Day address on September 1. "We shall do everything in our power to crush Hitler and his Nazi forces." He hoped some "future American Presi-dent" would say this generation had done its work "faithfully and well."

Telegram to Roosevelt
New Milford, Conn., September 1, 1941
THAT FUTURE PRESIDENT WILL CERTAINLY SAY IT ABOUT YOU. OUR AFFECTION-ATE REGARDS.

FELIX FRANKFURTER

The White House, September 3, 1941
Dear Felix:
How thoughtful of you to send me that message — and I appreciate it ever so much.

Always sincerely,
F.D.R.

Washington, D.C., September 12, 1941
Dear Frank:
After you had finished last night, there was that physical inhibition — that respectful period of silence — which always follows, the pause that succeeds, a tremendous performance. Whether it is a very, very rare musical performance, Toscanini conducting Beethoven's Fifth, or the kind of a speech that carried the verdict of history in its own utterance, one's facul-ties for a time are too concentrated and tense for words. And so, Marion and I sat silent for a stretch as your final words — "assault upon their de-mocracy, their sovereignty and their freedom" — kept ringing in our ears. "He never spoke better," Marion's voice at last quietly broke the silence,

"it was so lean, clean, cut to the bone, with an austere impressiveness equal to the awful gravity of the issue."

And now that I have read and re-read the speech, in the early morning freshness, I am still under its spell — and still feel Marion has given the key to its nobility and enduring history — you gave the occasion utterance worthy of the awfulness of the issue. You remember Dante's remark that true eloquence stands erect by the strength of its own substantive will. You voiced the hopes and the majesty and might of humanity. The event is with God.

Ever faithfully yours,
F.F.

Roosevelt, on September 11, announced that German or Italian vessels of war would enter at their own peril the waters whose protection is necessary for American defense. "The orders which I have given as Commander-in-Chief to the United States Army and Navy are to carry out that policy — at once."

He added: "I have no illusions about the gravity of this step. I have not taken it hurriedly or lightly. It is the result of months and months of constant thought and anxiety and prayer. In the protection of your nation and mine it cannot be avoided. The American people have faced other grave crises in their history — with American courage and American resolution. They will do no less today. They know the actualities of the attacks upon us. They know the necessities of a bold defense against these attacks. They know that the times call for clear heads and fearless hearts. And with that inner strength that comes to a free people conscious of their duty and of the righteousness of what they do, they will — with Divine help and guidance — stand their ground against this latest assault upon their democracy, their sovereignty, and their freedom."

Washington, D.C., October 2, 1941

Dear Frank:

After sleeping on the question about the big transports which you put to me last night, I awoke with a very definite answer. My feeling is perfectly clear — for what it may be worth — against the proposal.

Did the present procedures result in loss of life the public would be prepared for it — indeed it would be merely the expected. But loss of life on one of these transports — however legal the venture may be — will be wholly unexpected, will stir discussion easily leading to the exploitation of public confusion. I cannot believe that the gain would compensate for such dangerous consequences in public opinion. The tide is running much too strongly your way to be disturbed for such doubtful gains.

It was grand seeing you.

Ever yours,
F.F.

Washington, D.C., October 14, 1941

Dear Frank:

I should like you to see what Dean Acheson and I said at our leave-taking of Brandeis.

And when next we have free talk I want to tell you some of the things that Brandeis said of you the last time I saw him — a day before the blow came.

Ever yours,
F.F.

Mr. Justice Brandeis died on October 7, 1941. The funeral service was stripped of all religious symbolism and meaning. In the simple ceremony of leave-taking, Mr. Dean Acheson, a former law clerk, spoke briefly and Frankfurter, after a sentence or two, read from The Pilgrim's Progress. *The same passage from Bunyan, in praise of Great-heart, was read at Frankfurter's own funeral. Both deserved it.*

At their last meeting, Brandeis told Frankfurter that Roosevelt had never been such "a noble figure" as in these war years. "He is greater than Jefferson and almost as great as Lincoln."

Washington, D.C., October 20, 1941

Dear Mrs. Roosevelt:

When, the other night, I asked Eugene Meyer what were the dominant impressions which he brought back from England, he left no doubt in my mind that it was the role that the women play in the defense of the island. He was literally lyrical about the work of one particular leader among women's defense organizations. On the assumption that the British experience may not be without value for our Defense efforts, it occurred to me that you might have Eugene Meyer tell you at first hand, if you have not already heard from him, some of his observations in their relation to us.

Faithfully yours,
Felix Frankfurter

Mr. Eugene Meyer spent many years in public service, in various important positions, before he became the owner and publisher of the Washington Post.

Telegram to Roosevelt

Washington, D.C., October 24, 1941

AS ANOTHER NON-VOTER I SAY GRAND.

FELIX FRANKFURTER

Roosevelt had endorsed La Guardia for Mayor of New York. He said: "although my voting residence has always been up-state, I have lived and worked in the city of New York off and on since 1904. I have known and observed New York's mayors since that time. I am not taking part in the New York City election but, because the City of New York contains about half the population of my state, I do not hesitate to express the opinion that Mayor La Guardia and his Administration have given to the city the most honest and, I believe, the most efficient municipal government of any within my recollection."

Telegram to Roosevelt

Washington, D.C., October 28, 1941

LAST NIGHT I JUDICIALLY CHEERED. THIS MORNING AFTER A SOBER NIGHT'S SLEEP I CONTINUE JUDICIALLY TO REJOICE.

FELIX FRANKFURTER

Washington, D.C., October 24, 1941

Dear Mr. President:

Your omnivorous eye may have seen in the New York papers notice of the death of my revered uncle, Dr. Solomon Frankfurter, and therefore you may have noted a statement that upon Hitler's entry into Vienna this aged scholar was put in a concentration camp and his release was afterwards secured through our State Department. I write you this note on the assumption that truth has its own excuse for being.

Precisely because I wanted to avoid the criticism even of the evilminded and hardhearted against any charge of favoritism by your administration, I did *not* invoke the good offices of the State Department. On the contrary, I secured his release through the kindness of Lady Astor's intervention with her then German friends.

Faithfully yours,

FELIX FRANKFURTER

The White House, October 27, 1941

Dear Felix: —

I was really sorry to hear of the death of your uncle. I did not even know that he had been put in a concentration camp. There would have been no possible reason why the State Department should not have asked for his release. I think that even a Justice of the Supreme Court is entitled to ask his own Government to help out persecuted people, even though they be his own close relatives, in any part of the world. I hope this old gentleman died in his own home and in his own bed.

As ever yours,
F.D.R.

Washington, D.C., October 29, 1941

Dear Frank:

It was most sweet of you to write me about my uncle. He was truly a scholar and a gentleman, and to the very last of his eighty-five years lived a devoted and brave life. He kept his soul free — though violence and brutality sought to break it.

I would not have added a word — nor subtracted one — from your Navy Day speech. Every word told — and the whole had the power of action as well as of education.

I think much these days of all the burdens that rest on you — and pray for your continued strength and the indomitable example of your spirit.

Devotedly yours,
F.F.

The White House, October 29, 1941

Dear Felix:

Your message is really stimulating. I know it came from the heart.

Very sincerely yours,
F.D.R.

The strict formality of Frankfurter's opening letter, in salutation and structure and signature, is proof that he wished to place it on record that he sought no personal or private advantage from his friendship with the President. His silence may have been foolish, as Roosevelt's generous letter implies, but surely it was a noble foolery. His uncle had been the chief librarian and director of the library at the University of Vienna.

In his Navy Day speech of October 27, Roosevelt said: "Our American merchant ships must be armed to defend themselves against the rattlesnakes of the sea. Our American merchant ships must be free to carry our American goods into the harbors of our friends. Our American merchant ships must be protected by our American Navy. It can never be doubted that the goods will be delivered by this Nation, whose Navy believes in the tradition of 'Damn the torpedoes; full speed ahead!' "

Not even Frankfurter, when he had suggested that Roosevelt should use the colloquial phrase about "delivering the goods," had ever conceived that it would be used in these dramatic and historic circumstances. He praised the Navy Day speech by letter and by telegram. He went around Washington quoting the President's statement: "We Americans have cleared our decks and taken our battle stations."

Washington, D.C., October 29, 1941

Dear Grace:

The President probably has seen the article on The Psychology of Persecution in the *Commonweal* of September fifth last. If by chance he has not seen it, he will want to read it in connection with his speech on Monday concerning the hostility of the Nazis against the Church. In the interest of convenience I am sending it along.

You will notice that it belongs to the Library of Congress and therefore I will trouble you to have it returned to me so that I may return it to the Library.

Faithfully yours,
FELIX FRANKFURTER

Hyde Park, N.Y., November 1, 1941

Dear Felix:

Ever so many thanks for your note and for the copy of the *Commonweal*. I read the article with a great deal of interest.

With all good wishes,

As ever yours,
F.D.R.

P.S.   I am returning the article as you request.

Washington, D.C., November 6, 1941

Dear Frank:

You may be interested in these comments on the N.Y. election by shrewd Charlie Burlingham. Please return it at your convenience.

I know how risky it is to tell a prolific author how much one likes a particular brain-child of his. But I am too old, I find, to learn prudence. And so I shall stick my neck out and tell you that your talk to the Hyde Park Meeting simply delighted me. It was, of course, very charming — but it was much more. It had much wisdom tucked away in a casual-seeming way. I wish that address were printed in all books on civics. It gives more of the "innards" of government and of our democratic ways than books on civics usually contain. It *will* be in our books on government fifty years hence!

Marion and I were cheered that Missy left the hospital — and we now hope that Harry will keep fit for his great spirit.

Devotedly yours,
F.F.

Mr. C. C. Burlingham had written to Frankfurter to describe the divisions in the Democratic party in the city of New York. Governor Lehman had endorsed Mr. O'Dwyer because he was the candidate of the Democratic party. Roosevelt supported La Guardia even though he was the head of a coalition. Governor Lehman's supporters accused Roosevelt of trying to split the Democratic party by placing La Guardia first and the party second. Burlingham bluntly declared that most voters in New York were convinced that La Guardia was much better than the Democratic party and believed that Roosevelt had established the right priorities.

To everyone's grief, Missy LeHand had suffered a stroke in June 1941. Harry Hopkins, driven by a great spirit, insisted on punishing his frail body with overwork.

Washington, D.C., November 12, 1941

Dear Frank:

I'm a tough sleeper, but I became restless early this morning, and here it is, a little after seven, and I'm writing this note to you. For it's your cares that roused me from my sleep. As I came home last night and Marion and I saw those dreadful headlines, we could talk of nothing else except all the burdens that the selfishness and ignorance and shortsightedness of others cast upon you.

And so I woke — thinking of coal and rails, and wishing that I could lift ever so little from your shoulders. But all I can do is to send you my most heart-felt good wishes for your strength and health, and my devoted affection.

Ever yours,
F.F.

The White House, November 14, 1941

Dear Felix: —

Ever so many thanks for that sympathetic note. I wish I could put you in charge of this coal production problem but I am afraid that the legalities of what I fear I must do may come before you for final approval! Is there any way I can cut you in half, leaving your starboard side on the bench and putting your port side to work in the Executive Branch of the Government!

As ever yours,
F.D.R.

P.S.   The word "port" in the above is a nautical term and not spirituous. Never having been an admiralty lawyer, I thought you might need this clarification.

The "dreadful headlines" referred to threatened strikes, quarrels over production, and charges that some of the President's close friends and supporters were guilty of a conflict of interest. There was plenty of trouble in the coal mines and on the railroads, as the President's reply indicates, but the charges against the President's friends were false.

Washington, D.C., November 17, 1941

Dear Frank:

You doubtless know it already, but what follows will take you only a minute to read. Someone whom I have hitherto always found to know the difference between evidence and gossip professes to have reliable information as to the *specific* instructions of Kurusu. Because of scepticism as to the dependability of Nomura's warnings regarding the intentions of this country in case of new aggressions by Japan, Kurusu was sent here to find out if we mean business in case Japan moves. The rest of Kurusu's mission is all window-dressing.

BUT, even if this isn't the first time that I tell you something you already know, why must you make my nautical ignorance a matter of record — *you*, master of "off-the-record!" Anyhow, I shamelessly confess I care more for alcoholic than nautical port. Does that prove I am listing to starboard?

I hope that you have exorcised sinus and all the minor devils.

Ever faithfully yours,
F.F.

On receiving this letter, Roosevelt phoned Frankfurter to ask him in sheer amazement how he had found out about the dilatory diplomatic tactics and about a possible military strike by Japan. The President said this was the most closely guarded secret in Washington, the evidence was puzzling and contradictory, and a very small group was still laboriously examining the confused pattern emerging from the negotiations with Japan. Frankfurter chuckled and said he would be glad to give the President all his information — in person and alone at the White House. This was done. Pearl Harbor was on the horizon.

Washington, D.C., November 23, 1941

Dear Frank:

Your *suaviter in modo fortiter in re* has again been vindicated. How easy it is for people to solve a problem who do not appreciate its complexities. These "crack-down-on-'em" critics have not the wisdom to understand that the only abidingly "practical" way for a statesman is to mobilize and employ the spiritual resources of a nation for its practical ends. You have had to retain and still further gain the confidence and devotion of humble folk without alienating them from old and intimate loyalties. And you have done it.

Thereby you have won new good will and increased prestige to move for larger ends on a wider front.

We have cause for a second Thanksgiving Day.

Ever affectionately yours,

F.F.

As the year neared its end, Frankfurter wrote this tribute to the combination of patience and boldness with which Roosevelt had brought a half-reluctant nation to realize the stark challenges which menaced its safety and its freedom.

Washington, D.C., December 2, 1941

My dear Justice Frankfurter:

I have just written a note to Chief Justice Harlan F. Stone, asking if he would be willing to broadcast on December 15 which, as you know, is being celebrated as Bill of Rights Day.

We would like very much to have you and also Mr. Justice Murphy participate in the program which will take place at 9:30 P.M. As the District of Columbia celebrates the evening celebration, it would be a tremendously valuable thing if you gentlemen could do this. I am very anxious that this celebration serve to bring to the people of the country the fact that the Bill of Rights guards the liberties of all our citizens, and that we can not have real defense unless all of them work together and are equally protected.

Very cordially yours,

ELEANOR ROOSEVELT

Washington, D.C., December 6, 1941

Dear Mrs. Roosevelt:

Let me acknowledge your kind letter of the second inviting me to share in the Bill of Rights day celebration of the District of Columbia.

Knowing your concern in such matters, I need hardly say that any wish of yours calls presumptively for fulfillment. On the other hand, I know you will not think it stuffy if I say I have made it a fixed rule to indulge in no public appearance during Term time. A job on this Court calls for more than all that I have, and at least should not receive less. And a public speech, however short, takes it out of me. But, after all, the sesquicentennial of the Bill of Rights comes only once in one hundred and fifty years and one ought not to be a slave of any rule. Therefore, if it suits your purpose, I should be glad to speak the enclosed piece, or any part of it that may commend itself to you, on the night of the fifteenth. It was written for a small volume that will have such a limited circulation that, were this idea agreeable to you, I do not think there is any danger of making the talk over the radio a warmed-over dish.

Very cordially yours,
F.F.

Washington, D.C., December 8, 1941

Dear Mr. Justice:

Thank you for your letter of December 6. Mrs. Roosevelt has been called to the Pacific coast and has asked me to let you know that the Washington meeting on the Bill of Rights for December 15 has been called off as it was considered unwise to hold large assemblies at this time. We would appreciate it very much, however, if you could present over the air "The Paths Must Be Kept Open." Miss Meredith Howard has relinquished her time on December 15 over N.B.C. from 7:55 to 8:00. If you feel you can do this will you ask your secretary to call the Office of Civilian Defense, RE 5050, Extension 1282, so that final arrangements can be made.

Thanking you for your cooperation, I remain,

Sincerely yours,
BETTY G. LINDLEY

Frankfurter, in his article on the Bill of Rights, had written a paragraph in which he manifested a rare pride, for he had little pride of authorship. He wrote: "Lincoln magnificently illustrates that nature herself is democratic. The arrangements of society should not thwart her purposes. Tolerance for dissident views is not an exercise in benignity but a form of practical wisdom. Truth is an eternal chase. The history of man's endeavor to achieve truth shows the displacement of yesterday's dogma by today's skepticism. And today's folly may prove itself tomorrow's wisdom. The paths to the City of God must be kept open."

Washington, D.C., December 7, 1941

Dear Frank:

No one is now so ignorant as not to know that the whole American people are behind you. And one may venture to say, in all humility, that the God of Righteousness is with you — and you are His instrument. Our devoted prayers attend you.

Affectionately yours,
F.F.

Frankfurter's letter on the day of Pearl Harbor.

Memorandum for The President
                              The White House, December 7, 1941
    Felix Frankfurter suggested that if the President cannot get hold of
the Attorney General or the Solicitor General he might want to have a
good lawyer standing by in an advisory capacity and he suggests Dean
Acheson whose telephone number is Ashton 5572 or his caretaker Ashton
5271.
Pearl Harbor Day

Telegram to Roosevelt
                              Washington, D.C., December 9, 1941
IN THE COMPANY OF THE ADOLPH MILLERS, THE POLISH AMBASSADOR AND HIS
WIFE AND MRS. RALPH ELLIS, MARION AND I HEARD YOUR SPEECH WITH DEEP-
EST SATISFACTION. YOUR SOBERLY CONFIDENT VOICE MUST BRING CONFIDENCE
WITHOUT COMPLACENCY TO OUR PEOPLE AND YOUR APPEAL FOR PRIVILEGED
EFFORT AND YOUR ASSURANCE OF TRUST IN STAMINA ARE BOUND TO GIRD THEM
FOR THE GLORIOUSLY GRIM TASK AHEAD.
                                            FELIX FRANKFURTER

Roosevelt delivered his war message to Congress the day after Pearl Har-
bor. The speech began with the unforgettable sentence: "Yesterday, De-
cember 7, 1941 — a date which will live in infamy — the United States of
America was suddenly and deliberately attacked by naval and air forces of
the Empire of Japan." He asked that the Congress declare that since "the
unprovoked and dastardly attack" by Japan on Sunday, December 7, "a
state of war" had existed between the United States and the Japanese Em-
pire.
    The next evening the President delivered a fireside chat to the nation,
reviewing and explaining the events which had brought America into the
war. In this address Roosevelt said: "We are going to win the war and we
are going to win the peace that follows."
    On December 11 the President asked Congress to declare that a state of
war be recognized as in existence between the United States and Germany,
and the United States and Italy.
    "We live by symbols," Frankfurter often said, quoting Mr. Justice
Holmes, and he chose a symbolic way to hear the President's broadcast to
the nation on America's entry into the war. He listened to the speech in the
company of the Polish Ambassador; Britain and France had gone to war
because of Germany's attack on Poland. He listened to the speech in the

company of Adolph Miller; five Presidents had been served by this econo-mist and member of the Federal Reserve Board.

Frankfurter once wrote of Adolph Miller: "He served under five Presi-dents of varying temperaments and political outlook. With at least three of these he was on intimate personal terms; they drew upon his counsel in good season and bad. To all he gave that rarest aspect of devotion to the Presidential office — courageous candor. To each he told, with surgeon-like truthfulness, exactly what he believed, however unwelcome his analysis and explication of complex issues may have been, and of course always with exquisite courtesy."

And Frankfurter said he would think it the highest honor he ever could receive if he were one day deemed worthy of having these words applied to his own services for successive Presidents, and above all for his services with President Roosevelt.

One curious phrase in Frankfurter's telegram needs explanation — "ap-peal for privileged effort." Roosevelt had appealed to those in the army and navy not to regard it as a sacrifice to serve the United States but as a privi-lege; had appealed to everyone to regard it as no sacrifice to do without many accustomed things but as a privilege. It was in this sense that Frank-furter spoke of "privileged effort."

The next few letters left a deep imprint on history. They begin with a note to Harry Hopkins, expressing concern at his recent illness, and enclos-ing a copy of a memorandum sent to the President. That memorandum reviewed the problems which face a Chief Executive in wartime and urged the appointment of a man of great ability to whom vast powers could be delegated as the President's representative. This led to Mr. Justice Byrnes's resignation from the Supreme Court, in October 1942, and his appoint-ment as director of the Office of Economic Stabilization charged with the most extensive powers over the American economy and the home front. The delay of nearly a year was caused by the difficulty in persuading Con-gress to pass the required legislation. When the Byrnes appointment finally was made, Frankfurter wrote the President that this was the first time in his life that a suggestion which was good for the country was bad for himself. He was devoted to Mr. Justice Byrnes and was losing his "most congenial" colleague on the Supreme Court.

Washington, D.C., December 17, 1941

Dear Harry:

You know what it means to me to hear you are not well. It gives me the deepest possible concern and I hope to Pete it was just a passing thing and that your strength is already replenished and that you are set for the continuing fray.

There are some things that one feels with the utmost conviction and cannot gainsay. A memorandum that I have sent to the President is of that order of conviction. Of course I wanted to tell you about it and share my thoughts with you. Having been unable to do that, I want you to see it. I shall only add that I have naturally thought about *the* right man for the particular job and I have talked to Jim Byrnes about that too and he agrees with me.

Affectionately yours,
FELIX

Washington, D.C., December 17, 1941

Dear Mr. President:

The least I can do is not to waste your time and not be like the fellow whose memorandum Lincoln endorsed "From a young man on how to win the war."

That is not the purpose of this enclosure. But it may not be without value to summarize a good many talks I have had since September 1939 with some of the best brains who were intimately familiar with the defects and inadequacies of the British and French war effort, and to indicate the meaning of their experience to some of the problems that now confront you.

I did not feel justified in relying solely on my own judgment before sending this memorandum to you. I submitted it to Jim Byrnes who asks me to say that he entirely agrees with it and that he looks forward to an early opportunity of talking with you about carrying out the suggestion made in the memorandum.

With affectionate good wishes,

Faithfully yours,
FELIX FRANKFURTER

Frankfurter Memorandum for the President

I

A rapid summary of the basic conditions, familiar though they be, will give the setting to what follows.

All other belligerent countries have already mobilized practically all their resources and man-power. Little expansion of their forces can be expected. Only one major element would add greatly to the resources of the Axis, namely, the conquest of the oil resources of the Caucasus and of the Netherlands. The forces of Great Britain and Russia have also been mobilized. Apparently all that can be expected from them is that they maintain their effort in men and materials.

It is fair to assume that from now on the drive of the Axis will be to use as quickly as possible for some decisive results the instruments of war which they have accumulated. The events of the last ten days offer clear proof that the Axis believe that they have reached a point of maximum mobilization and that they can use these forces successfully before the potentials of this country come into effective operation.

The decisive shift in the development of the conflict is therefore due to the fact that the United States has entered it with its immense potentialities of men and resources, the mobilization of which is only partial as compared with that of the other belligerents. Inevitably, therefore, final victory depends on the speed with which the full forces of this country will be brought into being and how they will be used.

But before they can be used they must exist. This memorandum concerns itself with that problem.

II

Specifically, the experience of other countries since the beginning of the war in achieving effective mobilization of a nation's resources is believed to be relevant to the quickest translation of potentiality into actuality.

France and England were at war in September 1939. French manpower had certainly been mobilized before the war to the full. Her armament effort was far from being mobilized — indeed was only beginning to be mobilized when she was out of the war. England's forces did not begin to be mobilized in full until after the French disaster. Even then it took many months before the production of Great Britain and the utilization of her full resources began to bring real results.

Two fundamental weaknesses explain the course of Britain and French events, according to the analysis of those capable of judging and fearless in doing so:

(1) Lack of a definite goal set by either Great Britain or France at the beginning of their efforts;

(2) Slowness in execution, because the British and French war administration was not organized so as to make quick decisions possible.

The goals to be achieved were devised on the installment plan and the machinery of administration in both countries was constantly stalled because of failure to make or to obtain decisions on major questions in executing paper policies. Two causes were responsible for this state of affairs: (1) the substantial continuance of peacetime governmental machinery for the war effort; and (2) the failure appropriately to differentiate in action between the function of those charged with setting goals to be achieved — policies — and the function of those charged with carrying out these policies and reaching these goals.

Take the French situation. Daladier, at a time when he had almost full power for the conduct of the war, found himself crowded by requests for all sorts of decisions which should have been taken by people in charge of executing policies. As a result, his time and energy became absorbed with settling day-to-day questions leaving him no energy or freshness of thought for the vital problems of the conduct of the war. Daladier was pressed by the various agencies for these day-to-day decisions, partly because the French government had failed to determine in due time the main objectives to be achieved, but partly also because the questions that were put to Daladier involved conflicting or overlapping functions between various agencies of the government. It was necessary to arbitrate between them. Since no one was authorized to act on behalf of Daladier, these questions were constantly thrown up to him.

As to England. The peacetime provision of a system of coordination between the various departments on the one hand, and on the other hand the existence of a War Cabinet with a permanent secretariat, went a good distance toward avoiding the French confusion. But even the British system creaked and crawled because it did not face up to basic requirements, namely, the determination of objectives by the heads of governments not burdened by the responsibility for the details of their execution and the necessary delegation of authority to achieve relentless execution of objectives. British machinery is orderly but slow. While execution of policies has very much improved, the mechanism is still cumbersome and too often creaky.

III

The fact of the matter is that in times of peace the democratic system of administration is purposely so arranged as to assure that decisions are preceded by extensive discussion and their execution is constantly controlled. Ample debate not only enters into devising policy but into executing it. That is not a system designed for war. Problems arising in the mobilization of the resources of the country for the achievement of goals set must be disposed of promptly and the machinery of administration must be so organized as to make this possible. It is essential, therefore, that the organs of government which decide on policies or objectives be not saddled with the task of day-to-day decisions in the execution of policies. Otherwise, men soon find their energies absorbed in making all kinds of decisions, major and minor — deciding questions of policy as well as questions relating to their execution. And in making innumerable decisions on execution, major objectives imperceptibly but inevitably become clouded and lost to view.

IV

What concrete lesson can we learn from these British and French experiences?

The total mobilization of our resources will, of course, touch innumerable phases of our national life. But plainly, the most urgent need is to produce the necessary armaments for war. This is no time for paper plans. But adaptation of means to ends — how to translate policies into ammunition and armaments — is the most exigent and practical of questions. And as British and French experience proves, effective administration plays an indispensable part.

Apply the British and French experience to the realization of our Victory program. This is in process of formulation through the Army and Navy Departments and SPAB, in consultation with our allies. The scope of such a Victory program must of course be determined by the President. The goal once set by him will be turned over for administrative execution. At that stage the present administrative situation bristles with difficulties.

For the agencies dealing with various phases of production are many. But each is under a different authority, none has responsibility for achieving the over-all objective. Appropriations having been ordered by Congress, orders are placed by the Ordnance Divisions of the Army and Navy Departments because the money has been voted to the Army and Navy. But the task of increasing and, in many cases, of creating, the capacity for production of such orders belongs to OPM, while the authority to reduce the civilian production without which increased armament capacity cannot exist, belongs to SPAB. Each one of these agencies will thus deal with the part of the problem which concerns it, but responsibility for the main objective is nowhere except with the President. But in the execution of this objective questions are constantly bound to arise within these agencies but beyond the scope of any. Inescapably, they will be sought to be put before the President for decision. The result will be that many decisions of importance, but nevertheless merely decisions to be taken in carrying out objectives already set by the President, will be delayed or will not be taken without submission to the President.

Either multitudinous decisions will thus be put to the President, submerging him, slowing down execution and subordinating attainment of the main objective, or, if controversies are not brought to the President's attention and decisions upon them do not reflect his will, agencies will not consider them as final. Again delay and confusion are bound to arise.

There does not seem any escape from the conclusion that some one should be capable of acting for the President in seeing that the Victory program adopted by him is promptly and effectively carried out. Such a person would be charged with the over-all view of the program, the execution of which is in the hands of various agencies, and to such a person these various agencies would turn for day-to-day decisions. He would be acting for the President and as such there will arise occasionally great questions for which the President's direct judgment and decision would be necessary. He would be the eyes and ears for the President on the various phases of the program through whom the President would get a whole picture without himself doing the picture puzzle. He would be an instrument of the centralized execution of the President's will — an instrument of dispatch, concentration and responsibility.

As the war develops, there may arise other phases of the war administration for translating the President's will into day-to-day execution through a single channel of normal communication between him and the myriad agencies for achieving high objectives without unduly drawing on the strength and vision of the President for tasks that are his and his alone, not merely as President but as Commander-in-Chief. But the translation of the Victory program from things on paper to actualities is an immediate problem for effective administration.

Washington, D.C., December 18, 1941

Dear Felix:

I have read your note. I know it is important. Do not be impatient.

Very cordially yours,
HARRY

Washington, D.C., December 19, 1941

Dear Harry:

If what I wrote conveyed any impatience, it completely misrepresented my feelings. I am not "impatient." You know how deep my feelings of confidence have been right along. They are deeper than ever — considering the marvelous direction since December 7th.

It is not impatience that makes me so sure that the analysis I made is correct, and I know full well that no one has a keener sense than you that time is of the essence.

My best to you always,

Ever yours,
FELIX

Telegram to Roosevelt
Washington, D.C., December 18, 1941

YOUR KELLY LETTER WILL LIVE IN HISTORY WITH THE BIXBY LETTER.

FELIX FRANKFURTER

President Roosevelt's Kelly letter, which Frankfurter compared with Lincoln's letter to Mrs. Bixby, read as follows:

To the President of the United States in 1956:

I am writing this letter as an act of faith in the destiny of our country. I desire to make a request which I make in full confidence that we shall achieve a glorious victory in the war we now are waging to preserve our democratic way of life.

My request is that you consider the merits of a young American youth of goodly heritage — Colin P. Kelly III — for appointment as a cadet in the United States Military Academy at West Point. I make this appeal in behalf of the youth as a token of the Nation's appreciation of the heroic services of his father, who met death in the line of duty at the very outset of the struggle which was thrust upon us by the perfidy of a professed friend.

In the conviction that the service and example of Capt. Colin P. Kelly Jr. will be long remembered, I ask for this commission in behalf of Colin P. Kelly III.

FRANKLIN D. ROOSEVELT

Washington, D.C., December 23, 1941

Dear Mr. President:

The enclosed was dictated from New York over the phone by Dorothy Thompson. She feels deeply that a desperate feeling is now animating the German people and she is sure that it can be influenced enormously by what you say, and only by what you say.

Therefore she believes that you could utter a Christmas message that would have special influence with the German people while, at the same time, it would give the right spiritual pitch to our own purposes in the conflict.

I took this up with Bob Sherwood and was to have placed the enclosure in his hands but, through some unexplained mishap, an appointment between him and me miscarried.

I truly hate to break in on you now on a day like this, but Dorothy Thompson was so earnest in her conviction and what she has written can be so quickly appraised by you, that I am sending it to you.

With devoted regards,

Ever yours,
F.F.

Nearly two thousand years ago, in the days of the decline of a vast Empire that could truly boast that it ruled the world, a Child was born in a stable in a remote Roman province, a refugee Child whose mother bore Him among cattle because cattle were kinder than men. He lived obscurely amongst workers, he preached that God is a Spirit and that they worship Him who worship in spirit and in truth. He declared that there was one race — humanity; that the pure would see God and the meek inherit the earth. He told the poor and the downtrodden that they were the Sons of God and the heirs to His Kingdom. He prayed that men should be given their daily bread and forgiven their trespasses as they forgave the trespasses of others and that the Kingdom of God should come on earth as in Heaven.

He was martyred in order to appease His enemies. And he was thought to have been liquidated from history as He bled to death upon a cross.

But His life on earth did not end upon the cross, but upon the mountain. Only a handful of people has ever known Him. Yet they knew that God had walked among them in Him who preached that God lived in men. Caesar and Pilate, Herod and the men of the Sanhedrin all are dust, alive only in the pages of history books. But throughout the world, during an age longer than that of any Empire, men still acknowledge His sway, own His call, and test their lives by His.

Tonight on His birthday, while the battle rages over all the globe; while men freeze in their own blood in the depths of Russia; and mingle their sweat with blood in the African desert; and purple with their blood the seven seas; while hearts break at every fireside; while British boys and German boys repine in prison camps, and the lads of Italy fight a war long since senseless to them; and the children of France and Spain have no bread to break at a Christmas meal in His name; and American homes are under the darkness of the shadow that has come to us too, I remember that I am President of a country that acknowledges that there is but one King for men, and He is God.

It may seem strange that men should fight in order to take from other men the lands of their fathers, in order to take the bread from other men's mouths. Surely they are driven by some incomprehensible, some major delusion. Surely they must sometimes remember that those five loaves and three small fishes fed a multitude when they were gathered together in brotherhood. And surely they must now see that the riches of kingdoms, the wealth of all the nations, is insufficient to nourish starving children when men raise a sword between themselves.

I speak for a nation unique among the nations of men, representative of all the peoples of the old world, who set up a covenant in the wilderness, and pledged themselves to live as free and equal men in the light of God's law. I speak for Americans whose blood is that of Briton and French, Germans and Italians, Russians and Greeks, Serbs and Scandinavians, Chinese and Japanese, Jews and Spaniards, Portuguese and Irish, white and black, who here have sought to build a state in which men might find freedom in the brotherhood of life. That we have sometimes forgotten this covenant is true. That we have done much that we should not have done and left undone much that we should have done, is true. Yet in our hours of greatest trial we have been sustained by the covenant which we took in our beginnings with God and with mankind.

Now this nation, the last to be attacked, attacked like all the others, in a moment when we were striving for peace — peace and justice too — takes up the fight with all its strength and with all its heart and with all its soul — the fight for liberation and the fight for peace, the fight to dispel the darkness, and with the help of God, to bring redemption to the nation of His children, and a just and lasting peace to all mankind.

The Critical Year

1942

This was truly the critical year. Japan before the beginning of March had captured Singapore; landed on Borneo, the Solomon Islands, New Guinea, New Britain; sunk the Prince of Wales *battleship on which the Atlantic Charter had been drafted; and begun to menace the Mid-Pacific, India and Australia. In Europe, Germany still ruled the Continent, with Russia pleading in vain for an early Second Front, for which Britain and the United States were not yet ready.*

1942

January 15   *Inter-American conference opens in Rio de Janeiro to draw up plans for protection of American republics against aggression.*

February 1   *Quisling, a German puppet, becomes virtual dictator of Norway.*

May 26   *Churchill and Molotov sign twenty-year mutual aid treaty between Britain and Russia.*

June 9   *United States and Britain agree to pool all resources of food and production.*

June 18   *Churchill comes to Washington to confer with Roosevelt.*

November 8   *United States forces land in French North Africa.*

WITH 1942 the correspondence between Roosevelt and Frankfurter changes its character abruptly and irrevocably. The President becomes the Commander-in-Chief. As for Frankfurter, he no longer fears that Nazi Germany — "organized evil" to him — will be suffered to enslave Europe while America timidly purchases a temporary safety for herself by a selfish and shortsighted neutrality.

With 1942 we face a new agenda, new issues, a new vocabulary of politics, almost a new cast of characters. Gone forever is the old debate about embargoes and neutrality, appeasement and isolation. Those slogans are heard no more. They died when the guns roared at Pearl Harbor.

With 1942 we see Washington crowded with business leaders eager to give their genius for organization and administration to their country's cause. Many of them are Republicans. They had already opposed Roosevelt three times and perhaps a large number of them were to oppose him the fourth time. But in these tragic and embattled years he is their Commander-in-Chief and so they stand at his side.

With 1942 the Republican party puts aside selfish political sniping. Partisanship is not altogether adjourned for the duration. Human nature in politics is not quite capable of that nobility. But the political debate is cleansed of its ancient bitterness. Wendell Willkie towers into a great national leader. Months later Roosevelt could think for a time of a new party, combining the progressive Republicans and Democrats under the leadership of himself and Willkie. The change is so gradual yet so pervasive that Senator Vandenberg, once the unrepentant leader of Republican isolationism, can emerge by the end of the war as the supreme symbol of a bipartisan foreign policy dedicated to a partnership for peace in cooperation with many nations.

With 1942 the importance of trade unions becomes absolutely critical. Output soars until all records are broken; but sometimes the strain on labor-management relations becomes so harsh that the restraints of reason snap. Trouble in the factory, on the railroad, in the coal mines cannot be tolerated; but signs of trouble grow and spread. Frankfurter had spent his life as a friend of labor; he had helped write the Norris–La Guardia labor law; but he knew no loyalty to labor when the country was in danger and obstinate union leaders were blind to that danger. He consistently offered advice to Roosevelt that he summed up in these words — "Use your friendship with

labor to get tough with the unions when union leaders forget their duty."
There is a letter for this year in which Frankfurter speaks as roughly of
certain labor leaders as he ever did of some business leaders. He actually
advises Roosevelt to call the foremost union leaders in the country to the
White House and then "knock their heads together" to prevent the na-
tional cause from being injured by needless quarrels.

With 1942 the partnership between Britain and America is replaced by
the Grand Alliance. A year earlier, Churchill and Roosevelt signed the At-
lantic Charter. In 1942 we have the United Nations declaration.

With 1942 we also have the beginning of Russia's vehement demand for
an invasion of Europe. What is Churchill doing, Stalin asked, in keeping
all those troops in England when it is impossible for Germany to invade the
island while so many Nazi divisions are fighting in Russia? By what account-
ancy of statesmanship does Roosevelt equate the provision of guns and
tanks with the torrents of Russian blood? Russia is a necessary ally, a heroic
ally, but an ally troublesome beyond belief.

With 1942 we come to the year, as Roosevelt told Frankfurter, in which
it is easy to lose the war. For the dictator states are fully organized and
implacably strong while America is still only half-ready. The supreme task
before America is to buy time by giving up territory, if necessary, but to use
every minute of that precious time to prepare for the day when great battles
will produce the ultimate victory.

With 1942, even as the defeats and retreats multiplied, Roosevelt began
to feel the sinews of war growing in his hands. We have edited our memo-
ries, most of us, about what happened after Pearl Harbor. We have allowed
ourselves to imagine that we rushed at our tormentors with a roar of right-
eous anger and inflicted immediate and terrible retribution on them. The
real story is very different, and in its way even more heroic though less
dramatic. It is the story of how America worked and suffered, lost battles
but never its courage, and with agonizing cost swept forward always against
forces staking everything now on a supreme gamble for swift victory. It is a
year, for America, of defeat, of production, and of preparation. It is the year
which marks the slow and hard turning from the great defeats to the grand
advance.

Churchill and Roosevelt arranged for the declaration by the United Na-
tions to be published on the first day of the New Year to signify their faith
in the peaceful world that would follow the long months of ruin and blood-
shed. They wanted to give the subjugated nations the incentive of hope so
that they would not be broken by Nazi or Japanese tyranny. The phrase
the "United Nations" was invented by Roosevelt and met with Churchill's
eager approval. But victory was a distant prospect in 1942.

Washington, D.C., January 3, 1942

Dear Frank:

You saw the meaning of Hitlerism from the very beginning of his accession to power. When others, who should have known better, were blinder than bats — for they would not see — you realized that Hitler's treatment of the Jews was not just another pogrom, but the first stage of his warfare against civilization. You saw it all — and largely in lonely statesmanship.

And so, for eight years you had the task of educating your countrymen — and some of your close collaborators — to *your* insight, so that action could keep pace with insight. It's been a long, long trail — and only insight combined with *active* patience, resourcefulness, faith and courage could have achieved the wonderful goal of the Declaration by United Nations!

What a sure summons that is for the dedication of "our lives, our fortunes, and sacred honor" — but also what a harbinger of sure victory against the forces of brutal darkness and of hope that the awful cost has possibilities of a world more securely and more sanely founded than ever before.

With devoted good wishes,

Affectionately yours,
F.F.

Washington, D.C., January 5, 1942

Dear Frank:

"Martin, Barton and Fish" evokes most exciting memories. But that delectable volume of your campaign speeches does much more — it stirs me with fresh delight. Those speeches are alive, even on the printed page. And what an opening, that historic speech spoken to Chicago in the early morning hour — and the serenity of spirit in the Hyde Park talk to your friends: the people of the United States.

I shall treasure that volume all my days, and I shall treasure it for the past, present and future that it carries. Not least, because it epitomizes so beautifully and bravely the days and years that lie ahead:

"And I will not stop fighting."

Gratefully yours,
FELIX FRANKFURTER

Roosevelt sent Frankfurter a beautifully bound volume of some of his best speeches in his three Presidential campaigns. The first speech was his acceptance speech on July 2, 1932, to the Chicago convention which had nominated him for the Presidency. Breaking with tradition, he did not stay at home waiting for a delegation to tell him that he had been nominated. Instead, he flew to Chicago where the delegates, weary after a convention that had already lasted six days, waited patiently for the delayed plane. They were rewarded by hearing Roosevelt say, "I pledge you, I pledge myself, to a new deal for the American people."

In the 1940 campaign, Wendell Willkie, for some strange reason, singled out Rep. Joseph Martin for high praise. This irritated the President, who regarded Rep. Martin as a stubborn isolationist with a very bad voting record. He quietly meditated a stroke of revenge. In Madison Square Garden on October 28, 1940, he reviewed the record. He pointed out that the Republicans, despite what Willkie and others were now saying, had opposed the repeal of the embargo on the shipment of arms and munitions to nations at war, and to permit such shipments on a "cash-and-carry basis." In the Senate the Republicans voted 14–6 against repeal. In the House they voted 140–19 against it.

"The Act," said Roosevelt, "was passed by Democratic votes but it was over the opposition of the Republican leaders. And just to name a few, the following Republican leaders, among many others, voted against the Act: Senators McNary, Vandenberg, Nye and Johnson; now wait, a perfectly beautiful rhythm — Congressmen Martin, Barton and Fish."

And so it went on, with the crowd next time chanting the names of "Martin, Barton and Fish." The President was immensely proud of this thrust which was repeated for the rest of the campaign.

It was at this same meeting that Roosevelt first was greeted with huge banners bearing the slogan: "We love you for the enemies you have made." This was, he said, the people's reward for his pledge that "I have only begun to fight and I will not stop fighting."

Frankfurter deliberately tried to break the strain for the President, in these grim times, by showing him a letter from the Adjutant General, drafted with a shapeless lack of grace and knowledge, informing him that the work he was doing on the Supreme Court was sufficiently important to excuse him from military service.

The President needed a moment's ease, for 1942 was to be a year, as he said, of "formidable odds and recurring defeats." Only a man of Roosevelt's serene spirit could have relished lighthearted letters, at such a time, and written them himself.

Washington, D.C., January 13, 1942

My dear C-i-C:

Marion says that she is "relieved" by the assurances of the enclosed letter but that is not the way I feel about it. An Adjutant General who finds that what I am doing is "very important work" at this time is much too soft for my taste.

Respectfully and martially yours,
FELIX FRANKFURTER

The White House, January 16, 1942

Dear Major: —

This indecision on your part greatly disappoints me. As your Commander-in-Chief I want you to know that I believe you would look awfully well in uniform, for you have retained a remarkable figure considering your age. I suggest you leave this problem up to Marion. Borrow a uniform, show yourself to her in it, and let her infinitely greater wisdom decide on whether you should heed your country's call or continue your persistent evasion of the draft.

Incidentally, I need a Judge Advocate at Samoa. If you act fast you may get there just ahead of its capture by the Japs. Or, as an alternative, I will appoint you as a parachutist to drop in on Wake Island from the sky and re-capture it singlehanded. Then, you could be buried in Arlington — the ultimate goal of every good soldier.

As ever yours,
FRANKLIN D. ROOSEVELT

Washington, D.C., January 20, 1942

Dear C-i-C:

Correspondence with the Commander-in-Chief, even the most beloved, is bound to be a one-way street. The only possible chance for a poor Major, particularly a judicial major, is to shift the discussion to a more spiritual level. I can't quite do that — but I am eager to shift it to a spiritous level! This I can do — if you will let me.

I have in my keeping a really precious bottle, which I am charged with giving to you personally. I am yours to command any morning after breakfast — for Court is not now in session — or some night when you have time and desire for nothing in particular.

With devoted regards,

Ever yours,
F.F.

Washington, D.C., January 17, 1942

Dear Frank:

A fellow on the bleachers sometimes sees a good deal of the game. It is not wholly out of ignorance that I want to tell you how happy your anouncement on Production has made me — for your personal sake no less than the country's.

It took Lincoln three years to discover Grant, and you may not have hit on your production Grant first crack out of the box. But the *vital* thing is that you have created the function — the function of one exclusive, "final" delegate of your authority. It's simply grand — indispensable for *your* conduct of the war.

Ever yours,
F.F.

The War Production Board was established by Roosevelt on January 16 with Donald Nelson as its first chairman. This was really not all that Frankfurter had wanted in his memorandum to Roosevelt and Harry Hopkins advocating the selection of an official with the delegated authority from the President to make important decisions for the home front. But he had learned from the President that progress toward the full plan would have to be made by stages. He therefore welcomed the President's formation of the War Production Board, with wide powers to its chairman, as a necessary first measure. Donald Nelson turned out to be a useful and memorable official but no production Grant.

Washington, D.C., January 17, 1942

Dear Frank:

Owen Roberts is, as you well know, the most forthright of men. But he is not only — thank God! — very modest. He is also truly shy. And so I venture to suggest that you get him alone, and not with the other members of his Board, to tell you of things that have no proper place in their report — particularly on matters of personnel pertaining not to the past but to what lies ahead.

Gosh — what a truly wonderful thing your last address to Congress was. I have just re-read it before filing it. That was "On the State of the World" — and for all times!

Devotedly,
F.F.

Frankfurter was always quite impenitent about his part in arranging for Mr. Justice Roberts to make a personal report to the President on the immediate events that led to Pearl Harbor, and what happened after the attack began. He was afraid of a vindictive search for scapegoats diverting the nation's attention from more important tasks. He respected the right of Congress to conduct ample and vigilant investigations; but he was fearful that Roosevelt's authority might be compromised by a meddlesome Con-

*gressional committee as Lincoln's had been in the Civil War. The later
controversy over Pearl Harbor, and its echoes to this day, prove that his
fears were not without substance. As it happened, Roosevelt, after listening
to Mr. Justice Roberts, decided that all the really essential information
should be put in the written report and arranged for its early publication.
But to this day there is an obstinate suspicion in Congress, especially among
those who sat on the investigating committees, that Congress never got the
full story about Pearl Harbor.*

*Roosevelt's State of the Union Message had been a report on what had
now become a World War. "The militarists of Berlin and Tokyo," the
President said, "started this war. But the massed, angered forces of common humanity will finish it."*

The White House, January 21, 1942

Dear Felix:

You certainly know your cheeses! It is delicious and I am keeping it for
very special occasions. You were grand to think of me. My best to you.

As ever,

FRANKLIN D. ROOSEVELT

Telegram to Roosevelt

Washington, D.C., January 25, 1942

WARM CONGRATULATIONS ON YOUR IMMEDIATE RELEASE OF ROBERTS REPORT.
OF COURSE YOU WOULD.

FELIX FRANKFURTER

The White House, January 26, 1942

Dear Felix:

I am glad you approve so heartily of my release of the Roberts report.
Thank you for telling me as you do in your very kind telegram.

Very sincerely yours,

FRANKLIN D. ROOSEVELT

Washington, D.C., January 28, 1942

And what joy you would have given, Dear Frank, to T. Jefferson also in
your role of book-architect! But if it be arrogant to speak for Jefferson's
spirit, it is only simple truth to tell you what exquisite and enduring pleasure you have given me with that thin but noble volume of your devising —
so worthily giving physical permanence to utterances that summarize wonderful aspects of world history and that will fortify the spirit of man for all
time.

I rejoice, too, that you joined Churchill with you in your volume. If we

cannot resolutely be determined to work out the world's destiny together
with the British, what hope can there be of working it out *not* in comradeship with them?!

Many, many thanks for your so cherished token of your friendship.

Devotedly yours,
F.F.

Washington, D.C., January 30, 1942

Dear Frank:

You are the Nation's pace-maker, and so I too, am included. But you
are my pace-maker in a special sense. For in the race of your decade I am
also an entry — a late and limping entry, almost left at the post, but in it I
am. And so you have served for me, these many years, as a pace-maker of
how life should be lived — in joy and gaiety, in stress and sorrow, on the
sidelines and at the controls of destiny.

This is a day for thinking of you as a fellow human and as a friend who
has proven beyond compare that to him that hath life, life shall be given —
and life so abundant is the gracious gift to the world.

In simplest words, this brings you the love of Marion and Felix.

F.F.

*Frankfurter always used the occasion of Roosevelt's birthday to write to
him in terms of personal affection, a greeting to a friend as well as a salute
to the President.*

Washington, D.C., February 10, 1942

Dear Frank:

You asked me to remind you of the remark I made over the phone last
night that "this is a war for democracy, not for the Democratic party" —
with your etc.

Your return of H.R. 6269 without approval was an added good deed
on your heavy-laden Monday.

Marion and I hope that you have good news of Franklin. We send you
our affectionate thoughts.

It was grand to have had a few words with you.

Ever devotedly,
F.F.

*The President on February 10 had vetoed the alien registration act be-
cause it seemed to him that the amendments, if left unrebuked, would*

encourage repressive and illiberal measures. He remembered the intolerant years which followed the First World War, and he had no wish to leave a similar legacy. On the surface the issue was narrow and technical: the necessity of freeing aliens with non-diplomatic status, but often engaged in essential war work, from the restrictions that were appropriate in the days of peace. But Roosevelt so handled the entire controversy, and dramatized it for the public, that it became another lesson in tolerance.

Washington, D.C., February 12, 1942

Dear C-i-C:

Please let a mere and much reserved major tell you with what joy I read of your designation of the Dutch Admiral as Naval Chief in the Pacific area. I assume that he is the best equipped man for those difficult and treacherous waters. But it is also a fine, concrete proof in action that we *are* the United Nations, and that the common Cause, not national pride nor bigness nor history, will determine the execution of a unified strategy.

Respectfully and affectionately,
F.F.

Washington, D.C., February 24, 1942

Dear Frank:

Marion and I wanted to listen to you all by ourselves — we had such a sense of the intimate austerity of the occasion. There was a deep silence between us as you finished — as is the case when feeling and reflection commune all one's inner energies and nothing is left for words. The silence was at last broken by Marion's "What courage he has — and how it sustains our people."

The silence in words that fall upon us, as you finished, is still within me. I feel that the only adequate response to the strength that you instill is to put forth strength to the only Cause there is now, the only fit appreciation of the faith you fortify is to prove it by works. How I wish I might ease your burdens ever so little — serenely and gallantly as you bear them. And the United Nations shall call him blessed — as in the not too distant future the nations of the world shall call him blessed.

Ever yours,
F.F.

President Roosevelt chose Washington's Birthday to make what may well have been the greatest speech of his life. It was the Roosevelt equivalent of Churchill's "Blood, toil, tears and sweat."

Ever since Pearl Harbor, the tide of disaster had rolled on. Indeed, it seemed to grow worse. Meanwhile, the talk in Washington was of production charts and a long war. The American people, stung by the defeat and humiliation, were hungry for a dramatic victory. But no victory was in sight.

Roosevelt sensed this mood and knew its dangers. He decided to broadcast to the nation and speak with unprecedented candor on the course of the war — the losses, the casualties, the mistakes, the problems, the hopes. Above all, he wanted to explain, in words that every American home would understand, why it was necessary to give such urgent emphasis to the production of war goods.

Production was the key to victory. He had already pledged himself to preside over a production effort that would enable us to "out-produce our enemies" and maintain a steadily increasing and inexorable supply to "every theatre of the war." That was a formidable undertaking. It was, in fact, without precedent in the history of war. No other nation had ever tried it. Britain in the years of her world leadership had never accepted so extensive a commitment. Germany coveted the domination of Europe and the Atlantic community. Japan wanted to control Asia. But Roosevelt had pledged America to fight all the aggressive dictator states, to push them back from the lands they had shamed and plundered, to fight them everywhere, and at last to beat them all into submission. First Germany and Italy; then Japan. That was the scale of priorities. It also was a relentless commitment.

The first duty of the President, in these challenging anxieties, was to "trust the people." Americans could "hear the worst, without flinching or losing heart." For in a "time of crisis, when the future is in the balance, we come to understand, with full recognition and devotion, what this nation is, and what we owe to it."

Roosevelt had asked the newspapers to print maps of the world so that people listening to him could quickly follow his description of the countries in the various theaters of war. He was most anxious to have the country understand why it was necessary for the United States to fight over such vast distances, and how difficult but essential it was to sustain and nourish our supply routes with Britain and Russia and China — not to mention the embattled American garrisons fighting so gallantly against unbelievable odds in the Pacific.

This was the year when the dictators would make their strongest thrust for victory, since they knew that America would grow more powerful with every passing month, and they were resolved to strike first and strike hard. So the American people had to work hard, take their defeats, and work even harder — perhaps a harsher task than the one which faced the British *people during the Battle of Britain. For there would be none of the shared exultation of the British people when the bombs fell and the country braced itself to beat back the anticipated German invasion.*

Frankfurter heard all these thoughts from the President's own lips a few days before the great speech was delivered. In a brief memorandum of this conversation, Frankfurter said he had never seen such "solemnity" in the President. Roosevelt estimated that the war might last another three years — an amazingly accurate guess in early 1942 but one which depressed Frankfurter. At one point in the conversation Frankfurter said: "You remember Pascal's saying that force and right rule this world — force till the right is ready. Our task is to put force behind the right and make it prevail." The President asked Frankfurter to repeat these words, and then he wrote them down on a piece of paper and read them aloud to himself. "Yes, that's it. That's it exactly," the President said very slowly.

Roosevelt spoke to the nation, that somber night, while American troops were still fighting on Corregidor.

"Germany, Italy and Japan," he said, "are very close to their maximum output of planes, guns, tanks and ships. The United Nations are not — especially the United States of America. Our first job then is to build up production so that the United Nations can maintain control of the seas and attain control of the air — not merely a slight superiority, but an overwhelming superiority."

The closing words rang out like the chords of a great symphony:

The task that we Americans now face will test us to the uttermost.

Never before have we been called upon for such a prodigious effort. Never before have we had so little time in which to do so much.

These are the times that try men's souls.

Tom Paine wrote these words on a drum-head by the light of a camp-fire. That was when Washington's little army of ragged, rugged men were retreating across New Jersey, having tasted nothing but defeat.

And General Washington ordered that these great words written by Tom Paine be read to the men of every regiment in the Continental Army, and this was the assurance given to the first American Armed Forces:

"The summer soldier and the sunshine patriot will, in this crisis, shrink from the service of their country; but he that stands it now, deserves the love and thanks of man and woman. Tyranny, like hell, is not easily conquered; yet we have this consolation with us, that the harder the sacrifice, the more glorious the triumph."

So spoke Americans in the year 1776.

So speak Americans today!

Washington, D.C., March 4, 1933-1942

Dear Frank:

Just a word of affectionate greeting on your Presidential birthday. The unprecedented tenure is symbolic of the intrinsic uniquity (to use a Holmesian word) for which you are destined in history.

With deepest good wishes,

Devotedly yours,
FELIX FRANKFURTER

Frankfurter once found Mr. Justice Holmes's word in a dictionary, when challenged to do so by Mr. Justice Black, so it had better be accepted as valid verbal tender.

As Britain lost Singapore and Burma, and as Japan began to threaten the safety of Australia, anxious questions were asked in Australia about the wisdom of British strategy and the use of Australian forces. Churchill, burdened grievously as few statesmen have ever been burdened, was not always wise or conciliatory in his replies.

The Australian government began to think of a new association with the United States — an association which continues to this hour — and it made its first overtures through Frankfurter.

That should surprise no one who knew anything of his relationship with influential Australian figures over many years. He made the Australian law reports compulsory reading. Every Australian Ambassador in Washington, without exception, was his close friend; the last one before Frankfurter's death, Sir Howard Beale, being the closest of all. Sir Owen Dixon, Chief Justice of Australia, and one of the foremost judges of this century in the entire English-speaking world, was a deeply cherished friend. Frankfurter had a voluminous correspondence with Sir Robert Menzies, Australia's leading statesman. Mr. Herbert V. Evatt, a respected legal scholar before he entered politics and became Minister for External Affairs in Australia's labor government, was an old friend. Frankfurter eased the negotiations for the visits to Roosevelt of Prime Minister Curtin and Evatt — visits which were extremely successful, as will be seen. This letter to Harry Hopkins marks the beginning of Frankfurter's helpful intervention in putting Australia's case.

Washington, D.C., March 9, 1942

Dear Harry:

I have another long telegram from Evatt. It deals with the Australian–New Zealand proposals for command in the Pacific in view of the new situation. Churchill, I assume, has already put, or will put, these to the

President, so I shall spare you the details of Evatt's message unless you desire them.

Inasmuch as I am probably the only person in Washington with whom Evatt has a sense of intimacy, it is not too difficult to understand why, considering the pressures of his situation, he wires me. You will agree, therefore, that to cable him what I most feel like saying, namely, "What the hell — why do you turn to me?" would risk being wholly misunderstood across seven thousand miles. And so until I can talk to him face to face when he gets here, the wise thing seems to me to express appropriate sympathy, to give him my wholly private assurance that his situation is being impartially and sympathetically taken into account, and to withhold any comment on the merits of his proposals.

To that end I have drafted the enclosed cable and shall send it tomorrow morning unless in the meantime I hear from you to the contrary.

Ever yours,

F.F.

Washington, D.C., March 12, 1942

Dear Mr. President:

You once wrote me something that I deeply cherish. You called me "an independent pig," and added, "That is one reason why I like you." Therefore you do not have to be told that, much as I love Bob Sherwood, even he could not seduce me with a suggestion unless I truly believed it to be right. And so when he suggested Elmer Davis to head up Information something clicked in me and I just know it is right — and right for you from every angle.

I therefore venture to express the hope that you will put this through — not merely to beat Congress to it but as a positive and effective instrument of the psychological aspect of war. And of course Information, as all else in this total warfare, has to be total Information — domestic as well as foreign — recognizing the unity of the United Nations.

With warmest regards,

Faithfully yours,

F.F.

Robert E. Sherwood, the playwright who had become a speech writer for the President, was a favorite with Frankfurter, as was Elmer Davis, the courageous journalist and radio commentator. From this mixture it was almost inevitable, as Frankfurter suggested, that Elmer Davis should emerge as the head of the Office of War Information.

We come now to the letter in which Frankfurter lashes out at the blind bickerings of labor leaders. The three chief characters are Philip Murray,

Sidney Hillman, and John L. Lewis. The Secretary of Labor is Miss Frances Perkins.

Washington, D.C., March 20, 1942

Dear Frank:

Here are some notes for a program to be put up to Murray and Hillman. I feel more and more strongly that only by their *positive* action can foolish legislation and friction be overcome, and John L. kept in durance vile.

It was simply grand yesterday! I came away as though I had drunk from that '65 bottle — and was still under the "infloooence" when I came home in the evening and gave Marion an account of it. You seemed so superbly fit.

And Oliver told his sisters that "Uncle Felix says that the President sent all of us his regards!!"

Ever yours,
F.F.

Frankfurter Memorandum for the President

From those who are experienced in such matters, I get a sense of great confusion in the day-to-day relationship of labor with the government.

This confusion does not come from a lack of loyalty or devotion to the war among the workers. Nor is there wanting any confidence in your complete understanding and sympathy. Quite the contrary. Never before have the workers, and their leaders — with the one exception of Lewis — been so united as they are today under your leadership.

Yet there is a deep sense of dissatisfaction — a feeling that labor isn't yet giving its maximum contribution to the nation's effort. Labor's program is still considerably in a negative stage — that is, the labor leaders are relying on you to defend them from their enemies, rather than putting forward on the workers' behalf a positive program to help you deal with issues of inflation, wage and price policy and manpower allocation, etc.

Behind these inhibitions is primarily a conflict of two personalities, both loyal to you, both wanting passionately to win the war.

Murray, emotional, deeply devout, and somewhat mystical, is torn by inner conflicts. On the one hand, he is suspicious and jealous of Hillman, of whose position as your chosen labor representative in the government, he is deeply jealous. On the other hand, he has just broken a relationship of almost lifelong loyalty to John Lewis and the psychological effect of that relationship is etched deep in his personality.

Each step is haunted by the fear that somehow Lewis will be able successfully to say that by following you and supporting the war, he has obtained less for labor than Lewis would have got by fighting you and sabotaging the war. This explains, for instance, Murray's passionate unwillingness to deal with the "little steel" wage controversy as anything more than an individual dispute. He fears that Lewis may be able to say that the miners got one dollar a day wage increase under his leadership, while Murray was only able to get a pittance for the steel workers.

It is only when fear of Lewis reduces him to the last extremity, as in the case of the peace negotiations, that Murray turns to Hillman for help and attempts to cooperate with him. On other occasions, he snipes at Hillman and simply thinks of him in the same terms as Lewis thinks of Hillman.

On the other hand, Hillman has faults to which Murray can point in justification for his criticism. Unquestionably, his leadership during the past two years has not been so bold as the times required. This, however, is understandable. When he first went on to the Defense Commission, neither wing of labor was wholeheartedly back of your foreign policy. John L. Lewis, still the dominant figure in the CIO, devoted his entire energy to the destruction of Hillman, whom he characterized as "the President's stooge in the labor movement." There is no question but that these constant attacks have exasperated Hillman's inferiority complexes and produced in him an unfortunate timidity and ineptitude, deriving basically from lack of self-confidence.

Consequently, the government's whole dealing with labor is shot throughout with intrigue and petty political maneuvering.

A typical case is that of the Detroit Tool Makers. One of the severest labor bottlenecks in Detroit was that of tool and die makers and an intensive upgrading program was necessary. If this was to be achieved, it was necessary to have a wage stabilization agreement, so as to equalize wages in the various jobs and prevent the piracy of labor by one employer from another. Hillman went to Detroit and negotiated an agreement by which certain "captive shops" agreed to raise their wages to a level equal to that paid in the other shops. On the other hand, the workers agreed not to ask for further wage increases. The employers accepted this arrangement only on condition that these increases not be used as a precedent by other groups of workers in the industry in seeking for wage increases.

In direct violation of this agreement a group of workers in the same union persuaded the Secretary of Labor to call a similar conference in Detroit to effect a stabilization agreement for the maintenance workers. As a result of this action by the Secretary of Labor, the employers walked out on Hillman, and upgrading of tool makers was delayed for nearly a month until he could work out a new agreement.

The same thing has happened with the question of double time for

Sundays and holidays. Almost immediately after Pearl Harbor, Hillman worked out an agreement in the shipyards by which double time was eliminated unless the worker actually worked seven successive days. He planned to extend this to other industries. Meanwhile, the Secretary of Labor, acting at the instance of the Navy Department, called separate conferences to abrogate such overtime on a nation-wide basis, and as a result neither Hillman nor the Secretary of Labor was able to handle the problem which was tossed into the lap of the War Labor Board, where it still remains.

There is one promising solution. That is for you to call Hillman and Murray together privately and to knock their heads together. If labor is to play its role in this war, then these two men must be brought into cooperation. Only you, whom they both respect and to whom they are both devoted, can accomplish this. So far as the mass of workers are concerned, you are the only leader of the labor movement in the United States today. The strength and power of every labor leader is conditioned by your support and blessing. Only you, in a direct, intimate conference with these two men, can force them to overcome their petty inhibitions and small suspicions so that together they may lead labor effectively in cooperation with the Administration.

Washington, D.C., March 31, 1942

Dear Frank:

The attached letter was written yesterday to await your return. Although your action on the Australian Council has "killed" it, I send it as a way of expressing my happiness over your action.

Whenever you can run off for a few days to Hyde Park it's good for the Nation.

Ever devotedly,
F.F.

Washington, D.C., March 30, 1942

Dear Mr. President:

To use Churchill's phrase to Curtin in the reverse, I am *not* courting a rebuke in venturing to say a word about Evatt's mission.

You know how sensitive poor relations are — and the Australians feel like poor relations. What is needed is to satisfy them psychologically. In giving them the status of recognized and regularized participation in the process of making decisions that they deem vital to themselves, it seems relevant to recall Balfour's remark that equality of status does not mean equality of function. I really think you would be less troubled by some regular opportunity for Australia to have its views enter into ultimate decisions than to have irritations kept alive and intermittently renewed. As

Holmes used to say when a particularly difficult case was up, "Surely a form of words can be found."

It is perfectly plain that Evatt is most eager to play ball and has a fair perspective of the total situation. He said a poignantly moving thing the other night at a private dinner given him by the Council on Foreign Relations in New York, at which I presided. After stating the special situation of Australia, he said, very quietly, "Please, gentlemen, don't misunderstand me. If I have to choose between my country going under and England going under, I should want my country to go under. For England is the bastion of us all." And that is really his deep conviction, as I know from intimate talks with him on the basis of old friendship.

Needless to say, neither Evatt nor anyone else has the slightest notion that I am writing this to you, or will know that I have written.

Faithfully yours,
F.F.

Washington, D.C. April 15, 1942

Dear Mr. President:

The paragraph quoted below comes to me in a letter from Frank Buxton regarding a recent meeting at the Examiner Club — one of those old dining clubs in Boston going back to the days of the Adamses, the meetings of which were among the real pleasures I had to forego when I came down here. Dr. Park, to whom Buxton refers, is Dr. Charles E. Park, the minister of the First Unitarian Church in Boston:

"Dr. Park, whom you know as a cultured, fine-souled, able fellow, read a paper at the Examiner Club two or three months ago in regard to the evolution of the clipper ship. He began with the opium war in China and after sketching developments on the Chinese coast which were closely related to sailing vessels, told of the changes which the English and the Americans had made in their sailing craft. Among his slides was one showing the signature of the President's mother as supercargo on a vessel bound for China. He told what he knew about her and said that the log or a reproduction of it has come to the attention of the President — perhaps is in his possession. If the President cares to forget the trollops of the movies and the beguiling heroes when he wants to divert himself for half an hour, maybe he'd like to have Dr. Park and his good talk and his grand pictures at the White House some night."

Speaking of clipper ships leads me to express the hope that you will allow Sam Morison to be the naval historian of this war.

With warm regards,

Ever faithfully,
F.F.

Memorandum for Felix Frankfurter
                                    The White House, April 18, 1942
    I wish I had the time to see Dr. Park but there is not a chance just
now. I have a copy of the log of the clipper ship my Mother and her
Mother went to China on in 1863. They passed the Confederate commerce
destroyer "Alabama" in the night but were not seen.
    I have asked that Sam Morison be taken into the Navy, with a Com-
mission, in order that he may write the story.

                                                            F.D.R.

*The appointment of Mr. Samuel Eliot Morison as Naval Historian led to
the writing of a fourteen-volume history of classic greatness.*

                                    Washington, D.C., April 16, 1942
Dear Frank:
    You put an idea into my head and now I want to put it to you.
    I remember vividly my experience in hearing, while in England in July,
1936, your speech in French at Quebec. What do you say to your now
speaking *in French* to the people of France — not mentioning Vichy or
Laval or anything explicitly political, but speaking to the people of France
out of the heart, out of the cherished memories of past comradeships of our
two peoples, and with assurance of collaboration in the future among free
peoples, ourselves and them, explaining, perhaps, that bombings may be,
are, instruments of *their* deliverance, speaking to them, that is, as friend to
friend, a human being, who is the symbol of hope for all liberty-loving
peoples, to his fellow human beings, above all the chatter and maneuver-
ings of politicians. Ten minutes of simple, firm, kindly friendly talk — as
informal as to your Hyde Park folk last summer, or the good, informal talk
to the Pan-Americans the other day.
    I really think that some such thing broadcasted, recorded, and re-
peated again and again might have far-reaching influence.
    Anyhow, it has seemed worth while to put to you what your Quebec
French remarks stirred in me as important for the present situation.
                                                        Ever yours,
                                                        F.F.

                                    Washington, D.C., April 22, 1942
Dear Frank:
    You have doubtless heard of the reported intention of Laval to broad-
cast to this country in the near future. One's first thought — at least mine
was — to "wait and see" what he has to say. But my own second and more
satisfying thought is that psychologically it is much better to beat him to it

and put him on the defensive with his own and other people. I know how much you have on your mind these days — and how exigent these other matters are — but I really feel confident, down to the bottom of my insights, that a speech by you in French the next few days, and then repeatedly broadcast, through recording, in the various languages would really help the "softening" process for the effort and the events ahead of us.

Ever devotedly yours,
F.F.

The State Department was against this proposal in this form but the President's criticisms of French collaboration with Germany were translated and extensively distributed by leaflet over France, and repeated in many broadcasts. On November 7 he broadcast to the French people on the day of the North African invasion. He ended with the cry: "Vive la France éternelle!"

The White House, April 27, 1942

Dear Felix:

Ever so many thanks for that delicious Camembert cheese. I had some for dinner the other night and enjoyed it immensely.

My best to you,

As ever,
F.D.R.

Washington, D.C., April 28, 1942

Dear Frank:

Especially to one part of your Message yesterday would T.R. have said "bully" — the $25,000 limit. That goes way beyond his old horizon — but he would see its symbolic significance, its demonstration that it *is* "a people's war." The historians of 1992 will find that proposal an epitome of much that was and perhaps even more that will be. Good luck — and I too dare say "bully."

I'm glad you liked the Camembert — upstate New York! But, please don't spend time acknowledging things of mine.

Tonight we shall hear and cheer you.

Ever yours,
F.F.

In a seven-point economic stabilization program, Roosevelt, on April 27, had outlined various measures "to keep the cost of living from spiralling *upward." He said that in a period of "grand national danger," no American citizen ought to have a net income, after taxes, of more than $25,000 a year.*

Washington, D.C., April 29, 1942

Dear Frank:

And now that I have read the speech, in the cold grey morning after, it still warms the heart and engages the head. I know how foolish it is to tell an artist that a particular performance is especially fine, and yet I venture to say that last night's broadcast was one of your very best. It was simple, direct, comprehensive and compelling. Its wide range was not diffusive — and it evoked the right moods in the diverse audiences for whom it was intended, here and everywhere. And your simply told tales made vivid and convincing the demands you made upon us all, and the sober hopes that you aroused.

And them's not only my sentiments. Marion is a very severe critic — I, at least, can seldom meet her standards. She liked the speech immensely — and thought it was what it should have been.

Ever yours,
F.F.

The White House, May 1, 1942

Dear Felix:

That was a mighty nice note of yours. It was a hard speech to prepare particularly because newspaper men and newspaper owners, just like most citizens, are human and the little details of dividends, government bond coupons, wages of the hired man and prices of wheat and artichokes sometimes loom larger than turning out ships, planes and anti-aircraft guns. Those stories at the end were the result of Harry Hopkins' stroke of genius; he thought of it while the final draft was being prepared.

What worries me is that there are dozens of stories just like those in the War and Navy Departments and they have not been adequately used. I am thinking of resigning this job and taking on the job of Public Relations man for the Government.

Incidentally, I could do a swell job with Supreme Court decisions. There is a heart throb in most of them and I could get lots of background from you in regard to this. Seriously, I am not joking at all about the need for dramatization of the decisions of the Court. Newspapermen do not know dramatics when they see it. Why don't you all hire Bob Sherwood? Happy thought!

As ever,
F.D.R.

Speaking nearly five months after the attack on Pearl Harbor, Roosevelt on April 28 found himself addressing a nation conscious for the first time of shortages while American victories were still being deferred to a distant day. Japan held the Netherlands East Indies and threatened to cut the Burma Road, in its drive toward China and India. Corregidor by a miracle of courage still stood. In an effort to placate Stalin and the Russian government, Roosevelt admitted that Russian forces had destroyed and were destroying more armed enemy power — troops, planes, tanks and guns — than "all the other United Nations put together."

He then criticized Laval because Laval had become "Chief of Government" in a new French Administration and also Minister of Foreign Affairs, the Interior, and Information. Laval — "the only clean thing about him is his white tie," as John Gunther said — was a recognized German puppet.

"There is one front and one battle," Roosevelt declared, "where every one in the United States — every man, woman, and child — is in action, and will be privileged to remain in action throughout this war. That front is right here at home, in our daily lives and in our daily tasks. Here at home everyone will have the privilege of making whatever self-denial is necessary, not only to supply our fighting men, but to keep the economic structure of our country fortified and secure during the war and after the war."

Then, grimly and emphatically, on the larger issues — the nation must not shrink from "hard work and sorrow and blood."

Washington, D.C., May 18, 1942

Dear Frank:

You have, I know, a bigger load of visiting presidents and prime ministers than is good for a twenty-four-hour day in time of war to carry, and yet — might it not help in the long run if Curtin were to spend two or three days or a week in Washington. The trip of Evatt has been very educative, for the general cause. It made him, largely, a United Nationser instead of merely an Australian! And even if Curtin could not leave his country, an invitation from you would in itself do much.

I dare say you have thought of all this, but I feel it so strongly that it insisted on being written.

Ever devotedly yours,
F.F.

Washington, D.C., May 21, 1942

Dear Frank:

I ought to answer this letter of Cripps, and of course I shall give him merely my own notions regarding his inquiry. But it would help immensely if you could spare me a few minutes in the near future. Now that Court isn't sitting (except for conferences and for Monday opinions) I am free to come at any time.

> Ever devotedly yours,
> F.F.

Sir Stafford Cripps, a dominant figure in the British Labour party and in wartime Britain, had written to Frankfurter on a variety of subjects ranging from freedom for India to social justice in Britain. He was worried over the failure of Stalin and Roosevelt to meet — not knowing the facts and mistakenly blaming the President. After his conference with the President, Frankfurter wrote to Cripps with great care, expecting his letter to be shown to Attlee and to Churchill. Several letters then passed between Cripps and Frankfurter. The climactic letter on Anglo-American relations is given later.

> Washington, D.C., May 26, 1942

Dear Frank:

Here is something for you to try your 'prentice hand at putting Supreme Court jargon into FDRese.

It was a zestful joy to see you.

Yours more than respectfully —

> Affectionately,
> F.F.

With this note was enclosed, as a joke, a very complicated decision in a tax case to test the President's ability to find human interest material in the judgments of the Supreme Court. The President balked at the challenge: neither he nor Robert Sherwood ventured to turn the opinion into simple, direct prose.

> Washington, D.C., June 6, 1942

Dear Frank:

Because I know that the Battle of the Atlantic Seaboard is constantly on your mind, I venture to make a suggestion which it will take you only a minute to find either foolish or deserving of further consideration.

What everyone on the outside is asking is whether all the skill and resourcefulness of which our people are capable are being exerted and employed in the fight against the U-boat. Is there a better, shrewder more alert instrument of inquiry for your own information of naval affairs than Jimmie Byrnes? He has, of course, very considerable knowledge of naval affairs from his long experience as chairman of the Appropriations Committee for

Naval affairs. But way beyond any technical knowledge — I now know, after a year's close observation of him, that he has a razor-blade mind, at once sharp and tough, and a rare capacity for getting at the core of a complicated problem, penetrating and imaginative. He is wise — and discreet in his wisdom. I merely suggest him as a comprehensive eye and questioner for you.

Needless to say I have not said a word to him or anyone else about this.

Ever devotedly yours,
F.F.

Washington, D.C., June 6, 1942
Dear Frank:

These should have gone to you before — but I have been away for several days, getting our children off to England, in response to their mother's *cri de coeur.*

Since the enclosures were written, you so kindly arranged to see Dr. Weizmann. But I send this anyhow — inasmuch as Ben-Gurion is the head of the Jewish agency in Palestine and a man who has himself lived through all this — and a person in whom Isaiah had the greatest confidence.

The world is literally resting on your shoulders, and Palestine is only a very small part of it territorially — but in symbolic importance not the least part of the world.

So — please read what Ben-Gurion has written.

Ever yours,
F.F.

The enclosures on Zionist hopes in Palestine were written by Dr. Chaim Weizmann, Mr. Ben-Gurion, and Frankfurter himself. Frankfurter emphasized the importance of the Ben-Gurion memorandum because Roosevelt was much less familiar with him than with Weizmann. It was after this presentation of the Zionist case that Roosevelt reported to Frankfurter, regretfully, that he was finding increasing opposition to the Zionist cause not only from the State Department but from his military advisers. Frankfurter got the President's permission to give this disturbing new information to Weizmann and Ben-Gurion. They both asked Frankfurter to give the President another memorandum stating that in their judgment the Arab countries would do absolutely nothing to help the Allied cause until Italy and Germany were clearly approaching final defeat — a judgment which later events were to vindicate with complete precision.

Washington, D.C., June 7, 1942

Dear Grace,

I hope that you can put this into the President's hands before he sees Dr. Weizmann.

Thank you much,
F.F.

July 8, 1942

Dear Frank,

Isn't Stone the man to give you an authoritative report on the rubber situation? The Chief Justice knows more about scientific processes than all the rest of the Court, and he would, of course, carry the greatest weight. He is within easy reach — in New Hampshire — and I am confident that he could dispel the fog in which the rubber controversy is enveloped, and that you could make him take on this job. There is no decent reason why he should not do it — if you wanted him to do it.

Ever yours,
F.F.

As Chief Justice Stone's letter to Roosevelt shows, he had a different concept of his judicial functions and he declined to conduct this investigation into the uses of rubber under wartime conditions. His letter, in fact, expresses the ultimate convictions of Frankfurter on having the members of the Supreme Court avoid all public duties not strictly relevant to their judicial responsibilities. The great change in his attitude came after he had supported Mr. Justice Jackson's absence from the Court to prosecute the Nazi war criminals at the Nuremberg trials. This support almost caused an open breach with Judge Learned Hand, who said the trials at Nuremberg represented victors' justice and therefore they embodied no justice at all. At one point in the argument Judge Hand sadly observed that Frankfurter, on this one issue, was thinking like a Jew and not like a judge. The argument ended only when Judge Hand refused to continue the discussion lest it destroy their friendship.

Frankfurter never changed his mind about Nuremberg but, after this argument with Judge Hand, he became very austere in his attitude to the public duties of a member of the Supreme Court. If he were left to make the decision, he would have made it impossible for any Justice to assume any nonjudicial duties, even when asked to do so by the President on an issue of supreme national importance. Though he had already resigned from the Court by 1963, he was strongly opposed to having Chief Justice Warren head the investigation into the circumstances of President Kennedy's assassination. He predicted that the judicial process would suffer a loss of public respect, in the end, from this entanglement by the Chief Justice in what was essentially a political investigation.

Franconia, N.H., July 20, 1942

Dear Mr. President:

I have your letter of the 17th inst. Personal and patriotic considerations alike afford powerful incentives for my wish to comply with your request that I assist you in arriving at some solution of the pending rubber problem. But most anxious, not to say painful, reflection has led me to the conclusion that I cannot rightly yield to my desire to render for you a service which as a private citizen I should not only feel bound to do but one which I should undertake with zeal and enthusiasm.

At the outset, I may say to you in confidence, that during the administration of your predecessor in office, when I was an Associate Justice, I felt obliged to decline a somewhat similar request for reasons which are for me as persuasive now as they were then. Apart from the generally recognized consideration that it is undesirable for a judge to engage actively in public or private undertakings other than the performance of his judicial functions, there are special considerations which I think must be regarded as controlling here.

Although it can by no means be certain, I assume that I would have no occasion to pass upon proposals involving questions of constitutional power or other questions which would be subject to review by the courts. That of course would plainly be inadmissible. But the rubber problem must be solved in the first instance by executive and legislative action having important political implications, not to say repercussions. Any findings that I might make (which unlike judicial findings could not be restricted to evidence appearing of record) and any action I might recommend if adopted, would almost certainly become the subject of political attack.

A judge and especially the Chief Justice cannot engage in political debate or make public defense of his acts. When his action is judicial he may always rely upon the support of the defined record upon which his action is based and of the opinion in which he and his associates unite as stating the grounds of decision. But when he participates in the action of the executive or legislative departments of government he is without those supports. He exposes himself to attack and indeed invites it, which because of his peculiar situation, inevitably impairs his value as a judge and the appropriate influence of his office.

We must not forget that it is the judgment of history that two of my predecessors, Jay and Ellsworth, failed in the obligation of their office and impaired their legitimate influence by participation in executive action in the negotiation of treaties. True they repaired their mistake in part by resigning their commissions before resuming their judicial duties, but it is not by mere chance, that every Chief Justice since has confined his activities strictly to the performance of his judicial duties.

I hope, Mr. President, that you will fully understand how deeply I regret my inability to render this service for you and that it is only a sense of public obligation transcending all personal consideration which prevents. I console myself by the assurance that there are others, not judges, more capable than I, of doing this particular task, on whose disinterestedness and patriotism you and the public can rely.

With high personal regards, I am

Faithfully yours,
HARLAN F. STONE

Washington, D.C., July 9, 1942

Dear Frank:

You may be interested in this letter I am sending to Stafford Cripps.

You cannot take too many days away from Washington — for the country's good. We need your utmost freshness of body and spirit — and that means as much freedom as possible from the harassments of needless details.

We both send you our love.

Ever yours,
F.F.

Washington, D.C., July 9, 1942

My dear Stafford:

The question you raise in your letter of April 24th about Anglo-American relations concerning which you say you have had "unsatisfactory accounts," is not well suited for a letter — it needs talk. And since Graham Spry had hopes of returning to Washington before he went back I left your letter unacknowledged in the expectation of sending what views I had through Spry. But he now writes that he must leave for England without another visit here. Before I think out loud about Anglo-American relations, let me thank you warmly for letting me hear from Spry the full story of your Indian Mission.

I shall not bore you with a repetition of all the tittle-tattle and the petty stories of alleged grievances and irritations which you must have heard *ad nauseam* as explanation of the bad state of American feeling toward England. I refrain from doing so, because, in the first place, the dominant underlying feeling is not bad, and, secondly, these episodes and incidents do not seem to me to touch the core of the real difficulty. You also know that the tide of feeling is greatly influenced by the fortunes of war.

Victory, or an epic retreat like Dunkirk, or the unostentatious endurance of the unendurable, dissipates attention to the petty bickerings and frictions inevitable in human relations and taps the deep communities between our peoples.

But there is a central difficulty. It is, as I see it, a lack of continuing consciousness of comradeship between the two peoples — comradeship not only in staving off an enemy that threatens everything we hold dear, but comradeship in achieving a common society having essentially the same gracious and civilized ends. These are big words. But I am convinced that all talk about good Anglo-American relations, as an indispensable prerequisite to a decent world order, is shallow unless the feeling permeates both our peoples that the United States and Great Britain care essentially for the same things — that is, to give dignity and scope to Lincoln's "common people."

The real blocks to a more vigorous and persistent consciousness of the common-ness between the two peoples are ignorance, and distrust which derives from ignorance. Too many Americans are yet unsure that England is not fighting this war for the maintenance of a system of privilege and an imperialistic order and that the English people are a democracy and are toiling, suffering, and dying for a decent social order. Too many Americans still assume that England is ruled by a class of incorrigible Tories whose conversion to the ideals of a social and economic democracy is as temporary as it was tardy.

The problem would be easy if it were true that these distorting sentiments were largely generated by the Coughlins and the McCormicks. As a matter of fact, they are the deposit of history and reflect memories too easily brought to life. The American Revolution, the Boston Tea Party, the War of 1812, the policy of England during the Civil War, the miserable history of the debts, are events of the past whose consequences still endure. The intense anti-British feeling of Americans of Irish descent has fanned the flames. And then there is India. The enormous complexity of the Indian problem has doubtless been illuminated by your Mission. But the ultimate fact remains that to the simple understanding of the American masses Great Britain is the historic oppressor of India — particularly when compared with what they believe to be the relevant principle that has dominated our policy toward the Philippines.

All that I am saying is, I know, commonplace. But Anglo-American relations is an occasion for applying Holmes' wisdom that what we need is education in the obvious and not investigation of the obscure. Of course, I shan't pretend to sketch a detailed program, but what seems to be inescapably clear is that the problem of Anglo-American relations is a problem in mass education. What is essential is a more vivid realization by Americans of the actual makeup of the English people, the reality of their democracy, and secondly, a realization that the aims of the British people in waging this war are substantially our aims — instinctively enough felt however vaguely they may be formulated. Americans do not feel estranged from coal-miners, steel workers, cotton workers, or the rest of England's industrial millions. There is sympathy with the teeming multitudes who have created the cooperative movement, developed unionism, waged and won a hard fight for the building of a political party. Low, the cartoonist, is the sort of Englishman (to be sure adopted) who has pierced to the heart of this nation. Americans are at home with Low's cartoons. But until the right spokesmen are found for this hand-worker England — put to one side Churchill as the embodiment of resistance to Hitler — on whose production the struggle is being sustained, there will remain in too many American minds a featureless blur of dingy, underpaid hordes who are being strangled by the old school tie. The real democratic England needs exactly the same sort of elucidation as enlightened America wanted in the years 1914-1918. Graham Wallas, Nevinson, Massingham, Hobson, H. G. Wells, Brailsford, Norman Angell, and a dozen others did this job during the last war.

Realization of the actual England for the American mind has to be honestly constructed out of real stuff. There must be a fresh, singular, passionately sincere projection of the motives now evolved and the perceptions now arrived at, to assure a deep conversion to English purposes. For nothing less is needed than a full realization by us that it is not just survival that is concerning England. France was caught in that snare. English destiny has to be conceived afresh by the men who are remaking it. That is what will revivify Anglo-American relations. Let England face her adjustments publicly. Singapore was not a disaster. It was an adjustment. France lost Canada on the eve of its magnificent eighteenth century. Britain's new century will hardly be a naval century. But it will be a release of thirty million under-educated, under-developed, under-advantaged Britons into the exercises and adventures of a better social structure.

In other words, England and America must work to come together for an understanding of the system at which they are aiming in the world order, so that nationalism and democracy can fall into the place that a decent order — revolted by the despicable Nazi and Japanese systems — must suitably provide.

I speak my deepest conviction when I say that what is needed is to enlighten America on the inner magnificence of the English spirit.

From which it is a natural step for me to say that I wish you might come here. I have some realization of the burdens that are carried by a member of the War Cabinet who is also the Leader of the House. But I wish it might be possible for you to spend some time here, if only a fort-

night. I do not have to tell you what a warm welcome would meet you —
equally warm from the people and their President. You would, I know,
immensely further the process of spiritual cross-fertilization between our
two peoples.

We both send cordial regards to all the Crippses.

Ever yours,
FELIX FRANKFURTER

*Sir Stafford Cripps was the Leader of the House of Commons and a
member of the War Cabinet. Graham Spry, former chairman of the Canadian Broadcasting Corporation, was Sir Stafford's assistant. Father Cough-
lin, the rancorous radio priest, added a hatred of Britain to his other prejudices. Colonel McCormick was the publisher of the Chicago* Tribune.
*David Low had come to England from New Zealand. Graham Wallas,
Henry Woods Nevinson, H. W. Massingham, J. A. Hobson, Henry Noel
Brailsford, Norman Angell were all British journalists and scholars, of wide
renown and great eloquence. H. G. Wells requires no identification.*

*It is worth some considerable emphasis in pointing out that Frankfurter
in this letter foresaw not only the granting of independence to India but
also the reform of the British educational system by the Butler Act and the
establishment in Britain after the war of the Welfare State.*

The White House, July 17, 1942

Dear Mr. Justice:

The President asks me to tell you that he is very sorry he cannot see
Mr. David Ben-Gurion. He also asks me to tell you that, quite frankly, in
the present situation in Egypt, Palestine, Syria and Arabia, he feels that the
less said by everybody of all creeds, the better.

With all good wishes to you and Mrs. Frankfurter,

Always sincerely,
GRACE

*On the urging of Mrs. Roosevelt, to whom the problems and aspirations
of young people were matters of personal concern, the President agreed to
address the International Student Assembly on September 3. This was the
third anniversary of the entry of Britain and France into the war. By speaking to students, he was able to look forward as well as to look back on the
forces which had produced the world conflicts. He was grateful to Frankfurter for having put on paper, in the following brief memorandum, words
which the President had heard him use in the White House when this
speech was under discussion. The President told the students that "the bet-*

ter world will be made possible only by bold vision, intelligent planning, and hard work."

Frankfurter Memorandum for the President

Washington, D.C., August 30, 1942

Wisdom does not necessarily come with years; neither is wisdom the characteristic of youth. Old men may be foolish and young men may be wise. Among the Fathers of our country — the men who made the Constitution and thus fashioned this nation — were young men. I mean by young men, men in the thirties. But it is important to remember that these young men, Madison, for instance, had attained their convictions through responsibility for action. And it is also well to recall that the conflicting elements in the Philadelphia Convention would probably not have reached those wise compromises, which alone made possible the Constitution of the United States, but for the shrewd wisdom and tolerant good humor of Benjamin Franklin, the oldest member of the Convention, then past eighty.

Telegram to Roosevelt

New Milford, Conn., September 3, 1942

YOU COULD NOT HAVE ADDRESSED YOUTH EVERYWHERE MORE FITTINGLY. WHAT YOU SAID COULD NOT HAVE BEEN BETTER CONCEIVED, BETTER PHRASED, OR BETTER SPOKEN.

FELIX FRANKFURTER

The White House, September 6, 1942

Dear Felix:

I am delighted to have your wire. It was a difficult speech to put together, but it seemed to have jelled at the last moment. I wish I could see you both, but I fear it cannot be done, as I am in the throes of preparing an even more difficult air blast Monday evening on the high cost of living. Marion will understand what that means — you yourself know nothing about that subject, though you are rather good on the cost of high living!

As ever yours,
F.D.R.

At this time Mr. Archibald MacLeish was the Librarian of Congress. The interesting thing about this particular exchange of letters is Frankfurter's zeal in hunting out any article which might give the President some momentary solace and easement, especially when the war news was bad. Roosevelt, of course, had a veritable passion for ships and the sea.

New Milford, Conn., August 16, 1942

Sir:

I write to crave a favor.

Your world-famous Library of which you are so distinguished a head, has doubtless already received the July–September 1942 number of the *Political Quarterly*, an English periodical. I should be greatly beholden to you to place that number in the hands of the President of the United States, with the suggestion that, in the untutored opinion of this correspondent, the article entitled "The Admiralty," by Lord Winster, may interest the President, and may, indeed, be not without amusement to him.

With homage to your leadership, believe me, Sir, to be

Yours also respectfully,
FELIX FRANKFURTER

Mr. Archibald MacLeish

Washington, D.C., September 3, 1942

Dear Mr. President:

Felix has been very eager that I should secure for you the July–September issue of the *Political Quarterly*. He thinks that you would find both pleasure and amusement in the leading article on the Admiralty. I therefore have stolen this copy from the Central Serial files of the Library of Congress and I send it down in the hope that you may have a free moment in which to glance at it.

I attach Felix's note on the subject in which he emulates an Eighteenth Century style which seems to me deserving of notice — or something. I wonder what he has been reading.

Faithfully yours,
ARCHIBALD MACLEISH

New Milford, Conn., September 8, 1942

Dear Frank:

Merely because some of the matters dealt with in your Fireside Chat last night were outside my area of free opinion, is no reason why I should not tell you how very much I liked those as to which I have no judicial lockjaw. That opening with Lt. Powers — and the moral *his* performance has for us all — and the exposition of the four interdependent theatres of war were especially superb.

I hope that you are as fit as these last two speeches sounded to me.

Our affectionate regards,

Yours faithfully,
F.F.

Congress had marked time or adopted wrecking amendments to Roosevelt's seven-point plan to maintain economic stability, check inflation, and

prevent war profiteering. That plan had been submitted on April 27. An-
gered by what seemed to him an inexcusable delay, Roosevelt on Septem-
ber 7 issued a warning to Congress "to curb inflation before October 1 or I
will."

This is an important event in the war because it led at last to the resigna-
tion of Mr. Justice Byrnes from the Supreme Court to begin his new duties
as overseer and stabilizer of the economy. In 1944 he was to be a candidate
for the Vice-Presidential nomination — he would have become President if
the nomination had gone to him instead of to Senator Harry Truman —
and later he served as Secretary of State. The friendship between Byrnes
and Frankfurter suffered no impairment as the years passed. They grew to
have different views on racial problems, but that did not disturb their per-
sonal relations.

To make his warning against inflation more stringent, Roosevelt also
planned a broadcast to the nation to explain the problems burdening the
American economy. "If the vicious spiral of inflation ever gets underway,"
he said, "the whole economic system will stagger."

He began by telling the story of Lieutenant James Powers, United States
Navy, during three days of the battle with Japanese forces in the Coral Sea.
In the first two days, Lieutenant Powers demolished one large enemy gun-
boat, put another gunboat out of commission, severely damaged an aircraft
tender, and a twenty-thousand-ton transport, and scored a direct hit on an
aircraft carrier which burst into flames and sank quickly. On the third day,
Lieutenant Powers said to the pilots of his squadron, "Remember, the folks
back home are counting on us. I am going to get a hit if I have to lay it on
their flight deck." That is exactly what he proceeded to do, releasing his
bomb only when he was sure of a direct hit on the Japanese carrier. He had
dived so low, from an altitude of eighteen thousand feet through Japanese
planes and anti-aircraft fire, that his own plane was destroyed by the ex-
plosion of his own bomb. Lieutenant James Powers, missing in action, was
awarded the Presidential Medal of Honor.

"You and I," said the President, "are the folks back home for whose
protection Lieutenant Powers fought and repeatedly risked his life. He said
that we counted on him and his men. We did not count in vain. But have
not those men a right to be counting on us? How are we playing our part
back home in winning this war? The answer is that we are not doing
enough."

Washington, D.C., September 30, 1942

Dear Frank:

Let me tell you what I said to Jimmie — for the first time in my life
something *very* good for my country is very bad for me?!

You will know best of all people how deeply accurate I am in saying that I am sadly happy that you have put Jim Byrnes where you and the war should have him. He has that very rare faculty — sagacity, downright wisdom. Still rarer, his sagacity is never obstructed by the irrelevancies of self. And he lubricates the inevitable drudgeries and difficulties of life with gay and invigorating humor. For good measure, the Lord threw in a smoothly working brain. Oh — how we need him here. But with you — in the gruelling days so invigoratingly borne by you — is his place. First things, first!

And so — my gratitude to you for depriving me of my most congenial pal.

Ever yours,
F.F.

This letter was written three days before the Office of Economic Stabilization was established. Frankfurter, of course, knew all about Roosevelt's plan to ask Mr. Justice Byrnes to leave the Supreme Court so that he could be appointed to this position.

This is the beginning of Frankfurter's campaign to have Judge Learned Hand appointed to the Supreme Court to fill the vacancy left by Mr. Justice Byrnes's resignation. The campaign almost succeeded — the President directed Frankfurter to prepare Judge Hand's name for nomination to the Supreme Court and submission to the Senate for confirmation. Unfortunately, the campaign failed — and in this instance it is no exaggeration to say that it failed at the very last moment. The next few letters explain what happened. In addition to this correspondence, Frankfurter discussed the Hand appointment privately with Roosevelt, during this period, five or six times in person or on the phone. He was not quite sure of the exact number. The postscript to the third letter refers to the shattering of precedent by Roosevelt's third term and the decision about Mr. Justice Byrnes, and also to the vigor, despite their age, of Bernard Baruch and Admiral Leahy. Roosevelt, after agreeing to Judge Learned Hand's appointment and accepting the actual words in which the nomination should be made, finally and reluctantly decided that he could not appoint Hand, then seventy-one, after all he had said about judges over seventy in the court-packing fight.

Washington, D.C., September 30, 1942

Dear Frank:

You know how rigorously I have abstained from volunteering suggestions for nominations by you. But I ought not to be more of a damn fool than I can help being. And so, a word about the vacancy — I feel like saying the emptiness — created by Jim Byrnes's going.

Naturally, Jim and I talked about the effect of his going on the Court.

He and I agree, I believe, that you again have a chance to do something for Court and Country comparable to what you did when you made Stone the Chief Justice. And I have good reason for believing that Stone would agree with the notion that Jim and I have on this matter.

Needless to say, I am writing this solely on my own, and without anyone's knowledge.

Ever yours,
F.F.

Washington, D.C., November 2, 1942

Dear Frank:

I should like to put something to you — having nothing to do with the Court or the Conduct of the war. I'm sorry, but I'm not the author of any plan on "How to Win the War and Make Friends."

Since we're not in session this week, I'm not doing time in the marble prison and could see you at your convenience — if you can sandwich me in on your awful schedule.

Faithfully yours,
F.F.

Washington, D.C., November 3, 1942

Dear Frank:

After a good night's sleep, this bubbles up:

Item 1 — It was truly grand to see you. To have found you so fit and more than puckish, enabled me to listen even to dreary arguments with a gay heart.

Item 2 — Especially on the score of politics, L. Hand is the only lad who will create no headaches for you — or, if you will, break no eggs. He is *the* one choice who will arouse universal acclaim in the press — and the only one who won't make the adherents of other aspirants say "Why in the hell was X chosen and not my man who is just as good as X?" L. Hand would not rub old wounds — quite the contrary. He would prove that the past is past. *His* youth — *his* non-hardening of the social and modern veins, is established. By virtue of his work he has, as it were, been on this Court for years. This would only make it known of all men. Really — you could have a pleasant smile, beat others to the smile, and tell the Nation what a great thing you are doing for the Nation. Every other person would divide feeling and opinion, not to speak of other considerations. I never was more sure of anything — as a matter of *Politics*.

Item 3 — It was — and remains — truly grand to see you.

Ever yours,
F.F.

P.S.   Third term, Bernie at 72 +, Leahy at his age, Jimmie taken off Bench — all more extraordinary than the Hand business.

Washington, D.C., December 3, 1942

Dear Frank:

If you have decided on Jim Byrnes's successor do not waste your time reading the rest of this. But if not, truth and devotion to you compel me to say the following.

Knowledge of what greatness has done for Court and Country — and surely Holmes, Brandeis and Cardozo were the only truly great judges here since the Civil War — makes me covet for you that you give to the history of your presidency the only man worthy to rank with Holmes, Brandeis and Cardozo. Were you to name Learned Hand, five minutes after the news flashed to the country, all considerations of age, geography and the like will be seen to have had no relevance. If only for a few years, Hand could not but bring distinction to the Court and new lustre to the President who made it possible.

Devotedly yours,
F.F.

I have nominated Learned Hand, the Senior Circuit Judge of the Circuit Court of Appeals for the Second Circuit, as an Associate Justice of the Supreme Court in succession to James F. Byrnes.

In time of national emergency when each must serve where he can be most useful, it is fitting that in replacing a member of the Court who has been drafted into the war effort, considerations of age and geography — which in normal days might well be controlling — should yield to the paramount considerations of national need.

Judge Learned Hand enjoys a place of pre-eminence in our federal judiciary. His long experience as a judge, his deep knowledge of all phases of law, especially of federal law, make him uniquely qualified for the Supreme Bench. His choice at this time is clearly indicated. He will bring to the Court a youthful vigor of mind and a tested understanding of the national needs within the general framework of the Constitution.

Memorandum for F.F.
The White House, December 4, 1942

Private

The words "prayerful consideration" rarely mean what they say. In the present case they do. In the same way "the exception proves the rule" — but one of the requisites for the exception is the very important element of timing.

Sometimes a fellow gets estopped by his own words and his own deeds
— and it is no fun for the fellow himself when that happens.

F.D.R.

Washington, D.C., December 7, 1942

Dear Frank:

Your "private" note of December 4th, which has just come, was a
most generous thing for you to send me. I deeply cherish it. Now it only
remains to say that I think I appreciate the travail through which you have
passed, and therefore feel for you.

Devotedly yours,
F.F.

Frankfurter Memorandum on Judge Learned Hand

When Jim Byrnes resigned from the Supreme Court to become the
Director of Economic Stabilization (just before the opening of 1942 Term
of the Court), he left a big hole on the Court. While he had been out of
the current of law practice for some years, the Lord endowed him with an
excellent and quick brain whereby he easily mastered the technical aspects
of the Court's work. He brought to the Court, however, not only vast experience in the actual operations of Government, an understanding of which
lies so close to so much of the litigation that comes before the Court, but
also an uncommon sagacity — a sense of what matters and what does not, a
perspective which eliminates the irrelevant and the minor. More than that,
he manifested what surprised me greatly, namely, the real judicial temper,
that is, detachment from political or personal considerations, a disregard of
motives other than those wholly relevant to a judge's job. I was surprised at
this, not for lack of appreciation of his character, but because, after all, he
had for a long, long time been on the political side of life, with all its
accommodations and compromises, and almost inevitably these get a so-
called practical-mindedness, that is, a consideration of motives which ought
not to enter into a judge's way of thinking but almost inescapably do. I
soon became aware that there was no man on the Court who was more
truly judicial-minded than Jim Byrnes — and hardly any man as much.
Therefore his loss was a very considerable one in the present composition of
the Court.

The Court was also lacking — as Stanley Reed has come to express it
on more than one occasion — in legal learning and experience, more particularly in the domain of federal law. The outstanding judicial figure in the
country off the Supreme Court — and in my judgment a more distinguished mind than any man on the Court — is Judge Learned Hand of the
Circuit Court of Appeals for the Second Circuit. He enjoys an esteem sec-

ond to nobody in the country. And so I wrote to the President saying, if his mind were still open, he had a chance to do for the Court what Theodore Roosevelt did when he appointed Holmes, what Wilson did when he appointed Brandeis, and what Hoover did when he appointed Cardozo. I told him I was aware of Hand's handicap — that he is seventy years old — but that he has great vitality and what the country would fasten on was Hand's distinction and not his age, and that, in any event, he has the prospect of a number of years on the Court and that I was sure he is not the kind of a man who would linger on the Court beyond his time.

I wrote this letter in longhand and the note of December 4, 1942, from F.D.R. is a reply to it. The reference in it to a man being "estopped by his own words," etc., is of course to F.D.R.'s position in the Court fight in 1937 — his reference to the age of judges — which was the most foolish part of the whole Court fight. F.D.R. now well knows this to be so, and he should have known at the time, for the most liberal judges on the Court had been Holmes, although ninety, and Brandeis, although past eighty. But F.D.R., as he told one or two people, felt he could not get over his attitude in 1937 as to age and the use that would be made of it by his critics. I have no doubt that was an error of judgment on his part, for even though some wag might have poked a little fun at him, the acclaim that would have greeted Learned Hand's appointment would have drowned the fun-poking. In any event, to have a man of Learned Hand's stature on the Court would have been worth the price of a little fun.

On Learned Hand's death in 1961, Frankfurter wrote: "However full-throated one's appreciation of him, reference must be made to the fact that Judge Hand did not become Mr. Justice Hand. Of course he should have been on the Supreme Court. Holmes wanted him there while he was still District Judge. He would have met the spacious requirements for a seat on the Supreme Bench as very few men in his time.

"In addition to his other pre-eminent qualities, he would have added to literature as well as to the literature of the law by his opinions in the United States Reports. Not a little nonsense on why he was not named has been written by those who are ignorant of the fortuitous elements that determine Supreme Court choices. But for Czolgosz's pistol, Mr. Justice Gray's successor would have been not Oliver Wendell Holmes but Alfred Hemenway, a respectable Boston lawyer, whose chief recommendation was his law partnership with President McKinley's Secretary of the Navy. Learned Hand was not denied a place on the Court for any specific disqualifying reason — geography or partisan politics or judicial outlook — until, when he was past seventy, age was deemed a bar. Events cast a sardonic smile on this misjudgment, for Judge Hand continued his distinguished

judicial labors for more than a decade after the short tenure of the much younger man who was preferred to him."

Washington, D.C., October 19, 1942

Dear Frank:

This extract is a fair sample of comments I have had from several of my former students from different places of service. This one comes from Sioux Falls, S. Dakota.

The way these lads write — and I have had some wonderful letters from boys in England, in Australia, the Solomons — has put a thought into my head that doubtless has long since passed through yours. But I'll put it to you — briefly.

You doubtless will speak over the air on December 7th, next. Why is that not *the* day for you to speak directly and explicitly as Commander-in-Chief to the men on the Seven Seas, in the five continents and in all the airfronts. You are, to be sure, the Commander-in-Chief of us all, but in an intimate and immediate sense *theirs*. And at an hour appropriate for all the men everywhere to hear your warming, energizing voice — expressing anew the great heritage we defend, the faith that moves us, the determination to enrich the heritage and live the faith — it would be stirring and wonderful and inspiring and personal to every soldier, sailor and airman, in all the ranks and ratings, for you to address *them*. Of course the rest of us would listen — and the mothers, fathers, service husbands' wives and all who have personal ties in the armed forces would feel the significance that you speak to *their* men.

Someday, perhaps, you'll tell me how you attend to your correspondence. I wish I had extra hours to write to all these lads who write me — at least, to write adequately to them.

Ever yours,
F.F.

The White House, October 22, 1942

Dear Felix: —

I think that is a mighty good idea of yours and I am asking questions as to the best hour, method, etc.

I do wish I could get a glimpse of you. Every day seems more crowded than the last.

As ever yours,
F.D.R.

For the Press Immediate Release November 20, 1942

The President will not deliver an address on December seventh nor take official notice of that anniversary. The President does not feel that this attitude on the part of the Government need interfere with the carrying out of programs already arranged under private auspices. But in so far as notice of December seventh by the President is concerned, he feels that it should be observed as a day of silence in remembrance of a great infamy.

Washington, D.C., November 30, 1942

Dear Frank:

You will want to see this letter. The writer, a Naval Lieutenant, has just returned from the Solomons — he has been through it all, and he is going back just as soon as his squadron will be assigned to a new ship. I need only add, that he is one of the finest lads who ever left Cambridge. If I tell you that he is a very young lawyer but I charged him — before the war — with taking care of Marion's small affairs were I suddenly killed by a truck, you will have a sense of his qualities.

His letter stirs a thought. Silent observance of the seventh is fitting enough. But what about speaking to your forces on December the eighth the day that is *not* a day of sorrow and perfidy, but the day this country was summoned to action by you and so superbly responded.

Ever yours,
F.F.

And how Frankfurter loved these lads from Harvard!

Roosevelt asked Judge Rosenman to make extracts from these letters for a broadcast to the forces, then decided to remain silent on the anniversary of Pearl Harbor. The naval lieutenant was William DuBose Sheldon: his letter was also his testament, for he was soon dead.

Washington, D.C.,Thanksgiving Day, 1942

Dear Frank:

That was an exquisite thought of yours — to have such a Thanksgiving Service in the White House and to make the whole Nation part of it and, for the time being, part of your family. It was finely simple and quietly austere, as befits this Thanksgiving. Only next time I hope you will also be the choirmaster.

We are having a houseful of young lads — one of them just back from the Solomons — and we all drank your health and gave you a gay and grateful place of pride in *our* thanksgiving.

Marion and I send you our love,

FELIX

The White House, October 31, 1942

Dear Felix: —

I am awfully glad to have *Brandeis on Zionism*. What a great historical pity that Holmes and Brandeis were born, one of them thirty years too
soon and the other twenty years too soon! All mankind suffers therefrom.
I really think the world needs them more today than it did then.

By the way, did you note that H.M., Jr., was said by the papers to have
been chosen the next leader of Zion? Eleanor and I are telegraphing him
when he reaches Miami, on his way home, that we will not receive him
unless he arrives with a long black beard. Incidentally also, he will be
disowned by his old man.

Please do jot down that story of my namesake on the farm in Bethle-
hem — the greatest compliment I ever got.

As ever yours,
FRANKLIN D. ROOSEVELT

*Frankfurter had sent the President a collection of Brandeis's speeches on
Zionism.*

*Henry Morgenthau, Jr., the Secretary of the Treasury, was far more sym-
pathetic to Zionism than his father ever was; but of course the newspapers
were bizarrely wrong in their speculation.*

*A refugee family from Germany, grateful for the President's help which
had made it possible for so many refugees to live in Palestine, changed their
son's name in tribute to Roosevelt. The mother and father never quite
explained how "Franklin Delano" would sound in Israel.*

Washington, D.C., November 10, 1942

Dear Frank:

For a mere professor, one of the strangest aspects of the war is the
made demand of our press for "spot" news about military events. Newspapers whip up their readers, by all the familiar arts they excite incontinent
appetite for news, news, news, — and they insist that this is "a people's
war" and the people must have knowledge of events to come, and immediate news of their happening. Well — I don't know much about war, but I
have yet to learn that a basic principle of military science and, especially,
for licking Hitler, is open warfare openly arrived at.

The beautiful and effective synchronization of the African offensive
ought to make even the greedy press realize — and help the public to understand — that some things, and in war the most important, cannot be
told till they can be told! It's very grand news.

I re-read a lot of Lincoln this summer — and how often and how vividly so much of him in the Civil War reminds of you.

Devotedly yours,
F.F.

The invasion of North Africa, with the promise it gave of turning the flank of the enemy, brought a hint of better tidings as this hard year neared its end. There had, at last, been some victories too in the Pacific — the Battle of the Coral Sea, Midway, Guadalcanal. The tide was slowly turning in the war against Japan. In the struggle against Germany and Italy the greatest fact of all was that the Nazi armies had accepted defeat in the Battle of Stalingrad. Yes, the news was getting better.

Frankfurter's Memorandum on India, put in Roosevelt's hands on November 12, 1942

1. The immediate issue between Great Britain and the Congress Party of India is not one of post-war political reforms but of the transfer of power *now* to an Indian Government in order to secure full popular support for the prosecution of the war. That also is the issue in the forefront of most American thought and talk about India. Sir Stafford Cripps' plan of a wholly Indian Executive Council responsible through the Viceroy to Parliament, foundered on the fear by the Congress Party that such responsibility would, in effect, be subject to the control of the Government of India by Whitehall.

2. The British Government has so far refused to go beyond the Cripps Plan because:

(1) The utterances of important Congress leaders have created a genuine fear that any government in India controlled by them will seek to appease Japan;

(2) There was not at the time of the Cripps negotiations, and there is not now, justifiable ground for assuming that powerful minority groups in India, e.g. the Muslim League and the Depressed Classes, will enter a National Government. They fear that this will prejudice their position under the future permanent rule in India;

(3) In war time, it is impossible to devise constitutional changes which would allay the apprehension just referred to, even if there were agreement on appropriate safeguards among the main political parties, of which there is no sign;

(4) The Indian Army, eighty per cent of whose officers are British, cannot at this stage of the war be placed under the control of an Indian Cabinet.

3. Neither the Congress distrust of the British nor British and Muslim

distrust of the Congress can be lightly dismissed or deemed without cause. Dispatches from reliable American correspondents, such as Mr. Herbert Matthews of the New York *Times,* bear testimony to the reality of this mutual suspicion. Authoritative English testimony is equally conclusive.

> The first major impression, which any observer of the Indian scene in the winter of 1941-42 was bound to form, was the intensification of the old antagonism between the two great Indian communities, the Hindus and the Moslems.

So writes Reginald Coupland, the Beit Professor of Colonial History at Oxford University, who had made an intensive study of India and thereafter was attached to the Cripps Mission. (*The Cripps Mission,* page 22)

4. Any proposed solution, therefore, of the present deadlock must begin with this reality as the most important psychological starting point. The following plan reflects an attempt to overcome these difficulties:

(1) The Congress Party must first unqualifiedly call off the present movement of disorder.

(2) When that condition is satisfied, the British Government should accept for the duration of the war a provisional government, the personnel of which has been agreed upon by the principal parties in India.

(3) The British Commander-in-Chief in India shall be a member in this Cabinet.

(4) The Governor-General of India shall agree to accept the advice of the Provisional Indian Government except when, in his judgment, this is likely to interfere with the war effort of the United Nations.

(5) When any proposal of the Provincial Government raises such a concern about its effect upon the conduct of the war, the Governor-General shall request the Cabinet, through its Prime Minister or Defense Minister, to submit the proposal in question to a Defense Council. The Defense Council would consist of (i) the British Commander-in-Chief, (ii) the Indian Defense Minister, (iii) one ranking American military officer, and (iv) one such Chinese officer. It will be carefully provided, however, that the American and Chinese military officers do not represent their respective Governments, but serve merely as members of the Military High Command, associated with the Commander-in-Chief for the effective prosecution of the war.

(6) If the Defense Council accepts the disputed proposal of the Provisional Indian Government, or the Indian Government agrees to modify its proposal in accordance with the advice of the military members of the Defense Council, there will be no occasion for the Governor-General to exercise his veto. But if the Indian Government should give the stamp of approval to proposals which the military members of the Defense Council

consider inimical to the successful conduct of the war, the Governor-General may exercise his veto power.

5. If the professions of the Congress, that it seeks power now mainly to reinforce India's war effort, are to be accepted, the Congress cannot reasonably object to a plan which permits the Governor-General a veto only as to matters affecting India's war effort, and even then makes the exercise of that veto conditional on the advice of a body representative not merely of the British Commander-in-Chief but also of military experts of the two United Nations primarily interested in the war effort of India.

And if the successful prosecution of the war precludes the British Government from taking the risks of transferring power now to an Indian Government — risks as hazardous to the cause of the United Nations as to that of Great Britain — it would not preclude an arrangement by which the Governor-General's veto is maintained but its exercise made conditional on the determination of a Council including the military experts of the United Nations. And there is no legal difficulty in the way of adopting a convention by which the power of veto is to be exercised as suggested.

6. Indian history leaves no doubt that, to be acceptable to the controlling elements in India, a solution must be worked out in consultation with them. Any plan aiming at an Indian settlement must not be made public until it has been discussed with the Indian political leaders and their agreement to it secured.

Telegram to Roosevelt
Washington, D.C., November 17, 1942

SWELL!

FELIX FRANKFURTER

This telegram was in praise of Roosevelt's speech at the New York Herald Tribune *Forum. The President had said that criticism "actuated by political motives" had done less harm in the United States than might have been expected because of "the good old horse sense of the American people."*

Washington, D.C., November 25, 1942

Dear Frank:

There are all sorts of people whom you have to see, but there is a fellow in our midst whom business does not require you to see but who, if you saw him, would give you joy and stimulus. He is not a headliner — he is just a great man, if I know a great man after ample opportunities for judging. He is merely a scientist — but a scientist who has actually labored for years as effectively as anyone I know in the vineyard of your Four

Freedoms, "a man who" — but I will no longer keep you in suspense with my nominating speech. I will give you the name of Sir John Orr.

He is a hardheaded Scotsman whose burr you'd find engaging, who came out of the last war with a Military Cross and a Distinguished Service Order, who has had as much convincing experience to prove the wisdom of all your efforts in regard to agriculture and the relation of food and health in achieving a civilized world as any man I know.

I'll bet every penny I earn even below Jimmie Byrnes' ceiling, that you would find delight and profit in talking with Sir John Orr such as very few people give you. Orr will be here until December 6th, and I undertake to have him turn up at any time that you can manage to see him. Take me on faith for once — if Orr does not make good I shall gladly do whatever penance you may prescribe.

Faithfully yours,
F.F.

P.S.   In good British Embassy fashion I am enclosing a Who's Who on Sir John Orr.

Roosevelt agreed that Sir John Boyd Orr was "a great man" and got valuable ideas from his talk with him for the establishment of a World Food and Agricultural Organization (FAO) as part of the United Nations after the war.

Washington, D.C., November 30, 1942

Dear Grace:

Antoine de Saint-Exupéry, the famous French aviator and author of those wonderful books, *Wind, Sand and Stars,* and *Flight to Arras,* is anxious that the enclosed letter come under the President's own eye. And so he has asked me to serve as a conduit for its transmission. I am sure the President will want to read what Saint-Exupéry has written on the dominant French problem. He also hoped the President would accept his inscribed book.

It was a pleasure to have had at least a glimpse of you on Thanksgiving Day. I just couldn't let Baby Justice Jackson monopolize all of you.

Very cordially yours,
FELIX FRANKFURTER

Former Attorney General Robert Jackson was now on the Supreme Court.

Washington, D.C., December 8, 1942

Dear Frank:

Just a year ago this hour, in the presence of the people's representatives, you called the Nation to war. That awful and august experience will be the last to fade from our memories. Young men were asked to forfeit their lives — with all their promise — and the rest of us to give whatever may be required so that what gives life more than brutish significance may survive, so that civilization may become still more gracious and good and not be destroyed.

It was only a year ago — but how far you have led us in that short year and how gladly the people heard you and hear you whenever you summon to high endeavor.

Bless you,
F.F.

Telegram to Roosevelt

November 24, 1942

DELIGHTED TO SEE JUSTICE EVATT WEDNESDAY MORNING TEN-THIRTY. ASK HIM TO GO TO MAC'S OFFICE.

FRANKLIN D. ROOSEVELT

Washington, D.C. December 9, 1942

Dear Frank:

The photograph has just come — and I keep looking at it, as Marion will, when I bring it home tonight. It's most satisfying — it conveys as much as we can expect a photograph to convey, and the rest our combined affectionate imagination, especially Marion's, will fill in. You were good to take time to inscribe it — and we shall cherish it all our days.

You certainly have taken the Australian into port. Doc Evatt went off to Canada like a kitten that had wallowed in cream. I am urging him to go to London soon.

Fred Dumaine was lyric after leaving you. "How does he do it?" he kept chanting, in his hoarse soprano voice.

Ever devotedly yours,
F.F.

The President had inscribed this photograph — "To my friend Felix Frankfurter, with affection, admiration, and gratitude. Franklin D. Roosevelt."

Light at the End
of the Tunnel

1943

1943

January 14-24	Roosevelt and Churchill meet at the Casablanca Conference.
January 30	Russian victory in the Battle of Stalingrad.
February 7	Lieutenant General Dwight D. Eisenhower appointed commander of North African operations.
May 12	Churchill visits Roosevelt in Washington to discuss problems of a Second Front in western Europe to take pressure off Russia and break the Axis states.
July 26	Mussolini resigns, is arrested, but is rescued by German troops. Later Mussolini is caught and is killed by Italians who profaned his dead body in the street.
August 11-24	Quebec Conference between Roosevelt, Churchill, and Prime Minister Mackenzie King of Canada.
September 9	Badoglio government accepts terms of peace for Italy.
September 13	General Chiang Kai-shek is elected President of the Chinese Republic by the Central Executive Committee and is also confirmed as commander-in-chief of the Chinese army.
November 28 — January 12	Teheran Conference between Stalin, Roosevelt and Churchill. En route to Teheran, Roosevelt stops off at Cairo for a four-day conference with Chiang Kai-shek and Churchill.

THIS *was to be a year of conferences — Casablanca, Quebec, Cairo, Teheran. That in itself was a portent of victory. The miracles of production had given us the tools to finish the job. Now we had to use them with skill and power, with unity of purpose, with the restraints of world strategy preventing any premature or excessive commitment to any one theater of war. Only the great leaders, standing at the summit of power, could make the final decisions. Churchill and Roosevelt consolidated their unshatterable partnership. But Stalin stood aloof, resisting all entreaties, and only consenting to go to Teheran near the end of the year.*

"The Axis Powers," said Roosevelt, "knew that they must win the war in 1942 — or eventually lose everything. I do not need to tell you that our enemies did not win this war in 1942."

At the Casablanca Conference early in January it was agreed that the first major offensive would move from North Africa to the capture of Sicily and the clearing of the Mediterranean area. At the same time the decision was taken to increase the number and severity of the air raids on Germany. But the invasion and liberation of western Europe were put off for another year. The two rival French leaders, General de Gaulle and General Giraud, made formidable but embarrassing appearances at Casablanca. President Roosevelt committed Britain and America, with Churchill's approval, despite later doubts, to a policy of "unconditional surrender." This did not mean a pitiless peace. Germany, Japan, and Italy would be treated fairly, once they had fully admitted their defeat.

On July 25 Mussolini resigned — a strangely tame word for the discredited and frightened Fascist leader. "The criminal, corrupt Fascist regime in Italy is going to pieces," Roosevelt announced.

On August 17 Roosevelt and Churchill met in Quebec. They said the battle in the Atlantic against the submarines was finally being won by Britain and America. They agreed with great secrecy that in 1944 France would be invaded through Normandy. A four-power statement on the postwar organization of the world was to be prepared by Russia, China, America, and Britain. General Eisenhower was told to take Corsica and Sardinia. Lord Mountbatten, with General Stilwell as his deputy, became head of the Southeast Asia Command.

En route to Teheran in December, Roosevelt stopped at Cairo for a conference with Chiang Kai-shek and Churchill. To Churchill's surprise and

*concern, Roosevelt treated China, then writhing in the cruel grip of war
and dismembered, as if she had the full status of a great power. Coming
years would question the wisdom of this Cairo Conference.*

*Stalin was told at Teheran that the invasion of Europe across the English
Channel would take place on May 1, 1944. He said Russia would enter the
war against Japan — a promise he redeemed in the very last days of that
struggle. Stalin wanted to know the name of the commanding general who
would organize the European liberation. Roosevelt said it was too early to
give a definite answer. He seemed to favor the appointment of General
Marshall, his Chief of Staff. In the end the choice fell on General Eisenhower.*

*After Teheran came the second Cairo Conference at which Churchill
and Roosevelt met with the President of Turkey.*

*Roosevelt's State of the Union message on January 7 opened with a mix-
ture of grimness and confidence. "The past year," he said, "was perhaps the
most crucial for modern civilization; the coming year will be filled with
violent conflict — yet with high promise of better things."*

*The Nazis, he went on, always had the advantages of superior air power
and they used it to bomb Warsaw, Rotterdam, London and Coventry.
"That superiority has gone — forever. Yes — the Nazis and the Fascists
have asked for it — and they are going to get it."*

*Then came the statement for which the nation had been waiting. "I do
not prophesy when the war will end. But I do believe that the year of 1943
will give to the United Nations a very substantial advance along the roads
that lead to Berlin and Rome and Tokyo."*

*No one had been waiting for such an assurance more eagerly than Frank-
furter. Hence the tone of his congratulations.*

Washington, D.C., January 9, 1943

Dear Frank:

It is less than arrogant for me to be confident that your address will be
a most heartening message to "our boys at the front," no less than an exhilarating spur to the home front and fortification of the spirit to all the
millions the world over who, in effort and faith, are united to deliver mankind from the reality and the menace of enslavement.

Keep fit — and, continue to lead.

Ever yours,
F.F.

The White House, February 2, 1943

Dear Felix:

Many, many thanks to you and Marion for that delicious old Vermont cheese, which you sent to me for Christmas. I am guarding it carefully and enjoying it thoroughly.

This note takes to you both my affectionate regards and every best wish for the New Year.

As ever yours,
F.D.R.

Roosevelt had delayed his acknowledgment of the gift of Vermont cheese, among other reasons, because of the preparations for the Casablanca Conference and his absence from the country.

The White House, February 5, 1943

Dear Professor:

It is good to have your note and to see the really good editorial, which good old Fred sent you.

Believe it or not, it was not much of a stunt because I couldn't help thinking that thousands and thousands of equally good Americans have taken the jaunt I took.

I am naturally still keyed up a bit during the five days I have been here and I am going to the usual place for a four-day rest and sleep.

Next week will be bad until the end of it but I do hope that you and Marion can come in then and let me tell you some of the high spots.

Affectionately yours,
F.D.R.

Frankfurter had phoned Roosevelt to give him a quick summary of what people were saying about his part in the Casablanca Conference. The President asked to see an editorial in the Boston Herald written by Frank Buxton and sent on to Frankfurter by Fred Dumaine.

The Copernican Quadricentennial interested the President because Frankfurter wanted him to take part in it. There were two other reasons: Copernicus was a Pole, and the ceremony became an occasion to honor Americans of Polish descent; and secondly, the ceremony gave the President the chance to testify to the achievements of all races in liberating the human mind as against the Nazi doctrine of a master race. Frankfurter indulged himself in one brief play on words. "Copey" is Charles Townsend Copeland, the famous and beloved teacher of literature at Harvard.

Washington, D.C., February 5, 1943

Dear Mr. President:

You possibly know, and certainly know about, Professor Harlow Shapley, the Harvard astronomer, and I suppose as distinguished a one as this country has. The enclosed letter from him speaks for itself.

Would you like to indicate in a word what I should say to him?

Faithfully yours,

FELIX FRANKFURTER

Memorandum for F.F.

Washington, D.C., February 15, 1943

I have gone over the enclosed very carefully but I do not think I had better do it because I have declined accepting honorary chairmanships of practically all organizations and I think I will have to stick to the rule.

I would, of course, be glad to write them a letter which can be read at the celebration if they would like to have one.

I remember old Copernicus very well, although he was a little older than I was at College where he was a member of the Fly Club — because he discovered flies!

F.D.R.

The enclosed letter to Justice Frankfurter, by Dr. Harlow Shapley, written on the letterhead of Harvard College Observatory, invited the President to be honorary chairman of the dinner to be given by the Kosciuszko Foundation on May 24 in celebration of the four hundredth anniversary of the appearance of Nicholas Copernicus's book, Revolutionibus Orbium Coelestium.

Washington, D.C., March 9, 1943

Dear Mr. President:

Here I am again, serving as a post office between you and Professor Shapley. His letter speaks for itself. Of course I am at your disposal — if any need for me there be.

Faithfully yours,

FELIX FRANKFURTER

Cambridge, Mass., March 5, 1943

Dear Felix:

In further response to your letter, reporting on the President's interest in the Copernican Quadricentennial. I have had an opportunity to discuss the matter with the Kosciuszko Foundation. The President's willingness to cooperate, and your own valuable intercession, are deeply appreciated.

We should very much like to have you follow through, as you have offered to do, and ask the President to prepare a statement that can be formally presented at the beginning of the ceremonies in Carnegie Hall. Of course I could write to him directly, asking for this statement, but I believe it would be more comfortable for him to have you make the arrangements.

Naturally I would be glad to make a formal request of him, if that is best from the standpoint of the record. I know of course he does not give a damn from the standpoint of the dignities and formalities. Please advise me; but remember that this generous collaboration from the President is the making of the celebration.

Let me go just a bit further, in this personal communication to you. As the time approaches (May 24) I think we should seriously consider if it might not be wise to arrange to have the President speak by national radio hookup to the convention — that is, read the tribute that will be prepared. That of course is something one should not arrange or try to arrange far in advance, for obvious reasons. But the importance of this event not only in recognizing the birth of the modern scientific world but in saluting the contributions of small nations to the current civilization is such that the opportunity might be seized upon for a pregnant statement of world-wide, or at least nation-wide significance.

Secretary of State Hull has written (in what may be and certainly sounds like a personal letter) that the importance of the occasion is obvious and "I hope that I will be able to see my way clear to send you a message to be read on that occasion." Dozens of university presidents and leading scientists have given acceptances — I am actually dumbfounded by the response. Apparently a considerable number of them will be able to attend the meeting in Carnegie Hall.

My five days in Washington over the last week-end were terrifically laborious, and therefore I did not have the pleasure of bothering you personally. Mrs. Shapley and the forty young genius scientists of the "Talent Search" had lunch in your cafeteria; and Henry Wallace again met all the kids — this time with even greater pleasure than last because the girl winner was an attractive blond from Ames, Iowa, whose father is the professor of the Vice-President's son.

Thanks for everything.

As ever yours,
HARLOW SHAPLEY

Washington, D.C., March 11, 1943

Dear Felix: —

My old roommate Copernicus is a persistent cuss. I think you had better disabuse Shapley's mind, for I cannot possibly go on the air, but I will send a message — on condition that you prepare it for me. Something along the line of "Alas, poor Yorick, he would not have met his cruel fate had he not tried to count beyond ten!" If you want to write the message in rhymed verse it is all right with me.

Strictly between ourselves, I have little sympathy with Copernicus. He looked through the right end of the telescope, thus greatly magnifying his problems. I use the wrong end of the telescope and it makes things much easier to bear.

As ever yours,
F.D.R.

Washington, D.C., March 15, 1943

Dear Frank:

In due course I shall send you some profound observations on astronomy. But in the meantime you might like to see these handsome pictures of and about your buddy — no, not Copey — but Coperny!

Ever yours,
F.F.

Washington, D.C., May 5, 1943

Dear Frank:

Here are some notes for your Copernicus letter, the joint product of Harlow Shapley and myself. I hope that they may serve to save you time. Several States, including New York, have taken official cognizance of the event, which promises to be noteworthy.

I am glad that you had the refreshment of your recent trip. Washington seems to be running true to its historic form of being not a little enveloped in moral miasma. But like Lincoln, you can rely on the people — and the men in the services, on the seven seas, in the four continents, in the air, everywhere.

Marion joins me in affectionate greetings and good wishes.

Ever yours,
F.F.

Roosevelt had just returned from an inspection trip to army posts in the Western and Southern states.

The Copernicus Anniversary

Only recently we celebrated the three hundredth anniversary of Sir Isaac Newton, the two hundredth of Thomas Jefferson, and the one hundredth of William and Henry James. It is right that we memorialize these men and recall their gifts to us.

And so, I am happy to learn that scores of our learned societies, hundreds of our schools and colleges, are this year celebrating the four hundredth anniversary of the appearance of that epoch-making book which established the true place of the earth in the solar system. By thus freeing men's minds from the false egocentric view of the world, this discovery released the great ventures of modern science. To celebrate the author of this great book, Nicholas Copernicus, one of the founders of free thought, may seem at first not to be in keeping with the hard situation that confronts us and necessarily absorbs most of our thought and energies. But the pursuit of truth and of high ideals is the source that inspires our vast efforts to restore and extend freedom to all the peoples of the earth. Devotion to ideals and freedom for ideas have made us resist the brutal aggression of tyrants.

It is, therefore, highly appropriate that, in the midst of our dedication to the war and the sacrifice which it demands, we pause a moment to draw refreshment of mind and spirit by recalling that four centuries ago we were emancipated from one of our many bondages. To discover these restraining bonds, to loosen them, and to free the body and mind and liberate the spirit of man from such bondage, we must oppose without stint the decivilizing tendencies that too frequently scourge mankind.

We must oppose these vicious trends so that men with the genius of insight like that of Copernicus, assured freedom of thought and action, can freely develop their benign powers for breaking the shackles that cramp the forward progress of men. And we must oppose these vicious trends so that the ordinary man may come into the inheritance of a free and fuller life made possible by such men of genius.

For not only must great men and great nations be allowed to attain freedom. Liberty must be made progressively available to small states, to communities, and to the individual himself, if humanity is to march forward into light and life. The creation and operation of armies and navies require enormous organization and vast numbers that only a large state can provide. They require, as we all realize, tremendous financial resources. But (we must always remember) the creation and sweep of great liberalizing ideas may be the work of a single isolated (as it was in the case of Copernicus) Polish churchman.

By these reverent ceremonies, therefore, the people of America honor not only a great pioneer of our civilization. They recognize thereby the undying contributions that have come from the small nations of the world. I join with gratitude in these ceremonies. Copernicus serves to remind us that small nations have given for the common advantage of all people, many of the great enduring concepts which have enriched the life of man. This opportunity of living with the growing and unrestrained knowledge about man and his place in the universe places on us all so imperious a responsibility that we should pledge ourselves, in the name of those venerated great men of ideas, to strive to maintain that opportunity forever.

Washington, D.C., May 22, 1943

Dear Felix:

I am grateful to Dr. Shapley for that very fine edition of Dr. Mizwa's brochure on Copernicus, which he has been good enough to sign to me.

As ever,

F.D.R.

Washington, D.C., June 22, 1943

Dear Grace:

If the Copernican people have not already sent it to him directly, the President may care to have for his collection this interesting photograph of the audience at Carnegie Hall on May 24, 1943, standing while the President's message was being read.

Yours very sincerely,

F.F.

Washington, D.C., February 14, 1943

Dear Grace:

This is the letter — from little Oliver's taxi-driver friend — about which Marion spoke to the President. He may also want to see this picture of the lad, taken at Dark Harbor, Me. How fit the President is!

F.F.

P.S.   This is how the lad looked when Marion sent him back to his mother.

Dear Oliver:

Thinking that the Christmas card must not have reached you (the one that I mailed about November 1st, 1942, by ordinary mail), at Justice Frankfurter's suggestion, and with his aid, I am trying again.

We all miss your cheery "good morning," and your "sunny" presence. You have, to a marked degree, the rare quality of *liking other people so much*, that they just cannot help liking you. I feel proud to have known you; and just thinking of you creates in me a feeling of warmth and pleasure. *All* that have known you here have the same grand feeling about you! ! ! (Here's a tip — if you want to see Justice Frankfurter's face light up with exceptional pride and pleasure, just take a peek at him when somebody mentions your name.) So while we all miss you, we are glad that you can be with your parents again. We expect a lot from your future, young man, but we are confident in our expectations. The world is going to need a lot of fellows just like you! ! Does all this sound too serious to a boy only 5½ years old? No, not if I know Oliver Gates! ! !

Justice Frankfurter gave me a swell picture of you standing with a

background of barren trees (excepting one). It is a profile. I would appreciate, also, a picture of you, looking straight forward. My wife, my family,
and friends all liked your picture.

Enclosed is a picture of myself, dressed just as you have seen me, when
driving my taxicab. I think it flatters me. But I like to think that I look like
this when I am thinking of you.

Winter, here, is about half over. Spring is "just around the corner."
This is the season that I like best in Washington. I'll just bet 2 to 1 that
you will be missing our spring too. Remember how we used to listen to the
mocking bird in the morning. I'll be thinking of you, and missing your
"good morning" call too!

Well, take good care of yourself and your lovely sisters. Follow the
loving guidance of your father and mother. And don't forget us over here,
'cause we can't forget you!.

With sincere love, and best wishes from

Your cab-driver friend,
ROY M. ALLIN

Washington, D.C., February 25, 1943

Dear Frank:

I have to thank you for three things:

1st For recalling us to the Beatitudes.

2nd For reading them so beautifully.

3rd For applying them so effectively.

It was a great joy to Marion and me to see you so mobilized and so gay
on Sunday.

Ever yours,
F.F.

Washington, D.C., March 4, 1943

Please, Grace — what a day. If only Missy were also here to rejoice!

F.F.

Washington, D.C., March 4, 1933-1943

Dear Frank:

This *is* a day for thanksgiving and prayer. It is also a day for the affectionate good wishes from Marion, and your devoted friend.

FELIX F.

*Frankfurter had sent this brief note to mark the eleventh anniversary of
Roosevelt's first inauguration in 1933. But he grieved that Missy LeHand,
an invalid since 1941, was away from the White House. It was a time of*

personal grief for the President. He had learned while returning from the Teheran Conference of the death of Marvin H. McIntyre, his friend for more than twenty-five years.

Washington, D.C., March 27, 1943

Dear Frank:

You will remember my sending you a letter from a lad who had been through the Guadalcanal affair, and wrote about the feeling of those men. Well — that letter has turned out to be the testament of his thoughts, as you represented Bill Sheldon's confident hopes.

I have known literally thousands of fine boys, as they went through Harvard Law School for a quarter of a century. But there were very, very, few Bill Sheldons.

Ever yours,
F.F.

Frankfurter's Tribute to William Sheldon

The friends of Lieut. William DuBose Sheldon, U.S.N.R., who died March 10 from illness contracted at Guadalcanal and at other South Pacific engagements, will welcome the tribute paid him by the commanding officer of the Pacific Fleet Bombing Squadron because in that simple account they will recognize the authentic Bill. He had all the gentler qualities — loyalty, modesty, high courtesy, regard for the tender places in life — to a degree unusual in so young a person, and an unselfishness remarkable in a person of any age. In him selflessness came from a deep insight into the essential tragedy of life and a deeper dedication to its mitigation. But in Bill Sheldon these gifts of gentleness were united in rare measure with sterner qualities, likely to be missed by those who knew only his quiet voice, his shy, hesitating manner, his finely sculptured face and delicate physique. With time one became aware of deep reserves, of a strong even stubborn will, and a maturity far beyond his years. He was one of those whom William James called "the once born."

Ever since his student days he was a leader of men, affectionately called "Uncle Bill," and behind that name exercising a moral authority over his contemporaries which they rejoiced to recognize. Gifts of character are rarer than gifts of mind, and the sources of such moral sway as Bill held over men are not easy to fathom. If I may venture an explanation, Bill possessed such moral authority because he had moral superiority without moral snobbery. The clarity of his mind achieved its full powers because the motives of his actions and judgments were swept cleaner of dross than is true of most men.

The Greeks had such as Bill Sheldon in mind when they said the good die young. No one saw more clearly than he the moral issues of this war and he felt his life belonged to his country not as to a devouring state but to an organized way for leading civilized lives. It was like Bill to make his decision to be a part of the war swiftly, silently and alone. As it was like him to endure, after conspicuously gallant service in combat, the vicissitudes of illness far from home and friends, without letting them know. That is hard for his friends to bear now, but it was characteristic. He kept his troubles to himself.

If I have said anything exaggerated or false, if I have been guilty of the sentimentality which so easily overtakes one in the first shock of loss, I ask Bill's pardon. There is no swifter way to bury the dead. And Bill is someone to think back upon, to measure one's self by, to cherish in death as in life.

Frankfurter sent the President a copy of his tribute to Bill Sheldon.

Washington, D.C., April 9, 1943

Dear Frank:

Your "hold-the-line" order will become not the least memorable of your war acts, and your statement in its support not the least historic of your state papers.

Affectionately yours,
F.F.

Again worried about the threat of inflation, Roosevelt issued a memorable state paper pointing out how economic instability could be avoided.

Memorandum for Honorable Felix Frankfurter

The White House, April 10, 1943

Please read the enclosed and return for my files. I wish that Harold Laski would confine himself to things he knows about. On the things he writes about in this article, it is perfectly clear that he knows not whereof he speaks — and that is bad for Harold and his reputation. He is capable, but should stick to his line.

F.D.R.

Washington, D.C., April 16, 1943

Dear Frank:

I had already seen, and been saddened by, what the N.Y. *Times* printed last Saturday of Harold Laski's "Open Letter." You know how tenacious my friendships are, and what deep affection I have for Harold. But I try not to mix up head and heart in public questions, with the result that, for some time, I have not been able to see eye to eye with Harold on various phases of the war, its conduct and what is beyond.

But the Atlantic is hardly suited for exchange of letters dealing with serious divergence of view — with the result that Harold has known from my silences my disagreement. But the other day, when Gil Winant talked to me about Harold's worries in detail, I sent some specific messages by Gil, which, I'm afraid however, won't do much good. I wish I had him here to talk things over quietly and at length.

The poor lad is golden-hearted and his ardor is all for the right things. But I'm afraid the road to the Heavenly City is easier for him than for me.

Ever yours,
F.F.

Laski had written an "open letter" to Roosevelt criticizing American policy on Vichy France, Italy, and Spain. It must be understood, with the maximum force that can be given to these words, that Frankfurter loved Laski as if he were his own son, and Laski of course loved Frankfurter far more than his own father.

Washington, D.C., April 16, 1943
Dear Mr. President:
When the Library of Congress expressed the desire to have the manuscript of my Jefferson Bicentennial address with its longhand corrections, it suggested to me that you might want it for the Hyde Park Library. Needless to say, its significance is in the event celebrated and not in its authorship.

In suggesting that you may want this for the Hyde Park collection, I am taking the risk that you may think me humorless, but I hope not immodest — although, if I have to choose, I am not sure I would not prefer your thinking me immodest rather than humorless.

Faithfully yours,
FELIX FRANKFURTER
P.S.   In any event, you will want this brochure of the memorial exercises for Brandeis.

The White House, May 5, 1943
Dear Felix:
I am perfectly delighted to have the manuscript of your Jefferson Bicentennial Address with its longhand corrections. It will be a real addition to my collection of manuscripts in the Library at Hyde Park.

Also, I am glad to have the brochure of the memorial exercises for Justice Brandeis.

My best to you,

As ever,
F.D.R.

As an example of the thoroughness with which Frankfurter prepared himself for a great occasion, it may be said that he worked just over four months on this address, "The Permanence of Jefferson." In the first copy which Frankfurter sent him, the President marked this sentence about Jefferson: "He had that rarest of political talents, the capacity to organize a political party for the realization of his ideals."

Washington, D.C., May 3, 1943

Dear Mr. President:

This whole series of opinions may, I think, find proper lodgment in the Hyde Park Library. They ought to furnish to the future historian food for thought on the scope and meaning of some of the Four Freedoms — their use and their misuse.

You may find some diversion from your heavy burdens — some of which are needlessly put upon your shoulders — in Bob Jackson's opinion. It is really worth reading.

Faithfully yours,
FELIX FRANKFURTER

This simple letter introduces one of the most controversial decisions in Frankfurter's judicial career. For he had given the President the full text of all the opinions in the "flag-saluting cases." It should be noted, with emphasis, that Frankfurter commended to the President's special attention the opinion written by Justice Jackson. Yet that opinion had overruled his own opinion in the earlier case which the Supreme Court was reversing. Rarely does one find such fairness and magnanimity where deep issues are engaged. One night all these issues in the first flag-saluting case were discussed at the Roosevelt home in Hyde Park. Mrs. Roosevelt took the position later taken by Jackson; the President was with Frankfurter.

Lillian Gobitis, twelve, and her brother William, ten, were expelled from the public schools of Minersville, Pennsylvania, for refusing to salute the national flag as part of a daily school exercise. The Gobitis family was affiliated with Jehovah's Witnesses. The children had been taught to believe, as a matter of conscience, that such a display of respect for the flag was forbidden by command of Scripture. Speaking for the Court in an 8 to 1 decision,

Frankfurter in a 1940 judgment held that the exaction of such a pledge of respect to the flag was a proper exercise of legislative authority.

Three years later, in the Barnette case, this opinion was reversed. Speaking for a new majority, Justice Jackson said:

> *Freedom to differ is not limited to things that do not matter much. That would be a mere shadow of freedom. The test of its substance is the right to differ as to things that touch the heart of the existing order.*
>
> *If there is any fixed star in our constitutional constellation, it is that no official, high or petty, can prescribe what shall be orthodox in politics, nationalism, religion, or other matters of opinion, or force citizens to confess by word or act their faith therein. If there are any circumstances which permit an exception, they do not now occur to us.*
>
> *We think the action of the local authorities in compelling the flag salute and pledge transcends constitutional limitations on their power and invades the sphere of intellect and spirit which it is the purpose of the First Amendment to our Constitution to reserve from all official control.*

Frankfurter began his dissent with these words:

One who belongs to the most vilified and persecuted minority in history is not likely to be insensible to the freedoms guaranteed by our Constitution. Were my purely personal attitude relevant, I should wholeheartedly associate myself with the general libertarian views in the Court's opinion, representing as they do the thought and action of a lifetime. But as judges we are neither Jew nor Gentile, neither Catholic nor agnostic. We owe equal attachment to the Constitution and are equally bound by our judicial obligations, whether we derive our citizenship from the earliest or the latest immigrants to these shores. As a member of this Court I am not justified in writing my private notions of policy into the Constitution, no matter how deeply I may cherish them or how mischievous I may deem their disregard. The duty of a judge who must decide which of two claims before the Court shall prevail, that of a State to enact and enforce laws within its general competence or that of an individual to refuse obedience because of the demands of his conscience, is not that of the ordinary person. It can never be emphasized too much that one's own opinion about the wisdom or evil of a law should be excluded altogether when one is doing one's duty on the bench. The only opinion of our own even looking in that direction that is material is our opinion whether legislators could in reason have enacted such a law. In the light of all the circumstances, including the history of this question in this Court, it would require more daring than I possess to deny that reasonable legislators could have taken the action which is before us for review. Most unwillingly, therefore, I must differ from my brethren with regard to legislation like this. I cannot bring my mind to believe that the "liberty" secured by the Due Process Clause gives this Court authority to deny to the State of West Virginia the attainment of that which we all recognize as a legitimate legislative end, namely, the promotion of good citizenship, by employment of the means here chosen.

When Frankfurter circulated this dissent, two members of the Supreme Court, who need not be identified here, called formally on Frankfurter in his Chambers to plead with him to omit or soften this opening paragraph. They said it was too emotional and too personal for inclusion in a Supreme Court opinion. Frankfurter said they had given him very good reasons for taking these words out, but he had even better reasons for keeping them in; and in they stayed.

At the Hyde Park discussion of the Gobitis case, of which Frankfurter made a record, Mrs. Roosevelt said she would not presume to question Frankfurter's legal scholarship and reasoning. But there seemed to her to be something wrong with an opinion, both in logic and in justice, that forced little children to salute a flag when such a ceremony was repugnant to their conscience. Besides, she was apprehensive about the practical results. She feared that self-appointed, flag-waving patriots would now feel that they had a mandate from the Supreme Court to drive out every conspicuous sign of dissent and non-conformity, even when undertaken for conscience's sake.

The President disagreed. He said with great emphasis that what the local authorities were doing to the children was "stupid, unnecessary, and offensive" but it fell within the proper limits of their legal power. That was an exact statement of Frankfurter's own position.

E. F. Prichard, Jr., of Kentucky, endeared himself to Frankfurter by his refusal to become a reverent disciple. One day, while Frankfurter was expounding some policy or other at a dinner party, he noted that Prichard was counting his fingers and had almost exhausted his second hand. "What are you doing?" Frankfurter asked. "Oh nothing. Just counting your digressions." No one laughed harder than Frankfurter. Together with Mr. Archibald MacLeish, he edited Law and Politics, *a collection of Frankfurter's occasional articles and speeches for the period 1913-1938.*

The enclosure was a letter from the War Department, signed by General Cramer, advising Frankfurter that he was being put into the inactive reserve.

Supreme Court of the United States
Memorandum

From: "General" Felix
To: Dr. Watson
For: The C. in C.
Subject: Old Fashioneds and kindred matters.

Washington, D.C., September 15, 1943

My dear C-i-C:

From the enclosure you will learn that I have been placed, by your direction, on the martial shelf as a superannuated major, and the only chance now left for me to become a colonel is for Prichard to become Governor of Kentucky.

Respectfully but affectionately,
FELIX FRANKFURTER

The White House, September 28, 1943

My dear "General" Frankfurter:

I regret that you have been retired. You should always remember, however, that General Napoleon Bonaparte was retired to Elba while still in his forties.

I think there is an error in General Cramer's statement to you that you have been transferred to the "Inactive Reserve." I think he meant the "Inactive Preserve." The status is somewhat akin to the process of pickling in alcohol!

Always sincerely,
FRANKLIN D. ROOSEVELT

Washington, D.C., September 28, 1943

My dear C-in-C:

Allow me to say that your letter of even date is doubly gratifying, to wit: —

1. That you should compare my case to that of General Napoleon Bonaparte again proves how deeply rooted you are in legal tradition. Even in your military administration in time of war you rely on precedent.

2. More heartening still, is your correction of General Cramer's designation of my status. For you to assure me that I am transferred to the "Inactive Preserve," which gives me a status "somewhat akin to the process of pickling in alcohol," affords me justifiable grounds for assuming that I can rely on you for my good spirits in the future.

Respectfully and gratefully yours,
FELIX FRANKFURTER

Washington, D.C., June 30, 1943

Dear Pa;

By this time the President must be fed up even with potentates and premiers — and so he may well don't want to see jes folks. And the Lord and he and you know the last thing that Marion and I want to do is to add a feather weight to his chores these days. But if Marion and I would give him a few minutes of relaxation, before we go — we're at his command. We plan to leave this hell-hole on Tuesday, of next week, the 29th. But please — no "courtesy visit." We'll bid him our affectionate *au revoir* as heart speaks to heart.

Yours faithfully,
FELIX FRANKFURTER

Washington, D.C., July 1, 1943

Dear Frank:

Now that you've done it you must let me say how profoundly wise was your refusal to let the death sentence for Stephan be carried out. I speak not only as an old prosecutor but as one who studied the Stephan record. And I have no use for feeble sentimentalism toward grave criminal conduct even in peace-time, let alone while we're at war. But you have acted as the strong head of a strong nation — conscious of your strength and of ours, and confident of our security. And so you differentiated between evil deeds that do require the ultimate penalty and those that do not.

I congratulate you on, and rejoice over, your wise courage.

Marion and I had a joyous hour with you.

Ever yours,
F.F.

Frankfurter was an opponent of capital punishment. He rejoiced, as he told friends, that the President had so much compassion that he would worry over one life and try to save it, even amidst the daily carnage of war.

New Milford, Conn., August 26, 1943

Dear Frank:

The enclosed wire from the editor of the *Economist* speaks for itself. But on the chance that you may want to greet so important a publication on its centenary — for it has been a real friend of fruitful understanding between our two countries and consistently friendly (particularly considering that it is the great financial organ) toward your Administration — I have drafted a short message for your blue pencil.

The Quebec speech — which came beautifully to these Connecticut hills — executed the difficult job of generating the right mood by conveying purposes without revealing facts.

And you can't go fishing too often to suit me — even at the cost of having Pa tell me some whoppers when we get back. But he needn't try to tell me that you did your fishin' in Bessarabia. Even I know that Bessarabia isn't near Lake Huron!

Marion joins me in affectionate regards and good wishes.

Ever yours,
F.F.

August 3, 1943

CONFIDENTIAL

MR. JUSTICE FRANKFURTER:

THE 100TH ANNIVERSARY OF THE ECONOMIST WILL BE CELEBRATED AT A LUNCHEON SEPTEMBER 2ND. SPEAKERS WILL INCLUDE THE CHANCELLOR OF THE EXCHEQUER, THE GOVERNOR OF THE BANK OF ENGLAND, KEYNES AND OTHERS. A BRIEF MESSAGE FROM THE PRESIDENT WOULD CROWN THE OCCASION. YOU ONCE TOLD ME HE READS THE ECONOMIST. THEREFORE, MAY I ASK YOUR ASSIST-ANCE IN REQUESTING SUCH A MESSAGE? SIMILAR MESSAGES ARE EXPECTED FROM DOWNING STREET AND POSSIBLY THE PALACE. WHILE DELIGHTED TO LEAVE THE CONTENTS OF SUCH A MESSAGE UP TO YOU, I WOULD SUGGEST SOMETHING ALONG THE LINES THAT HE READS THE ECONOMIST WITH INTEREST AND PROFIT, APPROVING, IN PARTICULAR, THE COMBINATION OF ECONOMIC SOUNDNESS AND FORWARD-LOOKING VIEW, JUST IN THE UNLIKELY EVENT THAT YOU ARE DEVOID OF IDEAS. THE PRESIDENT MIGHT ALSO SAY HE THINKS ITS COMMENT ON AMER-ICAN AFFAIRS IS FAIR AND VALUABLE AS INFORMED OUTSIDE OPINION. HOPING YOU WILL EXCUSE THIS TRUMPET AUTOBLAST, BELIEVE ME, WITH KINDEST RE-GARDS, GEOFFREY CROWTHER.

Frankfurter's draft for Roosevelt follows:

For a hundred years the *Economist* has contributed effectively toward a better, that is a deeper, understanding of the forces which make for economic well-being. But even more than in the past, an adequate understand-ing of the economic interdependence of nations will be necessary to ensure peace in a free world. In the task of economic enlightenment we shall con-tinue to look to the *Economist* to play a significant part.

Frankfurter apparently thought more of the Economist *than did Roose-velt. The President modified Frankfurter's words before sending them off as his own message.*

Washington, D.C., September 1, 1943

Dear Frank:

I have a deep regret about your Message to Congress — regret that you did not speak it to the people over the air. For it is one of the most educational state papers you ever wrote. Your message put the panorama of world-encircling events in enlightening perspective, and thereby gave adequate basis for understanding the tasks that have confronted the country and the effectiveness with which the Government has met them. The Message once more proved how exciting a quiet narrative of great events and efforts can be made to be.

Ever faithfully yours,
F.F.

Once again Roosevelt chose the anniversary of Germany's attack on Poland as an occasion for a broad review of the war, and of the problems facing the American economy.

Washington, D.C., October 20, 1943

Dear Frank:

In reply to a note of sympathy on the plight of Denmark, comes this letter from the charming Danish wife of Francis Hackett.

The Brethren commented — this time it was a unanimous decision — on the grand form you were in yesterday.

A very good time was had by all — even on tea!

Affectionately yours,
F.F.

Bethel, Conn., October 16, 1943

Dear Felix,

You write that the Danish resistance should make me feel proud, and it does, and yet it seems to me the so absolutely obvious thing to do now, when it can be useful, that pride does not come in. But I am happy that the Danes were adamant also about refusing to save their own skins by throwing their Jewish fellow-citizens to the wolves. Hitler had hoped to force the King to form a Government by persecuting the Jews, but I know that they wouldn't themselves want him to do that. I've just learned that well over five thousand Danes with Jewish blood have reached Sweden, owing to the brilliant carrying-out of plans which the Danish "Underground" of course had ready.

All the news coming to me by way of my work confirms the faith I've had all along that the Danes would act even if no help was, or could be, expected. The work of sabotaging the vital Jutland traffic lines, etc., goes on undiminished.

I don't know if I should say it, but *how* it would cheer them in their loneliness if F.D.R. were to say even one little word to show that at least he personally were aware of Denmark's attempt to be useful actively. I can honestly say that nowhere in the world is he so admired, almost adored, as in Denmark. When we lived there we were always being asked about him; and his big view was praised. If he made a speech, there it was on the front page of all the newspapers with large headlines. I remember one editorial which said, "More than any one else the President of the United States speaks for the conscience of the world." The man who wrote that, the best informed journalist I know on world affairs, is now in a concentration camp, along with many of our most useful citizens.

Well, forgive so much talk, but my days and nights are brimming over with it all — and I know your sympathy for the oppressed everywhere. The size of a country matters not to you!

Much love to you and Marion.

Yours,
SIGNE

Of all his correspondents, and they included some of the most famous names in the world, Frankfurter regarded Francis Hackett as the best letter-writer. Mr. Justice Holmes agreed with that judgment. Frankfurter used to send quotations from Hackett's letters to the President and other friends. Hackett, a critic and biographer and man of letters in the classical meaning of those words, is best remembered for his biographies of Anne Boleyn, Henry VIII, and Francis I. His wife, Signe Toksvig, is an accomplished writer who has made her own distinctive place as a writer on diverse themes, from Hans Christian Andersen to the meaning of the spiritual world.

Frankfurter is referring in the latter portion of his letter to the annual official visit by the members of the Supreme Court to the President.

Washington, D.C., October 20, 1943

Dear Mr. President:

While searching for an old letter in my Brandeis files, I happened on the enclosed memorandum. Although it contains views expressed a quarter-century ago, they appear not wholly irrelevant for our day. But, in any event, the document may interest you as a historian.

A word about the origin of the memorandum:

Before Hoover left for Paris, he sent an intermediary to Brandeis with a view to eliciting any observations that Brandeis might have regarding problems that would come before the Peace Conference. Brandeis, in his characteristic way, said that there was only one problem on which he was glad to convey to Hoover his views. The memorandum herewith is a minute of what Brandeis then said, and I had his word that it accurately stated what he wanted to get to Hoover.

Faithfully yours,
FELIX FRANKFURTER

The following is Frankfurter's memorandum on Mr. Justice Brandeis's views on Russia as expressed on November 10, 1918. Herbert Hoover's emissary was Mr. Lewis Strauss, years later the Chairman of the Atomic Energy Commission.

Justice Brandeis believes that thus far we have misunderstood the Russian people and very much underestimated the situation. None of the Commissions which we have sent to Russia has, in his opinion, accomplished the least fragment of tangible result, and, in fact, he has some misgivings as to whether they have not been harmful to our prestige among the masses and confusing to the individual Russians who may be earnestly trying to discover a way towards stabilization and recovery. Neither military nor diplomatic missions are, in his opinion, capable of bringing the proper help and he believes what is needed is an economic mission which would offer its services in an attempt to promote economic recovery and heal the wounds which the transportation and production structures of the Empire have suffered as a result of war and revolution.

He distrusts the ability and disinterestedness of the Kerensky group as well as certain cliques of Russian ex-diplomats in Washington, London and Paris. These groups he believes are probably Czarist and autocratic at heart. He does not credit a large part of the information which has come to us concerning the present regime, fearing that it may be largely inspired by the group just mentioned. The present Government, he feels, should nevertheless be dealt with in the utmost caution until its intentions are clear and we are convinced of its honesty.

The urgency of the Russian question, and the fact that upon its settlement rest inevitably the proper functioning of economic interdependence in Europe, indicates to him the necessity that it should be the first matter to be settled by the powers at the forthcoming Conference in Paris. Any delay in facing the situation will postpone the restoration of normal world conditions and allow the focus of the disorganization to fester and spread.

Washington, D.C., October 29, 1943

Dear Mr. President:

All who truly care for the maintenance of our democracy should be grateful for your letter to the Speaker setting forth "the true facts concerning the deferment of Government employees." The present campaign of poison, which pictures the Federal Government as a haven for "draft dodgers" and "slackers" is part and parcel of a long campaign picturing the Government as a haven for peace-time slackers or worse. We badly need in this country a tradition of public service powerful enough to enlist its best brains. To get men of brains and character is sufficiently difficult in view of the greater worldly attractions that private enterprise offers. To add to this handicap the systematic attempt to surround work for the Government with discredit instead of with esteem is one of the subtlest and one of the surest forms of undermining the possibilities of effectuating our democratic purposes. It is because your letter serves as a counter-offensive against this menacing attitude against public service that I deem it one of the most important state papers to have come from you recently.

Faithfully yours,
FELIX FRANKFURTER

Washington, D.C., November 3, 1943

Dear Tree-grower:

Of course Moscow was a "triumph." But I'd bet a pre-war cookie that the real diplomatic triumph was very skilful grafting here so that there could be fruit in Moscow.

Good luck and serene confidence for all that is to come.

Ever yours,
F.F.

Frankfurter was sharing Roosevelt's sense of achievement over what appeared to be the success of the Foreign Ministers' Conference in Russia. A few months later one could not be so sure. Mr. Molotov represented Russia, Mr. Eden spoke for Britain, and Mr. Cordell Hull defended America's interests.

Washington, D.C., December 20, 1943

Dear Frank:

Just a word to tell you how relieved and happy Marion and I are that you are again on *terra Americana* — again home after a valorous voyage, on sea and in air, to further the opportunities for a home for a decent civilization for the whole world. With affectionate good wishes,

Ever yours,
FELIX FRANKFURTER

The White House, December 23, 1943

Dear Felix:

Ever so many thanks for your note and this carries affectionate greetings to you and Marion. After I come back from Hyde Park I hope to tell you both all about the trip. I realized on the trip what a dreadful lack of civilization is shown in the countries I visited — but on returning I am not wholly certain of the degree of civilization in *terra Americana*.

As ever yours,
F.D.R.

Roosevelt was back from the Teheran Conference in Iran with Churchill and Stalin. He returned to find the economic and political situation in the United States discouraging. On October 29, on behalf of the American government, he had felt compelled to seize the coal mines, shut down by a labor dispute. Now, on December 27, he seized the railroads to prevent them from being shut down by a strike. He wondered if slackers and profiteers and selfish men were creeping out of their holes. He would speak on this subject with blazing anger in his annual message to Congress next month.

Meanwhile, on Christmas Day, he reported on Teheran. He told the nation that General Eisenhower would be in command of the liberation forces for Europe, with Lieutenant General Carl Spaatz in command of the entire American strategic bombing force operating against Germany. In the Pacific theater of war, General Marshall had met with General MacArthur and Admiral Nimitz to plan new moves against Japan.

"On the basis of what we did discuss," said Roosevelt, "I can say even today that I do not think any insoluble differences will arise among Russia, Great Britain, and the United States. In these conferences we were concerned with basic principles — principles which involved the security and the welfare and the standard of living of human beings in countries large and small. To use an American and ungrammatical colloquialism, I may say that 'I got along fine' with Marshal Stalin. He is a man who combines a tremendous, relentless determination with a stalwart good humor. I believe he is truly representative of the heart and soul of Russia; and I believe that we are going to get along very well with him and the Russian people — very well indeed."

These were not Roosevelt's wisest words.

Washington, D.C., December 25, 1943

Dear Frank:

And what a Christmas remembrance! For I have the taste of a bibliophile even if without the means of gratifying it, and the drive of a historian though without his equipment. To have your Inaugural Addresses in such beautiful livery is pure joy — and to have them at your hands, with your warm inscription, is an enduring treasure.

I've re-read them — and not for the second time. What a panorama of history they unfold — the life, the hopes and anxieties and triumphs, dangers vaulted and ideals pursued and achievements yet to encompass, of the American people for more than a decade: the most fateful decade, perhaps, in the history of our country. A thin, almost austere little volume — as befits the expression of him who has the guidance of the nation that now, more than ever, is the last best hope on earth.

My deepest appreciation,

Devotedly yours,
FELIX FRANKFURTER

The Gleam of Victory

1944

1944

March 22	German troops occupy Hungary.
June 4	United States Fifth Army enters Rome, making it the first European capital to be liberated.
June 6	Invasion of Normandy begins under command of General Eisenhower.
July 24	Russia liberates Pskov, making possible an attack on German forces holding Estonia.
August 23-24	German troops in Paris surrender. Rumania accepts armistice terms.
September 4	Brussels is liberated.
September 8	Bulgaria accepts armistice.
November 7	First session of French National Assembly summoned by General Charles de Gaulle as leader of the Free French forces. Roosevelt is elected President for a fourth term, with Harry S. Truman as Vice-President.
December 25	Churchill and Anthony Eden arrive in Athens to arrange for the settlement of the Greek Civil War.

THIS *was to be a year of victories — and of surprises and paradoxes. In a military sense, the central event of the entire war was the assault on Europe to liberate it from Nazi domination. The Normandy landings had been pushed back by bad weather from May to June. D-Day on June 6 almost coincided with the fall of Rome to the allied armies. The weaker half of the European prison-house had cracked; but the Nazi fortress in Western Europe still had to be stormed and captured.*

On D-Day, so long awaited, so carefully planned, Roosevelt made no boasts of victory, indulged in no parade of American power. Instead, he prayed to Almighty God, before the whole nation, that our forces might be deemed worthy of victory, no matter how long the ordeal might be protracted. Never had an army of liberation and retribution been launched with such solemnity.

Politically, the dominant event was to be the Presidential campaign. Here again there was a great paradox. In 1940 there had been one consuming question. Would Roosevelt run for a third term? Frankfurter had played an important and perhaps indispensable role in helping him to reach his decision. But in 1944 the entire inner circle of friends and advisers took it for granted that Roosevelt would seek a fourth term. The one unanswered political question concerned the identity of the Vice-Presidential candidate.

Early in 1944 Frankfurter had a long talk with the President, who estimated that the war in Europe would be over by the latter part of 1945 and Japan would surrender within two years after Europe's liberation. He told Frankfurter that he had no choice in the matter: he had to run again, for only he carried in his head all the plans for military victory and the organization of the postwar world. Frankfurter accepted this statement, not as a proclamation of the doctrine of the indispensable man, but as a statement of undeniable fact. He also accepted with even more emphasis, and infinite sadness, the fact that Roosevelt was tired, desperately tired, and, left to his own unfettered choice, would like nothing better than to return to Hyde Park, and not seek another four years in the White House. The President told Frankfurter, with intense conviction, that he had already had far more than all the glory and power he had ever dreamed of; but he could not quit while the tasks of war were only half-done, and the work of peace was all to be done.

Like other close friends of the President, Frankfurter saw Roosevelt's fatigue. They saw him racked with a persistent cough, saw him go for months without wearing his steel braces on his legs, saw him deliver a speech while sitting in his wheelchair. But they had seen Roosevelt in a state of fatigue many times before, and then had seen him snap back in a firm recovery. They expected this resilience to assert itself again. It was no foolish hope. In the latter stages of the 1944 campaign against Governor Thomas E. Dewey the President took as many risks and made as strenuous speeches as he had ever done in his entire political career.

Frankfurter, who had seen at close hand the blunders which had led Woodrow Wilson to make peace in a partisan spirit, urged Roosevelt to bring some leading Republicans into the preparations for a peace settlement. Roosevelt agreed, and the bipartisan experiment in foreign policy soon began.

And looking solemnly at the President, and weighing his words very carefully, Frankfurter at this interview entered into an agreement with Roosevelt that he would cut down on the flow of his letters and written memoranda, and transact more business by phone or personal interview to lighten the President's burdens. That explains the abrupt contradiction in the number of letters that passed between the two men. There never was the slightest shadow on their unbroken friendship. Frankfurter wisely wanted to spare the President the trouble of examining lengthy memoranda and of replying to them.

Two exceptions were recognized — one on questions of atomic policy, the other on relations with Russia. Frankfurter agreed with Dr. Niels Bohr of Denmark, one of the pioneers and prophets of the atomic age, and with Mr. Henry L. Stimson, for long years one of Frankfurter's supreme heroes, that America should not try to hoard its atomic secrets but, instead, should use its atomic power to work for a general political settlement with Russia on many outstanding issues.

On Russia there was the greatest paradox of all. Frankfurter had thought Russia would hold when Germany attacked, even though almost everyone else had predicted that Russia would break. Now he was convinced that almost everyone, beginning with the President, was thinking too much of the personality of Stalin and not enough of the structure of power in the Soviet Union. He had already begun his campaign by invoking the high authority of Brandeis in emphasizing the importance of Russia in any lasting peace settlement. But he had to proceed slowly and warily, for the overburdened President desperately wanted to believe that he was right about Stalin and he would modify his position only gradually over a period of months. The debate between Roosevelt and Frankfurter was still going on, in their personal interviews, when the President's death in 1945 suddenly ended the discussion forever.

Washington, D.C., January 7, 1944

Dear Frank:

Marion has been down with a mild case of the flu and she tells me it affords a rather pleasant, even if debilitating opportunity of relaxation from chores. I hope yours is a similar experience — and, indeed, that you are prolonging your "house arrest" to gain some free time and freedom from bores beyond the exactions of the flu! Anyhow — I hope deeply that you are your complete self again.

Forgive the enclosed screed — your waste-basket is capacious.

Affectionately yours,
F.F.

Washington, D.C., January 7, 1944

Dear Mr. President:

After hearing it twice and reading it the next day, I have reflected much on your admirable Christmas address. Naturally enough, your announcement of Eisenhower's appointment furnished the headlines. But I suspect that the most important single sentence was your statement that "I do not think any insoluble differences will arise among Russia, Great Britain and the United States."

And it is over that statement that I have especially pondered these last two weeks. That the translation into action of the policy you thus announced is indispensable for a peaceful and a decent world as far as one can see ahead, there surely can be no doubt. But our appropriate relations with the other two leading nations of the contemporary world and the problems they present to you, have stirred in my mind a comparison with the problems that confronted Washington in relation to the two leading nations of his time — Great Britain and France. In Washington's time opinion was unduly divided between the partisans of England and France. Now appear dangerous signs of such partisanship among too many of our people as between Great Britain and Russia, instead of a determined effort to translate into action the policy which was symbolized at Teheran and which you expressed in your Christmas address. Such a policy is indispensable for our day fundamentally for the same reason for which Franklin urged cooperative action — if we don't hang together, we'll hang separately. And like every idea that displaces familiar habits of thought, it must be stated over and over again and made to reach the mind by every variety of avenue through which access to the mind is gained.

This policy of education is of course merely a continuation of your old "quarantine" speech. And just as you have insisted that the war front and the home front are parts of the same front, so our people must be made to see by unceasing reiteration that the foreign policy which you are espousing is indispensable to desirable domestic policies. In other words, unless we have the policies and arrangements that assure a decent and peaceful world, we cannot possibly have the necessary conditions for a forward-looking national life.

Inter-dependence and independence are thus two sides of our shield. And that is peculiarly true for this country. There are famous words of Burke very relevant to the role of the United States in the world of today. "We are on a conspicuous stage, and the world marks our demeanor." We are a power of hope and example in the world as the most successful democracy. As never before we are a power in the world, because for weal or woe we can bring more weight to bear than any other nation. Great power must be used for great purposes. And that is why the purposes we pursue at home give significance and meaning to the purposes we represent abroad. Conversely the purposes we represent abroad derive significance from the purposes we pursue at home.

These are generalities, I know, but they have been much on my mind, and therefore you will forgive me for putting them on paper.

Faithfully yours,
F.F.

In his State of the Union message on January 11, Roosevelt, speaking with anger, said:

The overwhelming majority of our people have met the demands of this war with magnificent courage and understanding. They have accepted inconveniences; they have accepted hardships; they have accepted tragic sacrifices. And they are ready and eager to make whatever further contributions are needed to win the war as quickly as possible — if only they are given the chance to know what is required of them.

However, while the majority goes on about its great work without complaint, a noisy minority maintains an uproar of demands for special favors for special groups. There are pests who swarm through the lobbies of the Congress and the cocktail bars of Washington, representing these special groups as opposed to the basic interests of the Nation as a whole. They have come to look upon the war primarily as a chance to make profits for themselves at the expense of their neighbors — profits in money or in terms of political or social preferment.

Such selfish agitation can be highly dangerous in wartime. It creates confusion. It damages morale. It hampers our national effort. It muddies the waters and therefore prolongs the war. . . .

Over-confidence and complacency are among our deadliest enemies. Last spring — after notable victories at Stalingrad and in Tunisia and against U-boats on the high seas — over-confidence became so pronounced that war production fell off. In two months, June and July, 1943, more than a thousand airplanes that could have been made and should have been made were not made. Those who failed to make them were not on strike. They were merely saying, "The war's in the bag — so let's relax!"

That attitude on the part of anyone — Government or management or labor — can lengthen this war. It can kill American boys.

Frankfurter had these words mimeographed, had three hundred copies sent to friends across the country, and asked that the President's statement be printed and framed and placed in a prominent place under the bold heading, "Don't let the Commander-in-Chief's words apply to you!"

Washington, D.C., January 30, 1944

Dear Frank:

Among the Presidents who have mattered decisively, you are the only one, barring T.R., who is — or has remained — a personal person for the people as well as for himself. And the thirtieth of January helps to renew and to vivify that sense of human being and not of an Institution.

To that end, Marion and I send you our affectionate good wishes. Since this may not reach you till tomorrow, it will come to you with compound interest.

Ever yours,
F.F.

The White House, February 3, 1944

Dear Felix:

That was a mighty nice letter which you sent to me on my birthday. Thanks very much.

I do hope you and Marion will come in and see me very soon.

Always sincerely,
F.D.R.

Washington, D.C., March 11, 1944

Dear Frank:

And now comes this letter from C.C.B. You will note his wish, in his last sentence — I shall be glad to serve as a post-office, but I sent him Marion's and my copy of the Order of Service.

Is it true that your Secretariat is out to lynch me for having stayed so long! But I assumed — and still do — that the Commander-in-Chief of a global war knows how to get rid of an old retired major.

It *was* very generous of you to indulge me in such a long, joyous, old-fashioned visit — and delectable it was. As a good reporter — Herbert Croly said that nature meant me to be a journalist and perversity took me into the law — as a good reporter I made Marion share very considerably in my pleasure. She returns affectionately your messages to her. I had a grand time — memorably so.

If only I could find a magic wand to wave away your sinus.

Ever devotedly yours,
F.F.

March 9, 1944

Dear Felix:

Thank you for the order of service in the White House. I am glad you were there and if I had ears to hear I should wish that I had been too.

Your interest in the origin of the prayers I share. Many of them, of course, are translations from the Latin, but in the first Book of Common Prayer in the reign of Edward VI there were comparatively few prayers. The earliest form of the *Prayer for the King's Majesty* is found in two little books from the press of Berthelet, who was the King's Printer at the end of the reign of Henry VIII and the beginning of Edward VI. I will have the prayer for Edward VI copied for you to compare with the prayer for the President and all others in authority. You will see how many phrases have been retained — and how beautiful they are — "Dooest from thy throne beholde on the dwellers upon earth: with mooste lowly hertes we beseche the vouchsafe with favourable regard to behold * * * and so replenysshe hym with the grace of thy holy spirite, that he alway incline to thy wil and walke in thy way * * * indue him plentifully with heavenly geftes. Grant him in health and welth long to live."

This morning I was talking with a man of God and I gave him the order of service and asked him to annotate it by giving the sources so far as he could, so that I might send it to you. If you can find another copy or two for me I should like them very much.

Ever yours,
C.C.B.

Herbert Croly was the first editor of the New Republic. *It is now a matter of record, on Frankfurter's own written authority and not casual reminiscence, that Croly and not Joseph Alsop is the author of this famous remark about him.*

The White House, April 25, 1944

My dear Mr. Justice:

There is enclosed a copy of a request Mrs. Roosevelt has received from a young man who is building up a library. Mrs. Roosevelt will be grateful for your suggestions as to books that would answer the purposes stated in this request, so that she may pass them along to the young man.

Very sincerely yours,
MALVINA C. THOMPSON

My wife and I are employed as record clerks by the Goodyear Aircraft Corp. of Phoenix, Arizona. Before we came to Arizona, because of my wife's asthma, we worked for the personnel department of the Kaiser Shipyard of Vancouver. I was raised in South Dakota and graduated from a small country high school. Due to the extreme difficulty of even earning a living I did not go farther in school . . .

Since my first high school days my friends and associates have considered me a radical. If hoping and seeking for a better world for the kind of people my mother belonged to — if wanting less burden and more light for the great masses in this world is being radical, then I plead guilty. Many of my associates look upon one as radical if he takes an interest in the Atlantic Charter, the Teheran Conference, Mr. Wallace, or decent treatment of the colored people. Sometimes I fear that American ideals as expressed in our "foundation documents" are too high for the average American working man, who, in turn, is too indifferent to try to study and learn the reasons he has been betrayed so many times in the history of this world.

I am permitting myself one extravagance. Since boyhood I have desired to have a small library of my own, of books that have proved to be a great value to mankind. So I have been buying copies of carefully selected titles which include classics, political science, economics, and history . . . I will be grateful to you all my life if you would just tell me what books you would feel that you would just have to have in your personal library if you were limited to just twelve volumes.

Washington, D.C., May 2, 1944

My dear Miss Thompson:

I am truly honored that Mrs. Roosevelt should turn to me for suggestions regarding the contents of a library for a young man who has the intellectual eagerness revealed in his letter to her. Such an inquiry is to me very serious business and deserves some thought, so please let me think about it and I shall write again.

Sincerely yours,
FELIX FRANKFURTER

Washington, D.C., May 18, 1944

Dear Mrs. Roosevelt:

As I wrote Miss Thompson, very few things have ever touched me as much as that you should turn to me to suggest a reply to the challenging inquiry from your correspondent who wished to have a list of a dozen books "if you were limited to just twelve volumes." Only a very foolish or very daring man would attempt to answer such a question, but I am self-indulgent enough to assume that that is not the reason you turned to me! Seriously the inquiry not only interested me much but it also brought back memories of my youth when a list of the fifty or hundred best books was one of the cultural games. And what a game it was!

Strangely enough I do not know why I do not promptly give the answer to your correspondent's question which I have often expressed for such a hypothetical question. In the course of idle conversation I have said on more than one occasion that if I were restricted to a single work on a desert island, it would be the Oxford English Dictionary, for through that I could reconstruct a good part of English literature. And that work as you know is precisely twelve volumes.

But any such list of course depends on the tastes and the interests of the reader. From the copy of your correspondent's letter I have tried to glean as best I could what manner of person he is, and I have drawn up a list for the manner of man that his letter pictured him to be, knowing full well there could be a dozen such lists. Well, without further ado I enclose a list of which at any rate it can be said that no one, I care not who, but would profit by making these volumes his companions.

Very sincerely yours,

FELIX FRANKFURTER

1. The Bible
2. Shakespeare's works in a single edition — edited by Dr. William A. Neilson
3. *The Oxford Book of English Verse*
4. Random House edition of *Greek Historians* (2 vols.)
5. Montaigne's *Essays*
6. Bacon's *Essays*
7. *Essays: First Series* — Vol. II of Emerson's Complete Works
8. Tolstoi's *War and Peace*
9. *The Federalist*
10. *The Heritage of America,* an anthology edited by Commager and Nevins

11. *Life and Writings of Abraham Lincoln,* edited by Philip Van
    Doren Stern
12. *The Complete Jefferson,* edited by S. K. Padover

The White House, May 25, 1944

My Dear Mr. Justice:

Mrs. Roosevelt asks me to thank you for the list of books you sent her
and which she has passed along to her correspondent. She is sure that the
list you suggest will be very helpful to this young man in building up his
library.

Very sincerely yours,
MALVINA C. THOMPSON

*It should be remembered that Frankfurter's list of books was prepared
for a young man at a certain stage of reading. Excluding books on the law,
his own three favorite books, measured in terms of their lasting influence
on him, were John Morley's* On Compromise; *Boswell's* Johnson; *and* The
Federalist. *Only a fourth book could venture to break into this sacred circle
— the three-volume biography of T. H. Huxley by Leonard Huxley.*

Washington, D.C., May 9, 1944

Dear Frank:

Your old vitality newly refreshed breaks through even cold print.
Nothing could be more heartening — so much depends on it!

On several counts this sketch of Holmes belongs in the Hyde Park
library. But before it gathers dust on the shelf you may care to glance at
it — you may find items of interest in it.

Marion joins me in fondest greetings.

Ever yours,
F.F.

The White House, May 29, 1944

Dear Felix:

Ever so many thanks for your nice note and for your pamphlet sketch
of the life of Oliver Wendell Holmes. I think it is grand and I am delighted
to have it for the Library.

My warm regards to you and Marion.

As ever yours,
F.D.R.

The President had sent Frankfurter a scorching letter, in private, attacking a New York industrialist for complaining that profits in war plants were too low.

The Democratic National Convention was to meet in Chicago on July 9. Early that month Mr. Robert E. Hannegan, Chairman of the Democratic National Committee, wrote formally to the President informing him that he already had enough pledged votes of the delegates to be nominated for a Fourth Term. Would he accept the nomination and serve for another term? On July 11 Roosevelt gave this answer:

Every one of our boys serving in this war has officers from whom he takes his orders. Such officers have superior officers. The President is the Commander-in-Chief and even he has his superior officer — the people of the United States.

I would accept and would serve. I would not run, in the usual partisan political sense. But if the people command me to continue in this office, I have as little right to withdraw as the soldier has to leave his post in the line.

For myself, I do not want to run.

All that is within me cries out to go back to my home on the Hudson river, to avoid public responsibility, and to avoid also the publicity which in our democracy follows every step of the Nation's Chief Executive. Such would be my choice. But we of this generation chance to live in a day and hour when our Nation has been attacked, and when its future existence and the future existence of our chosen method of government are at stake.

Therefore reluctantly but as a good soldier I repeat that I will accept and serve in this office if I am so ordered by the Commander-in-Chief of us all — the sovereign people of the United States.

On a piece of scratch paper, days later, Roosevelt gave Mr. Hannegan this message in his own handwriting:

Dear Bob,

You have written me about Harry Truman and Bill Douglas. I should, of course, be very glad to run with either of them and believe that either one of them would bring real strength to the ticket.

Always sincerely,
FRANKLIN ROOSEVELT

Mr. Truman knew nothing of this note. The men running the convention took it that Mr. Truman was the President's first choice because his name preceded the name of Mr. Justice William O. Douglas in the scrawled note. Mr. Truman came to the convention prepared to nominate Mr. James Byrnes for the Vice-Presidency. Mr. Byrnes, a strong candidate, finally withdrew when it became clear that labor was against him. So Mr. Truman became the choice. The rest is history.

What rang in Frankfurter's ears, and would not be stilled, was Roosevelt's statement: "All that is within me cries out to go back to my home on the Hudson river."

He knew, better than almost anyone, what that cry meant — and what it would mean in coming months. That explains the tone of the next letter to the President.

New Milford, Conn., July 12, 1944

Dear Frank:

Probably no letter you ever wrote, unless I am greatly mistaken, pulled you up more by the roots than your letter to Hannegan. No letter, in any event, ever spoke more eloquently — with the eloquence of undiluted sincerity. When, in the fulness of time, you will return to your congenial home on the Hudson, you will do so, because of this Hannegan letter, with the ultimate satisfaction of duty fulfilled in complete disregard of personal preference.

With every good wish,

Affectionately yours,
F.F.

As one can gather from Frankfurter's next letter, General Charles de Gaulle had come and gone.

But it is the Niels Bohr memorandum that is the important document. Its intense secrecy can be measured by the fact that Roosevelt enforced special security arrangements in its delivery to the White House. He knew in advance that it was coming, for Frankfurter had discussed Bohr's views with him several times. He had the memorandum, with Frankfurter's covering note, brought directly to him in a sealed envelope.

Work was proceeding on the manufacture of the first atomic bomb, still to be tested and exploded. When Senator Harry Truman, as chairman of the investigating committee into war expenditures, stumbled upon some curious expenditures and asked what they meant, no one could tell him. General Marshall, who did know, visited Senator Truman to ask him, as a patriotic matter, to take the expenditures on trust and make no more inquiries about them. He accepted the advice. Neither as Senator nor as Vice-President did Mr. Truman know anything about the bomb.

Inside the government, those who knew about it were few in number and pledged to total secrecy. One or two cabinet members might know something about it; but their knowledge would be limited to a few specific points; and the rest would know nothing. In the great departments, the utmost secrecy was observed, with only the bare minimum of indispensable people being brought into the affair.

Secrecy, in fact, was the root of the matter. The atomic age was being born not as an adventure in shared scientific knowledge but under the savage spur of military necessity. No one knew whether the bomb would work, or what its aftereffects would be, or whether Germany was going to lose the race to get the bomb first. Our worries about Russia's getting it came later. The secrecy paid off. That is what the President and his secret circle of advisers knew and remembered. They were conditioned from the very start of the atomic age to think in terms of secrets.

Had the secret work on the atomic bomb been tried and failed, or had it even been a less crushing military success, the President and Churchill might have been less obstinate in clinging to a policy of secrecy. As it was, Niels Bohr and Dr. Robert Oppenheimer found themselves talking to closed minds. They were arguing with the assumptions and presuppositions of Roosevelt and Churchill; they were arguing in fact against their inarticulate major premise. The political leaders did not understand what the scientists meant when they talked of an open world, and to the extent that they did begin dimly to understand, they did not like it.

Frankfurter knew little about science. But he knew a great deal about research and about scholarship. He knew that it was repugnant to the ethics and philosophy of scientific research to think of exclusive secrets and of building a barbed wire of security regulations to barricade and protect atomic secrets from the rest of the world. The scientists like Bohr and Oppenheimer, looking beyond the needs of war, saw the dangers in a policy of secrecy. Frankfurter merely believed, as a practical matter, that the policy of secrecy would not work very long. So he listened patiently to Niels Bohr, tried to understand, and hurried off to see the President in yet another private conference.

Niels Bohr knew the leading Russian scientists personally. He knew what they could do on their own, and of the stimulus that would come to the Russian program from captured German scientists once the war had ended. But the prevailing, uninstructed, primitive view in Washington was that Russia was a backward scientific country and could never match America's achievements. Hence it was easy for American policy-makers to accept the melodramatic myth that only traitors could help Russia enter the atomic age. Once again a gulf of misunderstanding separated the scientific leaders and the political leaders.

Niels Bohr, one of the most honored names in scientific achievement, was director of the Institute of Theoretical Physics in Copenhagen. In

1943, with the help of the Danish underground and the British secret service, he escaped from Denmark to Sweden from where he went to Britain. In Britain, he was welcomed by the director of the Cavendish laboratory and invited to join the atomic project.

Just before Bohr's arrival in England, Churchill and Roosevelt, at the Quebec Conference, agreed to a policy of cooperation on atomic problems. Canada was included in this agreement because of her possession of uranium.

Sir John Anderson, Chancellor of the Exchequer and in charge of Britain's uranium project, welcomed Niels Bohr's help and invited him to join the British and American scientists engaged in the joint project in the United States. Bohr arrived in this country late in 1943. Soon thereafter, he began his series of talks with Frankfurter and also with Lord Halifax, the British Ambassador. Following his visit to Los Alamos, Bohr again saw Frankfurter. By this time Frankfurter knew enough of the problem to begin his confidential discussions with Roosevelt.

The President charged Frankfurter to deliver an encouraging message to Bohr. Armed with this knowledge of the President's interest and support, Bohr returned to Britain where Sir John Anderson, later Lord Waverley, hoped to use Roosevelt's interest to strengthen his own campaign to make Britain's work on the uranium project less secret and exclusive. Churchill resisted any change. Throughout this whole affair, Anderson was Bohr's consistent supporter, Churchill his unyielding opponent.

Bohr returned to Los Alamos on July 3, 1944, and prepared a long memorandum, which Frankfurter promised to submit to the President. In fact, he gave Roosevelt an oral summary of the memorandum, printed here in full, before he delivered it. Roosevelt studied it; discussed it with Frankfurter on two separate occasions; and then in August had a conference with Niels Bohr himself.

Following the second Quebec Conference in September, Roosevelt and Churchill met at Hyde Park for further discussions. Churchill scented danger in Bohr's suggestion that the scientific community might help in promoting the process of political cooperation with Russia, and he infected Roosevelt with his suspicions of Bohr's purposes. This was the most preposterous thing of all. Bohr had already rejected an invitation from Peter Kapitza, Russia's leading atomic scientist, to work in the Soviet Union. He was as loyal to the democratic cause as Churchill himself. But strange weeds grow in the soil of secrecy, and they certainly grew here. Bohr was declared off limits. He was placed under secret scrutiny. For a time the most detailed watch was kept on his movements. Under Churchill's influence, Roosevelt's trust in Bohr was replaced by suspicion. Even Stimson, who agreed generally with Bohr, could not see him.

Frankfurter knew all about these developments and dreaded their portent. He did his best — it was never too successful — to keep Roosevelt's mind open to the larger implications of atomic policy as they would affect our relations with Russia and the organization of the postwar world. At least he succeeded in convincing Roosevelt that any stain of suspicion on Bohr's loyalty and integrity was both ridiculous and insulting.

At their Hyde Park Conference, Roosevelt and Churchill reached the tentative decision to use the atomic bomb on Japan, if tests proved the bomb feasible as a military weapon.

Even more important than this stupendous decision was the agreement to continue to keep the atomic program secret from Russia. Roosevelt's willingness to go along with this secrecy is the unanswerable proof that by late 1944 he had developed profound doubts about Russian policy and had begun to regret his praise of Stalin, though he never said so publicly.

The central issue, as Bohr saw it and as Frankfurter put it repeatedly to the President, can now be defined.

Continued secrecy would poison American-Russian relations and endanger the prospects for peace. Russia would have reason to think that she had suffered a gigantic and unexampled double-cross if the United States, while talking of the partnership of war, worked in unity with Britain but kept its entire atomic program an absolute secret from the Soviet Union. Perhaps a policy of disclosure would not produce the open world. But the failure to deal frankly with Russia would almost certainly produce a closed world, a world of division and discord, an armed world capable for the first time in history of reducing itself to a charred and poisonous rubble.

Frankfurter always held to the trembling hope — it was no stronger — that Roosevelt, even after the Yalta Conference in 1945, would agree to modify the policy of stern and unlimited secrecy. He hoped Stalin and Roosevelt would meet, with Churchill present, for the single and exclusive purpose of reviewing the entire range of issues involved in atomic policy. But death interposed its own sad veto on these hopes. Almost at the very hour that Roosevelt died at Warm Springs, on April 12, 1945, Frankfurter and Lord Halifax were walking in Lafayette Park opposite the White House talking of these very matters.

When President Truman, at the Potsdam Conference, overcoming the doubts and admonitions of his own advisers, finally told Stalin of the bomb, he was surprised by Stalin's calm. He need not have been. Russia had already begun her own atomic program, helped by traitors who had stolen the secrets which it was the purpose of our secret policy to protect. Russia had a grievance against America, a deep and angry suspicion of being badly used. The possibility of creating conditions of trust and cooperation with Russia had been grievously damaged.

The exchange of letters with Mrs. Roosevelt in 1950 rounds out the story with tragic finality. She was probably the only person, apart from Roosevelt himself, who knew of Frankfurter's deep and long-continued involvement in these atomic problems. Certainly Mrs. Frankfurter knew nothing about it. Even Mr. Acheson and Mr. Stimson, his two greatest friends, had only sporadic and broken glimpses of what was involved. In 1950 Mrs. Roosevelt, who had great sympathy with what Niels Bohr and Frankfurter and Oppenheimer had tried to do, wanted to see Frankfurter to report on a conversation with Bohr in Copenhagen. Frankfurter, then on holiday, asked for a delay in his meeting with Mrs. Roosevelt, for he knew, sadly, that by 1950 the urgency had gone. His own correspondence with Niels Bohr had given him ample evidence of that fact. When he saw Mrs. Roosevelt, they brooded over the strange and melancholy turnings of this whole story, on how one of the greatest achievements open to scientific genius had resulted in creating a world yet more divided and dangerous; and they wondered, knowing there could be no answer, if the result would have been the same if Roosevelt in 1944 and 1945 had been as vigorous and dominant as in 1940.

Niels Bohr was the Nobel Laureate in Physics in 1922 and the recipient of the first Atoms for Peace Prize in 1957. When he died in 1962, Frankfurter wrote of him: "One can confidently say that on no conscience did the potential menace of nuclear physics to mankind weigh more heavily than it did on Professor Bohr. Equally, I believe, is it true that no man was so preoccupied with thinking about means of alleviation of this menace than the persistent thought that Professor Bohr gave to this matter."

That is all. Even in 1962 Frankfurter did not want to tell the whole story or even to hint at its larger meaning. But when he decided to publish his correspondence with the President, on nothing was he more insistent than that his confidential involvement in the discussion of atomic policy should be revealed. He did not know whether Roosevelt had been right and he himself had been wrong. On this point he passed no judgment at all. He was utterly without interest in this personal question.

What alone concerned him was the importance of presenting the essential facts to the American people, making them see that on issues of this unprecedented magnitude it was possible for informed and patriotic men to differ profoundly, and to invite them to ponder the larger and still unresolved implications of atomic policy.

As stated earlier, the full text of Niels Bohr's memorandum of July 3, 1944, is given here, but only Frankfurter's covering letter of September 8, 1944, since it clearly summarizes what Bohr wanted to say in his second and much shorter letter. Frankfurter's September letter was written just before Roosevelt's conference with Churchill. Bohr's mastery of written

English was imperfect and his document is not always easy reading. But in all the sweep of the Roosevelt-Frankfurter correspondence, there is nothing to surpass its importance. For it confronts us with the central challenges of the atomic age as they affect American-Russian relations and the enduring hopes for peace.

New Milford, Conn., July 10, 1944

Dear Frank:

After my recent talk with you it occurred to me that, if by chance it should not be possible for you to see Professor Niels Bohr, you might like to have on paper the direction of his thoughts, in so far as these could be put on paper. Here is the memorandum which he wrote exclusively for this use by me. Indeed, as I told you, he has not spoken to a soul about these aspects of the matter to anyone except me on this side of the ocean — not even to the Danish Minister, whose guest he is. The memorandum is in his able but quaint English, and of course couched in the most abstract language for security reasons. Not even I have made a copy of this memorandum.

Since leaving Washington I have learned that Professor Bohr's stay here has been extended. He will be in Washington through Saturday, July, 15th.

But I hope that *you* won't have to stew in that hell's hole. Holmes used to speak of the "peculiar" heat of Washington. It sure is "peculiar."

From all that one can gather from the press, the visit of Jean d'Arc Clemenceau came off well. And what grand news from the fronts!

Take care of yourself! Marion and I send you affectionate regards.

Ever yours,
F.F.

Memorandum

July 3, 1944

Top Secret. Confidential

The project of releasing, to an unprecedented scale, the energy bound in matter is based on the remarkable development of physical science in our century which has given us the first real insight in the interior structure of the atom.

This development has taught us that each atom consists of a cluster of electrified corpuscles, the so-called electrons, held together by the attraction from a nucleus which, although it contains practically the whole mass of the atom, has a size extremely small compared with the extension of the electron cluster.

By contributions of physicists from nearly every part of the world, the

problems of the electron configuration within the atom were in the course
of relatively few years most successfully explored and led above all to a
clarification of the relationship between the elements as regards their ordinary physical and chemical properties.

In fact all properties of matter like hardness of materials, electric con-
ductivity and chemical affinities, which through the ages have been exploited for technical developments to an ever increasing extent, are determined only by the electronic configuration and are practically independent
of the intrinsic structure of the nucleus.

This simplicity has its root in the circumstance that by exposure of
materials to ordinary physical or chemical agencies, any change in the
atomic constitution is confined to distortion or disrupture of the electron
cluster while the atomic nuclei are left entirely unchanged.

The stability of the nuclei under such conditions is in fact the basis for
the doctrine of the immutability of the elements which for so long has been
a fundament for physics and chemistry. A whole new epoch of science was
therefore initiated by the discovery that it is possible by special agencies,
like the high speed particles emitted by radium, to produce disintegrations
of the atomic nuclei themselves and thereby to transform one element into
another.

The closer study of the new phenomena revealed characteristic fea-
tures which differ most markedly from the properties of matter hitherto
known, and above all it was found that nuclear transmutations may be
accompanied by an energy release per atom millions of times larger than
the energy exchanged in the most violent chemical reactions.

Although at that stage no ways were yet open of releasing for practical
purposes the enormous energy stored in the nuclei of atoms, an immediate
clue was obtained to the origin of the so far quite unknown energy sources
present in the interior of the stars, and in particular it became possible to
explain how our sun has been able through billions of years to emit the
powerful radiation upon which all organic life on the earth is dependent.

The rapid exploration of this novel field of research in which international co-operation has again been most fruitful led within the last
decenniums to a number of important discoveries regarding the intrinsic
properties of atomic nuclei and especially revealed the existence of a non-
electrified nuclear constituent, the so-called neutron, which when set free
is a particularly active reagent in producing nuclear transmutations.

The actual impetus to the present project was the discovery made in
the last year before the war, that the nuclei of the heaviest elements like
Uranium by neutron bombardment, in the so called fission process, may
split in fragments ejected with enormous energies, and that this process is

accompanied by the release of further neutrons which may themselves effect the splitting of other heavy nuclei.

This discovery indicated for the first time the possibility, through propagation of nuclear disintegrations from atom to atom, to obtain a new kind of combustion of matter with immense energy yield. In fact a complete nuclear combustion of heavy materials would release an energy 100,-000,000 times larger than that obtainable by the same amount of chemical explosives.

This prospect not only at once attracted the most widespread interest among physicists, but of its appeal to the imagination of larger circles I have vivid recollections from my stay in U.S.A. in the spring of 1939 where, as guest of the Institute of Advanced Studies in Princeton, I had the pleasure to participate together with American colleagues in investigations on the mechanism of the fission process.

Such investigations revealed that among the substances present in natural ores, only a certain modification of Uranium fulfils the conditions for nuclear combustion. Since this active substance always occurs mixed with a more abundant, inactive Uranium modification, it was therefore realized that in order to produce devastating explosives, it would be necessary to subject the available materials to a treatment of an extremely refined and elaborate character.

The recognition that the accomplishment of the project would thus require an immense technical effort, which might even prove impracticable, was at that time, not least in view of the imminent threat of military aggression, considered as a great comfort since it would surely prevent any nation from staging a surprise attack with such super weapons.

Any progress on nuclear problems achieved before the war was, of course, common knowledge to physicists all over the world, but after the outbreak of hostilities no further information has been made public, and efforts to exploit nuclear energy sources have been kept as military secrets.

During my stay in Denmark under the German occupation nothing was therefore known to me about the great enterprise in America and England. It was, however, possible, due to connections originating from regular visits of German physicists to the Institute for Theoretical Physics in Copenhagen in the years between the wars, rather closely to follow the work on such lines which from the very beginning of the war was organized by the German Government.

Although thorough preparations were made by a most energetic scientific effort, disposing of expert knowledge and considerable material resources, it appeared from all information available to us, that at any rate in the initial, for Germany, so favourable stages of the war it was never by the Government deemed worthwhile to attempt the immense and hazardous technical enterprise which an accomplishment of the project would require.

Immediately after my escape to Sweden in October 1943, I came on an invitation of the British Government to England where I was taken into confidence about the great progress achieved in America and went shortly afterwards together with a number of British colleagues to U.S.A. to take part in the work. In order, however, to conceal my connection with any such enterprise, post-war planning of international scientific co-operation was given as the object of my journey.

Already in Denmark I had been in secret connection with the British Intelligence Service, and more recently I have had the opportunity with American and British Intelligence Officers to discuss the latest information, pointing to a feverish German activity on nuclear problems. In this connection it must above all be realized that if any knowledge of the progress of the work in America should have reached Germany, it may have caused the Government to reconsider the possibilities and will, not least, have presented the physicists and technical experts with an extreme challenge.

Definite information of preparations elsewhere is hardly available, but an interest within the Soviet Union for the project may perhaps be indicated by a letter which I have received from a prominent Russian physicist with whom I had formed a personal friendship during his many years' stay in England and whom I visited in Moscow a few years before the war, to take part in scientific conferences.

This letter contained an official invitation to come to Moscow to join in scientific work with Russian colleagues who, as I was told, in the initial stages of the war were fully occupied with technical problems of immediate importance for the defense of their country, but now had the opportunity to devote themselves to scientific research of more general character. No reference was made to any special subject, but from pre-war work of Russian physicists it is natural to assume that nuclear problems will be in the center of interest.

The letter, originally sent to Sweden in October 1943, was on my recent visit to London handed to me by the Counsellor of the Soviet Embassy who in a most encouraging manner stressed the promises for the future understanding between nations entailed in scientific collaboration. Although, of course, the project was not mentioned in this conversation I got nevertheless the impression that the Soviet Officials were very interested in the effort in America about the success of which some rumors may have reached the Soviet Union.

Even if every physicist was prepared that some day the prospects created by modern researches would materialize, it was a revelation to me to learn about the courage and foresight with which the great American and British enterprise had been undertaken and about the advanced stage the work had already reached.

What until a few years ago might have been considered a fantastic dream is at the moment being realized in great laboratories erected for secrecy in some of the most solitary regions of the States. There a group of physicists larger than ever before assembled for a single purpose, and working hand in hand with a whole army of engineers and technicians are producing new materials capable of enormous energy release and developing ingenious devices for their most effective use.

To everyone who is given the opportunity for himself to see the refined laboratory equipment and the huge production machinery it is an unforgettable experience of which words can only give a poor impression. Truly no effort has been spared, and it is hardly possible for me to describe my admiration for the efficiency with which the great work has been planned and conducted.

Moreover it was a special pleasure to me to witness the complete harmony with which the American and British physicists, with almost everyone of whom I was intimately acquainted through previous scientific intercourse, were devoting themselves with the utmost zeal to the joint effort.

I shall not here enter on technical details, but one cannot help comparing with the Alchemysts of former days, groping in the dark in their vain efforts to make gold. To-day physicists and engineers are on the basis of well-established knowledge directing and controlling processes by which substances far more precious than gold are being collected atom by atom or even built up by individual nuclear transmutations.

Such substances must be assumed to have been abundant in the early stages of our universe where all matter was subject to conditions far more violent than those which still persist in the turbulent and flaming interior of the stars. Due, however, to their inherent instability the active materials now extracted or produced have in the course of time become very rare or even completely disappeared from the household of nature.

The whole enterprise constitutes indeed a far deeper interference with the natural course of events than anything ever before attempted, and its impending accomplishment will bring about a whole new situation as regards human resources. Surely, we are in a whole new situation as regards human resources. Surely, we are being presented with one of the greatest triumphs of science and engineering destined deeply to influence the future of mankind.

It certainly surpasses the imagination of anyone to survey the consequences of the project in years to come, where in the long run the enormous energy sources which will be available may be expected to revolutionize industry and transport. The fact of immediate preponderance is, however, that a weapon of an unparalleled power is being created which will completely change all future conditions of warfare.

Quite apart from the questions of how soon the weapon will be ready for use and what role it may play in the present war, this situation raises a number of problems which call for most urgent attention. Unless, indeed, some agreement about the control of the use of the new active materials can be obtained in due time, any temporary advantage, however great, may be outweighed by a perpetual menace to human security.

Ever since the possibilities of releasing atomic energy on a vast scale came in sight, much thought has naturally been given to the question of control, but the further the exploration of the scientific problems concerned is proceeding, the clearer it becomes that no kind of customary measures will suffice for this purpose and that especially the terrifying prospect of a future competition between nations about a weapon of such formidable character can only be avoided through a universal agreement in true confidence.

In this connection it is above all significant that the enterprise, immense as it is, has still proved far smaller than might have been anticipated and that the progress of the work has continually revealed new possibilities for facilitating the production of the active materials and of intensifying their effects.

The prevention of a competition prepared in secrecy will therefore demand such concessions regarding exchange of information and openness about industrial efforts including military preparations as would hardly be conceivable unless at the same time all partners were assured of a compensating guarantee of common security against dangers of unprecedented acuteness.

The establishment of effective control measures will of course involve intricate technical and administrative problems, but the main point of the argument is that the accomplishment of the project would not only seem to necessitate but should also, due to the urgency of mutual confidence, facilitate a new approach to the problem of international relationship.

The present moment where almost all nations are entangled in a deadly struggle for freedom and humanity might at first sight seem most unsuited for any committing arrangement concerning the project. Not only have the aggressive powers still great military strength, although their original plans of world domination have been frustrated and it seems certain that they must ultimately surrender, but even when this happens, the nations united against aggression may face grave causes of disagreement due to conflicting attitudes towards social and economic problems.

By a closer consideration, however, it would appear that the potentialities of the project as a means of inspiring confidence just under these circumstances acquire most actual importance. Moreover the momentary situation would in various respects seem to afford quite unique possibilities which might be forfeited by a postponement awaiting the further development of the war situation and the final completion of the new weapon.

Although there can hardly be any doubt that the American and British enterprise is at a more advanced stage than any similar undertaking elsewhere, one must be prepared that a competition in the near future may become a serious reality. In fact, as already indicated, it seems likely that preparations, possibly urged on by rumours about the progress in America, are being speeded up in Germany and may even be under way in the Soviet Union.

Further it must be realized that the final defeat of Germany will not only release immense resources for a full scale effort within the Soviet Union, but will presumably also place all scientific knowledge and technical experience collected in Germany at the disposal for such an effort.

In view of these eventualities the present situation would seem to offer a most favourable opportunity for an early initiative from the side which by good fortune has achieved a lead in the efforts of mastering mighty forces of nature hitherto beyond human reach.

Without impeding the importance of the project for immediate military objectives, an initiative, aiming at forestalling a fateful competition about the formidable weapon, should serve to uproot any cause of distrust between the powers on whose harmonious collaboration the fate of coming generations will depend.

Indeed, it would appear that only when the question is taken up among the United Nations of what concessions the various powers are prepared to make as their contribution to an adequate control arrangement, it will be possible for any one of the partners to assure themselves of the sincerity of the intentions of the others.

Of course, the responsible statesmen alone can have the insight in the actual political possibilities. It would, however, seem most fortunate that the expectations for a future harmonious international co-operation, which have found unanimous expression from all sides within the United Nations, so remarkably correspond to the unique opportunities which, unknown to the public, have been created by the advancement of science.

Many reasons, indeed, would seem to justify the conviction that an approach with the object of establishing common security from ominous menaces without excluding any nation from participating in the promising industrial development which the accomplishment of the project entails will be welcomed, and be responded to with a loyal co-operation on the enforcement of the necessary far-reaching control measures.

Just in such respects helpful support may perhaps be afforded by the world wide scientific collaboration which for years has embodied such bright promises for common human striving. On this background personal connections between scientists of different nations might even offer means of establishing preliminary and noncommittal contact.

It needs hardly be added that any such remark or suggestion implies no underrating of the difficulty and delicacy of the steps to be taken by the statesmen in order to obtain an arrangement satisfactory to all concerned, but aim only at pointing to some aspects of the situation which may facilitate endeavours to turn the project to lasting advantage for the common cause.

Should such endeavours be successful, the project will surely have brought about a turning point in history and this wonderful adventure will stand as a symbol of the benefit to mankind which science can offer when handled in a truly human spirit.

Washington, D.C., September 8, 1944

Dear Frank:

Here is a letter from my Danish friend.

From many long talks with him I gather that there are three solid reasons for believing that knowledge of the pursuit of our project can hardly be kept from Russia:

(1) they have very eminent scientists, particularly Peter Kapitza, entirely familiar through past experience with these problems.

(2) some leakage, even if not of results and methods, must inevitably have trickled to Russia.

(3) Germans have been similarly busy, and knowledge of their endeavors will soon be open to the Russians. Therefore, to open the subject with Russia, without of course making essential disclosures before effective safeguards and sanctions have been secured and assured, would not be giving them anything they do not already — or soon will — substantially have.

In a word, the argument is that appropriate candor would risk very little. Withholding, on the other hand, might have grave consequences. There may be answers to these considerations. I venture to believe, having thought a good deal about it, that in any event these questions are very serious.

My very best wishes for successful days in the talks immediately ahead.

Affectionately yours,

F.F.

Copenhagen, Denmark, June 18, 1950

Dear Mr. Justice:

Professor Niels Bohr asked me to see him alone while I was here, and he particularly wants me to talk to you on some things which he feels it is important should be done at home.

Will you be in Connecticut and could you and your wife drive over to Hyde Park for lunch with me shortly after I get home on July 3rd? Or is there any more convenient way in which I can arrange to see you?

Professor Bohr feels it very urgent and while I am not able to judge the situation, I feel I should see you and then proceed from there as you advise me.

Very sincerely yours,

ELEANOR ROOSEVELT

Washington, D.C., June 25, 1950

Dear Mrs. Roosevelt:

Your letter from Copenhagen comes just as we are about to take off for England. We shall not be back until about the 22nd of August. We shall make straight for New Milford, Connecticut, on our return. Of course I shall be subject to your call if it will still be your desire to see me.

We regret very much not to have the pleasure of lunching with you shortly after you get home, and the more so since the occasion of your desire for a talk is Professor Niels Bohr. He is altogether a noble creature, and what often may seem to be impractical suggestions by him may well be the wisdom of the long reach.

With cordial regards,

Faithfully yours,

FELIX FRANKFURTER

Late in the 1944 campaign, Roosevelt went before the Teamsters Union to make one of his most effective speeches — to put it with calculated understatement. The speech, a masterpiece, is known as the "Fala Speech" because of this passage:

These Republican leaders have not been content with attacks on me, or my wife, or on my sons. No, not content with that, they now include my little dog, Fala. Well, of course, I don't resent attacks, but Fala does resent them. You know, Fala is Scotch, and being a Scottie, as soon as he learned that the Republican fiction writers in Congress and out had concocted a story that I had left him behind on the Aleutian Islands and had sent a destroyer back to find him — at a cost to the taxpayers of two or three or eight or twenty million dollars — his Scottish soul was furious. He has not been the same dog since. I am accustomed to hearing malicious falsehoods about myself — such as that old, worm-eaten chestnut that I have represented myself as indispensable. But I think I have a right to resent, to object to libellous statements about my dog.

There was, of course, no substance whatever in the rumor. Thereafter Governor Dewey was running against Fala — and he lost.

Washington, D.C., October 2, 1944

Dear Frank:

Since even you agree that your Teamster's was a political speech, I can't tell you what I think of it. I'm not even sure that I can ask you to tell Fala how deeply I share your resentment on his behalf.

But not even my most judicial mood is able to suppress my feelings of affectionate regards and good wishes — and Marion says she ain't got no judicial temper.

Ever yours,
F.F.

Washington, D.C., November 14, 1944

Dear Frank:

Precisely a week ago — Election Day 1944 midnight — we drank your health in fizz water, as Holmes used to call it, worthy of the occasion. For, of course, the happy outcome of the Great Referendum gave Marion and me elation on your own personal account.

But as day by day the election gains the perspective of history, the scale of its significance becomes clearer and greater. By their extraordinary discriminating judgments, the American people in the various states vindicated on the whole as never before, I believe, our life-time faith in the democratic faith that Jefferson and Lincoln and you symbolize. And the American people averted a mean threat to the forward march of the world.

Marion and I send you our affectionate good wishes.

Ever yours,
FELIX FRANKFURTER

The White House, November 27, 1944

Dear Felix:

My warmest thanks for that grand letter. It means more to me than I can express in words.

Every good wish to you and Marion.

As ever yours,
FRANKLIN D. ROOSEVELT

Washington, D.C., December 24, 1944

Good wishes are especially appropriate this Season.
These come from

MARION AND FELIX FRANKFURTER

The Last Months

January 1945 – April 1945

1945

February 7-12   *Yalta Conference between Stalin, Churchill, Roosevelt. The Conference agrees that the United Nations should hold their first conference in San Francisco on April 25.*

March 3   *Finland declares war on Germany. In Cairo the Constitution for the Arab League is prepared.*

April 5   *Russia denounces her five-year non-aggression pact with Japan, thus making it possible for Russia to take part in the war against Japan. But Russia fought for only a few days before the final Japanese surrender.*

April 12   *President Roosevelt dies at Warm Springs. Harry S. Truman takes the oath as President.*

Roosevelt *left on January 22 for the Yalta Conference in the Crimea to meet with Churchill and Stalin. After the conference, he was so weary that it was almost a week before he could do any work. He played with his stamp collection. He reported to Congress on the Yalta Conference on March 1. Less than six weeks later, on April 12, President Franklin D. Roosevelt was dead.*

Washington, D.C., January 16, 1945

Dear Grace:

    All these years I have abstained from becoming that awful type of nuisance who bothers the President for autographs on photographs. But I do really believe he would not want to deny the great pleasure he will give to one of his staunchest and most effective supporters. Augustus L. Richards, who happens to be a classmate of mine, is one of those Republicans who for a dozen years has been in himself to no small degree a one man army for the President's purposes and policies. He is the best type of a New Englander and neither a photograph nor autograph collector, but it would give him great joy to have his hero's photograph in his home at Remsen, New York, where he lives in the famous Steuben place. And so I hope I shall be forgiven for putting the President to the trouble of autographing this photograph for Richards.

    With all good wishes,

Very sincerely yours,
FELIX FRANKFURTER

Washington, D.C., February 6, 1945

Dear Grace:

    Laryngitis has had me down for two weeks, or should have told you before this of my appreciation for getting the President's photograph duly autographed for Mr. Richards. I bet the fellow has been walking on air ever since its receipt!

    My warm regards,

Yours very sincerely,
FELIX FRANKFURTER

Washington, D.C., March 14, 1945

Dear Frank:

No one can truly feel another's grief. But Pa's death leaves such a void for me that I can at least in part realize what his going means to you. His shrewd humor, his energizing warmth, his unflagging affection, his non self-regarding environment — what a friend we have lost.

I say "we," but of course his feeling for you, his devotion to you, was a thing apart and unique. In his case, devotion came very close to consecration, but a consecration most human withal. He idealized you, as Marion says, without dehumanizing you into an idol.

Life seems to be thus — bitter-sweet at the core. That you should have had to bring back a heavy heart from your Yalta triumph — the triumph of accelerated justifiable hopes for a peaceful future world! But the strength that comes from the memory of Pa's devotion unto the last — his soldier's service — will continue to mingle with your indomitable will and the strength that you draw from the hopes of mankind.

Affectionately yours,
F.F.

The White House, March 16, 1945

Dear Felix:

That is a mighty nice note you sent to me about Pa and letters like yours are a great comfort. As I said in my statement after Pa's death, "there was never a cloud between us." I shall miss him much.

Affectionate regards to you and Marion,

Always sincerely,
F.D.R.

General "Pa" Watson, who had insisted that he was well enough to go to Yalta, died at sea on February 20 while the presidential party was returning home.

Washington, D.C., March 17, 1945

Dear Mr. President:

As you well know, there is a peculiar quality to the Washington grapevine and so it works its way even through the marble walls of the Supreme Court. If it be true, as the rumor goes, that there is a deadlock about a new Solicitor General, or at least that different people are pulling in different directions, you may care to know what follows.

In the first place, no new man could take hold of the major functions of a Solicitor General at this Term. There are only three weeks of argument

ink of Dean for Solicitor General? He would
Court.

F.D

t Frankfurter's last letter to Roosevelt should con-
son. Frankfurter and Mr. Acheson were friends for
lent agreed that Mr. Acheson should become the So-
e died before he could sign the appointment. Frank-
it in time Mr. Acheson would become Chief Justice of
rancis is Francis Biddle, the Attorney General. At this
heson was an Assistant Secretary of State.

e his own death, Mr. Justice Frankfurter had me sum-
He asked me to stand beside his bed so that I could hold
time we were together. He spoke of this book. "Tell the
said slowly and gravely. "Let people see how much I loved
much I loved my country, and let them see how great a
really was."

nore slowly, he said he had something to tell me. He did not
it was a dream or a vision. But that morning, in the early
felt he was in heaven, with Churchill coming forward to
and promising a good long talk with Roosevelt. Two days
shington's Birthday, Mr. Justice Felix Frankfurter was dead.

e his own death, President Roosevelt was working on a speech.
his last words:

ly limit to our realization of tomorrow will be our doubts of to-
move forward with strong and active faith."

Se
eneral
serves the
powers of
next few ye
but all the o
the courts, are

Thirdly, o
the matter is en
hunch that, while
many more month
General. He has be
because both Ned Bu
demand for Dean to t
siderable. And so I wou
it his duty to respond t
nantly a lawyer that the S
to him. He has the respect
advocate and he would bri
post. He would favorably con
held that office in the past.

Dean and Francis are wa
admiration for him. But you k
about his sovereignty, and it will
feel that I was butting into his pr
know what I have written.

P.S.   Of course no one — neither De
this letter.

Memorandum for the At
The

Private

I understand that there are only a few wee
this term of the Supreme Court and that the
have all been parceled out to members of the Solic

I hear a rumor that Dean Acheson feels he ou
soon *to* his firm, as Ned Burling and George Rub
years old.

What would you th
the definite liking of the

It is *appropriate* th
cern Mr. Dean Ach
fifty years. The Presi
licitor General but
furter had hoped th
the United States.
time Mr. Dean Ac
Two days befo
moned urgently.
his hand all the
whole story," he
Roosevelt, how
man Roosevelt
Then, even
know whether
dawn, he had
welcome him
later, on Wa
Just befor
These were
"The on
day. Let u

The Afterword

FRANKLIN DELANO ROOSEVELT*
by
Felix Frankfurter

"When a great tree falls, we are surprised how meagre the landscape seems without it. So when a great man dies. We may not have been intimate with him; it is enough that he was within our view; when he is gone, life seems thinner. . . . The happiest of us hardly can hope for a destiny so complete and fortunate as that which has just been fulfilled. We shall be fortunate enough if we shall have learned to look into the face of fate and the unknown with a smile like his." Said of another, it was prophetically true of Franklin Delano Roosevelt and the world that mourns him.

Writings about Napoleon fill sizeable libraries. Roosevelt will claim an even larger share of history so long as the civilization endures which he helped to save. Fluctuations of historic judgment are the common lot of great men, and Roosevelt will not escape it. What history will ultimately say, it is for history to say. Only one thing is certain; he will remain among the few Americans who embody its traditions and aspirations.

But if history has its claims, so has the present. For it has been wisely said that if the judgment of the time must be corrected by that of posterity, it is no less true that the judgment of posterity must be corrected by that of the time. Franklin Roosevelt cannot escape becoming a national saga. It is right that this should be so, for such sagas guide and sustain the high endeavors of a people. But the saga must not swallow up the man, whose vivid friendship gave hope to millions though they never knew him, and whose death brought a sense of personal loss to millions who never saw him. This deep identification with his fellowmen must be saved from the impersonality of immortal fame.

This identification with his fellowmen was Roosevelt's profoundest characteristic and the ultimate key to his statesmanship. He was a democrat in feeling and not through abstract speculation about governments. When he said, "we are all immigrants," it was not a phrase but a feeling. And this feeling was not merely gregariousness in a setting of charm. It was not an undiscriminating love of his kind. His friendliness was so inclusive that his discriminating and often uncanny perception of men's qualities was a less

* Reprinted from the *Harvard Alumni Bulletin*, April 28, 1945.

apparent trait. He was keenly aware of men's frailties and follies. But he identified himself also with their follies and frailties, and so escaped the corrosion of cynicism.

This permeating friendliness represented true feeling. But equally true were deep recesses that were accessible hardly to anyone. From the time he was a boy, according to his mother, he had the self-sufficiency and the strength that come from a reserved inner life. Thus, while to outward view he was usually debonair and had a gaiety at times easily taken for jauntiness, he had a will of steel well-sheathed by a captivating smile. His optimism was a phase of this resoluteness. For too many people optimism is an evasion, a Micawber's hope that something will turn up. In Roosevelt, optimism was not an anodyne, it was an energy — an energy to spur his resourcefulness, a force that gave creative energy to others. An official not given to idolatry was once heard to say, "After talking with the President for an hour, I could eat bricks for lunch."

There were thus fused in him, and to an extraordinary degree, qualities indispensable for leading his people out of a period of deepening economic and moral deterioration by invigorating the forces of democracy. The same qualities fitted him to serve as a symbol of hope for liberty-loving people everywhere, in resisting a seemingly invincible challenge to civilization. Franklin Roosevelt's sophistication gave him understanding of men, his simplicity gave him trust in them. His understanding enabled him to govern; his trustfulness made him the exponent of democratic government.

Public men, like other men, are moved by major and minor motives, and the art of government has its own logistics. Moreover, instead of being "after all a very simple thing," as one of our Presidents so tragically misconceived it, government is a very complicated enterprise, and democratic government the most difficult. Undoubtedly there were surface deviations and inevitable tacking from time to time in the course Roosevelt pursued. But one cannot read the first study about Mr. Roosevelt as a public figure, written in 1911 by that discerning journalist, W. A. Warn, without realizing that during the thirty-five years of his public life he steered a consistent course — the course of his dominant impulses. When Roosevelt first came to the Presidency, he could not escape the truth of Macaulay's dictum that we must reform in order to conserve. Events demanded a leader of social reform, and Franklin Roosevelt had the prepared mind and temper for it.

When Roosevelt became President, disillusionment about Europe, strong belief in disarmament rooted in idealism, preoccupation with domestic problems and the prevalence of influential opinion in favor of economic nationalism, combined to produce a good deal of blindness concerning the extent to which the fate of this country was bound up with that of the rest of the world. A strange juxtaposition of history brought President Roosevelt and Hitler to power at the same time. By the law of his nature Franklin Roosevelt from the first felt revulsion against Hitler and his cohorts as individuals, and hostility to the resurgence of barbarism which they represented as a system. He clearly saw that the new barbarism, if unchecked, would be a menace to civilized society, not excluding that of the United States.

The function of statesmanship is to endeavor to forestall untoward events or to prepare adequately against them. The President had to do both at the same time. He worked with might and main to avert a war which was bound to be infinitely more destructive and agonizing than the last one, and to avert it by saving and not surrendering freedom. Politics in a democracy means a continuous process of education. But education does not always mean exposition, and certainly not shouting. It involves much incubation. Not least of the arts of statesmanship is that of correct timing, of knowing what to say and when. The President was confronted with illusions highly creditable to men of good-will, but steadily rendered invalid by Hitler. He was also confronted by pressures of every kind, of which democracy is an amalgam. And in his own political household he must often have encountered hesitation rather than encouragement. But there came a time when he could no longer doubt that he had to shift from the task of social reform to war leadership, in order not only to maintain our spiritual heritage but to assure opportunities for further progress as a free society.

There came a moment when President Roosevelt was convinced that the utter defeat of Nazism was essential to the survival of our institutions. That time certainly could not have been later than when Mr. Sumner Welles reported on his mission to Europe. Certainly from the time that the fall of France seemed imminent, the President was resolved to do everything possible to prevent the defeat of the Allies. Although confronted with the obvious danger of attack by the Axis upon us, there came that series of bold and triumphant measures which Mr. Churchill authoritatively summarized in his moving speech on April 17, 1945, to the House of Commons — the shipment of arms to Great Britain, the stab-in-the-back speech, the base-destroyer deal, Lend-Lease, the smoothing of the difficult ways of the Allied purchasing missions, the encouragement of Mr. Willkie's trip to England, the assistance in a hundred ways of British economic warfare, the extraordinarily prompt and cordial support of Russia. Moreover, while engaged in this series of complicated moves, he so skillfully conducted affairs as to avoid even the appearance of an act of aggression on our part.

And so, in the hour of national disaster on that Sunday afternoon after Japan had struck, when the President gathered about him his Cabinet and his military chiefs, the most experienced statesman among his advisers, after watching the President's calm and resolute control of the situation, could say to himself, "there is my leader."

His silver voice is stilled but the pitch he struck in others will gather volume. For while his death comes as a cruel and monstrous loss, the creative energy which his life released throughout the world will continue, and, one is justified in believing, will even enhance his influence. He now joins the select company of those whose "home is in the minds of men, where their glory remains fresh to stir to speech or action as the occasion comes by. For the whole earth is the sepulchre of famous men; and their story is not graven only on stone over their native earth, but lives on far away, without visible symbol, woven into the stuff of other men's lives."

The ultimate mysteries of life are merely renewed. They remain the same. Franklin Roosevelt knew this well and he chose to express it at the Harvard Tercentenary Celebration in the words of Euripides:

> *There be many shapes of mystery.*
> *And many things God makes to be,*
> *Past hope or fear.*
> *And the end men looked for cometh not,*
> *And a path is there where no man sought.*
> *So hath it fallen here.*

On Memorial Day 1956, a ceremony was held at the graveside of Franklin Delano Roosevelt in Hyde Park, New York, at which Justice Frankfurter delivered the following remarks:

FRANKLIN DELANO ROOSEVELT

This is not a meeting of the American Historical Association. This is not an occasion for a documented account of the exercise of the Presidency by the only man in its history who held it for three terms and had begun the important fraction of a fourth. I shall not attempt even to sketch the significance of Franklin Roosevelt in relation to his times — the convulsions, national and worldwide, of which he was the center — the storms that he rode and how he surmounted them, the old problems that he solved, the new that he encountered and partly stimulated. I shall not indulge in the humorless impertinence of forestalling what is called the verdict of history. Indeed, Clio has the teasing elusiveness and seeming caprice of a much-wooed woman. Fluctuations of historic judgment are the common lot of great men, be they statesmen or poets — Jefferson and Lincoln, Shakespeare and Walt Whitman. It is not hazardous, however, to make one forecast. Franklin Roosevelt will meet what has been rightly defined as the final test of Presidential greatness: "To be enshrined as a folk hero in the American consciousness." He will continue to embody in an uncommonly gay and courageous manifestation the traditions and aspirations of Americans.

Franklin Roosevelt cannot escape becoming a national saga, enshrined in myths, if you will. Myths endure only when rooted in essential truth; as such they serve to guide and sustain the high endeavors of a people. Enduring myths do not survive detached from the man who calls them forth. As it was of Lincoln, so it will be of Franklin Roosevelt, vast as are the surface differences between them. They both had the common touch — a sense of kinship with their fellows, the sense of the deep things men have in common, not common in the sense of what is vulgar and unedifying. The Roosevelt saga will never swallow up Roosevelt the man, whose friendship gave hope to millions who never knew him and whose death brought a feeling of intimate, personal loss to millions who never saw him.

Identification with his fellow men was Roosevelt's profoundest characteristic and the ultimate key to his statesmanship. He was an instinctive democrat, a democrat in feeling and not through reflection; he was a spontaneous fellow-citizen and did not become one through abstract speculation about government. More than once I was asked after March 4, 1933, "Why does F.D.R. hate the rich? Why does he have a skunner against the J. P. Morgans?" Invariably I replied, "Nothing could be farther from the truth. He isn't against the rich and the powerful. He is merely not for them because they are rich and powerful. He has the same feeling about them that he has about his neighbors in Hyde Park, pursuing their modest callings. Wealth and the power that wealth confers seemed to him negligible, indeed irrelevant, to the right feeling about them as people. Nor should it cloud our judgment regarding the consequences of their actions to society." An episode which I had the good fortune to witness right here in Hyde Park illustrates this attitude of Roosevelt's in seeing men as men. He drove up to a neighboring farmer, who for all I know may be here today, with whom he was in negotiation about a piece of land. This was in the middle thirties, when the cares of office might well have weighed down the strongest of men. The President and his neighbor entered into converse, out of earshot of the rest of us in the President's car, when I suddenly heard, what I could hardly believe I had heard, this self-respecting and self-reliant fellow American say to the President of the United States:

"Mr. Roosevelt, you and I are both very busy men. Suppose we continue this talk at some other time when we both have more time."

The President accepted this, as though it were the most obvious remark to make to the head of the most powerful nation in the world, and with the utmost good humor, he replied:

"Very well, Peter, I'll try to get hold of you some other day when you have more time."

This little episode, it seems to me, reveals more about Franklin D. Roosevelt than does many a heavily documented doctoral thesis.

This permeating friendliness of Roosevelt expressed true feeling. Not less true were depths within him which were hardly accessible to anyone. From the time when he was a boy, according to his mother, he had a self-sufficiency and strength which comes from the reserves of an inner life. In the light of events, his qualities of character can be deducted from the first magazine article published about Roosevelt — a delineation of him as a young state senator, in the New York *Times* for January 22, 1911, by its Albany correspondent familiarly known as "Baron" Warn. In those early days, as thirty years later in the White House, while to outward view he had a gaiety at times bordering on jauntiness, Franklin Roosevelt had a will of steel, well sheathed by a captivating smile. These reserves, deep below his outward easy-goingness, were doubtless the source and sanctuary of his resolute determination in overcoming obstacles, both in his personal life and in the conduct of affairs, that so often make men falter and not run the course. Our friend had, no doubt, the common touch. But he had also another quality — that mystical touch of grace, a charismatic quality that stirs comfortable awe, that keeps a distance between men and a leader and yet draws them to him.

What was said of Benjamin Franklin may be said of Franklin Roosevelt, that he was "a harmonious human multitude." There were fused in him the qualities necessary for leading our people out of a period of deepening economic and moral deterioration by invigorating, through precept and example, the forces of democracy. The same qualities equipped him to serve as an energy of hope for liberty-loving people everywhere in resisting seemingly invincible challenges to civilization. His sophistication gave him understanding of men. His sympathy gave him trust in them. What Winston Churchill characterized as Roosevelt's "power of gauging the tide and currents of its mobile public opinion" enabled him to govern our heterogeneous democracy. His trustfulness in them made the people return the trust.

The public issues that aroused so much rancor and conflict in the Roosevelt era will eventually, and before very long, be things of the forgotten past, as public issues which gave rise to the bitterness and passion that swirled around the heads of Jefferson and Jackson and Lincoln have become things of the forgotten past. Most political issues are ephemeral. Those leaders of our people abide who represent some universal element in the long adventure of man, represent qualities that kindle the heart and fortify the spirit. Franklin Delano Roosevelt belongs to this very small band of men who, generation after generation, accompany mankind on its fateful journey, and each of us in the gladness and gratitude of his heart is here to bear testimony to the friend who abides with us.

Index

Historical events that occurred during the years covered by the Roosevelt-Frankfurter correspondence are listed chronologically at the beginning of each chapter. They are not included in the index.

Franklin D. Roosevelt is abbreviated FDR, and Felix Frankfurter, FF.